SCHOOL SOCIAL WORK

Practice, Policy, and Research Perspectives

Also available from Lyceum Books, Inc.

CASE MANAGEMENT: AN INTRODUCTION TO CONCEPTS AND SKILLS, by Arthur Frankel and Sheldon Gelman

MODERN SOCIAL WORK THEORY: A CRITICAL INTRODUCTION, 2E, by Malcolm Payne, foreword by Stephen C. Anderson

CROSS-CULTURAL PRACTICE: SOCIAL WORK WITH DIVERSE POPULATIONS, by Karen Harper and Jim Lantz

CLINICAL ASSESSMENT FOR SOCIAL WORKERS: QUANTITATIVE AND QUALITATIVE METHODS, by Catheleen Jordan and Cynthia Franklin

POLICY ANALYSIS AND RESEARCH TECHNOLOGY, by Thomas Meenaghan and Keith Kilty

STRUCTURING CHANGE: EFFECTIVE PRACTICE FOR COMMON CLIENT PROBLEMS, edited by Kevin Corcoran

WORKING WITH CHILDREN AND THEIR FAMILIES, 2E, by Karen Harper-Dorton and Martin Herbert

SOCIAL WORK EDUCATION IN EASTERN EUROPE: CHANGING HORIZONS, edited by Robert Constable and Vera Mehta

STRENGTHENING REFUGEE FAMILIES, by Daniel Scheinfeld and Lorraine Wallach

MARKETING STRATEGIES FOR NONPROFIT ORGANIZATIONS, by Siri Espy

COLLABORATION SKILLS FOR EDUCATORS AND NONPROFIT LEADERS, by Hank Rubin

SCHOOL SOCIAL WORK

Practice, Policy, and Research Perspectives

Fourth Edition

Edited by

ROBERT CONSTABLE
School of Social Work
Loyola University of Chicago

SHIRLEY McDONALD
Jane Addams School of Social Work
University of Illinois at Chicago

JOHN P. FLYNN, Emeritus
School of Social Work
Western Michigan University

LYCEUM
BOOKS, INC.

5758 S. Blackstone Ave.
Chicago, Illinois 60637

Dedicated to children in the American public school system, past, present, and future;
to the families and communities whose hopes they bear;
to teachers who nourish and protect the unique and living spark in each child;
to school social workers who struggle to make the partnership alive and effective.

© Lyceum Books, Inc., 1999

Published by

LYCEUM BOOKS, INC.
5758 S. Blackstone Ave.
Chicago, Illinois 60637
773/643-1903 (Fax)
773/643-1902 (Phone)
lyceum3@ibm.net
http://www.lyceumbooks.com

Library of Congress Cataloging-in-Publication Data

School social work : practice, policy, and research perspectives / edited by
   Robert Constable, Shirley McDonald, John P. Flynn. — 4th ed.
      600p   3 cm.
     Includes bibliographical references and index.
     ISBN 0-925065-50-1
     1. School social work.   I. Constable, Robert T. 1940–
  II. Flynn, John P. 1933–   III. McDonald, Shirley, 1934–
  LB3013.4.S365   1998   98-26474
  371.4′6—dc20   CIP

Carel Bailey Germain (1916–1995): In Appreciation

—

Carel B. Germain, professor emerita of the University of Connecticut School of Social Work, died on August 3, 1995, from pulmonary fibrosis. At the time of her death, we were editing the final manuscript of the second edition of the *Life Model*. Our collaboration began in 1972 as new faculty colleagues when the dean asked us to develop the school's first-year integrated practice courses to replace the former casework and group work courses. This project led to twenty-three years of writing collaboration and a close friendship. The struggle to develop and express our ideas about practice forged an enduring bond between us.

Carel, a native of San Francisco, was active throughout her childhood and adolescence in the Camp Fire Girls. Her early-found passion for nature had a profound impact on her later intellectual preoccupations. She graduated from the University of California, Berkeley, and began her career in public welfare agencies in San Francisco during 1937–47. She married her high school sweetheart, William, on his return from military service in World War II. When their twin daughters, Adrienne and Denise, were in high school, Carel pursued her social work degree, graduating from Columbia in 1961. Her brilliance was immediately evident to faculty and peers.

On graduating, Carel became an assistant professor and assistant director (later acting director) of psychiatric social work at the University of Maryland School of Medicine, Department of Psychiatry. She also served as a field instructor and then became a member of the faculty at the University of Maryland School of Social Work. In 1965, at age forty-nine, she entered the doctoral program at Columbia; she completed her advanced degree in 1971. Concurrently, beginning in 1968, she became successively associate professor, professor, and acting dean at the University of Connecticut School of Social Work. In 1972, she joined Columbia's faculty until she returned to the University of Connecticut in 1978.

In recent decades, Professor Germain has been a dominant social work theoretician, historian, and thinker. She was recognized internationally for her brilliant interdisciplinary scholarship. Her astounding contribution to the profession's literature began when she was a doctoral student with the publications of "Social Study: Past and Future," "Casework and Science: A Historical Encounter," and "An Ecological Perspective in Social Casework." These classics were followed with the publication of more than fifty articles and numerous books. In her scholarship, Professor Germain drew on numerous academic disciplines to develop her ideas. At her memorial service on November 10, 1995, I stated:

> Our profession has lost its major scholar and teacher, a cut above the mold. We do not have Carel any more to intellectually stretch us—to teach us about social work history; to make knowledge available to us from other disciplines: such as biology, to develop the ecological metaphor; the discipline of environmental psychology, to present ideas about the natural and built environment; and the disciplines of anthropology, sociology, and psychology, to create ideas about cohorts and the life course.
>
> Carel, a creative and rigorous intellectual explorer and discoverer, roamed the globe of ideas and discovered their relevance for a profession she deeply loved. Never satisfied with the intellectual status quo, she leaped forward into uncharted theoretical territory, found new concepts, and made them available to us. And when we resisted new ways of thinking and believing, she gently and firmly brought us along on the journey and steered and willed us to become fellow explorers and discoverers.

Her body of work reflected an uncommon intellect and erudition. She bequeaths a lasting gift to the profession.

Carel enriched the lives of her colleagues and friends with a wonderfully understated, playful sense of humor. When we were stuck on a chapter, she would send a note with a "smiley" face and a quote: "Writing is easy; all you do is sit staring at a blank sheet of paper until the drops of blood form on your forehead." When I wrote her a congratulatory note on receiving an honorary doctorate from Smith College, I ended it with "Congratulations! Congratulations! (Carel with two doctorates, I feel I should say everything twice.)" She wrote back thanking me for my note and signed it, "Love, Love, Carel, Carel."

And once in a while she would tell a joke. My favorite is Carel telling a story about an inhibited person who was so inhibited that for Thanksgiving she refused to stuff a turkey because she considered it an invasion of privacy.

Carel had an enthusiasm for life and a passion for the beauties of nature. She was graceful, gentle, and gallant in her ways. She held fast to her ideas, never cutting her cloth to suit the fashions of the day.

As social workers, we can continue to acknowledge and use her brilliant ideas, to remember her collegiality, loyalty, and elegance, and to appreciate the fact that her life touched and gave additional meanings to our lives. We can continue to visualize her beautiful face—the twinkle in her eyes and her enchanting smile. In these and other ways, Carel will always be with us and part of us.

Alex Gitterman

Florence Poole (1904–1980): In Appreciation

Florence Poole died suddenly on June 23, 1980. To those of us who were closely associated with Florence, the news came as a shock. The significant contributions that she made to both social work and education and the outpouring of time and energy she had invested in the work for which she was so fitted—the education of social workers—cannot be forgotten.

With careful deliberation I perused Florence's resume to cull some of the things that might be of interest to social workers. I recalled a phrase written by Heinrich Heine: "The actions of persons are like the index of a book; they point out what is most remarkable in them." Everything Florence Poole has done has been valuable to us and truly has pointed out what was most remarkable in her—elementary school teacher, camp counselor, social worker, supervisor, and finally the coveted titles of associate professor at the University of Pittsburgh School of Social Work, and professor at the University of Illinois School of Social Work in Urbana and at the Jane Addams School of Social Work in Chicago. For a half-century of her life, Florence Poole offered dedicated service to children, parents, teachers, social workers, and administrators in some capacity, and her writings have inspired all of us to perform more effectively.

Florence was an unusual person. In a profession that has been graced by so many wonderful people, she was still exceptional—in her shy, unassuming, and gentle ways. One of her outstanding characteristics was her belief that the dignity and worth of every human being were living, consuming realities, and this guided her every action. She possessed a fundamental commitment to social work as a service profession. If she wanted the best from her students, it was only that they might bring the best to the people they would serve.

Her accomplishments in the field of social work and education are many, and any attempt to recapitulate their significance would scarcely allow her the exemplary credits she deserves. Few in the field of social work have been as prolific in writing articles of such value to the field. Few have so graciously and unstintingly given of their time and talents. Florence wrote thirteen publications and papers and at least twenty-five unpublished papers and speeches. She had the enviable record of more than thirty-nine institutes and workshops that have given insight and impetus to social workers, teachers, parents, and administrators and have allowed us to profit immensely from what she has done. Universities sought her leadership and knowledge when having their schools of social work accredited. National and state organizations sought her help by asking her to assume an officer's position, to be a consultant, or to be involved in some capacity to assist them in functioning more appropriately. Many universities requested that she teach in their summer programs. Florence, who I am sure never knew what she was getting into when she entered a helping profession, was constantly engaged in making social work, and especially school social work, the profession it ought to be and did grow to be.

Among her memorabilia was found a Japanese proverb that was representative of Florence's outlook in life: "When I dig another out of trouble, the hole from which I left him is the place where I bury my own." Another article, entitled "Thought for Today," exemplified her pattern for daily living. It read:

On this day . . .
Mend a quarrel,
Search out a forgotten friend,
Dismiss a suspicion and replace it with trust,
Write a letter to someone who misses you,
Encourage a youth who has lost faith,
Keep a promise,
Forget an old grudge,
Examine your demands on others and how to reduce them,
Fight for a principle,
Express your gratitude,
Overcome an old fear,
Take two minutes to appreciate the beauty of nature,
Tell someone you love them,
Tell them again,
And again,
And again.

The personal and professional tribute that should be accorded to Florence can never be written adequately; out debt of gratitude can never be repaid; the generosity and support she has offered us cannot be duplicated. School social work will succeed in its undertakings because of the exemplary designs that Florence fashioned for us from its crude beginnings.

Few persons have spent as enriched a life as Florence did in her service to others. Few have made such dedicated contributions and left such a precious imprint on the social work profession. Few have so influenced the lives of others. The memory of Florence's conscientious and devoted efforts will always be enshrined in our hearts, and for these we are grateful.

Margaret Quane

CONTENTS

Preface to the Fourth Edition

This edition of *School Social Work* reflects a span of sixteen years during which this book has both served the field of practice of school social work and in many ways helped to construct it. School social work is essential to the work of education throughout the world as families and communities strive to make schools safe and inclusive places for children to grow. The substance and process of education has changed profoundly over the past decade and a half. Schools are concerned when their students are challenged by the complexity and risks involved in growing up today. Information is transmitted instantly and indiscriminately by the media. As a result, the most remote rural area is as much a part of the electronic community as any city neighborhood. No longer are certain problems uniquely "urban." Families, struggling for survival in a marketplace without borders and an ever more complex and demanding work system, are frequently unable to prepare their children for the future. Furthermore, shifts in society and the welfare system have placed greater demands on educational institutions. Schools, often finding themselves in the middle of a political battleground, have no choice but to respond in a highly differentiated way to the needs identified by their families and their communities. Over the past twenty years in many areas of the United States the school social worker has been the catalyst behind creative responses to these changes. The number of school social workers has often continued to increase even where pupil enrollment has declined.

A highly sophisticated model of practice is emerging, integrating research, policy, and different forms of intervention at the school community level. The model seeks to reconstruct the school as a safe place where family and school can work together and manage the evident risks to development experienced by our children. School social workers and others develop plans and programs to meet the particular needs of each school community. This vision of practice, which continues to shape the book, can be traced to the earliest days of school social work, to its later articulation by Florence Poole and others, and to its continuation through periods of fundamental changes in society and in school policy. As a result the school social worker is needed by schools as never before.

We have made changes in the fourth edition to reflect developments on these themes. More than a fifth of the articles are new. Of the remaining articles, more than half have seen substantial revision. Common elements of the school social worker's role are assessment and consultation, direct work with children and families, and work with the broader school community. These tasks and skills are the basis for everything the school social worker does. In this book, time-honored chapters, such as Carel Germain's on theory or Joy Johnson's on the no-fault school, continue to address the basic themes of school social work but also suggest areas and directions for current development.

Long concerned with the needs of children in general education, the school has also become the center of planning for children with special needs. Throughout the book we have substantially revised the discussion and the references to law, policy, and programs for children with disabilities in order to reflect new developments and the innovative responses of social workers. Adaptive behavior assessments and the social worker's contribution to the student's annual goals and objectives in the Individualized Education Program (IEP) are addressed in new chapters.

The revised policy section has been strengthened to reflect current developments. The discussion focuses on research that school social workers do when they are justifying, developing, or evaluating programs. Needs assessment, evaluation, the use of research for program development, and the relation of research to policy development at the school community level are major areas here. New chapters by John Flynn on policy analysis and the school social worker and by Ed Pawlak on organizational perspectives develop this integration of research and policy into practice.

A number of developments in education are given special emphasis in the fourth edition. Children are experiencing violence within their communities and in interpersonal relationships. Increasingly, this violence is spilling into the schools. Jay Callahan's new article, "School-Based Crisis Intervention for Traumatic Events," responds to this trend, as does Fineran and Bennett's article, "Peer Sexual Harassment and the Social Worker's Response." The treatment of group intervention, mediation, and conflict resolution has been strengthened with both new and revised chapters. In addition, the chapters on family, school, and community models of helping have all been enriched considerably.

The fourth edition of *School Social Work* represents the joint effort of forty authors, including the three editors. We are particularly appreciative of Mary Hathcoat, who made a real contribution to the book's development. Each of us acknowledges the patience and forbearance of our spouses, children, grandchildren, friends, and colleagues, who made the endeavor possible. To this list we add the many readers of the first, second, and third editions, who supported us in the belief that the content is worthwhile and usable and who urged us to refine and develop these ideas in a fourth edition.

Robert Constable
Shirley McDonald
John P. Flynn

History and General Perspectives in School Social Work

CHAPTER 1

Theoretical Perspectives in School Social Work

Robert Constable
Professor Emeritus, Loyola University of Chicago

- The Purpose of School Social Work
- The Field of Practice of School Social Work
- Whom Does the School Social Worker Serve?
- Where (in What Contexts) Does School Social Work Take Place?
- What Does the School Social Worker Do?
- School Social Work Practice Theory
- A Historical Analysis of School Social Work

There is not one school social work role, but a *cluster* of roles with a common theoretical foundation. In a general sense the school social work role is developed from the interaction of social work with the process of education. In a particular sense the role is developed by social workers and others, such as the principals and teachers, within each school building. Working from general policies and relating the particular needs of the school community to the role, a match is made between the needs of the school community and the possible contributions of the social worker. School social workers in concert with other members of the school team make assessments and develop appropriate programs and services within the school. To perform their duties successfully school social workers need to have a vision of what is possible, possess tools of analysis, be comfortable with the processes of negotiation, and coordinate their interventions with the life of the school. Assessment of needs and capacities of identified students and of the school and development of a distinct role within the school team are key competencies in school social work practice. Where in the school community do children's and families' learning and development and the response of the school community itself face break down? Where is the best place to intervene? What should the role of the school social worker be in this particular school community? Guided by the purposes and needs of education and the learning process, an effective, focused, and comprehensible school social work role can be negotiated within a school community.

The school social worker inevitably works in the most vulnerable parts of the educational process, where education can break down. Today neither schools nor families can alone succeed in the task of preparing children for productive adult lives. Families and schools need to discover partnership, yet this is precisely what eludes each of them. There are many possible roles the school social worker can play. The school social worker may work one on one with teachers, families, and children to address individual situations and needs. The school social worker may develop with the principal, teachers' representatives, and school nurse (a crisis team) such programs as a crisis plan for the school. The school social worker may work with that crisis team through a disturbing and violent incident, serving individual pupils and teachers experiencing crisis as well as working with the broader school population. He or she may develop a mediation program in a high school experiencing confrontations between students. The list continues through many variations. The school social work role rests on a wide range of skills that become crystallized in individual interventions and in school programs, but it takes shape through interactive teamwork.

THE PURPOSE OF SCHOOL SOCIAL WORK

School social work is a diverse and flexible response to the social and developmental needs implicit in the human learning process as it takes place within the educative environment of public school and in the family setting. The goal of school social work is to help young people accomplish appropriate developmental tasks in ways that best respect the values underlying our common human nature, our common human needs, and the human potential of each person, often needlessly wasted. The role can be flexibly developed to meet the variety of circumstances schools, families, and young people face.

The basic unit of attention in social work in the school is the constellation of teacher, parent, and child, in that order. The social worker must be able to relate to and work with all aspects of the child's situation, but the basic skill underlying all of this is assessment. The social worker needs to discover the units of attention in places where intervention will be most effective in each case. Then the social worker develops a plan to assist the total constellation: teacher and students in the classroom, parents in the family, and others need to work together to support the child in the successful completion of the developmental steps that lie ahead.

Stories of Practice: Models of School Social Work

A classic example of clinical school social work.   A child who speaks mainly Spanish in his family has a first experience of kindergarten in a predominantly Anglo school and every day spends the class hiding behind the piano. The more the teacher tries to move him from behind the piano, the more firmly he remains, and it has now become a struggle of wills between child and teacher. The school social worker first assesses the situation in a consultation conference with the teacher, and they develop a few joint strategies focusing on the child's experience in the class. They might shorten the exposure of the youngster to the class or help the teacher modify the educational focus and expectations. The youngster might get started in school with a supportive person from his own community. The teacher might help the youngster work with another child in the class who is less afraid and can be supportive. The teacher might invite the family to school to help them feel more comfortable and thus convey that feeling of comfort to the child. The social worker and teacher look for signs of the youngster's possible response. Chances are that the problem is at least partly one of language. Another possibility is that the youngster is not ready for kindergarten and should wait a bit. Or the youngster may need more detailed prekindergarten testing or different placement in school, one that accommodates his special needs. The social worker will also assist the teacher in his or her contacts with the parents, since in this case these contacts seem crucial.

So far the social worker has not seen the parents, and may not need to, if the situation can be managed by the teacher with the social worker's consultation. Consultation is the first, most effective, and least costly use of the social worker's time. However, in many cases, and especially in the case of a child entering school, it may be necessary to confer with the parents. Parents, especially from a different linguistic or cultural group, may be insecure and uncertain of their role in school. They may feel strange about being involved with the school. It is of course precisely these feelings that may be conveyed to their child, so that the child fears the school and can find no way to cope with it. The school social worker, aware of these likely fears, can take a normalizing approach toward them, with the intent of helping mother and father feel at ease. The school social worker, when entering the home, is entering the world of the family. In this story the parents gradually feel comfortable and trusting enough to discuss their real concerns. They are worried about letting the youngster go to school. They experience Anglo culture as distant, different, and threatening. Moreover, each parent has a different approach to discipline, and their difficulties with each other make them both feel helpless regarding some of the youngster's behavior. When the parents are in disagreement, the youngster always wins and this learned behavior is being brought to the school. The school social worker makes an assessment, jointly with the parents, of how the child is responding, what the dynamics of the home may be, and what type of agreement between parents, teacher, and child can be constructed. The school must also support the child's first steps to adapt appropriately. The school social worker's work with the parents would parallel work already done with the child's teacher. In this case the work between the teacher and the parents may suffice. In other stories the social worker will opt to work with the child also, but building on the work already done with teacher and parents.

A school crisis.   In another story the school itself is in crisis. A crisis happens in a school when too many things are taking place at once for the school to manage and still remain a safe environment for children or when children are having great difficulty processing a situation. When Christa McAuliffe, an astronaut and a teacher, died in the *Challenger* explosion before millions of children watching on television, schools throughout the country seized it as a teachable moment. It was an opportunity; indeed, there was a necessity to help children process their feelings about dying and about the meanings of their lives.

In our own particular story the school is in turmoil because of the violent death in a school bus accident of one of the children, an eight-year-old Korean girl. The school has a general plan for dealing with crises and specifically a detailed crisis manual that the school social worker helped create as a key member of the crisis team. Upon hearing about the death, the social worker makes an immediate assessment of the points of vulnerability in the school and meets with the school crisis team. They agree on a division of work. The principal works with the news media and community and makes an announcement to teachers and students as soon as there is a clear picture of what happened. The social worker has been in touch with the girl's family to learn what their wishes are and to assess how they are managing the crisis. The social worker agrees to work with the family, staying in touch throughout the crisis. She cancels normal appointments, except those that cannot be changed, and opens her office as a crisis center for students and teachers who want to talk about what has happened. She talks to the teacher of the student who died, and they discuss how the class is to be told. Later, people who were involved with the student or who feel the need attend a small Buddhist memorial service, and still later, students, teachers, and the family preserve the memory of the student in a more permanent way with a small peace garden in the school courtyard. School and community deal with the aftershocks of the death in a healing process that takes place over the next several years.

A child with special needs.   In another story a child with a disability needs to be moved from one class to another. In the first class she is more protected, but achieves less than she might be capable of and is mostly friends with other children with disabilities. She is moving to a class with a wide range of children with different levels of ability, where, if she feels safe and accepted, it is hoped she might achieve more. But she will experience greater stress whatever her level of achievement. The shift is carefully planned and is based on tests that say that the student will be able to achieve in this class with some special help. The new teacher and the old teacher are fully involved in the process. The student is also fully involved, and the social worker has developed a supportive relationship with the student and with the parents. When the day comes for the move, the social worker is there in case of unforeseen difficulties. The social worker works with the teacher, parent, and child in the months following the move, until it is clear that his services are no longer needed.

Consultation and placement of students.   In another story the social worker develops an active consultation program with teachers at a junior high school. One problem the school faces is that children are coming to the departmental structure of the junior high school from a self-contained sixth-grade class in a familiar building close to home. It is not unusual for such children to regress for a semester or more. Some never recover the achievement and feeling of safety they experienced when they had one teacher and knew the teacher and their classmates well. Through the classroom observation that is a normal part of her work in the school, the social worker gets to know the teaching styles of each of the teachers and the range of strengths each brings to his or her work with children. Before the 400 new students from feeder schools come to the junior high school in September, she reviews their records from elementary school and matches each at-risk child with a homeroom (language arts and social studies) teacher who fits well with that child's needs, making certain that there are only a few children with serious problems in each classroom and a balance of children with positive social adjustments and learning skills. Referrals of children for help the following year run at about half the normal rate, and children who need more intensive help are helped earlier.

Group work in a school.   In another story a group of seven twelve-year-old boys decide in their discussions with each other that they all have problems with their fathers. They appear at the social worker's door, asking to form a group to discuss their concerns. The social worker, who is male, calls each of the parents for permission and invites them to come in to discuss the situation. The parents come in, some individually, some in a group, and the boys are seen in a group with some individual follow-up. The result in each boy is a lowering of tension in his relations with his father and a measurable improvement academically and socially. No boy needs to be seen longer than three months.

Mediation.   In another example a high school is experiencing a large number of fights between groups of students of different ethnicities over insulting language, relations with girls (or boys), and accusations of stealing, among others. There is a particularly high level of tension around allegations of being gay or lesbian. Fights have usually been handled by the intervention of the vice principal, but this is not well accepted by the students and has resulted in escalations of punishment and students' experiencing shame and wishing revenge on the students who have shamed them and on the vice principal. The social worker and the principal develop both a mediation and an education program. Disputes between individual students are sub-ject to mediation by a panel of specially trained students, who are selected for their leadership ability and their interest in participating in the program. This program lowers tensions in the school as problems are resolved mutu-ally, collaboratively, and without escalation, and the dignity of each student is preserved. The education program normalizes the difficulties youngsters often have in resolving their sexual orientation and welcomes them to dis-cuss it with the social worker. The social worker and some teachers, with the social worker's assistance, maintain contact with different coalesced groups of Hispanic, Caucasian, and African-American students and with their leadership.

The examples that can be given of the role of the social worker are innumerable. In each case the social worker applies the basics of the school social work role to a different set of circumstances in concert with other members of the school team, finding collaborative ways for the school to solve problems. The work of the social worker is indeed the work of the school, and the effectiveness of the school social worker is the effectiveness of education wherever he or she is involved.

THE FIELD OF PRACTICE OF SCHOOL SOCIAL WORK

The rich correspondence of the fields of social work and education creates a unique field of practice in social work. School social workers use a multi-plicity of concrete skills, fitted to a picture of the needs and capacities of a particular school community, to contribute to the effectiveness of the educational process for vulnerable youngsters and their families. Because of the different ways the role can be developed, school social workers need to understand the possibilities within the field and to develop a high level of skill in carrying them out with other professionals on the school team.

The field of school social work has been developing consistently since the earliest part of the twentieth century. Toward the middle of the century, Florence Poole (1949) crystallized the diversity and unity of school social work as a social work field of practice. Her conceptual clarity and the sound-ness of her approach to the school social worker's role can best be seen in the following passage from her work: "At the present time we no longer see social work as a service appended to the schools. We see one of our most significant social institutions establishing social work as an integral part of its service, essential to the carrying out of its purpose. We recognize a clarity in the definition of the services as a social work service." She saw the clarity and uniqueness of social work service as coming from the societal function of the school. "[The worker] must be able to determine which needs within the school can be appropriately met through school social work service. She must be able to develop a method of offering the service which will fit in with the general organization and structure of the school, but which is identifiable as one requiring social work knowledge and skill. She must be able to define the service and her contribution in such a way that the school personnel can accept it as a service which contributes to the major purpose of the school.

Florence Poole's approach to practice was built on the parameters of the mission of the school, the knowledge and skill of social work, and the worker's professional responsibility to determine what needs to be done and to develop an appropriate program for doing it. For her, the "givens" of school social work were the rich interaction between the mission of the school and the knowledge and skill of social work. Built on these givens, the worker's professional judgment was the crucial ingredient in determining professional function. Changes have taken place over forty years in the societal mandate given the schools, but the issues that Florence Poole helped clarify so soundly are scarcely less important today: the legal and institutional base for practice, the institution as a target for service, the interprofessional team cooperation, and the relation of all of these filtered through professional judgment to determine the resultant action taken by the worker.

WHOM DOES THE SCHOOL SOCIAL WORKER SERVE?

The school social worker is concerned with every child whose coping capacity may not be well matched with the demands and resources of the education institution. Society places a heavy responsibility on education not merely to teach but, with the family, to prepare children for the future, to be the vehicle for aspirations, not only for children who may conform easily to external expectations, but for every child. Responsibilities are placed on the school, on the parent, and on the child to make the educational process work so that every child who goes to school may fulfill his or her potential for growth and contribution to others. At one time or other any of us could be vulnerable because of life circumstances, school realities, or personal developmental realities. In addition, certain burdens are felt by particular groups within society. Children come to school with messages from society, and sometimes from the school itself, that because of certain defining characteristics, such as gender, race, disability, ethnicity, or socioeconomic class, they cannot have the same aspirations as others or that objective conditions, such as poverty, will surely prevent them from achieving their aspirations. The school social worker can refute these messages by working with children and families one on one and by developing programs that may help remove some of the obstacles faced by such children. Each chapter that follows in this book addresses a particular concern for these populations, in the development of school policies affecting social work (section II), in the development of practice roles and skills (section III), and in the development of needs assessment and research as the basis for policy and program development (section IV).

WHERE (IN WHAT CONTEXTS) DOES SCHOOL SOCIAL WORK TAKE PLACE?

The School Community Context

The educational process is dynamic and wide ranging. Involving children, their families, and an institution called school, it is the context for school social work. School is no longer a building, or simply a collection of classrooms in which teachers and pupils work together. School is conceptualized as *a community of families and school personnel engaged in the educational process.* The school community, no longer simply bounded by geography, comprises those who engage in the educational process. As in any community, there are varied concrete roles. People fit into such communities in very different ways. Parents and families are members through their children. Teachers and other school personnel are members with a complex accountability to parents, children, and the broader community. Drawing on each person's capacities, the school social worker focuses on making the educational process work to the fullest extent. And so school social workers work with parents, teachers, pupils, and administrators on behalf of vulnerable children or groups of children. The success of the process depends on the collective and individual involvement of everyone. The social worker helps the school community operate as a real community so that personal, familial, and community resources can be discovered and used to meet children's developmental needs.

In the process of helping schools develop a broader concept of their own communities, the social work role need not be discovered anew. The traditional approach of connecting children with networks of community services has been evident from the earliest years of social work in schools. Beginning in the late 1960s, the parent involvement experiences through the War on Poverty and Project Headstart program added a new dimension to the relationship. More recently, there are the parent-sponsored school movements of the 1980s and 1990s. Each movement would find ways of developing a school community, although goals differed according to the conceptions of the times.

From Spanning Boundaries to Organizing School Communities

As long as it was taken for granted that home would be isolated from school, the role of school social work has historically been to span the boundary between home and school as expeditiously as possible, and this has taken place since its origins in the early twentieth century. Schools have generally operated in relative isolation from their constituent families, each protecting its functioning from "interference" from the other. This isolation is, of course, counterproductive in situations of vulnerability or difficulty. A need for someone like the school social worker to span, and even challenge, these boundaries is thus created.

Within the American context the mandate given public education provided a powerful legal and societal basis for the development of school social work. Public education in the United States is a social movement scarcely a century and a half old, conceived in the optimism of a young country and born in the still unrealized conviction that every human being has a right to the means to realize individual potential. The vision of Horace Mann and others would become clouded by the immense task of bringing the idea of democracy and equality to reality in a culturally diverse society where professed dedication to equal opportunity masks the realities of discrimination. The profundity of the charge to education in our society is succinctly expressed in the landmark case of *Brown v. Board of Education of Topeka, Kansas* (1954):

> If education is a principal instrument in helping the child to adjust normally to his environment, it is doubtful that any child may reasonably be expected to succeed in life if he is denied the opportunity of an education. The opportunity of an education, where the state has undertaken to provide it to any, is a right which must be made available to all on equal terms.

It is perfectly consistent with the ideology of democracy that education should eventually be considered a civil right. However, the *Brown* opinion lays bare a broader inherent mission for education. In a society based on individual achievement, a child must have education to adjust normally to his or her environment and to succeed in life. The court faced squarely what has in fact been the function of education for many years in an increasingly complex and individualistic society. An almost instinctive commitment and belief in education may seem naive to some observers. The manifest inequalities of our society seem to belie its promise. Nevertheless, the institution of education is closely linked to the energy and the dynamics of society. In the twentieth century, the state of education is very much a reflection of the state of society.

The American Societal Context

The connection of school social work to its school and community context is essential for the development of theory. The current legal and social policy context for school social work and the role of the school social worker in school policy development is discussed more fully in section II of this book. In the United States and in certain Western European countries there has been an erosion of state welfare systems and the supports they provide to families. As national government policies shift toward "market" approaches, a longer term development appears to be that the protections normally associated with childhood are declining while the risks are increasing. High rates of suicide, addiction, violence to and among children, early pregnancy, AIDS, and early exposure to the job market through economic necessity are among these risks, to some extent created and in any case sustained by the laissez faire attitude associated with the reigning free market philosophy. Nevertheless, some of the risks generated by the broader societal system may be buffered through schools and homes that work and that respect human dignity and worth—through good teaching and good parenting.

The effect of policy shifts on the national level demands a strengthening of social institutions at the local level, the most important for children being family and schools. While a weakening of national support for education may be experienced as an offshoot of the free market philosophy, schools have nevertheless continued their century-old quests, such as for greater inclusion of previously secluded groups of youngsters in the educational mainstream. Earlier expectations had been that persons with different capabilities would be segregated from one another, the extreme being the institutionalization of children with disabilities. The changes that have taken place in special education over the past thirty years are particularly important for school social workers and need to be thoroughly understood. They are also a useful metaphor for the complex relations between school policy and contexts and the school social worker's role. More recently, school reform experience in the United States has been bringing with it increased expectations for performance by children. Yet no progress can be made on school reform without dealing with the correlates of poverty and socioeconomic class. Many children are very much at risk and lack institutional, community, and family supports (Mintzies and Hare, 1985). Recent data on state achievement tests in mathematics indicate dramatic differences in achievement explainable mainly by the realities of poverty. Impoverished school districts working with impoverished families achieve at rates considerably lower than their more privileged neighbors (Biddle, 1997).

WHAT DOES THE SCHOOL SOCIAL WORKER DO?

The school social worker's role has often been conceptualized as primarily involving direct work with children and parents. However, job studies indicate that it is actually much broader. It includes highly skilled intervention with teachers in consultation, with parents, and with children, individually and in groups. In 1989 a group of nineteen nationally recognized experts in school social work were asked to develop and list the tasks that entry-level social workers would perform in their day-to-day professional roles. The result was a list of 104 tasks, evidence of the complexity of school social work. These tasks, when they were defined, fell along five job dimensions:

1. Relationships with and services to children and families,
2. Relationships with and services to teachers and school staff,
3. Services to other school personnel,
4. Community services, and
5. Administrative and professional tasks (Nelson, 1990).

Further research on these roles, tasks, and skills found four areas of school social work to be both very important and frequently performed:

1. Consultation with others in the school system and interdisciplinary team-work;
2. Assessment applied to a variety of different roles in direct service, in consultation, and in program development;
3. Direct work with children and parents in its many forms; and
4. Planning and implementation of school programs (Constable, Kuzmick-aite, and Volkmann, 1997).

Assessment

We have seen that a key skill, cutting across all areas, is assessment. *Assessment* is a way of understanding what is taking place in relations in the classroom, within the family, and between the family and school and looking for ways to make changes. The social worker looks for units of attention, places where intervention will be most effective. *Needs assessment,* a broader process, provides a basis for program development and policy formation in a school. It is often a more formal process, utilizing many of the tools of research, geared toward the development of programs and policies that meet the needs of children in school, and applying to the experiences of groups of children in school.

Role Development

It is not usual that beginning school social workers have a great deal of influence in the initial development of their roles. Indeed, the idea of ever influencing the development of their roles in particular schools may seem foreign to their experience. However, over a longer period of time, as they learn to respond in a more differentiated way to the needs of the school community, school social workers can influence the development of their roles in particular schools.

The process of influencing the development of a role may be conceptualized as resting on role conception and role perception. *Role conception* is how each person conceives of his or her role as a school social worker and his or her own initiative in developing that role. After all, if I do not clearly see possibilities or I am afraid to develop them, not much will happen. It will rest on my own theoretical clarity regarding the needs and capabilities inherent in the situation (including my own needs and capabilities). It will also rest on my self-confidence, my competence, my ability to develop a network of relationships, and, within this network, my ability to work with others to develop workable solutions to problems that have reached our thresholds of perception.

Role perception is the way others perceive my role and the way I reflect that perception in what I do. It reflects an assessment of the networks of the local school building and district and their preferred organization. It is profoundly influenced by national policies and laws. It is defined by standards of good practice as they have developed within the field of school social work and the relation of these to the needs of the school community.

Role development is the product of the interaction between what the school social worker brings to the situation, the perceptions of others, and the actual conditions of the school community. People's perceptions of a role are tested and evaluated in relation to the needs, capabilities, and social networks of a particular school and the outcome, the *product* that results and its influence on the experience students have of education.

SCHOOL SOCIAL WORK PRACTICE THEORY

The dynamic relation between school social work and education generates the purpose and scope of practice and the techniques used. When this relationship is clarified according to the needs of particular situations, practice then becomes free to grow in the directions that are consistent with its purpose.

The Fundamental Orientation of Social Work

In order to develop a theoretical base for school social work, we first need to articulate a concept of the fundamental orientation of social work across all fields of practice. A major achievement of the past several decades has been that a fundamental orientation to further professional differentiation has been clearly defined. This was done by the Task Force on Specialization, of which Carol Meyer and William E. Gordon were members. The task force was jointly sponsored by the National Association of Social Workers (NASW) and the Council on Social Work Education:

The fundamental zone of social work is where people and their environment are in exchange with each other. Social work historically has focused on the transaction zone where the exchange between people and the environment which impinge on them results in changes in both. Social work intervention aims at the coping capabilities of people and the demands and resources of their environment so that the transactions between them are helpful to both. Social work's concern extends to both the dysfunctional and deficient conditions at the juncture between people and their environment, and to the opportunities there for producing growth and improving the environment. It is the duality of focus on people and their environments that distinguishes social work from other professions (Garber, Gordon, Lewis, Meyer, and Williams, 1979).

The duality of focus in the above statement involves the integration of *personal* tasks and *social* tasks in the characteristic perspective of social work. The personal and the social can be brought together with a concept of relational work as it takes place on an interpersonal level and in every institutional area of society. This relational work is done by client systems and institutions with the social worker as a coach for what is being done, moving person and systems toward reflective understanding and action. The *work* of the social worker is to facilitate the relational *work* taking place in the context of human values. The practice of social work must deal *with values and in values.* It can never be composed of pure technique. Differentiation of social work is not based on different methods, but on a relation between method, social processes, and human purposes and values.

Social workers practice in the arena where human beings work with others to perform life tasks and achieve fundamental human goods where achievement or provision is at risk and where human vulnerability or circumstances make it difficult for the outcome of the work to reflect the full worth of persons and their membership unit. Risk and vulnerability come for many people with the performance of life tasks and with life transitions. Vulnerability may come in utilizing personal and institutional resources for coping. Personal and developmental vulnerabilities are compounded by the inevitable deficiencies of institutions. Paul Tillich commented on the philosophy of social work in confronting the influx of refugees in 1940. From his perspective, legal and organizational arrangements "inevitably fail" (Tillich, 1962) but social workers can intervene with people who experience those failures and with the systems that often fail. Changes and adjustments in persons and institutions in relation to each other are the province of the social worker.

The social worker is a catalyst for the personal, familial, and institutional work to be done for the best match between resources and life tasks, in accord with the essential values of human nature. The practitioner is skillful to the extent that he or she can bring a person or a set of persons to work on a problem, and in the process of that work to learn, to grow, and to change, while simultaneously influencing others in an altered transaction. Assessment of what is happening and what can happen between person and environment is the crucial skill in the change process. Personal and societal change comes from doing. Much of the catalytic effect of social work is through helping people to reflect and modify actions. This process of being a catalyst to action demands an assessment both of the process itself and of the limits of the possible within the situation in relation to purpose. Such assessment, used by the social worker and made available to those he or she works with—in fact done jointly with them—objectifies for the social worker and for the client the nature of the tasks, the risks, the process, and the persons. It thus begins to reconcile the subjective and objective aspects of helping; indeed, assessment could be seen as the master skill.

The Practice of School Social Work

With this understanding of the orientation of social work, how may we define school social work as a field of practice, related to other fields of social work practice, and to social work education and theory? The Task Force on Specialization defined specialization in relation to the institutions that society has evolved to meet common human needs. These needs and their institutions were seen to include:

The need for physical and mental well-being—Health

The need to know and to learn—Education

The need for justice—Justice

The need for economic security—Work/public assistance

The need for self realization, intimacy, and relationships—Family and child welfare (Garber et al., 1979)

In each area, the social worker works as a professional and mediates a relationship between persons and institutions. Fields of practice in social work grow around such transactions. Practice within each field is defined by a clientele, a point of entry, a social institution with its institutional purposes, and the contribution of social work practice, its knowledge, values, and appropriateness to the institutional purpose.

The school social worker makes education possible for many children who otherwise would have difficulty coping with the educational process as it takes place and is defined in school. The close association with education is not a limitation or narrowing of focus. In reality, it broadens the functions of the school social worker. If the mission of education is taken fully into account, the worker's efforts toward change in the school as an institution can be as fully explicated and developed as efforts toward change in the child and family. Again, changes in one will affect the other and vice versa. The nature of practice in school institutions brings social workers to accept fairly clearly a dual focus on individuals and environments. The school provides a natural setting for social work intervention, a setting that then calls forth a diversity of skills, working with individuals, neighborhoods, families, groups, teaching professionals, multidisciplinary teams, and educational decision makers. Thus within this framework there is an integration point from theories of individual helping, groups, families, school teams and organizations, and communities. The role, with its foundation in social work values and the values of American education, with its consciousness of the natural strengths in the ecological position of the school with families and children, becomes the point of integration of theory from all the above areas. The school social worker's role becomes a part of the latent natural dynamics of the educational process. The school social worker only needs to recognize this relation and work with it to create powerful tools for change processes. The school social worker assists each sector of the ecosystem—the community, the school organization with its teams and its classes, families, peer groups, and schoolchildren—to discover its own resources and helps all sectors find ways to work together. Versions of this role have existed since the earliest days of school social work, and it is a magnificent mission!

To understand how change takes place we must understand the ecological position of the school. A social worker who operates in relation to the mandate of the school is part of an institution that, in the most profound way, mediates success and failure, belongingness and nonbelongingness for children in our society. Only the family may have a more powerful influence. The centrality of the school to all natural ecosystems of childhood provides an opportunity for a unique blend of social work practice. The school is intertwined with just about everything that happens to children. The image of self developed in the classroom, among other places, is carried throughout a person's lifetime. Problems outside of school are reflected in the school environment. The ecological perspective is useful in developing an understanding of the child in school, in the community, and in the family precisely because it allows a focus on interaction with the environment and not on the person alone. Behavior in the classroom may be understood better by understanding its context, its relations to other settings, and the relation of these settings to each other. As one learns to develop an "ecological map" of the important transactions and relations between systems, one may build on the understanding developed. Choices can be made of where to intervene and, through an understanding of the developmental history of behaviors, *when* an intervention may be most effective.

Thus theory for school social work practice grows out of this constant interaction of *clientele, point of entry, institutional setting* and *social work knowledge,* and *values* in the context of human development and the education process. Such theory responds to changes in education and its mission and in the conditions and contexts of children's development as they concretely take place in particular schools.

Building on generic social work knowledge and values, there are then three levels of this learning of school social work practice. These three levels are *learning* a knowledge and theory base, *integrating* theory in practice, and *generalizing* from one's own and others' experiences to a personal practice model in school social work.

The knowledge and theory base is drawn from the following:

1. *Knowledge of the educational institution,* its legal and sociological base as an expression of community values; knowledge of its organization, including financing; familiarity with and understanding of the language and concepts used by educators;

2. *Knowledge of programs for schoolchildren with special needs,* the philosophy and methodology of these programs, and the implications of different types of special education programs for pupil adjustment;

3. *Familiarity with principles of curriculum development* and teaching methods; understanding of the differential effects of teaching styles on children; ability to contribute helpfully as a social worker in a consultative relationship with teachers and school administrators; and

4. *Deepened understanding of the nature of developmental crises* and children's responses to stress; understanding of familial, institutional, and community dynamics in relation to the behavior of children.

The student's integration of theory in practice takes place as theory is tested in a field experience in school. Again, building on generic practice theory, the student's integration of theory in practice should result in the following general outcomes:

1. *The ability to operate as a practitioner in the complex organization of the school* with parents, with teachers, and with schoolchildren, in carrying out a given intervention plan. The student should have tested experience working in the context of professional difference, familiarity with the role difference of other specialists, and ability to collaborate and communicate in a purposeful way.

2. *The ability to participate as a social worker in planning efforts* geared toward curriculum and program development; the ability to initiate planning efforts when necessary and provide professionally appropriate supervision and consultation; the ability to communicate regarding school needs from one's professional point of view to the community.

The integration of theory in practice and the process of generalization from one's own experience and that of their students into a *personal practice model* would take place through an integrative seminar in school that is closely related to the *field experience* and through the field experience itself.

A HISTORICAL ANALYSIS OF SCHOOL SOCIAL WORK

During the past eighty years of its existence, school social work as a field of practice has addressed the increasing expectations of education in a complex and modernized society. The problems confronted by the educational institution over its long history have ranged from the presence of old and continuing problems, such as large immigrant populations, truancy, and the tragic waste of potential in emotional disturbances of childhood, to newer problems, such as school disruption, homelessness, drugs, the new immigrants, and AIDS. The focus of school social work has followed the historic concerns of education. The diversity of problems the school social worker has dealt with historically, and faces at the present moment, is immense and ever changing.

Although we are only beginning to clarify a theory base for school social work, the function of the social worker in the school and the mandate for public education were closely intertwined from the beginning. Given the mandate for equal opportunity for all in a democracy, the exclusion of any person from participation in education is both a societal and an individual problem. The passage of the mandatory school attendance laws at the turn of the century is credited with beginning a revolution in secondary school education. Schools began to broaden their curricula to accommodate a greater diversity of students. The first social workers in schools, in 1907 in New York City, were hired in recognition of the fact that conditions that prevented the school from carrying out its mandate were its legitimate concern (Costin, 1978; Meares, 1986). School social work would draw its legitimacy and its function from its capability to make education work for groups of children who could not otherwise participate. It has reflected in its history the evolving awareness in education, and in society, of groups of children for whom education has not been effective—the children of immigrants, the impoverished, the economically and socially oppressed, the delinquent, the disturbed, and the disabled. It drew its function from the needs and eventually the rights of these groups as they interfaced with the institution of education and confronted the expectation that they should achieve to their fullest potential. In each circumstance, as school social workers defined their roles, there was a match of the social work perspective, its knowledge, values, and skills, and the missions and mandates of the school.

The first school social workers in Hartford, Connecticut, and New York City carried in their models of practice the unresolved questions of the broader social work field, for example, the differences between Mary Richmond and Jane Addams in their respective visions of practice. The Hartford group, established at the same time as the New York group, became part of a psychological clinic and dealt with the psychosocial problems that children brought to school and that impeded their educational perform-ance. They reflected Mary Richmond's approach to social work practice. In contrast, the New York group came from the settlement house tradition. They were primarily concerned with the environmental problems that pre-vented children of immigrants from using their opportunities for an educa-tion and reflected more the intellectual influence of Jane Addams than of Mary Richmond.

The basic issues and possible future direction in the maturation of school social work practice and theory were laid out in the Milford Confer-ence Report. By the end of the 1920s a wide range of fields of practice had organized themselves around the different settings of school, hospital, court, settlement house, child welfare agency, family service agency, and so forth. Social work education followed an apprenticeship model, teaching what were perceived to be highly specialized and segmented fields of practice. The question of what all of these fields had in common became extremely important. In 1929, at the Milford Conference, the basic distinction be-tween fields of practice, the *specific* practice that emerged from these fields and the *generic* base for practice in these fields—that is, the knowledge, values, and skills of casework—was established. This distinction was ex-tremely important for social work education and for the field of school social work in that it allowed each field of practice to flourish and develop on a common foundation of casework. The emergent field was indeed diverse. Furthermore, no theory had emerged that could do more than offer a gen-eral orientation to helping. It still was up to the learner-practitioner and supervisor to find a way to relate theory to practice. This situation would continue in various permutations of the history of theory for more than half a century. The casework theory identified as generic would not refer to a concrete practice separable from its manifestation in different fields. There was no "generic" practice but generic knowledge, values, and skills would be a foundation for a further differentiation of practice. The casework foundation of the 1920s and 1930s did not focus simply on individuals, as later versions did, but on persons and family units together. It was much more than a simple methodological base since it included knowledge and values, but it was still a conceptual foundation for specific practice. Free-standing practice took place in fields of practice that would develop from settings but would also be reflected in academic and field preparation. Prac-tice differentiation took place in relation to specific, identified fields, such as school social work, medical social work, psychiatric social work, child welfare, family services, and so on. Grace Marcus clarified the distinction between *generic* and *specific*:

The term generic does not apply to any actual, concrete practice of an agency or field but refers to an essential, common property of casework knowledge, ideas and skills which caseworkers of every field must command if they are to perform adequately their specific jobs. As for our other troublemaking word, "specific," it refers to the form casework takes within the particular administrative setting; it is the manifest use to which the generic store of knowledge has been put in meeting the particular purposes, problems, and conditions of the agency in dispensing its particular resources (Marcus, 1938–39).

The distinction was important, not only for its ability to permit professional differentiation on a common foundation, but also because later versions began to separate a body of method theory, such as casework, from its specific manifestation in fields of practice.

Considerable development of school social work as a field of practice had already taken place from the mid-1920s through 1955. This growth trailed off by 1955 with the consolidation of NASW which had merged then-existing organizations, representing different fields of practice, into one single professional organization. The *Bulletin* of the American Association of Visiting Teachers was merged into the new journal of the united social work profession, *Social Work*. The period of the 1950s and 1960s were centralizing years. School social work literature dropped off with the loss of the *Bulletin*. However, at that point, the major concern in the professional literature, in the profession, and in social work education had to do with what social workers had in common, not what made them different in different sectors of the profession.

By the late 1950s, and through the following decade, Harriett Bartlett's and others' work built the foundation for a reorientation of methods and skills to a clarified professional perspective of the social worker. Bartlett (1959, 1970) worked with William E. Gordon (1969) to elaborate the concept of the transaction between individuals and their social environments into a common base and a fundamental beginning point for social work. This concept was cited earlier in this chapter in the report of the NASW Task Force on Specialization (Garber et al., 1979). Shifting the focus to the person-environment transaction, it was no longer assumed that the individual was the primary object of help. The development and diffusion of group and environmental interventions and the use of a range of helping modalities in richly differentiated areas of practice would make Gordon and Bartlett's work useful.

During the late 1960s there arose a renewed interest in developing theory and practice in areas such as school social work. "Generic" approaches to practice in every field were no longer adequate for the practice that was emerging. There was a gradual redevelopment of literature, journals, and regional associations of social workers in different fields of practice. School social work had large numbers of experienced practitioners who were encouraged to remain in direct practice by the structure and incentives of the school field. These were some of the first and strongest advocates of a movement to develop practice and theory in their own area in the mid- to late 1970s. With the development of state school social work associations, and then school social work journals, the search for some balance between centralizing and standardizing thrusts and the thrust of specific practice began again. The profession in its development of theory revisited the balance of generic and specific in practice theory. Each student would struggle with this balance also in his or her attempts to match classroom theory with fieldwork in a school.

At present school social work appears to be most mature in regions where it has been free to develop its distinct model of practice in relation to the mission, process, and organizational and legal structure of *education* (as distinguished from a particular school). The difficult demands placed on present-day schools make school social work, not a luxury, but a necessity if schools are to accomplish their societal mandate. In special education, the rights of every child with disabilities to a free appropriate public education have been more and more explicitly defined over the past thirty years. The resulting role of the school social worker has shifted from a focus on youngsters who do not meet normative expectations to a focus on implementing individualized approaches to learning and influencing the norms themselves on behalf of youngsters. School social work service was a humane attempt on the school's part to help youngsters; it is now in many cases an entitlement, a civil right of every youngster with disabilities who needs this type of help in order to benefit from an education. The societal expectations for the present-day school have in turn demanded a more complete understanding and interpretation of the distinct contribution of the school social worker. It is no accident that a major portion of the literature has concerned itself with the parameters of the school social work role. The institution of education is not simply a backdrop for some type of standard practice. In the blending of social work with the mission of education, a distinct and different practice emerges. The characteristics of the educational institution are as integral a part of school social work practice as are the dynamics of the school community and the coping behaviors of the school's clientele.

REFERENCES

Bartlett, H. 1959. The generic-specific concept in social work education and practice. In A. E. Kahn (ed.). *Issues in American social work.* NY: Columbia University Press.

Bartlett, H. 1970. *The common base of social work practice.* NY: National Association of Social Workers.

Biddle, B. J. 1997. Foolishness, dangerous nonsense, and the real correlates of state differences in achievement. *Kappan* 79(1):8–13.

Brown v. Board of Education, Topeka, KS. 347 U.S. 483 (1954).

Constable, R., Kuzmickaite, D., and Volkmann, L. 1997. The Indiana school social worker: Parameters of an emerging professional role. Paper given at the Indiana State Association of School Social Workers annual conference, October 21.

Council on Social Work Education. 1992. *Curriculum policy statement for accreditation of schools of social work.* Alexandria, VA: Council on Social Work Education.

Garber, R., Gordon, W. E., Lewis, H., Meyer, C., and Williams, C. 1979. *Specialization in the social work profession.* NASW Document no. 79-310-08. Washington, DC: National Association of Social Workers.

Gordon, W. E. 1969. Basic constructs for an integrative and generative conception of social work. In G. Hearn (ed.). *The general system approach: Contributions towards an holistic conception of social work.* NY: Council on Social Work Education.

Marcus, G. 1938–39. The generic and specific in social work: Recent developments in our thinking. *News-letter* (American Association of Psychiatric Social Workers) 3/4.

Mintzies, P., and Hare, I. 1985. *The human factor: A key to excellence in education.* Washington, DC: National Association of Social Workers.

Nelson, C. 1990. A *job analysis of school social workers.* Princeton, NJ: Educational Testing Service.

Poole, F. 1949. An analysis of the characteristics of the school social worker. *Social Service Review* 23 (December): 454–59.

Tillich, P. 1962. The philosophy of social work. *Social Service Review* 36(1).

CHAPTER 2

The Contribution of Social Workers to Schooling—Revisited*

Paula Allen-Meares
Professor and Dean, School of Social Work, University of Michigan;
Chair, NASW Communication Committee

- Historical Development of Social Work Services in Schools
- Social Work Values
- Future Directions and Challenges

Many educators are unfamiliar with the services provided by social workers employed in the school setting. The purpose of this chapter is to describe the history of the service and those who shaped it, and its values and contribution to schooling with particular reference to entry level tasks required for professional practice. Relevant literature in education and social work is also reviewed.

The breadth and diversity of school social work is illustrated, to some degree, in the publication *Achieving Educational Excellence for Children at Risk* (Hawkins, 1987), which describes the goals and services offered by the profession. Examples include the provision of group work to gifted children, transitional programming for disabled children, forming partnerships with families of the disabled, early intervention to prevent truancy, a special project to prevent adolescent suicide, ways to facilitate racial integration, and expanding schooling to involve multicultural communities. A review of the history of school social work highlights its flexibility and adaptability as a field of practice.

HISTORICAL DEVELOPMENT OF SOCIAL WORK SERVICES IN SCHOOLS

Social work services in schools grew out of concern for underprivileged pupils. The service began during the school year of 1906–1907, indepen-

*SOURCE: *Urban Education*, 22(4), January 1988, 401–312. © 1988. Paula Meares. Reprinted by permission of Sage Publications, Inc. Adapted for this publication.

dently, in New York City, Boston, and Hartford. In New York City, settlement workers from Hartley House and Greenwich House thought that it was necessary to know the teachers of children who came to the settlements, so they assigned two workers to visit schools and homes in order to work more closely with schools and community groups to promote understanding and communication (Allen-Meares et al., 1986). In Boston, the Women's Education Association placed visiting teachers in the schools to foster harmony between school and home and facilitate the children's education.

The Psychological Clinic in Hartford initiated the first visiting teachers program (today frequently referred to as school social workers) in that area. It was the function of the visiting teacher to assist the psychologist to secure family and developmental histories of children and to implement the clinic's treatment recommendation (Lide, 1959). The first board of education to initiate and finance a visiting teachers program was in Rochester, New York, in 1913. The board of education at that time stated:

> This is the first step in an attempt to meet a need that the school system has been conscious of for some time. It is an undisputed fact that in the environment outside of school are to be found forces that will often thwart the school in its endeavors. The appointment of visiting teachers is an attempt on the part of the school to meet its responsibilities for the whole welfare of the child ... and to maximize cooperation between the home and the school (Lide, 1959: 108).

During the decades that followed, school social workers grew in number and the focus of the service changed in response to important influences of the times. For example, one significant influence in the field's early development was the passage of compulsory school attendance laws, which grew out of the concern for the illiteracy of immigrant children and brought needed attention to the child's right to at least a minimum education. The lack of effective enforcement of the school attendance laws led to such studies as that of Abbott and Breckinridge (1917) on nonattendance in Chicago schools. Their findings supported the need for attendance officers (another term to designate the school social worker) who understood the social ills of the community—poverty, ill health, and lack of secure family income—and their effects on attendance. Attendance workers played an important role, clarifying and sensitizing school personnel to the effects that children's out-of-school lives had on them. Thus the principal activity of the school social worker, at that time, was one of home-school-community liaison.

Oppenheimer (1925) carried out a study to obtain a detailed list of school social work tasks. The study involved the analysis of 300 case reports made by school social workers or visiting teachers, resulting in a list of 32 core functions. An appraisal of the nature of these tasks confirmed the school-family-community liaison as the primary role of these practitioners. Oppenheimer also concluded that the most important function of the school social workers was to aid in the reorganization of school administration and practices by supplying evidence of unfavorable conditions that underlie pupils' school difficulties and by pointing out needed changes.

As a result of the mental hygiene movement, the services expanded in the 1920s to include a therapeutic role (Lide, 1959). There was increasing interest on the part of the school social worker to understand behavior problems of pupils and techniques to prevent social maladjustment.

During the 1930s, the role of attendance officers gradually took on a new dimension: individual work with children and their families, later referred to as social casework. With the advent of the Great Depression, the provision of food, shelter, clothing, and emotional support for troubled pupils occupied much of the school social workers' attention. In addition, there were those at the time who saw the sources of problems not as inherent in the personality of the troubled pupil, but the result of a faulty school curriculum and policies (Reynolds, 1935).

During the 1940s to 1960s, home-school liaison and the attendance officer's role were essentially replaced by social casework. No longer would social change and neighborhood conditions be seen as targets of intervention.

The 1960s brought still another change in goals and methods of school social work practice (Sarri and Maple, 1972). Public schools were under attack. Several studies of public education documented adverse school policies. It was claimed that inequality of educational opportunity existed as a result of segregation; that public schools were reinforcing the myth that minority children and pupils from low-income backgrounds could not perform as well as their middle-class counterparts; and that the school was essentially a repressive institution (Kerner Report, 1968). Some parents claimed they felt alienated from the school. Simultaneously, the literature on school social work was advocating group work with parents and students, broader approaches to practice, drawing upon a social systems perspective, and methods and demonstration projects to bring the school and community closer together to facilitate the educational process (Sarri and Maple, 1972). The school was essentially singled out for the violence of the 1960s because it had failed to educate minority pupils.

For social work services in the schools, the 1970s were a time of great expansion. The numbers of programs and workers across the United States increased. There was an increased emphasis on family, community, and teaming with other school personnel, and broader models were encouraged (Alderson, 1972). One model, widely discussed in the literature and intended to address the problems of securing equal educational opportunity for all pupils, was the school-community-pupil relations model (Costin, 1975). This model emphasized the complexities of the interactions among students, the school, and the community. Its primary goal was to bring about change in the interaction of this triad and thus to modify to some extent those harmful school policies and practices and community conditions that undermined schooling.

Influences on the school social worker role have been explored by Constable, Flynn, and McDonald (1991), who found that litigation, federal legislation, and other influences have a profound impact on the activities of school social workers. Factors that have played a role include: legislation such as the Education for All Handicapped Children Act, 1975; changes in the theoretical perspective grounding social work practice; an increased emphasis placed on ecological and social systems approaches; and pressures from the social work profession to evaluate outcomes and to be accountable.

As the school setting became the institution targeted to rectify deprivation in the home, community, and family, once more its strategic position in the network of human services was recognized. A content analysis of social work literature over the period 1968–1978 found that school social workers were once again expanding their focus (Allen-Meares and Lane, 1982). Though more attention was given to children with disabling conditions, the liaison role was emphasized, as well as the role of promoting change in adverse school policies and practice. Consultation, teaming, and collaborative activities suggested a move away from long-term clinical treatment to an approach that had breadth in terms of tasks, and that was responsive to changing needs and conditions.

As social conditions (e.g., poverty, unemployment, and so forth) continued to place children and their families at greater risk and the federal government saw legislation as the mechanism to best address various groups who needed educational assistance, school social workers grew in number and so did their state associations. In response to this growth, the National Association of Social Workers held special school social work conferences as part of its annual meeting. A review of conference programs reaffirmed the expansion of the service and its resiliency to respond to changing needs. These special conferences focused on work with infants, the role of the school social worker in early childhood special education, school reform, how school social workers could facilitate a multicultural school environment, and social work practice with new populations (e.g., chemically exposed infants, youth infected with AIDS, and those who were homeless).

The debate about the quality of education from the report of the National Commission on Excellence in Education (1983) and the national cry to reform schooling led to a national study of state offices of education to identify reform initiatives to achieve excellence as well as conditions that were barriers to academic excellence (Allen-Meares, 1987). Allen-Meares (1987) maintained that the impetus for the study also evolved from concern about the erosion of federal support for social welfare programs for vulnerable children and their families. At the time, the call for school reform and improvement in the achievement of pupils ignored the consequences of racism, sexism, inadequate health care, poverty, and economic deprivation on the physical, emotional, psychological, and intellectual growth of children and adolescents. The study found that excellence was defined by having an effective school administrator; maintaining high expectations for students and staff; involving students in learning; and eradicating school problems. Reform initiates were: appointment of blue ribbon committees; pressure on the legislature to increase funding; an increase in scholastic requirements for teachers and pupils; and more attention to math and science. Barriers to excellence in education were: parental apathy, poverty, child abuse and neglect, family crisis; poor parenting skills; economic deprivation; poor parent-teacher relationships; lack of drop-out prevention programs and team work among school personnel; and lack of financial resources. It was clear that school social workers could play a variety of direct practice roles to minimize the impact of such barriers; however, systemic change was also in order.

During this time, the number of state associations of school social workers increased. Today there are 25 state associations, and many hold annual conferences and publish independent newsletters. Twenty state NASW chapters now have school social work committees. There are also four regional councils: the Midwest School Social Work Council; the Southern School Social Work Council; the Western Alliance of School Social Workers; and the Northeastern Coalition. In 1994, spearheaded by the school social work leadership, a School Social Work Association of America formed, independent of NASW. These state, regional, and national professional associations provide their members with educational opportunities for professional growth through the provision of yearly workshops, job networks, continuing education credit, and legislative advocacy. There are currently 12,000–15,000 school social workers nationally.

Also in 1994, NASW launched school social work as the first practice section. During the period of 1980 until the present, NASW has taken an active role in changing the credentialing requirements for school social workers. Many states upgraded their credentialing standards for school personnel as a part of their efforts to reform schooling. For example, in Illinois, social work practitioners seeking employment in the public schools must complete special graduate school social work courses and take two exams (one that tests knowledge of such areas as educational legislation, exceptional children, school code, models of school social work practice, social work values, ethics, and interventions, and another exam which tests for basic skills competencies, in reading, math, and English).

In anticipation of the proliferation of school social work credentialing exams, NASW, the Educational Testing Service in Princeton, New Jersey, and Allen-Meares developed the first national school social work credential examination. The exam was first administered in 1992. The content of the exam was developed from data obtained from a national sample of school social work practitioners (Allen-Meares, 1994). This study had essentially four purposes:

1. To collect information about the demographic and organizational contexts in which school social workers work;
2. To identify the most important job dimensions that school social workers must be able to perform as they begin their practice;
3. To ascertain whether these job dimensions correlate positively or negatively in terms of frequency performed; and
4. To identify and compare tasks school social workers prefer to perform and those that are mandated.

Preferred and Mandated Tasks

Respondents to the survey considered the following tasks in rank order as most important: 1) *administrative and professional tasks,* 2) *home-school liaison,* 3) *educational counseling with children,* 4) *facilitating and advocating families' use of community resources,* and 5) *leadership and policy-making.* The size of the employing school district significantly influenced the importance given to some tasks. An analysis of tasks contained in each job dimension was conducted to differentiate tasks that were mandated from those that were preferred. Mandated tasks would be to make home visits or to refer children and their families for service. Tasks school social workers preferred to perform would be to act as advocate with community agencies, to help new staff understand diversity, or to help develop prevention programs. Further analysis of these data led the researcher to conclude that the practice of school social work is influenced by a number of contextual variables that are beyond the control of the practitioner. Large caseloads, expectations by supervisors and administrators, multi-building assignments and too few workers were identified as variables that prevented practitioners from embracing their preferred tasks.

In 1994, known as the Year of Education Reform, school social workers were once more included in a major piece of legislation—Goals 2000: Educate America Act, P.L.102-227. This act was signed into law on March 31, 1994. The intent of the act is to promote research, consensus building, and systemic change to ensure quality of educational opportunities for all students.

This major piece of legislation targets reform initiatives particular to schools, but major social and technological-economic changes in the broader society may prevent it from achieving equity in educational opportunity. For example, an increasing number of children and female-headed households live in poverty; technological advancements require a more sophisticated labor force; reform in welfare and health care are still topics of debate

TABLE 1   Social Work Values

Social Work Values	Applications to Social Work in Schools
1. Recognition of the worth and dignity of each human being	1. Each pupil is valued as an individual regardless of any unique characteristic
2. The right to self-determination or self-realization	2. Each pupil should be allowed to share in the learning process
3. Respect for individual potential and support for an individual's aspirations to attain it	3. Individual differences (including differences in rate of learning) should be recognized; intervention should be aimed at supporting pupils' education goals
4. The right of each individual to be different from every other and to be accorded respect for those differences	4. Each child, regardless of race and socioeconomic characteristics, has a right to equal treatment in the school

SOURCE: Adapted from Allen-Meares et al. (1986)

without firm proposals for real change; there is a call for more community control of schools; and violence in the community and in schools is at an all-time high.

SOCIAL WORK VALUES

It can be readily seen from this brief account of historical development that the goals of the school social work profession have expanded greatly since its modest beginnings at the turn of the century. Examples of primary values of the social work profession and their applications in school social work practices are shown in Table 1.

Examples of other values compatible with those of the profession as a whole but having special relevance to school social work are (1) children are entitled to equal educational opportunities and to learning experiences adapted to their individual needs and (2) the process of education should not only provide the child with tools for future learning and skills to use in earning a living, but provide essential ingredients contributing to the child's positive mental health (Allen-Meares et al., 1986).

FUTURE DIRECTIONS AND CHALLENGES

Questions about the quality of schooling, reduced tax base, the increased demand on schools to serve a more diverse student population, increased poverty among children and families, and violence will challenge this field of practice to think critically and differently about school social work service delivery. For the twenty-first century, the integration of school social work and community services will be essential. It is clear that schools cannot respond to the social, emotional, and educational needs of all their pupils. The capacity of the community to devote its resources to enhance the availability and scope of social supports will be a decisive factor in the health and functioning of its children and families. Thus, collaboration between the different service delivery systems within the school, as well as those external to it, will also be essential.

What does this mean for school social work services? There will be an increased emphasis on developing a service delivery system involving collaboration between schools and community agencies both private and public. Clearly, practitioners will need to rethink and restructure their roles within the school. The challenge is to redefine school social work to meet such a major shift in our society.

REFERENCES

Abbott, E. and Breckenridge, S. 1917. *Truancy and non-attendance in the Chicago schools: A study of the social aspects of compulsory education and child labor legislation of Illinois*. Chicago: University of Chicago Press.

Alderson, J. 1972. Models of school social work practice. In R. Sarri and F. Maple (eds). *School in the community*. Washington, DC: National Association of Social Workers.

Allen-Meares, P. and Lane, B. 1982. A content analysis of school social work literature: 1968–1978. In R. Constable and J. Flynn (eds.). *School social work: Practice and research perspectives*. Homewood, IL: Dorsey Press. 39–49.

Allen-Meares, P., Washington, R.O., and Welsh, B. 1996. *Social work services in schools*. Needham, MA. Allyn & Bacon.

Allen-Meares, P. 1987. A national study of educational reform: Social work practice in schools. *Children and Youth Services Review* 9(3):207–19.

Allen-Meares, P. 1994. Social work services in schools: A national study. *Social Work* 39(4):560–67.

Constable, R., Flynn, J., and McDonald, S., (eds). 1991. *School social work: Practice and research perspectives*. Chicago, IL. Lyceum Books, Inc.

Costin, L. 1975. School social work practice: A new model. *Social Work* 20 (21): 135–39.

Education for All Handicapped Children Act. 1975. P.L. 94–142.

Goals 2000: Educate America Act. 1994. P.L. 103–227.

Hawkins, M. (ed.). 1987. *Achieving educational excellence for children at risk*. Washington, DC: National Association of Social Workers.

Kerner Report. 1968. The National Advisory Committee on Civil Disorder. Washington, DC: Government Printing Office.

Lide, P. 1959. "A study of historical influences of major importance in determining the present function of the school social worker." In G. Lee (ed.). *Helping the troubled school child in school social work, 1935–1955*. Washington, D.C. National Association of Social Workers.

National Commission on Excellence in Education. 1983. *A nation at risk: The imperative for educational reform*. Washington, DC: Government Printing Office.

Oppenheimer, J. 1925. *The visiting teacher movement, with special reference to administrative relationships*. 2nd ed. NY: Joint Committee on Methods of Preventing Delinquency.

Reynolds, B. 1935. "Social casework: What is it? What is its place in the world today?" *Family* 16 (December): 238.

Sarri, S. and Maple, F. (eds.). 1972. *School in the community*. Washington, D.C. National Association of Social Workers.

CHAPTER 3

An Ecological Perspective on Social Work in the Schools

Carel B. Germain
Emerita Professor of Social Work, School of Social Work,
University of Connecticut

- The Dual Function of Social Work
- Primary Prevention
- Influencing the School

One of the most difficult tasks for all of social work practice is to define its distinctiveness—what distinguishes the social worker from other professional helpers. In fact, this is not even a new task. In 1915 Abraham Flexner was invited to speak before the National Conference of Charities and Corrections. He was the social scientist who modernized medical education in this country, bringing it up from the depths of inadequate proprietary schools and into the universities. Because of his achievement and his resulting status in the arena of professional education, Flexner's appearance at the national conference was eagerly awaited. He would be speaking to an occupational group whose members called themselves social workers and who aspired to professional status. Imagine the consternation, then, as the speaker informed his audience that, indeed, they were not a profession nor could they reasonably aspire to becoming one because they did not have a distinctive professional knowledge base or skills that were transmissible (Flexner, 1915).

Furthermore, and this must have been the crowning blow, their only function was a mediating one for linking up their clients to other professions, and invoking their power in solving the client's problem. The impact on the audience can be sensed in the responses of those present as preserved in the conference proceedings. But the reponses echoed down the years as social work continually tried to define its distinctiveness and to establish its professional status. In particular, the casework segment devoted time, energy, and thought to developing a distinctive knowledge and value base and distinctive skills which then became confused with those of other pro-

SOURCE: Adapted from a paper presented at the New York State Conference of School Social Workers, White Plains, New York, May 22, 1978.

fessions on whom they were patterned, especially psychiatry. The efforts left undeveloped until the present day what might have been a truly distinctive function. Flexner's indictment of the mediating function, and Mary Richmond's refusal (1917) to accept it as a social work function, are particularly ironic in today's world. It is clear that what is needed in this dehumanized and depersonalized bureaucractic society is a profession that mediates between people in need—particularly the poor and other powerless groups such as children and the aged—and the institutions of society set up to serve them. Ironic, because this increasingly important function so ably performed by social work, does indeed rest upon an identifiable and transmissible base of knowledge, values, and skill.

In some ways, school social work followed the same historical trends of the larger professional group. Originally conceived as a response to problems of truancy created by free, compulsory public education, school social work was expected to uncover and to mitigate neighborhood and school conditions that gave rise to truancy (Costin, 1969). For many historical reasons, school social work, by the 1930s, had narrowed its focus to a casework service for children who were defined by the school as having emotional and behavioral disturbances attributable to early family experiences. The number of children thus served was necessarily small; there was little impact on adverse school structures and practices, and the service itself tended to become stigmatized.

By the 1960s and 70s, however, schools and school social work faced new imperatives generated by new social forces. The numbers of alienated pupils and high school dropouts increased. The school's ability to teach fundamental skills to many children declined, especially those pupils whose lifestyles and languages differed from the middle-class orientation of the school. Overt conflict between communities and schools for control of educational processes increased. The pain and stress accompanying the struggle for desegregation, the worry that schools might actually be undermining the creativity and spontaneity of all pupils, and the recognition that schools solidified the inequities of social class became salient forces in the field of school social work (Rist, 1970). In addition, every profession is now under attack on issues of effectiveness, ethical practice, and accountability. Insistence on public control of all professions is mounting and many of the consequent reforms, such as equal educational opportunities for the disabled, are long overdue. These reforms do pose new issues of formal and informal labeling, confidentiality, and even service provisions when so much time is required by the new accountability procedures and forms.

THE DUAL FUNCTION OF SOCIAL WORK

The profession's struggle for distinctiveness, that began in 1915, also influenced the development of school social work within this set of contemporary forces. William Gordon (1969) and Harriett Bartlett (1970), under the auspices of NASW, constructed a definition of social work practice that suggests social work's uniqueness lies in its location in the interface area where people's coping patterns interact with the qualities of their impinging environment. Thus, the social worker's function is to work in that interface with the person, the environment, or both, in order to secure a better match between coping needs and environmental requirements and people's coping abilities. This definition means that the social worker—in any field of practice—has a dual and simultaneous function: to strengthen people's coping patterns and their growth potential on the one hand, and to improve the quality of the impinging environment on the other. This interface position does not negate the importance of the personality and its motivational, emotional, cognitive, and sensory-perceptual elements. But neither does it overlook the complexity of the environment and its interacting physical, social, and cultural elements. Rather, it takes both into account simultaneously and seeks to improve the transactions between them. Thus the old polarity between social workers who favor social action, and social workers who favor service to people can become, instead, a complementarity of two essential functions. This view of professional purpose can correct the imperfections in our commitment to person-situation which are apparent whenever we overlook one or the other. Most often, it is the situation that is overlooked, perhaps because it is the more difficult of the two to change.

An ecological metaphor for practice can respond to this dual function in a way that the traditional medical or disease metaphor cannot do (Germain, 1979). Ecology is the science of organism-environment relations. It leads to a view of person and environment as a unitary, interacting system in which each constantly affects and shapes the other. This view directs our professional attention to the whole, so that we attend to the complexities of the environment just as we attend to the complexities of the person, developing skills for intervening with each and with their transactions. The ecological metaphor also shifts us from an illness orientation to a health orientation, and to engaging the progressive forces in people and situational assets, and effecting the removal of environmental obstacles to growth and adaptive functioning.

Most school social workers have been practicing in just this way, conceiving their social purpose to be helping children develop age-appropriate social competence, and influencing the school to be more responsive to the needs of the children. William Schwartz (1971) characterizes this as helping the children reach out to the school and helping the school reach out to the children since each needs the other. Perhaps the reason that school social workers seem to be ahead of other sectors of practice in fulfilling the distinctive dual function of social work is because the school is a real-life ecological unit, beyond the realm of metaphor or analogy. The child clearly is in intimate interaction with the school, second in intensity only to the interaction of the child and family. But the school social worker literally is located at the interface where school and child transact, in a way that the family agency social worker or child welfare social worker, for example, can never be located with respect to the child-family transactions.

Actually, the school social worker stands at the interface not only of child and school, but family and school, and community and school. Thus, s/he is in a position to help child, parents, and community develop social competence and, at the same time, to help increase the school's responsiveness to the needs and aspirations of children, parents, and community. Social competence as a human attribute or achievement is tied to ideas of self-esteem and identity. It includes effectiveness with respect to knowing and deciding when to take action in the environment, as opposed to a passive orientation to life and its events and processes. It is tied also to relative autonomy from internal pressures and external demands, while maintaining relatedness to other human beings, to the world of nature, and to one's own internal needs (Germain, 1978). This appears to be a nonnormative set of ideas fitting any cultural context in any historical era, for it is the culture and the times that define the actual substance of such competence.

Robert White (1959) speaks of competence as the human being's innate drive to have an effect on the environment. Piaget refers to competence when he describes how children's intellects develop through opportunities to take action upon the environment, assimilating and accommodating the external into internal cognitive structures (Evans, 1973). The ego psychologists, in tracing the development of integrated ego functioning, are describing competence. Erikson's notion (1959) of school children's tasks of industry is a case in point. How children deal with the task depends, in part, on what they bring to it, on how they handled the earlier tasks of trust, autonomy, and initiative, and on what their physical states provide in health, vigor, stature, coordination, and so on. It will also depend on their cognitive, sensory-perceptual, and motivational equipment for adaptation and coping. But, and this is the value of Erikson's formulation for social work, their ability to achieve competence will also depend upon the qualities of the impinging social and physical environments, particularly the family, the school, and the community. These environments must provide the growth-inducing conditions and the right stimuli at the right time and in the right amount if children are to achieve the tasks involved in establishing industry and competence. Otherwise, they may be left with residues of inferiority—social, intellectual, physical, or emotional inferiority—that may affect their ability to handle later tasks. Three examples of interface work on competence follow: First, an example from the child-school interface:

> Jim, age 13, a newcomer in a middle school, was referred to the social worker. He had no friends, rebuffed the other boys, and didn't return teachers' greetings. He often seemed angry in class, and he was failing several subjects. Yet,

he had been an average student in elementary schools and had had friends and interests. During our first few interviews there was little mutuality, and I learned the meaning of patience all over again. Then one day Jim told me the family secret that his mother is an alcoholic. He was very angry with her for drinking and for the way she treated him as a baby when she was drunk. He was afraid to make new friends and of bringing them to the house for fear he might divulge the secret. His interest in school work had all but disappeared. Mother had given Jim this permission to talk freely, which I interpreted as her call for help. I saw her alone, and with my encouragement she began attending AA. Soon Jim expressed interest in catching up at school, and we worked out a tutoring plan that seemed to go well. Yet, his teachers were not recognizing his efforts and his changed motivation and were treating him with seeming dislike and annoyance. This stimulated his anger, which then provoked their further negative responses. Jim's problems, though not caused initially by the school, were now being perpetuated by school staff. I asked the principal to call a conference in which I explained to his teachers that Jim had realistic problems in his family that were being handled. I wanted them to see that Jim had real courage in tackling his problems—first alone and now with help. He was trying hard, but marked change will require more time and patience. At the end, one teacher commented she had not really thought of Jim with such sympathy before. Jim's grades are now improving, the teachers' attitudes toward Jim and his attitudes toward them are more positive. He made several friends and was busy with them during the past four Saturdays. He also told me his mother drank only once over the last month, and my impression is that he is less involved now in his mother's behavior. His whole bearing reflects his returning self-esteem, sense of competence, and even autonomy (Shelling, n.d.).

Second, an example from the parent-school interface:

The social worker in an inner city school in Brooklyn was concerned about poor relations between parents and the school which compounded the problems children were having in school. She persuaded the principal to turn over an unused room as a parents' drop-in lounge for those mothers bringing their small children to school each morning. She decorated it with plants and had coffee and doughnuts ready. She made each mother feel welcome and valued, and soon had a number of regulars who looked forward to the respite, the warmth, and attention given them by the school. After a bit she was able to engage two separate groups in meeting to talk to their shared needs and tasks as single parents living on limited budgets in a harsh environment. In the process, the mothers developed a mutual aid system, exchanging ideas, resources, and social support. Through social work intervention, the mothers' competence was enhanced and the school's responsiveness was increased. Anon.

A third example is from the community-school interface:

The social worker induced the elementary school in a Hispanic neighborhood to extend its boundary beyond its doors and out into its neighborhood. It became, in effect, a community center. The parents planned family life education and ethnic programs. They held evening forums for discussion of neighborhood issues of housing, welfare and health care. After-school recreational programs for the children were provided in the school yard, supervised by older siblings and adult volunteers. It is not surprising that this school enjoyed the full support of its community, and its children, parents, teachers, and community enjoyed a strengthened sense of competence, self-esteem, and identity (Phillips, 1978).

PRIMARY PREVENTION

There is another implication to be derived from the school social worker's distinctive dual function. As a profession, we feel pressed to move into the arena of life itself in order to prevent problems before they arise. The school social worker's location in the child's ecological context is critical to undertaking preventive tasks. The state of our knowledge does not yet permit us to claim the same preventive success that public health professionals achieve through vaccination and sanitation measures based on known etiology. Nevertheless, we have reason to believe that emotional innoculation and life-oriented growth experiences can stave off disorganization in the child, the family, and perhaps within the community.

From an ecological perspective, all organisms use adaptive processes to change their environments and/or to change themselves in order to reach and maintain a goodness-of-fit. In human beings, adaptation is the active, creative use of social and cultural processes to change environments so they will conform to human needs and aspirations. Humans also actively change themselves to conform to environmental requirements and expectations through biological and psychological processes. Human beings, however, never fully achieve a goodness-of-fit or adaptive balance with their environments because their needs and goals forever change, environments constantly change, and also because what people do to physical and social environments is often detrimental to their own functioning (Dubos, 1968).

This evolutionary, adaptive view of people and environments lends additional support to Gordon's (1969) formulation of the social work function as strengthening adaptive potential and improving environments. But it also points to the usefulness of a growing body of stress theory which has an important bearing on primary prevention (Coelho, Hamburg, and Adams, 1974). Stress theory suggests that when the usual adaptive balance is upset by external or internal processes and events, the person and/or the environment will experience the upset as stress and will institute coping strategies to eliminate or reduce the stress or to accommodate to it. Stress and coping are mediated by age, sex, culture, physical condition, particular vulnerabilities, and previous experience. Stress is a part of living, arises from all facets of life, and is not necessarily problematic. In fact, some stress is pleasurable, or is generated by desired events, or is even sought after to alleviate tedium. Stress theory suggests, however, that problematic stress must be understood as a transactional phenomenon occurring in the interface between person and environment—again the area where the school social worker is located.

Coping, too, is a transactional phenomenon located in the interface area because it depends upon personality variables that are in reciprocal relation to environmental variables (Mechanic, 1974; White, 1974). For example, cognition and problem-solving skills used in coping depend on the quality and quantity of information and on the training provided by the environment of family, school, and other social institutions. Coping rests on a minimal amount of self-esteem and psychic comfort, but those qualities depend on emotional supports from the social environment. Motivation for coping depends, in part, on the incentives and rewards provided by the family, school, and community. And finally, coping requires some degree of autonomy, or having enough space and time in the physical and social environments in order to make decisions and take action. This suggests, again, that the interface area is indeed a strategic location for the school social worker. Typically, s/he strengthens coping by supporting self-esteem and identity, rewarding motivation and coping efforts, providing information, teaching problem-solving skills, working to relieve anxiety, depression, and other threatening affects that interfere with coping, and providing opportunities for decision making and action. S/he also directs his/her efforts to reducing stress imposed on the child, the parents, or the community by the procedures or personnel of the school.

So far this discussion of adaptation, stress, and coping merely reformulates what was said earlier about the school social worker's dual function. I would now like to suggest that ideas of stress and coping bear also on issues related to the primary prevention of difficulties before they arise. In general, social work is most often engaged in secondary and tertiary prevention to prevent further disabling from already present and often entrenched problems. As a result, we often feel we are engaged also in picking up the pieces after the damage has been done and have little to do with preventing those problems in the first place. Yet, school social work is moving more and more toward primary prevention. It can also point the way for social workers in other fields of practice who are interested in primary prevention.

Primary prevention has been defined as specific actions directed at specific populations for specific purposes (Goldston, 1977). It seeks to prevent problematic stress and maladaptation and to promote adaptive functioning and positive development. To reach these goals, primary prevention engages the positive forces in individuals, families, and groups, and works to change environmental properties that have an adverse effect on growth and adaptive functioning.

Knowledge of the developmental stages and tasks of the child, adult, and family, and of the environmental provisions required for those tasks enables the school social worker to identify populations-at-risk. These might include, for example, children whose parents are considering or moving into separation or divorce, children experiencing the serious illness or death of a parent or sibling, or children not reaching their intellectual potential. Parental populations-at-risk might include single parents, unemployed parents, parents living in poverty, or socially isolated parents. School social workers frequently offer group meetings to parents of children entering school for the first time, because initial entry represents a transitional point in the life cycles of both parent and child. Thus it has potential for stress and maladaptive response.

> In one such program, the social worker included the kindergarten teacher as a group member because she could provide immediate observations of the child's reactions in the classroom. Her presence also facilitated communication between parent and teacher which could then foster mutual trust and mutual decision making and problem solving as the parents moved through the elementary grades. In this particular program, the parents who participated were engaged in planning the next year's groups and then served as their co-leaders. Thus the roles of parents changed from recipients of the program to planners, then to recruiters of other parents, eventually to group co-leaders, and thus to providers of the service now intended to reach the entire population-at-risk (Santos, 1977).

In a middle-class school, with bused-in children from the inner city, the school social worker—with the principal's consent—developed a project she called "Concern for Community," utilizing a team made up of a teacher and several volunteers including a retired social worker. The project involved a series of fifth grade field trips for firsthand learning about institutions and agencies set up to meet human needs, including hospitals, adolescent group homes, and geriatric facilities. The children learned the community's layout by locating their own homes on a map in relation to the homes of the other group members and classmates. The children also met with the social worker in small groups during the school year to talk about human needs in their community and resources for meeting them. The project's objectives were to stimulate a greater concern in the children for one another, for human need, and for their shared environment, and to increase the children's sense of interdependence and mutual caring. The trips, and especially the small group experiences, were evaluated by the school as having met the objectives.[1]

Early adolescence, ages 12 to 15, is a critical period of development that involves coping with unique biological, psychological, and social demands. Because of hormonal and bodily changes, especially in girls, and sudden

---

1. I am indebted to Edna Bernstein, MSW, Stamford, Connecticut, for this illustration.

entry into the teen culture with its new pressures and demands, early adolescence can be a period of stress and increased vulnerability. Yet, the educational structure in many communities superimposes additional stress by the transfer from elementary to junior high at this very time. The security achieved in a small, self-contained classroom with a single teacher can be lost in the larger population, larger campus, rotating classes, multiple teachers, and increased academic demands (Hamburg, 1974). This appears to be an appropriate population-at-risk for primary prevention programs by the social worker. Such programs might include meetings with teachers and administrators to educate the educators about the age-related stresses of their pupils. These would be based on the teachers' interests and work-related needs so that desired structural changes might be achieved. Anticipatory guidance groups for sixth graders, mutual support groups of seventh grade teachers on how to help their students deal with demands of the transition, and mutual aid groups for parents on their shared tasks in understanding the early adolescent could also be offered (Work Group E, 1977). While we do not know for sure, such primary prevention might contribute to reduced dropout, drug use, and pregnancy and lead to better grades, less absenteeism, and fewer court referrals. Preventive programs will need to be evaluated, particularly in the light of such real constraints as insufficient funding, insufficient staffing, and value systems that tend to resist prevention efforts as invasion of privacy.

Opportunities for preventive work will depend upon the social worker's skill in establishing an ecological niche in the school, so that services are not limited to children who are referred. One social worker reported on efforts to begin relationships before problems emerge by creating an atmosphere that allows all students to confer with him about concerns and difficulties confronting many or most children, such as management of adult authority, peer group disruptions, and pressures of competition. He uses an open-door policy for children to drop in. He accepts advisory roles in student activities and participates in playground and lunchroom duties so that he can provide on-the-spot or life-space helping efforts. He suggests that this increases children's awareness of the social work service and their right to it when and where needed or desired, and without stigma (McGarrity, 1975).

INFLUENCING THE SCHOOL

Throughout this chapter, I have referred to the social worker's function as including professional responsibility to influence the school to be more responsive to the needs of child, family, or community and changing school practices that undermine self-esteem, autonomy, and competence or that add to the burden of depression, anxiety, passivity, or alienation already present. Those tasks are hard—which may explain why many social workers tend to give short shrift to the "situation side" of our person-situation commitment. Nevertheless there are two reasons for optimism: First, we are understanding our commitment better so we are more ready to accept the dual, simultaneous function. Second, real help with environmental tasks is on the way. Anderson (1974), for example, has developed a team model in school social work which has many advantages in addressing problems that affect large numbers of pupils. The team consists of the social worker, psychologist, and often the secondary counselor and nurse, and sometimes the teacher and principal who are, in any case, included in the planning and action. A team can exert greater influence than an individual, although Anderson acknowledges there are severe difficulties in team management just as there are in medical and psychiatric settings where team practice is commonplace.

By virtue of the interface position, however, even the individual school social worker can serve as an early warning system to the school regarding undesirable consequences of its policies and procedures. This collaborative role assumes there is consensus between the school and the practitioner about what is good or bad for children, families, and communities. Where there is such consensus, efforts of the social worker to bring about change in organizational elements can be relatively easy and relatively successful. Sometimes, however, there may not be consensus—perhaps because of such issues as power, authority, prestige, competing interests, personal commitments, or fiscal and political constraints imposed by the outside environment. Assuming the advocacy role in such situations demands "influencing skills" in addition to our helping skills (Brager, 1975). Advocacy in one's own system is a delicate task, since it must be done in such a way that the practitioner does not alienate the very system that employs him/her. A social worker trying to introduce change into the organization, who loses his/her job in the process, is of little use to his/her clients. Thus, political skills of influencing are needed including persuasion, bargaining, mediation, negotiation, and conflict management. Knowledge of a specialized kind is required in order to understand and to utilize the formal and informal systems within the school, its seats of power and decision making, channels of communication, its norms, customs, rules, and policies. Organizational theory and skills of influencing are now taught in many social work schools and in many agencies' staff development programs. They are also set forth in journal articles and books (Brager and Holloway, 1978; Germain and Gitterman, 1980; Patti and Resnick, 1972; Wax, 1968). All practitioners, however, must work at integrating them into our practice. School social workers, like many practitioners in other fields, are effective in working within the system on behalf of one child or one parent, getting the school to bend a rule, make an exception, grant a privilege here, or withhold a sanction there. This very important activity must be continued, but we must also maintain constant vigilance about the impact of the school on all its pupils and, where necessary, undertake knowledgeable, well-planned, skillfully implemented efforts to change adverse structures and practices in the school. That is the implication of the distinctive dual function of social work. It is the implication of primary prevention, and it may be the 1990s response to Abraham Flexner.

REFERENCES

Anderson, R.J. 1974. School social work: The promise of a team model. *Child Welfare* 53: 524–530.

Bartlett, H. 1970. Seeking the strengths of social work. In *The common base of social work practice*. NY: National Association of Social Workers.

Brager, G. 1975. Helping vs. influencing: Some political elements of organizational change. Paper presented at the National Conference of Social Welfare, San Francisco, CA.

Brager, G., and Holloway, S. 1978. *Changing human service organizations: Politics and practice*. NY: Free Press.

Coehlo, G. B., Hamburg, D., and Adams, J. (eds.). 1974. *Coping and adaptation*. NY: Basic Books.

Costin, L. B. 1969. An analysis of the tasks in school social work. *Social Service Review* 43: 274–285.

Dubos, R. 1968. *So human an animal*. NY: Charles Scribner's.

Erikson, Erik. 1959. The healthy personality: Identity and the life cycle. *Psychological Issues*. NY: International Universities Press. 1 (1): 50–100.

Evans, R. I. 1973. *Jean Piaget, the man and his ideas*. NY: E. P. Dutton, 78–79.

Flexner, A. 1915. Is social work a profession? *National Conference Charities and Corrections, Proceedings*, 576–606.

Germain, C. 1978. General systems theory and ego psychology: An ecological perspective. *Social Service Review* 52(4): 535–550.

Germain, C. B. (ed.). 1979. *Social work practice: People and environments*. NY: Columbia University Press.

Germain, C. B., and Gitterman, A. 1996. *The life model of social work practice*. NY: Columbia University Press.

Goldston, S. 1977. An overview of primary prevention programming. In Donald Klein and Stephen Goldston (eds.). *Primary prevention: An idea whose time has come*. Rockville, MD: U.S. DHEW Publication No. (ADM) 77–447.

Gordon, W. E. 1969. Basic constructs for an integrative and generative conception of social work. In Gordon Hearn (ed.). *The general systems approach: Contribution toward an holistic conception of social work*. NY: Council of Social Work Education.

Hamburg, A. 1974. Early adolescence: A specific and stressful stage of the life cycle. In G. B. Coelho, D. Hamburg, and J. Adams (eds.). *Coping and adaptation*. NY: Basic Books.

McGarrity, M. 1975. Building early relationships in school social work. *Social Casework* 56: 323–327.

Mechanic, D. 1974. Social structure and personal adaptation: Some neglected dimensions. In G. B. Coelho, D. Hamburg, and J. Adams (eds.). *Coping and adaptation.* NY: Basic Books.

Patti, R. J., and Resnick, H. 1972. Changing the agency from within. *Social Work* July, 48–57.

Phillips, M. H. 1978. The community school: A partnership between school and child welfare agency. *Child Welfare* 57: 83–92.

Richmond, M. 1917. The social caseworker's task. *National Conference of Social Work, Proceedings,* 112–115.

Rist, R. 1970. Student social class and teacher expectations: The self-fulfilling prophecy in ghetto education. *Harvard Education Review* 40: 411–451.

Santos, R. R. 1977. Developing primary prevention programs with major community institutions. In D. Klein and S. Goldston (eds.). *Primary prevention, an idea whose time has come.* Washington, DC: Department of Health, Education, and Welfare.

Schwartz, W. 1971. On the use of groups in social work practice. In W. Schwartz and S. Zalba (eds.). *The practice of group work.* NY: Columbia University Press.

Shelling, J. 1978. Unpublished case material. The University of Connecticut School of Social Work.

Wax, J. 1968. Developing social work power in a medical organization. *Social Work,* October.

White, R. 1959. Motivation reconsidered: The concept of competence. *Psychological Review* 66: 297–333.

White, R. 1974. Strategies of adaptation: An attempt at systematic description. In G. B. Coelho, D. Hamburg, and J. Adams (eds.). *Coping and adaptation.* NY: Basic Books.

Work Group E. 1977. Population at risk: Secondary school students. In D. Klein and S. Goldston (eds.). *Primary prevention: An idea whose time has come.* Washington, DC: Department of Health, Education, and Welfare.

CHAPTER 4

The Characteristic Focus of the Social Worker in the Public Schools

Marjorie McQueen Monkman
Professor Emerita of Social Work, University of Illinois at Urbana

- The Characteristic Focus of Social Work
- Ecological Perspective
- Social Work Knowledge
- T.I.E. Framework: Outcome Categories
- Concepts for Analyzing Resources
- Values
- Social Work Activities
- The Worker

Federal and state legislation and major legal decisions have given recognition to school social work services and provided an opportunity to broaden these services from the traditional roles. The recognition of school social work services in the laws and policies creates greater expectations for the worker and challenges the profession. The purpose of this paper is to conceptualize what is the focus of school social work and what is the role of the individual worker in utilizing this focus, in developing new techniques in practice, and in demonstrating desired change.

It is hard to overestimate the importance of the individual worker's contribution to change in the practice situation. Workers carry a heavy responsibility for what they bring to the practice situation. They bring a characteristic professional focus which is both broad and unique. The worker's focus makes it possible for him or her to identify knowledge needed for intervention. The worker brings activities and skills for bringing about desired changes. The worker brings values that lead to the selection of perspective, knowledge, and action. The worker brings the contribution of charisma and personal style. It is through the social worker that the professional focus, knowledge, values, and activities impinge on the practice situation. The role of the worker is formed from these attributes as they interact with the particular structure and expectations of the setting (see figure 1).

FIGURE 1   Contributions of the Worker

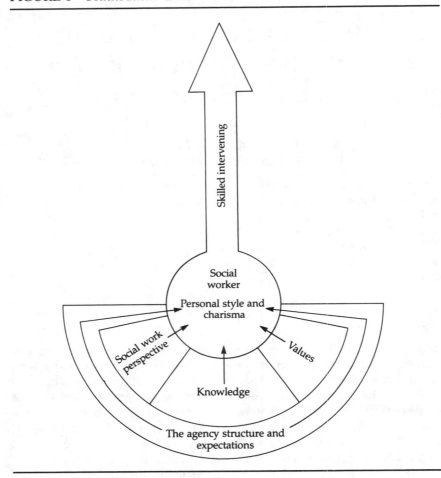

Skilled intervening

Social
worker

Personal style and
charisma

Social work
perspective

Values

Knowledge

The agency structure and
expectations

THE CHARACTERISTIC FOCUS OF SOCIAL WORK

From the beginning, the social work focus has been identified as resting on the person-in-the-situation, a dual focus. As a result of this focus, social workers work with persons in diverse aspects of life, perhaps more than any other helping discipline. The conceptualization of the person-in-the-situation has been enhanced for social work by the work of Harriett Bartlett (1970), William E. Gordon (1969), and others (Gitterman and Germain, 1976; Germain and Gitterman, 1980; Monkman, 1976, 1978, 1981, 1983, 1984; Pincus and Minahan, 1972; Schwartz, 1969). These theorists have conceptualized the traditional focus in a manner that more accurately reflects the roots and multiple avenues of practice. Their approach to defining the point of intervention in social work is to emphasize phenomena at the point where the person and the environment meet. Social work interventions take place in the transactions between the coping behavior of the person and the qualities of the impinging environment. The purpose of the intervention is to bring about a better match between the person and the environment in a manner that induces growth for the person and at the same time is remediating to the environment (Gordon, 1969).

In order to understand more clearly the characteristic focus of the social worker the concepts, *transactions, coping behavior, quality of the impinging environment, practice target,* and *outcomes of intervention,* need to be more clearly explicated.

Transactions

The activities at the interface may be termed transaction(s) between the individual and the environment. Transactions embody exchange in the context of action or activity. This action or activity is a combination of a person's activity and impinging environment activity; thus, exchange occurs only in the context of activity involving both person and environment. The transaction is created by the individual's coping behavior on the one hand and the activity of the impinging environment on the other (Gordon, 1969).

Coping Behavior

Coping behavior is that behavior at the surface of the human organism which is capable of being consciously directed toward the management of transactions. Coping behavior excludes the many activities that are governed by neural processes below the conscious level. It includes the broad repertoire of behavior that may be directed to the impinging environment and that potentially can be brought under conscious control. Coping behaviors include not only the behaviors directed to the environment, but also those efforts of individuals to exert some control over their behaviors—to use themselves purposively.

Coping behaviors are learned behaviors and, once learned, they become established as coping patterns. Significant repetitions in coping behavior by individuals or groups of individuals suggest coping patterns that may at times become the focus of the interventive action. Looking for these patterns in what people are experiencing and how they are responding to a set of environmental conditions takes us beyond our traditional concern for the uniqueness and integrity of each individual. If we know something about the conditions and about human coping, we can say something in some detail and substance about the response of a clientele to a social institution such as education and from this we can develop the appropriate response of school social work. In a relationship with any one individual, we respond to that person as a unique human being and as a part of a larger collectivity. We respect and encourage the effort of an individual with disabilities to overcome adversity, and/or social discrimination, but we know that some of the adversity and discrimination is shared with other persons with disabilities. This knowledge is as much a base for action as is our knowledge of his or her unique response to adversity and discrimination.

People cope with themselves as well as with the environment and this is also learned behavior. These behaviors, as they are developed over time, incorporate expectations and feedback from the environment. The ways individuals and groups cope are related to the information they have about themselves or their environment—how they perceive self and environment. This information is patterned into a cognitive structure which directs the coping behaviors and could even direct the perception of the environment in a manner that will make it difficult to receive further information as feedback from the environment. There is a circular relation between what we usually do to cope with the environment and how we perceive things. An understanding of this relation is the crucial assessment tool. If coping behaviors and patterns are not in keeping with the environment as we perceive it, we may then examine the information and the perceptions of the coping persons. This assessment is directed toward patterns of perception and action rather than seeking some type of single cause within the individual.

Coping is an active, creative behavior which continually breaks the boundaries of "the given." Adapting is seen as a passive concept that implies that the person simply takes in the output from the environment. Some writers connect coping with stress in adapting and refer to coping as those behaviors emitted when there is stress in adapting. We would say that stress is inherent in any growing process, but that it is important to assess the degree of stress to understand the coping patterns adopted. The person is considered able to cope when he or she is dealing with the stress and "making a go of it" (Gordon, 1969).

Quality of the Impinging Environment

The other side of the transaction field is the environment. Social work practice has not confined its concern to the person in any particular situation, that is, at home, in the hospital, in school, or in any other situation. No other profession seems to follow people so extensively into their daily habitats. We have been interested in how the qualities of any of these situations interact with the coping behaviors. As in the case of the coping behaviors, Gordon (1969) has given a way of partializing the qualities of a situation. He has defined the qualities of the impinging environment as those qualities at the surface of the environmental system that the person is actually in contact with, rather than "below-the-surface" structures, which are inferred to be responsible for the nature of what the human organism actually confronts.

FIGURE 2   T.I.E. Framework: Transactions between Individuals and Environments

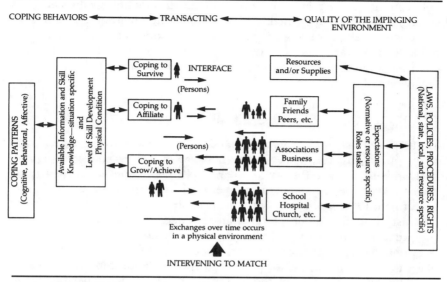

SOURCE: Monkman (1981).

While emphasis on the environmental side is on the impingements, it is recognized that it is through one's knowledge of what is back of the impingements that enables the person to arrange for changes in those impingements in desired directions. It is often necessary to work for change on several levels. For example, a worker may be working with a truant child in an effort to get the child to return to school. At the same time, he or she may find that the teacher is happier with the child truant and that the administration is indifferent. Intervention may be needed at all three levels if the child is to return and remain in school (see figure 2).

Practice Target

Transaction has been defined as activity which combines coping behaviors and the quality of the impinging environment. Through these transactions there is an exchange between the components of each side. The goal of social work practice is matching, that is, bringing about a fit which makes for positive outcomes both for the person and the environment. Professional intervention for bringing about a match may include efforts to change the coping behavior, the quality of the impinging environment, or both (Gordon, 1969).

Social work is concerned with what will happen to the coping behaviors and the quality of the impinging environment as a result of the exchanges between them. The relation of coping and environment is reciprocal. Thus coping behavior and/or quality of the impinging environment could become what we are seeking to change and thus our measures of outcome or dependent variables. To the degree that activity in the transaction changes, we may predict consequent changes in either or both the coping behavior and environmental side.

ECOLOGICAL PERSPECTIVE

We are essentially operating from an ecological perspective. Ecology seeks to understand the reciprocal relation between organisms and environment: how organisms shape the environment to its needs and how this shaping enhances the life-supporting properties of the environment (Germain and Gitterman, 1980). For social work, the ecological perspective appears to fit our historical view much better than the medical or disease perspective that we seemed to have adopted in past decades. The ecological perspective is essentially a perspective, a point of view, for relationships which take place in reality; it is a way of perceiving these relationships more clearly.

One of the reasons for the better fit of the ecological perspective to social work is that it is a multicausal rather than a linear causal perspective; that is, it makes possible a view of multifaceted relationships. From this perspective, our attention is called to the consequences of transactions between people and environment, but the metaphors, models, and/or theories we have previously borrowed have focused more on cause of action and have tended to be one-sided and unidirectional.

SOCIAL WORK KNOWLEDGE

A basic area of knowledge for social work is knowledge of the *needs of people and how these needs are met*. People individually and collectively have a need for physical well-being. These needs consist of food, shelter, and so on, which may be identified as needs for surviving. People have need for relationships, including intimacy and other forms of affiliating. People have need for growth, which may include their need to know, to learn, to develop their talents, and to experience mental and emotional well-being.

A second major area of knowledge for social work is knowledge of *the institutions or societal resources* which have been established to meet these needs. We need knowledge of the major structures and processes involved in resource provision and development. This area is quite complex and includes expectations, policies, procedures, and so on.

The third major area of knowledge is knowledge of *the match between these institutions and the needs of the people*. From the perspective of social work, this is knowledge of the transactions and the result of these transactions for people and their environments. For example, P.L. 94–142 and subquently P.L. 101-476 (IDEA, Individuals with Disabilities Education Act) is an environmental policy change that changes societal expectations and resources for exceptional children and, in turn, affects all children. The environmental impingements that individual children experience will change as these policies change. The difference in the transactions between pupils and their teachers, peers, and even the physical structure of the school have become a part of the general experience of children. However, these children continue struggling to cope with change and new events brought on by these policies. These transactions are particularized and occur in time and space (at a particular time and in a particular place), as do all living transactions.

The Purpose of Social Work Activity

The purpose of social work activity is to improve the match between coping behaviors and the quality of the impinging environment so that the stress in these transactions is not so great that it is destructive to the coping abilities of the individual or the environment. Changes are always occurring and people are always coping or striving to manage change. Not only is our purpose to bring a match that is not destructive but, if possible, one that makes the person better able to cope with further change and makes the environment less stressful to others.

As our focus becomes clearer, we could make the knowledge we have of transactions more explicit for social workers and other disciplines. To do this we need to develop our focus in a way that makes what we aim to change, coping behavior and the impinging environment, more explicit. Figure 2 illustrates the concepts we will be discussing.

T.I.E. FRAMEWORK: OUTCOME CATEGORIES

Coping Behaviors

Social workers basically deal with at least three categories of coping behaviors and three categories of the impinging environment (Monkman, 1978). This framework for dealing with the transactions between individuals and environments is called Transactions Individuals Environment (TIE). Surviving, affiliating, growing, and achieving form a continuum of coping. There are then three categories of coping behaviors: (1) coping behaviors for surviving, (2) coping behaviors for affiliation, and (3) coping behaviors for growing and achieving. These categories help us set priorities for practice intervention. Coping behaviors at any point in time are affected by information from past coping experience and build themselves over time. Our first consideration is whether the client has the capacity to obtain and use the necessities for surviving; second, for affiliating. Both surviving and affiliating skills seem to be prerequisites to growing and achieving.

Coping behaviors for surviving are those behaviors that enable the person to obtain and use resources that make it possible to continue life or activity. To survive we need to have the capacity to obtain food, shelter, clothing, and medical treatment, and to have access to these through locomotion.

Coping behaviors for affiliating are those behaviors that enable the person to unite in a close connection to others in the environment. Subcategories of affiliating behaviors are (1) the capacity to obtain and use personal relationships and (2) the ability to use organizations and organizational structure. Social workers would have great difficulty conceiving of a person apart from his or her social relations. Each individual experiences social relations through organizations and groups, families, schools, clubs, church, and such.

Coping behaviors for growing and achieving are those behaviors that enable the person to perform for, and to contribute to, him or herself and others. Subcategories of coping behaviors for growing are developing and using (1) cognitive capacities, (2) physical capacities, (3) economic capacities, and (4) emotional capacities.

Quality of the Impinging Environment

The environment can be seen as comprising: (1) resources, (2) expectations, and (3) laws and policies. The categories of the environment do not have a priority of their own. Rather, since our major value is the person, their priority gets established in the match with coping behaviors.

Resources. Resources are supplies that can be drawn on when needed or can be turned to for support. Pincus and Minahan (1972) have characterized resource systems as informal, formal, and societal. Informal resource systems consist of family, neighbors, co-workers, and the like. Formal resource systems could be membership organizations or formal associations that promote the interest of the member, such as AA, Association for Retarded Citizens, and so on. Societal resource systems are structured services and service institutions, such as schools, hospitals, social security programs, courts and police agencies, and so on. Resource systems may be adequate or inadequate and provide opportunities, incentives, or limitations. In many situations, there are no resources to match the coping behaviors for surviving, affiliating, and growing.

Expectations. Expectations are the patterned performances and normative obligations that are grounded in established societal structures. Expectations can involve roles and tasks. Social workers recognize these structures and recognize that a positive role complementarity usually leads to greater mutual satisfaction and growth. However, it is not our purpose as social workers simply to help people adapt to societal roles or perform all expected tasks. Roles are the patterned, functional behaviors which are performed by the collection of persons. Examples of roles are mother, father, social worker, physician, and so on. While these are normative patterns in our society, individuals do not always agree on the specific behaviors of a role. Roles do change, since they are socially defined and functionally oriented. Sometimes this societal change is not acceptable to the individual and creates a mismatch between coping behaviors and the environment.

The concept of task is a way of describing the pressures placed on people by various life situations. These tasks "have to do with daily living, such as growing up in the family, and also with the common traumatic situations such as bereavement, separation, illness, or financial difficulties" (Bartlett, 1970). These tasks call for coping responses from the people involved in the situation.

Laws and policies.   Laws and policies are those binding customs or rules of conduct created by a controlling authority, such as legislation, legal decisions, and majority pressures. Subcategories of laws and policies are rights and responsibilities, procedures, sanctions, and inhibiting or restricting factors. As a category, laws and policies are seen as necessary and positive components of the environment. Yet, it is also recognized that many single laws or policies have negative effects for groups of people. Some of our policies make survival more difficult. In some cases, particularly for welfare clients, to receive assistance from welfare agencies may make affiliation almost impossible.

Expectations, laws, policies, and procedures are communicated through resources. The quality of output from a resource, such as a school, is very much affected by the state and national policies that have been adopted. The ultimate test of these policies is the match they make with coping behaviors of those persons with whom the school transacts, namely children. Thus, if these transactions are destructive to the coping behaviors of children, the procedure for implementing or the policy itself is in need of change. This is another way of saying that policy is a legitimate target for change. Social workers are often in the best position for evaluating the match between policy and coping. The classroom is an example that may make the interrelationship of the environmental categories clearer. The expectations for tasks to be accomplished in the classroom come to the child through the teacher (and others). The teacher is a resource to the child, but unless he or she is able to bring the expectations in line with the coping behaviors of the child, there is no match. In some cases, the coping behaviors are so different from the expectations that other resources are necessary. Social workers might intervene in the environment and/or in coping behaviors of school children, that is, in the resources, expectations, policies, procedures, and/or in the coping. In some situations, however, change might be indicated in all six outcome categories.

Research Evidence

An exploratory study (Monkman and Meares, 1984) using a random sample of Illinois school social workers and utilizing the focus described in this manuscript (TIE Framework) lends evidence to the fit of this framework to practice. The data show that coping behavior and environment outcome categories were selected in approximately equal amounts. A national study using a random sample of direct practice MSWs from a variety of practice settings (Monkman, 1989) gave additional evidence that social workers outcomes are located in the categories described in this framework.

Matching Person and Environment

The discussion to follow will be an oversimplification of the interrelation between transaction and the matching process, but it is a first step in utilizing the framework developed thus far. Two populations will be used as examples (see figure 3).

The first population to be considered comprises unmarried teenage parents. To be of help to this group it is important to consider the match between behaviors for surviving, affiliating, and growing and each of the categories on the environmental side. To give a few specific examples: placing the teenage mother on homebound instruction may enhance cognitive achievement but may be destructive to affiliation in interpersonal relationships and affiliation with society and/or organizations. The student may not be aware of laws and policies that can affect her decision to have her baby and keep her baby. Knowledge of the task of being a mother is important both for the mother and for the child.

Another population would be developmentally delayed children. Again, we are concerned with matching in all six categories. Many of the programs presently developed for developmentally delayed children are geared to maximizing cognitive development—or more specifically, academic achievement. Most of these programs do not develop affiliating or surviving skills. Very little energy is put into making a better match between the coping behaviors of the developmentally delayed child and the wide range of tasks for daily living.

It is important to remember that our outcome variables are both coping behaviors and the quality of the impinging environment. We may affect either or both. In the case of the teenage parent, the social worker may have helped to change her behavior in all three categories, as well as increasing resources. The worker may have made information about expectations,

FIGURE 3   The Characteristic Focus of School Social Work

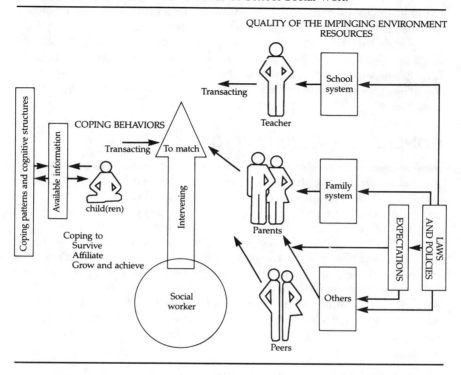

laws, and policies more available to her and may have changed some of the expectations emanating from her impinging environment; for example, the worker may have changed the demands to give up her baby or keep her baby. For the developmentally delayed child, he or she may have developed resources for increasing his or her affiliating behavior. He or she may even have measures of change in these behaviors. The worker may have helped his or her parents change their expectations so that they do not make impossible demands on the child.

Often, social work interventions include teaming with other social workers and other helping persons. For example, many growing and achieving behaviors for school children require teaming with teachers of these children. Teachers spend many more hours with children than social workers do. They have more direct opportunities to develop coping behaviors and skills in children. By teaming with teachers, social workers can increase their change possibilities for children. By bringing these two resources together, they can make a greater change in some aspect of the children's environment.

The point of these examples is to show that this framework makes it possible for us to partialize, generalize, and measure change in practice situations. It is possible to make each of these examples more explicit depending on the conditions of your practice situation. To bring about these changes a worker may, for instance, use knowledge of organizations, skills for working with groups, skills for data collecting, and skills for communicating. The worker must also determine the major critical exchanges in the transaction.

CONCEPTS FOR ANALYZING RESOURCES

Resources have been identified as a major component of the environment. Resources such as family, school, hospitals, and so on, may be viewed as systems. Concepts from the general systems model are useful for conceptualizing and organizing data in the various resource systems. These concepts may be used to call our attention to the skills necessary for the worker to get in and out of a resource system. This model calls to our attention such questions as (1) For what is the major energy in the system being used? (2) Is tension in the system a productive or destructive force? (3) What effect will change in one part of the system have on the other parts? Social workers, such as those employed in schools, become parts of systems. However, while the worker is a part of the system, the worker also intervenes in the system itself as a resource for children (Monkman, 1981).

Understanding Organizations

Workers need to understand what makes organizations operate if they will be able to use the school or other social agencies as a resource. For example, organizations have a managerial structure that is generally hierarchical. Organizational structure can be best understood in relation to organizational process. Workers need to understand the informal power that can be gained either from interpersonal relationships or from assuming responsibilities, as well as power that comes from the formal structural arrangements.

A second, but no less important, process variable is communication. Communication serves a linkage function. It links various parts of the organization by information flow. This may be individual to individual, individual to group, unit to unit, and unit to the supra structure, and so on. Communication has been called the "life blood" of organizations or systems. Social workers have a particular responsibility for developing and maintaining channels of communication if they are to accomplish their own missions.

The climate of an organization has a major effect on its productivity. Climate describes expectancies and incentives and represents a property that is perceived directly or indirectly by individuals in the organization. Climate is made up of such phenomena as warmth, support, conflict, identity, reward, and risk. For social workers, climate is seen as a major quality of resources and is often a target for change.

The earlier discussion makes clear that resources are dependent variables or targets for change for social workers. Resources for clients may take a variety of meanings and may in particular be the "setting" or places of employment for social workers. Thus, it is imperative for social workers to understand the systems or organizations of which they may be a part and to know and ask the essential questions for assessing resources.

In addition, organizational systems have external environments. The exchange between an organization and its environment is essential to the growth of the organization. Organizational environment may be thought of in two categories: (1) general environment, and (2) specific environment.

The general environment consists of conditions that must be of concern to all organizations. Examples of these would include political, economic, demographic, cultural, technological, and legal conditions. The specific environment includes other organizations with which the organization interacts frequently or particular individuals who are crucial to the organization. Examples of the specific environment of a school system are the parents of the children enrolled in the school, the local mental health center, the local child welfare services, the juvenile court, and so forth.

Social Networks

Environments are made up of networks of resources. An important, but sometimes neglected, network is the informal social network for the client: that is, peers, neighbors, friends, relatives, and so on. Each of the persons individually is an important resource for the client, but the linkage and relationship between these persons in the network is also important. Professionals are aware of the negative potential of peer influence on children. However, the positive aspects of these relationships are also useful to practice. Within these networks can be found members who serve as effective informal helpers. Knowledge of social networks and the ability to assess these in practice situations is becoming increasingly important as people become more mobile and lose continuing contact with their own roots. Mobility weakens these linkages, increases isolation and loss, and simultaneously makes network relationships more important.

Networks of Service Organizations

Social workers are often in the position of developing networks of service organizations for clients. Many of our practice situations involve a service network such as the school, family, state child welfare agency, and the courts or judicial system. Social workers are particularly concerned about the relations between these resource systems. This is a domain of social work practice. Social workers may develop and use these interresource linkages, establish channels of communication between these resources, and develop new resources. Thus, the school social workers are in the middle of a system, within an organizational structure, in an environment of social and environmental networks. In order to enhance the development of linkages between various human service organizations, they need to have knowledge of systems variables and organizational variables. Knowledge of the relations of change taking place in differing parts of the system, of the tendency of systems to maintain themselves, to tighten their boundaries, when threatened, can make the worker much more sensitive to the necessary steps in developing linkages between agencies.

We have reviewed concepts and knowledge applicable to the environmental aspects of school social work practice. Other areas of knowledge are equally applicable. These might be (1) knowledge of normal growth and development of children and the stress in coping that accompanies different growth stages, (2) knowledge of exceptional children, (3) knowledge of various learning processes, (4) knowledge of specific resources, (5) knowledge of major policy and policy issues affecting practices in the school setting, and (6) knowledge of positive and negative transaction patterns. Certainly, the earlier discussion gives evidence of the breadth of knowledge that social workers need to bring to practice in the school setting. While we borrow knowledge from psychology, sociology, economics, political science, education, and so on, we borrow from them in relation to our perspectives and to accomplish the purposes of social work.

VALUES

Values guide the action of social work from the preferred perspective to the preferred action. A clarification of types of values is helpful in determining the role of a specific value in practice. Siporin (1975) has defined ten different types of values; five of these are particularly useful to social work:

1. *Ultimate (conceived, or absolute) value* is a general, abstract formulation, such as liberty, justice, progress, self-realization, the worth of the individual.

2. *Instrumental value* is more specific and immediately applicable, such as acceptance of others, equality of opportunity for education, safeguarding the confidentiality of client information. This is also termed a utility value, in referring specifically to the property of things as good or beneficial because of their usefulness to an end.

3. *Personal value* refers to what an individual considers good and right for himself, or what is generally so considered as right or beneficial for an individual, such as individuality, self-respect, self-reliance, privacy, self-realization.

4. *Scientific value* is one to which scientists commit themselves and which they believe should govern scientific behavior: rationality, objectivity, progress, critical inquiry. Society is increasingly accepting these as general social values.

5. *Professional value* is one to which professional people commit themselves and accept as a basis for professional behavior, such as competence, impartiality, placing a client's interest first.

The primary and ultimate value in social work seems to be that "It is good and desirable for man(kind) to fulfil his/her potential, to realize himself/herself, and to balance this with essentially equal efforts to help others fulfill their capacities and realize themselves" (Gordon, 1962). This value represents our dual focus on people and their environment that has characterized social work practice from its beginning. From our ultimate values follow instrumental values that guide actions in practice. An example of an instrumental value is "the right to self-determination." This instrumental value guides our practice, unless it is in conflict with our ultimate value, that is, the individual's self-determination is destructive to himself/herself or others. Knowledge is usually required to make this determination. Thus, values and knowledge are different, but interrelated, in their application to practice. Values, however, give us purpose and ethical structure in social work.

We are careful not to inflict our personal values on others while we accept professional values as a basis for our professional behavior. Hopefully, our personal values are not in conflict with the professional and ultimate values. Yet, the professional values may not encompass all of our personal values. An example of this difference may be seen in relation to divorce. An individual worker may feel that divorce would be wrong for him or herself, but his or her professional values would enable the worker to help clients make this decision for themselves.

It is important to remember that social work has a philosophical base and continues to require judgment as to means and ends. The judgment, however, can be made with more explicit awareness of the *knowledge* and *value* implications.

Social workers must be able to understand the differences between knowledge and values and the relationship of the two. Value refers to what persons prefer or would want to be. This preference may involve all the devotion or sacrifice of which one is capable. Knowledge denotes the picture we have built up of the world and ourselves as it is, not necessarily as we would prefer it to be. It is a picture derived from the most rigorous interpretation we are capable of giving to the most objective sense data we are able to obtain (Gordon, 1962). The future of social work may be dependent on this discrimination. That is, if a value is used as a guide in professional action when knowledge is called for, the resulting action is likely to be ineffective. If knowledge is called on when a value is needed as a guide to action, the resulting action may be destructive. Thus:

> Both outcomes greatly reduce the potential for human welfare residing in the profession's heritage of both knowledge and values. Man's ability over time to bring some aspect of the world into conformity with his preferences (realize his values) seems to be directly proportional to his ability to bring his statements and perceptions into conformity with the world as it now is (develop the relevant science) (Gordon, 1962).

SOCIAL WORK ACTIVITIES

Social work activities involve assessing, relating, communicating, planning, implementing, and evaluating. *Assessing* is the bridging concept between action and knowledge and values. This does not mean to imply that assessing is a first step that occurs before any other activity. It is rather a continuous process as other data continue to be gathered. The social work perspective makes explicit the view of the phenomena into which we intervene. Knowledge gives us the most accurate picture of these phenomena that we are able to obtain in any one point in time. Values lead in the choice of perspectives, in the desire to obtain knowledge, and in the choice of action approaches. The first step in any practice situation is to assess that situation from our perspective, with our knowledge, and in relationship to our values. This step leads to change action.

In most practice situations, *assessing* occurs simultaneously with *relating*. The idea of establishing a relationship has been common in social work literature from the beginning. In more recent years, it has been discussed as a process activity that leads to an end change, resulting in the phenomena into which we intervene. At times in the past, it has been confused with an end in itself or an outcome variable. Certainly, to establish a relationship may be seen as an interim goal, but not as an outcome in the practice situation. Social work places considerable importance on the skill required to relate to the major factors involved in any practice situation, whether client or resource.

Communicating is an essential activity in practice. Most of our data is collected through communicating. To a large extent the accuracy of our data is dependent on our ability to ask questions and clarify answers. It is through communicating that we express our desire and ability to relate and to help.

Planning activities leads to change goals and tasks for each party involved in a practice situation. Plans need to be based on the assessment of the practice situation including the resources available to carry out these plans. Some plans include the development of other resources, as well as bringing about a match between person(s) coping behaviors and existing resources. Planning includes time lines and criteria for assessing change, and contracts are the tools used to bridge planning and implementation.

Implementing a change plan is the activity involved in accomplishing these various tasks and goals. Implementing may involve linking people with resources, changing expectations of the client or of the resource(s), developing or changing policy, changing the procedures in a resource system, or developing new or more effective coping behaviors in person(s), and so on.

Evaluating is part of the assessing process. In the beginning, we assess where the various parts of the practice situation are and, in the end, we evaluate or assess the changes in the various parts. We also evaluate activities that the change processes have accomplished. Evaluation is an assessment of both the outcome and the process. Assessment of outcome is not possible without a perspective that makes our outcome measures clear. It is because in the past this focus has not been explicit that we have been vague and inaccurate and/or confused the relating process with an outcome measure. Assessing and evaluating are continuous processes that should be linked to our characteristic focus, knowledge, and values. Our assessing and planning processes need to be done in a manner that makes evaluation possible.

Each of these process activities involves and includes many skills. They simply serve as a way of organizing our various skill areas. While there is a beginning and an ending to the change process, the steps in this process are not mutually exclusive or linear steps. They are rather interrelated and purposeful activities that together accomplish an end result.

THE WORKER

While workers may bring the characteristic focus, knowledge, values, and actions of the profession, they also bring themselves as resources to the change process. Workers, like clients, have past experiences, information, and cognitive structures or preferred views of transactions, and predictions about consequences of certain kinds of transactions. Each worker brings his or her own style of transacting. It is the responsibility of the worker to constantly change his or her perceptions in the light of new knowledge, more accurate facts from the situation, new resources, and so on.

Workers often tend to prefer particular practice activities. However, the workers' preferred skills should not blunt the awareness of what is needed in any particular situation. For example, some workers have knowledge of interventions to change coping behaviors of individuals. The specific knowledge, plus workers' preference for their individual activities, may lead to a limited practice. Various combinations of selected knowledge and individual preference may lead to a limited perspective for assessing and may lead workers to ignore the important aspects of the practice situation. Workers may fail to develop skills for working with groups, the school system, or other community resources.

Many school social workers were trained at a time when methods of practice were the major divisions of training. Workers were trained to do either casework, group work, community organization, and/or intervention at the policy or administrative level. The major method for a school social worker was casework. In more recent years, it has been recognized that there are many common activities in practice. It has also been recognized that change may be enhanced through collaboration and exchange with others who share common change goals. It is the responsibility of practitioners to keep up with changes in knowledge and to develop their skill level to incorporate new practice activities as they develop and are tested.

There is nothing, however, in the professional methodology or activities that can subordinate the unique, personal artistic contributions that each worker brings to the helping process. Certainly, the individual's sensitive capacity to experience and express empathy and caring are valued among social workers. It is, however, the responsibility of individual workers to evaluate the effects of their individual style on any change process. It is the worker's responsibility to recognize strengths and limitations. Unique qualities and personal style must be self-conscious and disciplined, just as discipline is inherent in the definition of art itself.

We have analyzed and specified the components, characteristic focus, the knowledge, the values, and the skills, that social workers contribute to the public schools. This contribution is significant and provides a response that can be uniquely useful to education in meeting the challenges of its changing mandate. In specifying the components of practice, we see the model developed as useful, both for clarification of the contribution of the social worker, and as a tool for building social work knowledge, and for research testing of theory. Since the construction of a model is the first step toward measurement and testing, we would see the elements of the model as a first step toward the measurement and testing of components of social work practice and we have developed them with that intention. For each social worker, the task of participating in the development of new knowledge is just as important as application of the characteristic focus of the profession and its knowledge, values, and skills. There is much creative work to be done. The responsibility may seem heavy, but the challenge is exciting.

REFERENCES

Bartlett, H. 1970. Seeking the strengths of social work. In *The common base of social work practice*. NY: National Association of Social Workers.

Germain, C. B., and Gitterman, A. 1996. *The life model of social work practice*. NY: Columbia University Press.

Gitterman, A., and Germain, C. 1976. Social work practice: A life model. *Social Service Review* December, 50: 601–610.

Gordon, W. E. 1962. A critique of the working definition. *Social Work* October, p. 9.

Gordon, W. E. 1969. Basic constructs for an integrative and generative conception of social work. In Gordon Hearn (ed.). *The general systems approach: Contributions toward an holistic conception of social work.* NY: Council on Social Work Education.

Monkman, M. M. 1976. A framework for effective social work intervention in the public schools. *School Social Work Journal* Fall, 1(1).

Monkman, M. M. 1978. A broader, more comprehensive view of school social work practice. *School Social Work Journal* Spring, 2(2).

Monkman, M. M. 1981. An outcome focus for differential levels of school social work practice. In *Professional issues for social workers in schools.* Conference Proceedings Silver Spring, MD: National Association of Social Workers, 138–150.

Monkman, M. M. 1983. The specialization of school social work and a model for differential levels of practice. In Miller, D. G. (ed.). *Differential levels of students support services: Including crisis remedial and prevention/developmental approaches.* MN: Department of Education.

Monkman, M. M., and Meares, P. A. 1984. An exploratory study of school social work and its fit to the T.I.E. framework. *School Social Work* 19(1): 9–22.

Monkman, M. M. 1989. A national study of outcome objectives in social work practice: Person and environment. Unpublished.

Pincus, A., and Minahan, A. 1972. *Social work practice, model and method.* IL: F. E. Peacock.

Schwartz, W. 1969. Private troubles and public issues: One social work job or two? *Social welfare forum.* NY: Columbia University Press.

CHAPTER 5

The Wonderland of Social Work in the Schools, or How Alice Learned to Cope

Sally G. Goren
Clinical Associate Professor, Jane Addams College of Social Work,
University of Illinois at Chicago

- Systems Theory
- Visibility
- Viability
- Value

A social worker entering a school for the first time may feel a bit like Alice as she tumbled into the Rabbit Hole and landed in the long corridor, finding it lined with locked doors. Only when she discovered the means by which she could change her size and shape did she begin her adventures in Wonderland. Throughout her experience in the pages of Carroll's book, Alice used her judgment, her feelings, and her integrity to deal with the characters whom she met. This paper will attempt to offer some guidance to the social worker who finds him or herself in the Wonderland of a school system. The worker may initially feel that his/her district or building resembles a series of locked doors with bits of the madness of Wonderland emerging through the cracks. To function effectively, it is essential that the social worker named Alice (or Alex) learn to identify within his/her setting the means by which he/she can achieve that optimal effectiveness that will prove his/her value to the system and meet his/her own professional standards and personal needs. Therefore, an evaluation of the system will be based on some understanding of systems theory. It is this writer's belief that each social worker in a school constitutes a "mini-agency" complete in one person. On such an assumption, we will examine the roles the social worker might play, the various constituencies with whom the social worker interacts, and the question of accountability.

SOURCE: Reprinted with permission from *School Social Work Journal*, Vol. 6, Fall 1981, pp. 19–26.

SYSTEMS THEORY

To flesh out this view of school social work, it is important to share some common understanding of systems theory. If we view any system as a complex, adaptive organization which is continually generating, elaborating, and restructuring patterns of actions and interaction, we see that the school, as a system, must be understood as an entity which is greater than the sum of its parts. It has discrete properties that need to be evaluated if we are to identify the points in which social work interventions may be made to ensure the maximum effectiveness mentioned above. To view the school as an *adaptive* organization supports the social worker's theoretical underpinnings in which linkage, environmental impact, and enablement of each individual's maximum development is held in high value. The systems definition also emphasizes the *interactive* elements which may impede or aid goal achievement. Thus the social worker is led to identify the junctures of interactions which bridge or fragment the discrete elements within the system (Costin, 1995).

Looking further into one's own school system, it is important to estimate its openness. An open system receives input, produces output, and interacts with all the actors within and outside of the system. The interactions may not always be agreeable, but there must be the opportunity for the school, its administrators, teachers, support staff, students, parents, and community to be heard and to hear one another. An important element of a viable system is, in fact, *tension*. This becomes the impetus for change and growth, for negotiation, for development, and for effective, productive relationships. Another element of the open system is that of *feedback* (Fordor, 1976). This speaks to a communications system that generates action in response to information which is the basis for constructive change.

As an employee of the school, it is critically important that the social worker define him or herself within the system. The opportunity to be a significant interactor rests on the social worker's ability to inform the other actors of the social work role, to accept the input from others within and outside the school, and to respond, to produce output which is designed to meet needs that have been identified. A systems understanding speaks emphatically to the need for the social worker to be visible, viable, and valuable. We will examine next how these qualities may be evidenced within the school.

VISIBILITY

To whom is the social worker important? In what ways is the social worker significant? The answers to these questions are to everyone and in every way. The social worker has an impact on any person with whom he or she interacts. To look at the possible breadth of the assignment, we will examine several factors defined by Lela Costin (1972) as a guide to visibility. The effective social worker will function as:

1. Provider of direct counseling services to pupils;
2. Advocate for specific pupils or groups of pupils whose needs are underserved or unmet;
3. Consultant to administrators in their task of program development and policy change;
4. Consultant to teachers to enhance their ability to create a productive climate for maximum learning;
5. Link to community services and facilitator between the school and community in obtaining necessary services for pupils and their families;
6. Leader in coordination of interdisciplinary teams providing service to pupils; and
7. Assessor of needs of individual pupils and of the school system as related to program development. (Costin, 1972)

All of the above demand that the social worker becomes known to the administrators, the teachers, and pupil services personnel who function within the school or school district. The social worker also needs to create an identity with the pupils in the school and, from these contacts, with the families whose children may be the recipients of social work services. How one fleshes out his/her visibility will vary but may include:

1. Informal meetings with teachers and other school personnel over lunch or coffee, before or after the pupils are in the building;
2. Regularly scheduled conferences with administrators and with teachers with whom the social worker shares responsibility for a child's welfare;
3. Initiation of contact with community agencies to whom the social worker may refer children or families for service;
4. Explanation of services to families via attendance at meetings of the PTA or other parent groups;
5. Responsibility for presentations at in-service meetings for teachers and/ or administrators;
6. Assumption of leadership at pupil services personnel team meetings; and
7. Attendance and presentations at school board meetings.

There are many ways that the social worker's visibility may be developed and the particular manner in which this is demonstrated will depend on the social worker's understanding of the politics of the school and the district. As early in one's entry into a district as possible, one must identify the power structure. Determining that will direct the worker toward the creation of relationships that will provide him or her with the support necessary for provision of service. To attempt to work without such support from the person or persons who wield power is an exercise in frustration and a sure diminution of the effectiveness of the efforts. These remarks are not meant to imply that all workers in all settings need to be allied with the power structure, but the worker does need to identify where the power lies in order to understand how his/her work may be enhanced or inhibited. The development of successful working relationships will depend on the clinical assessment skills and the use of relationship building skills that are in the educational and employment experience of all social workers. However, it must be stated that even the most highly skilled workers may be unable to achieve an alignment with the administrative power structure in some instances. Acknowledging that there may be more frustration than gratification in such settings, the social worker may still be able to function as an advocate for children and parents, particularly when the law supports necessary services. The social worker may be a mediator between teachers and administration on behalf of individual children or particular programs. In short, the social worker retains the responsibility to carry out the interventive roles fulfilled by workers in any field of practice (Compton and Gallaway 1979).

Visibility also implies availability. To be ready to assist a principal or nurse in handling a crisis such as child abuse is an excellent way to cement one's position in the school. To provide linkage to a neighborhood day-care center for a child whose parent has become seriously ill demonstrates the effectiveness of relationship building in the community. To educate parents regarding the symptoms of childhood depression or normal pre-adolescent behavior presents the social worker in an appropriate and useful educator role. To inform the school board of new legislation affecting the school and to present a plan for meeting the criteria demanded by the law again places the social worker in a position of enormous value to the school community. It is no longer possible to limit one's role to individual or group counseling of children, though only a few years ago studies indicated that many school social workers defined their responsibilities in just such limited terms (Costin, 1969). Fortunately, there has been a shift in this narrow definition and social workers in schools are engaging in the variety of tasks that have been mentioned above (Costin, 1969). All of this leads to an examination of the viability of the school social worker.

VIABILITY

Linked to visibility is viability. Not only does the school social worker need to be seen, the social worker needs to be seen in action. Creativity is the catch word and the ability to use oneself creatively with the interactors in the school system is imperative. No longer remaining in one's office counseling children, the worker must assess special needs of the system and develop programs to meet them. If a classroom appears to be out of control, how can the worker assist the teacher, the students, or their families? What will meet the needs of the greatest number? It might be regular consultation with the teacher or an effective education project with the class, or several small group meetings with a portion of the pupils in the classroom. Perhaps a need for systematic handling of truancy problems exists. The worker may develop a plan to meet this need in coordination with the principal or assistant principal. Families or some members of the school board may be included in the development of the plan. Time spent with community agencies may alter previous adversarial positions or simply establish a modus operandi that had not existed and which can be functional not only for the worker but also for other school personnel who identify children in need of particular services. We again see how assessment skills, organizational skills, and finally, treatment skills can be applied to a school system to provide maximum learning opportunities for the pupils served by that system.

Not only might the social worker be creative in relation to direct services to pupils with specific needs, he or she can be equally creative in identifying system needs and developing programs to address them.

A social worker who noted considerable distrust and low morale among teachers in a junior high school established a series of meetings and, assuming the role of facilitator, enabled the teachers to examine some of the system problems and the impact on their work. As concerns were shared and ideas for dealing with them were explored, the suspiciousness of the teachers declined and fruitful relationships soon developed. They admitted similar anxieties about their classroom performances and, as a unit, were able to prepare criteria for the evaluation of their work and advocate for their adoption by the administration.

In another instance, a social worker worked with a principal and pupil personnel staff to develop an enrichment program for minority first grade students. The social worker was able to provide some research expertise which aided the program's acceptance by the school board and by the families whose children attended the school.

Since Public Law 94-142 was passed in 1975 (now reformulated as PL 101-476, Individuals with Disabilities Education Act, IDEA) opportunities to expand social work services in the schools have increased. The law provides funding for districts to provide new services for children with disabilities and therefore has led to the hiring of new staff and the development of creative programs, to serve their target groups in ways previously not possible. In many instances, the guidelines of the law have been imaginatively and broadly interpreted in those districts which have seen the mandate as an opportunity rather than a burden. It behooves the school social worker to be in the lead in such program development and to take an active role in the execution of new programs.

Built into the law is the necessity for accountability, an ever increasing requirement in all fields of social work practice. Without minimizing the additional time this demands and recognizing that it can be regarded as a burden for an already overworked staff, there is also a chance to dramatically detail the breadth, content, and effectiveness of social work services. The law has provided us with the impetus to devise systems which can readily indicate who we serve, how we serve them, and the time allocation the various services require. This brings us to an examination of the final V: the value of the school social worker.

VALUE

Early in this paper the author commented upon the total agency concept implicit in each social worker in the schools. It is eminently clear to any reader who is employed in schools that this is true. Is it clear to teachers and administrators? As a professional working within a host setting, the requirement for interpretation of one's function is continual. This is so because the responsibilities are broad and change as needs of the school community change. Since the other professional staff is also continually changing, new staff need to be informed in order to best utilize our services. Implicit in the statement above is the responsibility of the social worker to have control of the definition of his/her role. While it will always be defined in relation to an accurate assessment of service needs, it is the social worker who has the most intimate knowledge of his/her own skills and training and this needs to be communicated to staff in a school setting. To expect that teachers, speech therapists, principals, psychologists, et al., know what one does is to permit any and all of the staff to dictate what to do, how to do it, and when to do it. Rather than allow the job to be defined by others, it behooves a social worker entering into practice in a school to view him or herself as that total agency with the intent of meeting the school and community needs. These needs will be addressed within the knowledge, skill, and ethics of the social work profession; therefore, it is incumbent on the social worker to have a comfortable professional identity that can be expressed soundly to delineate the functions the social worker may undertake in the setting.

Just as it is the responsibility of the worker to be visible and viable in the school building, it is even more important that the social worker, from the point of entrance into a school system, share in the control of the evaluation process. Defining one's role and the scope of the job establishes the basis on which an evaluation of the social worker will be made by the responsible administrator. If the social worker regards him or herself as that total agency he/she needs to think and act as administrator, supervisor, and line worker.

As an administrator, one partializes time to meet the needs of the organization. This determination of the allocation of one's resources should be cooperatively established with the school district official to whom the social worker is directly responsible. The breadth of function, client contact, and caseload management are all part of this role. In order to have realistic criteria upon which one's evaluation will be based, the social worker needs to be a participant in their development. If a district has a standard evaluation form for teachers, it might need to be adapted so that it is appropriate for a social worker or else another one be developed which will better judge the overall effect of social work services in the building. In the role of administrator, it might be well to establish regular conferences with the building principal, the special education coordinator, and/or any other administrative level personnel who might have an impact on the worker's position. This will continuously inform them of one's work, and, of course, of one's value.

There are a number of situations with which this writer is familiar, where administrators avoid contact with the social worker and reluctantly have any interaction. In other districts, the principal or assistant principals are intrusively involved in the case by case management of the social worker. In the first-mentioned situation, administrators must be informed via some method of one's overall work. This may be achieved by memos, weekly or monthly statistical and/or case reviews, and extensive written documentation of any cases wherein issues of legal responsibility may be a factor. The reasons for avoidance may be varied, but the worker must maintain professional linkage with administration by whatever means possible. In the case of the overly-involved administrator, some methods similar to those employed with the "absent" administrator may serve to satisfy the control needs of that person. If the administrator is convinced that the worker is sharing with him/her the case management issues which the administrator feels necessary to know, the worker may find him or herself freer to pursue the tasks as they have been assessed.

There are many suggestions for management of the system in this paper. Each may work in some situations and not in others. Many ideas have not been mentioned. Nonetheless, the message is to experiment with various means of engagement, reporting, integration of social work services within the educational milieu. Failure of one method does not foretell failure of another and perseverance will be rewarded in most circumstances.

As one's own supervisor, the social worker must determine individual and group needs of the pupils with whom he/she works. Judging the necessity of a referral, any indication of the need for consultation, and the type of interventive role which will most readily meet the assessed need are assists the line worker receives from a supervisor. In most school districts, the line worker must carry this dual responsibility. Some districts do provide social work supervision or consultation, some have access to psychiatric consultation, but many school social workers have no established avenue to obtain this kind of input. The need for input, feedback, and direction has led some social workers in schools to develop informal consultation groups. Without devaluing the autonomy the school social worker enjoys, the burden of such total responsibility for one's work can be shared with others. But the significance of the responsibility should be accorded adequate valuation by the district's administration.

There is no need to review the many, varied tasks the social worker, as line worker, undertakes. There is need, however, to account for them. The importance of *counting* contacts with children, with parents, with teachers, and with community resources cannot be overemphasized. Adding the time to fill out necessary reports and records is imperative. This kind of statistical record will provide the basis for the evaluation of effectiveness of service. Following the time keeping is the need to demonstrate effectiveness of one's action. If the social worker has shared in the development of goals with teachers and administrators, he/she will be able to share in the evaluation of his/her service. The fact that the social worker may not be effective in every instance should not deter him/her from creating an evaluation system which will demonstrate incremental change, diagnostic reassessments, and goal renegotiations. It is important to show that service plans are related to jointly-determined goals and to provide some rationale for success or failure of the plans. To reemphasize the importance of one's involvement in this evaluative process, one might consider designing a short form that could be used with any child, group, family, or teacher. The form might include goals, methods for achievement, and time spent in an effort to meet the goals.

This entire section on value may have been better entitled *evaluation.* It is the author's contention that one's value is best understood via evaluation of one's work and the plea is, therefore, for each school social worker to carry a major responsibility for the negotiation and creation of the criteria on which such an evaluation will be based. This is another way that one informs, educates, and indeed, determines the parameters of one's work. Control is shared, goals are shared, and power is shared. The social workers who can actively demonstrate their value will find that they have a strong advocate in the principal or other administrator and that kind of advocacy will agitate for more social work services and, hopefully, more social workers.

To be an effective participant in the creation of an atmosphere that will enhance learning opportunities for children, the social worker in the school must use all his/her best clinical and organizational skills. The social worker must first know who and what he/she is professionally. He/she must develop respect for the work of others. Trust will grow as hopes and expectations are shared and common goals are agreed upon. The social worker who creates a significant position for him or herself in a school system will have an accurate knowledge of the system and a clear knowledge of his/her position in it. The social worker will know the loci of power, the system needs, and the style of all the interactors within the system. This assessment will be the basis for the social worker's creation of an appropriate role. The social worker in a school, in essence, is always using professional skills. Whether meeting with a child or a teacher, arranging a contractual agreement with a family service agency, or consulting with a pupil services team, the effective social worker will be actively assessing and treating.

As Alice moved through her adventures in Wonderland and the Looking Glass, she became more assertive and gained control. Alice (or Alex) in the school system will find that active involvement in all aspects of that system will be the foundation for provision of service, acceptance within the system, and professional satisfaction for a job very well done. The social worker will also be very tired at the end of each day, recognizing that he/she has indeed used him or herself skillfully throughout every contact that he/she has had. The social worker will have been visible, viable, and of value to everyone he/she encountered during the day at school.

REFERENCES

Compton, B., and Galaway, B. 1994. *Social work processes*, 5th Pacific Grove, CA: Brooks/Cole Publishing Co.

Costin, Lela B. 1969. An analysis of the tasks of school social workers. *Social Service Review* 43: 274–285.

Costin, Lela B. 1972. Adaptations on the delivery of school social work services. *Social Casework* 53: 348–354.

Costin, Lela B. 1975. School social work practice: A new model. *Social Work* 20: 136.

Fordor, Anthony. 1976. Social work and system theory. *British Journal of Social Work* 6, Spring. Reprinted in Compton and Galaway, *Social work processes*, 2nd ed. Homewood, IL: Dorsey Press, 1979, 98–101.

Policies, Programs, and Mandates for Developing Social Services in the Schools

CHAPTER 6

Policies, Programs, and Mandates for Developing Social Services in the Schools

Richard S. Kordesh
Visiting Lecturer in Community Development and Family Policy,
Jane Addams College of Social Work, University of Illinois at Chicago

Robert Constable
Professor Emeritus, Loyola University of Chicago

- Policy and Program Development for School Social Workers
- The Unfinished Journey for Children with Disabilities and Their Families: From Civil Rights to School Programs
- The Educational Rights of Children with Disabilities
- Social Reform Programs, Communities, Families, and Schools: From Community Reform to School Programs
- Implications of Reform Movements for School Social Workers

Section I of this book examined the past, the present, and the possible future of the relation between social work and education and its impact on practice theory. This relation is made concrete and systematic through the development of social policy around the educational institution and function. Social policy in a social institution, such as education, is formulated through societal and professional values, through institutional structure and programs, and through a developing and growing body of law, expressing political realities. Social policy is manifested through the practice of the myriad professionals in a school in their daily encounters with students and through the concrete organization of the school itself. Thus the concrete organizational and economic realities of the school reflect the merging of law, public expectations, and what is humanly and organizationally possible. There is usually a gap between what is expected and valued and what at any given time becomes possible, but even the identification of such a gap is an important spur to change and may be prophetic of the future.

POLICY AND PROGRAM DEVELOPMENT FOR SCHOOL SOCIAL WORKERS

In this section of the book we will review policies, programs, and mandates for social work services in the schools and the relations between these and the school social worker's role. We will examine the process of policy analysis at the local community and school organizational levels. We will review some of the educational policy, program, legal, and value environments within which school social workers operate. Social policy has historically been conceptualized as national policy, far from the locus of practice. Practice theory usually developed in its own orbit, and the two rarely met. There is consequently some confusion about the relation of policy to practice. Traditionally, policies are considered to be developed through law, court decisions, and directives at the federal, state, and local levels, but mainly "from the top down." They are usually written in fairly general language. They prescribe and suggest common goal and means, but it is often up to the grass-roots level, the level of *implementation*, to develop ways to carry out these policies in concrete situations. The paradox is that any top-down policy, often developed far from its implementation point, may have an uncertain outcome. Its success depends on the real environment of service and the capabilities of those implementing it. Some policies exist mainly on paper because no one has found a way to implement them successfully. Some unfortunately may even accomplish the very reverse of their purposes. The limits of policy, which prescribes but does not deal with implementation, are becoming all too clear. Initiatives from the grass roots may also develop as experiments from the points of need and of service. They may become codified to a limited extent in more general programs, directives, and laws, at the level of *articulation*, but will retain a certain uniqueness. Whatever the origin of policies, whether from laws articulating rights or from grass-roots programs that resonate with needs and empower consumers to take action on these needs, any policy ultimately contains both levels in one way or another. School social workers are well situated to have access to both levels. In developing programs to meet the needs of the school community, they are in fact both implementing and developing policies. To prepare for this reality the language and theory of policy needs to be blended with the language and theory of practice.

There are two directions to policy development and its implications for the school social worker: from the national level to the local level and from the local level to the national level. Flynn's chapter on policy analysis at the local level (chapter 8) makes the connection between the policy development roles of the school social worker and direct practice roles of the school social worker, and Pawlak (chapter 9) provides a conceptual base for the analysis of school organizations. Hare and Harris Rome (chapter 7) analyze the economic, political, and social environments of school social work. Whitted and Constable (chapter 10) and Bishop (chapter 11) then explicate the implications for practice and policy of the Individuals with Disabilities Education Act. In chapters 9, 10, and 11 we will see the implications of the clarification of the rights of a child with a disability to a free appropriate public education. Throughout this section we will examine the implications for the school social worker of community- and family-based social reform efforts that are responsive to social needs. These needs become evident when, in the face of societal fragmentation, family and community structures deteriorate and become less capable of providing an adequate nurturing and socializing context for children. In both cases the position of the school makes it central to reform and the position of the social worker makes him or her crucial to implementation. In one example the direction is from civil rights and national school policy to its implementation at the state and local school level; the other is from communities reclaiming themselves at the grass-roots level to a broader movement at state and municipal levels.

The common thread in both examples is that school social workers need to understand the language and theory of policy as well as of practice. It is part of their role to develop policy and programs. School social workers help develop and implement crisis plans as members of the school crisis team. Social workers help create solutions with teachers, parents, and pupils to maintain youngsters with disabilities in classes with children without disabilities. School social workers and the school team *develop programs that make policy possible.* Working in the most difficult areas of education, their role inevitably is an innovative one that goes beyond the "givens" of the institution or the situation. The distance from such innovation to policy and program development is not great. When school social workers have the freedom to develop their role in such an individualized and professionalized way, the school becomes more responsive to societal and community conditions as they inevitably find their way into the educational process.

The process of program and policy development demands a foundation in research methods germane to the missions, structures, and concerns of schools. A natural extension of this section on policy is section IV of this book, on research and evaluation. Here a variety of research methodologies are discussed for needs assessment, analysis of community and organizational developments, and evaluation of effectiveness. The reader may want to skip from this section to section IV and back to develop a complete picture of the world of policy development around school services and to understand the methodologies that assist the analysis and development of policies and programs at the community level, the organizational level, and the level of service delivery.

It is important that school social workers see policy and program development as their participation in the school's active response to societal conditions in its own community and to more general mandates. It is the *translation* of policy into practice that needs first of all to become an essential part of the professional response of the school social worker. The field of children with disabilities is a clear example of this process as it has evolved for school social workers and educators over thirty years of professional experience. It is not the purpose of this section on education of children with disabilities to be the last word on a constantly developing field; other references do this better.[1] Rather the school social worker needs to understand how a language of law and of rights is translated into programs that the school social worker has a role in making possible.

THE UNFINISHED JOURNEY FOR CHILDREN WITH DISABILITIES AND THEIR FAMILIES: FROM CIVIL RIGHTS TO SCHOOL PROGRAMS

Over the past thirty years, laws and policies have been developed that clarify the civil rights of children with disabilities to a free appropriate public education. Social work has found itself at the center of the decision-making and procedural safeguards for these children. The extension of these rights to the area of early childhood in 1986 opened the opportunity for early intervention with families as well as with children. Finally, the Regular Education Initiative (REI) encouraged movement back into the regular classroom for youngsters with mild disabilities. Although the focus is on children with special needs, the thrust toward involvement with regular education is a trend that inevitably involves all children and the school as a whole.

THE EDUCATIONAL RIGHTS OF CHILDREN WITH DISABILITIES

In 1970–72, two court decisions were made that were destined to revolutionize the delivery of services to pupils with disabilities in schools. The effects of these decisions would reverberate for many years and in the process change the fundamental nature of social services to children in schools. These decisions, *Pennsylvania Association of Retarded Children (PARC) v. Commonwealth of Pennsylvania*[2] and *Mills v. Board of Education of the District of Columbia*,[3] each contributed to the revolution by defining the concept of rights of persons with disabilities to an appropriate education and to access to the same opportunities enjoyed in our society by the nondisabled. These court decisions acknowledged a set of civil rights for persons with disabilities and sketched out the boundaries in giving shape to those rights. In the several years following those decisions, other laws were passed, such as the Vocational Rehabilitation Act of 1973,[4] the Education of All Handicapped Children Act (P.L. 94-142), and the Individuals with Disabilities Education Act (P.L. 105-17).[5] These laws would define the rights more precisely and set down the mechanism for enforcement.

By the end of the decade and the beginning of the 1980s, there gradually emerged a refined body of court decisions, laws, ensuing regulations, Office of Special Education policies, and Office of Civil Rights findings that have defined what is an irreversible direction toward the enforcement of the rights of people with disabilities. The thrust of this cumulative body of law is becoming more clear. Whether it is clarified by a body of regulations that may serve to avoid litigation, or whether the clarification is achieved through court decisions, the direction is the same: toward the broadening of the traditional focus of the school in the process of providing and facilitating a free appropriate public education for all children. This right to a free appropriate public education was to consist of more than equal access to education or even compensatory education. For people with disabilities, neither opportunities nor objectives could be the same as for the regular education student. The new concept of the right to an education was to encompass, as Weintraub and Abeson clarified, "equal access to differing resources for differing objectives."[6]

Two major federal district court decisions dominate the many right-to-education decisions of this period and illustrate the definitive change taking place: *PARC v. Commonwealth of Pennsylvania* and *Mills v. Board of Education.* The PARC case was taken on behalf of thirteen school-age children with developmental disabilities placed in state institutions and the class of all other children with developmental disabilities in the state denied free access to public education opportunity by public policy as expressed in law, policies, and practices of the state education agency and school districts throughout the state that would postpone, terminate, or deny children with developmental disabilities access to a publicly supported education, including a public school program, tuition or tuition maintenance, and homebound instruction. The order struck down sections of the state school code and set dates by which the plaintiff children and all other children with developmental disabilities in the state were to be reevaluated and provided a publicly supported education. Local districts that provided programs of preschool education were required to provide the same for children with developmental disabilities. Furthermore, the court urged that these children be educated in a program most like that provided to nondisabled children.

Mills v. Board of Education followed PARC by several months and was basically similar except that a wider range of disabilities were represented and some of the children were residing at home. As in PARC, the court ordered that the plaintiffs and all others of the class receive a publicly supported education; the decision also specified that the plaintiffs were entitled to due process of law prior to any change in educational program. The District of Columbia Board of Education failed to comply with the court order, stating that it did not have the necessary financial resources and that to divert money from regular education programs would deprive regular education children of their rights. The court was not persuaded by that contention. The school has an obligation to provide a free public education to these exceptional children. Failure to provide this education could not be excused by the claim that there are insufficient funds. "The inadequacies of the District of Columbia public school system cannot be permitted to bear more heavily on the 'exceptional' or disabled child than on the normal child." The resultant court order, which was quite comprehensive, could be summarized under two basic sections:

1. A declaration of the constitutional right of all children, regardless of any exceptional condition or disability, to a publicly supported education; and

2. A declaration that the defendant's rules, policies, and practices, which excluded children without a provision for adequate and immediate alternative educational services, and the absence of prior hearing and review of placement procedures, denied the plaintiffs and class rights of due process and equal protection of the law.

With these two cases the rights of children with disabilities to free and appropriate public education and many of the procedural safeguards that were to find their way into later legislation and regulations were already manifest. Shortly following the court decisions, two closely related laws were to clarify further the rights of children with disabilities to an education. The first, Section 504 of the Vocational Rehabilitation Act of 1973, prohibited discrimination on the basis of disability in programs and activities receiving federal financial assistance. The second, P.L. 94-142, a "bill of rights for the people with disabilities," gave further definition to the right to a free appropriate public education for all children with disabilities aged three to twenty-one. The latter also provided for education in the environment of least restriction and spelled out the accountability and procedural safeguards that would ensure this right. The most recent certification of these rights can be found in P.L. 105-17, the Individuals with Disabilities Education Act (IDEA) of 1997. States that request funding under P.L. 105-17 now must file a state plan that assures that the state will comply with the requirements set forth in the legislation. The Office of Special Education and Rehabilitative Services reviews these state plans and conducts on-site visits to determine whether educational programs comply with the law. Furthermore, all states that accept federal funds for any educational purpose must comply with Section 504 of the Vocational Rehabilitation Act of 1973. A state may decide to reject funding under P.L. 105-17 but must still comply with Section 504 unless the state decides to reject all federal educational funds (this has not occurred). The Office of Civil Rights enforces Section 504 by investigating complaints and coordinating compliance reviews. Section 504 is somewhat broader in its coverage, covering youngsters who may be physically ill and have a disability but do not have an *educational* disability. They may need special accommodations, "aids and services," but not "special education and related services" as specified in IDEA.

P.L. 105-17 covers a wide range of disabilities affecting approximately 12 percent of the school-age population. Educational objectives for children with disabilities are arrived at by a multidisciplinary team and parents, following a "complete, multifaceted, nondiscriminatory evaluation." These objectives, together with the special education and related services needed to achieve them, become part of a written Individualized Education Program (IEP). The IEP needs to contain "appropriate objectives, criteria and evaluation procedures, and schedules for determining, on at least an annual basis, whether instructional objectives are being achieved." The IEP is a statement of resources necessary to achieve a goal, an agreement on what an appropriate education for the child is to be, and the central management tool for ensuring accountability and compliance with the purposes of IDEA.[7]

Children with disabilities have the right to special education and related services. *Related services* are defined in the regulations as "those additional services required to assist a child to benefit from special education." Without establishing a limit, the regulations of IDEA provided a long list of possible related services. This list includes psychological and school social work services and excludes medical services, except those needed for diagnostic and evaluation purposes. The concept of related services is also treated in the educational regulations of Section 504 of the Vocational Rehabilitation Act of 1973. The Section 504 regulations define nondiscrimination in education as "the provision of a free, appropriate public education to qualified persons with disabilities regardless of the nature and severity of the person's disability." These regulations extended the concept of *related aids and services* to apply to regular education as well as special education. Two passages from these regulations point out the purpose of "aids, benefits, and services" in regular education:

> For the purpose of this report, aids, benefits, and services, to be equally effective are not required to produce the identical result of level of achievement for disabled or for nondisabled persons but must afford disabled persons equal opportunity to obtain the same result, to gain the same benefit or to the same level of achievement, in the most integrated setting appropriate to the person's needs.
>
> A recipient shall place a disabled person in the regular educational environment operated by the recipient unless it is demonstrated by the recipient that the education of the person in the regular environment with the use of supplementary aids and services cannot be provided satisfactorily.[8]

There has been considerable discussion as to how extensive the application of the term "related services" should be. To what extent would the term include ongoing services, medical in nature? Would a language board or a hearing aid be related service? Is psychotherapy a related service? How extensive this right was to be would be a matter for the courts and ongoing federal regulations. In the following five years a body of judicial decisions and regulations would emerge that clarified the meaning and direction of this right. As in the *Mills* case, prior to any legislation on this right, the child's right to a free appropriate public education, and to related services as defined in the IEP, could not be abridged by ability or availability in the local district. In many cases, the needed special education and related services would be purchased from the outside, from special education districts designed to meet needs that the local schools could not meet, and from private schools and institutions. The development of ways to share costs for services between districts quickly followed the enunciation of the right.

According to the Office of Civil Rights, Congress did not intend to restrict the definition of the term "related services" to any list or category. What the child with disabilities needs to assist him or her in benefiting from an education is the essential criterion of related services. Developmental, corrective, or supportive services (such as artistic and cultural programs and art, music, and dance therapy) could be related services if they are required to assist a disabled child to benefit from special education. An ongoing medical service would be considered a related service if it is needed to enable a qualified student with disabilities to obtain the same result, to gain the same benefit, or to reach the same level of achievement as a nondisabled student to the maximum extent possible.[9]

An Office of Civil Rights ruling in the case of a Connecticut regulation on related services sheds light on whether a clear distinction between *educational* and *noneducational* could be made. The regulation would have allowed school districts to avoid payment for certain related services if they determined residential placements were for noneducational reasons. In this particular case, the school district refused to pay for room and board and the cost of psychological counseling as "other than educationally related aids and services." The Office of Civil Rights' finding was that the "critical element" in determining whether a local educational agency is responsible for paying the cost of related services is whether the disabling condition adversely affects the child's educational performance. As soon as the school district decided that a residential placement was necessary for the student "to meet with success in school," it became obligated to provide that education at no cost to the parents.[10]

Whether educational policy is made through regulations or through the courts, the effect of such policies and the direction taken by the courts in interpreting P.L. 105-17 and Section 504 is becoming fairly clear. It is crucial to analyze the effect of these provisions on school social work practice, on delivery of services to children with disabilities, and on the school itself as it has traditionally conceived of its mission. Along with the question of the effect of these developments on school and on school services is the larger and related question of implementation. How might schools absorb the changes in their traditional mission? How may the current service delivery system adapt to the current reality of entitlement to services through the schools? What models of school social work practice emerge from these mandates, which cover areas where school social workers have been serving for seventy years? What role might school social work play in the implementation of services to children based on educational rights? The other articles in this section and indeed in the book will begin to answer that question.

SOCIAL REFORM PROGRAMS, COMMUNITIES, FAMILIES, AND SCHOOLS: FROM COMMUNITY REFORM TO SCHOOL PROGRAMS

Problems of social fragmentation, increased risks, and savage inequalities in education have energized a variety of efforts at social and educational reform. A host of data identify family structures unable to socialize and fragmented, ineffective education. Youngsters coming from difficult family and social situations seem hardly ready for the challenge of the more rigorous curriculum imagined by school reform movements. These efforts at social and educational reform are converging on the schools and on families. Reform agendas in public policy are combining with local forces to create an expanding new frontier for human service delivery. The changes in public policy reflect a strikingly consistent reform agenda reshaping diverse arenas: education, child welfare, juvenile delinquency prevention, community development, and others. The reforms promote similar principles. They trigger what are now becoming familiar institutional changes in schools. And they have heightened the need for new working models of service coordination in schools. Over the coming years, these changes in schools will reconstruct radically the practice environment for school social workers. New skills and new knowledge will be demanded of them as these evolutionary trends reshape their roles.

Reform Principles and Their Diverse Origins in Policies

The reforms in policy that are leading to the development of human services in schools emanate from a variety of legislative and administrative actions. For instance, the Family Preservation and Support Services Act of 1993 provided states with new federal funding to change the child welfare system.[11] School-based services are viewed by that program as among the strategies necessary to effect the changes. Other federal policies, such as the Clinton administration's Empowerment Zones and Enterprise Communities, seek to make school-based services into part of the neighborhood revitalization process.[12] Some of the same reform principles, which will be enumerated below, are reshaping long-standing programs such as Headstart. With the support of federal Headstart State Collaboration grants, states are studying strategies for creating more seamless linkages between local Headstart programs and kindergartens in public schools. Relocating Headstart classrooms into schools and linking them with other school-based preschool programs are counted among the strategies. Virtually every field of human services is somehow creating new programs in schools, at least partly at the behest of the reform agenda.

Many school reform strategies are also leading to the placement of human services in educational facilities. For example, federal goals for educational reform espouse the routine objective of having "every child ready to learn" by the time he or she reaches kindergarten; this objective has been used to justify many new preschool initiatives in schools. The goal of making schools safer has prompted more juvenile delinquency and prevention initiatives to be based in schools.[13] The goal of increasing the job readiness of students has led to more integration of employment training and job counseling into the formal curriculum and in school-to-work programs. Moreover, health clinics and substance abuse prevention programs are increasingly repositioned into schools because they are seen as supportive of a healthy educational setting.

The principles reflected in the human service reforms essentially seek to break down barriers between categorical programs and to make formal service systems more responsive to families, communities, and diverse cultures.[14] Social work practitioners who have written grant proposals in recent years, and those who have attended training conferences on "building collaborations," "family centered" services, or perhaps "community based" strategies, will find the principles familiar. They are:

1. Services are to be designed and delivered with respect for the diverse cultures of clients, or, to use the term more predominant in reform language, "customers." "Culturally competent" practices are required by policies to ensure that human services help recipients utilize the strengths in their cultural traditions and institutions.

2. Services are to empower families to take active roles in the design, implementation, and evaluation of programs that serve them.

3. Services are to prevent problems from occurring, rather than to only respond to problems after the fact.

4. Services are to be accessible to people in the neighborhoods where they live.

5. Services are to be linked in comprehensive strategies, drawing on multifaceted resources from mental health, health, economic development, delinquency prevention, and other traditionally separate fields.

6. Services are to conduct assessments and provide interventions that address the problems and resources of whole families, rather than individuals only.

7. Services are to emphasize the strengths, or "assets," of the communities in which they are located, rather than stressing the deviance and deficiencies that might be present.

The school reforms referred to above dovetail with these principles. Like human services, schools also seek to improve their culturally appropriate practices. A vast array of methods for involving families in schools is being tested. More schools are experimenting with programs that keep them open into the evenings, on weekends, and during summers, allowing them to function as community centers for a wide range of populations with a wide range of services, rather than only as sites for classroom-based teaching. In short, schools and human services are reaching for many of the same goals. These shared aspirations have called forth new institutional models for school-based services.

Models for School-Based Services

Adopting the reform principles promoted by many policies requires new institutional arrangements in schools. Among the more widely used models for creating school-based services are family centers, complex prevention initiatives, and brokered service networks. Increasingly, the utilization of such models is seen by community leaders as a step toward the eventual establishment of "full-service schools."[15]

Family centers create places in schools for whole families to receive services, to deliver mutual support to one another, and to deepen the involvement of parents in the school itself. Complex prevention initiatives take advantage of the fact that the school provides the best setting in which to reach the greatest numbers of children who are at risk of failure or serious health or social problems. Brokered service networks, such as those established by Communities in Schools, reposition human services into schools in order to keep children in school and to allow teachers to focus on basic education.

Family centers.   Utilizing funds from federal early childhood programs as well as family support funds, many states have made the family center a leading tool in the implementation of human service reform.[16] Schools have often been the preferred sites for the creation of such centers. The centers hold several advantages: They allow for considerable expansion of the productive roles of parents in schools as well as in service delivery. They facilitate "one-stop shopping"—the colocation of diverse services in one setting. They encourage a focus on the whole family.

Pennsylvania is one of the states that has directed considerable investment into the family center model.[17] Since 1989, it has provided funding and training to new family centers serving all of its sixty-four counties. The majority of the family centers are based in public elementary schools. The centers are operated by local nonprofit organizations, usually those that already exist in their localities.

The Pennsylvania Department of Public Welfare describes the family center as a "process, a philosophy and a place." The "process" refers to the collaborative, egalitarian decision making it establishes between parents, service providers, and administrators. The "philosophy" stresses prevention, cultural competence, and bolstering of natural, helping relationships among families. The shared "place" buttresses a sense of community and ownership among families, staff, and other stakeholders.

The Commonwealth of Pennsylvania requires that each center be designed through intensive collaboration among parents, community leaders, service providers, local government representatives, and school representatives. The deliberations struggle to balance the goal of creating programs that the families themselves define as necessary with the goal of staying within the legally prescribed terms of various funding sources. This balancing of family preferences with policy objectives requires considerable flexibility on the part of state administrators, local program managers, and school officials.

This balancing act is illustrated by the outreach programs that many of the family centers offer to parents of young children. Most of the centers operate as a core program a family-visiting service structured on the Parents as Teachers (PAT) model for parenting education.[18] The program trains parents—usually mothers—from the surrounding neighborhoods to become certified in the PAT curriculum. Each "family educator" then begins building a caseload of up to twenty-five families with children under the age of three years. Home visits take place about twice a month. Visits cover many aspects of early child development. The family educator seeks to build a trusting relationship with parents and children, which hopefully will lead them to come to the center for family-to-family groups and seminars and even to participate in governing board meetings. Moreover, since the center is also supposed to structure community forums on broader school and neighborhood issues, educators and other center staff hope that families who visit the center will also feel more empowered to become involved in community activities.

The PAT model on its own is a straightforward expression of many early childhood policies, including the Child Care and Development Block Grant.[19] Thus the Commonwealth has no trouble justifying the use of public funds to support it. However, participation in the center triggered by the family-visiting operation or by other meetings with families in the center can generate requests from parents that the center undertake initiatives that might not dovetail so closely with regulations in existing funding streams. Or they might request that the center become involved in community crime prevention or community development, activities whose funding might not normally be earmarked for family centers.

Its philosophy requires the family center to respond to such preferences, even when doing so will challenge it to undertake initiatives with organizations—an economic development corporation, for example—with whom it is not accustomed to working. It might lead staff members to stretch their job descriptions to the point where they need to learn skills—community organizing or public advocacy—they do not initially possess. Or parents might seek a program—teen dance classes—for which there is not an obvious funding source among those currently allocated to family centers.

The family center's process demands that it evolve over time into an institution that expresses the visions and the cultures of the families in the surrounding neighborhood. Thus, in addition to the challenges it presents to staff, it can also present challenges to the school, for often the center will stimulate new activities—community meetings or after-school recreation—that might not have been anticipated by the principal or school board when they initially "signed on" to the concept of a school-based family center. It might expand the presence of new cultural groups whose families traditionally had not been visible in the school.

Nevertheless, such responsiveness is precisely what is required by the reform principles enumerated above. It is required by the imperative to be responsive to culture. It is called for by the need to integrate diverse programs into coherent initiatives. It is stressed by the emphasis on involving families in all levels of decision making. Because it is well suited to adopt reform principles, the family center has become one of the Commonwealth's favorite tools for instituting them in human services. Other states—perhaps most notably, Kentucky and Maryland—have also made family centers central to their school reform and human service system reform efforts.

The elementary school is in important respects a site well suited for a family center. The school is already "owned" by the entire community, rather than sitting under the control of a particular cultural group or income group. The school constitutes a "normalized" site for services—there usually is not any label of deviance or dependency associated with attending the public school. It is the single best place to reach most of a community's children and, through them, their families. It offers advantages for setting up one-stop shopping. And, of course, it can facilitate a more intensive integration of educational goals with human services goals, an integration especially important to children in vulnerable families.

Complex prevention initiatives.   Whereas a family center represents a relatively autonomous new institution in a school, another type of initiative—a complex prevention initiative—constitutes a more complex and multifaceted partnership among different individuals and institutions. Such a partnership seeks to involve formal and informal resources from within the school and outside of the school in mutually reinforcing, risk-focused prevention strategies. It is a major new approach to bringing human services into school settings.

A good example of a risk-focused prevention framework is the "Communities That Care" (CTC) model developed by David Hawkins and Richard Catalano of the University of Washington, Seattle.[20] CTC is fast becoming a widely used model for community risk assessments and community resource assessments.[21] It structures a multitiered method for community participation. And it offers many "best practice" examples of promising prevention strategies that a community can integrate into a school-based, as well as a community-based, project. Moreover, it has received considerable funding support from foundations, states, and the U.S. Department of Justice to train localities in its use.

CTC recommends that a locality form two participatory bodies. The first body is a "key leaders" group composed of the school superintendent, the mayor, a few major agency directors, and top leaders from government, business, and perhaps local foundations. This group commits various institutions to the process. The second group advocated by CTC is the "community policy board." This is a broadly representative body: it includes neighborhood residents, parents, agency professionals, community activists, principals, teachers, and often youth. The community policy board meets regularly to oversee and help conduct the risk assessment and resource assessment. It also devises the prevention strategies that will respond to findings from the assessments. The key leaders group and the community policy board work together to garner the resources necessary to implement the strategies.

The CTC risk assessment and resource assessment build schools directly into the process. For instance, the risk assessment gathers data on nineteen risk factors that can raise the likelihood of children and youth getting involved in harmful behaviors (dropping out, teen pregnancy, juvenile crime, substance abuse, and violence). Four of the risk factors focus directly on the school environment. Many of the other risk factors pertain to family, community, and individual characteristics that can also be related indirectly to conditions in the school. School-based risk factors include "early and persistent antisocial behavior," "lack of commitment to school," and others.

Schools and the services they offer are also prominent among the community's assets studied by the resource assessment. Resources include formal and informal institutions, programs, practices, and people who, in the view of risk-focused prevention, constitute the real and potential "buffers" between youth and the risk factors.

After the community policy board reviews data from the risk and re-source assessments, it selects (usually) three to five of what it considers to be the locality's highest priority, or most serious, risk factors. Then, after considering the resources already present, the board devises a set of diverse, complementary strategies for risk prevention. Many such multifaceted proj-ects take place wholly or partly in schools.

For example, a project might focus on risk factors exhibited in elemen-tary schools. Failure rates in third and fourth grades might be of concern. Suspension rates for violence or acting out in classrooms might also be rising. In such a case, a prevention initiative might include tutoring for the third and fourth graders by older, successful students, anger management seminars, a gang prevention project, and perhaps a parent support group to reinforce the positive roles of parents in each of the above areas. Such an initiative would be typical of the kind of school-based projects that are proliferating rapidly as a result of CTC and other prevention models.

Complex prevention initiatives reflect many of the same reform princi-ples espoused by the family centers. The resource assessment delves into the culturally based institutions and practices that might be drawn on to counteract the presence of particular risk factors. The risk assessment is comprehensive and virtually requires comprehensive strategies. The family, as well as the school, is viewed as a critical institution for prevention. And the community policy board, as well as the community-based research re-quired by the risk assessment, creates opportunities for families and resi-dents to participate meaningfully in all phases of the process.

Brokered service networks.   A third trend affecting schools through human service reform is the establishment of brokered service networks. While not as tightly coordinated as complex prevention initiatives, brokered service networks also reposition community resources into schools. Many schools engage in such brokering through their own personnel. However, some organizations, most prominently, Communities in Schools, Inc., work with schools and communities to help facilitate this repositioning.

Communities in Schools, Inc., based in Alexandria, Virginia, has affili-ates in many cities in the United States, England, and Canada. Virtually all of them see the task of repositioning human services and other community resources into schools as central to their missions. The Chicago affiliate presents a very straightforward example of how to create brokered service networks. It is also a prominent example: it works closely with thirty-five public schools in Chicago and is adding fifteen new schools per year.

Chicago Communities in Schools' (CCIS) mission statement reads as follows: CCIS *repositions existing community resources into school sites to help young people successfully learn, stay in school, and prepare for life.*[22] It repositions these resources through a finely honed process of negotiation

with the school, brokering between the school and other community institutions, coordination within the school, and assessment.

In order to work with CCIS, a school must demonstrate commitment
to the process by designating a "site coordinator" who will work with the
CCIS staff person, the agency coordinator, on a regular basis. Site coordinators must be full-time regular staff. Often they are assistant principals, school
social workers, or counselors who can make significant time commitments
to working with CCIS and the resources they help bring to the school.

The process begins with a team of staff and volunteers from the school
designating the ten most important issues with which it needs help if the
team is to make a substantial improvement in the educational environment.
The issues that have surfaced across the thirty-five schools vary considerably, but a few arise consistently. Among the most prevalent concerns are
the interest in supporting parents, gang prevention, and a variety of health
needs.

Once the top issues are identified, the CCIS agency coordinator (a
full-time CCIS staff member who works with up to seven different schools)
begins to search for, and negotiate with, organizations or individuals who
can deliver the needed services at the school. CCIS does not pay the entities
who move into schools. Rather, it emphasizes the advantages to the organizations of positioning some of their services into these new settings.

An example of a school that has made substantial use of the CCIS
brokering service is Victor Herbert School on Chicago's west side.[23] Providers currently working in this school include:

- American Red Cross: workshops on HIV/AIDS awareness,
- Bobby E. Wright Mental Health Clinic: culturally centered problem
  solving, life skills, and conflict resolution,
- Chicago Police Department: conflict resolution, safety, violence, and
  gang prevention,
- Cook County Children's Hospital: health services for students and
  families,
- Cook Country Sheriff's Department: drug awareness and gang
  awareness programs,
- Hartgrove Hospital: group and individual counseling,
- Junior Achievement: entrepreneurial curriculum,
- Sinai Community Institute: life skills, healthy decision making, and
  self-esteem, and
- Software for Success: computer-aided reading skills program.

Provider lists can grow and change as the school revisits its needs with
CCIS in an annual contract review and assessment.

CCIS staff also help to coordinate the repositioned resources once they are in the school. This is not the intensively managed collaboration required by a comprehensive prevention initiative; rather it is more an effort to ensure that providers know one another, that schedules are synchronized, that duplication is avoided, and that agencies can cooperate with one another when the need arises.

CCIS's goal is for each school to eventually be able to undertake the brokering and coordinating on its own. Thus CCIS staff pay close attention to developing a skilled, committed, and stable leadership base at the school. It is critical that the site coordinator develop the leadership capacity to maintain, build, and evaluate the networks of providers working in his or her school.

CCIS has received considerable financial support from foundations and corporations because what it does is seen as advancing school reform and human service reform. It advances school reform partly by opening up new relationships between schools and communities. It advances human service reform by making services more accessible to children and families and by encouraging cross-agency teamwork. By doing the above, it brings more of the community's resources to bear on keeping children in school and by helping them to address social and health problems that can place them at higher risk of school failure.

Full service schools.   Joy G. Dryfoos has studied the phenomenon of school-based services in considerable depth. Her book *Full-Service Schools* (1994) provides a sweeping view of the field. As Dryfoos puts it:

> Throughout the country, community agencies are locating programs in school buildings, mainly in low-income areas both urban and rural. Close to five hundred comprehensive school-based clinics have been identified, and many more are in the planning stage. . . . Hundreds of family resource centers (the number is unknown) provide other support services, including parent education, Headstart, after-school child care, case management, meals, crisis intervention, and whatever else is needed by parents and young children.[24]

Dryfoos's work, however, does not merely summarize the state of existing programs. Rather, it proposes a model for the "full-service school."

The full-service school goes well beyond family centers, prevention initiatives, and networks to fully transform the school into a comprehensive service center. As Dryfoos relates:

> The vision of the full-service school puts the best of school reform together with all other services that children, youth and families need, most of which can be located in a school building. The educational mandate places responsibility on the school system to reorganize and innovate. The charge to community agencies is to bring into the school: health, mental health, employment services,

child care, parent education, case management, recreation, cultural events, welfare, community policing, and whatever else may fit into the picture. The result is a new "seamless" institution, a community-oriented school with a joint governance structure that allows maximum responsiveness to the community, as well as accessibility and continuity for those most in need of services. The theme of integration of educational, health, and social welfare services reverberates through local, state, and national dialogues.[25]

A full-service school is a collaborative institution that realizes many of the reform principles described at the outset of this chapter.

A few schools can claim to have achieved the full-service status. Dryfoos describes how a middle school in the Washington Heights section of New York City teamed with the Children's Aid Society to create a full-scale settlement house in the school. Other schools are reaching for the comprehensiveness and strong community base that this school has established. In fact, a number of schools in New York City—the Beacons Schools and others—see themselves, and rightfully so, as "community schools": schools through which neighborhoods mobilize their resources not only to improve education, and not merely to provide services. Community schools seek to serve as the nerve centers for comprehensive neighborhood revitalization.

Community schools and full-service schools exhibit how far the movement to integrate human services, community development, and education can move. As the momentum to bring more services into educational facilities grows, more schools will begin to "measure up" as full-service schools. There are as yet no signs at the level of public policy or at the level of community service that the trend toward school-based services is slowing.

IMPLICATIONS OF REFORM MOVEMENTS FOR SCHOOL SOCIAL WORKERS

The implications of these developments for school social work are less clear at the moment than the implications of the educational rights of children with disabilities. School social workers again have an opportunity to articulate an appropriate professional role. If this articulation does not take place, they could be moved into marginal status, and the reform movements would be negatively affected. To some extent this has already happened in other social work fields of practice when faced with a similar challenge, although so far not in schools.

The first implication for social workers is the creation of a changing boundary between the school and the community. When the school is a service center for the community, its traditional boundaries shift to include the entire community, with a very different range of ages and needs. Education itself inevitably becomes redefined. While the school is the natural place for such a center of services, it is a radical change. The history of American education points out that it will take schooling a considerable amount of time to absorb these changes. The social worker, much more familiar with the broader community and its concerns, is in a most important position to make the concept work. Given this broadening of the school's identity into a community-wide institution, school social workers, with their generalist practice perspectives, might be best positioned among school-based professionals to play leading roles in the implementation of the reforms. Such leadership might entail monitoring policy changes in human services that would support new school-based services, facilitating planning groups to establish new school-based collaboratives, or utilizing the increased supports in policies to expand the generalist approaches in their own practice.

Along with the changing boundaries, the school also must deal with the inherent diversity of the communities it may encompass. Schools have often been the places where ethnic and class differences found some resolution, but their effectiveness in this has historically been mixed. The increased importance of school as a central resource for families may also make the potential for conflict greater.

The key to effectiveness of the programs will rest on whether they successfully assist and empower families. Such programs should be resources to help families develop the internal capacities needed to carry out their roles effectively. However, as history and experience attest, in the face of a weakened family structure, a program might further weaken families by attempting to "manage" their problems. The language and theory of practice and policy need to address these issues so that families remain in charge of their domains and partners with schools in a broadened education mission.

As alluded to above, school reforms and human service reforms are effecting a considerable diversification in the roles families can play in schools. School social workers seeking to empower families to play more meaningful and productive roles in their children's education as well as in service delivery will find new opportunities to do so. Family centers will constitute new institutional bases for parents in schools, allowing for better communication with school-based professionals as well as with one another. They will make it easier for family-centered, as opposed to student-centered, practice. They will create a legitimate base from which families can support one another, a process that group practice skills of social work can help facilitate. Mediation between families and professional specialists might also develop as a more common role for school social workers, given the increased presence of parents in many schools.

The role of the social worker, responding to community demands, could on the other hand become more specialized, with different types of social workers doing different things. This could become quite problematic. Inappropriate specialization may carry with it the possibility of deprofessionalization of the social work role. Deprofessionalization would reduce, simplify, and adapt the social work role so that it could be managed by a less well prepared (and less expensive) practitioner. If universities do not prepare students appropriately, or if school social workers do not adapt and develop their roles to meet these challenges at a high level of service, this could well take place. On the other hand the history of school social work has been one of active response and engagement with changing conditions, the most recent being the educational rights of children with disabilities. There is no reason to assume that they will not rise to this challenge as well.

Articles in this section and in the following sections follow the theme of policy development and implementation in the role of the school social worker. The chapters in section II review policy development in schools and the structure of services. This chapter has outlined the implications for school social work of two different developments: the rights of children with disabilities and the emergent forms of school community service integration and coordination. The following chapters in this section develop the theme of policy analysis with a focus on the current economic, political, and social worlds of school social work and the school organization. Section III, "Service Delivery in the Schools," focuses on the many possible elaborations of the school social work role in response to need. These elaborations all have some basis in policy, and much of the discussion is on implementation of these directions. In section IV the major focus rests on the uses of research, particularly needs assessment, at the school and community level toward program and policy development.

Changes in the expectations of schools and in school structure are profoundly influencing the purposes and functions of school social work. Furthermore, as the school social worker becomes more deeply involved with consultation on issues that have implications, not simply for single cases, but for entire school districts, an understanding of the roots of policy development in the schools will be essential. Even now, in many locales the knowledge and skills of school social work and its understanding of the school clientele are proving useful to the policy development process. Any further development will depend on the commitment of school social workers to seeing policy development as a natural direction of practice and to preparing themselves for the implications of this role.

In summary, the articles in this section provide in-depth explorations into crucial aspects of the school as an institution and its complex task of working and interfacing with other institutions around human service issues. There is no pretense of providing a comprehensive review of all aspects of the institution or all the vulnerable populations and institutions with which the school deals. Rather, the articles provide models for the type of thinking necessary if school social work is to achieve its appropriate match with the institution of education and provide a link to other elements in the community as a system.

REFERENCES

1. An example of this would be the excellent text, now in its fifth edition, H. R. Turnbull and A. P. Turnbull, *Free appropriate public education: The law and children with disabilities*, 5th ed (Denver: Love Publishing, 1998).

2. *Pennsylvania Association of Retarded Children (PARC) v. Commonwealth of Pennsylvania*, 334 F. Supp. 1257 (E.D. Pa. 1971).

3. *Mills v. Board of Education of the District of Columbia*, 458 G. Supp. 866 (DDC, 1972).

4. 29 U.S.C. 794.

5. 20 U.S.C. 11401 et seq.

6. F. J. Weintraub and A. Abeson, New education policies for the handicapped: The quiet revolution, in F. Weintraub, A. Abeson, J. Ballard, and M. LaVor (eds.), *Public policy and the education of exceptional children* (Washington, DC: Council for Exceptional Children, 1976), pp. 7–13.

7. U.S. Department of Health, Education, and Welfare, Education of handicapped children, *Federal Register*, August 23, 1977: 121a340–42.

8. U.S. Department of Education, Nondiscrimination on the basis of handicap in programs and activities receiving or benefiting from federal financial assistance, *Federal Register*, May 19, 1980: 33(6)(1) (34 C.F.R. part 104).

9. Office of Civil Rights, Letter of Findings, February 27, 1980, Illinois Board of Education, *Education of the Handicapped Law Review* 257:176. See also *Education of the Handicapped Law Review* Analysis and Comment, EHLR Perspective: Related Services, Supplement 28, July 25, 1980 (Washington, DC: CRR Publishing, 1980), A/C 20–21, *Tatro v. Texas*, U.S. Dist. Court, N. Dist. Texas, 12–21079, and *Tatro v. Texas*, 625 F.2d 557 (5th Cir. 1980).

10. Office of Civil Rights, Letter of Findings, June 16, 1980, Simsbury, Connecticut Public Schools, *Education of the Handicapped Law Review* 257:178.

11. Enacted as part of the Omnibus Budget and Reconciliation Act of 1993 (P.L. 103-66).

12. U.S. Department of Housing and Urban Development and U.S. Department of Agriculture, *Building communities: Together*, Empowerment Zones and Enterprise Communities Application Guide (Washington, DC: Authors, 1994).

13. S. M. McGroder, A. C. Crouter, and R. S. Kordesh, *Schools and communities: Emerging collaborations for serving adolescents and their families* (University Park, PA: PRIDE Project and Graduate School of Public Policy and Administration, March 1994).

14. National Commission for Children, *Beyond rhetoric: A new American agenda for children and families* (Washington, DC: U.S. Government Printing Office, 1991); C. Bruner, D. Both, and C. Marzke, *Steps along an uncertain path: State initiatives promoting comprehensive, community-based reform* (Des Moines,

Iowa: National Center for Service Integration, 1996); P. Adam and K. Nelson, *Reinventing human services: Community- and family-centered practice* (NY: Aldine de Gruyter, 1995).

15. J. G. Dryfoos, *Full-service schools* (San Francisco: Jossey Bass, 1994).

16. D. R. Dupper and J. Poertner, Public schools and the revitalization of impoverished communities: School-linked family resource centers. *Social Work* 42 (September 1997): 415–422.

17. Pennsylvania Children's Cabinet, *A blueprint for the future of Pennsylvania's children and families* (Harrisburg, PA: Author, 1994).

18. Parents as Teachers (PAT) is a nationally replicated program based in St. Louis, MO. For information, contact PAT at 9374 Olive Boulevard, St. Louis, MO 63132.

19. Child Care and Development Block Grant, P.L. 101-508. Enacted as part of the Omnibus Budget and Reconciliation Act of 1990.

20. J. D. Hawkins and R. E. Catalano, *Communities that care* (San Francisco: Jossey Bass, 1992).

21. Developmental Research and Programs, Inc., *Communities that care: A comprehensive prevention program, team handbook* (Seattle, WA: Author, 1995).

22. Chicago Communities in Schools, Inc., *Connections* (Chicago: Author, winter 1998).

23. Chicago Communities in Schools, Inc., *Service provider guide book for Victor Herbert School, school year 1997–98* (Chicago: Author, 1997).

24. Dryfoos, pp. 14–15.

25. Dryfoos, p. 12.

CHAPTER 7

The Changing Social, Political and Economic Context of School Social Work

Isadora Hare
Project Manager, Healthy Adolescents Project,
American Psychological Association

Sunny Harris Rome
Assistant Professor of Social Work, George Mason University

- School Reform and National Goals
- Demographic, Psychological and Socioeconomic Factors Influencing Educational Outcomes
- Federal, State, and Local Responses
- The Role of Social Workers in a Changing World

In 1987, Leila Costin wrote that the essential purpose of school is "to provide a setting for teaching and learning in which all children can prepare themselves for the world they now live in and the world they will face in the future" (p.538). As we approach the millennium this statement continues to ring true. Schools play an integral role in preparing our youth to become healthy, creative, and productive adults, workers, and citizens. Schools are a microcosm of the larger society in which they function. Because public schools are designed to serve all children, even in a society as vast, complex, and pluralistic as the United States, they inevitably reflect events and trends in society at large. Often schools exhibit a cultural lag in response to changing social circumstances, yet inevitably over time they become subject to those influences. As Germain has stated, social work in the schools is at the center of an "intricate transactional field of forces" (Germain, 1987, p. 510). This field includes demographic, social, economic, and political forces to which schools respond with both conservative and innovative strategies. Since its inception over ninety years ago, school social work's content and direction has been influenced by its social environment: conditions and events within society itself and particularly within the educational system where school social workers practice.

The United States is a free market democracy. As such, economic success and citizen participation at all levels of government are prime national goals. The extent to which our educational system prepares the upcoming generation to achieve these goals in the new global economy is therefore a matter of deep concern within our society.

SCHOOL REFORM AND NATIONAL GOALS

During the 1980s several national reports drew attention to serious problems in American education. Prominent among these was *A Nation at Risk*, which in 1983 pronounced that the United States faced a "rising tide of mediocrity" in education. These concerns and responses to them culminated in the enactment of Goals 2000: Educate America Act (P.L. 103–227) in 1994. This federal law put into place eight national educational goals. Six of these had been adopted by the nation's governors in 1990, after a historic summit convened by President Bush and the governors in Charlottesville, Virginia, in September 1989.

These national educational goals are defined in the law as follows (with goals 4 and 8 added to the original six):

"*Goal 1: Readiness:* By the year 2000, all children in America will start school ready to learn." Objectives include ensuring access to high quality and developmentally appropriate preschool programs for all disadvantaged and disabled children, facilitating parent involvement in education and providing the training and support required to perform this function, and supplementing education with nutrition and health care.

"*Goal 2: School Completion:* By the year 2000, the high school graduation rate will increase to at least 90%." Objectives include reducing the dropout rate and eliminating the gap in high school graduation rates between students from minority backgrounds and their non-minority counterparts.

"*Goal 3: Student Achievement and Citizenship:* By the year 2000, all students will leave grades 4, 8, and 12 having demonstrated competency over challenging subject matter including English, mathematics, science, foreign language, civics and government, economics, arts, history, and geography, and every school in America will ensure that all students learn to use their minds well, so that they may be prepared for responsible citizenship, further learning, and productive employment in our modern economy."

"*Goal 4: Teacher Education and Professional Development:* By the year 2000, the nation's teaching force will have access to programs for the continued improvement of their professional skills and the opportunity to acquire the knowledge and skills needed to instruct and prepare all American students for the next century."

"*Goal 5: Mathematics and Science:* By the year 2000, United States students will be first in the world in mathematics and science achievement."

"*Goal 6: Adult Literacy and Lifelong Learning:* By the year 2000, every adult American will be literate and will possess the knowledge and skills necessary to compete in a global economy and exercise the rights and responsibilities of citizenship."

"*Goal 7: Safe, Disciplined, and Drug-Free Schools:* By the year 2000, every school in the United States will be free of drugs, violence, and the unauthorized presence of firearms and alcohol and will offer a disciplined environment conducive to learning." Objectives include the implementation of firm and fair policies on drugs and alcohol, encouraging collaboration between parents, businesses, and community organizations, and developing comprehensive K–12 drug and alcohol prevention programs to be taught within health education, and organizing "community-based teams to provide students and teachers with needed support" (National Governors' Association, 1990).

"*Goal 8: Parental Participation:* By the year 2000, every school will promote partnerships that will increase parental involvement and participation in promoting the social, emotional, and academic growth of children." Objectives of this goal include developing policies and programs for increasing partnerships that respond to the varying needs of parents and the home, including parents of children who are disadvantaged or bilingual, or parents of children with disabilities; and engaging parents and families in a partnership that supports the academic work of children at home and shared educational decision making at school.

Since the inception of Goals 2000, individual states have adopted a variety of strategies to improve local education, including increasing efforts to prepare students for jobs; recruiting better educators; promoting more family, community, and business involvement; making schools safer; and increasing access to computers.

In 1996 the Goals 2000 legislation was amended. Local education agencies (LEAs) in states that had chosen not to participate in Goals 2000 were, with the states' permission, allowed to apply directly to the secretary of education for Goals 2000 funding. The legislation created a new focus on technology in schools, aimed at preparing all students to be technologically literate by the twenty-first century. Finally, it clarified that recipient states cannot be required to provide school-based health services, social services, or outcome-based education as a condition of receiving Goals 2000 assistance (P.L. 104-134).

The goals embody several important themes that are reflected in current educational policies. One is an emphasis on high standards of student academic achievement (goals 2 through 6). Another is the recognition that nonacademic, psychosocial factors also influence educational outcomes and must be addressed if high standards are to be reached and maintained. These factors influence school readiness, parental involvement in schools, and the ability to stay in school and not drop out (goals 1, 2, 7, and 8).

STUDENT ACADEMIC ACHIEVEMENT IN THE UNITED STATES

Since the formulation of the national educational goals in 1989, there has been an increased focus in the United States on setting high standards for student achievement both in mathematics and science and in other subjects. In March 1996, the nation's governors held a second National Education Summit at Palisades, New York, to "reaffirm their commitment to school reform" and to call for "an external, independent, non-governmental effort to measure and report each state's annual progress" ("Quality Counts," 1997, p. 3). The establishment of standards, the measurement of achievement, and the design and use of tests have become controversial topics among educators, politicians, business leaders, and the public.

Since 1969, the congressionally mandated National Assessment of Educational Progress (NAEP) has been the only ongoing national survey of students' educational achievement, periodically monitoring student achievement in a number of subjects in grades 4, 8, and 12. The NAEP does not provide results for individual students. Furthermore, it does not reveal whether students have mastered a challenging body of knowledge and skills because, as norm-referenced tests, the measures used only compare students to each other and not to an unwavering standard of performance" ("Quality Counts," 1997, p. 20). Other tests are used by individual states but yield such inconsistent results that they cannot provide a reliable measure of what students have learned.

President Clinton has emphasized education as a policy priority. The administration argues that national educational standards are essential to school improvement and that national tests linked to these standards, like those used in other countries, are essential as a consistent means of accurately measuring our educational progress as a nation (Froomkin, 1998).

In the United States education is locally controlled: there are almost 85,000 schools in approximately 14,500 school districts, all of which jealously guard their independence and decision-making power. The role of the federal government in education matters remains a highly controversial issue in the United States. Because of this, the Clinton proposal for a national testing program involves the following aspects:

- Tests would be voluntary with any state or local education agency (SEA and LEA) retaining the right not to participate.
- Tests would be basic, reflecting a common set of expectations rather than specified curriculum content (Froomkin, 1998).
- They would be based on the existing NAEP.
- The program would be administered by the twenty-six-member governmental bipartisan panel, the National Assessment Governing Board, which is also the governing body for the NAEP.

However, despite these assurances, the issue has remained politically divisive. Congressional Republican leaders have attacked the plan and some

House Democrats have joined the opposition on the grounds that minority students would be further prejudiced by testing. Strong support is coming from business leaders, particularly those in the technology sector of the economy, whose needs for a skilled workforce are increasing. However, the controversy continues to rage, and in January 1998, the National Assessment Governing Board postponed the first administration of the fourth- and eighth-grade tests until 2001 (Lawton, 1998). This is a clear example of how schools and educational policies are affected by the political and economic realities of the world around them. School social workers must be knowledgeable about such issues.

In spite of this debate and the resistance to change, the need for reform is accentuated by the performance of U.S. students on international tests. In 1995, the most comprehensive international study of mathematics and science performance ever was conducted. Known as TIMSS, the Third International Mathematics and Science Study tested half a million students in forty-one countries in thirty languages. These included some chief U.S. trading partners and economic competitors, such as Japan, Germany, Canada, Korea, Singapore, and Hong Kong (National Education Goals Panel, 1997). While U.S. fourth-grade scores were above the international average in both math and science, at the eighth-grade level U.S. students scored above the international average in science but below the average in mathematics. When compared to our chief economic partners, the United States is in the bottom half in mathematics and around the middle in science. Conclusions were drawn in three areas: curriculum, instruction, and teacher training needed change. The U.S. math curriculum is less advanced and less focused than in other countries; instructional methods are outdated, and teacher training methods should be revised (National Education Goals Panel, 1997, p. 12).

The twelfth-grade TIMSS results were reported early in 1998. These revealed that U.S. high school seniors ranked close to last among the twenty-one Western nations that participated in this phase of the study. Compared to their peers elsewhere, U.S. seniors study less than the reported average, spend more time at after-school jobs, and are less likely to take math and science for four years in high school. They do, however, use computers more often (Sanchez, 1998b).

While there is clearly reason for concern about instruction and curriculum in our educational system, other factors also influence the level of education in the United States.

DEMOGRAPHIC, PSYCHOSOCIAL, AND SOCIOECONOMIC FACTORS INFLUENCING EDUCATIONAL OUTCOMES

Demographics

The number of children under age eighteen in the United States has grown during the last fifty years. In 1996, there were 69.4 million children in this category (Federal Interagency Forum 1997, p. 1), representing almost 26 percent of the total population. There were approximately equal numbers—almost 23 million—in each age group: 0–5, 6–11, and 12–17 years. This number is expected to reach 72 million by 2005 (Annie E. Casey, 1997, p. 20). The extent and nature of population diversity is changing rapidly. The United States is currently experiencing its second great wave of immigration, this time not from Europe but from the economically developing worlds of Asia and Latin America (Booth, 1998). Already in states like New Mexico, California, and Texas, the numbers of children under age eighteen years who are African American, Latino, Asian and Pacific Islanders, and Native American together far exceed the number of white children. For example, in 1995 in California the total of "minority" children was just over 5 million compared to just over 3.5 million white children (Annie E. Casey Foundation, 1997, p. 42). The numbers of Hispanic and Asian children are projected to increase by 34 percent and 39 percent respectively by 2005, while the number of white children is projected to decrease by 10 percent. For the nation as a whole, the number of white children is projected to decrease 3 percent for the decade 1995 to 2005, while other groups are projected to increase by 8 percent (blacks), 30 percent (Hispanic), 39 percent (Asian and Pacific Islander), and 6 percent (Native American) Annie E. Casey Foundation, 1997, p. 20).

Because of these demographic factors, a lively debate is currently raging on the issue of bilingual education as opposed to English-only education. A recent multiyear study by Ruben Rumbaut of Michigan State University and Alejandro Portes of Princeton (1998) has shown that by the end of high school the children of immigrants prefer to speak English, and that socioeconomic status, in addition to ethnicity, affects dropout rates and school outcomes (Dugger, 1998).

Poverty

The child poverty rate for the country as a whole has hovered at or above 20 percent for more than a decade (Annie E. Casey Foundation, 1997, p. 16). In 1995, one in five children lived in families with incomes below the federal poverty line, which was $15,569 for a family of four people. In 1995, 24 percent of children under age six lived in poverty, compared to 18 percent of older children. Children living in households with two married parents are far less likely to live in poverty than children living in female-headed families: 10 percent compared to 50 percent in 1995. The child poverty rate is also much higher among African-American and Latino families. In 1995, 11 percent of white children were poor compared to 42 percent of black children and 39 percent of Hispanic children. If poverty is redefined as a family income one and a half times the federal poverty level—that is, $23,353 for a family of four—the child poverty rate rises to 32 percent (Federal Interagency Forum, 1997, p. 15).

> Despite the enormous wealth in the U.S., our child poverty rate is among the highest in the developed world. One study which examined child poverty rates in 17 developed countries indicates that the child poverty rate is 50% higher than the next highest rate. . . . The gap is greatly accentuated by the enormous differences in the role government plays in alleviating child poverty (Kids Count Data Book, 1997, p. 17).

As the Federal Interagency Forum on Child and Family Statistics stated in 1997:

> Childhood poverty has both immediate and lasting negative effects. . . . Research suggests that children who are poor are more likely than [others] to have difficulty in school, to become teen parents, and, as adults, to earn less and be unemployed more (p. 14).

Substance Abuse

Drugs. The National Education Goals Panel reported in 1997 that overall student drug use has increased. Between 1991 and 1996, the percentage of tenth graders who reported that they used any illicit drug during the previous year increased from 24 to 40 percent. Thirty-two percent of tenth graders reported that someone at school had offered to sell or give them an illegal drug at school during the past year (1996). This represented a significant increase since 1992, when 18 percent made similar reports (pp. 61–62).

The 1997 survey of teen drug use conducted by the University of Michigan found that marijuana use had dropped slightly for eighth graders but continued to rise for both tenth and twelfth graders. Almost half the seniors who graduated in June 1997 reported having tried marijuana at some time in the past. Of these, 5.8 percent reported that they had smoked marijuana daily during the previous month (Wren, 1997, p. 24), but 25 percent said they had smoked it during the previous month (Federal Interagency Forum, 1997, p. 37). Cocaine use among twelfth graders dropped from 6.7 percent in 1985 to 1.8 percent in 1995 (U.S. Department of Health and Human Services, Office of the Assistant Secretary [DHHS-ASPE], 1996, p. 157).

Alcohol. Studies have confirmed that alcohol is a more serious threat to adolescents than illicit drugs. The National Education Goals Panel (1997) found that 65 percent of tenth graders reported that they had used alcohol during the previous year, a percentage that has remained fairly stable since 1993. Twenty-five percent reported binge drinking—defined as taking five drinks or more in a row—in the past two weeks. Among twelfth graders,

31 percent reported binge drinking, up from the percentage for 1993 (Wren, 1997, p. 24). Binge drinking has also risen for eighth graders: from 12.9 percent in 1991 to 15 percent in 1997 (DHHS-ASPE, 1996, p. 152; Wren, 1997, p. 24).

Tobacco.   Research has now demonstrated that smoking cigarettes has serious long-term health consequences and that many adults who are addicted to tobacco began smoking as adolescents. Yet each year in the United States over one million adolescents begin smoking. The percentages of eighth, tenth, and twelfth graders who reported that they smoked cigarettes daily increased between 1992 and 1996. In 1996, 22 percent of twelfth graders, 18 percent of tenth graders, and 10 percent of eighth graders reported smoking daily (Federal Interagency Forum, 1997, p. 35). The federal government and organizations in the private sector are now mounting active campaigns to reduce teen smoking. Legislation is pending in the Congress to determine the terms of a monetary settlement between the major tobacco companies and the states who won a legal suit against them for expenses incurred from tobacco addiction and its adverse health consequences.

Teen Sex and Pregnancy

Most adolescents begin having sexual intercourse in their mid- to late teens. Fifty-six percent of young women and 73 percent of young men have had intercourse by age eighteen, compared with 35 percent of women and 55 percent of men in the early 1970s. While the likelihood of having intercourse increases steadily throughout the teen years, 18 percent of adolescents (almost one in five) do not have intercourse during their teen years (Alan Guttmacher Institute, 1996).

The teen birthrate has declined steadily for five years. In 1996 it was 57.7 per 1,000 females aged 15–19 years (a 12 percent decline since 1991; Child Trends, 1997). Each year almost one million teen women—11 percent of all women aged 15–19 and 22 percent of those who have had intercourse—become pregnant. Of these pregnancies, 14 percent end in miscarriage, 32 percent are aborted, and over half, 54 percent, end in live birth. Teens who give birth are much more likely to come from poor or low-income families (83 percent) than are teens who have abortions (61 percent) or teens in general (38 percent) (Alan Guttmacher Institute, 1996).

In 1995, for the first time the teen birthrate was highest among Hispanic girls (107 per 1,000 females aged 15–19), followed by non-Hispanic African-American girls (99 per 1,000) and non-Hispanic whites (39 per 1,000).

There is a close association between teen pregnancy and parenthood on one hand and school factors on the other. Child Trends, Inc., has identified four risk factors for teen births: early school failure, early behavior problems, family dysfunction, and poverty. In contrast, involvement in school activities after the birth of the first child or receipt of a high school diploma or GED were strongly associated with postponing a second teen birth (Child Trends, 1997).

Child Abuse and Neglect

In 1995, more than one million children were identified as victims of abuse or neglect. Nationwide, the rate of victimization of children was approximately 15 per 1,000 children under age eighteen. Twice as many victims suffered from neglect (52 percent) as from physical abuse (25 percent). About 13 percent were sexually abused. More than half of all victims were age seven or younger, and about 21 percent of the victims were teenagers. Forty-five states reported in 1995 that almost one thousand children known to Child Protective Services agencies died as a result of abuse or neglect. (DHHS, National Center on Child Abuse and Neglect, 1997).

Violence

The National Education Goals Panel (1997) reported the following:

- In 1996, 36 percent of tenth graders reported that they had been threatened or injured at school during the previous year. This represented a 4 percentage point reduction since 1991.
- Fifteen percent of school teachers reported in 1994 that they had been threatened or physically attacked by a student in their schools during the previous year. This was a 5 percent increase since 1991, when 10 percent made this report.
- In 1992, 17 percent of tenth graders reported that misbehavior by other students interfered with their learning at least six times a week. No reduction in class disruption occurred over the next four years of studies.
- In 1994, 46 percent of all secondary school teachers reported that student misbehavior interfered with their teaching. This was a 7 percent increase since 1991.

In March, 1998, the White House released survey results that reported that one in ten American public schools experienced serious violent crimes such as rape or robbery in the past year (Associated Press, 1998). The prevalence was higher at large schools and at schools in urban areas. This study was commissioned after a thirteen-year-old boy in Paducah, Kentucky, opened fire on a group of his schoolmates who were holding a prayer meeting, killing three and seriously wounding five.

Community violence among youth is at alarming levels. In 1994, almost 2.6 million youths aged 12–17 were victims of violent crime (Federal Interagency Forum, 1997). African-American males are at particular risk. Homicide is the leading cause of death for African-American men aged 15–24. The rate rose almost 200 percent between 1985 and 1991 (46.5 to 134.6 per 100,000; National Adolescent Health Information Center, 1995).

A 1998 study by the Centers for Disease Control and Prevention showed that the suicide rate for 10–19-year-olds rose between 1980 and 1995. Although suicide is still highest among whites, the increase was particularly dramatic among black youths. The suicide rate for this latter group increased by 114 percent since 1980, especially in the South. A total of 3,030 young African Americans have committed suicide since 1980, and nearly all of those studied involved the use of a firearm (Sanchez, 1998a).

Dropouts

Goal 2 of the national education goals aims to increase the high school graduation rate to at least 90 percent by the year 2000. In 1996, 86 percent of 18–24-year-olds had completed a high school credential. This was the same as in 1990. However, in 1996 the proportion of young adults who completed an alternative credential because of leaving high school before graduation doubled from its 1990 level. Further, disparities in high school completion rates between white and minority youth did no improve between 1990 and 1996. For example, the gap between Hispanic and white 18–24-year-olds who had a high school credential remained constant at 31 percentage points between 1990 and 1996 (National Education Goals Panel, 1997, pp. 30, 39).

Parental Participation

The recognition that parental participation is an important factor in assuring high standards of academic achievement led to the inclusion in 1994 of goal 8 in the Goals 2000: Educate America. Objectives for the goal include developing state policies to assist school districts and schools to establish programs for partnerships "that respond to the varying needs to parents and the home, including parents of children who are disadvantaged or bilingual, or parents of children with disabilities" and actively engage parents and families "in a partnership which supports the academic work of children at home and shared educational decisionmaking at school." Additionally, parents and families are charged with the responsibility of holidng schools and teacher to high standards of accountability (National Education Goals Panel, 1997, p. vii).

Measurement of core indicators showed that in 1996 parental attendance at parent-teacher conferences decreased from 84 percent in elementary schools to 47 percent in middle schools. Forty-one percent of elementary and middle schools reported that parental input is considered when making policy decisions in three or more areas. Though 62 percent of parents of students in grades 3–12 reported that they participated in two or more activities in their child's school, this percentage dropped from 73 to 53 percent between the elementary and high school grades. This low level of parental involvement is cause for concern. The first findings from the large-scale National Longitudinal Study of Adolescent Health (Add Health), published in September 1997, provide substantial evidence of the importance of "parental connectedness" in providing protection against a range of risk behaviors. Such "connectedness" involves frequency of activities with parents, perceived caring, and high expectations of school performance (Resnick et al., 1997).

In an attempt to further foster parental involvement, the Clinton administration has begun an initiative to explore the role of fathers as well as mothers in influencing their children's school performance. A report issued by the U.S. Department of Education in October 1997 showed that it is not merely contact between fathers and children that is important but rather "active participation in their children's lives through involvement in their schools that makes a difference in school outcomes (U.S. Department of Education, National Center for Education Statistics [NCES], 1997b, p. xi).

FEDERAL, STATE, AND LOCAL RESPONSES

Federal Policies

A number of federal policies enacted or amended in recent years are designed to promote student achievement by addressing the needs of children challenged by adverse physical, social, and economic conditions. Highlights are outlined below.

Individuals with Disabilities Education Act.   The Individuals with Disabilities Education Act (IDEA), formerly known as the Education of All Handicapped Children Act, established the right of all children with disabilities to a free and appropriate public education in the least restrictive environment. Subsequent amendments to the law extended services to infants, toddlers, and preschoolers, identifying social workers as qualified providers of early intervention services including home visits, psychosocial assessments, counseling, and coordination of community resources (P.L. 99-457). In 1990, "social work services in schools" were officially added to the list of "related services" required to assist children in benefiting from special education (P.L. 101-476).

Additional important changes were brought about by passage of the Individuals with Disabilities Education Act Amendments of 1997 (P.L. 105-17). Among the most controversial were provisions allowing school authorities greater latitude (including suspension, expulsion, and transfer) in disciplining special education students who display severe behavioral problems. Another change increased the membership of the team responsible for developing a child's Individualized Education Program (IEP), requiring the inclusion of the child's regular classroom teacher and, at the discretion of the parent or agency, related services personnel (including school social workers). Finally, the 1997 amendments require more parental involvement in the continuum of special education services and relax somewhat the qualification for personnel in districts experiencing shortages (National Association of Social Workers [NASW], 1997).

Elementary and Secondary Education Act. The Elementary and Secondary Education Act (ESEA) was originally enacted in 1965, as part of the War on Poverty. Its primary aim, through Title I, was to assist states in providing compensatory education to low-income, educationally disadvantaged children. The Improving America's Schools Act of 1994 (P.L. 103-382) amended ESEA to emphasize the need for children in Title I programs to attain the same high standards of performance demanded of students in the general population. Under the act, services have been extended to teen parents, migratory children, and neglected or delinquent youth in state institutions and community day programs (U.S. Department of Education, 1998b). A new focus on Latino children (32 percent of those served under Title I) has led to a proposed funding increase of $393 million for Title I in the president's FY 1999 budget request (U.S. Department of Education, 1998a). The Improving America's Schools Amendments also emphasize new opportunities for schools to operate schoolwide programs (serving all children in high-poverty schools), facilitation with transitions from preschool to school and from school to work, participation of private school students, and coordination of education with health and social services (U.S. Department of Education, 1998b). Title I remains the largest existing federal education program.

Through its other titles, ESEA creates opportunities for the professional development of school staff (including school social workers). It promotes technology and distance learning, educational equity for women, and school reform and innovation (including magnet schools and public charter schools). The act provides grants for school construction, promotes efforts to reduce drugs and violence, and addresses the needs of children with limited English proficiency, Native American children, homeless children, and gifted and talented children. It also supports character education, civic education, arts education, and education in science and foreign languages (U.S. Department of Education, 1998b).

Headstart. The Headstart program, begun in 1965 as part of the War on Poverty, is now being implemented in approximately 1,400 community-based nonprofit organizations and school systems (Administration for Children and Families [ACF], 1998). Headstart provides learning activities for economically disadvantaged preschool children; comprehensive health care services; and social services including community outreach, referrals, family needs assessments, and crisis intervention. It also promotes parental involvement in the educational process.

Despite widespread bipartisan support, the program has never been funded at a high enough level to reach all eligible children (Ginsberg, 1995). During the Clinton administration, however, funding was increased from $2.2 billion (FY 1992) to $4.355 billion (FY 1998). The President's most recent budget (FY 1999) requests funding at the level of $4.66 billion (ACF, 1998).

Amendments to Headstart in 1994 (P.L. 103-252) contained new performance standards, along with quality assurance measures designed to identify and aid deficient grantees. It also established a new Early Headstart Program, expanding the program's benefits to families with children under age three and to pregnant women. Services include early education in and out of the home, home visits, parent education, comprehensive health and nutrition services, case management, and peer support for parents (ACF, 1998).

Additional initiatives.   In his 1997 state of the union address, President Clinton outlined additional initiatives in the area of education. Like the National Education Goals, they emphasize student achievement and include strategies for addressing barriers to success. They include national standards, reading tests in the fourth grade, and math tests in the eighth grade; additional teachers and the certification of master teachers; volunteer tutors (parents, teachers, college students, senior citizens, etc.) to ensure that all children can read by the end of third grade; expansion of Headstart; public school choice through the creation of additional charter schools; safe, disciplined, and drug-free schools; funding of school construction; assistance with college costs; adult education and training; and efforts to increase technological literacy among students (U.S. Department of Education, 1998c).

The president's FY 1999 budget proposal included tax credits to assist local communities in the building and renovation of public schools; class-size reductions in grades 1, 2, and 3 to a nationwide average of eighteen students, by helping school districts hire and pay an additional 100,000 teachers; grants to urban and rural school districts to support standards-based, districtwide reforms; and grants for creating or expanding quality before- and after-school programs.

Two specific initiatives are of particular interest. The first is a proposed $600 million Hispanic Education Action Plan, designed to help Latino students and adults learn English, reduce dropout rates; improve educational programs for migrant youth and adults, and prepare disadvantaged youth for success in college through programs such as Upward Bound. The second is an initiative called High Hopes, designed to promote partnerships between colleges and middle school students in low-income communities. Its goal is to involve the community in efforts to provide support in the form of mentoring, tutoring, college visits, summer programs, after-school activities, and counseling to help students stay on track through high school. The White House requested $140 million for High Hopes in FY 1999, and an additional $70 million in each of the years 2000 and 2001 (U.S. Department of Education, 1998a).

As these and other innovations are implemented, state and local governments will be facing additional challenges brought about by devolution. The new welfare law, the Personal Responsibility and Work Opportunity Reconciliation Act of 1996 (P.L. 104-193), for example, gives states the primary responsibility for meeting the needs of low-income children and families—including making key decisions about welfare benefit levels, eligibility criteria, work requirements, time limits on receipt of assistance, and exemptions. Some states have, in turn, passed this responsibility on to their individual counties. These new pressures on state and local governments will surely challenge the ability of states, communities, and school personnel to meet an ever increasing array of needs.

State Reform: School Finance

Another area of intense activity, intended to address one of the primary barriers to student achievement, has been the litigation of lawsuits pertaining to school finance. The exact nature of the relationship between educational spending and student achievement is a matter of some controversy (Biddle, 1997). Yet it is undeniable that financial resources contribute in important ways to our educational system to maximize student success. Even more than family poverty, schools with high concentrations of poverty are associated with adverse student outcomes (Kennedy, Jung, and Orland, 1986, as cited in Treman and Behrman, 1997). High rates of poverty and low rates of school funding conspire to affect student achievement in areas including science and math (Biddle, 1997). This is particularly acute in urban school districts where the cost of educating children is highest.

Resources affect the entire educational climate, including the quality of buildings and facilities, equipment and technology, curriculum materials, availability of gifted and talented or extended day programs, teacher salaries, teacher training, and teacher-student ratios (Biddle, 1997). Teachers in high-poverty schools report more student misbehavior, disruption, weapons, and violence; more absenteeism; and less parental involvement in education. Racial and ethnic minority students are more likely than whites to attend high-poverty schools and thus are particularly disadvantaged by resource discrepancies (NCES, 1997a).

Although the U.S. Supreme Court has rejected the notion of a right to equality of education under the federal constitution (*San Antonio Independent School District v. Rodriguez*, 1973), courts in over forty states have considered the constitutionality of their own educational system, focusing on the adequacy of educational opportunity or the equity of resource distribution. Though not all of these challenges have been successful, many have. These lawsuits continue to serve as catalysts for states to examine, refine, and, in some cases, redesign their school financing schemes.

Sources of funds.   Historically, education was financed almost exclusively by local property taxes. Over time, this system became increasingly inequitable, with wealthier districts enjoying the dual advantages of a larger tax base and fewer school-age children among whom the proceeds must be spread. After the depression, state governments dramatically increased their contributions. Drawing on state income and sales taxes, they now match local government in their overall share of education spending (Howell and Miller, 1997), which typically supports priorities including curriculum materials, special education, reduced class size, facilities improvement, teacher training, and textbook acquisition (Mond, Pijanowski, and Hussain, 1997).

The federal financial contribution to education, though well publicized, remains quite small at approximately 7 percent. It takes the form of categorical assistance to aid schools in meeting the needs of specific populations of children, such as those with disabilities or the economically disadvantaged (Howell and Miller, 1997).

On national average, elementary and secondary schools receive approximately half of all locally generated taxes. Yet individual states vary considerably in the degree to which they rely on federal, state, and local funding. Data from 1995–96 show Hawaii, for example, drawing 8.4 percent of its educational budget from federal funds, 89.5 percent from state funds, and only 2 percent from local funds. New Hampshire, on the other hand, uses 3 percent federal funds, 7 percent state funds, and 90 percent local funds. Mississippi shows the greatest reliance on federal funds, at 15.3 percent (Howell and Miller, 1997). As a general rule, wealthier states and districts derive more of their educational budgets from local taxes, while poorer states and districts rely more heavily on state and local funds. Some states are also turning to new sources of revenue, including proceeds from lotteries, private payments, contributions, or corporate sponsorships.

Interestingly, the allocation of educational dollars is very similar across jurisdictions. Typically, 60 to 65 percent is spent on instruction, 11 percent goes to administration, 10 percent goes to facilities operation and maintenance, 9 percent to transportation and food services, and 7 percent to student services, including health, attendance, guidance counseling, speech and other special education services, and school social work services (Monk et al., 1997).

Discrepancies in spending.   Although overall spending per pupil has increased in the United States over time, discrepancies in school funding—between states, between districts within a state, and between schools within a single district—can be staggering. For example, while the average national per pupil expenditure in 1995–96 was $6,853, New Jersey spent an average of $10,825 per pupil, while Utah spent an average of only $4,499 per pupil (Howell and Miller, 1997). At one time, in Texas and California, the highest spending school districts had average per pupil expenditures that were more than ten times those of the lowest spending district (Guthrie, 1997).

The story told by these numbers is complicated by the fact that *equity* is a difficult concept to define. The nation's 14,772 school districts vary tremendously in both size and composition; some have concentrations of students who are considerably more costly to educate because of poverty, disability, mobility, or limited English proficiency. For example, Dade County, Florida, reports that it costs $1,141 more per year to educate a foreign-born student than a native one (Visiedo, 1995). In terms of students with disabilities, although federal assistance is provided through IDEA, it covers only about 7 percent of the actual costs of educating these children (Parrish and Chambers, 1996). This has a particularly strong impact on schools with high concentrations of children in poverty, since poor children are more likely to be diagnosed as having a disability (Terman and Behrman, 1997).

Legal remedies.   Since the mid-1960s, courts in many states have entertained law suits based on the inequitable distribution of resources across school districts. In some, they have found the state's school financing scheme in violation of the state constitution. These states include Arkansas, California, Connecticut, New Jersey, Washington, West Virginia, Wyoming, Kentucky, Montana, New Jersey, Texas, Arizona, Massachusetts, and Tennessee. One case has resulted in a single school district (Los Angeles Unified) agreeing to equalize spending across its 564 individual schools (Augenblick, Myers, and Anderson, 1997). In the vast majority of cases, states have attempted to remedy financing inequities by increasing their overall educational budgets and targeting the increased resources to low-spending districts. This way, they are able to avoid taking resources away from higher-spending districts. In most cases, budgets are being enlarged by increasing the state's contribution, and by requiring an increased local contribution or rewarding school districts that make a strong local tax effort.

Kentucky, whose entire system of public schools was declared unconstitutional in 1989, entirely revamped its financing scheme: It introduced a system whereby the projected cost of educating students includes a differential reflecting special educational needs ("pupil weighting"). It capped the amount that districts would be permitted to raise locally. It supplemented local taxes raised above a certain foundation amount so that efforts by poorer districts would net the same amount as efforts by wealthier districts. It created new categorical grants for high-priority activities. And it increased the state contribution by increasing the sales tax. These and other innovations have reduced by 55 percent the relationship between a school district's wealth and the amount its students receive (Adams, 1997).

In the early 1990s, Michigan took the bold step of completely abolishing its property tax, which had provided two-thirds of the state's educational budget. Instead, it increased the state sales tax, and the bulk of its school financing now comes from state, rather than district, coffers—resulting in increased equity across the state (Center for Education Reform, 1997).

Finally, inequities in the financing of school facilities has recently become a source of litigation. In 1994, Arizona was the first state in which the court found the school finance system unconstitutional because it failed to provide equitably for the construction and maintenance of school buildings. The existence of these inequities is not surprising, since 80 percent of school construction nationally is paid for by local taxes (Terman and Behrman, 1997). Litigation around school finance continues in Florida, Louisiana, New Hampshire, North Carolina, Pennsylvania, South Carolina, and Virginia. Efforts to rectify inequities in education funding are an important strategy as we seek to minimize the effects of poverty and maximize student success.

Local Innovations in Education: Social Services and Health Care

The 1990s have seen a plethora of changes in the educational, health care, and social services sectors that are influencing the practice of social work in schools. Schools are experimenting with various innovations in pursuit of better educational outcomes, and new models of delivering a variety of services to children and families are emerging. Most of these involve decisions and implementation at the local level.

Educational innovations.   School systems at the state and local levels are introducing a variety of nontraditional measures in the hope that these will raise student standards of achievement. Charter schools and vouchers, for example, are both designed to increase parental choice. Other examples include contracting with private, for-profit corporations, single-sex classes, and school uniforms.

Charter schools: Finn (1994) defined charter schools as "independent public schools, often run by a group of teachers or parents, innovative or traditional in content, and free from most regulations and external controls." Most charter schools emphasize a particular academic philosophy ranging from "back to basics" to newer pedagogical approaches. Minnesota was the first state to enact charter school legislation in 1991. As of March 1998, twenty-nine states and the District of Columbia had charter school laws. Nationwide there are now almost 800 charter schools (Schnaiberg, 1998), a majority of which are in Arizona and California. Charter schools are regulated at the state level and face a number of complex financial, governance, regulatory, and management challenges (Koppich, 1997). President Clinton has provided in his 1999 budget request for increased funding for charter schools through state block grants. However, views are divided on the schools' potential to improve student outcomes (Orfield, 1998).

Voucher programs: Koppich (1997) defines vouchers as "government payments to households, redeemable only for tuition payments at authorized private schools" (p. 105). Vouchers are extremely controversial because private schools can select which students they will accept, thereby potentially leaving only the most disadvantaged students in the public schools. It is also unclear whether vouchers to faith-sponsored schools violate the constitutional requirement of separation of church and state. Eighty-two percent of private schools are religiously affiliated. Currently only two voucher programs are operational: Milwaukee and Cleveland. Legal challenges to both programs are pending.

Contracting for services or privatization: This involves the use of public education funds to purchase services from for-profit or not-for-profit organizations in the private sector. The most controversial form involves hiring for-profit firms to manage entire public schools. A private firm, Minnesota-based Education Alternatives Incorporated (EAI) contracted with the city of Baltimore in 1992 to operate nine public schools, but the contract was cancelled after three and a half years of its expected five-year period. EAI also operated schools in Hartford, Connecticut, and Dade County, Florida, but thus far these schools have not demonstrated improvements in academic results. Another national for-profit firm, the Edison Project, is managing schools in six states, but it is still too early to demonstrate results.

Single-sex schooling: Experimentation with single-sex education is gaining momentum in public schools. This too is a controversial subject, and a 1998 report from the American Association of University Women found no consistent evidence that single-sex education is better for girls than coeducation. The report emphasized that small classes and schools, unbiased teaching, and a focused curriculum are more important to gender equity than separating the sexes (Reinhard, 1998). In the past few years, individual public schools in New York, Virginia, Maine, New Hampshire, Illinois, and California have created single-sex classes or all-girls academies such as the two-year-old Young Women's Leadership Academy in Harlem (Lewin, 1998).

School uniforms: In recent years, schools have begun to require elementary and middle school students to wear uniforms. The New York City school board voted unanimously in March 1998 to require uniforms in the elementary grades as a means of "bringing greater discipline, unity, and seriousness of purpose to schools, though there is little research to date supporting those claims" (Keller, 1998, p. 3). A survey of principals in ten states conducted by the National Association of Elementary School Principals in 1997–98 found that 11 percent of respondents require uniforms and 15 percent were considering introducing such a policy. In New York, the new policy allows both individual schools and students to opt out of the policy. School committees can vote to ignore the policy, and parents can exempt their children by making a written request and then meeting with an administrator.

   Implications for social workers.   These developments reflect a shift in school policy development to the local level. The executive summary of a recent, national report reflects this shift: "All of these models reflect the belief that a substantial part of budgeting, decision making, and accountability should occur at the level of individual schools, rather than at the school district level" (*Future of Children: Financing Schools* 7[3]: 7). In some cases, new models of schools may eliminate school social work services, or may increase them. James Comer's model developed a decade ago involves broad-based governance and management teams who focus on creating a desirable climate of social relationships in the school. It also involves groups of support staff including social workers. Whatever the alternative model employed, school social workers must be assertive and active in contributing to policy decisions and the design of programs to implement these policies.

   School-linked services.   The emergence of new models of delivering health and social services to children and families is also changing the context of school social work (Franklin and Streeter, 1995). Usually called school-linked services, these models developed in response to two forces: first, educational reform's recognition that the presence of numerous risk factors could place many students at risk of educational failure because of complex economic, social, and psychological problems (National Commission on Children, 1991); and second, the concern that services to children and families in general are insufficient because the delivery system is fragmented, difficult to access, confusing, and uncoordinated.

   In January 1994 more than fifty national organizations concerned with the well-being of children, youth, and families gathered in Washington, D.C., and reached a consensus regarding principles for developing integrated service systems. Such systems should be community based, school linked, family centered, culturally competent, comprehensive, and prevention focused. They should also feature ongoing needs assessment and program evaluation and should be collaborative in nature, merging categorical funding streams for most efficient service delivery to families and children.

As the U.S. Department of Education stated in 1996:

> In school-linked comprehensive strategies, schools are no longer isolated providers of a single component—education for children and youth—but active partners in a broader effort. As partners, schools have increased cooperation, communication, and interaction with parents, community groups, service providers and agencies, local policymakers, and other stakeholders (p. 7).

There are many models of school-linked services based at the local school level. Some are called full service schools (Dryfoos, 1994), others are called family resource centers, or one-stop shopping centers (Hare, 1995). Another model is the school-based health center, which is expanding rapidly around the country. Once considered controversial, these centers, first established in Dallas, Texas, and St. Paul, Minnesota, in the 1970s, now total 900 in forty-three states and Washington, D.C. The centers provide comprehensive physical and mental health services to underserved youth in high schools (41 percent) and middle schools (17 percent). The remaining 10 percent are found in K–12 or other types of schools, such as alternative schools, or Headstart programs (national survey of state school-based health centers, 1997).

These various models provide both an opportunity and a challenge to school social workers. Often they bring social workers and other professionals from community agencies, both public and private, into the schools. Ironically, problems of communication and coordination have arisen between practitioners hired by outside agencies and those employed by the school. School social workers must be proactive in overcoming such problems since they are "strategically placed to act as bridges connecting agencies and schools, to provide a *glue factor* in collaborative work" (Pennekamp, 1992; University of California at Los Angeles, 1996).

Howard Adelman (1998) has conceptualized the whole network of supportive services to help students overcome barriers to learning as the *enabling component*. It is essential, according to Adelman, that schools recognize this component in addition to the instructional and management components identified as crucial to school reform. Emergence of a cohesive enabling component requires

Weaving together what is available at a school,

Expanding what exists by integrating school and community resources, and

Enhancing access to community programs and services by linking as many as feasible to programs at the school.

Enabling activity can be clustered into six program areas. These encompass interventions to

Enhance classroom efforts to enable learning,

Provide student and family assistance,

— Respond to and prevent crises,

— Support transitions,

— Increase home involvement, and

— Outreach to the community (University of California at Los Angeles, 1996, pp. 6–7).

Adelman recognizes school social work services as one element in the enabling component of schools. Adelman and Linda Taylor are codirectors of the Center for Mental Health in Schools, at the University of California, Los Angeles, which has been funded by the federal Maternal and Child Health Bureau for a period of five years. A second center, the Center for School Mental Health Assistance, is based at the Department of Psychiatry, University of Maryland, Baltimore. Both centers are exploring new models of enhancing mental health services in schools.

Changes in health care.   School social work will also be increasingly affected by other developments in the health care delivery system. Medicaid (Title XIX of the Social Security Act) funding for students living in poverty is being used in many school system to finance those social work services that can be classified as part of the Early and Periodic Screening, Diagnosis, and Treatment provisions of the Medicaid law, or the targeted case management provisions (Farrow and Joe, 1992). This may require that school social workers have clinical credentials to enable them to be recognized as providers of Medicaid-funded services. As Medicaid patients are mandated to utilize managed care health services in order to stem the rising costs of Medicaid on a fee-for-service basis, and as managed care plans develop so-called behavioral health services to provide mental health and substance abuse services, it is likely that these developments will cause social work services in schools to evolve in different and challenging ways in the years ahead.

Many poor children in the United States lack health insurance altogether. Among all children under age eighteen in 1995 (approximately 10 million children), 13.8 percent were not covered by health insurance. Among children in poverty, 21.8 percent had no coverage. Nearly 30 percent of uninsured children (about 3 million) are eligible for Medicaid but are not covered (DHHS, Health Resources and Service Administration, 1997, p. 6). To partially overcome these problems, the 105th Congress enacted the State Children's Health Insurance Program (S-CHIP) as part of the Balanced Budget Act of 1997 (P.L. 105-33). This law constitutes title XXI of the Social Security Act and makes $20 billion over five years available to states that choose to participate. CHIP targets low-income children whose family incomes do not exceed 200 percent of the federal poverty level. States have the option of providing "child health assistance" by expanding Medicaid or by establishing a new program. It is estimated that CHIP will cover 2.8

million previously uninsured children and another 660,000 who will be enrolled in Medicaid through CHIP outreach and eligibility screening efforts (Rosenbaum, Johnson, Sonosky, Markus, and DeGraw, 1998, pp. 76–77). This outreach effort and program expansion have implications for social workers in terms of identifying eligible children in school and providing increased funding for services to newly covered children.

During the 1990s the relationship between health and education has received increased emphasis. This trend may be interpreted as increasingly casting social work in schools as a health—as well as an education—related service. Two major books published in 1997–98 explore health programs in schools: one generated by the Institute of Medicine (Allensworth, Lawson, Nicholson and Wyche, 1997) and the other sponsored by CDC-DASH, the U.S. Government Centers for Disease Control and Prevention Division of Adolescent and School Health (Marx, Wooley, and Northrop, 1998). Both recognize the role of social workers as part of comprehensive and coordinated school health programs and services. The latter elaborates on an eight-component model of comprehensive school health programs first conceived in a groundbreaking 1987 article by Allensworth and Kolbe. This system is designed to prevent and combat priority health risk behaviors among children and adolescents that would potentially result in HIV-AIDS, sexually transmitted diseases, pregnancy, alcohol and other drug use, unintentional and intentional injuries, tobacco use, and risky patterns of diet combined with insufficient physical activity. The eight components are health education, health services, physical education, nutrition services, staff wellness, healthy school environment, family and community involvement, and school counseling, psychological, and social services (Adelman, 1998).

THE ROLE OF SCHOOL SOCIAL WORKERS IN A CHANGING WORLD

School social work is included in the Goals 2000: Educate America Act, ESEA, and IDEA. Goals 2000 uses the definition of related services found in IDEA, in which school social workers are specifically mentioned. "Related services personnel" are cited as participating in many school reform activities at the state and local level.

The Improving America's Schools Act, which amended ESEA in 1994, retains the definition of pupil services and pupil services personnel that was first formulated in the 1988 amendments. "Pupil services" and "Pupil services personnel" are defined as "school counselors, school social workers, school psychologists, and other qualified professional personnel involved in providing assessment, diagnosis, counseling, educational, therapeutic, and other necessary services (including related services as such term is defined in Section 602(A)(17) of the Individuals with Disabilities Education

Act) as part of a comprehensive program to meet student needs, and the services provided by pupil services personnel."

The 1977 amendments to IDEA expand references to "related services," which include social work services in schools, mostly in conjunction with the increased focus on disciplining special education students who display serious behavior problems. The National Association of Social Workers sought to ensure that the rights of students with disabilities and their parents were adequately protected by the new law.

> Key social work roles under IDEA include: participating in a student's initial evaluation for special education and in decisions on reevaluations; designing and managing behavioral interventions; providing support services called for in a student's IEP; participating in IEP team meetings; supporting parental involvement in the mediation efforts called for by the new amendments; helping to determine whether a student's disability was the cause of an infraction that could lead to removal from school; and assisting in developing alternative 45-day placements for students who are removed from school ("Expanded IDEA Role," 1998).

As we approach the year 2000, school social workers are facing a changing world. Society itself is changing. Technology is advancing rapidly, and the social implications of many developments are yet to be explored, for example, the psychosocial effects of reproductive technology or assisted conception. At the level of the local school district or individual building, school social workers will have to adapt to changing models in education, social services, and health. The political forces of devolution are already propelling decision making, policy formulation, program design and program implementation downward from the federal to the state level, or from the state to the local or community level.

School social workers must project their image not only as providers of clinical services to individual students and their families but also as informed change agents with contributions to make to crafting policies and programs in the local education agency. School social workers must always be aware that they are school employees paid for by educational dollars. They must be able to define their contribution to the educational mission of the school. They must assist in translating educational policies emanating from various levels—federal, state, or local—into effective, outcome-oriented programs in individual school buildings.

School-linked service models require too that they enhance their team-building skills, both with other school professionals and also with other social workers and members of other disciplines entering the school from the community. They must learn the skills required for collaboration and services integration. They must learn to become experts in community and school needs assessments: how to do community scans and resource mapping. School social workers will have to demonstrate their competencies as

Activists and advocates,

Brokers,

Case managers and consultants,

Diversity specialists,

Enablers and evaluators, and

Facilitators of systems change.

As change occurs in the worlds that surround the school, social workers in schools must be prepared to change their roles and the focus of their professional practice.

REFERENCES

Adams, J. E. 1997. School finance policy and students' opportunities to learn: Kentucky's experience. *Future of Children: Financing Schools* 7(3): 79–95.

Adelman, H. 1998. School counseling, psychological and social services. In E. Marx, S. F. Wooley, with D. Northrup (eds.). *Health is academic: A guide to coordinated school health programs* (pp. 142–168). NY: Teachers College Press.

Administration for Children and Families. 1998. *Headstart: Fact sheet.* [On-line]: Department of Health and Human Services, February. Available: http://www.acf.dhhs.gov.

Alan Guttmacher Institute. 1996. *Teen sex and pregnancy: Facts in brief.* NY: Author.

Allensworth, D. and Kolbe, L. The comprehensive school health program: Exploring an expanded concept. *Journal of School Health* 57(10):409–412.

Allensworth, D., Lawson, E., Nicholson, L., and Wyche, J. (eds.). 1997. *Schools and health: Our nation's investment.* Washington, DC: National Academy Press.

Annie E. Casey Foundation. 1997. *Kids count data book: State profiles of child well-being 1997.* Baltimore: Author.

Associated Press. 1998. Study: Violence hits 10% of public schools. *Washington Post*, March 20, p. A3.

Augenblick, J. G., Myers J. L., and Anderson, A. B. 1997. Equity and adequacy in school funding. *Future of Children: Financing Schools.* 7(3):63–78.

Biddle, B. J. 1997. Foolishness, dangerous nonsense, and real correlates of state differences in achievement. *Phi Delta Kappan* 79(1):9–13.

Booth, W. 1998. One nation indivisible: Is it history? Soon, no single group will comprise majority. *Washington Post*, February 22, pp. A1, A18–19.

Center for Education Reform. 1997. *Education reform nationwide: State by state summary.* [On-line]: Author. Available: http://edreform.com/pubs/stxsts97.htm.

Child Trends, Inc. 1997. *Facts at a glance.* Washington, DC: Author.

Costin, L. B. 1987. School social work. In A. Minahan (ed.) *Encyclopedia of social work* (18th ed., pp. 538–545). Silver Spring, MD: National Association of Social Workers.

Dryfoos, J. 1994. *Full service schools: A revolution in health and social services for children, youth, and families*, NY: Jossey-Bass.

Dugger, C. W. 1998. Among young of immigrants, outlook rises. *New York Times*, March 21, pp. A1, and A11.

Expanded IDEA role throughout regs urged. 1998. *NASW News* 43(3).

Farrow, F., and Joe, T. 1992. Financing school-linked integrate services. *Future of Children: School-Linked Services* 2(1):56–57.

Federal Interagency Forum on Child and Family Statistics. 1997. *America's children: Key national indicators of well-being*. Washington, DC: Author.

Finn, C. E. 1994. What to do about education 2: The schools. *Commentary*. October: 30–37.

Franklin, C., and Streeter, C. L. 1995. School reform: Linking public schools with human services. *Social Work* 40:773–782.

Froomkin, D. 1998. Tests are key to the Clinton education agenda. *Washington Post* [On-line], March 3. Available: http://www.washingtonpost.com/wp-srv/politics/special/testing/testing.htm.

Germain, C. B. 1987. Social work services in schools [Book review]. *Social Casework* 68:510–511.

Ginsburg, L. 1995. *Social work almanac* (2nd ed.). Washington, DC: NASW Press.

Guthrie, J. W. 1997. School finance: Fifty years of expansion. *Future of Children: Financing Schools* 7(3):24–38.

Hare, I. 1995. School-linked, integrated services. In R. L. Edwards and J. G. Hopps (eds.). *Encyclopedia of Social Work* 19th ed., vol. 3, pp. 2100–2109. Washington, DC: NASW Press.

Howell, P. L. and Miller, B. B. 1997. Sources of funding for schools. *Future of Children: Financing Schools* 7(3):39–50.

Keller, B. 1998. New York City approves plan for uniforms in early grades. *Education Week* 20:3.

Koppich, J. E. 1997. Considering non-traditional alternatives: Charters, private contracts, and vouchers. *Future of Children: Financing Schools* 7(3):96–111.

Lawton, M. 1998. National panel delays tests in reading, math. *Education Week* 20: 18.

Lewtin, T. 1998. All-girl schools questioned as a way to attain equity. *New York Times*. March 12, p. A12.

Marx, E., Wooley, S. F., with Northrup, D. 1998. *Health is academic: A guide coordinated school health programs*. NY: Teachers College Press.

Monk, D. H., Pijanowski, J. C. and Hussain, S. 1997. How and where the education dollar is spent. *Future of Children: Financing Schools* 7(3):51–62.

National Association of Social Workers. 1997. *Individuals with Disabilities Education Act Amendments of 1997 (IDEA): Implications for social workers*. Washington, DC: Author, June.

National Commission on Children. 1991. *Beyond rhetoric: A new American agenda for children and families.* Washington, DC: National Commission on Children.

National Education Goals Panel. June, 1997. The national education goals report: Building a nation of learners, 1997. Washington, DC: U.S. Government Printing Office.

National Survey of State School-Based Health Centers. 1997. *1996 Survey.* [On-line], March 1. Available: http://www.gwu.edu/~mtg/sbhc/96survey.html.

Orfield, G. 1998. Charter schools won't save education. *New York Times.*, January 2, p. A19.

Parrish, T. B. and Chambers J. G. 1996. Financing special education. *Future of Children* 6:121-138.

Pennekamp, M. 1992. Toward school-linked and school-based human services for children and families. *Social Work in Education* 14:125-130.

Quality counts: A report card on the condition of public education in the 50 states 1997. *Education Week Supplement* 16(January 22).

Quality counts '98: The urban challenge. Public education in the 50 states. 1998. *Education Week Supplement* 17(January 8).

Reinhard, B. 1998. Report casts doubt on the value of single sex schooling,. *Education Week* 27:8.

Resnick, M. D., Bearman, P. S., Blum, R. W., Bauman, K. E., Harris, K. M., Jones, J., Tabor, J., Beuhring, T., Sieving, R.E., Shew, M., Ireland, M., Bearninger, L. H., and Udry, J. R. 1997. Protecting adolescents from harm: Findings from the National Longitudinal Study of Adolescent Health. *Journal of the American Medical Association* 278:823-832.

Rosenbaum, S., Johnson, K., Sonosky, C., Markus, A., and DeGraw, C. 1998. The children's hour: The State Children's Health Insurance Program. *Health Affairs* 17:75-89.

Sanchez, R. 1998a. Black teen suicide rate increases dramatically . *Washington Post,* March 20, pp. A1, A17.

Sanchez. R. 1998b. U.S. high school seniors rank near the bottom: Europeans score higher in math, science test. *Washington Post,* February 25, pp. A1, A12.

Schnaiberg, L. 1998. In midst of skepticism and scrutiny, NEA's five charter schools push on. *Education Week* 17(26): 1, 14.

Terman. D. L. and Behrman, R. E. 1997. Financing schools: Analysis and recommendations. *Future of Children: Financing Schools* 7(3):4-23.

U.S. Department of Education. 1996. *Putting the pieces together: Comprehensive school-linked strategies for children and families.* Washington, DC: Author.

U.S. Department of Education. 1998a. January 27. *A biweekly look at progress on the Secretary's priorities* [On-line]. February 6. Available: http://www.ed.gov/pubs/EDInitiatives/98/98-01-06.html#1.

U.S. Department of Education. 1998b. *Elementary and secondary education: Overview of key provision in the Act* [On-line]. Available: gopher://gopher.ed.-gov.10001/00/OESE/legislative/ESEA.over.

U.S. Department of Education. 1998c. *President Clinton's call to action for American education in the 21st century: Ensuring educational excellence in 1998 and beyond* [On-line]. January 27. Available: http://www.ed.gov/updates/inits98/overview.html.

U.S. Department of Education, National Center for Education Statistics. 1997. *The condition of education 1997* (NCES 97-388), by T. M. Smith, B. A. Young, Y. Bae, S. P. Choy, and N. Alsalam. Washington, DC: U.S. Government Printing Office.

U.S. Department of Education, National Center for Education Statistics. 1997. *Fathers' involvement in their children's schools* (NCES 98-09), by C. W. Nord, D. A. Brimhall, and J. West. Washington, DC: Author.

U.S. Department of Health and Human Services, Health Resources and Services Administration, Maternal and Child Health Bureau. 1997. *Child health USA '96–'97* (Publication No. HRSA-M-DSEA-97-48). Washington, DC: Author.

U.S. Department of Health and Human Services, National Center on Child Abuse and Neglect, 1997. *Child maltreatment 1995: Report from the states to the National Abuse and Neglect Data System.* Washington, DC: U.S. Government Printing Office.

U.S. Department of Health and Human Services, Office of the Assistant Secretary for Planning and Evaluation. 1996. *Trends in the well-being of America's children and youth: 1996.* Washington, DC: U.S. Government Printing Office.

University of California at Los Angeles, Center for Mental Health in the School. 1996. *School-linked services and beyond. Addressing Barriers to Learning* 1:1–2, 5–9.

Visiedo, O. 1995. Something has to give. *Education Week* 14(17):34.

Wren. C. S. 1997. Survey suggests leveling off in use of drugs by students. *New York Times*, December 21, p. 24.

CHAPTER 8

Policy Analysis and the School Social Worker

John P. Flynn

Professor Emeritus, Western Michigan University School of Social Work

- Policy Defined
- Policy Analysis—Why Bother?
- Functioning in the Policy Space
- A Framework for Policy Analysis
- The Analysis of Existing Policy in a School System

Social work has clearly established its practice focus to include schools in the community. It has honored its practice skills through recognition of the interrelatedness of political, economic, and social tasks in the development of children and families. The service orientation of the profession has been enabled to perform its critical function in school systems because it is in concert with the fundamental legitimizing power of social policy as it is developed in the educational institution. Any profession serving social institutions does so only at the pleasure of society at large, and social policy is the vehicle that conveys and provides for that legitimacy. At the broadest level, such social policy is evident in federal educational legislation and regulatory measures. Below that comes legislated policy established by the states. However, the classical focus on policy developed at the central government level is shifting in many fields, education included.

The responsibility for shaping educational policy is clearly shifting "downward" (hierarchically speaking) from the national to the state and local levels. There is a shift away from nationally mandated specifications toward encouragement of state guidelines and local discretion in design of programs and services for students and families. The task of education is to draw on a range of competencies to facilitate the process and to minimize barriers to learning. The school social worker is in a unique position to make valuable contributions to the developmental opportunities afforded by this shift. The school social worker has an extensive repertoire of skills to contribute that comes from the profession's base in both clinical or direct services as well as its resources in policy, planning, and administration of human services. Social work's forte is the development and maintenance of functional linkages in human systems, a logical necessity for school systems aimed at educating the whole child and engaging families and community services. With education defined more and more as engagement with the whole person-in-environment, social work experiences and skills bring unique perspectives and competencies to the team and to the school system.

The school social worker initiates, shapes, modifies, and applies organizational or school system policy in a number of ways. These opportunities lie in the ability to conceptualize, organize, and communicate systematic analysis of policies and the skill to know how and when to advocate for a policy's implementation. This is true for enforcement of an existing policy, revision of a dysfunctional policy, or proposal and communication of new policy options that meet student, family, and organizational needs. These policies can affect students positively or negatively, particularly vulnerable or troubled students at risk. Depending on the content and implementation of such policies, opportunities or resources can be made available or taken away from students.

POLICY DEFINED

"Policy" might be said to undergird all that is legitimate and sanctioned in organizations such as school systems. Dollars are not spent unless there is adequate authority in "budget policy." Individuals are only free to act in ways that are commensurate with "building policies." Teachers are free to improvise with instructional methods, as long as those approaches are within "curriculum policy." And so forth. These phrases are commonplace in school, and their corollaries can be found in any organization. But what is "policy?"

First, *policy* defined in its most general terms in the social welfare context, *refers to those principles that give expression to valued ends and provide direction for appropriate action.* That is, policy announces value preferences and provides a (verbal or nonverbal) statement of the broadest expectations and boundaries of intent and action. Some examples might be found in general institutional or organizational preambles, in mission statements, or in the annual performance objectives of a department such as a special education unit. These might be broad statements of intent that speak to equality, fair play and fair treatment, equal opportunity, or open enrollment, for example. Each of these concepts are statements of principle, indicate valued ends, and suggest a range of actions to be taken to achieve desired ends. On the other hand, policy statements may be specific, rather than general, as with requirements for eligibility, specification of parental rights or obligations, or expectations of staff performance.

Second, *policy increases or reduces the number of probable outcomes that are possible in social interaction.* Policy limits choices and opportunities and narrows the range of possible action. This is what is meant by the "stochastic nature" of social policy in which predictability and order are created and fostered, reducing random possibilities, drawing order from possible chaos. When the expectations of behavior are not clear, no limits exist and the environment becomes unpredictable and, at times, chaotic. On the other hand, clarification through policy (assuming it is monitored and implemented) is a powerful way to communicate the values intended by the organization. Policy that is effectively implemented can make order out of chaos and increase the likelihood that behavior will be directed toward desired ends. Policy makes the outcomes of a social process much more predictable—people know (generally speaking) how to behave, what is expected of them, and what the likely outcome is to be when policies are clearly stated and implemented and outcomes are monitored. Policy channels or influences human behavior in that way. For example, a school system's requirements on earliest age of entry into the school system, or policy statements limiting the size and nature of any object that may be perceived as a weapon brought into a school building, or rules governing who is welcome in the school building and under what conditions all limit the range and number of possible outcomes. Consequently, policy is a means whereby influence is exercised over participants in the school system and over those in the school's significant environments.

Third, *policies may be embodied in formal statements or in informal actions of school staff.* Common examples of formal policy are rules and regulations, board resolutions, and administrative directives from a central office. Informal policy is exemplified in the behavior or professional actions of school staff (such as a social worker's willingness to undertake home visits, a teacher's availability to meet with parents "after hours," or a principal's acceptance of certain errant behaviors and total rejection of others). The important point here is that these examples—both formal and informal manifestations of policy—are all illustrations of valued ends that give rise to personal desired actions as exemplified by school personnel.

Some would argue that policy is not "policy" unless it is formally ratified by some legitimate body or office. But that characterization applies only to formal policy that has been properly legitimated or sanctioned by those who have the right to take action. On the contrary, the fact cannot be denied that individuals and groups in social systems, schools included, establish policies by their own choices and behaviors within or in spite of formal policy boundaries. School personnel do this through their conscious and unconscious choices and preferences in interaction among themselves, with students and their families, or with other organizations in the community.

Consequently, the school social worker must be aware of the power inherent in implementing or even creating policy within the school system. Policy is a tool that cannot be neglected and must be used appropriately. This is why the school social worker should have facility in the use of that tool in conducting a systematic analysis of policy affecting everyday practice of the profession and be prepared to make that contribution to the team.

POLICY ANALYSIS—WHY BOTHER?

The ability to make or apply policy is the ability to influence the behavior of others. Power over another person or situation, to influence the probabilities of outcomes just discussed, carries no small ethical obligation. Consequently, it is essential for the social worker in the schools to be aware of this power, as much as of the ethical obligation to conduct technically sound behavioral assessments or to assist parents in making informed decisions. Policy analysis skills enable the social worker to examine the efficacy of a particular system-level or building-level policy, assist in offering credible arguments for change, and provide a framework for constructive or creative proposals for new policy. To appreciate the reality of this power, the school social worker must (a) recognize what a particular policy is or could otherwise be, (b) be aware of how policy does or could influence a situation, and (c) understand the fact that policy is both formal or informal in its impact on stakeholders in the school environment. A clear understanding of these aspects of policy in a school system is fundamental in fulfilling the social worker's membership in the professional team in the school.

FUNCTIONING IN THE POLICY SPACE

Social workers can bring about change in the shape and content of policy in schools in a number of ways, discussed later in this book. Some examples are the using organizational analysis, conducting research and evaluation projects, or implementing needs assessments to bring about changes in how services are supported or implemented. The focus for the present, however, is on the shape and content of policy itself.

The social worker in the schools has a unique opportunity to function as both a policy practitioner and a policy analyst. That is, the social worker applies school policy in bringing services to the student or family or in bringing the student or family to the services. This role of providing *linkage* is an aspect of practice that makes the school social worker unique among team members. Social workers, given their assignment in schools, are in a position to observe and assess the utility or disutility of many policies (and their resultant procedures) from many sides due to that linkage position. In other words, the social worker in a school system or in a particular building has the opportunity to occupy a "policy space" in the course of providing services to students and families and in working within the school system. Consequently, direct practice and the delivery of services are intricately interwoven with opportunities for policy analysis. By way of illustration, perhaps a school system has particular guidelines on eligibility for special education services. There is likely some latitude left to the discretion of school staff (i.e., the policy space) on how the criteria shall be met (such as what documents must be offered or available to determine eligibility) or how the eligibility data will be prepared and presented. The social worker has the opportunity to assist the classroom teacher and other ancillary personnel as well as the family to come to a productive decision for the child. At the same time, important information is generated concerning the adequacy of policies and procedures governing decision making on special education placements. On the clinical level, the nature and style of the social worker may color or shape the policy space, such as how active or supportive a role the social worker might play in developing the information for an eligibility claim or in monitoring any resultant plans agreed to by the parents and the school system. In other words, the school social worker has opportunity to create her or his own "minipolicies" over time, as does the service team to which the social worker may be attached. Informed policy determines how and in what manner professional decisions are systematically or routinely carried out. Stated another way, school social workers and their team colleagues have tremendous discretionary power in many situations, and their decisions and their behaviors speak loudly of principles that give expression to valued ends and provide direction for appropriate action.

The school social worker has many opportunities to monitor, implement, modify, or promote school policy. In the first instance it is essential for the analyst to realize the difference between policy that *authorizes* an action, program, or procedure as opposed to the actual *implementation* of that policy. The social worker as *policy monitor* is in a position to identify disparities between authorization or enactment of a policy. Any failures or shortcomings of policy implementation can be brought to light through thorough analysis and credible argument for change. The social worker can also use the analysis for other policy roles, such as acting as a *policy expert* on external policy mandates, acting as a *constructive critic* in voicing the policy options to be found in existing or proposed school policy, serving as a *conduit or sounding board* for students or families on the impact of school policies, or becoming a *policy change agent* within the school system itself or with the external environment (e.g., mental health agencies) regarding administrative or operational procedures in enacting school policy. Taken together, these roles provide a constellation of policy-relevant activities that constitute the role of the social worker as a *policy practitioner* in the school. Nevertheless, whether one is fulfilling the role of policy monitor, expert, constructive critique, conduit or sounding board, or policy change agent, it is absolutely necessary that the role be supported by sound systematic analysis of the policy driving the professional activity (see e.g., Jansson, 1994). Such analysis gives credibility to what is advocated by the social worker and lends to the power of any recommendations that might be accepted or implemented by others.

A FRAMEWORK FOR POLICY ANALYSIS

A disciplined and well-prepared professional person sets forth his or her theoretical perspective and plan of intervention prior to taking action. That is, professionals do not just "come off the wall," as the saying goes. A true professional is aware of what theoretical model is to be used and what techniques are to be employed before taking action. This is obvious to the clinical practitioner who can easily identify what theory or model she or he might be employing in working with a client. The need for conscious choice of tools to be used for assessment or analysis of policy is no less important for those doing such analyses. This chapter will set forth suggested elements for the analysis of the content and process of policy and will provide illustrations by using examples relevant to social work services in the schools. This framework is an abridged version of one provided in more detail in Flynn, 1992. A number of detailed examples and illustrations may be found in that publication.

The elements for analysis are grouped into five categories and may generate different information depending on whether the policy under analysis is:

a. currently in place as a formal policy,
b. a proposed policy,
c. a proposed revision of an existing policy, or
d. an operational reality or informal policy.

The five categories of elements for analysis are operationalized:

A. Identify the policy problem, the policy goals, and the policy statement (as written or published, or as might be inferred from behavior).
B. Assess current and anticipated system functioning due to present policy or as a result of any proposed policy.
C. Determine implications for selected values embedded or implied in the policy.
D. Establish feasibility of the policy and resources needed for the desired outcomes of the policy.
E. Provide recommendations for wording and action for the new or revised policy.

These categories are relevant to examining the substantive *content* of a policy or the *process* by which a policy is implemented or has been developed. In real life, one may not need to examine every element of each category or all content and all process. In all instances, however, it is absolutely necessary to examine the *values implied* in the policy as stated or as proposed.

THE ANALYSIS OF EXISTING POLICY IN A SCHOOL SYSTEM

In the following pages of this chapter, a hypothetical policy statement—a policy established by a fictitious school system, called "Middleville Schools"—will be used throughout to provide a basis for illustrating the elements of an analysis of policy. The reader could, of course, speculate about the use of these analytic elements on any particular existing policy or any policy that might be proposed for analysis or adoption. For heuristic purposes, we will assume that Middleville Schools has heard some concern in the community about the extent to which parents and guardians are properly involved in matters concerning their children. There is some question whether anyone other than school personnel are welcome. (A caution: the author will go through each element and provide an illustration or comment on each. This seems fair if one is to put forth a framework that presumably is of value. However, those who read this and apply the framework to an actual analysis need not be so complete. In real life, use "what fits." Use the framework to discipline your data collection, analysis and your own conclusions. It is up to you to be as "complete" as is reasonably possible.)

A hallmark of any analytic framework is to set forth, in advance, the elements or characteristics of any phenomenon that will be studied or subjected to analysis. The reader will see that our first task is to identify the actual policy statement involving the policy under question, followed by groupings of explicitly stated elements that will be examined.

A. Identify the Policy Problem, the Policy Goals and the Policy Statement

What is the problem, the goal desired, and how should the policy be stated?

Meaningful participation of parents in their children's school experience and in the overall life of the school itself is often stated as a goal and a desirable condition in many school systems. This is often pursued by support for formal teacher-parent organizations, systematic use of volunteer parents in the classroom, augmentation of a school's technical or professional resources by involving particularly talented parents, and so forth. The goal, in those instances, is generally to weld the interdependence of school and families or school and community in some instances. The goal may also be to maximize the use of resources in the school's environment. Other situations involve parents in decision making, such as handling of disciplinary measures for a particular student or placement planning and individualized service plans for special education services. While there has been some feedback from the community that parents are not adequately represented, the Middleville School Board does have the following policy in place:

> In all instances involving disciplinary action for a student and those events considering a student's placement in a special education program, the parents or legal guardian of such student will be informed, consulted, and actively participate in the decision process and any resultant determination. (Original date, 19XX)

In this instance, the policy is formally stated, rather than being merely an informal but prevailing expectation, and is formally legitimated by the school board. As will be noted later in our analysis, formalization and legitimation may not necessarily mean that the policy is promulgated and enforced.

1. Bases of legitimacy of the policy and source or location.   Is the location of the policy within or external to the school system? Who provides the right to take action, and where is that documented (i.e., in written form where it can be easily documented or in the repetitive or patterned behavior of significant actors observed in the system)?

The policy has clearly been legitimated (i.e., the right to take action has been established) by the Middleville School Board. In fact, the documentation is available in writing and dated in board minutes. Furthermore, additional legitimacy is obtained in state and federal guidelines regarding parental participation in development of individualized service plan processes for special education evaluation and placement decisions. Parental notification (though not necessarily parental participation) is also required by state regulation involving a child's suspension or expulsion.

2. Targets or clients of concern.   Who is the object of change, and whose interests will be served by the policy?

The "target" of a policy may be seen as that element (person or persons) *in whom* desired behavior is being sought. In this sense, the target of the policy may be seen as all staff of the school system and the parents as well, since it is clear that the assurance of participation is both a right and a responsibility across the board. All parties are obligated to behave in ways that significantly involve parents.

On the face of it, every policy is presumed to benefit the client, and "the client" is widely assumed to be the customer, the guest, or the citizen, or in this case the student or the parent. However, if one assumes that the client is truly that element *on whose behalf* the goal is being sought, then the school system itself, or its staff, could also be seen as a beneficiary or a client in a number of ways. On one hand, assurance of parental participation allows the school system to satisfy state and federal requirements and, consequently, obtain outside funding, serving then the interests of the system as a whole. On the other hand, such a policy surely serves the interest of those parents who might otherwise find it difficult to participate in a meaningful way in key decisions affecting their children. This policy legitimates parental entry.

3. Factors of eligibility.   Who is or what will be included or covered in the policy and under what conditions?

Any one claim to eligibility under this policy is rather vague. For example, the policy states that "in *all instances* . . . the parents or legal guardian will be informed." The policy gives no direction or suggestion as to whether "all instances" includes the first incident or first formal action or even the first informal discussion of the propriety of taking action. On the other hand, one could logically conclude that parental participation was mandated only when formal consideration of action is first considered or when final decisions are on the table. Some of this same vagueness can be detected in the policy's wording "will be informed, consulted, and actively participate in the decision." Consequently, the policy is vague and weak in this area and certainly provides a good example of the utility of having *policy guidelines*. Guidelines may be thought of as less formal, less restrictive signposts or suggested ways to operationalize policy so that policy is consistently applied. Guidelines are not generally published in formal policy and are generally developed after a policy has been established. The analyst may need to determine whether such guidelines exist and whether they are adequate.

4. Effect on system maintenance, change, or control.   What is the intended or unintended effect on issues of maintenance, change, or control within or for the school system? Who has a vested interest in the policy's initiation or continuation?

It would appear on the face of it that the intent of the policy is to bring about system change. The presumption is that parental participation has been inadequate and is desirable. A question here is whether parental or guardian participation is actually the norm in this school system or whether there is some misperception about the policy's implementation. One would have to examine the data on actual levels of participation of parents. For example, one needs to know the rate of participation at the present time in the various buildings, grade levels, and neighborhoods in the entire school district to determine whether there are differential rates of participation. Also, those rates might have to be examined both before and after enactment of the policy to observe any change in participation rates. Another aspect of examining change would be to observe or document the behavior of school staff. Are various staff groups any more or less conscientious in fostering parental participation? Analysis of these data may offer some suggestion whether or not the policy serves the purpose of social control of staff or parents or both in bringing about desired participation within the system as a whole.

5. Explicit or implicit theories.   What theoretical foundation gave rise to or supports the policy?

The fundamental theoretical foundation of parental participation can be found in the basic democratic theory that citizens have the right and responsibility to fully participate in decisions affecting their own (or their children's) lives. Furthermore, the policy is entirely in concert with common and case law regarding the primacy of parental responsibility for the welfare of their children. Hence, this criterion is, generally speaking, unassailable as a policy feature.

There may be some significant actors within the school system who hold the theoretical or philosophical view that participation beyond the school's walls by others in the community (including members of the family) actually broadens and enriches the educational process and aids in individualized planning. On the other hand, some may view parental participation in "professional affairs" as an unnecessary burden. Those persons should be identified, and their positions and influence should be examined; the resultant information may have implications for the change or control questions raised above.

6. Topography of the policy system.   Can you "map the terrain" of who is involved in this system? What offices or units are logically included as being affected by this policy as it stands or as any changes might be proposed? Who might constitute a viable "action system" to provide support for or opposition to such a policy? Who are some of the key participants?

If one were to sketch out a conceptual map there would be a number of relevant actors. The map would certainly include the building principal(s), the classroom teachers involved, any special education personnel having professional knowledge of a particular situation, and perhaps other community agencies providing services relevant to the student and the parent or guardian. It would be necessary, then, to examine the information on the actual range and variety of opportunities for participation. Are there potential advocacy groups involved? Are certain staff groupings or certain building principals especially interested in or opposed to investing in this issue?

7. Contemporary or antecedent issues.   What are some of the issues embedded in this particular policy within or around the school system that should be considered? Are there other relevant past events that explain the existence of this policy or how the policy was developed or stated?

It would be very important to identify any prior incidents related to the conditions covered by the policy (e.g., children bringing weapons to the school, controversial disciplinary actions, or the general and actual practice—or lack of consistency, on the other hand—in involving parents or guardians in individualized service planning). There may be some historical "baggage" that gave rise to the policy's adoption, or it may have been hastily crafted; or it may have been carefully considered and debated.

There may also be contemporary issues that place this issue on the system's agenda. For example, perhaps there are other issues in the community also involving matters of informed consent of parents, alleged arbitrary decisions being made by public officials in other arenas, such as adolescents gaining access to health care without parental knowledge or counseling services being provided to students without parental approval. These factors may suggest something about the potential for amending the policy or how firm a base of community support the policy has in its present form.

B. Assess Current and Anticipated System Functioning

To some extent we have already moved into the domain of the second category of elements. In real life, it is impossible to deal with human systems in a linear fashion. Real-life interaction is circular and iterative. However, this second set of the elements emphasizes an assessment of the current structural state of a system. Consequently, the elements or questions involve the following.

1. **State of communication and system boundaries.** What is the nature of communication and interaction between key elements in the system as a result of this policy?

For policy to be effective and to have the power to bring about predictable behavior, it must be clearly published and implemented. Do families actually have clear and frequent communication with, from, and to the school? Do the boundaries between home and school, in general, seem permeable or impermeable? That is, is there generally a free flow of interaction or communication between home and school, or are the barriers and gates firm and protected? It is essential to determine the extent to which publication and implementation of this policy has actually occurred. Then, too, have divisional and departmental level administrators and supervisors adequately monitored the implementation of this policy? Has communication been *unilateral* by way of mere policy pronouncements from above? Or, rather, has communication been *bilateral* in that those who manage and supervise staff have engaged in practical discussions with those staff implementing such policy in order to get corrective feedback?

From a practical point of view, have parents been informed sufficiently far in advance that their participation is reasonably convenient? Have professional staff appropriately assisted parents or guardians to be adequately prepared for whatever participation might be needed? In this particular policy, the parent would need to become familiar with the decision process and the range of options available in advance, in coming to decision about an individualized educational plan for a student, for example. Do staff assist them in meeting the spirit and intent of this policy? In the case of pending disciplinary action by the school, do staff assist parents in joining the school in productive problem solving, or is the parent brought in only to be informed of decisions already made?

It is useful to examine the *direction* of the feedback by observing whether any difficulties encountered by staff in achieving full participation have been taken into account in changing the policy or in developing guidelines. This might have been done by examining staff experience with the policy or by allocating more resources to achieving the policy goal. For example, have the boundaries between home and school been altered through increased funding for staff transportation for home visits or by publishing informational materials that familiarize parents with basic information on procedures?

It is sometimes instructive to identify key system points for communication. Are there various groups that have opportunity to influence one another concerning this policy? Are any particular bargaining, negotiating, or collaborative groups or coalitions likely to be forming as a result of this policy? Do psychologists, speech therapists, and social workers tend to have a position on informing and including parents that differs from that of most building principals, or do those groups work together on this?

Here it might be beneficial to see if any advocacy groups have communicated their interests in this matter, for example, when the rate of expulsions or suspensions appears to weigh more heavily on a particular neighborhood or segment of the community. What channels are used? Do these groups tend to bring their concerns to staff who work at the implementation level, or do they tend to bring their concerns about the policy directly to the board at public meetings?

It could also be instructive to examine the school's posture on parental participation in general—not just as it applies to special education or disciplinary action. Some examples might be the school's overall use of parent volunteers in the classroom, logistical support given by the school system to parent-teacher organizations, or other ways that the school might give the metamessage that parents or guardians are welcome or unwelcome. In practical terms, how frequently do the home and the school interact in this school system?

2. **Authority, influence, and leadership.**   What authority, exercise of power, or leadership is given to or needed to effect this policy? Who holds power, and who actually can or does exercise that power?

Assuming that the policy is functioning effectively, by whose or what authority and influence is the policy held to the line? Is the system's superintendent involved and aggressive? Is there monitoring by that office?

On the other hand, is there actually little support but for the outreach initiatives of staff at the lowest levels? Could it be that the policy is failing because support is lacking at the departmental level(s) or because few building principals are cooperating? On the other hand, it is building principals who are generally advocates for meaningful parental involvement and service staff who are lax in taking initiatives to involve parents or guardians in any meaningful way? In any case, why is this happening? One might examine the extent or manner in which the system's administrative leaders in the persons of departmental directors, program heads, coordinators, or other significant actors play roles in leadership in implementation of this policy.

3. Strains and constraints.   What effect does the policy have on tension, variety, and entropy (i.e., the natural tendency of a system toward disorder or the inability to do work in a system) within the system? Is it dysfunctional or functional?

Some variety and variability in human systems is good. Groups and organizations thrive on sustainable variety, school systems included. In fact, it might be argued that the greater the variety of inputs into the educational process, input from the home included, the stronger the overall educational process. However, when tension is not managed and variety leads to chaos or a school's response is no longer predictable, then entropy sets in. That is, the system has less functional order and less ability to do its work. Remember that the main purpose of policy is to give order and direction.

Some forms of tension are caused by *strains* in the system that (at least theoretically) can be corrected. Some examples in this instance might be inadequate numbers of service-level staff, overworked teachers with classes that are too large, and principals with responsibility for too many buildings. The variety of points of view provided by parents contributes more information for decisions about children, but it also adds to the quantity of information that staff have to deal with. Also, when policy is published but not implemented, it may sometimes be due to the lack of support of guidelines giving direction to system personnel. A well-intended but unimplemented policy can become minimized or practically nonexistent in this instance.

Other factors may be more in the form of *constraints*, defined here as barriers that cannot be moved (except under unusual circumstances) because they are part of the nature of the phenomenon. In a school system, one constraint may be labor agreements that limit the length of the workday, though this factor is sometimes erroneously used as an excuse for inactions. Another example might be the lack of adequate physical facilities to accommodate some meetings, though this factor could be more of a short-term barrier, given newly assigned resources in the future.

4. Resistance to change.   How salient is this policy (i.e., how many groups or other issues does this policy affect, or does it cut across many boundaries)? What are the issues, forces, or factors that might resist or mitigate change as a result of the policy?

A key question here is, How many different groupings or categories does this policy affect? The likely answer is that this is a very salient policy in that regard. The superintendent and the school board are in touch with a variety of publics who likely see themselves as stakeholders who should have a meaningful say in the system. There are currently nonprofit foundations interested in fostering family and community participation in local schools. State and federal statutory regulations require such participation in certain circumstances. And some school personnel value broad participation highly, as suggested above. Consequently, there would appear to be a very high probability of political leverage here to promote a salient issue.

The next level of questions, then, searches for any resistance or counterresistance to policy implementation or change that might exist within specific pockets or positions of school personnel. Is implementation of this policy in competition for financial resources with other needs in the system? Also, there should be some examination of whether particular segments of the community do not or cannot fully cooperate in seizing their opportunities to participate. Some examples of such groups might be those who have been alienated by school experiences in the past, those who are limited by inadequate transportation, or those who lack adequate substitute child care. Implementation of the policy may require allocation of new or altered resources to reach out to those parents.

In terms of bringing about system change for the policy, it is essential to determine where or to whom (i.e., what person or office) any informal and formal presentations of analysis and recommendations might best be brought forward. Might it be at the lowest level nearest the problem (i.e., using the principle of subsidiarity), such as a department having the most direct dealings with parents and families? Might it be in open discussions, such as at board meetings? Which point of entry is likely to have the greatest leverage, or the ability to engender meaningful discussion and change?

5. Feedback devices.   What channels exist that provide information to guide the system toward corrective action based on the policy's outputs?

"Good" policy has built-in mechanisms for providing self-corrective feedback. While we have had some discussion of feedback, this characteristic of policy needs additional attention. Some policy statements assign monitoring duties to a particular position or office within the organization. A "sunset" law—a law designed to expire at a time specified before continuation legislation is again considered—is an excellent example of a built-in feedback mechanism. Furthermore, both positive and negative feedback should be systematically sought. Middleville Schools' policy in our hypothetical example on participation is lacking in this regard. There is no suggestion in the policy statement itself that such feedback is desired or required.

Hence, this policy analysis will likely recommend, in its summary analysis, that appropriate feedback devices be established.

6. Impact on the system's dynamic adaptation.   To what extent does the policy enhance the system's ability to be more adaptive and self-corrective?

Organizations must alter their forms over time in order to survive. This is what is meant in systems literature as "dynamic adaptation." However, absent the feedback mechanism noted above, there is nothing to suggest that the parental participation policy has any impact on the system's capacity for dynamic adaptation. While Middleville School may be very dynamic in their forward movement, no evidence can be found in this particular policy.

7. Environmental impact.   What impact is there (or will there be) in the general educational climate as a result of the policy's being in existence?

It is reasonable to assume that this policy will engender more positive feeling in the community, not only among parents and guardians of the system's students but in the broader community as well. After all, such a policy communicates the metamessage "This system is an open system." The school is open to the community, so to speak. Input is welcome. In fact, a parent's being informed and fully participating could easily be interpreted as also welcoming anyone who might appropriately inform and advocate for a particular student, parent, guardian, or family in given problem-solving situations. Other community agencies might well perceive that there are open doors in this school system.

C. Determine Implications for Selected Values

The third category of elements involves an assessment of the congruence of the policy and its implementation with selected values. The word "selected" is carefully chosen here, for who is to say what set of values should be brought to the analysis? First, since the values of adequacy, effectiveness, and efficiency are so much a part of American folklore, it would be foolish to omit them. Second, inasmuch as this discussion is for and about the practice of social work, the framework has drawn heavily on the Code of Ethics of the National Association of Social Workers (1996)—hence the inclusion of the values of social justice, self-determination, identity, individualization, nonjudgmental attitude, and confidentiality. Consequently, the following elements and questions should be considered.

1. Adequacy.   To what extent is the goal achieved when the policy is carried out, both in terms of "coverage" for individuals and for the system as a whole?

The elements of adequacy, effectiveness, and efficiency are often invoked together in popular analysis as if the phrase were a mantra for responsible citizenship. However, each of these elements differ in the sense of what is examined and expected. *Adequacy* is defined here in terms of the question stated above: adequacy is the extent to which a goal is achieved if the policy is carried out. Adequacy may be thought of as "horizontal," or as the degree or extent to which all those meant to be "covered" are covered. In this instance, all are parents or guardians found to be included when it comes to participation in designated decisions? On the other hand, adequacy may be thought of as "vertical," or as the extent which particular targets or clients or individuals are affected. In this case, do different socio-economic segments in the community receive differential support in their participation, or does the school encourage parental involvement only for certain types of decisions, such as placement for gifted children or planning for special education, or only for participation in the parent-teacher organization? The issue with adequacy is *coverage*, who is covered and how sufficient that coverage is.

2. **Effectiveness.**   To what extent is there a logical connection, if any, between the means or techniques employed by the policy and the policy goal that is to be achieved?

Effectiveness is related to what most people generally consider the "outcome" and its relation to the employed to obtain that outcome. In this instance, one must examine the means or methods whereby Middleville Schools personnel assured and obtained full participation as mandated by the policy. As just noted above, the presence and impact on specific target populations might be examined in this regard. While pure cause-and-effect relationships are rarely documented in social phenomena, correlations between methods employed and participatory outcomes would likely be valid and should certainly not be ignored.

3. **Efficiency.**   To what degree are the means employed in goal achievement maximized with the use of the minimum amount of necessary resources?

The useful concept of *efficiency* has recently been clouded by the contemporary dialogue between "managed *care*" and "managed *cost*," which the emphasis is either on efficiency in *cost* or on level of *effort*. Efficiency as an evaluative concept refers to the degree to which the means employed in achieving the goal are maximized (i.e., use judiciously) while using the minimum amount of necessary resources. Put another way, did the job get done with minimum effort or cost?

This criterion suggests that the analyst should examine costs to both parents and guardians and the school system as well as benefits to both parents and guardians and the school system. This analysis would likely be highly speculative in nature but worth the effort in determining how, to whom, and to what extent any recommendations for action might be shaped. Furthermore, such analysis is likely to suggest both tangible and intangible costs and benefits that may be difficult to make concrete. Many of the costs could be psychological or social in nature. Nevertheless, this is a very important part of the analysis, and the analyst will have to be creative. The analyst will likely have to operationalize such concepts as time, effort, satisfaction, improvement, quality of relationships, commitment, sharing, and even "participation" itself.

4. **Impact on rights, statuses, and social issues.**   What is the policy's impact on individual, group, or organizational rights and statuses, particularly in terms of equity, equality, and fairness?

These elements are at the center of this analysis, since examination of these values and their presence or absence in the policy or its implementation is likely to shed light on much of the rest of the analysis. Policy can vitally impact a person's or a group's status and position in any social system, including a school system. Policy and its implementation can affirm proper rights and obligations, duties and responsibilities, prerogatives or privileges, or rewards or punishment. Aside from food and shelter, there are the factors that sustain life.

This policy illustration on parent and guardian participation surely assigns status and rights to some members of the community, whether the policy is operationalized adequately or not and whether it is enforced or not. A real test at the level of application may be found, however, in the extent to which people are treated equitably, equally, and fairly.

Equity may be defined as the extent to which people in similar circumstances are treated similarly. This is not to be confused with *equality*, in which people are treated the same in all circumstances. The policy analyst should try to determine whether all people were informed of the policy and whether all parents and guardians were given the same opportunity to participate. That would be evidence of essential equal treatment. At the same time, it should be determined whether the principle of equity prevailed: some children and families in differential situations may need differential treatment to achieve reasonably similar results. This would entail, for example, aggressive outreach to some, additional time before coming to joint decisions for others, possible inclusion of additional aides, advocates, or spokespersons in still other cases. Achievement of both equity and equality increases the likelihood that the policy was implemented with fairness.

Fairness is concerned with whether people or situations were dealt with in a manner that is reasonable and just as a result of application of the policy. Consequently, carefully considered decisions, jointly arrived at, in an open process without arbitrary rules are likely to promote just or fair treatment. The analyst should look for evidence of realization of this value or be prepared to provide either rewording for the policy or a set of guidelines that would honor such outcomes.

5. Self-determination.   Does the policy honor the right of citizens to a voice in the determination of those matters that vitally affect themselves?

Surely self-determination must be honored if justice and fairness are also to be achieved. Self-determination does not provide one with a unilateral right to establish the rules of conduct or the rights of choice beyond what is the generally acceptable in a social contract. A central question here is whether the school system "takes over" for the family by unilaterally making decisions that should properly be made by or shared with the family.

6. Identity.   What effect does this policy have on the self-image of the client or the target of the policy and on the need for and right to human dignity?

This criterion speaks to the extent to which the policy or its application allows the target of the policy's intent to accept its impact with dignity. That is, human dignity should not be reduced by unreasonable and inappropriate policy directives. The purpose of policy is to support and enhance human interaction, not to demean any participants. On the face of it, one might assume that the mere fact of inclusion is important decision-making processes would respect and enhance one's sense of identity. However, to obtain data for this part of the task, the analyst will likely have to gather personal opinions from past and current, nonparticipating and participating parents and guardians. The views of third-party observers could also be of value.

7. Individualization and nonjudgmental attitude.   To what extent is the need for individuals (or groups or organizations) to be treated in terms of their unique nature, needs, and qualities recognized by the policy?

This criterion is akin to the question of the policy's impact on identity. The emphasis in this criterion, however, is on the means or manner by which the system carries out its implementation of the policy, whereas identity speaks more to the outcome effect on the target persons who presumably are the beneficiaries of the policy.

Individualization speaks to the need for the individuals or groups to be treated in their unique nature, needs, and qualities. The nonjudgmental attitude speaks to the quality of behavior or demeanor of those who carry the policy out as representatives of the school system. Is the policy put into practice by person-to-person contact informing families of the parents' or guardians' rights and opportunities, or are families merely informed by memo or by general reference to school system policies? It could also be worthwhile to see how and whether participation as a concept is presented. It is characterized as a pro forma requirement or an inconvenience to the staff, or is it described as a positive opportunity to share or collaborate in a child's school experience?

8. The GRADES test.   What are the implications of this policy for matters of Gender, Race, Age, Disibility, Ethnicity, or Socioeconomic status?

It can reasonably be said that most school personnel are not racist, or sexist, or guilty of a number of isms, at least in terms of their conscious intentions and behaviors. Nevertheless, as patterns of behavior are established and routines set in, it is easy for the collective behavior of organizations and individuals to become institutionalized. Consequently, it is essential that the policy analyst consciously and explicitly press the analysis against a number of similar questions. The questions would go something like: "Given what has been observed, or given what might take place during the implementation of this policy, what implications are there for those of a particular *gender or sexual orientation?* . . . for persons of a particular *racial identity* or for *people of color?* . . . for a particular *age group* . . . for a person with a *disability* . . . for people of a particular *ethnic group?* . . . for those of a particular *socioeconomic status?*" Here is where you can do more than give lip service to advocating for those who might be disadvantaged by policy as a result of their GRADES identity.

In our fictitious policy in the imaginary Middleville Schools systems, could it be that the task (and perhaps even burden) of participation will more likely fall on female caretakers? It is widely known, for example, that mothers are generally more active in relating to schools than fathers. In particular, mothers more often attend conferences regarding their children. Could this mean that more aggressive efforts have to be made to involve fathers in the home-school collaboration?

Or how about the fact that there are increasing numbers of grandparents now raising their grandchildren? It is possible that grandparents are less familiar with the culture of current school systems and even school buildings inasmuch as it has been some time since they have been active with the schools. Perhaps different assumptions may have to be made regarding what needs to be communicated to grandparents or how the school might be perceived by grandparents raising school children.

Then there are those families in which one person's disability sometimes limits the extent to which they can freely participate in a whole range of activities in the community, including the schools. Perhaps there are special needs for transportation for the person who might otherwise visit the school, or perhaps an inordinate number of visits to the home are needed as a substitute for some of the conferences on site at the school. Perhaps the disability of a family member means that respite care is needed to facilitate a family caregiver's visits to the school. There are just a few possibilities that could be considered in the policy analysis.

Then there is the question of implications for the ethnic identity of the family. In carrying out the policy, are all staff adequately sensitive to unique subcultural factors such as those families in which only the male has authority to speak with those who might "intrude" on the family? Or how about those families in which any formal external institution is seen as a manifestation of authority—to be feared or to be obeyed or to be revered?

Finally, what might seem the most obvious is often overlooked: the socioeconomic status of the family and what opportunities might have to be forgone due to lack of supports available to the "average" family. This would include considerations of the availability of a telephone, transportation, general good health, availability of clothing in which a family member feels comfortable in public, access to substitute child care, and so forth.

The main point of the GRADES test is that not all people have equal ability to enjoy what is offered to them, even when a social policy is sound and positively motivated. Consequently, the professional person who is really committed to responding to the unique needs of individuals must consider the gaps and inequalities, not only in professional clinical practice and service, but in any adequate policy analysis and policy implementation.

D. Establish Feasibility and Resources Needed for the Desired Outcomes

The fourth category of elements in the framework involves an assessment of the feasibility and availability of resources necessary to implement the policy. There are obviously a myriad of possible considerations, but we will limit our framework to the following.

1. Technical capacity. What particular technology, skills, or talents are available to the school system internally or externally to achieve the goal? Does that technology consist of people or equipment?

Implementation of our sample policy would require very little hardware. Some support might be needed in terms of distribution of newsletters, use of advertising, media, and maintenance of mailing lists and phone lists. However, this policy is more likely to focus on consideration of people power.

People are resources in an organization. Foremost would be some assessment of the attitudes and commitment of administrators and service staff toward assertive implementation of this policy. If the assessment is positive or affirmative, then the need would be primarily to facilitate and provide support. If the assessment is negative or questionable, it may require in-service training or a different approach to supervision and performance evaluation of administrative and staff functioning. In situations wherein it is particularly difficult to obtain cooperation of parents or guardians from certain groups or areas of the system, outside consultation may be needed from those who have also faced this problem but have achieved successful outcomes.

2. Finances.   Are the financial resources available or likely to become available? Use of staff time, whether in training, retraining, or even in reallocation of staff resources devoted to the goals of most any set of policy priorities, can be seen as a financial cost. An obvious cost of aggressive outreach is a likely increase in reimbursable travel time for staff, or possibly a decrease in alternative reimbursable services provided by that same staff. It is important that the analyst try to determine, if only speculatively, what the real cost might be to focus or refocus staff direction on implementing this policy. At the same time, the analyst must try to estimate the opportunity cost of not implementing the policy by not appropriately involving the targets of the policy. There may be long-term and broader systemic costs that have a financial price tag. Psychological costs must also be considered, such as impact on morale, stress, and community relations.

3. Time.   To what extent is time a resource or a hindrance in achieving the policy goal? There appears to be no obvious implication for time as a factor in this policy in terms of any urgency for implementation. As just noted, there is an implication for the reallocation of staff time. If the school system has a history of discouraging participation by parents and guardians, the policy surely will demand more time of families. Time is a resource for families as well as for organizations. Consequently, there could be an increased demand on family resources in pursuit of a common mission, the adequate educational experience.

4. Rationality.   In the final analysis, to what extent is or will the policy be perceived as being rational? Does the policy, as conceived, forge a link between the perceived problem and its logical solution?

It is hard to think of an argument for *not* perceiving this policy as being rational, unless one adopts a narrow or erroneous view of what constitutes "efficient" use of staff time. As noted above, the concept of assuring full participation of people in affairs having personal implications in their lives is rooted in basic democratic theory. However, there might be those who would argue from a philosophical point of view that the purpose of the school is "to teach" and that teaching is a technical function to be performed only by those prepared in a particular way. However, this view is surely not prevalent today.

5. Power of the policy.   To what extent is the policy actually likely to shape or alter the behavior of those it is intended to affect?

Finally, one must question the extent to which this policy will actually have an impact on those for whom it is intended. This is the ultimate measure of the "power of the policy." Will it actually shape the administration's or the staff's patterns of behavior in fostering and effectively using the benefits of more complete family participation? Will the policy actually do anything to increase or enhance the frequency or quality of participation by parents or guardians? Are there any sanctions related to compliance to bring about the desired outcomes?

On the face of it, "participation," being "informed," being "consulted," "decision process," and "determination" are words and phrases in our illustration with a positive valence. Few people would be frightened of the concepts and values generally implied. Put another way, who could argue with these concepts in a wording of a policy statement? On the other hand, participation by family members can be rewarded but surely not punished. Regarding staff, however, certain incentives and disincentives can be tied to their support for this policy.

E. Provide Recommendations

The fifth and final step of the analysis is, of course, to provide a clear and cogent statement of recommendations for (a) wording of the policy (if any changes) and (b) key action elements. This statement should focus on both strengths and weaknesses, on any factors peculiar to the issue, and on those factors suggested by the data generated by the analysis. In this context, there are a number of considerations for communicating or conveying a policy analysis and any recommended action. For convenience, the original policy is stated again.

Original Policy Statement
In all instances involving disciplinary action for a student and those events considering a student's placement in a special education program, the parents or legal guardian of such student will be informed, consulted, and actively participate in the decision process and any resultant determination. (Original date, 19XX)

The most problematic aspects of the original policy statement are those that are vaguely or poorly operationalized. Here are some of the issues.

1. The policy refers to "all instances" involving disciplinary action. One questions whether this is appropriate. Surely there could be situations that are best handled within the classroom, and in some instance, those events could be shared with parents or guardians at a later time if appropriate. For example, minor infractions of school building rules may give the opportunity to build positive rapport between the principal and the student if they are handled informally in the interest of developing more constructive behavior in the future.

Consequently, the analyst may suggest a rewording to something like "all instances involving probable disciplinary action in which suspension, expulsion, or removal of a student's privileges" to replace "all instances involving disciplinary action."

2. The reference to "special education program" may be interpreted in different ways by different people in the community. This term is used as jargon by many within the system and most often refers to programs for students with learning and behavioral difficulties. However, to others it might appear to include programs for gifted children. The analyst might suggest the substitution of "in programs other than the student's regular classroom or curriculum schedule" for the phrase "in a special education program."

3. Presuming the school board is committed to its goal of family participation, it is important to build a feedback mechanism directly into the policy statement rather than leaving this matter up to future development of adequate guidelines. Consequently, the following could be added to the "Implementation of this policy shall be monitored regularly by the assistant superintendent for community affairs, and progress reports will be provided quarterly to the Board of Education."

4. Perhaps the most difficult concepts to operationalize in the policy statement are encompassed by the phrase "will be informed, consulted, and actively participate in the decision process and any resultant determination." Experience suggests that these policy provisions are not likely to be satisfied or clarified by mere words in one reworded policy statement. This is where development of more explicit policy guidelines would be appropriate. Guidelines are not part of the actual policy statement but are necessary statements of intent and behavior that are aimed at achieving the goal of the policy. The following guidelines could be considered as suggestions for action elements and content:

a. Special consideration should be given to encouraging input from (a) individuals who have been active in and may be assumed to represent any parent-teacher organization *and* (b) any individual who may be presented as an advocate for a student or family.

b. The issue of "informed" should include development of additional guidelines that specify organizational procedures to provide evidence of a persons having been informed. Such activities could include (a) a record of having met face-to-face with a parent or guardian or designee, (b) presentation with written procedures of review of a student's status and performance, (c) specification of types of issues and procedures for appeal and participants' right to be accompanied by advocates of choice, and (d) opportunity for dialogue with staff for purposes of clarification, and so forth. These alternatives should be considered in any drafting of guidelines.

c. The question of operationalizing "consulted" should speak to the manner and frequency with which contact will be initiated and pursued by school personnel. This would include fostering participation by both postal and telephone invitations or personal visits to the home, allowing sufficient notice, and convenience in time and place of meetings, and the like.

d. "Actively participate" will, of course, be up to the participant to determine its extent and nature. However, the school could develop guidelines that communicate the high value placed on family members' suggestions, comments, or statements of preference. It should be noted in writing (nonverbal behavior of staff is not sufficient) that family members' input is not only necessary but valued.

e. Reference to "resultant determination" could be clarified through guidelines and will depend on the type and nature of the decision or problem under consideration. For example, issues of disciplinary action may require reference to legal limitations or mandates of state law, as in the case of weapons or drugs being brought into a school building. Such matters may require certain written commitments by both the school and the parent. In the case of special programming for a particular student's unique needs, some agreements may be informal and a monitoring process agreed upon; in other instances, there may need to be an official "sign off" by both the school and the parent or guardian in order to satisfy mandatory regulations or funding and reimbursement considerations and to otherwise formalize agreements.

f. Development and promulgation of guidelines shall be mandated within the policy statement, and the office responsible for that task shall be specified.

Given this analysis and the changes just suggested, the modified policy to be recommended to the superintendent for ultimate consideration by the board would be as follows.

Proposed Amended Policy Statement

In all instances of (1) suspension, expulsion, or removal of a student's privileges for a student and (2) those events considering a student's placement in programs other than the student's regular classroom schedule, the parents or legal guardian of such student will be informed, consulted, and actively participate in the decision process and any resultant determination. Implementation of this policy shall be monitored regularly by the assistant superintended for community affairs, and progress reports will be provided quarterly to the Board of Education. Guidelines necessary for implementation of this policy shall be developed and promulgated by [date specified]. (Amended 19YY)

Additional Proposed Action

Other actions in support of the policy changes have been introduced in the course of the analysis, provided above. To summarize, the school social worker, individually or in cooperation with others, as indicated, should:

1. Move to obtain the endorsement of all key administrative or service departments within the school system for the policy changes.

2. Liaison with community advisory and advocacy groups, such as the Association of Retarded Citizens, the Council for Exceptional Children, and the like.

3. Participate in any inservice training for teachers and other ancillary service staff to adequately prepare them and to prepare parents for effective participation.

4. Obtain directives pertaining to the policy in writing.

5. Review such directives and policies, where possible, with new staff and new families as part of orientation routines.

6. Facilitate, support, initiate, support, and encourage all those who embrace the policy and its purposes.

Fair Warning to Conscientious People

The foregoing is merely an illustration of how an analytic framework might be used. It is not an instruction book. An analytic framework gives a list of *possible* considerations. This chapter has added a few possible mind teasers to those considerations in order to offer illustrations if this approach is to be used. In real life, the process is not so linear. It is, instead, circular, with a lot of back and forth filling. Moreover, in real life one will not be able to gather information for every element, nor is it absolutely necessary to do so. Any analytic framework should serve primarily as an instigator, stimulating further creative thought for the imaginative professional trying to take responsibility for constructive criticism.

A Few Final Words about Presentation of Policy Analyses

Effective analyses of policy are not hidden under bushel baskets. They need to see the light of day, of course, because they are done in order to be communicated. Such analyses are meant to teach, inform, or persuade. Consequently, policy analysis can be seen as fundamentally and honestly a political act, even under the most disciplined and objective circumstances. How best to communicate a policy analysis is a topic in and of itself; however, a few generalities can be stated to serve as reminders.

1. The form and style, written or oral, should be comfortable. The presentation should not be made in the laborious manner of the analysis we have just completed. Clarity and brevity are essential. The manner should be objective and should not be perceived as attacking any individual or group.

2. The content must be accurate and informative; the reader or listener must be assured that the analysis contributes to his or her understanding and increased confidence in understanding the issues.

3. The analysis should show working familiarity with all relevant antecedent and contemporary issues impinging on the policy choice.

4. Argument must be balanced, with the analysis identifying potential points for and against key choices to be made.

5. Speculation must be offered on the probable impact of key choices.

6. The presentation must use language appropriate for the reader or listener target group, language that helps those targets form a clear mental picture of what is being communicated. Clearly label sections, number key points or choices, and provide clear and concise summaries.

7. Last, the presentation must be consistent with professional values and ethics. Special emphasis must be given to accuracy or information. No attempts at manipulation must be made.

A comprehensive policy analysis, communicated with these considerations in mind, will add to the credibility of the analyst and the analysis that is provided.

REFERENCES

Flynn, J. 1992. *Social agency practice: Analysis and presentation for community practice* (2nd ed.). Chicago: Nelson-Hall.

Jansson, B. S. 1994. *Social welfare policy: From theory to practice* (2nd ed.). Belmont, CA: Brooks/Cole.

National Association of Social Workers. 1996. *Code of Ethics*. Silver Springs, MD: Author.

CHAPTER 9

School Social Work: Organizational Perspectives

Edward J. Pawlak
Professor of Social Work, Western Michigan University

Linwood Cousins
Assistant Professor of Social Work, Western Michigan University

- People Processing and People Changing Perspectives
- Formal Organizational Structure
- Informal Structure and Relations
- The School as an Organizational Culture
- Imaginization: Metaphorical Perspectives of Schools
- Managing Organizational Change

Schools are organizational entities that have structures, processes, policies, and cultures. These factors affect school officials, teachers, staff, students, and their families. Accordingly, school social workers have a responsibility to understand and influence these factors—especially on behalf of students and families who are clients. School social workers cannot understand and influence what they cannot see. Therefore, they must use several organizational lenses—conceptual frameworks—to discern organizational structures, processes, policies, and culture. A review of all organizational frameworks would take us far afield; thus we have selected those that we believe are particularly useful to school social workers.

PEOPLE PROCESSING AND PEOPLE CHANGING PERSPECTIVES

Hasenfeld (1983, pp. 134–143) analyzes human service organizations as entities that rely on *people processing* and *people changing* operations. As applied to schools, these perspectives direct attention to several processing tasks (Lauffer, 1984, p. 94): (a) assessing and classifying student attributes, qualifications, and circumstances to decide eligibility for particular programs of study, special services and benefits, or participation in athletics and other extracurricular activity; (b) exploring those attributes, qualifications, and circumstances to decide appropriate program and benefit alternatives; (c) selecting among the alternatives; and (d) referring or placing the student in a curriculum or program, or providing a benefit. The key elements that a school social worker must address are organizational decision making, school modes of operation, patterns of processing and changing students, and whether these patterns are appropriately or inappropriately different among students with particular attributes.

School social workers can use people processing and changing perspectives to explore several questions. What are the rules and procedures used by school officials and faculty in transactions with students? Are these rules and procedures applied equitably among students who, for example, face discipline, suspension, or expulsion? What are the consequences experienced by students of decisions made or not made by school officials or teachers (e.g., the decision to refer or not to refer for testing or to special services; the decision to place a student in one academic track rather than another; the decision to not sponsor "Saturday school" as a form of in-school suspension for students who are truant or have behavioral problems)? Do students with particular characteristics experience different and less favorable school career paths (e.g., low-income vs. upper-income students, girls vs. boys, white students vs. minority students)? Are students with particular characteristics screened in or out of particular programs (e.g., what kinds of students with what kinds of behavior in the primary grades are more likely to be screened into the early identification program)? Are some groups of students often inappropriately classified? Are students with particular characteristics or circumstances likely to have favorable or unfavorable labels? Do students with particular attributes have equal access to school curricula, programs, and activities? Is stigma attached to participation in some school programs and activities? Which teachers or staff members are working with which students? These and other questions can be raised about the school's processing operations and how the school goes about making decisions about teachers, staff, and students.

The answers to these questions might lead school social workers to engage in one or more types of intervention (Jansson, 1994, pp. 36–40): (a) policy-sensitive practice—for example, alerting a parent to her rights at an upcoming Individualized Educational Program (IEP) meeting; (b) policy-related practice—for example, informing a principal that a student who was qualified for a program was excluded; and (c) policy practice—for example, advocating to elementary school administrators a change in school policy where previously some students with behavioral problems were disciplined by removal from class and placement on "the bench" in the main office.

FORMAL ORGANIZATIONAL STRUCTURE

Formal structure refers to official, established patterns in an organization. Several dimensions are used to describe the formal structure of organizations: formalization, standardization, centralization and decentralization, and horizontal and vertical complexity (Hall, 1996). These dimensions can be manipulated or altered such that aspects of the organization or its programs can be designed to be more or less formalized, standardized, centralized, or complex. Variations in organizational and program structure lead to variations in consequences (positive or negative) for school administrators, teachers, students, and parents. Although some school organizational and program structures are not accessible to and manipulable by school social workers, some are. Practitioners have a responsibility to figure out which ones are and try to alter them. Some illustrations are provided below.

Formalization refers to the degree to which rules, policies, and procedures that govern behavior in the organization are officially codified and set forth in writing (e.g., rules governing how IEP meetings should be conducted, criteria governing discipline of students, guidelines for conducting locker searches, protocols for recording and reporting unexcused absences). Formalization prescribes behavior and usually reduces discretion (e.g., in a particular school district, principals may suspend students, but only the superintendent can expel a student). However, formalization may legitimate discretion, (e.g., in one school district, a school social worker is charged with helping children in their roles as students, but may provide counseling to parents if such assistance will facilitate a child's school adjustment).

Standardization is a type of formalization in which organizations have uniform ways of dealing with uniform situations; rules or definitions are established that cover a particular set of circumstances and apply invariably. For example, schools have standardized forms and practices to record student absences and report them to parents; school officials often follow a steplike protocol in which the frequency and intensity of interventions vary as absences increase.

Each of these concepts can be used to analyze several aspects of a school's formal structure. Such analyses are useful for several reasons. Formalization and standardization can be functional if they reduce role ambiguity, document rights, duties, and expectations, and hold school officials, staff, teachers, students, or parents accountable. For example, formal structures that entitle students and parents to appeal a counselor's assigned program of study promote due process, fairness, and opportunity to negotiate and champion academic preferences, which may also ease strong feelings. The lack of due process is likely to cast school administrators and teachers as authoritarian and arbitrary officials. Such perceptions held by students and parents may contribute to strained relationships, and lead to student behavioral problems, or parental defamation of the school in the community. Formalization and standardization may eliminate or constrain arbitrariness, and may promote equitable treatment and equal opportunity for programs, services, or benefits. Standardization may promote consistency among staff members who have similar decision-making or processing tasks.

Formalization and standardization can be dysfunctional if they promote "bureaupathologies" such as "red tape," inflexibility, and devotion to method and discourage innovation and appropriate discretion (Patti, 1982, p. 153). When school rules and procedures are contested, a school social worker might ask whether they have been formalized or are informal and a matter of convention (e.g., experienced teachers have probably heard a student or parent say, "Where does it say that students can't do that?"). Formalization and standardization may be dysfunctional when they lead to routinization or ritualistic behavior in situations that call for individualizing the interpretation and implementation of a policy. For example, some states have a zero tolerance for weapons in the school, with severe penalties such as automatic expulsion from school for an academic year—no exceptions. A fourth-grade student in a small town school brought a knife to school to cut brownies for her classmates. Her behavior came under the stipulations of the law, and she was barred from school. Some proponents were concerned that a precedent might be set if an exception was made, while others maintained that an exception does not drive out the rule. The student was suspended for a week after the superintendent and school board reviewed her case, and the incident was used to educate the school community about zero tolerance.

Centralization refers to the concentration of power, authority, and decision-making at the top of the organization. As applied to a school district or system, centralization refers to the board, superintendent, or what is commonly known as the "central office" or "central administration." As applied to a particular school building, centralization refers to the principal, assistant principal, and office staff. *Decentralization* refers to the distribution of power, authority, and decision-making down through the organization. As applied to the school district or system, decentralization refers to arrangements such as regional offices or centers, or the delegation of some functions to local school principals and faculty. As applied to a particular school building, decentralization refers to the delegation of some functions to individual teachers, faculty committees, parent-teacher advisory councils, or teacher-student work groups. Within a particular school building, principals can make decisions about discipline, suspension, and access to services, or they can involve staff and parents in developing guidelines for such decisions or rely on a faculty advisory committee. Whatever the case may be, school social workers must first learn what is concentrated or distributed before they can engage in organizational change.

Centralized and decentralized structures can be functional or dysfunctional; it all depends. For example, centralizing decisions regarding expulsion in the superintendent's office is functional because dismissal has profound consequences for the student and could lead to litigation; decentralizing decisions to local school officials regarding which students should be referred for school social work services is functional, because the predominant needs of students vary from school to school. Generally speaking, centralization of authority, power, and decision making may be functional when schools have to manage boundary relationships with the external environment, (e.g., the press, police, juvenile court, community advocacy groups), when scarce resources have to be rationed and carefully allocated, or when there are threats to the school (e.g., protests, litigation, complaints). Decentralization enables teachers, student, or their parents to gain ownership of policies and programs and increases the likelihood of their legitimacy and successful implementation. For example, a decentralized decision-making structure, such as a joint faculty-student committee on student conduct, might promote student ownership of the code of conduct, whereas a centralized top down imposition of the code might generate resistance. Decentralization is also suited to managing change and uncertainty at the front lines of the organization and promotes bottom-up innovation and adaptation (Wagoner, 1994).

Horizontal complexity refers to the type and degree of organizational segmentation, such as departmentalization and specialization of positions, roles, jobs, or duties. The degree of specialization and departmentalization can be functional or dysfunctional. High specialization sometimes leads to fragmented and uncoordinated delivery of services, but it also might contribute to efficiency and the availability of high levels of expertise. Sometimes school social workers have to run interference for students and parents who are overwhelmed by their problems and the bureaucratic maze of services.

Vertical complexity refers to the number of levels in the hierarchy from the top to the bottom of the organization. Vertical complexity may be functional or dysfunctional from the standpoint of a school social worker or parent interested in promoting change. If a change proposal has to traverse many hierarchical levels for approval, the structure may not be functional; if officials are accessible and there are few levels between the top and the bottom, organizational change may be more easily influenced.

Some aspects of formal structure are often depicted in pyramidal organizational charts or tables of organization that identify hierarchical relationships, preferred communication paths, and the complexity of the organization in terms of the different divisions, specializations, departments, or programs. However, these traditional organizational charts are being replaced by circle diagrams that partially overlap or are drawn in concentric fashion to depict interdependencies, collaboration, and participation in decision making among organizational units (Tropman, 1989). Linear, rational approaches to horizontal and vertical coordination in organizations are being supplanted by flatter organizations, negotiated political orders, fluid and dynamic structures, and combinations of loose and tight coupling among organizational units (Fennell, 1994, pp. 23–25). A variety of geometric shapes and diagrams are used to graphically depict these nontraditional organizational structures and relationships (Mintzberg, 1983, pp. 20, 22, 85, 103, 115).

As school social workers begin their assignments in a new school, they should devote time to comprehending the school's horizontal and vertical complexity, or its negotiated political order, often found in school manuals or handbooks. If such documentation is not available, school social workers are advised to be observant, to check out the arrangements with opinion leaders, and to map the structure or negotiated order for themselves. Such understanding is important because school social workers are required to integrate, coordinate, link, and communicate with different departments, units, positions, or roles in the school's structure. The role of school social worker gives practitioners legitimate, unique access to most if not all segments and roles within schools—structural mobility. Thus school social workers must figure out their niche in the school and must identify which individuals in which positions might facilitate or hinder work with officials, teachers, students, and families.

INFORMAL STRUCTURE AND RELATIONS

People in schools—in fact, in all organizations—develop social relationships that are not prescribed by organizational officials. These social relationships evolve into patterned group processes and social structures that are known as "informal organization" or "informal structure and relations." These social relationships are informal in that they are unofficial, not mandated, and not planned. Informal structure is rarely, if ever, documented (so don't ask your principal for a copy of the school's informal organizational chart, because it doesn't exist; but as we will point out shortly, you can draw one on your own).

There are four types of informal structure: affectional, communication, decision-making, and power. These structures are not mutually exclusive and the same participants may be involved in all structures but in different ways. *Affectional structure* refers to patterns of social relationships based on friendship, mutual attraction, similar interests, common experiences— for whatever reason, people like each other and spend time together when it is not formally required by the organization. Affectional structure manifests itself in several ways: two or more staff members frequently have coffee breaks or lunch together, sit next to each other at meetings, attend professional conferences together, play volleyball together after school, or socialize off the job. *Communication structure* refers to patterns of social interaction among staff members based on giving and getting information, opinions, viewpoints, or feelings (even when they are not within an affectional structure). Some common metaphors for communication structure include "the rumor mill," "the grapevine," "the talk on the street," "leaks," and "inside information" or "inside track." Informal communication structure can be detected by observing who talks with whom after a controversy or a staff meeting. Who are the confidants, the listeners? Whom do teachers depend on to figure out and report "what's going on?" *Decision-making structure* refers to patterns of social interaction among school personnel based on the solicitation or provision of analysis, insights, and advice leading up to a decision. Decision-making structure can be detected by observing who consults with whom during deliberations. Is there a small group of experienced teachers who are often consulted "on the side" by the principal? Do particular teachers meet informally in an attempt to sway opinion prior to a formal meeting? *Power structure* refers to patterns of social interaction based on ability to influence. There are four types of power: referent, expertise, reward, and coercive (French and Raven, 1968). A teacher may have referent power because she is liked, and another may have expertise power because she is a respected English instructor. Some teachers have reward power because they support colleagues and praise them for their contributions, and others have coercive power because they have years of experience, they are abrasive, and colleagues are intimidated by them.

School social workers must strive to discern informal structure because they will inevitably become a part of it, and they may have to work with or against it. School social workers must figure out who is included in which informal groups. Who is the "power behind the throne"? Who are the quiet "shakers and movers"? Who has the "ear of the administration" and who is "wired in"? Who really runs this place? Who are the insiders and outsiders? Is there an inner circle?

If mapping relevant informal structures and relations is essential or desirable, school social workers can easily do so with a formal organizational chart and highlighters of different colors. Assume that the school has an organizational chart in which each school official's, staff member's, and teacher's name and position is posted within its own rectangular box. Assume that an assistant principal and two teachers are an affectional group and that the principal relies on the school secretary and head of the physical plant to "keep their ears to the ground and keep her posted on goings-on." Different colored highlighters can be used to visually map these two informal structures. Such mapping may help demystify the complex informal operational structure and relations within a school and their congruence with formal structure.

Several factors contribute to the development and maintenance of informal structure and relations: (a) the characteristics or attributes of individuals, such as gender, race, age, and religion; (b) common life experiences (e.g., among teachers and staff—single parenthood, caring for an adult parent, attendance at the same university) or shared values, interests, and memberships in organizations external to the school (e.g., conservative orientation, quilting, fishing, political activity, church membership); and (c) sharing a common fate such as working under an authoritarian, domineering principal. When informal structure is detected, school social workers should try to determine the factors that bond members together.

Informal structures not only involve administrators, teachers, and staff in varying combinations but may include students and parents. Teachers sometimes have "favorites," both parents and students. Some students and parents are insiders because they have high participation rates in school activities; some students, teachers, and parent volunteers are involved in the ski club or play basketball together in the school gym on Sunday afternoon. Students detect informal structure and have names for some aspects of it—teacher's pets, brown-noses, suck-ups, grungies, preppies, nerds.

Informal structure serves several functions in organizations: (a) It provides informal linkages between departments, positions and roles (e.g., the school social worker and attendance officer worked together in another school district. (b) It sometimes compensates for problems in the formal structure (e.g., when a school principal was of little help to teachers who had to manage classroom behavior problems, they turned to a tenured experienced teacher for assistance. (c) It socializes and orients new school personnel and students to life in the organization—what are the "DOs and DON'Ts?" (d) It provides a network for the circulation of information. (e) It provides social support and alleviates stress and frustration. (f) It meets interpersonal and associational needs. In examining a school's informal structure, school social workers should try to figure out the functions that it serves and determine whether it supports or undermines the students served.

THE SCHOOL AS AN ORGANIZATIONAL CULTURE

The organizational culture of a school impacts all school functions. This fact is particularly relevant to social workers who practice in schools where there is difficulty in understanding the mutual influence and effect on intraschool relationships of social and academic processes occurring between schools and society at large. Posing several questions brings the issues into focus: What is the nature of organizational culture in schools? Why is this information important to social workers? What do social workers need to know about organizational culture in schools to function effectively?

What is cultural about the organization of schools? Culture can be defined as the *beliefs, values, traditions,* and *attitudes* that are the basis of the *frames of reference* or *meanings* people use to organize reality and direct their behavioral actions. In deciphering the culture in how schools work as organizations, two pathways are important.

Schools are transmitters of dominant cultural standards, norms, and values emanating from society at large. Dominant cultural norms are infused into schools through federal regulations, state and local boards of education, and universities as institutions for knowledge development and training. These institutions define, design, and organize educational material that becomes a part of the educational and social activities that have to be administered in a school. For example, the selection and enforcement of reading, writing, and arithmetic curricula, as well as the methods to teach these subjects, are artifacts of Western cultural beliefs about learning and socialization rather than universal facts of human nature.

Interpersonal transactions occurring between students and teachers or staff provide another pathway for culture to permeate schools as organizations. Culture operates in schools in this way by providing a blueprint for the meaning and interpretation of acceptable and unacceptable behavior, attitudes, emotions, and beliefs. For example, students generally understand that when they enter the classroom, the teacher is in charge. She makes the rules and enforces them. She decides who can talk and when. And when a student violates rules, the consequences generally fit the norms that have been sanctioned in school. As such, culture in schools manifests in an organized way various frames of reference or meanings associated with compliance and violation of official policies and regulations.

Both pathways of culture in the organization of schools are alike in reflecting varying degrees of influence by dominant cultural norms in society at large. When there is a high degree of compatibility and homogeneity among students and school officials, there is likely to be less conflict within the organizational milieu of the school. However, such compatibility and homogeneity in schools have never fully been the case for nonwhite groups (e.g., African Americans, Native Americans, Hispanics) and are becoming even less the case because of the increasing ethnic, religious, and economic diversity of groups residing in the United States.

School social workers must be abreast of the influence and impact of organizational culture through dominant beliefs, values, attitudes, and behaviors that are embedded in the *customs, traditions,* and *notions of common sense* forming the basis of *administrative policy* and *regulations* in schools. For example, social workers should examine disciplinary and evaluative activities occurring between social workers and students, between students and staff, and among parents, staff, and social workers. When observing disciplinary activities in school, social workers can ask themselves the following questions: Do the infractions that led to disciplinary action reflect commonly held beliefs, values, and attitudes between the student and school official about the rule or standard that has been violated? When there is a lack of commonality, are the differences labeled dysfunctional rather than as variations in how people understand the multiple meanings of the rules and standards being enforced? These questions are especially important to consider when the outcomes are detrimental to the social, emotional, and academic well-being of students.

Understanding and Action

What do social workers need to know in order to understand and effectively engage in situations in which dominant cultural frames of reference that organize schools do not work. We refer to cases in which the organizational culture of a school is not held together by common frames of reference, leaving students, teachers, and staff acting, thinking, and feeling incompatible and alienated. For example, many African Americans have experienced strain in relation to dominant cultural norms in school and have responded with resistance. Many African Americans have questioned the relevance of the subjects taught in school to their plight as a stigmatized group. Being able to read, write, and do arithmetic have not directly lead to less racial discrimination and increased economic and political liberation. Mastery of these academic subjects can help, but not always. In this context, when frames of reference operating in the organizational culture of a school are juxtaposed, compliance and noncompliance are better understood.

Another example is the kind of etiquette required in classroom interactions among students and between students and teachers. Many, but certainly not all, African Americans have been socialized in environments that value a high degree of expressiveness and animation through language and the body in communicating with people. However, classroom etiquette generally requires that students sit still when speaking, stay in their seats, only address the teacher, and so forth. When students do not or cannot comply with these social and behavioral norms, they are punished or labeled dysfunctional.

Social workers must understand that organizational cultures contain meaning processes manifested in terms of beliefs, values, attitudes, and behaviors that constitute frames of reference. Whether it is minority or majority groups, meanings and frames are influenced by, among other things, historical and contemporary experiences in the United States and beyond. Minorities specifically tend to experience school norms as extensions of the social, economic, and political inequality they experience in American society. Many studies have documented this, coupled with the finding that such relational strain between minorities and school staff influences the academic performance of the students and the evaluations of students by teachers and staff (Gibson and Ogbu, 1991; Spindler, 1997). Consider that social workers tend to perform evaluations and assessments that serve as the basis of various forms of psychological, social, and educational intervention with students in school. These activities serve an important social and cultural function for schools and society at large. This predicament requires social workers to understand the complicity of their roles and activities in enforcing dominant, and often oppressive, societal norms that function as parts of the organizational culture in schools. The full extent of what is meant here is more acutely realized in schools with significant numbers of minority students or students from low-income backgrounds.

What commonly happens, for example, is that social workers interact with school staff who believe unquestioningly that academic processes and contexts are free of culture or cultural bias. Noncompliance and low academic performance, in their view, reflect psychosocial dysfunction and cognitive or intellectual abnormality, respectively. School personnel and even some social workers may have difficulty seeing beyond the seemingly natural and just plain commonsense processes of most social and academic aspects of schooling. Taking these processes for granted, however, is partially a product of the blinding nature of a dominant culture. Taken as a whole in a contemporary context, these beliefs, traditions, and notions of common sense form parts of a frame of reference that maintain currently dominant organizational cultures in school and widespread social, economic, and political inequality in society. They have contributed to (a) racism or the belief that minorities fail in school because of their inferiority as a people and (b) beliefs that minority students simply need to persevere in their work and tolerate or overcome their feelings and perceptions of being treated inequitably by assimilating to or accommodating dominant cultural norms.

Social workers can do something about this. They can individually engage in accessible levels of the organizational culture of the school and collectively engage in advocacy, public education, and political action. Individual engagement begins with asking and answering the questions raised earlier: What are the beliefs, values, attitudes, and behavior that form the basis of social and academic compliance and noncompliance by students? Answers to such questions can lead to interactions with students and staff in which one is guided not only by the surface or manifest understandings of disagreements between students and teachers but also by the underlying or latent meanings that are the cultural foundation of such incompatibilities. The next step is to conduct educational, social, and psychological interventions that reach both levels of the problem without leaving students and teachers with understandings that limit them to a traditional arsenal of labels, diagnoses, and other disciplinary actions and reactions.

The second application as a social worker is a matter of scale. That is, the focus is on those legislative and academic policy practices that provide *unidimensional approaches* to education in the first place. Activities in these domains require social workers to participate in advocacy and public education through community dialogues and political actions that directly or indirectly address official policy-making bodies. School staff meetings, board meetings, state legislatures, and tracking federal bills in consort with the National Association of Social Workers' lobbying arm are excellent sites of practice.

In conclusion, the understandings and actions regarding the organizational culture of schools proposed in this discussion offer a way in which social workers can become transformative professionals. We can begin by understanding and refusing the notion that academic and social functions in schools are neutral transactions in organizational culture. Acting as such, social workers contribute to the realization of the overall interdependence between American institutions such as schools and social, economic, political, and cultural processes in society at large.

IMAGINIZATION: METAPHORICAL PERSPECTIVES OF SCHOOLS

Imaginization is the name for organizational assessment and development as created and practiced by Gareth Morgan, an academician and consultant (Morgan, 1993). Imaginization, the word, is the result of the fusion of the concepts of imagination and organization. Imaginization, the concept, refers to the creative use of metaphor to interpret and shape organizational life and develop shared understandings of organizational structure, processes, roles, and culture. Metaphors enable "new ways of thinking about management styles, organizational design, approaches to planning and change, and basic products and services" (Morgan, 1993, p. 265). One imaginizes by invoking metaphorical images to frame and reframe organizational situations in new ways: "We don't teach in a school; we teach in a military organization with a principal who acts like General Patton." "Faculty and students are like an extended family." "The school is an oasis in a community beleaguered by gang fighting, drug dealing, inadequate housing, with many single parents hanging on by their fingernails." School cultures are often characterized through metaphors: "The teachers approach their work as if it were a calling, not just a job." "The only time you see those teachers move is when it's time to go home, and they usually beat the students out the door." Metaphors send a strong metamessage that influences student and parental attitudes and behavior toward the school.

These examples reveal how the process of imaginization begins—with metaphorical characterization and images that serve as the point of departure for assessing the organization. Imaginization is not codified in behaviorally specific steps that one could mechanically follow. Metaphorical language is used to describe the basic protocol of imaginization: "Get inside." "Adopt the role of a learner." "Map the terrain." "Identify key themes and interpretations (to produce an evolving 'reading' of the situation)." "Confirm, refute, and reformulate throughout." The method is exploratory yet deliberative; it is free flowing yet anchored in organizational realities; it is directive yet participative; it is subjective yet objective. Nevertheless, there is sufficient structure and direction in the method for open, venturesome practitioners to begin imaginizing (Pawlak, 1994, p. 133).

The fundamental processes of imaginization are not foreign to social workers. We intuitively rely on metaphor in our everyday organizational lives to "read into" and characterize what is going on. However, we seldom "play out" the "readings" to use them as heuristic devices to analyze and solve problems. School social workers will find imaginization congruent with their professional values and education. The process has a primacy of orientation toward organizational members' definition of the situation, ownership of organizational problems, and responsibility for change (Pawlak, 1994, p. 134).

Images of schools created through metaphor development have been used to study school climate and environment. Grady, Fisher, and Fraser (1996) developed a questionnaire to gain "insight into teachers' mental images of their school as it is and as they think it should be." The questionnaire was used in a workshop with teachers who were led through five steps that can be adapted by school social workers to assess their schools:

1. Identify several most favored and least favored images of the school.
2. Identify positive and negative aspects of these favored and nonfavored images.
3. Identify assumptions/beliefs/values/philosophies which underpin these favored and nonfavored images.
4. Identify "examplars of language, rituals, ceremonies, stories, heroes, schedules, decision-making/delegating/accountability processes and so on which ought to be fostered in the school in light of the exercise" (Grady, Fisher and Fraser, 1996, p. 51).

As an exercise, formulate a metaphor about your school. Run with it. Where does it take you? What does it reveal about the school as an organization? What corrective action or change is suggested by the metaphor? What are the factors that might facilitate or hinder change? This delightful approach provides a refreshing counterpoint to traditional yet essential approaches to organizational analysis.

Thus far we have presented several conceptual frameworks that we believe are useful in understanding and analyzing schools as organizations: schools as people processing and changing organizations, schools as formal and informal structures, schools as cultures, and schools viewed from metaphorical perspectives. Each framework enables school social workers to understand schools from different organizational viewpoints. We believe an eclectic approach is essential. No one perspective is adequate to penetrate the complexities of schools as organizations. If the application of one framework does not yield insight into organizational problems, then another should be tried.

School social workers are not interested in organizational analysis for its own sake. The results of organizational analysis must be transformed into change efforts. In the final section of this chapter, we offer some general guidelines for introducing and managing change. Detailed discussions of organizational change models, strategies, tactics, and development abound in the literature (Pawlak, 1998, Smithmier, 1996; Flynn, 1995; Burbach and Crockett, 1994; Netting, Kettner, and McMurtry, 1993; Brager and Holloway, 1992; Mulkeen and Cooper, 1992; Bailey, 1992; Gottfredson, 1987; Holloway and Brager, 1985).

MANAGING ORGANIZATIONAL CHANGE

Organizational analysis yields insights or findings about organizational conditions or problems. These insights and findings are essential to the planning and implementation of change efforts. The following guides are offered as one way to approach changing schools from within.

1. Describe the organizational problem, condition, or opportunity for change. What are the features of the problem or change opportunity? How is the problem distributed in the school? What are the key groups affected by the problem?

2. What factors contribute to or sustain the condition or problem? What factors brought about the change opportunity at this time?

3. What is the goal of the change you propose? What are the reasons for changes?

4. Identify the key persons, groups, roles, positions, and units affected by the proposed change.

5. What are the sunk costs in the status quo? There are two kinds of sunk costs—financial and psychological investments (e.g., "this program is my baby"). What are the likely sources of resistance to change, what is the degree of resistance, and how might resistance be expressed? (Patti, 1980).

6. Identify possible approaches to change and possible positive and negative effects.

7. Think through the change that you want to introduce by anticipating potential adverse consequences and how they might be overcome. (Don't make your chess moves one at a time.)

8. Anticipate the reactions of school officials, staff, teachers, students, or parents.

9. Explore these matters with trusted colleagues, and ask for ideas.

10. What resources, time, support, or training are needed to implement change?

11. Develop a plan to influence change and a work plan to implement change so that influentials can envisage the feasibility of change. Strive to develop shared ownership of the change proposal and process.

School social workers have a primacy of orientation toward helping students and their families through individual or group counseling, and often such approaches are appropriate. However, when organizational conditions contribute to or sustain student problems, helpful interventions on behalf of students must be directed at the school as an organization. The roles and status of school social workers, as well as their professional education, enable them to take holistic perspectives and to legitimately engage the many different units, roles, and personnel within schools. School social workers have more opportunities to leverage change than they might realize. Carpe diem.

REFERENCES

Bailey, D. 1992. Organizational change in a public school system: The synergism of two approaches. *Social Work in Education* 14(2):94–105.

Brager, G., and Holloway, S. 1992. Assessing prospects for organizational change: The uses of force field analysis. *Administration in Social Work* 16(3/4):15–28.

Burbach, H. J., and Crockett, M. 1994. The learning organization as a prototype for the next generation of schools. *Planning and Change* 25(3/4):173–179.

Fennell, H. A. 1994. Organizational linkages: Expanding the existing metaphor. *Journal of Educational Administration* 32(1):23–33.

Flynn, J. P. 1995. Social justice in social agencies. in R. L. Edwards and J. G. Hopps (eds.). *The encyclopedia of social work* (19th ed.; pp. 2173–2179). NY: NASW Press.

French, J. R. P., and Raven, B. (1968). The bases of social poser. in D. Cartwright and A. Zander (eds.). *Group Dynamics* (3rd ed.); pp. 215–235). NY: Harper & Row.

Gibson, M. and Ogbu, J. 1991. *Minority status and schooling: A comparative study of immigrant and involuntary minorities.* NY: Garland.

Gottfredson, D. C. 1987. An evaluation of an organization development approach to reducing school disorder. *Evaluation Review* 11(6):739–763.

Grady, N. B., Fisher, D. L., and Fraser, B. J. 1996. Images of school through metaphor development and validation of a questionnaire. *Journal of Educational Administration* 34(2):41–53.

Hall, R. 1996. *Organizations: Structure, process, and outcome* (6th ed.). Englewood Cliffs, NJ: Prentice-Hall.

Hasenfeld, Y. 1983. *Human service organizations.* Englewood Cliffs, NJ: Prentice-Hall.

Holloway, S. and Brager, G. 1985. Implicit negotiations and organizational practice. *Administration in Social Work* 9(2):15–24.

Jansson, B. 1994. *Social welfare policy: From theory to practice* (2nd ed.). Belmont, CA: Brooks/Cole.

Lauffer, A. 1984. *Understanding your agency* (2nd ed.). Beverly Hills, CA: Sage.

Mintzberg, H. 1983. *Structure in fives: Designing effective organizations.* Englewood Cliffs, NJ: Prentice-Hall.

Morgan, G. 1993. *Imaginization: The art of creative management.* NY: Sage.

Mulkeen, T. A., and Cooper, B. S. 1992. Implications of preparing school administrators for knowledge work organizations: A case study. *Journal of Educational Administration.* 30(1):17–28.

Netting. E. F., Kettner, P. M., and McMurtry, S. L. 1993. *Social work macropractice.* NY: Longman.

Patti, R. 1980. Organizational resistance and change. the view from below. In H. Resnick and R. Patti (eds.). *Change from within* (pp. 114–131). NY: Haworth.

Patti, R. 1982. Analyzing agency structures. In M. Austin and J. Hershey (eds.). *Handbook on mental health administration.* (pp. 137–162). San Francisco: Jossey-Bass.

Pawlak, E. J. 1994. [Review of the book *Imaginization: The art of creative management.*] *Administration in Social Work* 18(4):132–134.

Pawlak, E. J. 1998. Organizational tinkering. In B. Compton and B. Galaway (eds.). *Social work processes* (4th ed.). NY: Allyn & Bacon.

Smithmier, A. 1996. Schools and community-based collaboration: Multiple resistances and structural realities. *Planning and Change* 27(1/2):15–29.

Spindler, G. (ed.). 1997. *Education and cultural process: Anthropological approaches.* Prospect Heights, IL: Waveland.

Tropman, J. E. 1989. The organizational circle: A new approach to drawing an organizational chart. *Administration in Social Work* 13(1):35–44.

Wagoner, R. V. 1994. Changing school governance: A case for decentralized management. *Planning and Change* 25(3/4):206–218.

CHAPTER 10

Educational Mandates for Children with Disabilities: School Policies, Case Law, and the School Social Worker*

Brooke R. Whitted
Partner, Foran and Schultz, Chicago

Robert Constable
Professor Emeritus, Loyola University of Chicago

- What Are the Educational Rights of Children with Disabilities?
- How Does the Special Education System Work?
- What Is the Role of the Local School System?
- Who Is the Child with Disabilities?
- What Is Special Education?
- What Are Related Services?
- What Services Must the School Provide?
- What Is Placement in the Least Restrictive Environment?
- What Are Placement Procedures?
- Can Students with Disabilities Be Suspended or Expelled?
- What Are Provisions for Mediation and for an Impartial Due Process Hearing?
- What Are Due Process and Judicial Review?
- What Is an Individualized Education Program?

This chapter is one of several in the book that focus on the implementation for school social workers of the mandate to provide a free appropriate public education (FAPE) to children with disabilities. Chapter 6 focused on the court decisions that defined the right. Here we provide an overview of the law and its interpretation in court decisions. Chapter 11 will focus on clinical and educational program development for preschool children with disabilities. Section III will discuss least restrictive environment and inclusion, the social developmental study, and the Individualized Education Program.

*The authors acknowledge the assistance of Bobby Silverstein in the updating of this article.

The Individuals with Disabilities Education Act (IDEA) and its accompanying regulations requires that every state and the District of Columbia ensure FAPE is available to all children with disabilities. The education of unserved or underserved children with disabilities has a clear priority over the education of children already receiving services. Such services must be provided to *all* qualifying children with disabilities without regard to their particular ability to benefit from special education and with no financial needs test. The act is heavily parent/guardian oriented and requires states to maximize parental involvement in educational decision making every step of the way. A formal administrative system for the resolution of disputes may be invoked by the schools or the parents of pupils with disabilities. Throughout this system, detailed steps of identification, evaluation, determination of eligibility, planning, service, and administrative appeals are set forth. The school social worker, as a school staff member, is an important figure throughout. Working knowledge of the requirements of the act is a necessity for school social workers, who inevitably work with children with disabilities and the special education system.

WHAT ARE THE EDUCATIONAL RIGHTS OF CHILDREN WITH DISABILITIES?

Over a period of twenty-five years a cumulative body of law, court decisions, and policies has developed in relation to the educational rights of children with disabilities to a FAPE. These became summarized in IDEA and its amendments, the most recent being P.L. 105-117, signed into law June 4, 1997. When we refer to the law, we are referring to legal principles in the law, codified in 20 *United States Code*, sections 1401–1468 (cited as 20 U.S.C. 1401–1468). When we refer to regulations, we are referring to 34 *Code of Federal Regulations* parts 300 and following (here cited as 34 C.F.R. 300 ff). These are frequently updated, as the law and its regulations develop, and can be found in any law library. For the school social worker in the United States, the contents of this book furnish a general update on the most recent provisions of the law through 1997. It is important for social workers in the United States to be familiar with this evolving body of law and its updates in order to design school social work roles that help the school respond to these mandates. For the international reader, practicing in a different legal orbit, it is important to see the relation of law to school policy and from this to the school social worker's role. The legal context for schooling needs to be taken into account to develop the school social worker's role. A large part of the law deals with the protection of vulnerable groups. It is out of this legal framework, as well as the educational mission of the school in any particular society, that the school social worker's role is constructed.

In the face of some neglect of children with disabilities prior to 1968, the rights of these children to a FAPE have had considerable development in the United States. In a classic statement of this tradition, culminating in the 1997 amendments to IDEA, Turnbull and Turnbull summarize it in the form of six rights:

1. The right to attend school—the principle of *zero reject*. Each school-age person with a disability has the right to be educated in a system of FAPE. Agencies and professionals may not expel or suspend students for certain behaviors or without following certain procedures; they may not exclude students on the basis that they are incapable of leaning; and they may not limit the access of students to school on the basis of their having contagious diseases.

2. The right to a fair appraisal of their strengths and needs—the principle of *nondiscriminatory evaluation*. Socioeconomic status, language, and other factors need to be discounted and must not bias the student's evaluation; agencies and professionals must obtain an accurate, nonbiased portrait of each student. Decisions need to be based on facts, not simply categories: on what students are doing and are capable of doing, in relation to behavioral outcomes individualized for the student. The resulting education would remedy the student's impairments and build on strengths.

3. The right to a *beneficial experience* in school—the principle of free appropriate public education—means that schools must individualize each student's education, provide needed related services, engage in a fair process for determining what is appropriate for each student, and ensure that the student's education indeed confers a benefit. Education must have a positive outcome for each student. The emphasis of this discussion is not simply on provision of access to education but on adapting the system and on building capacities in the person with a disability so that certain results are attained.

4. The right to be *included* in the general education curriculum and other activities—the principle of the least restrictive environment—means that the schools must include the student in the general education program and may not remove a student from it unless the student cannot benefit from being in that program, even after the provision of supplementary aids and services and necessary related services.

5. The right to be treated fairly—the principle of *procedural due process*—means that the school must provide certain kinds of information (notice and access to records) to students, special protection when natural parents are unavailable (surrogate parents), and access to a fair hearing process.

6. The right to be included in the decision-making process—the principle of *parent and student participation*—means the schools must structure decision-making processes (including policy decisions on a statewide level) in such a way that parents and students have opportunities to affect meaningfully the education the students are receiving. A related principle of enhanced accountability to pupils and parents is moving in the direction of report cards related to individualized goals and educational programs[1]

Building on this concept of educational rights, the term "free appropriate public education" means special education and related services that:

A. Have been provided at public expense, under public supervision and direction, and without charge;

B. Meet the standards of the state educational agency and secondary school educational agency;

C. Include an appropriate preschool, elementary, or secondary school education in the state involved; and

D. Are provided in conformity with a student's individualized education program (20 U.S.C. 1401(8)).

HOW DOES THE SPECIAL EDUCATION SYSTEM WORK?

It is important to understand the impact of laws, court decisions, and policies on state and local educational systems. To respect the rights of children with disabilities to a FAPE and to qualify for federal financial assistance under IDEA, a state must demonstrate that it "has in effect a policy that assures all handicapped children the right to a free appropriate, public education" (26 U.S.C. 412(l)). That policy must be written in the form of a "state plan" and is subject to reapproval every three years by the U.S. Department of Education.[2] Children receiving no education are to have priority over those receiving some form of education (20 U.S.C. 1412(3)). Children with disabilities must be educated to the maximum extent appropriate with children who are not disabled. This is called the "least restrictive environment" mandate " (20 U.S.C. 1412(5)). The FAPE required by IDEA must be tailored to the unique needs of each child, through a document called an "individualized education program" (IEP) prepared at a formal meeting between a qualified representative of the local education agency(LEA), the child's teacher, the child's parents or guardian, and, where appropriate, the child.[3] Parental involvement and consultation in this process must be *maximized*.[4] IDEA also imposes on the states detailed procedural requirements, that is, a set of rules outlining exactly how the educational rights of children with disabilities are to be protected. The rights of parents to consent to the provision or termination of special education services, to question the decisions of educational personnel, and to invoke a highly specific administrative hearing process are all outlined in IDEA (20 U.S.C. 1415 et seq). Parents may request mediation or an "impartial due process hearing" to appeal virtually any educational decision.[5] Any party dissatisfied with the results of the initial due process hearing may request and receive an impartial review by the state agency,[6] and if not satisfied with that review, may then go to court.[7]

Although IDEA leaves many details to the states concerning development and implementation of particular programs, it imposes substantial requirements to be followed in the discharge of the states' responsibilities. Noncompliance with federal procedural requirements—either in the state plan document or in implementation of federal requirements—may be sanctioned by the withholding of federal dollars flowing to the offending agency.[8] For example, a state's educational system might be investigated by the U.S. Department of Education for failing to educate children in the least restrictive environment. Such a failure would be evidenced by a pattern of educating physically disabled children in separate facilities even though the children in question may have no problems other than the physical ones that challenge them. The federal law requires education of children with disabilities to the maximum extent *appropriate* with nondisabled children. The failure of a particular state to meet this requirement raises a risk of sanctions.

WHAT IS THE ROLE OF THE LOCAL SCHOOL SYSTEM?

The impact of the law is ultimately to obligate the LEA to provide a FAPE with related services to all children with disabilities. The federal legal mandate requires the local school district to be the "agency of last resort" for the provision of specialized services to this population of children. Although other child welfare agencies might engage in interagency squabbles concerning who should pay for or provide services, LEAs and the respective state boards of education are not able to engage in such fingerpointing.[9] Under the Illinois school code, for example, special education services not provided by another agency *must* be provided by the LEA or the state board of education.[10] Thus the educational sector—even in a time of shrinking resources— is and has been a consistent source of dollars for children's services.

WHO IS THE CHILD WITH DISABILITIES?

IDEA defines *children with disabilities*

> as those children evaluated . . . as having mental retardation, hearing impairments including deafness, speech or language impairments, visual impairments including blindness, serious emotional disturbance, orthopedic impairments, autism, traumatic brain injury, other health impairments, specific learning disabilities, deaf-blindness, or multiple disabilities, and who because of these impairments need special education and related services (34 C.F.R. 300.7).

Eligibility runs from birth to age twenty-one. The key to eligibility is both having a listed disability and needing special education and related services. Having a disability implies difficulty in dealing with one's environment and indeed with the very programs and supports intended to help. The purpose of IDEA cannot be achieved without a profession, such as school social work, that focuses on child, family, and learning environment, each in relation to the other, and views the child as a whole.

WHAT IS SPECIAL EDUCATION?

A key to the definition of the child with a disability is that because of that disability and as a result of a complete, multifaceted, nondiscriminatory assessment (hereafter assessment), there is a need for special education and related services. We need to define these more precisely. According to IDEA, special education means

> specially designed instruction, at no cost to the parent, to meet the unique needs of a disabled child, including classroom instruction, instruction in physical education, home instruction, and instruction in hospitals and institutions. The term includes speech pathology, or any other related service, if the service consists of specially designed instruction, at no cost to the parents, to meet the unique needs of a disabled child, and is considered "special education" rather than a "related service" under State standards (34 C.F.R. 300.17).

WHAT ARE RELATED SERVICES?

Related services means transportation and such developmental, corrective, and other supportive services as are required to assist a child with a disability to benefit from special education, and includes transportation, speech pathology and audiology, psychological services, physical and occupational therapy, recreation, early identification and assessment of disabilities in children, counseling services, and medical services for diagnostic or evaluation purposes. The term also includes school health services,[11] social work services in schools, and parent counseling and training (34 C.F.R. 300.16).

Social work services in schools include:

1. Preparing a social or developmental history on a child identified as possibly having disabilities;
2. Group and individual counseling with the child and family;
3. Working with those problems in a child's living situation (home, school, and community) that affect the child's adjustment in school;
4. Mobilizing school and community resources to enable the child to receive maximum benefit from his or her educational program (34 C.F.R. 300.16 (12); 20 U.S.C. 1402 (29)).

In a particular situation special education and related services are defined individually by a multidisciplinary team, which must include the parents. The team prepares the resulting IEP. IEPs will be discussed in some detail later in this chapter and in the book.

Social work addresses the fit between schooling and the needs of children with disabilities and their parents. A particular group of children who experience difficulties in school, and usually need social work assistance, are those who are *seriously emotionally disturbed*, defined as

> a condition exhibiting one or more of the following characteristics over a *long period of time* and to a *marked degree*, which adversely affects educational performance:
>
> An inability to learn which cannot be explained by intellectual, sensory, or health factors.
>
> An inability to build or maintain satisfactory interpersonal relationships with peers and teachers.
>
> Inappropriate types of behavior or feelings under normal circumstances.
>
> A general pervasive mood of unhappiness or depression.
>
> A tendency to develop physical symptoms or fears associated with personal or school problems (34 C.F.R. 300.7 (9)).

There is some current discussion about changing this definition to a more functional orientation.

WHAT SERVICES MUST THE SCHOOL PROVIDE?

The LEA is obligated to provide special education and related services and supplementary aids and services required so that the pupil can attain the objectives stated in the IEP. The components of an IEP are special education, related services, supplementary aids and services, program modifications, and personal support. These are to benefit the student so that he or she may:

1. Advance appropriately toward attaining the annual goals;
2. Be involved and progress in the general curriculum and participate in extracurricular activities and other nonacademic activities; and
3. Be educated and participate with other children with disabilities and nondisabled children in those extracurricular and nonacademic activities (20 U.S.C. 1414 (d)(1)(a)(3)).

The mandate for use of related services is broad, going beyond special education to include what is necessary for the child to participate in general education and extracurricular activities.

Social Work Services

Under IDEA the educational sector is required to pay for related services, which may include any services required to assist a child to benefit from special education. A key issue has been what *level* of related services is necessary for a child to "benefit" from special education. The *Rowley* case involved a hearing-impaired girl who understood only about half of what was occurring in class, but who nevertheless received As and Bs because of her high intelligence.[12] Her parents wanted the school to provide a full-time sign language interpreter to attend class with her, but the Supreme Court held that the student was not so entitled, as she was already receiving an "educational benefit" without the interpreter.

[Rowley] generally is used by schools to back up the argument that they are not required to provide the "best" education—only an education that is minimally appropriate and available. Social workers should likewise be aware that the recommendations contained in their reports should address services necessary to minimally enable the child to benefit from educational programming. For instance, some depressed students may need nonmedical psychotherapy to attend to instructional tasks. In some cases such psychotherapy has been held to be a related service that must be provided by the schools.[13] The distinction between a fundable service and a nonfundable service would turn on whether mental health services, psychotherapy, or social work services (as they are defined above) would assist a particular student to benefit from special education. In a number of decisions the courts further defined a "service-benefit" standard.[14] The standard involves evaluating two criteria: (1) whether the program is designed to improve the student's educational performance and (2) whether the program is based on the student's classification as having a serious emotional disturbance.[15]

Psychotherapy

On the other hand, in another decision it was held that the service-benefit standard for determining whether psychotherapy is a related service is overbroad and inordinately encompassing. When the justification of the services is only psychological improvement, the LEA is not responsible for providing mental health services to the student.[16] It must be clearly demonstrated that social work services would assist students to benefit from special education. In school social work the general language for demonstrating this is found in the above definition of school social work services. For many years school social workers have defined their practice in relation to education both in practice and in theory, as the present volume will attest. Further court decisions will clarify these boundaries.

Children Unable to Benefit from Education

A law review article has stated that there are several thousand children in the United States so lacking in brain capacity that they are unable to benefit from any educational services, no matter how elementary they are.[17]

The U.S. Supreme Court has declined to review a hotly contested case in which a child "lacking any cortex" was held to be entitled to related services even though he was unlikely to benefit from services.[18] The *Timothy W.* case originated in Rochester, New Hampshire, where the school district argued that providing *any* services to such a hopelessly disabled child would be a waste of tax dollars better spent on less disabled children.[19] In their pleadings to the Court, the attorneys for the schools, astonished by the decision of the appellate court, said that such decisions requiring school personnel to provide services to children who cannot benefit from any services "may have unfortunate consequences for families of uneducable children because [they] raise false hopes, which in turn often lead to bitterness and disillusionment" and ultimately to intensive family therapy or marital counseling.[20] The U.S. Supreme Court will not, however, "read in" any exceptions to IDEA that are not present—and no exception was drawn for so-called uneducable disabled children.[21]

If a child needs a residential setting in order to benefit from educational programing, the schools must pay for such a setting, and there can be no charges to the parents or guardian.[22] If other agencies are active and are able to pay part of the cost, such payments are allowed as long as such agencies do not charge the parent.[23] When a school district writes an IEP stating that another agency is to provide some of the services, the school district is still the "agency of last resort," and parents may rightfully turn to the schools for recompense.[24]

A well-known U.S. Supreme Court case has held that clean intermittent catheterization (CIC) is a related service.[25] Amber Tatro needed CIC several times daily in order to stay in class and to benefit from educational services. In *Tatro* the schools argued that CIC was a medical service and therefore not a related service. The U.S. Supreme Court did not agree, noting that CIC was not exclusively within the province of physicians and could be administered easily by the school nurse. The school district was thus required to provide this service.

WHAT IS PLACEMENT IN THE LEAST RESTRICTIVE ENVIRONMENT?

One further principle, outlined above as one of Turnbull and Turnbull's six points, governs the all-important placement process. This is the principle of *least restrictive environment*. This principle is defined in the law as follows:

> To the maximum extent appropriate, children with disabilities . . . are educated with children who are not disabled, and special classes, separate schooling, or other removal of children with disabilities from the regular education environment occurs only when the nature or severity of the disability of a child is such that education in regular classes with the use of supplementary aids and services cannot be achieved satisfactorily (20 U.S.C. 1412 (5) (A)).

This principle is extremely important in achieving the general purposes of IDEA. Related services in the IEP (including the school social worker's contribution) are intended to assist the pupil to advance appropriately toward attaining his or her annual goals, to be involved and progress in the general curriculum, to participate in extracurricular and other nonacademic activities, and to be educated and to participate with other children with disabilities and nondisabled children in the general curriculum. The principle of *inclusion*, outlined above, presumes that the child with disabilities should participate in the general curriculum and requires the IEP to explain the extent, if any, to which the child will *not* participate with nondisabled children in regular classes and in extracurricular and other nonacademic activities (20 U.S.C. 1414). However, the term "inclusion" is not to be found anywhere in the IDEA legal mandate.

WHAT ARE PLACEMENT PROCEDURES?

Placement procedures make the connection between the assessment and the IEP. Disabilities are inevitably connected with social functioning in one way or another. If assessments are to be complete, multifaceted, and nondiscriminatory, as the law prescribes, the school social worker should participate in most assessments. In some states the social worker is the person responsible for the *social developmental study* of the child. The social worker's understanding of the child's current adaptation to home and school environments, the child's previous developmental steps, and the culture and functioning of the family is essential to any assessment. In the same vein, the annual goals for the child, the corresponding educational program and related services, as developed in the IEP, often explicitly involve tasks for the social worker with the child, with the family, and with education professionals. In the process of interpreting evaluation data and planning an IEP, the multidisciplinary team needs to:

1. Draw on information from a variety of sources, including adaptive and achievement tests, teacher recommendations, physical condition, social or cultural background, and adaptive behavior;

2. Ensure that information obtained from all of these sources is documented and carefully considered;

3. Ensure that the placement decision is made by a group of persons including persons knowledgeable about the child, the meaning of the evaluation data, and the placement options;

4. Ensure that the placement decision is made in conformity with the least restrictive environment rules;

5. Understand that if a child needs special education and related services, an IEP must be developed for the child (34 C.F.R. 300.533).

CAN STUDENTS WITH DISABILITIES BE SUSPENDED OR EXPELLED?

On January 20, 1988, the U.S. Supreme Court issued its opinion in *Honig v. Doe*.[26] This strongly worded case set forth guidelines that educators have actively and hotly debated ever since. Two California cases related to Honig involved violent, acting-out pupils who were suspended "indefinitely" and later expelled under the California statute that allowed indefinite suspensions. The school district's attorneys argued, when the cases finally reached the judicial level, that Congress could not possibly have intended that the schools be required to keep serving dangerous, emotionally disturbed pupils, when staff members and other students were at peril. The Court held that Congress "very much meant to strip schools of the unilateral authority they had traditionally employed to exclude disabled students, particularly emotionally disturbed students, from schools."[27] The U.S. Supreme Court, in this case, demonstrated clearly its reluctance to read into IDEA meanings never expressed by Congress.

The net effect of this case is that a school may not remove a pupil with disabilities from school for behavior that is a manifestation of the disabling condition without the consent of the parents. If the parents refuse to consent to a relocation of the child, the school's only recourse is to have its attorneys file a petition in a court of proper jurisdiction to obtain the permission of a judge. Although it has been argued that school authorities may make some attempt to determine the "relatedness" of the behavior to the disability, any attempts at expulsion or exclusion for behavior claimed to be unrelated to the disabling condition leaves educators on very unstable legal ground.[28] Almost invariably, a court will determine that the exclusion is a "change of placement" pursued outside the mandatory multidisciplinary process and therefore in violation of federal law. The Supreme Court has clearly expressed its feeling that allowing schools to suspend pupils who are dangerous to themselves and others for up to ten days cumulatively per school year gives educational authorities sufficient time to seek parental consent, negotiate alternatives, or go to court. The 1997 amendments to IDEA have created certain circumstances (students bringing guns to school, etc.) wherein the school may go beyond the ten-day limit. Social workers facing these circumstances should consult further the complex procedures that have emerged in and from the new law.

Social workers should become familiar with the basic law of suspension and expulsion of pupils with disabilities, as they may find themselves in the position of mediating disputes between schools and families of disabled students.[29] Moreover, social workers are commonly called as experts in due process hearings for the purpose of establishing whether the behavior in question is or is not related to the pupil's disabling condition. Finally, current law relating to suspension and expulsion is a powerful tool for families of the disabled in persuading school authorities to consider more restrictive alternatives for the child, such as private extended-day school programs or residential placement, when appropriate.

WHAT ARE PROVISIONS FOR MEDIATION AND FOR AN IMPARTIAL DUE PROCESS HEARING?

It is not surprising that there can be differences between parents and others on the multidisciplinary team over a possible recommended placement for a child. Indeed the due process protection of the Fifth and the Fourteenth Amendments to the United States Constitution demands formal procedures. After all a civil right is being defined. It was the intent of the framers of P.L. 105-17 that parents and educators be encouraged to "work out their differences by using nonadversarial means" (*Congressional Record*, May 12, 1997, p. S4298). The resulting amendments to IDEA, passed in June 1997, prescribe a two-step process to resolve disputes prior to taking them to the courts. The first step is mediation, the second step is the impartial due process hearing. In most cases it is only after these steps have been taken, and the issue is still unresolved, that the case would go to court.

Mediation is a voluntary process conducted by a "qualified and impartial mediator who is trained in effective mediation techniques" (20 U.S.C. 1415 (e)). Mediation cannot be used to deny or delay a parent's right to an impartial due process hearing. The state education agency would have a list of approved mediators. It would carry the cost of the mediation process. Any agreement reached by the parties to the dispute would be set forth in a written mediation agreement. Discussions in the mediation process are confidential and cannot be used as evidence in subsequent due process hearings or civil proceedings. Both parties may be required to sign a confidentiality pledge prior to the mediation process (20 U.S.C. 1415 (e) (A through G)).

The *impartial due process hearing* is conducted by either the state education agency or the LEA, although not by an employee involved with the education of the child. It is a somewhat more formal process than mediation. Any evaluation completed in relation to the pupil must be disclosed at least five days prior to the hearing. There are procedural safeguards: the right to be accompanied or advised by counsel and by experts, the right to present evidence and confront and to cross-examine and to compel the attendance of witnesses, the right to a verbatim record, and the right to written findings of fact and decisions. If the hearing is conducted by the LEA, its outcome may be appealed to the state education agency, where another hearing may take place. If the problem is not resolved at this point, it may be brought to court (20 U.S.C. 1415 (f) (g)). During due process hearings the child's placement would remain the same unless he or she has not been admitted to public school. In the latter case the child would be, with the parents' permission, placed in the public school until the completion of the proceedings.

WHAT ARE DUE PROCESS AND JUDICIAL REVIEW?

Once the second review is completed, any party dissatisfied with the result may appeal it to either state or federal court (20 U.S.C. 1415 (e) (2)) by filing a lawsuit against the other party, requesting appropriate relief.[30] It is important to note that the "stay put" provision operates while all proceedings are taking place (20 U.S.C. 1415 (e) (3)). This provision requires that the child remain in his or her then-current placement during such time as due process proceedings are pending. During this time, the district must pay for all educational services in the then-current placement, and the *Burlington* case clearly provides that even if the parent loses at each stage of the process, the district cannot obtain reimbursement from the parent.[31] The stay-put provision is thus a powerful tool for parents if proceedings commence when the pupil is in an educational setting that satisfies the parents. Most commonly, the child will be in a school-funded residential placement while the district seeks to return him or her to a local or mainstream setting, which it is important to note is one of the goals of the "inclusion" trend. If the parents request due process at this point, the child must remain in the residential setting at district expense during the pendency of all proceedings, through and including appellate court review.

Conversely, when the current placement is one that the parents feel is not appropriate, the stay-put provision operates to the benefit of the school district. In this instance, the parents' goal is to effect an alternative placement that they and their experts feel is more appropriate than the current setting, whereas the school district usually seeks to maintain the status quo. The school district continues to pay the cost of the child's educational placement, regardless of who requests due process.[32] For younger pupils entering school for the first time, the "current" placement is interpreted by most states to be the setting in which the child would be placed in the absence of any disability. For a student with disabilities transferring from one school district to another, the current placement is determined by the student's most recent IEP.

WHAT IS AN INDIVIDUALIZED EDUCATION PROGRAM?

The IEP is the blueprint for all that happens in the education of a child with disabilities. School districts must write an IEP before they can provide services (20 U.S.C. 1401 (18)). IDEA is quite detailed in its specification of the contents of this document (20 U.S.C. 1401 (19)). All IEPs must be reviewed annually, and parents or guardians, as outlined previously, are always entitled to question IEPs through the due process procedures (20 U.S.C. 1414 (a) (5)). Many state boards of education publish manuals on how to write an IEP, and all states have organizations and resource centers to assist parents and guardians in understanding the process of writing an IEP. The input of the social worker during the drafting of the IEP often has a substantial effect on the recommendations made, and social work services are often among the crucial "related services" in the IEP. School districts sometimes list their recommendations for the pupil prior to drafting an IEP. *This is a significant procedural error.* IDEA requires the IEP to be written first, on the logical assumption that recommendations for a particular educational setting and specific services cannot possibly be made until the needs of the child are determined. When recommendations are made before the IEP is drafted, this is sometimes a good indicator that school authorities are simply offering the program they have available, rather than creating a customized program to meet all of the needs of the child. It is legally improper and a violation of IDEA for recommendations to be based on administrative convenience, costs, waiting lists, or any factor other than the needs of the child with disabilities in question.[33]

The parent or guardian of a child covered by IDEA must be given prior notice whenever the school district proposes a change in the educational placement of a child, or a change in its provision of a FAPE for the child (20 U.S.C. 1415 (b) (1) (c)). This notice must, at the minimum, contain a complete description of available procedural safeguards, an official explanation for the change being proposed, and the reasons why other less restrictive options were rejected (20 U.S.C. 1415 (b) (1) (d)). Although the consent of a parent or guardian is required for the initiation or termination of educational benefits, consent is not required when a district seeks to change the program for a child already in special education (34 C.F.R. 300.504(b)). Notification of proposed changes, regardless of their magnitude, is required in all instances under IDEA because the right to demand a hearing is always vested in the parent or guardian who disagrees with the changes (20 U.S.C. 1415 (b) (1) (E) to (d)). "Complete failure" to implement an IEP has been held to constitute a change in the child's educational placement, as well as a failure to provide a FAPE.[34] An IEP is not, however, a contract, nor is it a guarantee that the child will achieve the results contemplated. An IEP is a blueprint, a series of guidelines for educators to follow in conferring educational benefit and a useful document for parents to follow in determining whether those benefits are being made available.

Legislation and case law on the civil right to a FAPE for children with disabilities have created new structures of service for these children. The social worker's services are framed in a developing body of law. It is important to understand that this law is not simply a set of procedures. It places a mandate on the school district and on the social worker to provide services that will enable children with disabilities and their families to survive in an initially unequal struggle. Here the language of the law can be translated into the language of service. The more familiar social workers are with both languages, the more able they will be to translate them into services that can redress this inequality.

In recent years, some advocates have said that the special education system is not working and that to benefit from educational services, students must be "fully included" in the mainstream. Many have gone so far as to present this concept as a "part of the law" and to tell parents this new "law" says they must cooperate in the full mainstreaming of their children. Nothing could be further from the truth. The law governing the least restrictive environment has not changed and merely requires that to the maximum extent *appropriate*, children with disabilities should be educated with nondisabled children. Although there is a presumption that the child with disabilities should participate in the general curriculum when appropriate, no federal law has ever mandated "full inclusion" without consideration of educational needs. Inclusion as such, discussed in Chapter 20, is often a matter of state policy. Federal law requires all school districts to make available a full continuum of alternatives from the least restrictive (such as complete mainstreaming with one resource period per day) to most restrictive (private residential placement). Part of the school social worker's role in these cases is to work between pupil, parents, and the school to construct this environment, as we shall see in later chapters.

REFERENCES

1. H. R. Turnbull and A. P. Turnbull, *Free appropriate public education: The law and children with disabilities* (Denver: Love, 1998), pp. 273–274.

2. 20 U.S.C. 1412; 20 U.S.C. 1413. The state plan describes the goals, programs, and timetables under which the state intends to educate children with disabilities within its borders.

3. 20 U.S.C. 1401 (18). The IEP must include at the minimum statements of present levels of educational performance, annual goals, short-term instructional objectives, specific services to be provided to the child, the extent to which the pupil will be able to be educated with nondisabled students, the projected date of initiation and anticipated duration of services, a statement of needed transition services, and various criteria for evaluating progress. 20 U.S.C. 1412(3), 1412(5), 1401(1), (19).

4. *Board of Education of the Hendrick Hudson Central School District, Westchester County, et al.*, v. *Amy Rowley, et al.*, U.S. 176, 73 L. Ed.2d 690, 102 S. Ct. 3034 (1982). Excluding parents from the process has, pursuant to *Rowley*, often been held by courts to be a "fatal flaw" committed by educators. *Spielberg v. Henrico*

County, E.H.L.R. 441:178. E.H.L.R. refers to *Education of the Handicapped Law Review* (Washington, DC: CRR Publishing).

5. 20 U.S.C. 1415(b)(1)(D) and (E). Complaints can be brought "about any matter relating to" the child's evaluation and education.

6. *Mayson by Mayson v. Teague*. 749 F.2d 652 (1984).

7. 20 U.S.C. 1415 (b)(2) and (c), 20 U.S.C. 11415(e)(2). A party may go to either state or federal court. Recently, plaintiffs filing in state court have been "removed" by the school district to the federal district court. This is only a good strategy where a state board of education seeks removal, as these entities are protected by Eleventh Amendment sovereign immunity, while local school districts are not protected. *Dellmuth v. Muth*, 109 S. Ct. 2397 (1989), *Gary A. v. New Trier High School District and the Illinois State Board of Education*, 796 F.2d 940 (1986.)

8. 20 U.S.C. 1414(b)(2)(A). Noncompliance may also be sanctioned by judicial review. U.S.C. 1416.

9. *Parks v. Pavkovic*, 753 F.2d 1397 (7th. Cir. 1985). In the district court opinion, Judge Prentice Marshall said that such fingerpointing was one of the most heinous violations of federal law he could imagine.

10. Ill. Rev. State. Ch. 122 [14-8.02].

11. Except nondiagnostic medical services, such as ongoing medical treatment. The federal government says medical services are defined by who must provide the services, not by the specific service. If a particular nondiagnostic medical service can be provided only by a physician, the LEA need not cover it as a related service. 20 U.S.C. 1401(17); also see *Kelly McNair v. Oak Hills Local School District*, H.E.L.R. 441:381 (6th Cir. 1988–89), in which the court held that special transportation need not be provided to a deaf child because the need for it was not related to her disabling condition. The statute specifically required a connection between the related service and the unique needs of the child.

12. *Rowley*, 458 U.S. at 184.

13. *Max M. v. Thompson*, 592 F. Supp. 1450 (1984). This student's neurotic anxieties prevented him from attending school, and the school social worker, among others, recommended psychotherapy. The school district did not provide the therapy. The parents paid for two years of treatment and then asked for reimbursement from the district. The court held that the school was responsible for the services to the extent that a nonphysician could provide them. The district, then, had to reimburse parents for the equivalent of psychologist-provided therapy, a lower amount than the actual cost, since a psychiatrist had been the therapist. See also *In the Matter of "A" Family*, 602 P.2d 157 (S.C. Mont.), holding family therapy is a related service; and *Gary B. v. Cronin*, 625 F.2d 563, n. 15: "While psychotherapy may be related to mental health, it may also be required before a child can derive *any benefit from education*" (emphasis added).

14. See *Papacoda v. Connecticut*, 528 F. Supp. 68 (D. Conn. 1981). *Vander Malle v. Ambach*, 673 F.2d 49 (2nd Cir. 1982), further proceedings 667 F. Supp. 1015

(S.D.N.Y. 1987). *Mrs. B. v. Milford Board of Education*, 103 F.3d 1114 (2nd Cir. 1997).

15. See also the discussion of these points in Turnbull and Turnbull, pp. 161–164.

16. *Clovis Unified School District v. California Office of Admin. Hearings*, 903 F.2d 635 (9th Cir. 1990).

17. R. Rothstein, Educational rights of severely and profoundly handicapped children, *Nebraska Law Review* 61 (1982): 586. See also *Parks v. Pavkovic*, 753 F.2d at 1405, in which the Court speculated about what type of child might not ever be able to benefit—and concluded that such a child would have to be in a coma.

18. Current decisions, E.H.L.R. 441:393; *Timothy W. and Cynthia W. v. Rochester, N.H. School District*, E.H.L.R. Summary and Analysis, pp. 265–266 (December 1989). Federal appellate court citation: 875 F.2d 954 (1989); U.S. District Court citation: E.H.L.R. 509:141 (1987). See also article by B. R. Whitted, "Educational benefits after *Timothy W.*: Where do we go from here? *Illinois Administrators of Special Education Newsletter*, Winter 1990.

19. 875 F.2d at 954.

20. *Petition for Writ of Certiorari to the United States Supreme Court of Rochester NH School Dist. v. Timothy W. and Cynthia W.*, E.H.L.R. Summary and Analysis, 226 (November 1989).

21. *Honig v. Doe*, 484 U.S. 305, 108 S. Ct. 592 (1988). Note that the Supreme Court, in refusing to review a decision, does not in the process issue an opinion covering its reasons. The citation in this note refers to the Court's tendency to read IDEA rigidly, and in *Honig*, it refused to read in a dangerousness exception to the principle that restricts exclusion of pupils with disabilities from school.

22. *Parks v. Pavkovic*, 753 F.2d 11397 (7th Cir. 1985), cert. denied at 473 U.S. 906 (1985). Interprets 34 C.F.R. 300.302, among other regulatory provisions.

23. See, e.g., the Disabled Children's Program of the Social Security Act, 42 U.S.C. 1382 et seq.

24. *Kattan v. District of Columbia*, E.H.L.R. 441:207.

25. *Amber Tatro et al. v. Irving (Tx.) Independent School District et al.*, 4568 U.S. 883 (1984).

26. *Honig v. Doe*, 484 U.S. 305, 108 S. Ct. 592 (1988), interpreting the "stay put" provision of the Education of the Handicapped Act, 20 U.S.C. 1415(e)(3). The authors strongly recommend that social work students read this case in its entirety. *Honig* is a powerful tool for advocates of special education, and a thorough knowledge of the procedures set forth by the Supreme Court is crucial.

27. 484 U.S. at 321.

28. M. L. Yell, *Honig v. Doe*: The Supreme Court addresses the suspension and expulsion of handicapped students, *Exceptional Children* 56 (1989) 69; also see M. L. Yell, The use of corporal punishment, suspension, expulsion, and timeout with behavioral disordered students in public schools; legal considerations, *Journal of Behavior Disorders* 15 (1990): 2.

29. For further information on mediation, see C. B. Gallant, Mediation: A unique due process procedure which utilizes social skills, in R. J. Anderson, M. Freeman, and R. L. Edwards (eds.), *School social work and P.L. 94-142: The Education for All Handicapped Act* (Washington, DC: National Association of Social Workers, 1980). Many states have implemented the mediation process as a technique for lowering the volume of hearings, and most of the mediation systems have been quite effective. Frequently, social workers are called upon to act as impartial mediators as well as to utilize their skills in facilitating communication between the school and family.

30. A practical note: If the parents lose and can afford an attorney, there is no reluctance to sue the district. If the district loses, there is a fair degree of reluctance on the part of the school boards to proceed with a lawsuit. One reason is that the child usually has to be sued as a "necessary party." Another reason is expense. Insurance carriers for districts resist providing coverage for these matters, so a school board must vote to proceed knowing that the district will expend precious local dollars with no hope of recoupment. Finally, even if the district wins on the administrative level, if it is sued by the parents, the insurance carrier will resist coverage for any reimbursement costs or Protection Act attorney fees, since these are not "damages." *Tonya K. v. Chicago Public Schools et al.*, 551 F. Supp. 1107 (1988). The greatest pressure on a district for settlement, then, is at the end point of the administrative proceedings.

31. See *Burlington School Committee v. Department of Education*, 471 U.S. 359 (1985).

32. Note here that it is not just parents who can request due process. Schools sometimes seek to provide a service that the parents oppose. For instance, the district may want to place the child in a classroom for the retarded, while the parents may feel that their child is not retarded, but learning disabled. The parents' refusal to consent to the "MR" placement may be met with the district's request for due process. From a liability point of view, this is the only alternative for districts in such a position. Parents are frequently unable to accept that their child is so low functioning. The social worker is called upon to assist the parents in working through their shame and guilt, among other feelings.

33. *Timothy W.*

34. *Lunceford v. District of Columbia Board of Education*, 7455 F.2d 157, 1582 (D.C. Cir. 1984).

CHAPTER 11

Services to Families of Infants and Toddlers with Disabilities

Kathleen Kirk Bishop
Associate Professor of Social Work, University of Vermont

- The Purpose of P.L. 105-17, Part C
- Analysis of Selected Aspects of the Law
- Implications for Social Workers
- Who Will Be Served?
- Early Intervention Services
- Requirements for a Statewide System
- Individualized Family Service Plans
- Procedural Safeguards
- State Interagency Coordinating Council
- Old and New Developments: Part C's Continuing Impact

When P.L. 99-457, Part H, was signed into law by Congress on October 8, 1986, it signaled a new concern for the health and well-being of infants and young children with disabilities and their families. The new law created a discretionary program to help states plan, develop, and implement statewide, comprehensive, coordinated, multidisciplinary, interagency systems of early intervention services for all eligible infants and toddlers from birth to age three and their families. This groundbreaking piece of legislation also initiated a paradigm shift in the way professionals would provide services to families. These approaches have placed families at the center of the planning, design, and implemenation of service systems; encouraged interprofessional collaborative practices; recognized and supported the strengths of families; and encouraged the delivery of services in the natural environments of infants and toddlers.

Reauthorized in 1991 as P.L. 102-119, the Individuals with Disabilities Education Act (IDEA), and most recently signed into law by President Clinton on June 4, 1997, as the IDEA Amendments of 1997 (P.L. 105-17, Part C, which pertains to infants and toddlers) this law continues to pose new challenges to all professionals and parents to go beyond their traditional roles and to work collaboratively with one another, and with others in health, education, social services, mental health, and other public and private agencies in order to realize the potential of this landmark legislation (Bishop, 1987). Clearly, school social workers are essential partners in the implementation of this legislation. The purpose of this chapter on P.L. 105-17, Part C, of IDEA is to present a brief extrapolation of key parts of the law that have the most relevancy for social work education and practice, to suggest areas where social workers can assume a leadership role in the continued interpretation and implementation of the law, and to describe and highlight best social work practice with this special population.

There are significant revisions in the latest version of Part C that require careful study and thoughtful action. The most important of these are the provisions that

1. Urge identification, evaluation, and services to historically underrepresented populations, particularly minority, low-income, inner city and rural populations (Sec. 631, 632);

2. Relate to early intervention services in natural environments (303.16 (c), 303.344(d)(1)(ii);

3. Provide services to infants and toddlers with disabilities and their families residing on a reservation geographically located in the state (303.160); and

4. Establish a relationship between the Goals 2000: Educate America Act and the provision of services under Part C.

As this chapter goes to press, the final regulations, issued on April 14, 1998, for Part C continue to be debated ("Early Intervention Program," 1998).

THE PURPOSE OF P.L. 105-17, PART C

IDEA, Part C, reauthorizes the original authorization (P.L. 99-457, Part H, 1986) and subsequent versions of the federal program for infants and toddlers with disabilities and their families. It provides formula funding on a voluntary basis for all states to fully implement a comprehensive, multidisciplinary, interagency, statewide system of early intervention services. As stated in Part C, Congress finds that there is an urgent and substantial need:

1. To enhance the development of infants and toddlers with disabilities, thus minimizing the potential for developmental delay;

2. To reduce the educational costs to our society, particularly to our nation's schools, by decreasing the need for ongoing special education

and related services after infants and toddlers with disabilities reach school age;

3. To minimize the likelihood of institutionalization of individuals with disabilities and maximize the potential for their independent living in society;

4. To enhance the capacity of families to meet the special needs of their infants and toddlers with disabilities;

5. To enhance the capacity of state and local agencies as service providers to identify, evaluate, and meet the needs of historically underrepresented populations, particularly minority, low-income, inner city, and rural populations (P.L. 105-17, Part C, Section 631(a));

6. To establish a policy of providing financial assistance to states;

7. To develop and implement a statewide, comprehensive, coordinated, multidisciplinary, interagency system that provides early intervention services for infants and toddlers with disabilities and their families;

8. To facilitate the coordination of payment for early intervention services from federal, state, local, and private sources (including public and private insurance coverage);

9. To enhance their capacity to provide quality early intervention services and expand and improve existing early intervention services being provided to infants and toddlers with disabilities and their families; and

10. To encourage states to expand opportunites for children under three years of age who would be at risk of having substantial delay if they did not receive early intervention services (P.L. 105-17, Part C, Section 632(b); references to Part C in the following text will only be by section).

ANALYSIS OF SELECTED ASPECTS OF THE LAW

Although the entire IDEA and the accompanying regulations have important implications for social workers in their many areas of practice, this discussion will be limited to Part C, the legislation that focuses on serving infants and toddlers with disabilities and their families. In particular, this section will use two key components of the law and the regulations the Individualized Family Service Plan (Section 636(a)-(e)) and service coordination services (Sections 632(e)(vii), 633(a)(4), 636(d)(7) to illustrate components of best practice that have major implications for social workers.

Before discussing particular foci for social workers, it is important to understand the philosophy of Part C, as it was originally authorized and subsequently revised as P.L. 102-119. Perhaps the philosophy is best reflected in the fact that families are mentioned at least thirty-one times in the 1986 legislation, beginning with the opening policy statement: "Congress finds that there is an urgent and substantial need to enhance the capacity of *families* to meet the special needs of infants and toddlers with disabilities" (Section 631, 4). These statements directed to the needs of families throughout the legislation (Sections 632(e)(xiv) and (g), 635(a)(3)-(4), 677) signal a change in philosophy from a child-centered approach to a family-centered approach for early childhood intervention services; that is, services to infants and toddlers with disabilities must be provided within the context of their families and other natural environments.

This family-centered philosophy recognizes that the family is the constant in the child's life while service systems and personnel fluctuate. It suggest recognition, respect, and support for the pivotal role that families play in the care (and nurturance) of their children (Shelton and Stephanek, 1994) and directs professionals to work as partners in securing the best possible early intervention services for families who have infants and toddlers with disabilities. The goals of family-centered service and family-professional collaboration should guide the social worker as he or she participates in the implementation of all aspects of Part C, whether working directly with children and families or developing policy, programs, and practice. In whatever arena social workers participate, families must be involved with everything from planning through evaluation, in all aspects of Part C.

Individualized Family Service Plan

As stated in the legislation, a requirement of the Individualized Family Service Plan (IFSP) is a family-directed assessment of the resources, priorities, and concerns of the family and the identification of the supports and services necessary to enhance the family's capacity to meet the developmental needs of the infant or toddler. It also requires collaboration with the family on major outcomes expected for the child and family and a clear and specific statement of the services to be given to the infant or toddler and the family (Section 636(a)(2)-(3) and (c)(2)-(5)).

Although there is a considerable literature pertaining to the value of family-centered approaches to children and families, and many programs emphasize the importance of being family centered, families and professionals continue to report difficulties in translating the family-centered philosophy into concrete actions. A major issue with the IFSP is to assure that the family is an integral part of the plan from the beginning of its development to the end of its implementation. Some concrete examples of exemplary practice include (1) collaborative agenda development for IFSP meetings, (2) openness to holding meetings in places and at times that honor family choice, and (3) use of language that is strengths-based, respectful of families, and easily understandable by all participants.

The IFSP is revolutionary in its conception. It is a single plan that addresses the child and family as a unit, regardless of who delivers and who pays for the services. It is a plan that reflects a strong component of family-professional collaboration in a manner that honors the wishes of the family. While there may be a tendency to see the IFSP as another form of Individualized Education Program (IEP) as required in P.L. 94-142, it is important to conceptualize the IFSP very differently. The IFSP is not an IEP with a couple of family goals added. It is not a group of plans from a variety of agencies located in a single folder labeled "IFSP." The IFSP, though conceived almost twelve years ago, continues to be a model for the kinds of plans that could be implemented for all students, regardless of age or grade level, and school social workers must take the lead in modeling exemplary family-centered and collaborative practices. The IFSP is an ideal instrument for this purpose.

Social workers have a long history of concern for families (see Richmond, 1917; Germain, 1968; Hartman and Laird, 1983). Family-centered practice is a model of social work practice that locates the family in the center of the unit of attention or field of action (Germain, 1968). As conceptualized within the "life model" of social work practice (Germain and Gitterman, 1980), the domain of family-centered social work practice is in the transactions between families and their environments. Within the past ten years, new theories and new ways of conceptualizing and contextualizing the issues and challenges for children and families within their social environment have emerged. These approaches include empowerment (Cochran, 1992; Pinderhughes, 1995), strengths-based practice (Weick and Saleebey, 1995), social constructionism (Laird, 1995), narrative therapy (White, 1995), collaboration with families (Bishop, Woll, and Arango, 1993), and partnership with communities (Bishop, Taylor, and Arango, 1997; Ewalt, Freeman, and Poole, 1998) and with multiple organizations and systems (Gray, 1989). Embedded in social work's mission of securing social justice and human rights for those families most oppressed and marginalized by issues of poverty, racism, and "ableism," Part C provides new opportunities to apply these emerging approaches to early intervention services for infants and toddlers most at risk or with a disability.

Within these frameworks, social workers have a leadership role and a major contribution to make as they work in collaboration with families in the development and implementation of an IFSP that reflects a family's concerns and desires for their child with a disability as well as the concerns and desires of the entire family. They must advocate for systemic changes that support families' efforts to be successful with their children, regardless of their social, cultural, political, and economic status in society. In addition, social workers have a role to play in assisting other professionals in understanding the values, knowledge, and skills needed to work with families in a family-centered manner.

Service Coordination

Part C states that the IFSP must identify the service coordinator from the profession most immediately relevant to the infant's or toddler's and family's needs (or who is otherwise qualified to carry out all applicable responsibilities). This person will be responsible for the implementation of the plan and coordination of services with other agencies and persons (Section 636(d)(7)).

Service coordination is an active, ongoing process. The service coordinator is responsible for:

1. Assisting parents of eligible children in gaining access to early intervention services and other services identified in the IFSP,
2. Coordinating the provision of early intervention services (such as medical services for other than diagnostic and evaluation purposes) that the child is being provided,
3. Facilitating the timely delivery of available services, and
4. Continuously seeking appropriate services and situations necessary to benefit the development of each child being served for the duration of the child's eligibility.

Specific service coordination activities may include:

1. Coordinating the performance of evaluations and assessments;
2. Facilitating and participating in the development, review, and evaluation of IFSPs;
3. Assisting families in identifying available service providers;
4. Ensuring that services are delivered in the natural environments for infants and toddlers where possible, and occur elsewhere only when the services cannot be achieved in the natural environments;
5. Coordinating and monitoring the delivery of available services;
6. Informing families of the availability of advocacy services;
7. Coordinating with medical and health providers; and
8. Facilitating the development of a transition plan to preschool services, if appropriate.

These service coordination activities recognize the multidisciplinary, collaborative, interagency nature of the services that are required for this population of children and families and emphasize the importance of the coordinative function necessary to integrate and implement the services effectively.

While the law suggests that the service coordinator come from the profession most immediately relevant to the infant's or toddler's or family's needs (Section 636(d)(7)), in reality this choice may not be workable. What is critically important in the choice of a service coordinator is that it is someone (a) who families are comfortable working with, (b) who believes in and supports families as experts on the care of their child, (c) who has experience using a collaborative process with families and who sees families as integral members of the team, (d) who can and will be responsible for the implementation of the IFSP, and (e) who has the skills and experience to coordinate with other agencies and service providers. In addition to the criteria stated above, other qualifications of service coordinators might include knowledge about infant, toddler, and family development and knowledge and experience in implementing Part C services.

For social workers, the service coordination functions and activities described in the law and regulations are integral parts of what social work students in MSW programs learn and practice and are natural and expected components of social work services (see Rose, 1992; Kisthardt, 1997). Social work as a profession traditionally has supported the values of client self-determination and participation in the development of plans for service, including giving voice to families and advocating for structural and systemic change. Social workers are recognized in many settings as the link between clients and community services and resources. It would seem, then, that social workers are a natural choice to assist families with the service coordination of activities they identify as useful for their child and family.

IMPLICATIONS FOR SOCIAL WORKERS

Within the context of P.L. 105-17, Part C, the responsibilities of social workers in partnership with families are multiple and varied. Some social workers will be involved in direct service, others will be involved in preprofessional preparation programs and in the continuing education of personnel, while others will be involved in the policy arena. All social workers working in any arena with infants and toddlers who are at risk for, or have, a developmental delay have a responsibility to participate in Part C activities.

Social workers (unlike in P.L. 94-142) have been defined as qualified providers of early intervention services (Section 632(F)(vi)), and social work services are defined as eligible services that children and families may receive (Section 632(E)(xi)) as part of the services designed to meet the developmental needs of their infant or toddler and their family.

The children and families to be served under P.L. 105-17, Part C, will need a great variety of services from many different providers and agencies. Because social workers focus on the child and family as a unit in the context of their social environment, social workers are in an excellent position to join in partnership with families, as well as other disciplines, public and private agencies, and communities in implementing Part C (Bishop, 1987), as well as securing services that families identify as essential for the child with a disability or other family members.

Social workers have a leadership role and major contributions to make as advocates for individual families as well as for systems' changes. The social work responsibility could be conceived of as threefold within the context of (1) families; (2) other service providers, agencies, and communities; and (3) at the systems change and legislative level.

First, within the context of *families*, social workers should:

1. Provide early intervention services to families that reflect a family-centered, community-based, culturally responsive, and coordinated approach;
2. Develop and model family-professional partnerships (Bishop, Woll, and Arango, 1993) in all aspects of service provision, especially in the development of an IFSP and the provision of case management services;
3. Assure that family support services are available to all families who desire them, including such services as respite care, sibling support, parent-to-parent support, and father's groups;
4. Provide services to families that reflect the principle of normalization as close to home as possible in the most natural environment;
5. Support a family's participation in all meetings that concern their child and family;
6. Develop IFSPs in partnership with families and other service providers;
7. Serve as service coordinators at the request of the family;
8. Assure the participation of families in all aspects of the development of early intervention services; and
9. Advocate for services that are accessible, flexible, culturally sensitive, and responsive to the diversity of family desires and styles (Rounds, Weil, and Bishop, 1994).

Second, within the context of coordinating services from *other providers*, such as agency and community organizations, social workers should:

1. Assist other professionals in understanding the cultural and social experience of the child in the family and community (Clark, 1989);
2. Assure that services are family centered, not agency centered or provider centered, and fit the unique needs of each individual child and family;
3. Facilitate collaboration between and among service providers and agencies in the family's local community;
4. Identify, with the family, service gaps in their communities and work with agencies to fill the gaps;
5. Work on confidentiality procedures that will assure maximum protection of families while facilitating information sharing that will benefit families and protect them from duplicative procedures and services;

6. Participate with other providers and agencies in the multidisciplinary assessment of families;

7. Work with providers and agencies to assure that infants, toddlers, and their families are offered a menu of services that reflect a variety of choices and options, always, if possible, in their natural environments; and

8. Develop collaborative training programs in which parents and professional have opportunities to educate each other.

Within the context of *legislative* and systems change, social workers should:

1. Call the contact person at the designated lead agency in the state and volunteer to participate in the discussion of the state's plan for implementation of P.L. 105-17, Part C;

2. Offer consultation on such issues as the state's definition of who is served, on personnel training and standards, and on the range of services offered to families;

3. Identify families, providers, agencies, and community groups who are concerned about infants, toddlers, and their families and develop coalitions to monitor and evaluate all phases of Part C;

4. Provide recommendations to the governor on the composition of the state interagency coordinating council and offer to serve;

5. Advocate for the necessary financial resources to facilitate full implementation of the law, particularly including serving at-risk infants and toddlers; and

6. Request review of all policies and procedure for Part C to insure that a family-centered approach is implemented.

Social workers have a special responsibility to this population of children and families. Infancy and toddlerhood are critical and vulnerable times in the lives of children times of rapid growth and change. They are critical and vulnerable times for families too. Families who have infants and toddlers with disabilities face the additional challenges of responding to the unique needs that their child has and discovering how to learn about and find the appropriate services and supports they and their child require. The provisions of family-centered, appropriate, timely intervention services is essential, and helping families come to grips with their real needs and connecting them to appropriate agencies will increase their chances of obtaining and effectively using these services.

As we know so well, no single provider, no single agency, and few communities can provide all the services families with infants and toddlers with disabilities need. "Collaboration with families and . . . other(s) is a necessity and an obligation of professional leadership" (Corrigan and

Bishop, 1997). P.L. 105-17, Part C, presents an important opportunity for social workers to join hands with families, other professionals, agencies, and communities within the health, education, mental health, and social services delivery systems in assuring that this law will improve the quality of life for infants and toddlers with disabilities and their families.

WHO WILL BE SERVED?

In the context of the law, infants and toddlers with disabilities are defined as children under three years of age who need early intervention services because:

1. They are experiencing developmental delays, as measured by appropriate diagnostic instruments and procedures, in one or more of the following areas;
   (a) cognitive development,
   (b) physical development,
   (c) communication development,
   (d) social or emotional development, and
   (e) adaptive development: or
2. They have a diagnosed physical or mental condition that has a high probability of resulting in developmental delay.

   Developmental delay takes the meaning given such term by the state. The law, therefore, requires each state to adopt a definition of developmental delay that will be used in implementation. Each state may define this term to be comprehensive or as restrictive as wished (Section 632(3)). Perhaps the most pressing challenge for each state continues to be the inclusion of "at risk" children and their families for eligibility in such categories as biologically, socially, emotionally, and medically, and environmentally at risk.

EARLY INTERVENTION SERVICES

In the context of the law, *early intervention services* are developmental services that:

1. Are provided under public supervision;
2. Are provided at no cost except where federal or state law provides for a system of payments by families, including a schedule of sliding fees;
3. Are designed to meet the developmental needs of an infant or toddlers with a disability in any one or more of the following areas:
   (a) physical development,
   (b) cognitive development,

(c) communication development,

(d) social or emotional development, or

(e) adaptive development;

4. Meet the standards of the state in which they are provided, including the requirements of this part for:

(a) family training, counseling, and home visits;

(b) special instruction;

(c) speech pathology and audiology services;

(d) occupational therapy;

(e) physical therapy;

(f) psychological services;

(g) service coordination services;

(h) medical services (only for diagnostic and evaluation purposes);

(i) early identification, screening, and assessment services,

(j) supportive health services to enable the infant or toddler to benefit from other early intervention services;

(k) social work services;

(l) vision services;

(m) assistive technology devices and assistive technology services; and

(n) transportation and related costs that are necessary to enable an infant or toddler and the infants's or toddler's family to receive early intervention services;

5. Are provided by qualified personnel, including:

(a) special educators,

(b) speech and language pathologists and audiologists,

(c) occupational therapists,

(d) physical therapists,

(e) pyschologists,

(f) social workers,

(g) nurses,

(h) nutritionists,

(i) family therapists,

(j) orientation and mobility specialists, and

(k) pediatricians and other physicians; and

6. Are, to the maximum extent appropriate, provided in natural environments, including the home and community settings in which children without disabilities participate, and are in conformity with an IFSP adopted in accordance with Section 636 (Section 632).

REQUIREMENTS FOR A STATEWIDE SYSTEM

In general, a statewide system of coordinated, comprehensive, multidisciplinary, interagency programs providing appropriate early intervention services to all infants and toddlers with disabilities and their families include the following minimum components:

1. A definition of the term "developmentally delayed" that will be used by the state in carrying out programs under this part;

2. A state policy that is in effect and that ensures that appropriate early intervention services are available to all infants and toddlers with disabilities and their families, including American Indian infants and toddlers and their families residing on reservations geographically located in the state;

3. A timely, comprehensive, multidisciplinary evaluation of the functioning of each infant and toddler with a disability in the state and a family-directed identification of the needs of each family of such an infant or toddler, to appropriately assist in the development of the infant or toddler;

4. An IFSP in accordance with Section 636, including coordination of services in accordance with such service plan;

5. A comprehensive child-find system, consistent with Part B, including a system for making referrals to service providers that include timelines and provide for the participation by primary referral sources;

6. A public awareness program focusing on early identification of infants and toddlers with disabilities, including the preparation and dissemination by the lead agency designated or established under item 10 (below) to all primary referral sources, especially hospitals and physicians, of information for parents on the availability of early intervention services, and procedures for determining the extent to which such sources disseminate such information to parents of infants with disabilities;

7. A central directory that includes early intervention services, resources, and experts available in the state and research and demonstration projects being conducted in the state;

8. A comprehensive system of personnel development (see Section 635(8)(A)-(D) for a full discussion of personnel development);

9. Policies and procedures relating to the establishment and maintenance of standards to ensure that personnel necessary to carry out this part (Part B) are appropriately and adequately trained (see (9)(A)-(B));

10. A single line of responsibility in a lead agency designated or established by the governor for carrying out the program (see (10)(A)-(F));

11. A policy pertaining to the contracting or making of other arrangements with service providers to provide early intervention services in the state;

12. A procedure for securing timely reimbursement of funds expended;

13. Procedural safeguards;

14. A system for compiling data requested by the secretary of education (Section 618);

15. A state interagency coordinating council (see requirements, Section 641);

16. Policies and procedures to ensure that (a) to the maxmimum extent appropriate, early intervention services are provided in natural environments and (b) the provision of early intervention services for any infant or toddler occurs in a setting other than a natural environment only when it cannot be achieved satisfactorily in a natural environment (consistent with Section 636 (d)(5)).

INDIVIDUALIZED FAMILY SERVICE PLANS

Assessment and Program Development

Each infant or toddler with a disability and the infant's or toddler's family is entitled to receive:

1. A multidisciplinary assessment of the unique strengths and needs of the infant or toddler and an identification of services appropriate to meet such needs;

2. A family-directed assessment of the resources, priorities, and concerns of the family and an identification of the supports and services necessary to enhance the family's capacity to meet the developmental needs of their infant or toddler; and

3. A written individualized family service plan (IFSP) developed by a multidisciplinary team, including the parents.

Periodic Review

The IFSP shall be evaluated at least once a year and the family shall be provided a review of the plan at six-month-intervals. The evaluation will occur more often where appropriate, based on infant or toddler and family needs.

Promptness after Assessment

The IFSP shall be developed within a reasonable time after the assessment is completed. With the parents' consent, early intervention services may commence prior to the completion of such assessment.

Content of Plan

The IFSP shall be in writing and contain:

1. A statement of the infant's or toddler's current levels of physical development, cognitive development, communication development, social or

emotional development, and adaptive development, based on objective criteria;

2. A statement of the family's resources, priorities, and concerns related to enhancing the development of the family's infant or toddler with a disability;

3. A statement of the major outcomes expected to be achieved by the infant or toddler and the family, and the criteria, procedures, and timelines used to determine the degree of progress being made toward achieving the outcomes and whether modifications or revisions of the outcomes or services are necessary;

4. A statement of specific early intervention services necessary to meet the unique needs of the infant or toddler and the family, including the frequency, intensity, and method of delivering services;

5. A statement of the natural environments in which early intervention services shall appropriately be provided, including a justification of the extent, if any, to which the services will not be provided in a natural environment;

6. Projected dates for initiation of services and anticipated duration of such services;

7. Identification of the service coordinator from the profession most immediately relevant to the infant's or toddler's and family's needs or any qualified person who will be responsible for the implementation of the plan and coordination with other agencies and persons; and

8. The steps to be taken supporting the transition of the toddler with a disability to preschool or other appropriate services (Section 636).

The contents of the IFSP shall be fully explained to the parents, and informed written consent from the parents shall be obtained prior to provision of the services described in the plan.

PROCEDURAL SAFEGUARDS

The procedural safeguards required to be included in a statewide system (Section 635(a)(13)) would provide, at minimum, the following:

1. Timely administrative resolution of complaints by parents. Any party aggrieved by the findings and decisions regarding an administrative complaint shall have the right to bring a civil action with respect to the complaint in any state court or competent jurisdiction or in a district court of the United States without regard to the amount of controversy (Section 639(a)(1));

2. The right to confidentiality of personally identifiable information, including the right of parents to written notice of and consent to the exchange

of such information among agencies consistent with federal and state law;

3. The right of the parents to determine whether they, their infant or toddler, or other family members will accept or decline any early intervention service without jeopardizing other early intervention services;

4. The opportunity for parents to examine records relating to assessment, screening, eligibility determinations, and the development and implementation of the IFSP;

5. Procedures to protect the rights of the infant or toddler with a disability whenever the parents of the infant or toddler are not known or cannot be found or the infant or toddler is a ward of the state, including the assignment of an individual (who shall not be an employee of the state lead agency, or any other state agency, and shall not be a person providing early intervention service) to act as a surrogate for the parents;

6. Written prior notice to the parent of the infant or toddler whenever the state agency or service provider proposes to initiate or change or refuses to initiate or change the identification, evaluation, or placement of the infant or toddler with a disability, or the provision of appropriate early intervention services to the infant or toddler;

7. Procedures designed to assure that the notice required by item 6 (above) fully informs the parents, in the parents' native language, unless it clearly is not feasible to do so, of all procedures available pursuant to this section; and

8. The right of parents to use mediation (see Section 639(8)(a)-(c) for some exceptions).

STATE INTERAGENCY COORDINATING COUNCIL

Any state that desires to receive financial assistance under this law must establish a State Interagency Coordinating Council, whose members shall be appointed by the governor. In making appointments to the council, the governor shall ensure that the membership of the council reasonably represents the population of the state. The composition of the council must satisfy the following conditions:

1. At least 20 percent of the members shall be parents of infants or toddlers with disabilities, or children with disabilities aged twelve or younger, with knowledge of, or experience with, programs for infants or toddlers with disabilities. At least one such member shall be a parent of an infant or toddler or a child with a disability aged six or younger.

2. At least 20 percent of the members shall be public or private providers of early intervention services.

3. At least one member shall be from the state legislature.

4. At least one member shall be involved in personnel preparation.

5. At least one member shall be from each of the state agencies involved in the provision, or payment for, early intervention services to infants and toddlers with disabilities and their families and shall have sufficient authority to engage in policy planning and implementation on behalf of their agencies.

6. At least one member shall be from the state educational agency responsible for preschool services to children with disabilities and shall have sufficient authority to engage in policy planning and implementation on behalf of such agency.

7. At least one member shall be from the agency responsible for the state governance of health insurance.

8. At least one representative shall be from a Head Start agency or program in the state.

9. At least one representative shall be from a state agency responsible for child care.

The council may include other members selected by the governor, including a representative from the Bureau of Indian Affairs (BIA), or where there is a BIA-operated or BIA-funded school, from the Indian Health Service or the tribe or tribal council.

Meetings

The council must meet at least quarterly as it deems necessary. The meeting must be publicly announced, open, and accessible to the general public. Subject to the approval of the governor, the council may prepare and approve a budget using funds under this part to hire staff, conduct hearings and forums, reimburse members for expenses, and obtain the services of such professional, technical, and clerical personnel as may be necessary to carry out its functions (Section 639).

Functions of the Council

The council shall have the following functions:

1. Advise and assist the lead agency in the identification of the sources of fiscal and other support for early intervention programs, the assignment of financial responsibility to the appropriate agency, and the promotion of interagency agreements, and advise and assist the lead agency in the preparation of applications and amendments;

2. Advise and assist the state educational agency regarding the transitions of toddlers with disabilities to preschool and other appropriate services; and

3. Prepare and submit an annual report to the governor and to the secretary on the status of early intervention programs for infants and toddlers with disabilities and their families operated within the state (Section 641).

OLD AND NEW DEVELOPMENTS: PART C's CONTINUING IMPACT

Since 1986 when Part C was enacted (then known as Part H), the complexity of service systems education, social services, and health has continued to grow and expand in a manner that makes it increasingly difficult to provide family-centered, community-based, culturally responsive services in a coordinated and seamless manner. New parents of an infant or toddler with a disability face this complexity and disarray in services at a point when they may have the least time and energy to find services for their child and themselves.

Using Part C as a catalyst for change, there has been considerable leadership from federal agencies, particularly the Maternal and Child Health Bureau's Programs for Children with Special Health Care Needs (Brewer, McPherson, Magrab, and Hutchins, 1989). In 1993, the Maternal and Child Health Bureau, under the leadership of Merle McPherson, awarded three interprofessional development grants (1) Partnerships for Change at the University of Vermont Department of Social Work, (2) Health and Education Collaboration of the Hawaii Medical Association, and (3) the Western Oregon State College Teaching Division. In January 1994, more than fifty national organizations concerned with the well-being of children, youth and families—including the National Association of Social Workers, American Academy of Pediatrics, and National Education Association—developed a set of principles that would pave the way for unprecedented collaboration among essential services at the local, state, and federal levels (see Principles to Link By, 1994). The Federal Interagency Coordinating Council has also provided leadership by using family-professional collaborative processes and developing materials that describe and encourage family-centered, community-based, culturally appropriate early intervention services. Around this same time, the National Commission on Leadership in Interprofessional Education (NCLIE), founded to promote interprofessional collaborative practices and training, developed the following purpose statement:

> Through a family/professional partnership, the Commission will support the preparation of a new generation of interprofessionally oriented leaders in health education, and social work, who possess the knowledge, skills, and values to practice in new community-based integrated service delivery systems (NCLIE Executive Board minutes, 1995).

More recently, accrediting bodies, such as the Council on Social Work Education, have begun to study issues of certification, licensing, and accreditation for interprofessional practice. Families have been active leaders and participants in all of these developments and continue, through their organizations (e.g., Family Voices and parent-to-parent organizations), to influence the Congress and federal, state, and community agencies to fulfill the promise of Part C and encourage the family-directed provision of early intervention services.

While much of this emphasis on interprofessional education and practice (Kane, 1975, 1982) is not new to social work education and practice, the emphasis on a family-professional partnership in the planning, implementation, and evacuation of services is new (Bishop, Woll, and Arango, 1993). Families are now recognized as having critical knowledge and experience about the care of their children and are viewed as equal partners on the team. Part C has been instrumental in the implementation of this philosophy of care.

Finally, the emphasis on natural environments (see policies and procedures on natural environment, regulations 303,167(c) and 303.344(d)(1)(ii)) coincides with a rededication to the concept of community as an important source of supports and resources for children and their families. This "new era of community renewal has dramatically changed the role of social workers in community practice. Social workers once assumed the role of change agent . . . Today, greater emphasis is placed on encouraging community members . . . to participate and assume leadership roles in all phases of community capacity development" (Ewalt et al., 1998, xi).

REFERENCES

Bishop, K. K., Taylor, M. S., and Arango, P. (eds.). 1997. *Partnerships at work: Lessons learned from programs and practices of families, professionals and communities.* Burlington, VT: University of Vermont, Department of Social Work.

Bishop, K. K., Rounds, K., and Weil, M. 1993. P.L. 99-457: The preparation of social workers for practice with infants and toddlers with handicapping conditions and their families. *Journal of Social Work Education* 29(1):36–45.

Bishop, K. K. 1987. The new law and the role of social workers. *Early Childhood* 3(2):6–7.

Bishop, K. K., Woll, J., and Arango, P. 1993. *Family/professional collaboration for children with special health needs and their families.* Burlington, VT: University of Vermont, Department of Social Work.

Brewer, E. J., McPherson, M., Magrab, P. R., and Hutchins, V. L. 1989. Family-centered, community-based, coordinated care for children with special health care needs. *Pediatrics* 83(6):1055–1060.

Clark, J. 1989. Proposed roles and mission for professionals working with handicapped infants and their families. Unpublished comments, Iowa, January 17.

Cochran, M. 1992. Parent empowerment: Developing a conceptual framework. *Family Sciences Review* 5:3–21.

Corrigan, D., and Bishop, K. K. 1997. Creating family-centered integrated service systems and interprofessional educational programs to implement them. *Social Work in Education* 19(3):149–163.

Early intervention program for infants and toddlers with handicaps: Final regualtions. 1998. *Federal Register* 63(71).

Ewalt, P. L., Freeman, E. M., and Poole, D. L. (eds.). 1998. *Community building: Renewal, well-being, and shared responsibility.* Washington, DC: NASW Press.

Germain, C. B. 1968. Social study: Past and future. *Social Casework* 49:403–409.

Germain, C. B., and Gitterman, A. 1996. *The life model of social work practice.* NY: Columbia University Press.

Gray, B. 1989. *Collaborating: Finding common ground for multiparty problems.* San Francisco: Jossey-Bass.

Hartman, A., and Laird, J. 1983. *Family-centered social work practice.* New York: Free Press.

Kane, R. A. 1975. *Interprofessional teamwork.* Syracuse, NY: Syracuse University School of Social Work.

Kane, R. A. 1982. Lessons for social work from the medical model: A viewpoint for practice. *Social Work* 27(4):315–321.

Kisthardt, W. 1997. The strengths model of case management: Principles and helping functions. In D. Saleebey (ed.). *The strengths perspective in social work practice.* NY: Longman.

Laird, J. 1995. Family-centered practice in the postmodern era. *Families in Society* 76(1):150–162.

Pinderhughes, E. 1995. Empowering diverse populations: Family practice in the 21st century. *Families in Society* 76(3):131–140.

Principles to Link By. 1994. Integrating education, health and human services for children, youth, and families: Systems that are community-based and school-linked. Final report. Available from the American Academy of Pediatrics, 601 Thirteenth Street, NW, Suite 400 North, Washington, DC 20005.

P.L. 105-17. Infants and Toddlers with Disabilities, Part C.

Richmond, M. 1917. *Social diagnosis.* NY: Russel Sage Foundation.

Rose, S. 1992. *Case management and social work practice.* NY: Longman.

Rounds, K., Weil, M. O., and Bishop, K. K. 1994. Practice with culturally diverse families of infants and toddlers with handicapping conditions. *Families in Society* 75(1):3–15.

Shelton, T. L., and Stephanek, J. S. 1994. Family-centered care for children needing specialized health and developmental services. Bethesda, MD: Association for the Care of Children's Health.

Weick, A., and Saleebey, D. 1995. Supporting family strengths: Orienting policy and practice toward the 21st century. *Families in Society* 75(1):141–149.

White, M. 1995. Reauthoring lives: Interviews and essays. Adelaide, Australia: Dulwich Centre Publications.

SECTION THREE
Service Delivery
in the Schools

CHAPTER 12

Developing and Defining the School Social Worker's Role

Robert Constable
Professor Emeritus, Loyola University of Chicago

- The Function of the School Social Worker
- The Characteristic Perspective of the School Social Worker
- Assessment in School Social Work
- Clinical Social Work in a School
- Units of Attention and School Social Work Role(s)
- The School as a Unit of Attention

School social work practice models have tended to reflect the dominant methods of the broader social work profession as well as the needs, conditions, and strengths of the school setting. Social workers coming into a school setting usually feel there is a gap between what they were trained to do and the demands of the setting. The school social work role is often quite fluid and involves a heavy emphasis on transactions with school and school people on behalf of groups of students as well as traditional direct services to individual children in schools. When social workers enter the school, they give up the security of conducting a practice with individuals within the confines of an office. They find themselves in a broader practice arena where there is a need to understand both individuals and the broader system of the school, family, and community. If change takes place, it takes place within these many systems as well as on the individual level. The diverse needs of the school and its pupils appropriately generate multiple avenues of response by school social workers. The traditional focus on helping individual pupils to cope remains strong and seems to run parallel to the widening breadth of school social work interventions, in the classroom, within the multidisciplinary team, in school policy development, and with families. Practitioners themselves have different proficiencies, whether with individuals, classroom groups, families, consultation relationships, or the community of resources. There is a match between pupil needs as the school defines them and the practice modalities with which the individual school social worker feels most capable, but for the most part the school social worker learns to develop a wide repertoire of modalities to fit the needs of children and families in the school community. In this sense the school social worker is not a solo practitioner but a key team member who develops programs and carries out policies. School social workers develop their roles in relation to the needs of people involved in the process of education. This demands a good deal of skill and familiarity with what potentially can be developed with parents, children, and others on the school team. To do this school social workers need to develop a deepened theoretical base and a practical familiarity with the potential elaborations of this role.

The role of the school social worker was outlined in some detail in chapter 1, "Theoretical Perspectives in School Social Work." Clarifying the purpose of school social work and its relation to the process of education, we reviewed stories of practice and models of school social work services. These were *clinical school social work, school crisis work, children with special needs, consultation and placement of students, group work,* and *mediation.* These are not the only ways the school work role may be elaborated, but they illustrate possibilities. Taking these models of possibilities, the key questions are:

1. How is the role defined in relation to the way the school social worker and others in the school community see problems, needs, and possible units of attention?
2. What theories does the social worker draw on to develop this role? (Foundation theories in the *ecological systems perspective* are treated in section I. Theories underlying *elaborations* of the school social work role and the resultant practice are treated in this section.)

The basic skills of school social workers are *assessment* and *role development.* These are treated in section I, in this chapter, and in chapters 13 and 14. Chapters 13 and 14, "The Dynamics of Working with Children in School from a Systems Perspective" and "Working with Families," are meant to be read in relation to this chapter. Together with section I, the three chapters present the basics of clinical social work in a school and become a foundation for the rest of the book. Starting with chapter 15, the clinical model is elaborated and the focus broadens to include work with the school and the school community.

THE FUNCTION OF THE SCHOOL SOCIAL WORKER

Florence Poole noted that the traditional function of the school social worker is derived from the rights of every child to an education. Pupils who could not use what the school had to offer are, as she put it almost fifty years age, "children who are being denied, obscure though the cause may be, nevertheless denied because they are unable to use fully their right to an education." Educators have turned to social workers for help with children who were "having some particular difficulty in participating beneficially in a school experience." The school social worker is concerned with every child whose coping capacity may not be well matched with the demands and resources of the education institution. The *goal* of school social work is to assist young people in accomplishing appropriate developmental tasks in ways that best respect the values underlying our common human nature, our common human needs, and the human potential of each person. The *function* of the school social worker is to use his or her professional skill to help the school fulfill its primary purpose and mission. In using this as her starting point, Poole (1949) is shifting from a focus on the problem pupil, who could not adjust and adapt to the dynamic relation of pupil and school in the context of each child's right to an education. The conditions that interfere with the pupil's ability to connect with the educational system are diverse, and the school social worker's role is correspondingly broad. Poole's explication of the function of the school social worker through analysis of the societal function and the mandates of the school in relation to the practice of social work is an essentially sound and farsighted approach. Her concept of multiple roles taken by the school social worker on behalf of a single pupil and of working with the school, as well as with the child, is still valid.

What has changed is the school itself and its consciousness of its mandates, and this has helped to develop further the role of the school social worker. We may use the focus on children with disabilities as a metaphor for this process of role development in school social work. In this sense practice theory verges on and includes school policy development because practice makes policy possible and the school social worker, as an advanced practitioner, helps design the school policy and program framework from which practice is derived. In special education, for example, the right of every child with a disability to a free appropriate public education has been more powerfully defined. Over the past thirty years, the role of the social worker has shifted from a focus on children who did not meet normative expectations to a focus on influencing the norms themselves on behalf of children, developing and implementing individualized approaches to learning. The service itself has shifted from a humane attempt on the school's part to help children who were out of the mainstream to an entitlement, a civil right of every child who needs help to benefit from education. With these changes has also come a concern for whole groups of children encountering similiar conditions as well as for individuals.

The function of the school social worker is developed from the dynamic encounter of the social work perspective with the problem and needs to be addressed and the mandates given the social institution of education. Changing school conditions and conceptions of social work have led to many different definitions of what the school social worker should do, but the elements of this encounter have remained the same over many years.

When the school was concerned mainly with cognitive development and the meeting of fixed expectations, social workers worked with pupils who could not meet these expectations or whose needs required careful planning with family, medical, or other systems in the community to meet existing expectations. Social work is the only profession that has the depth of experience in dealing with all of these systems while remaining in close, intimate, and sensitive contact with the pupil and family, helping them to choose, to discover, and to use community, family, and personal resources. The whole legal tradition associated with children with disabilities clarified the mandate of the school in relation to a vulnerable population to be provided an education. The profession is responding with the gradual development of a clearly rationalized set of tasks that can assist the individual and the school in carrying out this mission.

The school social work function that emerges from the present legal commitments and needs of the school and its pupils is a complex one. It can be divided into two main responsibilities: (1) a responsibility to help pupils use available services and resources to develop a workable connection with school, family, and community environments and (2) a responsibility to develop networks of services and support systems in school, community, and family. In both cases, at whatever level the school social worker is involved, with individuals or larger environments or both, the concern with the match between individual and environment is the same. A focus on the larger environment is still related to individual coping, and a focus on individual coping is still related to quality of the environment.

THE CHARACTERISTIC PERSPECTIVE OF THE SCHOOL SOCIAL WORKER

If school social workers are to succeed in the complex challenges of integrating children into communities and helping to maintain social integration, an ecological perspective must be taken. Within this perspective, there is a dual focus on the individual and on his or her transaction with an environment. This characteristic perspective of the social worker has been developed in the articles that keynote each section of this book and in chapters 3 and 4, in section I.

ASSESSMENT IN SCHOOL SOCIAL WORK

The ecological systems perspective leads the social worker to make institutional and psychosocial assessments that address the transactions of individuals with the environment. *Assessment* is a systematic way of understanding what is happening in relations in the classroom, within the family, and between family and school and the places where interventions will be most effective. It involves looking for possible change, even small changes, in the relations, tasks, and expectations in the classroom and in the home, and in the child's patterns of learning to cope. Working between the worlds of home and school, and the corresponding psychosocial tasks of child and family and the mission of the school, the worker assists teachers and parents to discover their own personal repertoire of ways to assist the child's coping, often modifying their own expectations of themselves and their own educational approaches in relation to the real needs of the child. When intervention with the child is necessary, the social worker can assist the child in relation to these changes and assist parents and teachers to respond to the child's present efforts at coping. Understanding the relation of education to the psychosocial tasks of child and family and the possible parameters of the helping process in school gives focus and definition to the assessment, clarifies the possible units(s) of attention, and develops the consequent role of the social worker.

What conditions in the individual, in the environment, and in their transaction may be causing breakdown? What networks of services, what support systems, might make it possible for the individual to survive, to cope, to form satisfactory interpersonal relationships, and to experience some level of success in the community and family environment? The answers will depend on individual needs and capacities. Individual survival, affilation, and achievement depend on the sum total of what individuals may be experiencing in their living situations, at school, and in the community. Work with individuals to help them take hold must relate to how they are coping with these conditions. In many cases no amount of individual work can counterbalance what may be taking place in these crucial sectors of a person's life.

The school social worker often has the best access to these sectors, as well as to individual pupils. This access to individuals and to major sectors of life activity allows for a practice approach that emphasizes interaction with the individual and with important sectors of the environment. The social worker does problem solving with teachers, administrators, and parents to help them to cope with the implications of their relations with the pupil and, when necessary, with pupils to help them to cope with the challenges of home, school, and community. The social worker knows that intervention may only be a temporary support in the situation and can at best help individuals discover their own resources for coping. The social worker needs most of all to have a broad understanding of the many acceptable ways people can discover and use their capabilities, can communicate with each other, and can be resources for one another. It is the social worker's willingness to help people discover the many possibilities for healthy relationships and to facilitate this process with crucial resource systems and agencies, as well as with the individual and family, that can make the difference between survival and breakdown in the relations of vulnerable individuals.

CLINICAL SOCIAL WORK IN A SCHOOL

To illustrate the emergent function of the school social worker, we take a deliberately simplified example of social work services to a child, Jorge Oliverez, with a moderate disability in a regular educational setting. Jorge is a twelve-year-old Cuban-American child with physical disabilities who has just moved to a new school district and is seeking entry into Blake Junior High School. In response partly to the manifest anxiety of Jorge's middle-aged parents, for whom Jorge is the youngest child by eight years, and partly to Jorge's own irascible behavior, his previous school, Dorian Elementary, gave Jorge considerable attention but protected him from the effects that his hostile, demanding behavior had on others. Jorge did not understand his own specific needs and preceived them as all or nothing. His demands for attention from adults led to estrangement from other children. The problem tended to be reinforced by the parents, who, in their unqualified support for Jorge's demands, undercut any positive, socializing effects the school might have. Jorge's new seventh-grade homeroom teacher, Mrs. Beall, found his constant demands for attention difficult to deal with in an active classroom.

From the beginning in the new situation, she responded by ignoring Jorge in the hope that he would modify his behavior. Jorge responded with increased self-destructive alienation and by looking for support from other places. He found allies in his parents and his gym teacher. With the implicit approval of his parents, Jorge had not turned in an assignment in language arts for several weeks and was beginning to fail the subject despite close to average ability. His classmates reacted to what they saw as Jorge's increasingly unusual behavior. The teacher felt that Jorge needed to learn to take the consequences of his behaivor but remained aloof from him. The principal was informed that Jorge's parents had been using the situation to mobilize other parents of children with disabilities in a parents' organization around the issue of districtwide neglect of programs for children with disabilities. Mrs. Beall decided that, if the principal backed the parents, she in turn would file a union grievance. She took the step of referring Jorge for placement out of his current regular class into a special class that generally has children with more severe disabilities. The parents, although conflicted, were partially in agreement with the idea of placement. What would a social worker, who had specific responsibility for conducting a social study, do in this situation? How would a worker make recommendations regarding school placement to the multidisciplinary team?

We can map four components in this case: Jorge's actual behavior, the conditions behind Jorge's behavior, the impinging environment in the classroom, and the conditions behind the impinging environment (see table 1). Social workers have a dual focus on person and situation. A variety of methods may be used to provide a better match between a person and his or her environment. A social worker could conceivably work with Jorge, his family, or the teacher, in program development in the school and in the community. At one point or another the social worker would probably have some direct or indirect influence on all of these systems and could intervene selectively in a few of them, according to his or her assessment of the situation, his or her competence, and the time available.

UNITS OF ATTENTION AND SCHOOL SOCIAL WORK ROLES

The locus of concern for the social worker may be Jorge and his family and their relations with the teaching-learning environment or more broadly children with disabilities as a group in school. One way to organize these complex choices for assessment and for intervention is to think of them as *units of attention*. A unit of attention is a chosen point of most effective change, a point or set of points in the system where, if change takes place, other positive changes will also become possible. For example, the social worker might work with the Oliverez parents and other parents of children with disabilities to promote greater awareness of the needs of children with disabilities in the school district. The worker might use the strong connections in the Cuban-American community as a resource. The worker might collaborate with school administrators to plan better services for children with disabilities. The worker might act as a consultant to Jorge's teacher, Mrs.Beall, helping her come to a better understanding of Jorge and his relations with the other students in the class. The social worker might develop a close collaborative relationship between Jorge's homeroom teacher and gym teacher as a support system, without incurring the resentment of his homeroom teacher. The focus depends on the school social worker's assessment of the needs in the situation. The worker's competence in different areas, the time available, and the extent of development of the social work program in the school—in other words the realistic limitations and opportunities of the situation as perceived following a professional assessment—may affect the focus.

In actual practice the social worker will with a variety of units of attention at the same time, and the focus of the social worker on these units of attention will also change over time. The case of Alan, his family, and his teachers, managed over a period of five years (described by Helen Wolkow in chapter 13), is a classic example of clinical social work in a school. There were various permutations of units of attention over the years as Alan's family situation, teachers, and Alan himself changed. A paradox is that while over the years the worker actively shifted her role to fit the developing situation, most of the "work" was done by Alan, his family, and the school, as all of them shifted over time and in relation to each other. Their tasks in relation to each other were so compelling that the worker used this energy

TABLE 1   Transactions, Impingement, and Source Environments in the Case of Jorge

Source Environment (conditions behind behavior)	Transaction		Source Environment (conditions behind behavior)
	Coping Behavior	Classroom Impingement	
Jorge: Fearful; dependent; compensates by demands for attention; uses disability to control and manipulate adults around him	Irascible; inordinate demands for attention; isolate; physical limitations; turns in no work; "building a case" against teacher	*Homeroom teacher:* Ignores; has referred to special class placement	Likes independent children; feels should achieve at class level without special attention; resents Jorge's demands
Parents: Disability has had deep impact on own feelings of adequacy, feel guilty also; react by overprotection; but basically feel quite helpless and angry to have this responsibility	Alternate between high defensiveness and helplessness	*Peers:* Steal pencils; call him names	Don't understand Jorge's behavior or rejection of them; his disability bothers them
		Gym teacher: Sympathetic to Jorge; spends time with him	Had a minor disability that he overcame when he was young; has had special training to prepare for working with physically disabled; feels competitive with Jorge's homeroom teacher
		Principal:	Concerned about image of school in community and with parents' organization; schools are being closed; tax revolt on
		Parents' organization:	Looking for test case to express concern about needs of children with disabilities

as the main tool for change, and so in fact, she did not need to be centralized at any time to give an exhaustive amount of energy to the situation. Accurately assessed, the principal actors did the work. The task of the social worker was to develop situations in which this work could be done most productively, using a variety of interventive modalities. Thus effectiveness did not come from the use of a single modality but from matching modalities with the situation and the energies and capabilities of its participants. This approach to assessment is more complex, but undoubtedly more effective. As any team member will recognize, effective interventions are accomplished, not by the school social worker alone, but by all the participants in the arena. Ineffective interventions are likewise a product of the participants in interaction and are not simply the fault of one team member.

Jorge's and Alan's stories provide examples of clinical social work in the school. They illustrate a range of interventions that can develop with a mildly challenged child from an involved family. A child with a more severe disability or a more vulnerable family would demand other responses on the part of the social worker. A child with a severe disability is usually more vulnerable and depends on complex relations with systems external to the family, as well as the family itself, to meet his emergent needs. These external systems provide special education, physical and mental health services of different sorts, job training, transportation, and a variety of temporary or permanent care arrangements when family care is no longer adequate. The family of the child with disabilities is under considerable pressure and cannot really function without some assistance from the outside. The school social worker will need to negotiate networks of service agreements with the family and the appropriate providers. Considerable professional skill is necessary to keep such a network going, but these networks could make the difference between a child's remaining in the community and going to an institution.

The emergent school social work function with children having moderate to servere disabilities is a blend of the social and the individual. To ignore people's very personal ways of coping and the complex needs of the child and family for services is to court certain failure. These needs, of course, are not merely individual but are shared with other children and families, and the social worker, planning with the school or appropriate educational resource and with external agencies, can affect large populations of pupils. It is undoubtedly in the exchange of individual and social, in the unique and personal transaction with the resources and systems that are available, that the social work function can most clearly find itself.

THE SCHOOL AS A UNIT OF ATTENTION

Much of the work of the school social worker focuses on the school community itself and all of the children in it as units of attention. The social worker assists the school community to develop and support programs that are carried out in school. Much of the discussion in this section of the book focuses on the practice that emerges. In one instance the school may be in crisis. The social worker is part of the crisis team, having helped prepare a general crisis plan, and will take part in work with different parts of the school community as it copes with the crisis. In another instance the social worker may be assisting in the development of regular education classroom environments that appropriately accommodate certain children with special needs. He or she may be involved in transition planning for these children and consultation on placements. The social worker may design special group experiences to meet the needs of diverse populations, such as young parents, children of divorce, pregnant adolescents, developmentally disabled eighth graders learning social skills, or teachers finding an appropiate role for themselves in dealing with children who tell them about abuse. The social worker may develop a mediation program to help the school find better and fairer ways for adolescents to deal with disputes and fights. These examples are developed further in this section.

In the chapters that follow, authors will explore the multiple and complex dimensions of the function of the social worker in the school. The chapters trace a continuum of intervention from individual through organization and community. In chapter 13 Helen Wolkow examines the role of the school social work practitioner from the perspective of a case history spanning part of a child's elementary school years. There is a direct link between the theoretical discussion in section I of this book and practice as it emerges in section III. Building on this base, the chapters following treat social skills development (chapter 23); partnership between home, school, and community (chapter 14); and the social work role in the implementation of the right to a free appropriate public education for students with disabilities (chapters 16 through 20). The picture broadens to include the development of consultation skills (chapter 21). The school and its networks of people becomes the setting for change in the following chapters on conflict resolution (chapter 26), mediation (chapter 27), student forums (chapter 24), the no-fault school (chapter 28), crisis intervention (chapter 25), and peer sexual harassament (chapter 29). Finally, the section ends with the relations of school and community networks (chapter 30).

Each chapter in this section discusses in depth one aspect of the application of the theoretical base developed in section I and the emergent function of the school social worker. For the school social worker, these aspects and the emergent function represent a development beyond generic practice theories. The school social worker in actual practice will shape and hew his or her practice to meet the needs and possibilities of the actual situation, the school, and its community environment. As a result of this shaping and hewing, the practice of one social worker will emphasize resource development and teamwork facilitation, another will emphasize the traditional treatment model, and so on—each becoming an adaptation to an environment of expectations and a professional decision on the worker's part about what is the most efficient, effective, and timely investment of self in service to a common social work commitment and perspective.

REFERENCE

Poole, F. 1949. An analysis of the characteristics of the school social worker. *Social Service Review* 23(December):454–459.

CHAPTER 13

The Dynamics of Systems Involvement with Children in School: A Case Perspective

Helen S. Wolkow
School Social Worker, Southwest Cook County,
Cooperative for Special Education

- Reason for Referral
- Case Study Findings
- Family History
- Educational Background and Evaluation
- Services Offered, Progress, and Results
- Current Progress
- Summary

If we are to view students in their environment, then we must examine the many facets of that environment: academic, social, developmental, and emotional. It is often difficult for educators and administrators to recognize that all parts of that environment must be attended to if learning is to proceed effectively. If a student is having difficulty at home, or with peers, his or her academics almost invariably will suffer. Working with a student on emotional needs when there is also an academic problem is not enough. Working on academics when a student is emotionally upset is not enough. If we are to view the child as a whole, then we must attend to all of his or her needs so that he or she may develop and function at his or her optimum.

The following is an example of a case quite common to the caseload of the school social worker. It involves a child with whom the social worker worked over a period of three years (second through fourth grade), his parents, his teachers, the school administration, and outside agencies.

REASON FOR REFERRAL

Alan was referred for evaluation by his second-grade classroom teacher toward the end of September, about five weeks after the start of school. He was a transfer student from another school district and was experiencing great difficulty with reading and spelling. He also had difficulty following directions and concentrating on his work, he was easily distracted, and he had poor fine motor coordination and poor visual perception. Alan often would try to copy from his neighbors, or just sit and not attempt to do his work. At times he would sit and suck his fingers. Teachers described him as shy and withdrawn.

The teacher presented the situation to the pupil personnel service team, and they agreed testing should be done. The parents were contacted and agreed to the evaluation. As part of this evaluation, or case study, I completed a Social Developmental Study. This provided us with some insight into possible etiology for some of his academic development and social difficulties.

CASE STUDY FINDINGS

Alan, a nice looking, blond, blue-eyed Caucasian male, was age seven at the time of our initial interview. When interviewed, he had a very quiet and shy manner, almost withdrawn. He spoke very softly, and at times it was difficult to understand what he said. A lot of his emotional energy seemed to be tied up with his parents' divorce process, which had started a year-and-a-half earlier. He felt school was rather difficult, especially reading, but math was okay. He believed his older brother had learned to read as a baby. Later I found out his older brother had been retained, had reading difficulties, and still seemed to be having some academic problems. He felt that his parents yelled a lot, both at him and his brother. He talked quite a bit about this and many of his answers to my questions referred to this. He was able to say that he felt angry when he could not get his way.

FAMILY HISTORY

Alan, at the time of the evaluation, lived with his mother, his ten-year-old brother, and his three-year-old sister. His mother and father had separated at the end of Alan's kindergarten year. Initially, the mother stayed home with the children during the day, but went to her parents' home for the night when the father returned from work. The mother attended school at a local junior college at the time. The father works as an accountant and recently had become a born-again Christian; the mother is Catholic and attends church on a weekly basis. The divorce became final the summer after Alan completed first grade. That summer, mother and children moved to the same mobile home park where her parents resided. This move placed them within our district boundaries. The park had many children in residence and was comprised mostly of working-class people. The family fit within the norms of that community. During this time, the father usually would take the children on weekends. He was most consistent in doing so, and both children and father seemed to enjoy the time very much. Both sets of grandparents were involved with Alan and supportive of the family situation. Alan often would visit a country cottage with the maternal grandparents, and he was quite fond of those times.

EDUCATIONAL BACKGROUND AND EVALUATION

Alan attended preschool a few days a week at age four and then kindergarten and first grade in a standard educational placement. He came to his present district at the beginning of second grade, and he was evaluated shortly after entry.

The assessment pointed out that his support systems were eroding and that his self-concept was rapidly deteriorating, along with his academic performance. To shore up this deterioration and to assist in rebuilding him to former levels of functioning, resources needed to be utilized within the educational system, within the family, and within the community. Coordination of resources would be essential, or there was the potential for systems to impact negatively on the efforts of the others, even when each support system is working within its individual sphere toward the best interests of the child. Such a case normally requires an extended period of time, both because of the amount of work indicated and also because of the nature of the goals of the service delivery plan. This case extended over six years, during which this student was enrolled in the second through the eighth grade.

As a result of the evaluation, Alan was placed on a learning disabilities watch status, which meant that the learning disabilities specialist consulted with his classroom teacher weekly about possible interventions in the classroom for the perceived problems. Also, Alan was placed with the reading specialist in a small group to see if this would strengthen his reading skills. The social worker was identified as the interim case manager because it was clear that case management was going to be crucial to Alan's case. As a case manager, I met jointly with the classroom teacher, learning disabilities specialist, and reading specialist to arrange mutual consultation. With regard to direct social work service, Alan needed help with divorce issues, self-esteem, socialization skills, and learning appropriate ways to express his needs. I explored the possibility of outside counseling with his parents. They did not agree to this, so I monitored him on a consultative basis until further direct work could be arranged.

It is important to look at the developmental stage Alan had been moving through in order to understand his sense of failure and defeat. Considering Erikson's model of developmental stages, Alan would be well within the stage described as industry versus inferiority (Erikson, 1963). If we look at Piaget's stages of cognitive development, he would be in the middle of the concrete operations stage (Campbell, 1978, p. 8). According to some developmental theorists, he has been in a stage of fear. The five-year-old is fearful that his mother will not return home. Age six is also a fearful stage, in particular that something may happen to mother and she may not be there or may die. (Ilg et al., 1981, p. 160). Alan had been wrestling with events in his life with which his cognitive abilities were not yet capable of dealing. Efforts to soothe himself or put events in perspective generally had met with failure. Thus, he was becoming increasingly overwhelmed and anxious, and as a result some regressive behavior was noted (finger sucking, passivity, and disengagement). Emotionally he had been challenged by events that went right to the core of his worst fears, both in terms of potential abandonment and of his sense of self-competence.

SERVICES OFFERED, PROGRESS, AND RESULTS

Alan's second-grade teacher was highly structured and somewhat inflexible. She was not, initially, very encouraging with him, nor did she recognize his artistic and creative strengths and his good problem-solving skills. She found his slow pace of working, which was part of his perfectionistic need, difficult to relate to. This teacher was not particularly receptive to direct suggestions from me, so I had to develop some alternative strategies to implement through our already established consultation with the reading specialist. In these meetings, by explaining what my goals were in my work with Alan and discussing some parallel goals that might be implemented by the reading specialist, the classroom teacher was able to discuss her approach. She was able to draw upon an approach that she had used with a similar student a few years back. In fact, the earlier situation was close enough to be useful, and she felt she could use the same approach with Alan. By seeing the similarities between students she was able to accept other suggestions.

At the end of February of second grade, Alan's classroom teacher went on maternity leave. Alan's new teacher was very warm, caring, and creative. She liked Alan and wanted suggestions on how to help him. The consultation meetings continued. We soon agreed that Alan needed more intensive academic support. We requested a new Individualized Educational Program conference to amend the findings of the original case conference. Alan was changed from the learning disabilities watch list to direct learning disabilities services and started with thirty to sixty minutes a week in a small group. In order to arrange this meeting in a timely manner, the school administration had to be consulted about Alan's high-priority status. Given this information, the special education director in particular put in extra effort to reschedule the team and the parents so we could meet within the following week.

A week after this meeting and Alan's being placed in the learning disabilities program, his teacher brought to my attention a picture Alan had drawn of himself with a noose around his neck. When I questioned him about it, he said he had just been kidding around, but then did admit he had some very sad feelings. I told him that I wanted to check in with him every day for a while because his being this sad concerned me. I also told him I needed to talk to his mother and father because it was important that they also know about it. When I approached his mother regarding my concerns, she said that she felt it really was not serious and that in fact Alan seemed to be doing much better. His father felt it was serious and wanted Alan in outside counseling. I suggested to both that I continue to work with him until school was out in June and that then he should see an outside therapist. Both agreed. I felt that I needed to have another conference with his mother to support her awareness that in many ways Alan was doing much better, but that this new development was still something I hoped she would take seriously. She listened attentively, asked some very perceptive questions, and although she did not seem as convinced about the seriousness of Alan's situation as I had hoped, her attitude did seem to be much more open and cooperative.

Alan started to do much better after he started seeing the learning disabilities teacher. She continued to consult with me and the classroom teacher until the end of the year, and the classroom teacher began implementing similar strategies in the classroom to speed his progress. Likewise, he became more outgoing and started displaying improved social skills, first in our group and then in the classroom setting. When it was determined that he was starting to generalize the skills he was learning in our small group, I met with each of the personnel who worked with him to request that they encourage his fledgling efforts to become more assertive and outgoing. Most of them were indeed cooperative and actively helped him with this. They regularly reported to me informally. Retention still was considered at the end of the year because his academic progress was not as great as we had hoped, but the parents agreed that they wanted to wait to see how things would progress for him in third grade. I then went to the principal to encourage him to consider placing Alan with the more flexible and care giving third-grade teachers. He said he would take my request into consideration when making class assignments.

When the school year was nearly ended, I contacted the mother and father about making arrangements for Alan to see an outside therapist and gave them some names I could recommend. I asked that when they had made arrangements, they give the therapist permission to call me regarding Alan's case, and that they give me permission to discuss the case with the new therapist. The mother was very uncomfortable about the whole arrangement, stating that Alan would not be comfortable talking with a stranger, just as she would not be. Because I felt that my relationship with the mother was fairly strong by this time, I encouraged her to at least meet with the people I had recommended; then, if she wished, she could call me to talk further about her concerns. She thanked me, but did not act on this offer. In two weeks, just at the end of the school year, I received a call from the therapist whose named topped the list, who mentioned that the father had made the arrangements for the meeting, and only the father had come. However, the therapist had called the mother, and she had agreed to cooperate in getting Alan to his appointments. At the beginning of third grade, I met with Alan and his parents separately after discussing his progress with his outside therapist. We all agreed that, following a few visits to assist in his adjustment to the new school year, direct social work service would not be indicated at this time.

Third grade generally went well for Alan. He made good academic progress. He was seen by the reading specialist and the learning disabilities specialist two times a week, with one other student. I had regular contact with his classroom teacher to make sure he was progressing both academically and socially. Initially, I discussed with her his previous struggles, and alerted her to watch for signs of depression. I also helped her to institute a behavior modification plan for the whole class, focused on positive social interaction, as a way of keeping a handle on Alan's real social progress, aside from his teacher's impressions. Alan finished third grade on a positive note and was promoted to fourth grade.

Alan continued doing well in fourth grade. He had a male teacher whom he seemed to enjoy. The teacher noted that Alan improved greatly in his academic, organizational, and social skills after entering fourth grade. Alan improved several grade levels in reading, health, and social studies. Grades in other subject areas stayed the same or went up slightly. He became more organized and began writing his assignments down each day; his homework assignments were consistently completed daily. My work with his teacher that year was less intense than previously. I consulted with his teacher weekly for the first few weeks of school, giving him essentially the same background information as I had done for the third-grade teacher, though not in such detail. This was followed by monthly check-ins, except when the occasional brief concern arose.

Alan became more involved in class discussions, although he still was shy about sharing experiences. One thing he did share, slowly, with each of us involved with him, was his mother's remarriage at the end of the summer. He was beginning to enjoy his stepfather, although he felt the stepfather sometimes was not confident when problems arose, but, as Alan suggested, perhaps this was because he had never had children before. I learned of this by asking Alan if he would like to come to talk with me a few times once I learned from his teacher of this new development. I also asked him for permission to contact his mother and stepfather to ask them if they would like to come in to talk to me about any issues surrounding their relationship with the children, especially with Alan. Surprisingly, they agreed and came in the following week. We decided to keep in contact throughout the rest of the year. I also agreed to start seeing Alan again in a small group of boys. He interacted with the other students, but he still needed work on social skills. At times he reacted in a negative way physically to others when annoyed; however, he eventually learned to walk away from those situations. I thus recommended that Alan return to therapy for the summer months, given those latest developments, more to prevent backsliding than because of the former concerns regarding serious depression.

Alan became more comfortable with his academics and the school setting. He would have liked more friends. He enjoyed being with his stepfather and no longer thought so much about the divorce. He visited with his father every weekend and also became involved with outside activities, such as Boy Scouts. His mother then started to work part-time in the office of one of the district schools.

Alan completed his middle and junior high school years successfully. He was placed on a consult basis for LD/R services the last two years of junior high, and continued in the Chapter I reading program through sixth grade. Socially he interacted well with others and was involved in the chess club. He was very involved with the youth group at his father's church.

CURRENT PROGRESS

Alan is now a freshman in high school and doing well academically. He does not seem to have many friends in the mobile home park but does have friends in his father's neighborhood, which he visits regularly. He is still somewhat shy and a "loner." Mother states he may move in with his father, after his junior year, as did his oldest brother. The move will be prompted by the fact he would be attending a much smaller and more personal high school in a small town setting. Alan continues to maintain the progress he made, academically, socially, and emotionally—the progress begun when he first came to the attention of the multidisciplinary team many years ago.

Alan is a good example of the importance of having several subsystems of the larger educational system work together. Success never would have been achieved by attacking only one component of this case. Alan needed to have his academics attended to, via the reading specialist, the learning disabilities specialist and the homeroom teacher. He needed the social work component to address his emotional and social needs, as well as to make his parents aware of those needs. He needed the outside support of the therapist at the mental health agency to carry on the therapeutic goals identified by the school when school was not in session. He needed the cooperation of the administration and staff to have these needs met appropriately and in a timely manner. Any of these component parts without the others would have compromised the outcome, with potentially serious results for Alan.

REFERENCES

Campbell, Sarah F. 1976. *Piaget Sampler.* New York: John Wiley & Sons, Inc. pp. 8–11.

Erikson, Erik. 1963. *Childhood and Society.* New York: W. W. Norton.

Ilg, Frances L., Louise Bates Ames, and Sidney M. Baker. 1981. *Child Behavior* (revised edition from Gesell Institute of Human Development from Birth to Ten). New York: Barnes & Noble.

Perlman, Helen Harris. 1974. *Social Casework.* Chicago: University of Chicago Press.

CHAPTER 14

Working with Families

Robert Constable
Professor Emeritus, Loyola University of Chicago

Herbert Walberg
Research Professor of Education, University of Illinois at Chicago

- School Effectiveness and Parent Involvement
- Educational Productivity
- Conception of the School as a Community of Families
- The Necessary Arrangement of Relations between Family and School
- Family Conditions and Family Risks
- The Family and Its Institutional Ecology
- The School Social Work Role: Findings from Research
- Choosing the Unit of Attention

The family and school, two critical institutions in the ecology of childhood, have long maintained a studied disregard for each other, paying cautious inattention to the extent of their real interdependence. Such cautious and strategic inattention works well when family and school are in implicit agreement, when the pupil is succeeding in school, and when the family is in control of the socialization processes outside of school hours. However, assumptions that such an ideal picture of family life is usual are no longer valid for a great many pupils. Changes in the structure of families and fragmentation and atomization of communities have increased the incidence of vulnerable children and pupils at risk in the educational process.

The school social worker's role is built on the centrality and interdependence of family and school in the normal ecology of childhood. This means that in order to help children cope better with developmental needs and life circumstances it would probably be ineffective to work with the child without working with the teacher, who can influence the school environment, and the parents, who can influence the home. Actually sometimes it is not necessary to work with the child at all if the changes in the child's world are sufficient. In any case it is important to begin with environmental changes. Even small changes taking place in the classroom environment, or with the teacher, or in the home environment, or with the parents, may be enough to give the child an opportunity to cope more effectively. A child who experiences a shift in social or learning patterns may see himself or herself differently. Analyzing the changes from a systems-based, social interaction point of view, we know that the child will inevitably be a part of these changes and that children are for most part very responsive and flexible. They often use well what opportunities they perceive. On the other hand, to focus on the child alone, in the absence of a focus on school or family, would be to expect heroic changes in the internal patterns and the external worlds the child inhabits. It is likely to be ineffective and an exercise in frustration. Small changes in the worlds that children inhabit, and corresponding changes in their relations to each other, create larger changes in the total environment supporting the child's learning to cope differently. When there are changes in classroom and family relations, working with the child individually, when necessary, becomes much less complicated. Additionally the social worker may be less prone to take over for a teacher and parents when the parents are already implicitly part of the team. Once changes, however small, are taking place in the child's real environments, the social worker can assist the child to change in relation to those environments. The power of these tools for change depends first of all on the social worker's ability to assess a situation and each part of the situation in relation to the other, to the way the child could perceive and use them, and to his or her next possible developmental steps. Assessment involves understanding the relationships, tasks, and expectations in the classroom and in the home, and the child's patterns of coping, and looking for ways to make even small changes. Such assessment leads to intervention. Working between the worlds of home and school, the school social worker needs to learn to assist teachers and parents to discover their own personal repertoire of ways to assist the child's coping, often modifying their expectations of themselves in relation to the real needs of the child. Much of school work intervention is working to assist parents and teachers to find different ways of responding to and working with the child's active coping strategies. If they are to respond together, they need to understand and accept each other's styles and work with other as part of a team. When intervention with the child is necessary, the social worker can assist the child in relation to those changes and assist parents and teachers to respond to the child's present efforts at coping, and his or her efforts to respond to the changing environment in new ways.

Social workers have not always understood their roles in terms of this balanced assessment and intervention between school, home, and pupil. In many cases there has tended to be an emphasis on one part or another and not so much on the relations between these parts as illustrated above. Often the perception is that one part—whether the child, the teacher, or the parents—is enough to think about. The paradox is that it takes less effort to focus on the whole, and then respectfully intervene where needed, than to exclude someone from the assessment and the joint effort and then attempt to compensate for what the exluded person might have offered. The habit of making a good broad assessment and the skill of assisting parents and teachers in their roles will save a great deal of the social worker's time. Both before intervention takes place and while it is taking place, there needs to be a constant developing assessment of each part in relation to the child's perceptions and capabilities for change and in relation to what the social worker might do to assist the change process. How the social worker assists parents and teachers in their roles is based on that assessment.

This chapter seeks to address assessment and intervention with families in the context of developing partnerships between home and school, and to place the family into a broader and more developed context of social work practice theory. There is first of all a discussion of emergent research findings on the relation parents have to the determinants of effective education. The goals of more effective schooling and greater achievement emphasized in diverse educational reform movements are not possible without family support and involvement. However, beyond knowing that families are essential to education, one needs to understand the structural problems and the multiple risks experienced by most families today, particularly by families of children with disabilities. Without intervention and appropriate community support, these structural problems and multiple risks will prevent many children from achieving, coping, and maturing to their potential. In order to construct relationships between school and vulnerable families, the school social worker needs to have all the assessment and intervention abilities of a good family therapist.

SCHOOL EFFECTIVENESS AND PARENT INVOLVEMENT

That in order to be effective schools need to work as partners with parents is simply a fact of life, especially in light of the demands on today's schools and on families in our postindustrial society. Over the past thirty years, educators have had to become more involved in the socialization of vulnerable children, but they have not been formally prepared for this. In addition, evidence continues to emerge showing that schools cannot accomplish their mission effectively without developing significant, ongoing connections to families. Parents, the first educators of children, continue to have major influence on their later development. In research on national assesssment samples of adults, stimulating educative experiences in a person's family and school predicted adult knowledge more decisively than did adult motivation and effort. Those who had educative beginnings gained knowledge at faster rates as adults and attained cumulative advantages throughout their lives (Walberg and Tsai, 1983). Those who did not have such beginnings were correspondingly disadvantaged. An important corollary is that early work at the interface of family and school might reverse the otherwise inevitable disadvantages of some children. Through the formative years until the end of high school, parents nominally control 87 percent of the student's waking time. There are surprisingly large differences in family time investments in children. Even before school age, children differ by as much as five to one in the imputed value of parental care invested.

Findings from a poll of 568 parents, done for the national PTA, *Newsweek*, and Chrysler Corporation, suggest that the involvemnt of parents in school may be more extensive than orginally imagined. Seven in ten parents talk to their children about school, and more than a third help with homework every day. Seventeen percent talk at least weekly with their child's teacher, and 71 percent attend parent-teacher conferences (Oronevsky, 1990). Paradoxically, school social work experience does not seem to confirm this level of involvement for more vulnerable children. Kurtz's review of the literature points out that parent participation in public education would produce some notable benefits in terms of improved preschool pupil achievement, better parent emotional well-being, and increased child care skills (Kurtz, 1988). Such difference in parent involvement may go a long way in accounting for children's varying capacities to profit from schooling and other educational experiences.

EDUCATIONAL PRODUCTIVITY

Syntheses of 2,575 empirical studies of academic learning show that parents directly or indirectly influence the eight chief determinants of cognitive, affective, and behavioral learning (Walberg, 1984; Walberg and Lai, 1988). These determinants include four essential factors: student ability, student motivation, quality of instruction, and amount of instruction. Four indirect or supportive factors are the psychological climate of the class, academically simulating conditions in the home environment, characteristics of the student's peer group outside school, and, inversely, exposure to low-grade mass media, in particular, television.

Student ability and motivation and the amount and quality of instruction all appear necessary for classroom learning. Without a minimum level of each, the student learns little. Large amounts of instruction and high degrees of ability, for example, may count for little if students are unmotivated or instruction is unsuitable. The other determinants—the psychological climate of the classroom group, enduring affection and stimulation from adults at home, a peer group with academic interests, goals, and activities, and minimal exposure to low-grade television programs—influence learning in two ways. Students learn from them directly, and these factors indirectly benefit learning by raising student ability, motivation, and responsiveness to instruction. Other social and economic factors influence learning in school, but less directly. These factors, such as class size, financial expenditure per student, and private governance (independent or sectarian, in contrast to public control of schools), weakly correlate with learning, especially if the initial abilities of students are considered.

Improvements by parents and educators in the eight factors described above hold the best hope for improving learning. Because children spend so much time at home or under the nominal control of parents, it appears that altering home conditions and the relationship between homes and schools produces large effects on learning, particularly in the early grades. Analysis of the High School and Beyond national survey data shows that during the school year American high school students average about four or five hours of homework and about twenty-eight hours of television per week (Walberg and Shanahan, 1983). An obvious place where home and school come together is in the area of assigned homework, with the amount, quality, and usefulness potentially determined jointly by educator, parents, and students.

Home Environment

In addition to partnership on homework, school-parent programs to improve academic conditions in the home have an outstanding record of success in promoting achievement (Walberg, 1984). In twenty-nine controlled studies of the past decade, 91 percent of the comparisons favored children in such programs over nonparticipant groups. Although the average effect of school-parent programs—what might be called "the curriculum of the home"—on achievement was twice that of socioeconomic status, some programs had effects ten times as great. The programs appear to benefit older as well as younger students. Because few of the programs lasted more than a semester, the potential for programs that continue over the years of schooling is great.

This home "curriculum" would consist of informed parent-child conversations about everyday events; encouragement and discussion of leisure reading, monitoring and joint analysis of television viewing and peer activities, deferral of immediate gratifications to accomplish long-term goals such as school achievement, and expressions of affection and interest in the child as a person and in his or her academic achievements (Walberg, 1984). Some research suggests other roles for parents, such as audience for the child's work, home tutor, colearner with the child, school-program supporter, advocate before school boards and other officials, committee member, and paid school staff worker (Walberg, 1984).

CONCEPTION OF THE SCHOOL AS A COMMUNITY OF FAMILIES

From the origins of public education, schools in the United States have generally operated in relative isolation from their constituent families, thus protecting their functions from "interference." This isolation is counterproductive in situations of individual and family vulnerability or student difficulty in coping. As long as this isolation has been taken for granted, the school social worker's role has historically been to span the boundaries between schools and families as expeditiously as possible. In some cases the boundaries themselves have been challenged by school social workers and parents.

An alternative is to conceive of school as a community of families with teachers and parents in a socializing partnership with one another, having both shared and separate functions. Parents have challenged barriers to participations in numerous and ongoing experiments with parent-sponsored schools. The conception of school as a community of families is a major departure from conventional thinking and practice. However, it is a trend that, given the realities families and children experience, is now becoming very important.

School social workers have long used community organization skills to create a community (composed of families) around the learning process (Nebo, 1963). The results reinforce partnership and appear to generally enhance the effectiveness of each child's education. In the late 1960s Project Headstart, reflecting a general philosophy governing community action programs, was the first to initiate planned parent participation as an essential dimension of schooling. Schraft and Comer (1979), in a widely copied school model addressing inner city education (the "Comer" model), reflect on the experience of parent involvement in an impoverished community where parents were perceived as "unmotivated" or "hard to reach." They reviewed how social workers took the lead in developing activities that, over time, involved a community of parents in the schools. In their review of their experience in New Haven, Connecticut, there were three levels of parent participation. The first level comprised general activity geared to involving the majority of the parent body, such as potluck suppers and fun fairs. The second level was designed to involve parents specifically in the daily life of the school, as classroom assistants or as participants in workshops to make materials for teachers. The third level enabled parents to participate meaningfully in the decision-making process in the school. Parents might move from level to level, but Schraft and Comer caution against expecting involvement in the third level without much development of the first two levels over a relatively long period of time.

Adolfi-Morse (1982) applied the above concepts to her work in a school for emotionally disturbed children in Fairfax County, Virginia. The school, which served a wide geographic area with many ethnic differences, is conceived of as a community of families. Events such as back-to-school night, potluck dinners, and parent-teacher organization meetings are used to reinforce this concept. Parents of children with disabilities, who may have been less involved than others, were often able to find important roles for themselves with their children as they were making the school community work. Their involvement seemed to bring about a change in their children's estimate of their own roles.

More recently, one of the authors did qualitative research at Argonne, a parent-run provate school in Milan, Italy. The school is emblematic of a trend in many parts of the world toward a redeveloped concept of family solidarity. Children are admitted to the school on the condition that the parents agree to be involved with the school and its activities in a partnership in the education of their child. Educational goals are individualized for each pupil in a process that is shared by parent, pupil, and school.

The resultant goals build toward developmentally appropriate strengths and capacities of children, which are much broader than the academic. Some children need help in developing friendships; others need to develop more consistent work habits. The effect of one child's changing and developing positive qualities is felt by classmates in many different ways, and this diffusion of one child's change through the student community is reinforced by peer friendship networks. The same friendship networks are encouraged among parents. Most parents needed to overcome their fear and reluctance involved in becoming friends with and resources to each other. The normality of development with all of its pitfalls and small triumphs is the theme of the shared experience of systematically organized friendship networks. Each child (ages ranging from six through nineteen in three schools) attends class with teachers, but works with a tutor on individual goals geared to normal developmental stages. The "tutor" coordinates the educational program with the parents, the teachers, and another set of parents that is more experienced and has a child at the same grade level. This other couple is specifically delegated to assist the family through their friendship, support, and ability to be candid about their own struggles in being parents and the normality of developmental crisis. Tutors are trained to include the family in their picture of the child. When asked to describe a particular pupil, they would, without being asked, also describe the family situation. The emergent structure presents exciting possibilities for a very different conception of education. It is one that appears, allowing for growing pains, to be working well and producing good results. Parent involvement is estimated by the teachers at 90 percent. Both parents generally come to conference and involve themselves in school meetings, as they had agreed to do.

THE NECESSARY ARRANGEMENT OF RELATIONS BETWEEN FAMILY AND SCHOOL

There appears to be a necessary arrangement of relationships among families, other mediating systems, and societal institutions such as schools. Families cannot educate their children in a complex modern society without the assistance of schools, and schools cannot educate without the cooperation of families. Each can prevent the other from accomplishing its proper function. This is particularly true for vulnerable children and families. There is a necessary order in the relationship of family and school. Family functions as "educator" take place in a child's life prior to school functions. School functions exist to help the family carry out its prior functions in accordance with the needs and standards of society and the rights of members of the family.

Children are in a recognized position of vulnerability and require protection from their environments. They have a right to recieve adequate nurturance and socialization whenever possible in their own families. The community, often represented by the school, is obligated to ensure that families have all those aids—economic, social, educational, political, and cultural assistance—that they need to face all their responsibilities in a human way. It is not the role of the school to take away from families the child-rearing functions that families can perform on their own or in cooperative associations.

The relationship of the family unit to the school and the community can be expressed by three principles:

1. The family has primary functions in the care and socialization of its children. It has rights and responsibilities derived from this function. These responsibilities include the economic, social, educational, and cultural provision for the needs of its members. As such, the family is the basic social unit of society.

2. The school's primary functions are helping the family to accomplish its responsibilities and supplying certain cognitive instruction that the family cannot take on. The work of the family is always personal. Transactions *en famille* are expected to be based on affection and respect for the other person. Particular types of learning would be distorted if they excluded the personal dimension. In families this personal dimension is experienced and learned in work, worship, gender roles, respect for others in social relations, and respect for one's developing sexuality. When affection and respect break down, the partnership of home and school can be developed through social work services that assist the family in developing or redeveloping respect and affection among members.

3. A secondary function of the school (and in a broader sense, the community) is to monitor potential abridgment of rights of children as pupils and citizens when external conditions of society or internal conditions within the family make it impossible for the family to accomplish its primary function. This must be done, as in the first principle, without inappropriately abridging the family's exercise of those functions it is able to accomplish.

These principles involve a balance between family and school, an order and a defined relation between their respective functions. The increased awareness of the importance of effective families, the increasing numbers of vulnerable families, and the increasing school responsibility for the education of vulnerable children inevitably lead to the need for more integrated relationships between school and family. On the other hand, the development of school services closing the gap between family and school could pose a threat to family autonomy and effectiveness. The danger is that, in the face of the weakness of the family and the complexity of the child's problems, schools might attempt to *substitute* for family functions. This never works well. When services take over, rather than empower families to carry out their duties, they limit the effectiveness of the partnership. Schools need to redefine their relationship with families so that true collaboration emerges with all families so that vulnerable children in vulnerable families are helped to make the most of what school has to offer. Balancing the need for collaboration is the need to protect the rights of children to appropriate family nurturance and socialization. Both need to be done in such a way that the family is appropriately supported in carrying out its responsibility.

FAMILY CONDITIONS AND FAMILY RISKS

The conditions families and children experience often make a mutually supportive relationship between families and schools difficult, but also further necessitate the relationship-building role between home and school in which the school social worker is the key player. This is particularly important for children with disabilities, whose high demands for caregiving, often felt in isolation from community support systems, add to the normal stresses encountered by all families. The literature of risk is useful in conceptualizing social conditions that demand greater development of support to manage losses and buffer stresses. Severe family stresses and losses are ordinary experiences for many children. A recent review suggests that among white children born since 1980, the percentage spending all or part of their childhood with one parent due to parental death, divorce, or being born out of wedlock is projected to rise approximately 50 percent by 2020; the corresponding percentage for African-American children is projected to rise to 80 percent (Hernandez, 1994). Even parents of children under age six predominantly balance the demands of participating in the workforce with child care responsibilities (Hanson and Carta, 1995; Children's Defense Fund, 1994). The unmarried teen birth rate increased by 119 percent between 1969 to 1991 (Children's Defense Fund, 1994). Children of these younger parents are at risk for cognitive, emotional, and physical difficulties (Smith, 1994).

Poverty is associated with great risks for children. These risks are greater for single-parent families and persons with lower job skills. In addition, the gap between relatively well off and poor people is increasing, with children the largest age group caught in poverty. Children born in poverty have their risks compounded: illness, family stress, lack of social support, health and environmental risks (Hanson and Carta, 1995; Schorr, 1988). Further risks are experienced by children in families where there is substance abuse or violence (Hanson and Carta, 1995). On the other hand, certain children, often described as "resilient," seem to maintain cognitive skills, curiosity, enthusiasm, goal-setting behavior, and high self-esteem and appear less vulnerable to some of these adverse environmental factors (Hanson and Carta, 1995). In some instances, family characteristics, such as rule setting, respect for individuality and parental responsiveness can "inoculate" children against adverse environmental factors (Bradley, Whiteside, Mundfrom, Casey, and Pope, 1994). Social support from the larger community or kinship group can also act as a buffer (Keltner, 1990). Usually a resilient child will identify some significant adult in their environment who encouraged their positive growth. Such family or extended family arrangements, which can occur naturally and in spite of very difficult circumstances, can also be constructed and encouraged with the assistance of professionals, such as school social workers.

The Child with Disabilities and the Family

All families experience some stress; however, families of children with disabilities face special levels of stress, frequently related to increased child care demands. As a result, there is an extensive literature on the stresses that disabilities place on families. These are examined to deepen our understanding of what *all* families encounter.

The special needs of a child with a disability levy a heavy physical, financial, and emotional tax on the family. Most obvious are the financial burdens (Moore and McLaughlin, 1988). There are also needs for information, particularly medical and diagnostic information (D'Amato and Yoshida, 1991; Bailey, Blasco, and Simeonson, 1992). Moreover, parents must develop the skill to manage the specialized services needed; otherwise these services might seriously intrude on other aspects of the child's development, sense of mastery, and self-esteem and on the family's ability to function independently. Reviews of research point out increased divorce and suicide rates, a higher incidence of child abuse, increased financial difficulties, and a variety of emotional manifestations, such as depression, anger, guilt, and anxiety in these families. Different types of disabling conditions may create different types of secondary problems. But all such conditions are exacerbated with increased age and caregiving demands as the child develops physically and emotionally (Gallagher, Beckman, and Cross, 1983; Hanson and Hanline, 1990; Harris and McHale, 1989; McLindon, 1990). Families of children with difficulty in communication (Frey, Greenberg, and Fewell, 1989), delay in developmental tasks, difficult temperament, need for constant supervision, or repetitive behavior patterns all experience increased family stress.

Parents of children with serious permanent disabilities go through a mourning process that includes all the usual stages of anger, guilt, depression, and grief over loss of the "ideal child who never came." A realistic acceptance of the child may be reached. Yet chronic sorrow is often experienced in the day-to-day struggle to meet the needs of the child while maintaining personal self-esteem, integrity as a family, and a meaningful place in the community (Bristol and Gallagher, 1982; Olshansky, 1962; Lachney, 1982; Turnbull and Turnbull, 1978; Bernier, 1990). The initial grieving may return, continue, or intensify when the child is unable to accomplish developmental milestones adequately or at the prescribed times (Davis, 1987).

Intense and unrelieved involvement in caregiving for a special needs child can put severe pressure on parents and siblings. If family members cannot adaptively share the caring role, the result is often rejection of the child or a split in the family into caregivers and noncaregivers, with the child empowered only by the disability itself. The effect on spousal relations can be dramatic. Increased caregiving demands and perhaps excessive feelings of personal responsibility for a disability may cause parental roles to split into caregiving and noncaregiving specialties. One parent (often a woman) assumes the caregiving role to the (often voluntary) exclusion of the other parent. Without constructing shared responsibility together, the stress becomes overwhelming for the caregiver or can lead to other pathological relationship outcomes. The effect for parents of such an overadequate-underadequate relationship is to seriously split and distort the spousal relationship and to carry the distortion to the siblings, generating caregiving and noncaregiving specialists. Such families often need professional help to balance caregiving over the entire family and to use the support of other informal or formal caregiving systems in the community. For various reasons connected with feelings of personal responsibility, families of children with disabilities may have real difficulty aaccepting help from the outside and suffer profound isolation at the time they most need workable social relations with friends, kin, and neighbors as well as extended community resources. Such informal support can be a source of respite care, advice, information, and material assistance, as well as empathy and emotional support. This support can be a buffer against the stresses of child care (Beckman, 1991; Beckman and Pokorni, 1988), but it still may not be sufficient to prevent parental dysfunction (Seybold, Flitz, and MacPhee, 1991).

Tavormina and Associates noted four major parental styles of adapting to the reality of raising a child with disabilities:

1. One parent emotionally distances himself or herself from the child, leaving the care of the child entirely up to the other parent, and concentrates entirely on outside activities unrelated to the child, such as job and organizations.

2. The parents draw together in rejecting the child. The child in this type of family is most apt to be institutionalized, regardless of the severity of his or her disability.
3. The parents make the child the center of their universe, subordinating all of their own desires and pleasures to the service of the child with disabilities.
4. The parents join in mutual support of the child, and of each other, but maintain a sense of their own identities and create a life as close to "normal" as possible (Bristol and Gallagher, 1982).

The relations of such parents with formal social support systems, such as schools, may become complicated. Despite an assumed community sanction to assist families in their functions, formal social support does not seem to have a significant effect in reducing stress in parents of young children with developmental delays (Beckman, 1991; Beckman and Pokorni, 1988). Indeed, parent-professional relations can be a source of additional stress (Gallagher et al., 1983). These paradoxical findings challenge school social workers to assist families to construct appropriate relationships with formal resources, which they desperately need, without distorting their own internal relations. Bristol and Gallagher (1982) suggest a number of different ways schools can develop effective partnerships with parents. Programs can be made more flexible, with individualized family plans, the establishment of meaningful parent roles, and the involvement of the father as well as the mother. Programs should focus on goals important to the family and should expect something of the parents. Parents often need help to see the importance of the often small gains made. The school social worker might help the parents develop their own support network of friends and relatives or assist them in building an expanded network.

THE FAMILY AND ITS INSTITUTIONAL ECOLOGY

There is increasing evidence that we are far less independent than we ever imagined. We depend on one another first of all through family units, and also through informal support systems, networks of friends and neighbors, and membership in informal groups in the workplace. Family, friends, work groups, and neighbors can be "mediating systems" that connect and stand between public and private life. These systems help us relate to the necessary institutional worlds of modern life, such as schools, workplaces, and health care organizations, and they supply the preconditions for our doing and acting in a fully human sense. Family, including the extended family, the most important of the mediating systems, has been expected to contain within itself the primary means to supply human needs. Although the family still is delegated this mission in modern society, the family's own support systems or structural adequacy are often sorely lacking. The combination of family, informal support systems, and formal institutional structure constitutes a network that allows each person to cope with the complexity of modern society. Coping and adaptation are clearly related to one's access to and ability to call upon and use such support systems. The comparative social isolation of the modern family, together with breaks in generational linkages, may cut off access to support and collective experience and create social pathologies. When a society is composed of relatively privatized family units, close connections with friends, extended family, and neighbors can deteriorate.

School is the essential institution in the institituional ecology of a family with children. Schools may not accomplish their particular missions without their own connections with families and informal support systems. Mismatches often occur between a social instituition, such as health care, education, or justice, and the needs of the school's clientele of individuals in families. Hospitals, courts, and schools can forget that their clientele are members of families, but they do so at their own risk. The renewed stress on the family has led institutions to begin shifting orientation from clients as individuals or consumers to the family unit.

THE SCHOOL SOCIAL WORK ROLE: FINDINGS FROM RESEARCH

A good fit exists between the school's need for a specialist in promoting a partnership with families and the school social work role as it has emerged in the research of the previous two decades. In a period of great role specialization in the schools, the social worker's role has remained quite broad. School social workers are invloved with pupils, teachers, parents, and the broader community and use methodoligies as diverse as casework, group work, family intervention, consultation, and community organization. Practice theory in school social work has generally pointed out a broad role linked to the mission of the public school. The constants is this picture are the person-environment perspective of social work and the mission of the school. The match between the two in the context of changing societal conditions allows for a flexible use of methodology in the service of the broadly conceived educational process.

Studies of the school social worker's role have found a similar richness in actual practice. Building on the traditional focus on schoolchildren and their families, the areas of consultation to administrators, resource development and community change, group work, and general consultation with and on behalf of students are very much a part of the school social work role (Chavkin, 1985; Constable, Kuzmickiate, and Volkmann, 1997). The breadth of this role definition is perceived and agreed upon not only by school social workers but also by school administrators who work with social workers (Constable and Montgomery, 1985).

CHOOSING THE UNIT OF ATTENTION

The social worker is in the school to help family, school, and community work with one another and with the pupil, and to help the pupil find his or her own resources and make use of what the family, school, and community have to offer. To accomplish this, the most important part of the role of the school social worker is choosing the unit of attention, discovering where to focus and what to do to enable the best match to take place between pupil-family needs and school-community resources. The unit of attention should be the point of most effective change, a point or set of points in the systems where, if change takes place, other positive changes will also become possible. The social worker may work with a pregnant adolescent and her family on issues of planning and coping with the pregnancy, with her teachers on issues of inclusion in an appropritae instructional program, and with community resources to provide appropriate child care—all so the adolescent can continue in school through graduation. In another community, the social worker may work with other combinations of the groups in this picture. In another, work with individual children and families may be the major focus. In another, the school social worker may spend time developing a truancy program or out-of-school resources for latchkey children. Again, the emphasis would be on helping teachers to be more effective with socially vulnerable children. The role as developed differs somewhat from school to school, and these differences are geared to the circumstances of each school and to agreements worked out between the social worker and the school administrators. Whatever the major thrust of the school social worker's role, the components of working with pupils, teachers, families, and community need to be there. Methods of working with each of these systems have been clearly established in social work education for many years, and over the past two decades much theory development has focused on integrating these essential components.

Using this framework, each unit of attention determines its own special demands on the social worker. Choosing the most effective focus, in the context of the time available, is a complex professional task for the school social worker. However, it is by no means a random process. There is a certain logical progression to it, reflecting principles of efficiency and family partnership with the school. A case study follows, to highlight each unit of attention described and to relate it to the school-family constellation.

The School Program as a Unit of Attention

The first unit of attention of the school social worker is the school program offered to pupils. Here the school social worker may work with others in the school to develop programs for particular groups, such as pregnant adolescents or children being mainstreamed from special education programs, or for individual students. In individual circumstances the social worker will work as a consultant to teachers. Many times, developing a program or consulting with teachers is enough to accomplish desired change. The change in the classroom affords the pupil an opportunity to accomplish learning and social developmental tasks. Nothing further is needed in this case. Extending intervention to the parents or pupil would be unnecessary and therefore intrusive. On the other hand, when intervention with parents and pupil is necsssary, it should first of all be built on continuing consultation with the teachers and other resources in the school.

> Jimmy B. is a seven-year-old boy with learning disabilities whose parents were going through a divorce. Jimmy was having great difficulty staying on task in class. He cried readily and was very dependent on adults in his environment. His classroom teacher, Ms. T., found him quite difficult and believed that he was simply avoiding the expectations of her class. His resource room teacher, Mr. G., saw more of what Jimmy could do in individual sessions but seemed to be protecting him from the expectations of Ms. T.'s class. The social worker, in consultation with both teachers and after observing Jimmy in class, saw a child who was withdrawing from learning tasks, probably because of generally slow development and inconsistent, sometimes conflicting school expectations. In cooperation with both teachers, tasks that could be expected of Jimmy in both classes were worked out. Both teachers developed a better understanding of the problems by sharing perspectives and by gaining a better understanding of the relation of his parents' divorce to Jimmy's efforts to concentrate. Both agreed on a program of support to encourage more mature functioning with gradually increased expectations of more independent functioning. The social worker agreed to contact the home, helpthe parents understand the educational goals,and solicit their help in supporting the new plan, especially when helping with Jimmy's homework.

The Family as a Unit of Attention

The second unit of attention is the family of the pupil. In harmony with the work begun by the teacher, the potential alliance of the school with the family may need to become explicit. With many students, contact with the family and some ongoing work with teachers is enough to accomplish a goal. In any case, the family's involvement is usually necessary before going on to the next step.

> In her contact with Jimmy's home, the social worker learned that his parents were at the point of seperation. Mrs. B., a clerk, felt very close to Jimmy, who was her youngest child. She had always enjoyed his sweet and babyish qualities, whereas his father tended to have high expectations of him. This difference was a cause of marital difficulty. Mrs. B. had relied on Mr. B. to set limits and was having difficulty setting controls of her own. The social worker had several contacts with Mrs. B. and one with both parents together. She helped them see some of the effects of their conflict on Jimmy and referred the couple to

a family service agency for more extensive family counseling. Both parents became concerned about the extent to which Jimmy was reacting to their difficulties. Mrs. B. worked out an agreement so that she could be reached by phone away from her place of employment, and building on this, Mrs. B. was able to work more closely with the school regarding expectations of Jimmy. Mr. B. was willing to support this work. Both parents requested that Jimmy be seen by the social worker, and the social worker agreed to do this, providing she could remain in contact with both parents regarding developments at home and school. In her observations of Jimmy and in her contacts with the parents, the social worker noticed that Jimmy himself drew out either protectiveness or rejection from people around him in the same way he had experienced this division from his parents. This is not unusual in children experiencing marital conflict. She decided to develop a contract between the parents and the teachers so that their efforts to work together and set common rules and expectations were supported.

Because of the parents' divisiveness over Jimmy the worker was careful to see them together in a joint session. She had assessed the role of Jimmy in the couple's dynamics and did not want the contract between parents and teachers to accelerate the couple's division, but to be a first step toward their getting help. She was careful to focus on Jimmy but knew that in working out details of the agreement with them, she was bringing them to a first step in dealing with their marital issues. While the parents' differences in relation to Jimmy came out immediately in the joint session, the worker did not probe into the couple's relationship or attempt to do marital counseling. Within the concrete framework of an agreement with the school over Jimmy, she patiently guided them to an initial agreement that included ongoing communication between the social worker and the couple. The agreement set expectations of gradually more mature functioning on Jimmy's part but, with the worker being in touch with both parents, also allowed for some shifts in Mom's and Dad's relationships with Jimmy. As the worker communicated with the parents over the ensuing months, she was able to help them differentiate their issues with each other from their parenting of Jimmy. Later, both were able to begin marital counseling in a community agency to which she had referred them.

In the above example the focus remained on Jimmy and how his parents could assist his maturation. The focus was safe enough for the parents to process many of their issues with each other, to differentiate Jimmy's needs from theirs, and eventually to get help with their marriage. The work of the school social worker with both parents needed to be as sophisticated as any family therapist. Actually, if the focus of the work were mainly Jimmy's maturation there would be little difference between the worker's work with the family and therapy in an outside agency, except that, in Jimmy's case, the concreteness of the focus on Jimmy's school difficulties provided a safe metaphor for the personal and family work that needed to be done. The worker had been prepared and was ready to assess the relation of the parents' dynamics as a couple to Jimmy's maturation and to school dynamics. She knew that intervention with the parents on Jimmy's behalf would inevitably deal with their dynamics as a couple. She could help them maximize their new awareness of this situation. Essentially, she had translated a knowledge of developmental and family dynamics to a knowledge of school tasks as a multilevel stage for these dynamics to be played out and to some extent ameliorated.

Granted the diversity of units of attention for the school social worker, what has centrality is (a) the learning process of the student, Jimmy, and (b) the family and school worlds that surround Jimmy's learning process. These family and school worlds are often quite dysfunctional in relation to the child's attempts at active coping. To understand this more deeply, one must consider some paradoxes within the educational process itself. The action of the learner is inevitably central to this process. A whole environmental world, from parent through school secretary, janitor, school psychologist, social worker, teacher, and principal, waits to see whether and how Jimmy will engage. When necessary, the social worker moves between all the parts of this world to help it work for Jimmy, and to help find and share the best of himself to work with the environment and mature appropriately. The more the social worker can adapt methodology to the particular needs in the situation and use diverse approaches that help Jimmy make sense of his world and discover what he can offer to it, the better. But ultimately Jimmy does the work, and multiplied by each student in the school, the educational process succeeds or fails on this. On the other hand, from Jimmy's perspective the learning process in school is a central developmental event. If he fails and denies its importance, even to himself, it is no less important an event. Buried, in a thousand efforts to compensate in different ways by doing other things, is the consciousness that he has failed in this social task. He will repeatedly try to succeed in his own way until he is discouraged and retreats in confusion. His surrounding world must help him find a match between "his own way" and the ways of the school, but the task for Jimmy and for the school demands flexibility, experimentation, and support for the process until some match is made. Educational tasks are so important and so central to the maturation of many children that there may be no more powerful way to help Jimmy grow. This will be particularly true if his family world can participate in and support the process.

The Pupil as a Unit of Attention

The third unit of attention is the pupil. Whatever changes take place in the classroom environment and in what the school is able to offer, the pupil needs to utilize them and to deal with personal issues of change. Building on the sound base of a connection with home and school, the combination of small home, school, and pupil changes is often much more powerful than an intensive focus on a single factor.

Jimmy was willing to see the social worker after his parents discussed it with him. He enjoyed working with clay, making elaborate log houses and little people, but could get teary-eyed if the social worker made any association in the play sessions with home or with a mother or father. He eventually was able to talk about his feelings regarding school. The social worker was able to involve Jimmy in the contract with his teachers and his parents on assignments and expectations and reinforce improvements with him. She decided that she would go slowly with Jimmy, helping him deal with the positive changes in the classroom and home that she had been encouraging.

The Community as a Unit of Attention

A fourth unit of attention is the agencies and resources in the community. The community provides a variety of resources, such as child care, health care, employment, and so on, that may make it possible to achieve certain goals. In most cases, the social worker would have difficutly making the connection without first establishing a firm base with school, family, and pupil.

Jimmy's parents requested marital counseling at a family service agency. The school social worker collaborated with the counselor they were seeing. Jimmy was clearly triangulated and inappropriately involved with the marital issues, and only with considerable effort were his parents able to refocus their discussion. Both parents were concerned about Jimmy's reaction to their problems, but the school's work with Jimmy gave them insights that enabled them to get to issues more related to their actual marital problems.

In addition to helping people to use existing resources, frequently the school social worker is in a position to develop resources in the community. An example is the use of a student volunteer in a park system to help an extremely isolated thirteen-year-old move into group game activities and eventually get reinvolved in the school environment, which he had not attended for many years. Social workers frequently advocate for the client to secure services or act as the coordinator of a network of services.

The above example illustrates a logical progression, moving from the pupil's school and family world to the pupil. An adolescent who asks for help may have fears of getting the family involved, particularly when his or her independence from the family is precarious or secrets are involved. Nevertheless, it is generally better practice to skillfully involve the family early in the helping process, in ways that will be helpful to the pupil and with the pupil's involvement. The longer one waits, the more difficult this involvement will be. Often the adolescent wants the family involved at some level, but does not know how that could be accomplished and is afraid. In the case of a secret, such as pregnancy, they have to find ways to tell the parents what is happening, but the social worker needs to be available to assist adolescent and parents to process the implications of the situation in as nondestructive a way as possible. In the author's experience with adolescents, they have always assented to the social worker's contact with the parents when it became a matter of the school social workers giving the student the best professional help possible, when they understood that the contact would be managed so as not to be harmful to them, and when they were involved in planning for their parents' involvement, including how the request for help would be framed with the parents and what information would be given. Many serious ethical and practice issues are involved in such contacts, and it may take a number of sessions with the adolescent to develop a workable plan. These contacts, managed differently to accomodate different concerns and realities, have always been fruitful, even with severely troubled parents. Often the act of making a connection where there is a considerable level of fear is a tremendous impetus for change for both parents and adolescents.

Final Notes

In actual practice the social worker will work with a variety of units of attention at the same time, and the focus of the social worker on those units of attention will also change over time. Helen Wolkow's case illustration in chapter 13 is emblematic of the type of long-term work with child and family frequently encountered in school social work. Over a period of five years the social worker worked at different times with Alan's school situation as it changed and developed, with Alan as he coped with and adapted to his own difficulties in learning and his reactions to his parents' divorce and mother's remarriage, and with Alan's family, mother, father, and stepfather as their own changes unfolded. This practice is quite different in several very important ways from freestanding practice in the community, family therapy, or work in a mental health clinic.

Practice in the community usually focuses on a set of problems. The family therapist assists parents and child in session to deal with their relationship issues, and when there is sufficient progress, the therapeutic relationship is ended. This gives intervention and episodic flavor but also limits much of what can be done to in-session work. Problems usually have become fairly serious by the time the family identifies them and asks for help. In Alan's case, the school social worker's relationship with Alan and with his parents continued in different ways through Alan's learning difficulties in early grades, suicidal ideation during his parents' divorce, postdivorce adaptation, and later struggles to learn better social skills with other children. Since Alan's relationship with the school continued through all of this, the social worker was available for direct early intervention to the point five years later of doing secondary prevention. The social worker and the teacher were the first to know about the suicidal ideation. The social worker was able to respond to this crisis with Alan and his parents at a time when his parents were still in denial. Ths school social worker had many intervention options. She adapted her intervention only to what Alan and his family needed and no more. The intervention was both minimally intrusive and an extremely efficient use of her time and energy in relation to the outcome. The centrality of the school's support for Alan and for the family meant that skilled help could be given in an unobtrusive way, related to the normal developmental tasks Alan and his family were dealing with, but also at the point where they would be able to invest their greatest energy. In Alan's case the family was for the most part unable to use the help of an outside practitioner or community agency but worked fairly well with the school social worker. The worker was able to involve the family as much as possible but was also respectful of the fears, particularly of the mother, that impeded deeper involvement. Even without much involvement of community agency practitioners and with a less intensive level of family involvement, the social worker helped Alan and his family work through a tumultuous period in their lives with a good outcome. Much of the work was accomplished without working directly with Alan, and this approach was less intrusive, and more efficient, than what a community-based practitioner might have achieved in the same situation. In the period of five years first through fifth grade Alan learned to adapt to school learning tasks, worked through his suicidal feelings, developed social skills and friendships with other children, retained a relationship with his father, and also maintained an acceptable relationship with his mother and his stepfather. A wide range of help was offered in a minimally intrusive way, using Alan's and his family's own adaptive efforts to cope with the life tasks connected with experienceing learning disabilities in the early school years and during a difficult period of family transition. The ordinary "work" of a social institution, the school, was used to enhance the positive coping skills developed by Alan and his family.

The new aspirations for excellence in education cannot be satisfied without family involvement. Family units, however, have become generally more vulnerable to multiple social pressures. School social workers have a wealth of experience in working with vulnerable families and vulnerable children in the context of the educational process. These skills can be applied to the development of partnerships between school and parents, not only for the most vulnerable, but for the general condition of family vulnerability experienced today, a vulnerability that can overwhelm efforts to achieve excellence.

REFERENCES

Adolfi-Morse, B. 1982. Implementing parent involvement and participation in the educational process and the school community. In R.T. Constable, and J.P. Flynn, (eds.). *School social work: Practice and research perspectives* (pp. 231–234). Homewood, IL: Dorsey.

Bailey, D., Blasco, P., and Simeonson, R. 1992. Needs expressed by mothers and fathers of young children with disabilities. *American Journal on Mental Retardation* 97:1–10.

Beckman, P. 1991. Comparison of mother's and father's perceptions of the effect of young children, with and without disabilities. *American Journal on Mental Retardation* 95:585–595.

Beckman, P., and Pokorni, J. 1988. A longitudinal study of families or preterm infants: Changes in stress and support over the first two years. *Journal of Special Education* 22:55–65.

Bernier, J. 1990. Parental adjustment to a disabled child: a family system perspective. *Families in Society* 71:589–596.

Bradley, R. H., Whiteside, L., Mundfrom, D. J., Casey, P. H., and Pope, S. K. 1994. Early indicators of resilience and their relations to experiences in the home environments of low birthweight, premature children living in poverty. *Child Development* 65:346–360.

Bristol, M. M., and Gallagher, J. J., 1982. A family focus for intervention. In C. T. Ramey, and P. L. Trohanis (eds.). *Finding and educating high risk and handicapped infants* (pp. 137–161). Baltimore: University Park Press.

Chavkin, N. F. 1985. School social practice: A reappraisal. *Social Work in Education* 8:1.

Children's Defense Fund. 1994. *The state of America's children 1994*. Washington, DC: Author.

Constable, R., Kuzmickaite, D., and Volkmann, L. 1997. The Indiana school social worker: Parameters of the emerging professional role. Paper given at the Indiana State Association of School Social Worker annual conference, October 21.

Constable, R. T., and Montgomery, E. 1985. Perceptions of the social worker's role. *Social Work in Education* 7(4):244–257.

D'Amato, E., and Yoshida, R. 1991. Parental needs: An educational life cycle perspective. *Journal of Early Intervention* 15:246–254.

Davis, B. 1987. Disability and grief. *Social Casework* 68:352–357.

Frey, K., Greenberg, M., and Fewell, R. 1989. Stress and coping among parents of handicapped children: A multidimensional approach. *American Journal on Mental Retardation* 95:240–249.

Gallagher, J. J., Beckman, P., and Cross, A. H. 1983. Families of handicapped children: Sources of stress and its alleviation. *Exceptional Children* 50(1):10–18.

Germain, C. G. 1982. An ecological perspective on social work in the schools. In R. T. Constable and J. P. Flynn (eds.). *School social work: Practice and research perspectives*. Homewood, IL: Dorsey.

Hanson, M. J., and Carta, J. J. 1995. Addressing the challenges of families with multiple risks. *Exceptional Children* 62(3):201–212.

Hanson, M. J., and Hanline, M. 1990. Parenting a child with a disability: A longitudinal study of parental stress and adaptation. *Journal of Early Intervention* 14:234–248.

Harris, V., and McHale, S. 1989. Family life problems, daily caregiving activities, and the psychological well being of mothers of mentally retarded children. *American Journal on Mental Retardation* 94:231–239.

Hernandez, D. J. 1994. Children's changing access to resources: A changing perspective. *Society for Research in Child Development Social Policy Report* 8(1):1–23.

Keltner, B. 1990. Family characteristics of preschool social competence among black children in a headstart program. *Child Psychiatry and Human Development* 21(2): 95–108.

Kurtz, P. D.1988. Social work services to parents: Essential to pupils at risk. *Urban Education* 22(4):444–457.

Lachney, M. E. 1982. Understanding families of the handicapped: A critical factor in the parent-school relationship. In R. T. Constable and J. P. Flynn (eds.). *School social work: Practice and research perspectives.* Homewood, IL: Dorsey.

McLindon, S. 1990. Mother's and father's reports of the effects of a young child with special needs on the family. *Journal of Early Intervention* 14:249–259.

Moore, J., and McLaughlin, J. 1988. Medical costs associated with children with disabilities or chronic illness. *Topics in Early Childhood Special Education* 8:98–105.

Nebo, J. 1963. The social worker as community organizer. *Social Work* 8:99–105.

Olshansky, S. 1962. Chronic sorrow: A response to having mentally defective children. *Social Casework* 43:190–192.

Ordonevsky, P. 1990. Parents report high involvement in school. *USA Today*, March 5.

Schorr, L. B. 1988. *Within our reach.* NY: Doubleday.

Schraft, C. M., and Comer, J. P. 1979. Parent participation and urban schools. *School Social Work Quarterly* 1(4):309–326.

Seybold, J., Flitz, J., and MacPhee, D. 1991. Relation of social support to the self-perceptions of mothers with delayed children. *Journal of Community Psychology* 19:29–36.

Smith, T. M. 1994. Adolescent pregnancy. In R. J. Simeonson (ed.). *Risk, resilience, and prevention: Promoting the wellbeing of all children.* Baltimore: Brookes.

Turnbull, A. P., and Turnbull, H. R. 1978. *Parents speak out: Views from the other side of the two-way mirror.* Columbus, OH: Merrill.

Walberg, H. J. 1984. Improving the productivity of America's schools. *Educational Leadership* 41(8):19–27.

Walberg, H. J., and Lai, J. S. 1988. Meta-analytic effects for policy. In G. J. Cizek (ed.). *Handbook of educational policy.* San Diego: Academic Press.

Walberg, H. J., and Shanahan, T. 1983. High school effects on individual students. *Educational Researcher* 64:75–92.

Walberg, H. J., and Tsai, S. L. 1983. "Matthew effects" in education. *American School Research Journal* 20:359–373.

CHAPTER 15

Classroom Observation:
An Instrument for Assessment

David Sanders
School Social Worker, Macon-Piatt Special Education District, Illinois

- Teaching Styles and Classroom Dynamics
- The Classroom Observation Form

Classroom observation is a key assessment tool of the school social worker. In order to decide on the unit of assessment the worker must understand the educational process in a concrete way. School social workers cannot understand a student's educational experience in any other frame of reference until they understand the concrete interaction that takes place between teacher and child in the context of a class group. When this is understood, assessment becomes somewhat quicker and more effective, and positive consultation with teachers becomes possible.

TEACHING STYLES AND
CLASSROOM DYNAMICS

The experienced social worker knows that differences in *teaching style* can profoundly affect students' development and learning. Teaching styles differ from one teacher to another, but within a somewhat limited range of possibilities. Each teacher develops a personal teaching style, compatible with his or her personality, that generally works for certain kinds of students. Some teachers, for example, have a no-nonsense, limit-setting style that lets students know exactly where they stand. Other teachers are less directive, more accepting of difference, but less clear about their expectations. These styles will have different effects on students. At best, the students who do well with one style may do less well with another. Good, experienced teachers may have more than one style, indeed a repertoire of teaching styles to match the needs of different students. They may vary their styles with certain students without undermining their effectiveness with the rest of the class. They may keep students on task in different ways, use other members of the class group to help a student, or manipulate rewards in different ways.

An experienced social worker also gets to know *classroom dynamics*. Having some formal preparation in group dynamics, the social worker learns to apply this knowledge to the classroom. Just as teachers are different, so is each class different in the dynamics of interaction between its members and the effect of these dynamics on individual students. Group contagion among students with certain behavior problems is particularly challenging to the teacher and dangerous for the educational process. Frequently teachers have no formal training in dealing with the dynamics of the class as a group, and so the problem is particularly disabling.

Understanding how teaching styles and classroom dynamics interact, the social worker needs to examine both in relation to individual students, who may be less responsive to a particular teaching style, or who may become negative targets of classroom dynamics. This examination is at best a prelude to a more developed understanding of alternative ways of working with classroom dynamics or the needs of individual students. This understanding is necessary for consultation and educational planning.

To acquire this skill, the school social worker needs to spend many hours unobtrusively observing classes. The teacher's permission to do this must be received. Teachers will grant permission willingly only if they see the observation as supportive and helpful to them, as a part of team problem solving, or as a part of a consultative relationship in which teacher and social worker put their heads together to help a student and to assist the teacher to be helpful. Some teachers will resist having school social workers in their classes. Social workers often find themselves beginning with the more personally secure members of the teaching faculty until their confidence and positive reputation increases. As the social worker begins to understand teaching styles and classroom dynamics through observation, work with teachers and students will go more quickly.

The school social worker needs an objective way of understanding the often complex interactions in a classroom and its effect on individual students. The instrument described in this chapter provides a way to measure the behavior of individual students in a classroom context. It provides a useful foundation for a report to the multidisciplinary team but also can be an excellent vehicle for consultation with teachers, helping them match their repertoire of teaching skills to the needs of the classroom situation and the individual students at the same time.

Classroom observations are also used when evaluating children with dysfunctional classroom behaviors for eligibility to receive special services, when assisting physicians who are diagnosing attention deficit disorders or measuring the effectiveness of a treatment plan, and when documenting the results of a specific classroom intervention strategy. It is important to know how the target student compares to a particular criterion: for example, he was "aggressive" three times more often than the average student in the room, or his "on task" performance went from 58 to 82 percent after beginning a medication regime, or his "off task" behavior dropped from 32 to 18 percent after a new classroom management plan was implemented. This kind of precise information gives practitioners confidence in their decisions and helps them make good decisions.

But classroom observations do not usually produce this kind of precision or uniformity. Typically, an observer—most often a school psycholgist, social worker, administrator, or supervisor—arranges to visit a classroom, sits in as unobtrusive a position as possible, observes as long as her schedule permits, and then departs with notes to assess what has happened. The ensuing staffing report goes something like this: "He appeared to be off task much of the time. He fidgeted around a lot in his seat and fiddled with objects in his desk. He got up and moved around the room quite a bit and bothered his neighbor many times. He was certainly more active than the rest of the students."

This format has served well enough, usually because of the integrity of the participants and the needs of the process, but mostly because there were few alternatives. Where this anecdotal and essentially casual approach fails is in its objectivity, reliability, and precision.

It is not objective because it allows the observer too much latitude, either intended, coincidental, or subliminal: What, precisely, is "off task" behavior? How are "fidgeting" and "bothering others" interpreted? And is the observer too much influenced by peripheral issues that may distort the conclusion? For instance, is he or she under pressure from administrators to "do something" with a troublesome student? Is the observer's relationship with the classroom teacher too close, or strained? No matter how mature and professional we think we are, we often respond, sometimes unwittingly, to subtle and disquieting pressures. And in the absence of an objective and standardized observation procedure, they are often difficult to resist.

And reliability? Can the observation process be duplicated, either by new personnel or by the same professional at another time and place, with enough consistency and uniformity to produce meaningful results that can be fairly compared? Criteria for such classroom behaviors as "fidgeting," "bothering others," and being "off task" were mentioned earlier as examples that can have various meanings. This lack of a common reference base can result in misleading conclusions and poor understanding of critical classroom behaviors. Can we expect decision makers to have any faith in our conclusions when our methods are so varied and haphazard?

And precision is totally lacking. How much more "off task" was Billy than Joey? Was it enough to be significant? And how much more "on task" is Tommy after starting his medication? A lot? Quite a bit? These terms are not helpful and do not build confidence. To ameliorate the present state of confusion and uncertainty with this important diagnostic tool, and to give it some uniformity, consistency, and definition this chapter suggests an observational procedure.

THE CLASSROOM OBSERVATION FORM

The procedure itself is nothing more than the well established, universally accepted timed-interval technique. But to provide a framework for collecting, organizing, standardizing, and presenting the data, the classroom observation form is introduced. (See figure 1.)

The first line of the form has spaces for all pertinent identifying information: the student's name, grade, teacher, and school and the date. Next, the legend gives brief explanations of the four critical student behaviors that will be observed (on task; off task, passive; off task, active; off task, severe), as well as two important observations about the classroom (group on task; transitions). Starting time, finishing time, notation interval, and observer's identification are noted on the next line.

Conduct the process as follows: First, complete all preliminary consultations with the teacher, administrator, parent, or physician to legitimize the observation. Then, confer again with the classroom teacher to set a date and time, and during these conferences emphasize that you will be measuring time on task and that lessons should be presented as usual and the classroom management plan followed—no special changes should be made just for the observation.

Tell the teacher that you will be observing two students: the target student and a sample student. The sample student should be of the same sex and selected at random from the seating chart. Allow the teacher to veto your selection if he or she feels the student you have choosen has similar symptoms (there are often several students in a classroom with attention deficit disorders, e.g.). After selecting the sample student, decide on a place from which to observe. You should be comfortable and as unobtrusive as possible, and you will need to be in a position to see their facial expressions (you will need all the cues you can get to analyze their behavior).

You will need two forms: one for the target student and one for the sample student. Fold the target student's at the top arrows (with the identifying information folded under) and place it over the sample student's at the bottom arrows so that you can easily make entries under "class" and "student" for both. You need to keep the target student's form on top because you wil be making frequent notes in the spaces below.

You need to decide on a time interval to record your observations. The more data you collect, the more reliable your conclusion will be, provided of course the data are good. The most comfortable time interval is thirty seconds. This requires a notation every fifteen seconds: one for the target student, then one for the sample student, alternately. At fifteen-second intervals the pace is lively but still manageable, unless you fall behind with

FIGURE 1   Classroom Observation Form

CLASSROOM OBSERVATION FORM

NAME:_____   GRADE:_____   TEACHER:_____   SCHOOL:_____   DATE:_____

LEGEND: For "Student":
For "Class":
O-On Task (attentive, productive)
O-Group on Task (clear direction and purpose)
P-Off Task, Passive (distracted, daydreaming)
X-Transitions (changing subjects, unmanageable interruptions)
A-Off Task, Active (aggressive, interfering)
S-Off Task, Severe (interventions needed, time-out)

STARTING TIME:_____   FINISH:_____   NOTATION INTERVAL:_____   OBSERVER:_____

CLASS:	O	OOOOOOOOOO OOOOOOOOOO OOOOOOOOOO OOOOOOOOOO OOOOOOOOOO
	X	XOOOOOOOOO OOOOOOOOOO OOOOOOOOOO OOOOOOOOOO OOOOOOOOOO
STUDENT:	O	OOOOOOOOOO OOOOOOOOOO OOOOOOOOOO OOOOOOOOOO OOOOOOOOOO
	P	OOOOOOOOOO OOOOOOOOOO OOOOOOOOOO OOOOOOOOOO OOOOOOOOOO
	A	OOOOOOOOOO OOOOOOOOOO OOOOOOOOOO OOOOOOOOOO OOOOOOOOOO
	S	OOOOOOOOOO OOOOOOOOOO OOOOOOOOOO OOOOOOOOOO OOOOOOOOOO

NOTE REF:

ACTIVITY:

NOTES:

COMMENTS:

TOTAL:_____

O:_____   " _____ %O:
P:_____   " _____ %P:
A:_____   " _____ %A:
S:_____   " _____ %S:
X:_____   n _____ %X:

TEACHER'S INTERACTIONS WITH STUDENT, VERBAL AND/OR PHYSICAL:

Positive:_____   Neutral:_____   Negative:_____
(encouragements, acknowledgements)   (clarifications, cues)   (reprimands, scoldings)

TEACHER'S OPINION OF OBSERVER'S PRESENCE ON STUDENT'S BEHAVIOR:

_____ NEGLIGIBLE (typical behavior)   _____ POSITIVE (improved behavior)   _____ NEGATIVE (worse behavior)

SOURCE: © 1990 David Sanders, LCSW.

your note taking. This interval also allows you to complete the form's one hundred spaces in fifty minutes; this is a good time period for most classrooms and you can always return for more information later, if needed—and it makes the math calculations easy.

Position your timepiece where you can watch the seconds go by. At the minute, observe the target student for a few seconds, make a decision about his or her behavior, then mark the form. At the quarter-minute, do the same for the sample student, and mark his or her form. Then, at the half minute, back to the target student. Every fifteen seconds you will be observing either the target student or the sample student, alternating between them, analyzing and categorizing their behavior into one of the four categories mentioned earlier:

1. *On task (attentive, productive)*. This is the "O" line under "student." All clues tell you that the student is attending to the given task. Obvious clues such as thoughtful engagement in completing the assignments or responding to a discussion question, are easy to assess, but others, such as apparent daydreaming or looking about the room, can be misinterpreted. Contextual information will help you make a good decision here. None of your decisions will be isolated from the ones you made thirty seconds ealier; if the student has established a pattern of listening and participating in a discussion, then his sudden, daydream-like appearance is probably due to his trying to recall the correct response to the question. You will never know, of course, but acknowledging habits and patterns will help you make the best decision possible at each observation interval when the clues are not obvious.

2. *Off task, passive (distracted, daydreaming)*. This is the "P" line. All clues here tell you that the student is detached from the given task and has little interest in completing it—his or her mind is somewhere else. Obvious clues are looking about absentmindedly, playing with things in or on the desk, having an unusual preoccupation with his or her thumb, and so forth. The same cautions apply here as for the previous category.

3. *Off task, active (aggressive, interfering)*. This is the "A" line. This behavior is usually easy to identify because it is likely to be obvious, at least to you. It often escapes the teacher's attention because the student may be quite clever concealing it until the teacher's back is turned or he or she is busy helping other students. Common behaviors that fall under this category are whispering or talking with neighbors; aggravations, teasing, or otherwise disrupting a classmate's attention; out of seat or moving about the room without permission; talking out, silliness, throwing things, or other classroom disruptions.

4. *Off task, severe (interventions needed, time-out)*. This is the "S" line. This category is for those times when the student's behavior is severe enough that the teacher has to confront the student, invoke a time-out, or give

a negative consequence to preserve enough control and authority to continue te lesson. As mentoned earlier, it is impotant to reassure the teacher that you want to observe the student under normal classroom conditions and under the management plan in place. Some teachers feel you need to see the student at his or her worst, so they will alow unruly behavior to go unchecked, but it is more important to see how the student responds to the teacher's classroom methods.

The line for "class" (above the "student" line) is there to record any disruptions in the classroom routine, because only students with exceptional self-discipline and control can remain "on task" when the teacher is distracted. If the task is well defined and the directions are clear, note the "O" line, but when there is an interruption of the lesson and the teacher is preoccupied (such as when the principal interrupts to confer the teacher, or during transitions to new subjects), note the "X" line. (You will save time by noting the "O" line once and then noting the "X"s only as they occur because there are usually few of them.)

This division of classroom behaviors into four basic categories will suffice for nearly all behaviors you will witness. When you have made your observation and categorized the behavior, darken the circle on the line corresponding to its code letter at the interval. If necessary, you can also make other supplement notations on the form using the following guidelines:

The line for "note ref" is used to refer to an explanation in the "notes." You may want to describe in detail a particular student behavior so you can refer to it later during your report. These spaces are provided to organize those observations. For example, during one interval you see the student poking his neighbor with a pencil. At that moment you would darken the circle on the "A" line and in the "note ref" space below it you would jot down a reference number (1, 2, etc.) Then in the space for "notes," you would write, "1. jabbed neighbor with pencil." Usually, these details are only important to note for the target student.

The "activity" line is important because it provides a reminder of what the classroom activity was during the observation. But more important, it sometimes gives clues about how students react differently to various teaching methods and learning activities. For instance, it may reveal that the student maintained good attention during a cut-and-paste activity but lost all interest during a classroom discussion, or that the student was on task when doing desk work but became very active during a small-group activity. This kind of information is helpful when planning intervention strategies.

The "comments" space is good for general comments on the observation period and physical classroom features, as well as any unusual events that occurred to minimize or alter the legitimacy of the conclusion.

There is space at the bottom of the form to tally the teacher's interactions with the target student. Positive interactions are clearly encouraging and rewarding. "Good job, Billy." "That's exactly right, Sally." Neutral interactions are informative, inquisitive: "Did you bring your note back, John?" "It's time to put your book away, Doris." Negative interactions are usually reprimands or warnings: "I told you to sit down!" "Put that back in your desk!" Be aware that "interactions" are not just verbal; also count physical interactions (looks, smiles, frowns) when you observe them. Try to note all interactions you witness, not just the ones that occur during an observation interval.

This information is important for two reasons: first, it reveals the frequency, or lack of, such interactions; second, it reveals the nature (positive, neutral, or negative) of such interactions. This will be helpful when discussing strategies for amelioration, because if positive interactions are infrequent, then a legitimate recommendation can be made to increase them, but if they are frequent, then the teacher can be commended and valuable time spent brainstorming other strategies.

The final notation to record is whether the student's behavior during the observation period was typical. Some students love to "perform" for guests while others seem unaware of visitors in the room. When naturally curious students ask, "What are you doing here?" probably the best response is simply to say, "I'm here to visit for a while and I promised Mr. Jones I wouldn't talk to anyone." Check with the teacher on this final question and mark his or her response; if the behavior appeared to be much different than typical, you will have to make a decision about how valid the results are.

The table in the lower right-hand corner is to summarize the data you observed and to record the final percentages. As mentioned earlier, this will be easy when all one hundred spaces are used because the calculations can be done quickly; otherwise, a pocket calculator will be useful to speed things up. Since it would be unfair to penalize a student for general class transitions and interruptions, observations made when the class "X" line is noted are overridden and calculated as an "X" percentage.

Another difficult time to assess is when students finish their work and are not sure what to do next. For instance, should the sample student be marked "off task" when he or she completes the work and has nothing to do while the target student is still working on the assignment? Typically, this is when students begin to talk with their neighbors and "active" behaviors begin, even for otherwise compliant students. Most teachers anticipate this with clear directions about what to do when work is finished, but not all. It might be wise to bring this to the teacher's attention before the observation begins. Your previous experiences will be your best guide. (See figure 2 for an example of a completed form.)

FIGURE 2 Example of Completed Classroom Observation Form

CLASSROOM OBSERVATION FORM

NAME: Billy Student   GRADE: 3   TEACHER: Jones   SCHOOL: Castle Hill   DATE: 9-26-97

LEGEND: For "Student":
  O–On Task (attentive, productive)
  P–Off Task, Passive (distracted, daydreaming)
  A–Off Task, Active (aggressive, interfering)
  S–Off Task, Severe (interventions needed, time-out)

For "Class":
  O–Group on Task (clear direction and purpose
  X–Transitions (changing subjects, unmanageable interruptions)

STARTING TIME: 9:10   FINISH: 10:00   NOTATION INTERVAL: 30 sec   OBSERVER: Smith

NOTE REF:

ACTIVITY:	reading (vocabulary)	math (telling time)		math pages (work in group)

NOTES:
1. distracted (daydreaming symptoms)
2. distracted (playing with pencils) (crayons)
3. whispering to neighbor
4. called on for answer, didn't know
5. out of seat
6. reprimand (back to desk)
7. reprimand (back to work)
8. bothering neighbor
9. time-out

COMMENTS: teacher gave clear directions; tasks were well defined; teacher encouraged on-task behavior; time-out given for "bothering others"; interruption at 9:47 when specialist conferred with teacher.

TEACHER'S INTERACTIONS WITH STUDENT, VERBAL AND/OR PHYSICAL:

Positive: IIII ④   Neutral: IIII IIII IIII I ⑪   Negative: II ②
(encouragements, acknowledgements) (clarifications, cues) (reprimands, scoldings)

TEACHER'S OPINION OF OBSERVER'S PRESENCE ON STUDENT'S BEHAVIOR:

X NEGLIGIBLE (typical behavior) ___ POSITIVE (improved behavior) ___ NEGATIVE (worse behavior)

TOTAL: 100

O: 47   = % O: 47%
P: 26   = % P: 26%
A: 16   = % A: 16%
S: 7   = % S: 7%
X: 4   = %X: 4%

By using a standard procedure for classroom observations, social workers and diagnosticians will be able to give intelligent, reliable, precise information about a student's classroom behavior, specifically about time on task. They will be able to present this information in percentages, an easily understood and readily accessible format. Percentages make comparisons with previous observations practical and allow baselines to be established for future comparisons. Observers will be able to repeat the process in a standardized format, which will enhance uniformity and reliability, and they will be able to share these results with other practitioners with the confidence only consistency provides.

CHAPTER 16

Adaptive Behavior
Assessments

Richard Van Acker
Associate Professor of Education, University of Illinois at Chicago

- Why Social Workers Do Adaptive Behavior Assessments
- Defining Adaptive Behavior
- The Assessment of Maladaptive Behavior
- The Assessment of Adaptive Behavior
- Reasons for Assessing Adaptive Behavior
- Common Measures Used in the Assessment of Adaptive Behavior
- Problems with Current Assessment Measures of Adaptive Behavior

For many years, social workers, psychologists, educators, and others have attempted to identify accurately those behaviors related to competence that distinguish individuals as they interact with their physical and social environments, that is, their *adaptive behavior* (Schmidt and Salvia, 1984). Adaptive behavior assessments fall into two major types: formal and informal. This chapter will primarily discuss the formal, usually semistructured interview style of assessment; the art of informal assessment is discussed in chapter 17. Understanding how individuals adapt themselves to the requirements of their physical and social environments is the goal of many of our social sciences. The ability to function effectively across a range of adaptive skill areas is essential for personal success and adjustment in life, and maximizing adaptive behavior skills for individuals with physical, mental, or emotional challenges is often a goal for social work intervention. Thus the construct of adaptive behavior is becoming increasingly important in the identification and treatment of individuals with various disabilities, such as cognitive impairments, emotional disturbance, and mental impairments. For example, the American Association on Mental Retardation (AAMR), The international leader in the conceptualization, definition, and classification of mental retardation, has included adaptive behavior as a critical factor in defining mental retardation since the late 1950s (Heber, 1959, 1961). Unfortunately, operationalizing the concept of adaptive behavior is no easy task.

WHY SOCIAL WORKERS DO ADAPTIVE BEHAVIOR ASSESSMENTS

Social workers have assessed people's functioning in their various environments throughout the history of the profession. Assessments are made in comparison to others in the same cohort, controlling for age, gender, ethnicity, community, environment, socioeconomic status and any perceived or suspected disabilities, as well as other defining characteristics. For most people functional abilities are relatively stable across various settings, but for some there is significant variation. Describing this variability is an essential component of a social developmental study and is identified as the *adaptive behavior assessment*. It is important that in school settings the social worker take responsibility for the adaptive behavior assessments, for three reasons:

1. Social workers are well trained in the interviewing process.
2. The professional focus of social work is on how the person functions in the environment, and social work practice has centered on how to improve the "fit" between the person and the environment. See chapter 4.
3. Finally, one of the fundamental concepts, and indeed requirements, of the Individuals with Disabilities Education Act (IDEA, P.L. 105-17) is the multidisciplinary approach to assessment and decision making in determining each referred student's learning needs.

Thus, both through training and theoretical framework, the adaptive behavior assessment falls well within the professional responsibility of the social worker.

DEFINING ADAPTIVE BEHAVIOR

Over the past three decades, there has been much discussion and frequent professional disagreement regarding what specifically constitutes adaptive behavior (Clausen, 1967; Gresham, MacMillan, and Siperstein, 1995; Halpern, 1968; McGrew and Bruininks, 1989, 1990; Zigler, Balla, and Hadapp, 1984). At this time, there is no single definition of adaptive behavior that is universally agreed upon in the professional community (MacMillan, Gresham, and Siperstein, 1995). Adaptive behaviors are those that allow the individual to live successfully, avoid life-threatening dangers, and interact with the physical and social environment in a manner that is safe. Effective adaptive behavior skills will allow the individual to thrive and find acceptance within his or her social environment. Adaptive behavior reflects the ability to meet the immediate physical and social demands of the environment as well as prepare for probable future environments.

Adaptive behavior is an inherently developmental and social construct. That is, adaptive behavior skills change over time and are defined by inter-personal, environmental, and societal expectations. So what behaviors or skills are important to measure when assessing adaptive behavior? The current AAMR definition for mental retardation, which is perhaps the most widely held, identifies ten critical adaptive skill areas: (1) communication, (2) self-care, (3) home living, (4) social skills, (5) community use, (6) self-direction, (7) health and safety, (8) functional academics, (9) leisure, and (10) work (American Association on Mental Retardation [AAMR], 1992). This is a rather comprehensive list of adaptive skill areas. And, as we shall see, the list includes behaviors that are difficult to assess reliably given the current status of our measures. Nevertheless, one major criterion for the identification of mental retardation calls for "limitations in two or more" of these adaptive skill areas (AAMR, 1992, p.1)

Adaptive Behavior as a Function of Age

Obviously, the age of the target individual must be considered when assessing adaptive behavior. Not all of the ten adaptive skill areas identified by the AAMR may be relevant at a given age. For example, when assessing early elementary-age students, skills related to work will be significantly less important than those related to functional academics, communication, and self-care (Gresham et al., 1995; Reschly, 1987). The nature of the expecta-tions placed on the individual for the display of adaptive behavior changes dramatically over the life span. As children grow, assessment of adaptive behavior targets learned behavior. We expect young children to communi-cate socially with others, to demonstrate social skills as they play together. We anticipate that children will demonstrate increased independence in self-care (e.g., dressing, feeding), community use (e.g., mobility in their neighborhood), self-direction, and engagement in leisure time activities as they mature. With adolescence come expectations for transition into the adult world of work.

When assessing adaptive behavior, care must be taken to ensure that the person completing the measure is sensitive to the realities of child development. As most assessment measures call for the respondent to rate the frequency with which the target individual displays a given behavior (e.g., usually, sometimes, never or seldom), knowledge of what is develop-mentally appropriate is assumed.

Adaptive Behavior as a Function of Cultural Expectations

Cultural awareness and sensitivity play a critical role in the assessment of adaptive behavior. Culture, by definition, affects the display of language, behavior, and beliefs. For example, some cultures support personal independence and individual achievement to a far greater extent than others. The age at which children are expected to display specific behaviors related to self-care, self-direction and independent community use differ dramatically across cultures. The respondent must be aware of the cultural background of the individual being assessed. Moreover, the validity of the score obtained will depend on the similarity or difference of the person being assessed to those individuals included within the normative sample of the measure being employed. That is, if the target individual differs significantly in level of acculturation from those individuals used to norm a particular measure, the score should be interpreted with great care.

Adaptive Behavior as a Function of the Environment

What is considered adaptive in one environment may prove maladaptive in another. A behavior that proves adaptive in a rural setting may have quite a different outcome in a urban setting. For example, as children mature, greater independence is expected and greater self-directed mobility within and between neighborhoods in the community. For many children growing up in the inner cities of our large urban centers, such mobility might significantly increase the personal danger to which these children are exposed. Movement through rival gang territories can lead to confrontation, assault, and death. Therefore, increased mobility and independence could be viewed as maladaptive.

Successful adaptation requires a good "person-environment fit." The individual's capabilities must match the environmental demands. The concept of environment in the assessment of adaptive behavior includes those specific settings in which the individual functions, in particular, the home, school, work, and community environments.

THE ASSESSMENT OF MALADAPTIVE BEHAVIORS

When assessing adaptive behavior, some measures include a rating of maladaptive behavior. For obvious reasons, the identification of maladaptive behavior is important in its own right. The relationship of adaptive to maladaptive behavior, however, is not that of behaviors at opposite ends of a continuum. In fact these behaviors can appear to exist quite independently of one another. An individual can display both adaptive and maladaptive behavior in the same area. For example, many individuals who practice many acts of great care in the area of health and safety (e.g., good diet and exercise) also will engage in significant levels of substance abuse (e.g., smoking and alcohol consumption). Moreover, the absence of maladaptive behavior does not imply the presence of adaptive behavior.

The inclusion of maladaptive behavior often increases the confusion and difficulty in the interpretation of findings. Like adaptive behavior, maladaptive behavior suffers from the lack of a clear and agreed upon definition.

THE ASSESSMENT OF ADAPTIVE BEHAVIOR

Adaptive behavior is measured across multiple environmental settings using typical, everyday functioning rather than optimal performance. Adaptive behaviors are those that are performed regularly (habitually and customarily), spontaneously and without prompting or assistance from others. When assessing adaptive behavior, we are not interested in what the target individual can do (*ability*), but rather what the individual typically does (*performance*). This is an important, and often misunderstood distinction. Often individuals who have the knowledge and skills necessary to perform a given response fail to do so riutinely in their everyday interactions with their environment. For example a student might know how to solve a given social problem (e.g., peer conflict) in an acceptable fashion (e.g., verbally expressing his feelings in a calm manner). However, when confronted with a peer conflict, the student might routinely respond with aggression. The assessment of his adaptive behavior is not aimed at the discovery of his potential response (verbal problem solving), but rather at a measure of his typical response (aggression).

The most common method of assessing adaptive behavior involves the report (e.g., interview) or rating of a target individual by a third person (respondent). Rather than employing systematic observation of the behavior of the target individual, the examiner relies on the cumulative observations of a respondent who is familiar with the target individual. This method of assessment is susceptible to various types of limitations, errors and biases. The respondent is limited to those behaviors he or she has had the opportunity to observe. Often different respondents will observe individuals in only a limited number of contexts (e.g., the school classroom, the lunchroom, the home setting). Students will often display quite different behavior in these various contexts. Thus assessments provided by different respondents can report significantly divergent results.

There also is a concern that respondents can differ significantly in their awareness or tolerance for some behaviors. Most assessments of adaptive behavior ask respondents to rate on a Likert scale the frequency or seriousness of various behaviors with an underlying assumption that various respondents will employ a similar standard. Thus one respondent's "sometimes" is assumed to differ from another respondent's "usually." This may not be a safe assumption.

Another problem results from the method used to calculate the target individual's scores (subscale, domain, and composite scores). These scores are obtained by assigning numbers (e.g., 0, 1, or 2) to the various ratings and manipulating these numbers mathematically. Remember, what are really being added are subjective ratings (e.g., a "sometimes" + a "usually" + a "seldom" = _____). This should be kept in mind as one interprets the results of any assessment.

Another concern with the traditional approach to assessing adaptive behavior is that the individual being assessed may conceal important behaviors from the respondent) (e.g., due to cultural demands, fear of consequences or other personal agendas). Thus the respondent may not report the presence of a potentially important adaptive or maladaptive behavior; or a respondent might be less than truthful when completing an assessment. This is especially true if the respondent has a stake in the outcome. For example, parents might be more willing to give their child the benefit of the doubt or provide responses based on ability rather than typical performance if they are concerned that their child might be classified as mentally retarded or emotionally disturbed. On the other hand, a teacher might be inclined to magnify the frequency or magnitude of a maladaptive behavior if it will increase the likelihood of removing a particularly challenging child from the classroom setting.

Given these potential limitations, errors, and biases, the examiner is advised to seek information and assessments of adaptive behavior from multiple people across a variety of settings within which the target individual interacts. The goal of multiple measurements of adaptive behavior is the identification of patterns in responding and the development of a reliable understanding of the target individual's adaptive and maladaptive behavior. As mentioned above, however, multiple ratings by third parties can often produce significantly disparate profiles for the target individual. One procedure recommended in the 1992 AAMR manual for reconciling disagreements among third-party respondents in assessing adaptive behavior and reducing error is to average ratings. (Most measures of adaptive behavior are designed to be administered individually. I.e., each respondent is to complete the measure independently. Thus, to assess a child's adaptive behavior in the school, a given measure might be completed by two or three relevant teachers independently of one another. The teachers are not to discuss the child and then provide a response that constitutes the consensus of the group. The same is true for assessments by parents. Each should complete an independent rating of their child.) Specifically, the 1992 AAMR manual states: "The use of at least two raters to score an individual on the same scale and derivation of an average of the results will increase the validity of the results" (p. 43). This statement has come under considerable attack as being psychometrically incorrect (Gresham et al., 1995). The averaging of two disparate scores does nothing to reduce measurement error and does not assist in the achievement of consensus. Perhaps a better strategy involves collecting additional data (e.g., additional third-party ratings, direct observational data, anecdotal records) and engaging in a triangulation of the data to identify consistent patterns of behavior (Gable, Magee-Quinn, Rutherford, and Howell, in press). One has to keep in mind that disparate ratings do not necessarily indicate error but could signal the differential behavior of an individual in various settings or in similar settings with different people (respondents).

REASONS FOR ASSESSING ADAPTIVE BEHAVIOR

There are a number of reasons for assessing adaptive behavior. One of the most frequently used reasons involves the identification or clarification of an individual's skills and deficits when attempting to determine if a disability exists. As mentioned above, the current AAMR definition of mental retardation states:

> Mental retardation refers to substantial limitations in present functioning. It is characterized by significantly subaverage intellectual functioning, existing concurrently with related limitations in two or more of the following applicable adaptive skill areas: health and safety, functional academics, leisure, and work. Mental retardation manifests before age 18. (AAMR, 1992, p.1)

In response to this definition, since about 1975 (passage of P.L. 94-142) federal regulations and state school codes began to require that adaptive behavior be assessed before a pupil could be considered eligible for special education services under the category of mental retardation or cognitive impairment. Adaptive behavior also is typically assessed for students being considered for other types of disabilities. For example, when exploring the possibility of an emotional disturbance an assessment of adaptive and maladaptive behavior is frequently recommended.

Another reason for assessing adaptive behavior relates to program planning. The recent reauthorization of IDEA in 1997 specifies the need to develop educational objectives and behavior management plans for students with disabilities whose behavior interferes with their own learning or that of others. Thus the assessment of both adaptive and maladaptive behavior has an increased level of importance in the identification of target behaviors. This new legislation also specifies increased responsibility in the development of educational objectives to promote the transition of students with disabilities into the workplace. Again, the assessment of adaptive behavior can play an important role in the identification of appropriate goals and objectives.

COMMON MEASURES USED IN THE ASSESSMENT OF ADAPTIVE BEHAVIOR

In the next section of this chapter, the most frequently used measures of adaptive behavior will be reviewed (see table 1). The 1992 AAMR manual

TABLE 1   Common Measures of Adaptive Behavior

Measure (Authors)	Age Range	Informant	Type of Measure
AAMD Adaptive Behavior Scale: Residential and Community Scale (Hihira, Leland, and Lambert, 1993)	18–79 years	Staff member or other professional	Interview questionnaire
AAMD Adaptive Behavior Scale: School 2 (Nihira, Leland, and Lambert, 1993)	3–21 years	Teacher	Interview questionnaire
Adaptive Behavior Inventory (Brown and Leigh, 1986)	6 years to 18 years, 11 months	Teacher	Interview questionnaire
Scales of Independent Behavior—Revised (Bruininks, Woodcock, Weatherman, and Hill, 1996)	3 months to 90 years	Parent, teacher, or significant other	Interview checklist
Vineland Adaptive Behavior Scales—Interview editions (Sparrow, Balla, and Cicchetti, 1984a, 1984b)	Birth to 18 years, 11 months	Parent or significant other	Interview
Vineland Adaptive Behavior Scales—Classroom edition (Harrison, 1985)	3 years to 12 years, 11 months	Teacher	Checklist

clearly states that a valid determination of adaptive skills requires the use "of an adaptive skill assessment to evaluate the person's adaptive skill profile on an appropriately normed and standardized instrument" (p. 25). The purpose of this section, therefore, is to familiarize the reader with some of these measures and to point out some of the important features related to the domains including issues related to scoring the measure, information on the normative samples available for interpretation, and critical psychometric properties of the measure. This information should help the reader select the appropriate measure for a specific need and aid in the interpretation and generalization of results for any particular target individual.

AAMD Adaptive Behavior Scales

As an organization, the AAMD has developed their own rating scale, titled Adaptive Behavior Scales (ABS), which correlates with the ten behaviors they identify as key. The revised AAMD Adaptive Behavior Scale—School 2 (ABS-S2; Nihira, Leland, and Lambert, 1993), and a residential and community edition. AAMD Adaptive Behavior Scale: Residential and Community Scale, 2nd edition. Both are individually administered measures. The school edition is designed for children and youth aged three to twenty-one, while the residential and community version is normed for individuals aged eighteen to seventy-nine. The ABS has undergone numerous revisions since first introduced in 1969. The latest versions comprise items selected from previous editions based on the item's interrater reliability and its ability to discriminate among various levels of adaptation.

These scales are divided into two parts. Part I examines ten domains related to independent and responsible functioning, language development, physical development, socialization, and domestic activity. Part II explores eight domains of maladaptive behavior that are manifestations of personality and behavior disorders. On the school version of the ABS, one domain has been dropped from each part of the measure, domestic activity from Part I and sexual behavior from Part II. Table 2 list the domains of the ABS.

The scoring procedures for both versions are identical. In Part I, two administration formats are used. The first format employs a series of statements denoting increasingly higher levels of adaptation. Items are scored by circling the highest level of functioning demonstrated by the target individual. The second format involves a series of statements that are an-

TABLE 2 Domains and Factors of the Adaptive Behavior Scales

Part I	Domains	Number of Items	Factors
I	Independent functioning	24	Personal self-sufficiency
	Physical development	6	Community self-sufficiency
	Economic activity	6	Personal-social responsibility
	Language development	10	
	Numbers and time	3	
	Domestic activity	6	
	Prevocational/vocational activity	3	
	Self-direction	5	
	Responsibility	3	
	Socialization	7	
II	Social behavior	7	Social adjustment
	Conformity	6	Personal adjustment
	Trustworthiness	6	
	Stereotyped and hyperactive behavior	5	
	Sexual behavior	4	
	Self-abusive behavior	3	
	Social engagement	4	
	Disturbing interpersonal behavior	6	

swered yes or no. Part II of the measure presents multiple statements and is scored by rating the target individual on a three point scale (never = 0, occasionally = 1,frequently = 2). All raw scores for the various domains on the ABS can be converted into percentiles or standard scores (mean = 10, standard deviation = 37). While no composite score is available, one can determine quotient scores for the underlying factors for each part of the measure (three factors for Part I—personal self-sufficiency, community self-sufficiency, and personal-social responsibility; two factors for Part II—social adjustment and personal adjustment). Age-equivalent scores are available for Part I. Part II scores are not related to age.

The residential and community version of the ABS was standardized on 4,103 individuals with developmental disabilities stratified on living arrangements (living at home, small group homes, community-based residence, and large institution). Sample members represented individuals from 46 states and the District of Columbia and were predominantly between the ages of eighteen and thirty-nine. The norm sample was generally representative of the nation as a whole with regard to race, ethnicity, and geographical region.

Adaptive Behavior Inventory

The Adaptive Behavior Inventory (ABI; Brown and Leigh, 1986) is an individually administered, norm-referenced measure to assess the behavior of students who range in age from six years, zero months to eighteen years, eleven months. The typical respondent when using the ABI is the target student's classroom teacher or other professional with whom the child frequently interacts. The ABI is specifically developed to explore the adaptive behavior skills of a given target individual. Both a full-scale and a short form (sometimes referred to as a "screening" instrument) of the ABI are available.

The ABI consists of 150 items divided among five subtests: self-care skills, communication skills, social skills, academic skills, and occupational skills. Individual items are scored using a four-point scale (0 = the subject does not perform the behavior, 1 = the subject is beginning to perform the behavior, 2 = the subject performs the behavior most of the time, 3 = the subject has mastered the behavior). Raw scores can be transformed into percentile ranks or standard scores (mean = 100, standard deviation = 15). The short form of this measure contains selected items from each subtest.

Two distinct samples were used to develop norms for the ABI. One sample was made up of students with mental retardation from special education programs or residential facilities. The second norm sample included students representing the general U.S. population. The methods used to identify subjects for these samples is poorly described, and much of the information needed to evaluate the quality of the norm samples is not provided in the test manual.

Scales of Independent Behavior Revised

The Scales of Independent Behavior—Revised (SIB-R; Bruininks, Woodcock, Weatherman, and Hill, 1996) is an individually administered measure to be used with individuals from three months of age through ninety years. There are three forms of the SIB available: the full-scale form, the short form, and the early development form. (The short form of the SIB-R is intended to serve as a screening device that consists of 40 items selected from the 259 items of the full-scale version. The early development form has been developed to assess "the development of preschoolers and the adaptive skills of youths or adults with serious disabilities." Bruininks et al., 1996, p. 16). The SIB-R is specifically intended to be used to assess independent functioning within various settings such as the home, school, community or workplace. The SIB-R lends itself well to purposes such as the establishment of appropriate instructional goals, making placement decisions, and evaluating program outcomes. This measure is frequently employed for both clinical and research purposes.

The full-scale form employs fourteen subscales of adaptive behavior, grouped into four clusters. Each item is scored on a four point scale:

0. the person never or rarely performs the skill even when asked;

1. the person performs the skill; however, the person does not perform the task well or performs the task about a quarter of the time; the person may need to be asked to perform the skill;

2. the person performs the skill fairly well or about three-quarters of the time; the person may need to be asked to perform the skill and;

3. the person performs the skill very well always or almost always without being asked.

Maladaptive behavior is assessed by interviewing the respondent about six broad cluster areas of problem behavior: three internalized problem behavior clusters and three externalized problem behavior clusters. The measure does not employ specific items to assess maladaptive behavior. Each area is assessed on two dimension: a frequency scale and a severity scale. The frequency scale is a five point scale:

1 = less than once a month;

2 = one to three times a month;

3 = one to six times a month;

4 = one to ten times a day and;

5 = one or more times an hour.

The severity scale also employs a five point scale:

0 = not serious or not a problem;

1 = slightly serious or a mild problem;

2 = moderately serious or a moderate problem;

3 = very serious or a severe problem and;

4 = extremely serious or a critical problem.

Table 3 presents the subscales and the clusters for the SIB-R.

Subscale scores, cluster scores, and a composite score (the combination of cluster scores for a measure of broad independence) are available. The age-equivalent scores for each subscale are readily calculated. The calculation of additional typical scores (e.g., standard scores, percentile ranks) for this measure are problematic. Computer scoring programs are available.

The SIB-R is normed on a sample of 2,182 individuals ranging in age from three months to ninety years of age. Norms are a composite of those established for the first edition of this measure ($N = 1,764$) and a separate standardization conducted for the revised edition ($N = 418$). The sample approximates the population as specified in the 1990 U.S. census in terms of gender, race, and community size.

TABLE 3   Clusters and Subscales of the Scales of Independent Behavior—Revised for the Assessment of Adaptive Behavior

---

Cluster and Subscale

Motor skills
   Gross motor skills
   Fine motor skills
Social interaction and communication
   Social interaction
   Language comprehension
   Language expression
Personal living skills
   Eating and meal preparation
   Toileting
   Dressing
   Personal self-care
   Domestic skills
Community living skills
   Time and punctuality
   Money and value
   Work skills
   Home and community orientation

Vineland Adaptive Behavior Scales

The Vineland Adaptive Behavior Scales (VABS) result from a significant revision and update of the Vineland Social Maturity Scale (VSMS; Doll, 1935, 1965) that was completed in 1984. The VABS is administered individually and is completed by a respondent familiar with the target individual. There are three separate forms of the VABS each with its own technical manual. Two of the forms are termed interview editions: the expanded form (Sparrow, Balla and Cicchetti, 1984a) and the survey form (Sparrow, Balla, and Cicchetti, 1984b). The survey form includes fewer items than the expanded interview form and consequently requires less administration time. Interviews are conducted in a semistructured format with the interviewer asking questions in his or her own words to probe the respondent about the target individual's functioning (rather than simply reading the interview items). When the interviewer has gathered enough information about a given skill area, he or she rates the individual on the scale's items. Thus the VABS requires that the interviewer gain familiarity with the instrument before administering it and provides a manual with a good deal of data about scoring the items. The interview forms of the VABS are designed for assessment of children from birth to eighteen years, eleven months of age.

The third form of the VABS provides a classroom edition of the measure (Harrison, 1985). This printed survey is completed by the student's teacher and requires approximately twenty minutes. This edition is suitable for children aged three to twelve years, eleven months.

All three forms of the VABS assess four domains of adaptive behavior. Each domain comprises several subdomains. Each is listed in table 4 along with a sample question from each subdomain. The interview editions also contain maladaptive behavior as an optional domain.

The adaptive behavior domains of the VABS are scored 2 (yes or usually), 1 (sometimes or partially), or 0 (no or never). These items also may be scored "DK" (respondent does not know) or "N" (no opportunity). Items on Part 1 of the maladaptive behavior domain are scored 2 (usually), 1 (sometimes), and 0 (never or very seldom). In Part 2, items are scored for their intensity (severe, moderate, or absent). Standard scores (mean = 100, standard deviation = 15) are available for each of the adaptive behavior domains and for the composite score, a summary of the four domains. Percentile rank scores, age equivalents, and adaptive levels also can be determined for each domain and for the composite score.

Depending on the form employed, a variety of norming groups were employed for the VABS. The interview editions were standardized with a national sample of 3,000 individuals ranging in age from newborn to eighteen years, eleven months. The classroom edition was normed on 1,984 children between the ages of three and twelve years, eleven months. These

TABLE 4   Summary of Information Related to the
Vineland Adaptive Behavior Scale

Domains and Subdomains	Sample Item	Internal Consistency (range for fifteen age groups)	
		Odd-Even Correlations	Split-Half Correlations
Communication		.73 to .94 six ≥ .90)	.84 to .97 (five ≥ .90)
Receptive	Listens to a story for at least 20 minutes		
Expressive	Uses *around* as a preposition in a phrase		
Written	Addresses letters correctly		
Daily living		.83 to .92 eight ≥ .90)	(all exceeded .90)
Personal	Dresses self completely, except for tying shoelaces		
Domestic	Puts clean clothes away without assistance		
Community	States current date when asked		
Socialization		.78 to .94 two ≥ .90)	.88 to .97 (two ≥ .90)
Interpersonal	Shows desire to please caregiver		
Play and leisure time	Shares toys or possessions without being told to do so		
Coping skills	Does not talk with food in mouth		
Motor skills		.70 to .95 (only for the 0-0 to 0-11 age groups is reliability greater than .89)	.83 to .97 (three ≥ .90)
Gross motor	Can jump over small objects		
Fine motor	Can unlock key locks		
Maladaptive behaviors		.77 to .88	.77 to .88
Minor behavior problems (27 behaviors)	Is stubborn or sullen		
Serious behavior problems (9 behaviors)	Displays inappropriate sexual behavior		

samples were selected to represent the population of the United States as described by the 1980 census with respect to racial/ethnic group. The sample was unrepresentative with regard to geographical region (underrepresenting the north central region), community size (underrepresenting rural communities) and parental education (overrepresenting parents with a college education). A supplementary sample of individuals with disabilities also was employed for the interview editions. This sample included individuals with mental retardation, emotional disturbance, visual impairment, and hearing impairment. These supplementary norms are not described very well but must be employed when exploring the maladaptive behavior domain (Part 2).

PROBLEMS WITH CURRENT ASSESSMENT MEASURES OF ADAPTIVE BEHAVIOR

A number of concerns should be acknowledged related to our current efforts at assessing adaptive behavior. To date, relatively few adaptive behavior scales have adequate national norms and sufficient psychometric qualities to warrant use in diagnostic and placement decisions (Gresham et al., 1995; Kamphaus, 1987).

Ability To Assess Potential Adaptive Behavior Domains

The AAMR definition specifies ten adaptive skill areas that should be considered when attempting to assess a child suspected of displaying cognitive impairments. Again, these ten adaptive skill areas are: (1) communication, (2) self-care, (3) home living, (4) social skills, (5) community use, (6) self-direction, (7) health and safety, (8) functional academics, (9) leisure, and (10) work. The 1992 definition specifies, "if two or more adaptive skill limitations fall substantially below the average level of functioning (as determined by either formal comparison to a normative sample or through professional judgment), then the individual would meet this second criterion for a diagnosis of mental retardation" (p.49). In 1985, Holman and Bruininks conducted a content classification analysis of thirteen adaptive behavior scales. They identified forty-five content areas and concluded that these scales vary markedly in content coverage. For the most part, each of the adaptive behavior scales currently available appear to measure a general personal independence factor. None of these measures, however, provide a comprehensive coverage of potential adaptive behavior domains (McGrew and Bruininks, 1989).

Technical Adequacy of Adaptive Skill Domains

The current standardized measures of adaptive behavior in many cases have inadequate subscale reliabilities for making diagnostic decisions (i.e., reliabilities of .70 to .75). In 1927, Kelly established standards for minimum reliabilities that are still applicable today. For measures that are employed to evaluate the level of individual accomplishment a .94 level of reliability is recommended. Examining the reliabilities for the various subdomains of any adaptive behavior scale is important when selecting a measure. The error of measurement for any subdomain increases as its reliability decreases. For example, the median split-half reliabilities for the self-care and leisure adaptive skill areas of the VABS are .69 and .71, respectively. Given these reliabilities and standard error of measurement (approximately 8.2), and adopting a 95 percent confidence interval, almost 33 percent of the general population could be identified as displaying limitations in these two adaptive skill areas. Any score attained on either of these skill areas could be off by as much as ± 16.4 points due to error and poor reliability. Thus a person with a subscale score as high as 93 could have a true score of 77. Table 4 provides the reader with a summary of the reliabilities for the commonly employed measures of adaptive behavior discussed above.

The assessment of adaptive behavior is an increasingly important activity for teachers, social workers, and psychologists. When assessing adaptive behavior, the examiner is generally interested in how well a target individual meets the needs of his or her physical and social environment. Does the individual function well enough not to represent a significant risk to self or others? Unfortunately, there is lack of agreement as to exactly which behaviors need to be assessed. Adaptive behavior is greatly influenced by societal expectations. The developmental level and cultural heritage of the individual must be taken into consideration when assessing adaptive behavior.

Adaptive behavior is usually not measured directly, but rather through information provided by a third-party respondent familiar with the target individual. When assessing adaptive behavior, one is interested in what the target individual does on a regular basis (not what the individual can demonstrate under optimal conditions).

The assessment of adaptive behavior suffers from a lack of adequate measures. There is a lack of reliability across many of the subscales in the various measures that results in serious error measurement. Moreover, the norms available are often inadequate.

Care must be taken when selecting measures for assessing adaptive behavior. Examiners may wish to select scales, or parts of scales, from any number of measures to maximize the validity and reliability of the results. When conducting an assessment of adaptive behavior, seek multiple respondents that are very familiar with the target individual. Look for patterns of behavior displayed in the target individual as reported across respondents. When behavior varies across respondents, the evaluator attempts to identify

TABLE 5   Reliability Estimates for Common Measures of Adaptive Behavior

Measure (Authors)	Reliability Estimates
AAMD Adaptive Behavior Scale: Residential and Community Scale (Nihira, Leland, and Lambert, 1993)	Coefficient alpha was employed to estimate the reliability of each item. In Part I, alphas from domains ranged from .80 to .98; forty-one of the fifty domain alphas met or exceeded .90. Alpha for Part II ranged from .80 to .95; only thirteen of the forty alphas met or exceeded .90.
AAMD Adaptive Behavior Scale: School 2 (Nihira, Leland, and Lambert, 1993)	Reliability was estimated separately for each normative group. Reliability estimates for items (coefficient alpha) were assessed. For the sample with individuals with cognitive impairments (mental retardation), alphas for the 171 domain-age reliabilities in Part I ranged from .81 to .98; 42 of the 171 coefficients were below .90 (primarily found in the prevocational/vocational and responsibility domains. In Part II, alphas for the 133 domain-age reliabilities ranged from .80 to .96; 49 of the 133 coefficients were below .90. Factor scores for both parts exceeded .90. For the sample without individuals with cognitive impairments, reliability estimates were lower. In part I, alphas ranged from a low of .79 to a high of .97; 100 of the 144 alphas fell below .90. For Part II, alphas ranged from .80 to .98; 69 of the 112 coefficients fell below .90. Domain scores should be used with caution because many have a reliability below .90.
Adaptive Behavior Inventory (Brown and Leigh, 1986)	Coefficient alpha was used to estimate internal consistency. For the normal intelligence standardization group, forty-two coefficients were computed (five subtests and total score for seven age groups). Coefficient alphas ranged from .86 to .97, thirty-two of the forty-two coefficients met or exceeded .90. All of the total score coefficients exceeded .90.
Scales of Independent Behavior— Revised (Bruininks, Woodcock, Weatherman, and Hill, 1996)	Estimates of internal consistency (corrected split-half correlations) of each subscale are provided for ten age ranges. Reliability coefficients for subscales range from .40 to .96; about 15 percent of the coefficients meet or exceed .90. Cluster reliabilities range from .67 to .97; twenty-five of the forty cluster-by-age coefficients meet or exceed .90. Broad independence (total score) for each age group meets or exceeds .90.
Vineland Adaptive Behavior Scales— Interview editions (Sparrow, Balla, and Cicchetti, 1984a, 1984b)	See table 4 for domain-specific reliability estimates.
Vineland Adaptive Behavior Scales— Classroom edition (Harrison, 1985)	See table 4 for domain-specific reliability estimates.

elements in the contexts assessed that might affect behavior. The ultimate goal of an assessment of adaptive behavior is to identify both the strengths and deficits displayed by an individual as he or she interacts with the world. With care and understanding of the potentials as well as limitations of current measures of adaptive behavior, one can proceed to identify possible areas of both adaptive and maladaptive behavior.

REFERENCES

American Association on Mental Retardation. 1992. *Mental retardation: Definition, classification, and systems of supports* (9th ed.). Washington, DC: Author.

Brown, L., and Leigh, J. 1986. *Adaptive behavior Inventory manual.* Austin, TX: Pro-Ed.

Bruininks, R., Woodcock, R., Weatherman, R., and Hill, B. 1996. *Scales of independent behavior, revised, comprehensive manual.* Chicago: Riverside.

Clausen, J. 1967. Mental deficiency: Development of a concept. *American Journal of Mental Deficiency* 71:727–745.

Doll, E.A. 1935. A genetic scale of maturity. *American Journal of Orthopsychiatry* 5:180–188.

Doll, E.A. 1965. *Vineland Social Maturity Scale* (rev. ed.). Minneapolis, MN: American Guidance Service.

Gable, R.A., Magee-Quinn, M., Rutherford, R.B., Jr., and Howell, K. in press. Addressing problem behaviors in schools: Use of functional assessments and behavior intervention plans. *Preventing School Failure.*

Gresham, F. M., MacMillan, D.L., and Siperstein, G.N. 1995. Critical analysis of the 1992 AAMR definition: Implications for school psychology. *School Psychology Quarterly* 10:1–19.

Halpern, A. 1968. A note on Clausen's call for a psychometric definition of mental deficiency. *American Journal of Mental Deficiency* 72:948–949.

Harrison, P. 1985. *Vineland Adaptive Behavior Scales: Classroom edition manual.* Circle Pines, MN: American Guidance Service.

Heber, R. 1959. A manual on terminology and classification in mental retardation [Monograph]. *American Journal of Mental Deficiency* 56(Suppl.).

Heber, R. 1961. Modifications in the terminology and classification in mental retardation. *American Journal of Mental Deficiency* 65:499–500.

Holman, J., and Bruininks, R. 1985. Assessing and training adaptive behaviors. In K. Lakin and R. Bruininks (eds). *Strategies for achieving community integration of developmentally disabled citizens* (pp. 73–104). Baltimore: Brookes.

Kamphaus, R. W. 1987. Conceptual and psychometric issues in the assessment of adaptive behavior. *Journal of Special Education* 21(1):27–35.

Kelly, T. 1927. *Interpretation of educational measurements.* Yonkers, NY: World Book.

MacMillan, D.L., Gresham, F.M., and Siperstein, G.N. 1995. Heightened concerns over the 1992 AAMR definition: Advocacy versus precision. *American Journal on Mental Retardation* 100:87–97.

McGrew, K., and Bruininks, R. 1989. Factor structure of adaptive behavior. *School Psychology Review* 18:64–81.

McGrew, K., and Bruininks, R. 1990. Defining adaptive and maladaptive behavior within a model of personal competence. *School Psychology Review* 19:53–73.

Nihira, K., Leland, H., and Lambert, N. 1993. *Examiner's manual, AAMR Adaptive Behavior Scale—Residential and Community* (2nd ed.). Austin, TX: Pro-Ed.

Reschly, D.J. 1987. *Adaptive behavior in classification and programming with students who are handicapped.* St. Paul, MN: Minnesota Department of Education.

Schmidt, M., and Salvia, J. 1984. Adaptive behavior: A conceptual analysis. *Diagnostique* 9:117–125.

Sparrow, S., Balla, D., and Cicchetti, D. 1984a. *Interview edition, survey form manual, Vineland Adaptive Behavior Scales.* Circle Pines, MN: American Guidance Service.

Sparrow, S., Balla D., and Cicchetti, D. 1984b. *Interview edition, survey form manual, Vineland Adaptive Behavior Scales.* Circle Pines, MN: American Guidance Service.

Zigler, E., Balla, D., and Hadapp, R. 1984. On the definition and classification of mental retardation. *American Journal of Mental Deficiency* 89:215–230.

CHAPTER 17

The Social Developmental Study

Marguerite Tiefenthal
School Social Worker, Retired, District 181, Hinsdale, Illinois;
Field Liaison, Loyola University at Chicago

Rita Charak
School Social Worker, Retired, District 102, LaGrange, Illinois

- Purposes of the Social Development Study in the Public Schools
- Components of a Social Developmental Study

Studying the social functioning of a child in his or her home, school, and community environment is an essential part of the total assessment of a student's functioning when referred for a case study evaluation. This information, along with an investigation into the child's general development, learning achievement, and behavior patterns, creates a relatively complete picture. Decisions about the extent of the child's special education needs can be safely based on such findings. Also, this assessment satisfies the mandate of the Individuals with Disabilities Education Act (P.L. 101–476, and reauthorization, P.L. 105–17) for nonbiased multidisciplinary assessment of children. The mandate also requires an assessment of the cultural background of the child and family with the parent's or guardian's views, when available, about the child's development and current functioning within the expectations of the child's broader environment (adaptive behavior assessment). Federal legislation also mandates the use of trained professionals from several different disciplines as well as the view of the parent or guardian in assessing children referred for evaluation.

This chapter will discuss mandates related to the content of social developmental studies, the components of a comprehensive social developmental study, the adaptive behavior assessment as an integral part of the study, how information gathered through the study is integrated to describe the child's background and current functioning in the environment, and how recommendations are developed to support the child's identified learning needs.

PURPOSES OF THE SOCIAL DEVELOPMENTAL STUDY IN THE PUBLIC SCHOOLS

Definition

Although the social developmental study (SDS) is sometimes referred to as the "social history," a tool often used by social workers to understand client dynamics, the SDS has additional components that make it more comprehensive. It should not be confused with the social history, which is only one of its components, albeit a major one. The SDS includes a basic description of the following:

1. The child,
2. The child's current social functioning and the presenting problem,
3. Observations in classroom(s) as well as other less structured school environments,
4. A private interview with the child,
5. An assessment of the child's adaptive behaviors,
6. The child's sociocultural background,
7. Any events or stressors possibly contributing to the problem,
8. Other significant life experiences, and
9. Current abilities of the child.

It is a compilation of information that, through this broad assessment, provides a comprehensive baseline of functioning and environmental realities used for planning and intervention. To fulfill the legislative mandates, the SDS must provide information on the cultural background of the child and family, an evaluation of adaptive behaviors, and a deepened understanding of the student's strengths and needs compiled from interviews and observations. The SDS includes information from many sources, including the student, parents, foster parents, teachers, other involved school personnel, significant people outside the school, such as extended family or other caretakers, and involved agencies. Each is significant in developing a profile of the student's current social and developmental functioning.

Illinois State Board of Education Form 34–57B (5–87) describes the SDS:

> This study allows the evaluation team to understand your child by assessing in-school and out-of-school behavior, and assessing how the environment affects your child's ability to learn. This study includes an assessment of adaptive behavior (how your child functions independently and meets standards of personal and social responsibility) and cultural background. This (adaptive behavior) study may include formal (tests) and informal procedures.

More and more states are developing policies encouraging the inclusion of the child in meetings where the reasons for the referral will be discussed. When the results of the assessment are reported, the child should also be included, unless the school team and parents agree this is not productive or the child declines to attend.

Purposes

Since the SDS is a compilation and analysis of information concerning those life experiences of the child, both past and present, that pertain to the child's problems or to the possible alleviation of those problems, it serves several purposes in the school setting. One major purpose is to assist the parents and school personnel (and the child) in understanding life circumstances as they relate to the child's school performance or behavior. A second major purpose is to aid the selection of an educational environment conducive to optimum learning and development of the child.

Although P. L. 105–17 does not specifically refer to a "social developmental study," it requires a comprehensive evaluation of a child that necessarily involves the collection of information from a variety of sources concerning their perception of the child's behavior.

The SDS, by including information from sources outside the school, helps to assess the whole child, focusing on identified strengths as well as areas in need of support. It brings into focus the developmental systems and ecological factors that affect the child's learning and behavioral patterns. By involving the family in this information gathering the school social worker begins a cooperative working relationship between parents or guardian and the school that may not have been present earlier. In addition, ideally a relationship is established through which emotional support, counseling, information about community resources, and legal rights can be discussed and the mediation of significant differences can begin. The relationship with the family formed by the social worker when compiling an SDS continues through the development and implementation of the educational plan. This relationship frequently has a therapeutic impact on the parents or guardian, helping them to address feelings of anxiety or alienation from their child's educational experience. During this process the social worker helps parents gain an understanding of the implications of the assessment for their child's long-range educational needs and helps them understand their rights under the due process procedures of their state. Thus the importance of the relationship begun when the information is gathered for the SDS can hardly be overstated. Giving parents or guardian the chance to vent frustration, anger, or fear of the future for their child is time well spent. In a few cases this may lead to more than one meeting, but it will pay off later when active parent or guardian cooperation will be necessary for the success of the child. Because the parents' rights and the child's need for their active participation are discussed during the assessment, the parents may feel better prepared, more empowered, and less threatened.

The SDS provides information that can guard against inappropriate labeling or placement of a child, which can occur when test scores and school performance evaluations are the only data used to make such a determination. The inclusion of developmental and ecological information provides a more complete view of the child and expands the range of possibilities appropriate to address the needs of the child (Goldstein, Askell, Ashcroft, Hurley, and Lilley, 1976).

COMPONENTS OF A SOCIAL DEVELOPMENTAL STUDY

The SDS assembles the evaluations done by the school social worker into a single written statement. With the addition of a professional judgment, the foundations for the social worker's recommendations emerge. The SDS is written in educational language (behavioral descriptions, not psychological diagnoses) and should include the social worker's recommendations for interventions that address the stated concerns. *Specific identification of a special education category or recommendations for placement are not appropriate.* A special education category designation, such as behavior disordered, learning disabled, and so forth, is the result of the compilation of the findings of the full multidisciplinary team, including the parents, as an outcome of the multidisciplinary conference. Only when the child's learning needs have been identified can the multidisciplinary team determine the most appropriate and least restrictive environment in which these needs can be met.

Eight components contribute to the gathering of information for an SDS:

1. Child interview(s),
2. Parent interview(s),
   a. Social history and current functioning,
   b. Adaptive behavior assessment,
3. Socioeconomic and cultural background,
4. Assessment of the child's learning environment,
5. Observation of the child in the school (classrooms, playground) and in a less structured setting (ideally in the home environment),
6. Adaptive behavior assessment (formal or informal),
7. Consultation with the child's current and previous teachers or review of files,
8. Consultation with other staff and agencies having knowledge of the child and the family.

Although the potential wealth of descriptive information gathered through this process may go beyond the scope of your assessment focus, only information directly pertinent to the child's educational progress that does not breach the confidentiality of the parent or child may be included in the written report. This report has eleven elements.

I. Identifying Information

A. The child's name, birth date, school, grade, teacher
B. Each family member's name, age, relationship to the child, educational background, occupation, employment, address, marital status
C. Names of other persons living in the home and their relationship to the child
D. Race/ethnicity of the family
E. Brief impression of the child at your initial meeting

II. Reasons for Referral

A. The stated reasons for the referral and any specific questions that should be addressed
B. The problem (the child's learning or behavior) as described by the teacher, parent, or others
C. What has been done to try to correct the situation (should include at least three significant interventions)
D. What the immediate precipitating events were that prompted the referral
E. A checklist citing specific behaviors that interfere with the learning process

III. Sources of Information

A list of dates and sources of data obtained should include, but not be limited to the following:

A. Home visit(s) or alternative modes of interviewing parents or guardian
B. Contacts with other relatives
C. Social worker's or other's interview(s) with the child
D. Review of school records
E. Outside evaluations
F. Formal or informal adaptive behavior assessment
G. Other observations of the student

IV. Developmental History

Developmental milestones may be significant and can include problems that occurred during pregnancy or delivery or any unusual conditions at birth. This information enables the social worker to consider the child over time in order to determine whether development is progressing appropriately. Lucco's (1991) tables of developmental evaluation provide an excellent developmentally informed guide for this phase of assessment. In addition, for a child between ages three and five, the social/developmental profile may include an assessment of the following:

Infancy to five years of age

A. Degree of independence

B. Quality of and types of interpersonal relationships experienced

C. Self-image

D. Adaptability

E. Play behavior

Children five years and older

A. Level of independence

B. Interpersonal relationships, including quality of
   1. Peer interactions
   2. Adult interactions

C. Range and intensity of play activity

D. Self-image
   1. Self-awareness
   2. Self-esteem
   3. Self-confidence

E. Coping and effectiveness in social situations

F. Sensitivity to others

G. Adaptability and appropriate persistence

H. Problem-solving abilities

V. School History

The school history for young children begins with day care, nursery school, preschool, and early childhood classes and experiences. Increasingly often, children experience group learning and daycare facilities from infancy on. This section should include a chronological account of informal and formal learning experiences, including their changes and interruptions and the progress or lack of progress the child has made to date.

School records reveal attendance patterns, progress rates, special instructional assistance, and testing results. Parents frequently recall significant changes, problems, traumatic experiences and the like, that have affected their child's learning progress over the years or difficulties making transitions to new, more advanced programming. The parents' attitudes toward early learning situations, their involvement with their child's learning, and their expectations of the school are all important data. The educational system's understanding of, and sensitivity to, parental feelings and level of willingness to support the child's education may make the difference between a successful plan for the child and one in danger of failure, while knowledge of the parents' interest and ability to be supportive can help in developing realistic plans.

VI. Cultural Background, Family History, and Current Issues

This is a mandated section and should stand separately in the report. The discussion should be substantial. A child's understanding of his or her cultural background may include ethnic customs, special observances, and unique dress or food, not shared by others their age, but also how they are taught and how they experience fitting into the larger society. This section may include the realities of the family's socioeconomic status, especially their status relative to community norms. Since these qualities frequently change (for better or worse) over time as the child matures it will be useful for future evaluators to understand all these factors even if currently none is unusual in relation to community norms.

Thus the child's understanding of his or her place culturally, socially, and economically and the evident realities of the family's position in the local community are both relevant. An appropriate assessment might read, in part:

> Jane's family is of East Indian origin, and they observe the traditions of the Sikh faith. They currently reside in a community with about 25 percent minority population; however, only one other family is of East Indian background, also of the Sikh faith and traditions. Economically, Jane's family seems to be about average in this solidly middle-class community. Though the family is close-knit and relatively quiet, they feel well respected by their neighbors.

In addition, this section may include information specific to this family's history or dynamics—for example, separations, divorces, deaths, remarriages, moves, transfers, changes in child care, absence of various family members, and other significant events. The atmosphere within the family (which may be temporarily in crisis) should be noted, along with the family's methods and abilities, individually and as a unit, to cope with stressful situations. Since, as mentioned above, some of this information may be highly sensitive and confidential, an agreed-to substitute statement may be needed, such as "Some current difficulties in the home make sufficient parental support difficult at this time."

VII. Adaptive Behavior

It is important to examine the extent to which the presenting problem influences the general behavior of the child. A simplified definition of adaptive behavior is the effectiveness with which the individual functions independently and meets culturally imposed standards of personal and social responsibility. The concept of adaptation historically has been used to differentiate a person's general functioning from his or her measured intellectual functioning (IQ) and was in use before the term "adaptive behavior" was adopted.

The social worker is usually identified as the professional responsible for conducting this assessment because of the social worker's training in interviewing and knowledge of patterns of normative behavior and of likely effects created by cultural differences. Adaptive behavior assessment information is typically gathered about the child either formally through instruments measuring specific adaptive behaviors or informally through observations and interviews.

Informal and formal adaptive behavior assessments may be chosen depending on the degree and focus of the problem. Informal assessments compare the child's functioning in the classroom with his or her functioning out of the classroom: at home, in the community, and during external school activities. The areas of functioning include independent functioning, personal responsibility, and social responsibility. When addressing independent functioning, the assessment will answer the question, Does he or she have (or can he or she acquire) the necessary skills in each area? When assessing his or her personal responsibility, the assessment will answer the question, Does he or she use the skills in each behavior setting? When assessing social responsibility, the question to be answered is, Does he or she use the skill appropriately, that is, in the appropriate place and at the appropriate time? Table 1 presents a conceptual model that may be used in acquiring this information systematically. The child's age and sociocultural background are, of course, essential ingredients in such an informal assessment, as they are in formal assessments.

VIII. Current Functioning

Sensitivity of family members to the child's problem and the family's ability, time, temperament, and willingness to be helpful are important. The parents' view of the child's personality, the interrelationships between family members, the family's interests, activities, hobbies, and leisure activities all give clues to possible recommendations to help the child. Special

TABLE 1   Informal Adaptive Behavior Assessment: A Conceptual Model

	Areas of Functioning		
Environmental Setting	Independent Functioning	Personal Responsibility	Social Responsibility
	Does he or she have (can he or she acquire) the necessary skills?	Does he or she use skills?	Does he or she use the skills appropriately (time and place)?
Academic school: subject areas			
Nonacademic school: playground, halls, gym, to and from school and classes			
Out of school: home, neighborhood, peers, parents, other adults			

attention is given to a child's interests at home, how he or she seems to learn best, areas of giftedness, hobbies, and special opportunities the child has for learning. Any maladaptive tendencies toward temper tantrums, fears, impulsivity, enuresis, sleep disturbances, stealing, or other difficulties should be noted.

IX. Additional Information of Interest

The SDS can include any traumas, hospitalizations, accidents, health problems or chronic conditions, disabilities, unusual problems, or chronic need for medication, if relevant to the child's educational functioning. The reasons for absences from school need to be considered. The child's stamina, energy level, and length of attention span in specific situations or times of day can be significant. The child's physical appearance and conduct while in the company of the social worker should be noted. This information can form the basis for an evaluation of the child's strengths and areas of need and will be useful for the team, particularly if the information modifies teacher reports.

Developmental history should include tolerance of frustration from infancy on, causes of frustration, and what parental coping strategies have been employed. Emotional development includes the ability to successfully get needs met and to develop satisfying age-appropriate relationships.

Observations on the child's role in the family, family expectations, opportunities for friends outside of school, and sense of humor can all contribute to understanding the child as a person in the environment.

X. Evaluation, Summary, Conclusions, and Recommendations

The final part of the SDS is a concise summary of the meaningful information, including how these experiences affect the child's educational progress. This forms the basis for the social worker's recommendations regarding the educational needs of the child, the best learning environment, parent counseling, available school-based services, and further diagnostic evaluations. Specific recommendations about how parents can be helpful and supportive are appropriate. Since the SDS is a diagnostic tool and is often essential in assessing severity of emotional problems and mental retardation, the data must be carefully collected and evaluated to ensure their accurate contribution to a differential diagnosis.

Confidentiality is a frequent concern in writing SDS. The social worker may be given sensitive information that has a direct bearing on the child's problem, but it may be inappropriate to share the information with other school personnel. "Sometimes social data is very personal and its potential prejudicial effect may outweigh its diagnostic values" (Byrne, Hare, Hooper, Morse and Sabatino, 1977, p. 52). One approach to this problem is to assure the parents early in the initial interview that this confidential information will not be shared with the school unless the parents give their permission or withholding it would endanger the health or welfare of the child. One procedure in keeping with this approach is to prepare the study in the form in which it will be presented and give the parent(s) the opportunity to read it and correct factual inaccuracies. In addition to technically fulfilling the confidentiality commitment, this procedure gives the parents concrete emotional assurance that confidentiality will be honored and adds trust to the social worker–parent relationship. Often the social worker and parent can collaborate on wording that will convey concern without revealing sensitive details. In rare cases, information to which the parents object may need to be included. Such information is only included if it is accurate and critical to decisions to be made abut the child's educational needs.

Social workers may be pressured to complete SDSs at the expense of direct service to students and may question the use of their time. Since the SDS is time consuming, this is a frequent concern among school social workers. Reserving time for these activities on a routine basis may help alleviate this pressure. Also, if recommendations from the study are drafted carefully so that they are useful in developing future intervention plans, the work will be more relevant, and the time spent more reasonable. Forms mailed to parents are sometimes used, but good practice dictates that additional information be secured through direct interviewing.

XI. Signature

The SDS ends with the name and professional qualification of the writer (Susan Smith, MSW and/or LCSW), and date of completion of the document.

This chapter has discussed the SDS as a dynamic instrument, a tool for delineating strengths and needs, a compilation of data from many sources, and a required component in the evaluation of the child. The purpose of the SDS is to assist the school, the multidisciplinary team, and the parents in providing the best, both educationally and emotionally, for the child.

Since adaptive behavior assessments are intended to be nondiscriminatory in areas of culture, race, and ethnicity (as is true of all other assessment data gathered by the team), assessing children's levels of adaptive behavior is a significant step toward assuring (1) that children from minority and culturally diverse groups are not overrepresented in special education designations as a result of cultural influences rather than true disabilities and (2) that children of all ages and cultural backgrounds are appropriately diagnosed and placed. Generally speaking, formal adaptive behavior assessments cover the following areas: perception, gross and fine motor coordination, communication skills, self-help skills, socialization skills, intellectual functioning in the home and community, and age-appropriate independence. There are numerous well-researched instruments, some more appropriate to assess particular presenting conditions, such as retardation.

Formal instruments for assessing adaptive behaviors are developed from sample populations to derive "normal" or average age scores that are then converted to standard scores. Informal assessments can include instruments categorized as "screening instruments" that are usually only one or two pages in length. Most formal instruments are administered through "semistructured" interviews, and most recommend that the person interviewed be the adult most familiar with the child's performance in the home or community environment. The choice of instrument depends on the child's age and the areas identified as needing evaluation. It is not good practice to use one instrument for all ages and situations.

It is recommended that a formal instrument for measuring adaptive behavior be administered by a person trained in the administration of that instrument. Some instruments used currently in the United States have equivalent Spanish-language translations, but few if any other language translations are available, making formal interviews in other languages difficult and probably not valid.

A discrepancy between the child's assessed intellectual achievement and the child's score on a formal adaptive behavior assessment can modify the recommended special education category. Particularly when it is possible that a child may be designated as mentally retarded or otherwise developmentally delayed, a formal adaptive behavior assessment will yield data with equivalency to the intellectual assessment, and this can either effectively confirm or deny the designation of developmental delay and differentiate such a child from a child who is functioning poorly in the school environment, but is competent in the home or community environment.

REFERENCES

Byrne, J. L., Hare, I., Hooper, S. N., Morse, B. J., and Sabatino, C. A. 1977. The rile of a social history in special education evaluation. In R. J. Anderson, M. Freeman, and R. L. Edwards (eds). *School social work and P.L. 94–142 the Education for All Handicapped Act* (pp. 47–55). Washington, DC: National Association of Social Workers.

Goldstein, H., Askell, C. Ashcroft, S. C., Hurley, O., and Lilley, M. S. 1976. In N. Hobbs (ed). *Issues in the classification of children.* San Francisco: Jossey-Bass.

Lucco, A. A. 1991. Assessment of the school-age child. *Families in Society: The Journal of Contemporary Human Services* 81(5):394–407.

Reschly, D. 1980. *Non-biased assessment.* Ames, IA: Iowa State University, Department of Psychology.

CHAPTER 18

The Individualized Education Program and the IFSP: Content, Process and the Social Worker's Role

Robert Constable
Professor Emeritus, Loyola University of Chicago

- The Individualized Education Program (IEP)
- The Process of Setting Annual Goals and Short-Term Objectives
- What is the IEP Team?
- Developing Agreements and Integration of Resources
- The Contents of an Individualized Education Program
- Involving Children in the IEP
- The Individualized Family Services Plan (IFSP)
- Major Outcomes Expected to be Achieved by the Child and the Family
- Service Coordination

The Individualized Education Program (IEP) and the Individualized Family Service Plan (IFSP) are central to the school social worker's work with any disabled child or infant. The IEP and the IFSP grow out of P.L. 105-17 and focus on the disabled child from birth to twenty-one and even beyond through transition planning and his or her right to a free, appropriate, public education. Parents are essential partners with the school in education. The IFSP deals with infants and toddlers, birth through five years of age. In the IFSP, the family is more than just a partner; it is a principal agent in management and implementation of a plan that may use a variety of resources to meet the very young child's educational needs. The education of the child with disabilities from birth through age two is not at this point conceived to be a civil right. The procedure and the involvement of the IFSP could certainly be adopted in the IEP. In both cases the social worker plays an important role, and the greater the need and complexity of family involvement, the more important this role becomes.

THE INDIVIDUALIZED EDUCATION PROGRAM (IEP)

The IEP is the central management tool used to ensure the child with disabilities the right to a free, appropriate, public education. The IEP assembles recent evaluation, present decision making, and future expectations in one document. It is a synopsis of the service efforts of the multidisciplinary team. It is built upon and thus reflects the evaluation effort that has previously taken place and the areas of need identified in the multidisciplinary conference (MDC). It involves the people who have interest in the child's education and who attend the IEP staffing: the parents, differing members of the multidisciplinary team (e.g., the teacher, administrator, psychologist, and other specialized personnel), when appropriate, and the child. It would be a mistake to view the IEP as merely another document. It is the living record of a process. The success of the IEP is dependent on the process itself. It is important to note that only when the students learning needs are determined, and special services required to meet these needs are determined, can possibility of placement be entertained.

The IEP is a record of the completion of a number of complex evaluative and decision-making processes and is a product of common collaboration. The social worker's input into the decision-making process will be based in part on the social developmental study. The social worker who participated in the IEP staffing generally has important responsibilities, which go beyond the report and which address the decision-making process itself.

The decision-making process aims for an agreement in five crucial areas. These are (1) the child's present level of performance; (2) annual goals and short-term objectives or "benchmarks"; (3) the special education and related services to be provided the child; (4) the means of evaluation; and (5) the needed transition services, including a statement of the interagency responsibilities or linkages, before the student completes his/her school experience (34 C.F.R. 300.346; 20 U.S.C. 1414 et seq.). The IEP is more than a set of reports of plans. It encapsulates the entire provision of special education and related services as well as the evaluation of effectiveness. It is ultimately a list of services to be provided to reach agreed-upon goals. Although the IEP cannot guarantee the child will actually reach these particular goals, it is an agreement on the school's part to provide or purchase (if it cannot directly provide) the special education and related services listed in the document. The completed agreement reflects that a complex evaluation and goal-setting process has taken place among parents, school, and child—and, if signed and not contested, is concrete evidence that consensus has been reached among all parties.

The full potential of what social work can offer to children in schools cannot be achieved without some significant level of participation by the social worker in the IEP process. No social worker can expect to offer services to children with disabilities in the school without IEP involvement. Although survival in the schools demands participation, the unique contribution of the social worker to the IEP process needs to be well understood. This contribution takes place in at least three major areas. The social worker (1) participates in the process of setting annual goals and short-term objectives; (2) helps the multidisciplinary team to develop sufficient consensus among itself and with parents to proceed; and (3) is involved with case management and integration of school and outside agency resources.

THE PROCESS OF SETTING ANNUAL GOALS AND SHORT-TERM OBJECTIVES

The social worker makes the education system work for children where it might not otherwise be effective. The education of the child with disabilities is in large part a preparation for his or her best level of social functioning outside of the school situation. Particularly for the severely disabled, a large part of this preparation has to do with the learning of life skills: those skills that promote appropriate independence, appropriate and satisfying interpersonal relationships, problem-solving skills, an appropriate self-image, and tolerance for unavoidable stress. These are areas where social workers have particular expertise and can make a crucial contribution to the educational process. For many children with disabilities, education is dependent upon achievement of these goals. The general areas listed earlier can be broken down into instructional objectives shared by teacher and social worker. These shared objectives can be achieved through consultation with the teacher, direct intervention with the child and parents, and through the social worker's involvement in the classroom itself. The instructional objectives often reflect the confluence of educational and social goals.

WHAT IS THE IEP TEAM?

The IEP is the crucial document in defining and ensuring the right of the pupil to a free appropriate public education. The membership of the IEP team has been defined by law. The *IEP team* means a group of individuals composed of:

a. The parents of a child with a disability;
b. A regular education teacher of the child (if the child is, or may be, participating in the regular education environment);
c. At least one special education teacher (or provider) of the child;
d. A representative of the local educational agency who provides or supervises special education and who is knowledgeable about the general curriculum;

e. An individual who can interpret the instructional implications of evaluation results.

"Parents" may also include an individual who may have special knowledge
or expertise regarding the child. Also, whenever appropriate, the child with
a disability should be included. The IEP team is easily confused with the
multidisciplinary team, which develops a multifaceted nondiscriminatory
evaluation and determines disability. The IEP process is quite different,
and the law prescribes the minimal membership of this team. But of course
it is inevitable that many of the same players will have a part on both teams
and indeed they may be identical.

DEVELOPING AGREEMENTS AND INTEGRATION
OF RESOURCES

Many school districts routinely use the social worker as a coordinator of
the initial multidisciplinary team and in the later IEP staffing with the
parents. Most social workers have developed problem-solving and consen-
sus-building skills through their professional education. These skills are
often crucial to the successful completion of the IEP process. The high
level of professional specialization within the school and the different interests often represented by parent and school create the potential for conflict.
Agreements, if reached, are frequently perceived as accommodations between weaker and stronger sets of interests. The social worker, who is the
most likely member of the school team to have a holistic perspective on
the child, generally has the best contact with all elements of the process
and is quite accustomed to working with potential conflict.

Attainment of IEP goals, particularly with the more seriously disabled
children, often demands coordination and integration of a variety of services
outside the school as well as inside. Disabled children receive services from
a variety of agencies: medical services, respite care, child welfare, mental
health, financial assistance, transportation, vocational education, and so on.
In addition to formal agency services, they can receive a variety of helps
from neighbors, kin, informal groups in the community, and so on. The
social worker is usually the only member of the multidisciplinary team who,
as a matter of choice, is in everyday contact with these resources and whose
educational preparation does include concepts of problem solving and coordination among these services.

The social work role has been defined in the law as:

1. Preparing a social or developmental history for a child who possibly has
disabilities;
2. Group and individual counseling with the child and family;
3. Working with problems in a child's living situation (home, school, and
community) that affect the child's adjustment in school;

4. Mobilizing school and community resources to enable the child to receive maximum benefit from his or her educational program (34 C.F.R. 300.186(12); 20 U.S.C. 1402(29)). The U.S. Department of Education in a document discussing the IEP listed the social worker as one of three professionals (the others were counselor and psychologist) who might serve as coordinator or case manager of the IEP process for an individual child or all disabled children served by an agency. Examples of the kinds of activities that case managers might carry out are (1) coordinating the multidisciplinary evaluation; (2) collecting and synthesizing the evaluation reports and other relevant information about a child that might be needed at the IEP meeting; (3) communicating with the parents; and (4) participating in or conducting the IEP meeting itself (U.S. Department of Education, 1981).

THE CONTENTS OF AN INDIVIDUALIZED EDUCATION PROGRAM

The IEP for each child must include:

A statement of the child's present levels of educational performance in academic and nonacademic areas that specify the effect of the disability on the student's performance. The child's baseline levels in various areas of educational performance (for example, academic performance, classroom behavior, social skills) are used in determining the appropriate goals and objectives for that child. The comparison of the present levels of performance with the levels at which the child should be functioning reveals the areas of deficit. It is the responsibility of the multidisciplinary team to provide input that establishes the child's present levels of performance. These baseline data are the result of collaboration among the various persons who deal with the child and his or her education. Identifying present levels of performance is necessary so that there is a basis for judgment in establishing goals as well as for later evaluation and adjustment of goals and program.

A statement of annual goals and short-term instructional objectives or benchmarks. Goals and objectives should reflect present levels of performance and provide a way for educators and parents to track the child's progress in special education. They should not be confused with the goals and objectives that are normally found in daily, weekly, or monthly instructional plans. Otherwise there could be hundreds of educational goals for one IEP. Annual goals are statements that describe what a disabled child can reasonably be expected to accomplish within the framework of the school year. Short-term instructional objectives or benchmarks are measurable intermediate steps between a disabled child's present levels of educational performance and the annual goals that are established for the child. The objectives must be based on a logical breakdown of the major components of the annual goals and can serve as milestones for measuring progress toward meeting the goals (U.S. Department of Education, 1981). They are concrete elements that in total will guide the education process toward the achievement of particular goals.

A statement of the special education and related services to be provided to the child and a statement of the program modifications or supports for school personnel that will be provided so that the child attains the annual goals and participates, whenever possible and appropriate, in the general curriculum: a statement of the extent to which the child will not be able to participate in general education programs. The statement of needed special education and related services is derived directly from the annual goals and short-term objectives. If necessary resources are unavailable within the school, the school must contract with outside agencies, individuals, or other school districts to ensure their provision. Parents, as part of the multidisciplinary team, must be included in the decision-making process that determines these resources. The law also requires a statement of the extent to which the child cannot participate in regular education with or without support services, underlining the importance of the process of developing the least restrictive environment for the child with disabilities. The negative wording (not participate) is meant to bring the team to justify nonparticipation in a general education environment, rather than assume an environment, directly matched to the child's learning needs, but more restrictive. This is some of the legal language that is now being addressed in state policies around inclusion.

The projected dates for initiation of services and the anticipated duration of the services. These time guidelines are established concurrently with the annual goals and initiation of services is proscribed by law. The length of duration of short-term objectives is based upon an estimate of the time necessary for completion of the goals and objectives.

An Individual Transition Plan (ITP), which is a statement of the needed transition services (to facilitate movement to post-secondary education, employment, or additional schooling or training) including, when appropriate, a statement of the interagency responsibilities or linkages before the student leaves the school setting. Generally applying to students fourteen or older, transition services mean a coordinated set of activities for a student, designed within an outcome-oriented process, that promotes movement from school to postschool activities. The coordinated set of activities is based upon the individual student's needs, taking into account the student's preferences and interests. It includes instruction, community experiences, the development of employment and postschool adult living objectives and, when appropriate, acquisition of daily living skills and functional vocational evaluation. Where a participating agency other than the educational agency would fail to provide agreed-upon services, the educational agency would reconvene the IEP team to identify alternative strategies to meet the transition objectives.

While the law specifies an ITP for pupils fourteen or older with certain variations as the students grows older, the term *transition* has also been applied to all movement from one level to another. For example, as a five-year-old child with severe disabilities moves from early childhood special education to kindergarten, an appropriate transition plan should be developed. Whenever there is a delicate transition from one environment to another, possibly somewhat more stressful, there needs to be planning, and the social worker probably should be involved.

A statement of how the child's progress toward the annual goals will be measured and how the parents will be informed (by means of periodic report cards) of progress toward annual goals. These would involve objective criteria and evaluation procedures and a schedule for determining, at least on an annual basis, whether the short-term instructional objectives (or benchmarks) are being achieved. Objective criteria are components of the child's behavior that may be observed and measured. Objective criteria may be used to compare the child's current performance with previous levels of performance or they may be compared with a classroom norm that is typical of children his or her age. The results of these comparisons indicate whether or not short-term objectives are being achieved or whether new and different objectives may be in order (20 U.S.C. 1414(1)).

We may break down the steps that should be followed to arrive at those goals and objectives in the school social worker's contribution to the IEP. The steps represent a way of clarifying our own goals and involvement in developing the IEP.

The Presenting Problem

In order to be eligible for P.L. 105–17 funding, the problem must relate to the categories of disabilities written into the regulations. The fact that the child fits into one of the categories, for example, hearing-impaired, does not automatically make him or her a candidate for social work intervention. The inability to deal with stress, potential breakdown of social functioning, or needed improvement of social functioning are general reasons for referral to a social worker. The additional stress of a disability and the need for individualized environmental support systems are reasons that many exceptional children need social work help. The child with a particular disability may have difficulty coping with the educational and social skill demands of the school. He or she may need help in acquiring such skills and/or in dealing with experiences that are new.

A Hypothetical Case Study

Let us follow a simple referral for a case study evaluation, the IEP process, and service sequence through each of the stages of the process. The reader should keep in mind that this is a hypothetical case study and that the type and extent of the school social worker's involvement in a particular case will depend on the individual child's needs as determined by the multidisciplinary team. We may begin with the presenting problem. Jimmy is a multiply physically disabled twelve-year-old who is borderline educable mentally disabled. He was referred because of his teacher's concern that his excessive demands for attention were impeding his learning process in several general education classes, particularly in gym. It should be noted that in this case we have deliberately used the example of a child who is taking a partial general education program.

The problem as a whole.   The school social worker's conference with teacher and parents resulted in a picture of a boy whose performance in school has been quite uneven and whose ability to function adequately in school has been hampered by parental overprotectiveness and disagreement on the degree of independence he should be allowed. He is currently enrolled in both special and regular education classes with poor adjustment to some of these classes, overwhelming needs for attention from adults, and withdrawal from relations with other children. In the family the parents have had difficulty agreeing on the tasks he could be involved in and on his expected level of self-care. As a consequence, Jimmy's participation in the family and in care of himself is considerably less than his potential. The parents are in conflict about this, and his two brothers and a sister reflect this ambivalence in their relationships with him. On the basis of this and other information gathered, the social worker makes a diagnostic statement that draws some connections between Jimmy's role in the family, the parents' feelings, and the way Jimmy has played out some of these family role interactions in school behaviors, particularly with parent-like school figures and teachers. The statement also includes alternative plans for working with the family, Jimmy, and his teachers. The results of the social worker's assessment, combined with the information gathered by the other team members, will be used by the team in the MDC and later to formulate the statement of present levels of educational functioning in the IEP.

The problem as it is experienced in the context of education.   The next step is to define the problem as it is being experienced in the classroom and in relation to the goals of education. At the risk of oversimplifying, we may provide several social parameters of the educational problem. One parameter is that of engagement or withdrawal from educational tasks appropriate to the child's capabilities. The child may either engage in the learning process with distracting, attention-getting, inappropriately aggressive behavior or may withdraw from the process, attempting to compensate in other ways for the withdrawal. A second parameter is that of engagement or withdrawal from relationships with other children. Pupils need to learn social skills appropriate to their own maturational level. The learning of these social skills influences the performance of educational tasks. Thus, there is a direct relation between the learning environment and the child's social maturation.

To follow our example, the school wishes to place Jimmy in a particular gym class with nondisabled children. We can predict with some certainty that Jimmy will place high demands on the gym teacher and the other pupils, and that the parents, while accepting of the idea, might endanger the arrangement because of their own anxiety and worries about Jimmy. Failure in the gym class could generalize to several other classes where he has recently made some adjustment. There is particular concern with the gym class due to dressing, showers, and inherent physical competition. Any one of these factors might place Jimmy's use of what the school could offer him at risk. What we know about the problem allows us to predict with some degree of accuracy the chances of goal achievement within a behavior setting and some ability to generalize to the overall ecology of the school. This understanding allows us to move to the next stage, definition of the problem in behavioral terms.

The problem as behavior.   The purpose of this stage is to state the school social worker's formulation of the problem in behavioral terms and to relate it to the educational goals established earlier. Behavioral terms are statements of the client's present functioning, or what Jimmy is presently doing. These terms establish a baseline for goals and objectives and must be specific.

Behavioral objectives risk fragmentation and meaninglessness if they do not flow from the process of problem definition discussed earlier. The school social worker may find him or herself in the position of choosing from a seemingly infinite range of behaviors for any child. Actually, a few well-chosen examples are much better, particularly if they may serve as indicators.

To go back to our example, Jimmy has difficulty dealing with a situation that seems competitive and draws attention to his poor functioning. Under stress he has tended to retreat into social relations with adults from whom he demands high levels of attention. He is particularly uneasy with the dressing and showering aspects of gym. His parents' anxiety reveals another set of needs in the situation. Teachers also can tend to overreact to the situation, increasing the chances of failure. To enumerate specific aspects of the problem:

1. Jimmy withdraws from situations involving physical competition. Without intervention, the pattern is expected to continue or increase in gym class.
2. Jimmy tends not to interact with nondisabled peers.
3. Social interaction with disabled peers is limited.
4. Jimmy has no close friends.
5. Jimmy makes excessive demands on adults, especially teachers, but doesn't function in the classroom up to his own capacities without constant support from the teacher.
6. Jimmy is particularly self-conscious concerning dressing and showering aspects of gym.
7. His parents have tended to protect Jimmy from situations that demand independence or involve any risking of self. Jimmy's home patterns are related to his school patterns.
8. Teachers have tended either toward excessive protection or excessive expectations of independence with Jimmy.

Annual goals, short-term objectives, and resources.   Finally, we may define goals and objectives. Annual goals are specific statements of the skills the student should be progressing toward within the framework of the school year. Annual goals evolve out of the assessment of the child's needs and abilities and should be an index of student progress. Although there are different formats that may serve as examples for a particular child's individualized education program, most would probably contain:

1. The *direction* of change desired—to increase, to decrease, to maintain.
2. *Deficit* or *excess*—the general area that is identified as needing special attention.
3. *Present level*—what the child now does in deficit or in excess.
4. *Expected level*—where the child realistically could be or what he could gain, with proper resources.

5. *Resources needed*—to accomplish the needed level of performance. Resources could be specialists, materials, situations, or methods required to bring about the desired change.

In Jimmy's case, there are two major annual goals. The components are listed in brackets.

Annual Goal 1: For Jimmy to increase [direction] positive social relations with nondisabled peers [deficit] from limited [from] to more informal [to] through interaction experiences in a group with the social worker and regular social work contacts with the parents and teacher [resources].

Annual Goal 2: For Jimmy to maintain [direction] his current academic adjustment.

Note that the direction set in the second goal is maintenance of current functioning. Maintenance equates present and expected levels of functioning.

Short-term instructional objectives. Short-term instructional objectives can be thought of as benchmarks or steps toward achievement of the annual goals. These steps are milestones through which progress toward the annual goals can be assessed. They should specify the conditions under which the behavior is to be exhibited by the student in his class, in unstructured group tasks, the lunchroom, gymnasium, etc. For the social worker, these can be indicators or changes in behavior and do not have to reflect every single objective that might be defined for that goal. For Jimmy, our hypothetical case example, some short-term instructional objectives might be:

1. Jimmy's level of class participation and quality of assignment completion in his regular education classes will be maintained at his current level through January 15.
2. Jimmy will interact compatibly with nondisabled peers in an unstructured group task by March 15.
3. Jimmy will interact comfortably and spontaneously with nondisabled peers in an unstructured lunchroom situation by May 15.
4. Jimmy will form casual friendships, with both disabled and nondisabled peers, by June 15.
5. Jimmy's distractibility and talking out in class will reduce by 50 percent by June 15.
6. Jimmy will be able to dress for gym without special arrangement by January 15.

Resources.   There may be external barriers to Jimmy's accomplishing these goals and objectives.[1] For example, teachers and parents may need help to avoid overprotecting Jimmy or some modifications in the gym program may be necessary. A list of the specific educational services required must be written into the IEP so that the goals and objectives can be implemented. The list of services and persons responsible is essentially a resource statement. Parents have a right to request that educational services that are included in the IEP, but are not available in the school, be purchased by the school district for the child or otherwise be provided at no cost to the parents.[2] Examples of such services might include:

1. The social worker will see Jimmy once a week for a forty-five minute period with a group of other children with disabilities who are also dealing with a mainstreamed class. The appropriateness of whether Jimmy should continue in the group will be reevaluated on or about January 15.

2. The social worker will monitor Jimmy's group progress and act as liaison between the multidisciplinary team and the family service agency working with Jimmy's family, as well as informing Jimmy's parents of progress.

3. The teacher will monitor Jimmy's achievement of the above objectives, reinforcing independent and peer-affiliative behavior.

INVOLVING CHILDREN IN THE IEP

It is a good practice to involve the school child in IEP plans. Sometimes these goals may seem abstract and so a mechanism, such as the car-in-the-garage technique, developed by Fairbanks (1985), is useful. This technique involves the following steps:

1. The school social worker draws a rough sketch of a garage on a piece of paper, connects it to a road, indicates that the garage is to be the child's destination, and asks the child to identify what should be placed in the garage as goals.

2. The child tells the school social worker what changes are desired, and the social worker or the child writes these goals inside the garage.

3. The child places one or more cars at various points along the road to the garage, symbolizing how far away from the goals and objectives he or she is. Sometimes the child leaves one or more cars off the road completely, indicating extreme lack of progress toward the goals represented by those cars.

4. The social worker asks the child for additional information about the cars and records the responses. The child's stated goals and objectives then become part of the IEP that is formally drafted at the planning team meeting.

FIGURE 1   Using the Car-in-the-Garage Technique to Clarify Objectives

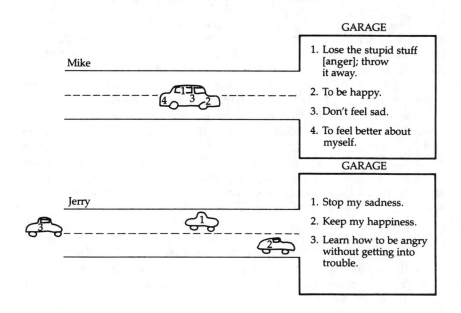

SOURCE: Nancy Mcdowell Fairbanks. 1987. Involving children in the IEP: The car-in-the-garage technique. Reprinted with permission from *Social Work in Education*. Vol. 9 (3).

5. The child draws new cars on the road as treatment progresses, relocating the cars on the road either closer or farther away from the garage.

6. The child places one or more cars inside the garage when particular objectives are attained and either establishes a new set of objectives or terminates treatment.

Figure 1 illustrates use of the technique in clarifying initial objectives for Mike, age twelve, and Jerry, age eight, in a public school day treatment program. Following the clarification of objectives, the technique can be used to measure progress and change objectives. In some cases it can be used with a group, because the technique becomes a visual and verbal metaphor for their accomplishments.

THE INDIVIDUALIZED FAMILY PLAN (IFP)

The IEP framework addresses education with the parents as partners in developing the education program. For a family-oriented social worker this may seem incomplete. A number of social workers and educators, particularly Betty Welsh (1985), developed the Individualized Family Plan (IFP) as a supplement to the social work IEP. In Jimmy's case the problem in school was related to a long-established pattern of inconsistent expectations at home that caused Jimmy's self-care and participation in the family to be far below his capabilities. If parents and family are treated, not only as partners, but as the first educators and the first context for education of the child, a quite different approach to goal setting and consequent practice can be developed. The IFP is a formalized plan worked out with the family to assist it and the child with disabilities in accomplishing certain goals. In Jimmy's case the social worker works with the disabled child and the parents and indirectly with siblings to develop an agreement on specific aspects of participation and contribution in family, through chores, helping with younger siblings, learning more responsibility in maintaining his room, choosing his clothes, and dressing himself. These become objectives to the general goals of enhanced contribution to the family and self-care. In the process of planning with the parents and with Jimmy, some marital and family issues are touched upon. The family deals with aspects of these with reference to wanting to help Jimmy in his efforts to grow up. On the other hand, the persistence of these strains may prompt parents or family to go more deeply into marital counseling or family therapy in their efforts to deal with the problem. In any case, the IFP becomes a framework for a more focused family practice that is related to the goals of education (Welsh, 1985). Because in many situations the school absolutely cannot accomplish its goals without family involvement, the IFP becomes a necessary tool of the school social worker.

THE INDIVIDUALIZED FAMILY SERVICES PLAN (IFSP)

The IFSP grows out of early intervention programs for infants and toddlers and the obvious necessity of family involvement with children from birth through two years of age, especially children with multiple disabilities. The family often has heavy involvement with the health care system, and this system is often an important source of referral to early childhood or parent-infant programs. Parents are mourning the loss of the perfect child and of their hopes and expectations (Lachney, 1982). The heavy caretaking demands can split even well-established marital relations into overadequate and enmeshed roles or underadequate and disengaged roles, and these roles often follow conventional gender expectations. The resulting marital and family patterns are disruptive of other aspects of family living and may account for the higher rates of divorce, suicide, and child abuse among families of children with disabilities (Gallagher, Beckman, and Cross, 1983). Working with the parents while they are actively mourning their losses and when care patterns have not been completely solidified may prevent the most crippling effects of these disrupting patterns on the family and especially on the disabled child.

The IFSP must contain:

1. A statement of the child's present levels of development (cognitive, speech/language, psychosocial, motor, and self-help)
2. A statement of the family's strengths and needs relating to enhancing the child's development
3. The criteria, procedures, and timelines for determining progress
4. The specific early intervention services necessary to meet the unique needs of the child and family, including the method, frequency, and intensity of service
5. The projected dates for the initiation of service and the expected duration
6. The name of the case manager
7. Procedures for transition from early intervention into the preschool program

The IFSP must be evaluated at least once a year, and must be reviewed every six months or more, where appropriate.

Many of the principles underlying the IEP are also applicable to the IFSP and need not be repeated. There are several differences, because the IFSP is more comprehensive than the IEP and takes in a wider universe. The focus of the IFSP is first of all on *development*, rather than a more static focus, appropriate to the older child. This is evaluated through a variety of means and instruments. In addition, a statement of the family's strengths and needs relating to enhancing the child's development is needed. A statement of the family's strengths and needs requires a family assessment, and is best carried out by the school social worker. An agreement on goals, objectives, and tasks needs to emerge from this mutual assessment between social worker and family. Also, the coping and adaptation of parents, siblings, and support systems in an extended family and friendship network need to be assessed. A certain amount of inactivity associated with being overwhelmed and with mourning, and the potential distortion of relationships inherent in heavy care-giving demands often can be expected in these situations, and thus the risks should be assessed. The teaching role of parents can be distorted by the loss of hope implicit in a mourning process, and by the same relational distortions involved in the discussion of care-giving roles. Parents may be reluctant to accept help and may isolate themselves from other potential support systems in the process. Success in this process presupposes a good contact between the social worker and parents when the pressures and risks are discussed in a normalizing context.

Thus, an agreement can develop with the family as the foundation for a statement of major outcomes expected to be achieved by the child and family.

MAJOR OUTCOMES EXPECTED TO BE ACHIEVED BY THE CHILD AND THE FAMILY

Based on the assessment and the particular contacts developed with the family, major expected outcomes now can be stated in a way that reinforces the primary roles of parents as educators as well as care givers and the appropriate assistance of the school in carrying out their mission. A key outcome will unavoidably be the family's participation in the teaching and care-giving roles and ability to use the case management process. The outcomes are largely based on (1) the assessments previously made of the child's present levels of development; and (2) the new coping and adaptation patterns becoming established in the family. Although educational and medical specialists have an important role in setting achievable developmental outcomes, social workers should be involved in setting achievable family outcomes and showing their relation to developmental outcomes.

These outcomes become more specific through (1) the criteria, procedures, and timelines for determining progress; (2) the specific early intervention services necessary to meet the unique needs of the child and family, including the method, frequency, and intensity of service; and (3) the projected dates for the initiation of services and the expected duration. As in the IEP, these set the parameters of the services to achieve the named developmental and family outcomes. Again, school social work services are the most appropriate (and available) external services in assisting families to meet the desired outcomes.

SERVICE COORDINATION

The IFSP must contain the name of the service coordinator from the profession most immediately relevant to the infant's, toddler's, or family's needs who will be responsible for the implementation of the plan in coordination with other agencies or persons. He or she coordinates services to the family of an infant or toddler with a handicap to assist in gaining access to early intervention services identified in the IFSP. Service coordination includes:

1. Coordinating assessments and participating in the development of the Individualized Family Service Plan
2. Assisting families in identifying available service providers
3. Coordinating and monitoring the delivery of services, including coordinating the provision of early intervention services with other services

that the child or family may need or is receiving, but that are not required under this part

4. Facilitating the development of a transition plan to preschool services where appropriate (*Federal Register* 52(222):303.6)

The coordinator then assists parents in gaining access to these services. However, parents themselves should take responsibility as much as possible for the coordination roles (Garland, Woodruff, and Buck, 1988) or at least have a major role in the selection of a service coordinator. The social worker's role places him or her closest to the parents in carrying out service coordination responsibilities.

The final part of the IFSP is that of the child's transition from an early intervention program to the preschool program. Although this is frequently the domain of the educational specialists, the process and the timing of the entry of the child from a family context into a new program with new demands may be an area in which the school social worker needs to participate.

The family involvement projected in the IFSP need not be confined to infants and toddlers. When children present complex vulnerabilities and long-established patterns that inevitably affect the educational process, it is simply good practice to involve the parents in the work of the school. The IEP and the IFSP can be no better than the process of thinking, communication, and decision making they represent. They certainly are accountability documents, but they also are vehicles for collaboration with parents and for coordination of resources and development of the working agreements necessary for complex goals to be achieved. The IFSP and the IEP are challenges for social workers in developing clarity about what they will be offering students, parents, and the school, while providing an opportunity to work systematically with all of the influences on the full educational process. It is an opportunity that we cannot afford to let pass.

NOTES

1. See *Federal Register*, Education of Handicapped Children, Tuesday, August 23, 1977, 121a.552(d). "In selecting the least restrictive environment, consideration is given to any potentially harmful effect on the child or on the quality of services which he or she needs." While the concept of external barriers is not highlighted in the law, it is a traditional concept in dealing with persons with handicapping conditions. Lack of focus on such tangible or non-tangible barriers would be in effect "blaming the victim" for a condition which he or she did not create.

2. A free appropriate public education is defined in the law as special education and related services that (A) have been provided at public expense, under public supervision and direction and without charge; (B) meet the standards of the state educational agency; (C) include an appropriate preschool, elementary, or

secondary school education in the state involved; and (D) are provided in conformity with the individualized education program (20 U.S.C. 1401(8)).

REFERENCES

Fairbanks, N. M. 1985. Involving children in the IEP: The car-in-the-garage technique. *Social Work in Education* 7(3):171–182.

Gallagher, J. J., Beckman, P., and Cross, A. H. 1983. Families of handicapped children: Sources of stress and its alleviation. *Exceptional Children* 50(1):10–18.

Garland, C., Woodruff, G., and Buck, D., 1988. Case management. *Division for Early Childhood White Paper*. Council for Exceptional Children: Reston, VA.

Lachney, M. E. 1982. Understanding families of the handicapped: A critical factor in the parent-school relationship. In Constable, R. T., and Flynn, J. P., (eds.). *School social work: Practice and research perspectives*. Homewood, IL: The Dorsey Press.

U.S. Department of Education. 1981. The Case Study Evaluation.

Welsh, B. L. 1985. The individualized family plan (IFP): A social work component to the IEP. Paper presented at the NASW School Social Work Conference, Philadelphia, PA.

CHAPTER 19

Annual Goals and Short-Term Objectives for School Social Workers

David Sanders
School Social Worker, Macon-Piatt Special Education District, Illinois

- Taxonomy of Needs
- Annual Goals and Short-Term Objectives: A Sample Taxonomy

Both student development and the educational process involve important areas of student need that are broader than or underlie academic areas as the school identifies them. These areas of personal and social functioning are directly related to the role of the school social worker. They underlie education and thus are necessary for education to take place. Because of this, they are not easily and concretely identified as subject areas. The school social worker is usually responsible for assembling a service strategy, often providing direct services so that the student may take developmental steps in these areas. It is very important that the social worker find realistic and achievable annual goals and short-term objectives matched with an appropriate strategy. However, writing such goals and objectives under staffing pressures can be stressful because participants find themselves trying to do two things simultaneously: listening and contributing to the discussion while trying to concentrate on writing the goals and objectives.

This chapter is intended to provide busy school social workers with an accessible taxonomy of frequently identified nonacademic needs, suggested model language for annual goal statements and short-term objectives to meet those needs, and ideas for objective criteria that will be needed to evaluate progress toward those goals. Having these prompts available during the staffing will reduce stresses, increase participation in the conference discussions, and speed up the entire staffing process by compressing the time needed to complete this essential task.

Educators, as well as support staff, should follow two obvious, but sometimes overlooked, guiding principles when completing Individualized Education Program (IEP) documents. First, all services provided to students should enhance their chances of success in the public schools. Second, those services should be provided using accepted, well-established practices.

Using this as the basis for any decisions recorded on a student's IEP, supervisors and school social work practitioners can be confident that they are serving the best interests of the student.

Guidelines from the Individuals with Disabilities Education Act require that the IEP:

a. Include a statement of the student's present levels of educational performance in academic and nonacademic areas;
b. Include annual goals to describe what the student can be expected to achieve;
c. Include short-term objectives designed to meet each annual goal;
d. Ensure that these short-term objectives are specific; and
e. Specify the objective criteria, the evaluation procedures, and a schedule for determining whether the objectives are being achieved.

Educational placement and any necessary related services must also be specified, including the frequency, length, and type of such services; and any necessary modifications to the general educational program to implement the services must also be clarified.

In addition, the prospective guidelines require the inclusion of appropriate *positive behavior strategies, interventions,* and *supports* for those students whose behavior impedes their learning or the learning of others. This will create additional opportunities for school social workers to share their skills and knowledge of behavior management strategies, and hopefully to provide the leadership necessary for creating and implementing the behavior plans that will be needed to meet this requirement. Often these behavior plans are too lengthy to write directly on the IEP. They are often written separately as an addendum and referred to on the IEP itself.

TAXONOMY OF NEEDS

Nonacademic needs that impede a student's functioning in school typically fall into four basic themes, or categories:

1. *Motivation*—referring to desire to achieve and develop within school expectations,
2. *Behavior*—referring to actions dysfunctional to own learning and development or the learning and development of others,
3. *Social skills*—referring to skills in relation to others, difficulties making friends, or problems fitting into groups positively,
4. *Self-image*—referring to difficulties in self-esteem or self-confidence.

Identifying the appropriate basic need category is the first step for using this taxonomy efficiently. The task of identification should focus on underlying needs as well as the presenting behavior. It is only after careful evaluation of the pertinent data that a confident decision can be made. Aggressive and defiant behaviors are illustrative. At first, fighting may indicate that *behavior* would be the appropriate basic category. But aggressive behavior is often symptomatic of weak or nonexistent, *social skills*, or of a profound and pervasive feeling of inferiority, in which case *self-image* would be the more appropriate category.

After the basic category is identified an *annual goal* must be written. The IEP guidelines require that the annual goals be measurable, meet the student's needs resulting from his or her disability, and enhance the student's ability to participate in the least restrictive education environment. "Measurable" implies markers of present performance and of anticipated performance. Both need to be obtained similarly, objectively, and consistently. In academic areas, such markers are readily available (test scores, report cards, achievement tests, etc.), but in nonacademic areas, they are often difficult to obtain or have to be created from scratch. In the above example, the daily record of office referrals for disciplinary measures could be used as a marker, as could inclusion in play groups during recess, which might be a better marker for self-esteem.

Expected levels can be documented for such nonacademic phenomena as *motivation* (teachers' daily records, charts), *behavior* (charts for documenting classroom behavior, time-out compliance, office referrals, detentions), *social skills* (self-rating scales, questionnaires, surveys), and *self-esteem* (self-reporting instruments, self-esteem scales, journal entries). Once a criterion is established, an expected level that is workable and achievable by the student over the period of an academic year can be developed. Once this is developed, any "increase" can be measured.

After the annual goal statements are written, short-term objectives must also be written. These should be specific and measurable benchmarks of progress toward the annual goals. To make the taxonomy even more useful, each annual goal statement is divided into several relevant subordinate *profiles*. Each profile, such as "homework completion," "school attendance," and "classroom behavior," further defines the basic, nonacademic need area. Each has its own sequential short-term objectives. There should be at least two short-term objectives for each profile.

Most of the short-term objectives begin with the generic phrase "With social work intervention, the student will . . ." and this may be the introduction of choice when writing the objectives on the IEP because it does not restrict a service plan to particular methods or strategies that may later be confining. In some situations, however, it could be important to identify a specific methodology, such as "With casework intervention, the student will . . ." or "With group work intervention, the student will . . ." or to identify a specific strategy, such as "With a conflict resolution program, the student will . . ." or "Using rational-emotive therapy techniques, the student will . . ." Circumstances unique to each student's IEP will dictate how precisely each objective should be written.

ANNUAL GOALS AND SHORT-TERM OBJECTIVES: A SAMPLE TAXONOMY

The following list of annual goals and short-term objectives is not exhaustive and is not intended to cover every student need certain to manifest itself during staffings. With the use of the taxonomy, however, the school social worker or special education supervisor will be able to quickly locate applicable goals and objectives either to write on the student's IEP, when appropriate, or to use as a prompt to generate more precise language (alternative phrasing is given in parentheses).

Annual Goals and Short-term Objectives List for Nonacademic Areas

I. **Motivation Annual Goal Statement:** *Student* will increase compliance to academic responsibilities to expected levels.

A. **Profile:** Poor homework completion, weak organization skills, poor study skills

1. With social work intervention, *Student* will learn the importance of completing homework assignments and being prepared for class.   Tests (content based)

2. With social work intervention (With an incentive plan), *Student* will complete homework as assigned and be prepared for class.   Charting (contracting incentive plans)
Daily log (teacher's records, assignment notebooks)

3. Independently (With social work intervention), *Student* will complete homework as assigned and will be prepared for class (receive passing grades in* class, maintain credits to graduate with class).   Charting (contracting, incentive plans)
Daily log (teacher's gradebook)
Other (midterm reports, report cards)

B. **Profile:** Off-task behavior

1. With social work intervention, *Student* will learn the importance of listening and being on task at school.   Tests (content based)

2. With social work intervention (With an incentive plan), *Student* will begin in-class assignments and (with appropriate cues from the teacher) will be on task for * minutes (until work is completed).

Charting (contracting, incentive plans)
Observations (documented)
Other (formal classroom observations)

3. Independently (With social work intervention), *Student* will be consistently and appropriately on task.

Charting (contracting, incentive plans)
Observations (documented)
Other (consultations, formal classroom observations)

C. **Profile:** Poor school attendance, truancy
1. With social work intervention, *Student* will learn the importance of daily school attendance.

Tests (content based)

2. With social work intervention (With an incentive plan, With a behavior modification schedule), *Student* will decrease school absences to less than one (two) per month.

Charting (contracting, incentive plans)
Other (attendance records)

3. Independently, *Student* will be at school each attendance day unless ill (excused, etc.)

Other (attendance records)

II. **Behavior Annual Goal Statement:** *Student* will increase acceptable classroom behaviors to expected levels
A. **Profile:** For students with behavior plans the above annual goal statement should suffice; review the following suggestions for short-term objectives
1. With social work intervention (With an incentive strategy) *Student* will follow the behavior plan specifically written as part of his IEP.

Charting (contracting, incentive plans)
Daily log (teacher's records)

2. Independently, *Student* will follow the behavior plan specifically written as part of his IEP

Charting (contracting, incentive plans)
Daily log (teacher's records, office records)

B. Profile: Poor listening skills, not following directions

1. With social work intervention, *Student* will learn why paying attention and following directions are important in the classroom (on the playground, in the cafeteria, etc.).

   Tests (content based)

2. With social work intervention (With an incentive plan), *Student* will listen for and follow directions in the classroom with appropriate cues from the teacher).

   Charting (contracting, incentive plans)
   Observations (documented)
   Other (consultations, formal classroom observations)

3. Independently, *Student* will listen for and follow directions.

   Observations (documented)
   Other (consultations, formal classroom observations)

C. Profile: Chronic classroom misbehavior

1. With social work intervention, *Student* will understand the importance of rule systems in school and will know the classroom (school, playground, cafeteria) rules and consequences of noncompliance.

   Tests (content based)

2. With social work intervention, *Student* will learn the purpose of time-out and will learn and practice correct time-out behavior.

   Tests (content based)
   Daily log (record of practice sessions)

3. With social work intervention (With an incentive plan), *Student* will take time-out correctly in the classroom in compliance to the classroom behavior plan.

   Charting (schedules, contracting)
   Daily log (teacher's behavior records)
   Observations (documented)

4. Independently (With social work intervention, With an incentive plan), *Student* will accept and follow the classroom behavior plan (increase acceptable classroom behaviors, decrease classroom disruptions to * or less per *).

   Charting (schedules, contracting)
   Daily log (teacher's behavior records)
   Observations (reports from teachers, staff)
   Other (office discipline records)

D. Profile: Bothering others, aggressive behaviors

1. With social work intervention, *Student* will learn why every student should feel safe and be safe at school.

   Tests (content based)

2. With social work intervention, *Student* will learn to identify motivations and causes of aggressive behavior (teasing, baiting).

   Tests (content based)

3. With social work intervention (With a conflict resolution program), *Student* will learn and practice a conflict resolution strategy (assertive, nonaggressive problem solving techniques).

   Tests (content based)
   Daily log (record of practice sessions)

4. Independently (With social work intervention, With an incentive plan), *Student* will decrease incidents of physical aggression at school (in the classroom, in the cafeteria, to less than * per *).

   Charting (contracting, incentive plans)
   Daily logs (teacher's behavior logs)
   Other (office discipline records)

E. Profile: Accepting consequences, respecting authority

1. With social work intervention, *Student* will understand cause and effect relationships as they relate to behavior and prescribed negative consequences.

   Tests (content related)

2. With social work intervention, *Student* will be able to explain how his/her behavior precipitates a prescribed negative consequence.

   Tests (content related)
   Observations (reports from staff)

3. With social work intervention (Independently), *Student* will cooperatively accept prescribed negative consequences of his/her behavior.

   Charting (contracting, incentive plans)
   Observations (reports from staff)

4. Independently (With social work intervention), *Student* will accept legitimate direction, criticism, and/or negative consequences.

   Observations (reports from staff)
   Daily log (daily record of incidents)

III. **Social Annual Goal Statement:** *Student* will increase cooperative interpersonal social skills to consistently predominate levels.
A. **Profile:** Uncooperative, dysfunctional social behavior
  1. With social work intervention, *Student* will learn the importance of cooperative social behavior.   Tests (content based)
  2. With social work intervention (Using a conflict resolution strategy), *Student* will learn and practice a conflict resolution (problem solving) strategy.   Tests (content based) / Daily log (record of practice sessions)
  3. Independently (With an incentive plan), *Student* will decrease incidents of social conflict in the classroom (school environment, on the playground) to one (two) or less per day (week).   Charting (contracting) / Daily log (teacher's behavior records) / Other (office discipline records)
B. **Profile:** Poor social skills, difficulties making friends
  1. With social work intervention (With group work intervention), *Student* will learn and practice basic social skills (taking turns, waiting politely, saying nice things, sharing, respecting differences, accepting others, good manners, controlling teasing and name calling).   Tests (content based) / Daily log (content based)
  2. Independently (With social work intervention), *Student* will use (increase) positive, cooperative interpersonal social skills in the classroom (on the playground, at school, that can be observed by *).   Observations (documented)
C. **Profile:** Anger control
  1. With social work intervention, *Student* will be able to identify telltale feelings and body signals when becoming angry.   Tests / Charting
  2. With social work intervention, *Student* will develop an under-   Tests / Charting

standing of reactions to and
perceptions of anger.

3. With social work intervention, *Student* will learn a self-talk (cool-down) technique to reduce angry feelings.

Tests (content based)
Charting

4. Independently, *Student* will use a self-talk (cool-down) technique to reduce and control his/her anger.

Observations (documented)

IV. **Self-image Annual Goal Statement**: *Student* will increase self-esteem to a consistently positive level

A. **Profile:** Poor self-esteem, elementary, intermediate

1. With social work intervention, *Student* will successfully complete a copyrighted esteem-building curriculum.

Tests (content related)

2. With social work intervention, *Student* will keep a personal journal and will enter one positive statement about self each *.

Charting (entries)
Daily log (record of entries)

3. Independently (With social work intervention), *Student* will increase and maintain positive feelings of self-esteem.

Charting (self-evaluation)
Other (Piers-Harris base and intervals)

B. **Profile:** Poor self-esteem, intermediate, secondary

1. With social work intervention, *Student* will recognize unique positive personal attributes.

Tests

2. With social work intervention, *Student* will learn and practice personal goal-setting strategies.

Charting (contracting)

3. With social work intervention, *Student* will experience success by setting and achieving realistic personal (educational, social) goals.

Charting (contracting, incentive plan)

4. Independently (With social work intervention), *Student* will increase and maintain positive feelings of self-esteem.

Charting (self-evaluation)
Other (Pier-Harris base and intervals)

C. **Profile:** Poor self-confidence

1. With social work intervention,   Tests
   Student will recognize unique
   positive personal qualities and
   attributes.
2. With social work intervention   Charting (contracting, incentive
   (With an incentive plan), *Stu-*   plans)
   dent will volunteer positive   Observations (documented)
   statements about self to (ask   Daily log (record of occurrences)
   clarifying questions of) teacher
   (familiar staff) when asked
   (with prompts).
3. With social work intervention   Charting (contracting, incentive
   (With an incentive plan), *Stu-*   plans)
   dent will ask clarifying ques-   Observations (documented)
   tions and/or make appropriate   Daily log (record of occurrences)
   declarative statements sponta-
   neously in the classroom.
4. Independently (With social   Charting (self-evaluation)
   work intervention), *Student*   Observations (documented)
   will gain self-confidence,   Others (Piers-Harris base and in-
   increasing participation in play-   tervals, consultations)
   ground activities (Joining a
   school club, starting a conversation with a familiar staff person, eating lunch with classmates * days of the week,
   applying for a job).

D. **Profile:** Poor hygiene and weak self-care skills

1. With social work intervention,   Tests (content based)
   Student will learn the impor-
   tance of good grooming, appearance, and personal hygiene.
2. Independently (With social   Observations (documented)
   work intervention), *Student*
   will show increased healthful
   personal hygiene habits in the
   classroom (school, cafeteria)
   (that will be noticed by *).

E. **Profile:** Drug use

1. With social work intervention,   Tests
   Student will learn the consequences of drug abuse.

2. With social work intervention, *Student* will learn strategies for assertively refusing offers from others to participate in drug use.　Tests

3. With social work intervention, *Student* will set healthful personal goals about drug and substance use.　Charting (contracting) Other (consultations with student)

4. Independently, *Student* will abstain from harmful drug use.　Other (consultations, medical, parental)

F. **Profile: Gang involvement**

1. With social work intervention, *Student* will identify his social and emotional needs and how those needs are met through gang affiliations.　Tests

2. With social work intervention, *Student* will identify potential dangers and hazards of gang affiliations.　Tests

3. With social work intervention, *Student* will identify satisfying and healthy alternatives to gang affiliations.　Observations (documented)

4. Independently, *Student* will choose satisfying and healthy alternatives instead of gang affiliations.　Charting (contracting) Observations (documented) Daily log (record of specific behaviors) Other (consultations with significant others)

CHAPTER 20

Least Restrictive Environment and the Trend toward Inclusion

Shirley McDonald
*Clinical Associate Professor, Jane Addams College of Social Work,
University of Illinois at Chicago*

Robert Constable
Professor Emeritus, Loyola University at Chicago

William Holley
School Social Worker, Orland Park School District 135, Orland Park, Illinois

- Placement in the Least Restrictive Environment
- Continuum of Services
- Report to U.S. Department of Education
- Implementaion Guidelines
- Challenges to the School
- The Ecological Perspective and the Role of the School Social Worker
- Least Restrictive Environment and Inclusion—Final Notes

School districts are making more levels of integrated special education services available to students with disabilities in response to the current trend to more strictly interpret the mandate for placing students in the least restrictive environment (LRE). When strictly interpreted, the concept of *least restrictive environment* holds that when in the best interests of the child, placement of the child in the general education classroom with children who are not disabled, with additional services as needed and appropriate, is preferable to services delivered outside of the general classroom. The terms "regular education" and "general education," the more recent usage, will be used interchangeably in this text, often reflecting the usage at the time the material being discussed was initially conceptualized. The legal statement is:

> To the maximum extent appropriate children with disabilities . . . are educated with children who are not disabled, and special classes, separate schooling, or other removal of children with disabilities from the regular education environ-

318

ment occurs only when the nature or severity of the disability of a child is such that education in regular classes with the use of supplementary aids and services cannot be achieved satisfactorily (20 U.S.C. 1412(5)(A)).

Research suggests that placement of children with disabilities in the general education classroom can be successful if general education teachers are able to modify or adapt their instruction to meet the range of sudent needs (Stainback, Courtnage, and Jabel, 1986). The unique skills and abilities of the school social worker are now called as never before to assist teachers in making such placements successful, and school social workers must be ready for the challenge.

PLACEMENT IN THE LEAST RESTRICTIVE ENVIRONMENT

The placement of children with disabilities in the LRE has considerable benefits, provided school personnel can adjust to any new procedures and adaptations necessary to support the child's educational needs. If, for example, developmentally disabled children are to be given the opportunity to acquire, maintain, and improve their life skills (adaptive behavior functioning), they may do this best by being placed with the main flow of students in the general classroom in their neighborhood schools. Such placements could also allow their neighborhood peer groups to be more accessible to them.

One of the most serious problems in placing students with disabilities in a specialized school setting is that frequently these settings are further from home, creating for the students a feeling of isolation from their neighborhoods and general school environments. Also, students routinely experience such a protected, controlled environment in these specialized settings that they may lose abilities to negotiate socially with the more free-wheeling environment of their age-mates.

Process of Making Placement Decisions

The decision about placement of children with disabilities in settings that can meet their educational needs in the LRE is the final decision to be made by the Individualized Education Program conference (IEP conference). In the multidisciplinary conference determination has been made that the child is eligible for special services, and now the IEP conference has determined what services the child will require to meet his or her special needs. Once these decisions are made, a *range of placement decisions* are considered in the process of determining how these services can be delivered to the child in the least restrictive environment.

The concept of a *continuum of services* is implicit in this decision. If the child's general education program is to be interrupted in any way to receive these services, then the less restrictive options that were considered and not agreed to, must be justified as not being sufficient to meet the child's educational needs.

CONTINUUM OF SERVICES

Federal regulations mandate that a continuum of placement possibilities be available through each local education agency for children with disabilities who live within its boundaries. The continuum of services must include instruction in general classes, special classes, home instruction, and instruction in hospitals and institutions. Schools must also make provision for supplementary services, such as a resource room where a child may receive special instruction for learning disabilities, behavior disorders, speech and language instruction, and so on, or itinerant instruction to be provided in cooperation with general class placement (Department of Health, Education, and Welfare, 1977, p. 121a, 441). In response to the court decisions and the federal regulations, states have further defined and established their own continua of placement alternatives.

The LRE amounts to a right to be educated to the maximum extent possible with children who do not have disabilities. Factors idiosyncratic to school districts (such as organizational arrangements, technological differences in delivery systems, agency jurisdictional problems, or lack of adequate local, state, or federal financial support) may not be considered as reasons for abrogating the right to the LRE. Ultimately, school districts bear the responsibility for providing the LRE appropriate for each of their children with challenging educational needs, especially providing adequate supports for children to be educated in their general classrooms.

We will be using Illinois as an example of the continuum of services developed by one state in accordance with the federal regulations:

1. *Standard program with modifications.* The child receives his or her basic educational experience through the general program. However, these experiences are modified through:
   a. Additional or specialized education from the teacher,
   b. Consultation to and with the teacher,
   c. Provision of special equipment and materials and,
   d. Modification in the instructional program (e.g. multiage placement, performance output expectations)

2. *Standard educational program with "resource programs" or "related services."* The child receives the bulk of his or her educational experiences in the general program. However, these experiences are augmented by one or more resource programs or related services delivered either in the classroom or elsewhere, but at his or her local school.

3. *Special education program (self-contained).* The child receives most of his or her basic educational experience through an instructional program in a special class that is largely self-contained, or in a special school, but with inclusion or mainstreaming in those parts of the general program that are appropriate, with supportive services provided as needed.

4. *Cooperative community educational program.* The child receives most of his or her educational experiences through either the general or the special program of the public school. However, this educational curriculum is supplemented through work experience programs or shared agency involvement (sometimes a component of "transition planning," e.g., school-to-work planning).

5. *Home or hospital educational program.* The child, who is eligible for either the general or a special education program but is unable to attend such programs, receives instructional or resource programs and related services in the home or in the hospital.

6. *State-operated or private program.* The child whose exceptional characteristics are so profound or complex that no special education program offered by the public schools can adequately or appropriately meet his or her needs can be placed in either a state-operated or private facility, preferably one in the state in which the child resides, but in some cases in another state, for either a day program or full-time residential placement (Illinois Office of Education, 1979).

School social workers have many skills to employ in assessing the degree to which environmental factors in the classroom and school milieu are effective in meeting the needs of children with disabilities. Social workers can make a careful appraisal of the child's environment, including the various situational and interactional processes in these settings. Social workers need to shift their thinking to one child in many different groups and classroom situations, and how the child relates to the different students and teachers as well as how the different students and teachers relate to the child. Social workers need to assess the feelings of students in the general classroom toward the student with special needs and how these, in turn, affect the child with disabilities, who may have previously experienced many negative feelings from peers and adults. As school social workers assess the total environment of the child with disabilities, they must attempt to understand the dynamics of all groups within which the child is functioning and how they interact to influence the child. These groups can enhance or impede the child's potential for change. The possibility of providing alternative group experiences within the school may also be considered. Social workers can appraise these different situational factors and assist not only the child but also the other students in the involved groups. They must use a variety of skills that involve understanding individual personalities, teacher capabilities, the dynamics of different class groupings, and the effect of the interactional processes on each person involved. These assessment skills are usedfor consultation with teachers and the principal and for intervention planning in the case of the child's transition to a new environment or maintaining a child in a less restrictive environment.

Prior to the passage of P.L. 94-142, the right to be educated in the LRE was recognized by the same landmark court decision that acknowledged the right of the child with disabilities to an education. "Among the alternative programs of education and training required by statute to be available, placement in a regular school class is preferable . . . to placement in any other type of program of education and training" (PARC v. Commonwealth of Pennsylvania). The principle takes into account a variety of alternative learning environments in which the child may be educated. Thus, for the child with disabilities, there is a continuum of placement possibilities ranging from the least restrictive (i.e. being placed in a general classroom setting with ample opportunity to interact with children with no disabilities), through a variety of combinations of regular and specialized class assignments, to the most restrictive placement setting, which might include a special school or even a nonpublic program, such as an institution with very little, if any, contact with children who are not disabled.

In addition to "least restrictive environment" as a federal mandate, LRE is also a concept that has given birth to yet another concept, that of "full inclusion." While no definition for "full inclusion" has been offered, to date, at the federal or state level, it is generally understood as the practice of serving students with a full range of abilities and disabilities in the regular education classroom, with appropriate in-class support (Roach, 1995). A recent ruling by the Fourth U.S. Circuit Court of Appeals indicates that "mainstreaming is an IDEA preference, not a mandate." This was a reversal of an earlier decision made by a district court that the least restrictive environment for a child who has autism is the more inclusive placement in a general education classroom. This decision appears to indicate that general education is not appropriate for every student, this intensifying the REI/inclusion debate (1997 L.R.P. Publications, Vol. 4, Issue 9).

REPORT TO U.S. DEPARTMENT OF EDUCATION

The document generally cited as the declaration for the Regular Education Initiative (REI) is titled *Educating Students with Learning Problems—A Shared Responsibility* (Will, 1986). Madeleine Will, who was then assistant secretary to the Office of Special Education and Rehabilitative Services, U.S. Department of Education, wrote:

> Although for some students the "pull-out" approach (taking a child out of class to receive special education and then returning the child to the regular classroom) may be appropriate, it is driven by a conceptual fallacy: that poor

performance in education can be understood solely in terms of deficiencies in the learning environment. . . .

This challenge is to take what we have learned from the special programs and begin to transfer this knowledge to the regular education classroom. . . . There is increasing evidence that it is better academically, socially and psychologically to educate mildly handicapped children with non-handicapped children, preferably within the regular classroom (pp. 10, 11-12).

Thus, the REI/inclusion discussion originally focused on the mildly disabled child. Interpretations of inclusion that include returning all or most children in special education settings to general education classrooms probably expand this concept beyond what Will originally intended.

Will (1986) explained that the REI/inclusion focus is not intended to deprive special education students of institutional protections or to place regular and special education students in the same classroom without *redeploying* resources and strategies. Instructional approaches, such as "the availability of consulting teaching models, Teacher Assistance Teams, and cooperative learning strategies, are intended to provide sufficient options to accommodate all children with learning problems in the regular classroom" (p. 18). Recent developments—for example, "clustering" small numbers of students that benefit from special education services into general classrooms, peer teaching whereby resource teachers coteach with the general education teacher, cooperative learning strategies, and extra team planning time to develop such teaching interventions—are intended to provide options to accommodate all children with learning problems in the general classroom. She emphasized that "in no case should existing protections be diminished, nor should the rights of individual children be denied" (p. 19).

Will's admonishment is important. One of the concerns of those observing the outcomes of emerging general education initiatives is whether it is more difficult to monitor special education students receiving required services when these services are incorporated into the general classroom routine than when they are delivered in the admittedly more restrictive arena of the special education setting. Once a student must share the educational setting with higher functioning students, the service provider is less able to focus on the special education component of the lesson because of the discrepancies in student learning needs. Even if time were not a factor, this monitoring would be difficult for the classroom teacher or other in-class support personnel, including the social worker. Some teachers in general education settings tend to "split the difference" in considering student abilities when presenting or reinforcing materials. This practice is directly challenged by special education mandates requiring individualization of instruction for each student identified as eligible for special education; and these individualized plans are specifically written into the student's IEP. The desire to spare a child embarrassment by avoiding any direct reference to discrepancies in his or her learning abilities may put further pressure on professionals to downplay a child's specific educational needs in a general education setting. In any case, maintaining the needed level of intervention and reinforcement of learning for a special education student adds programmatic and planning complications to the general education setting.

IMPLEMENTATION GUIDELINES

In 1989, the Illinois State Board of Education published the *Illinois Special Education Policy and Procedures Training Manual,* which prescribes the process for determining placement and access to regular education experiences. The manual includes the following guidelines:

- Handicapped (read *disabled*) children must, to the maximum extent appropriate to their needs, be educated with children who are not handicapped.

- Removal of a handicapped child from the regular education environment may only occur when the nature or severity of the child's handicap is such that education in regular classes cannot be achieved satisfactorily, even with the use of supplementary aids and services.

- Each handicapped child shall participate in nonacademic and extracurricular services and activities with nonhandicapped children to the maximum extent appropriate to the needs of the child. If the child is unable to participate in nonacademic and extracurricular activities with nonhandicapped peers, comparable activities must be provided.

- The handicapped child should be placed in the least restrictive environment.

Though no federal or state definition exists, and there are no mandates for implementation of inclusion, Dianne Ferguson (1995) in her article "The Real Challenge" offers the following:

> Inclusion is the process of meshing general and special education reform initiatives and strategies in order to achieve a unified system of public education that incorporates all children and youth as active, fully participating members of the school community; that views diversity as the norm; and that insures a high-quality education for each student by providing meaningful curriculum, effective teaching, and necessary supports for each student.

Ferguson percives that "inclusion" is "not about the eliminating of the continuum of services," rather the incorporation of the philosophy and benefits of "inclusion" along the continuum, while still accepting the benefits of more restrictive environments to allow for the specific needs of particular students with disabilities and their families. She further states that "every child should have the opportunity to learn in a variety of different places—in small groups and large, in classrooms, in hallways, in libraries, and in a wide variety of community locations." Ferguson includes in that statement students who do not have disabilities, for she believes that their segregation from peers who do have disabilities results in drawbacks for both populations. Inclusion, she concludes, is a "new challenge to create schools . . . where typical classrooms will include students with more and more kinds of differences . . . where the learning environment will be a constant conversation involving students, teachers, other school personnel, families, and community members, all working together" for the common goal of a successful educational experience for all students.

For inclusive efforts to be effective, the following is necessary:

- Ongoing teacher training about the specific needs of each disabled child in the classroom;

- Regular instruction for teachers regarding the appreciation of differences in students, and ways to understand and enjoy working with disabled children;

- Instruction for teachers to help them learn about the parents of children who have special needs, and the emotions behind decisions that they must make for their children, along with the unique challenges they face in rearing them;

- Additional teacher's aides to support the functioning of seriously disabled children in general education classes;

- Smaller class sizes determined by a formula that accounts for the increased challenge to the teacher due to the additional needs of disabled students;

- Increased special education staff to offset the loss in efficiency (e.g.; due to increased travel time to and from each school, complexities of maintaining a home office or satellite offices) of itinerant service providers;

- Parent education to inform about the strengths and weaknesses of the continuum of programs available; and

- A sophisticated and carefully monitored system of accountability for the delivery of quality services to special education students.

CHALLENGES TO THE SCHOOL

Many children with special needs, as a result of these fundamental policy shifts, spend all or part of their school hours with children with no disabilities. The philosophy of mainstreaming a variety of students in the general classroom necessitates adapting the environment of the school and the classroom on an ongoing routine basis to meet the special needs of children with disabilities. Certainly, students in the general classroom are involved as part of the environment in which the student with specific needs resides. Because all children are unique, the ultimate payoff often is more effective educational environments for everyone. However, this new emphasis on more flexible programming with larger class sizes can also awaken confusion, uncertainty, fear, and anxiety among school personnel, particularly the teaching personnel. The school social worker, who has traditionally dealt with socioemotional factors that hinder or promote the process of education, has much to offer in helping education personnel learn to understand and adapt to this challenge.

Temporal, Instructional, and Social Integration

There are three focuses in integrating children with disabilities with their peers who are not disabled: *temporal* integration, *instructional* integration, and *social* integration.

Temporal integration refers to the amount of time the child with disabilities spends with peers who are not disabled. The underlying assumption is that the greater the amount of time children with disabilities spend with peers without disabilities, the more socially adaptive will be their social and instructional growth experience. Children with disabilities need time and participation with all children to acquire essential socialization skills. Time spent with peers without disabilities is not necessarily formal instruction time. It may involve the lunchroom, recess, shared field trips, or other shared activities. Such programming also provides an opportunity for children with no disabilities to relate informally with children with disabilities and form friendships. Temporal integration is more than developing detailed schedules for both groups of children. It involves an informed estimate of how the groups of children will interact in informal situations. Occasionally, some preparation may be necessary for both groups and some monitoring of the experience is usually necessary.

Instructional integration refers to the extent to which a child with specific needs is integrated into the general classroom instructional environment. Three conditions of compatibility must exist for instructional integration to occur:

- Compatibility between the child's needs and the learning opportunities available in the general classroom;

- Compatibility between the child with challenging physical or behavioral needs, learning characteristics, and education needs and the general education classroom teacher's ability and willingness to modify instructional practices; and

- Provision by general and special education personnel of an appropriate, coordinated, and well-articulated educational program.

One of the tasks of the social worker in helping to meet conditions for instructional integration is to consult with the teacher regularly regarding the child's essential needs so that these can be met within a general learning environment. An example of such consultation might be arranging for a volunteer parent, a classmate, or an older student to act as a tutor. Other examples might involve consultation regarding a child who needs a quiet place, a child who requires an opportunity for verbalizing, or a child who could benefit from more direct interaction with classroom materials or classmates. The social worker may help the teacher determine how he or she will provide these opportunities within the classroom to the benefit of the target student and often others as well.

Social intergration refers to the placement of children with disabilities in situations where informal relations and friendships with their peer group with no disabilities is possible. Qualities of social integration may be expressed in terms of psychological and physical closeness, interaction with peers, and assimilation or acceptance of children with disabilities in the general classroom. In facilitating the social integration of children with identified needs into the general classroom, the social worker's knowledge and expertise in social and emotional areas can be the key to maintaining them in an integrated environment.

The school social worker may assist the teacher in planning the physical location of the children within the classroom. Using the social worker's knowledge of patterns of interaction, the students may be regrouped to make the climate more conducive to learning for all students in the room. The social worker may be asked to use his or her skills to work directly with all of the children in the classroom in order to help them accept the child with disabilities and assist in the integration of that child into the group. The three basic formats that the social worker may use are (a) an educational format: films, bibliotherapy, or discussion or specific disabilities; (b) an affective educational approach to help children know and understand one another better so that they can function more comfortably as a group; and (c) a problem-solving approach through formal classroom discussions of problems that affect students. The social worker can enable the classroom teacher to develop the necessary skills to use these formats in the classroom by modeling and co-leading these groups with the teacher, and then consulting regularly in a supportive educational role.

THE ECOLOGICAL PERSPECTIVE AND THE ROLE OF THE SCHOOL SOCIAL WORKER

Consultation with the Teacher

Social work consultation with teachers and other professionals is also a relevant means for adapting the environment to better meet the special needs of children with disabilities. A social worker needs to take time to develop an empathic, supportive, and trusting relationship with the teacher, and to become knowledgeable about the problems between the child with disabilities and the general education children with which the teacher is dealing. The social worker needs to listen to the teacher's perception of the situation, to be aware of the teacher's strengths, to be sensitive to his or her personality, and to be aware of the total educational milieu within which the teacher is functioning. Social workers must become knowledgeable about the educational process so that their unique skills and understanding of human interaction may be properly applied within the context of the educational situation. As experts in social functioning, social workers will be able to offer the teacher skills and techniques that will assist him or her in classroom management and in dealing with individual behavior, as well as support ongoing efforts at modification of the social and educational environment.

Janney, Snell, Beers, and Raynes, in a 1995 article in *Exceptional Children*, reported that after questioning teachers involved in pilot projects in several rural and urban Virginia school districts, their research team identified a few clearly significant factors in the successful integration of moderately to severely disabled students in general classrooms:

1. Teachers need top-down administrative support, guidelines and technical support, as well as demonstrated appreciation for their effors in implementing the guidelines.

2. Their parallel, if somewhat contradictory need is to be given freedom to individualize and create their own adaptations, to be allowed to take ownership of the process.

3. Hands-on support of teachers by "coaches" with personal experience in integrating disabled students in their classrooms, and getting to know these coaches who would be providing hands-on support to them and the integrated students, is preferable as initial preparation than more traditional, didactic presentations through workshops.

4. Once the students are integrated, the experience of working with and thus getting to know these students well is what makes the final overall response to the integrative experience universally positive. This is true even for teachers who feel that significant extra work is involved in making the inclusion or integration of these students successful—"more work, but worth it."

5. Finally, a sense that they are not alone in the endeavor, that they have supportive people to turn to, even to lean on, helps teachers work through difficult adjustments, particularly the adjustment of sharing their classrooms with other professional personnel (Janney et al., 1995, p. 437).

Interprofessional Cooperation

Including students with widely diverse needs in a single classroom is a big task. Teachers often cannot deal easily with the wide array of student's needs simultaneously. The social worker and other support personnel may help most by forming teacher assistance teams. Such teams may provide a variety of individual and group interventions. For example, the social worker and speech pathologist may conduct social skills groups. The psychologist, teacher, and social worker may offer role-playing exercises and include students as participants. Any of these specialists may enhance classroom integration of the disabled student by adapting their interventions to current lessons. The social worker may use playtime as a social group learning experience in the classroom. Through this team approach the social worker and other specialists can provide students with activities and experiences that they can share or model with peers in the general classroom. The support personnel can share their expertise with a wide array of other professionals, who in turn can share what they learn with others (Stainback, Stainback, and Forest, 1989, pp. 134-135; Welsh and Goldberg, 1979, pp. 271-284).

Work with the Family

In addition to evaluating the educational environment of the child with disabilities, the social worker will have primary responsibility for assessing the nature of the child's interactions within the family environment. This assessment involves understanding the family's expectations and their methods of child-rearing and determining whether these are conducive to the child's effective functioning in his or her current school placement. The social worker can be a vital factor in mobilizing the strengths of the family to help the child adjust to his or her disability and adapt to recommended school programs. The social worker also is important in assessing the child's relationship structures outside the immediate family. For example, babysitter, neighborhood, and peer-group relationships may affect the child's adjustment. The social worker needs to understand how the child with disabilities functions in each particular group and to assist him or her in fulfilling these roles. All of these factors will affect the child's adjustments in the classroom and the total educational environment.

Work with the Pupil

The child with disabilities may have difficulty in accepting or participating in a plan that introduces new and different situational realities. If this occurs, it may be very helpful for the school social worker to provide a support base for the child to help him or her feel more comfortable in the general classroom situation. In some cases, the social worker may need to work with the child regularly over an extended period of time. Children with behavioral and emotional problems may need extensive counseling, which a school social worker may provide. If in the social worker's judgment the child requires an individual treatment relationship, there will likely need to be communication with other staff regarding at least a general profile of the needs of the child, the problems to be addressed, and how activities on the child's behalf can assist other team members in their work with this child.

LEAST RESTRICTIVE ENVIRONMENT AND INCLUSION—SOME FINAL NOTES

The dangers inherent in a strenuous, rapid move toward inclusion of more and more seriously disabled students in the general education classroom is that few if any preparations discussed previously in this chapeter will occur and that students will reenter the general education system with little or no support, eventually dropping out after falling far behind. Transitions into different settings and sysems within the school are, of course, crucial tasks to school social work service delivery.

Perhaps the students most at risk for failure are those with what are sometimes labeled "invisible disabilities"—learning disabilities, behavior disorders, communication deficits, or mild fine motor dysfunctions. Such students have previously experienced significant difficulties in the general education setting and will be understandably anxious about reentering the system.

As the social worker appraises a child's total milieu, it may become apparent that environmental factors cannot be restructured sufficiently in a given general education classroom to meet the needs of a particular child. If the available resources of the general classroom and teacher cannot be restructured sufficiently to meet the child's needs, continuing to retain the child in a general classroom, which had been identified as the LRE, might adversely affect the student. For example, for the hearing impaired child, if the environment in a general education classroom is not sufficiently stimulating, possibly because there is insufficient social interaction through the lack of pupils skilled in signing, an appropriate recommendation may be to provide a more restrictive environment socially, but an environment with more hearing impaired children with whom, through signing, a child can have more social interaction.

When a child requires a more restrictive program, the social worker's task as a member of the special education team is to plan for a smoother transition to the new program, and to provide for the necessary resources during this process. In planning this transition, it is essential to explore both the child's and his or her family's reactions, concerns, and general feelings about recommended programs. With this knowledge, the social worker needs to work with other team members to identify alternative programs or environments appropriate to the child's adaptive and educational needs. Next, the social worker's support and understanding can be key factors in helping the child to adjust satisfactorily to another educational setting. If a child is placed in a specialized setting, the social worker may continue to see him or her individually. Also, the social worker may work with new teachers to help them understand how a particular child functions and how to deal with the child's needs. It must be stressed frequently that follow-up services are essential to the child, family, and teacher for a successful transition to be completed.

For students remaining in a general education setting, adequate preparations will ensure that the inclusion of the special education student will benefit all students because:

- Children who otherwise would receive special resource services outside the general classroom will experience less disruption by the services being given in the classroom.
- Provision of services in the classroom may spill over and benefit children who do not currently receive special services and, though identified as having some need, may "fall through the cracks" of the current system.
- More frequent monitoring by special education personnel of all classroom students may facilitate initiation of interventions when symptoms first appear.
- Increased understanding by general and special education personnel of problems students encounter can generate increased consultation and cooperation.
- A broadened exposure to other methods, techniques, and knowledge bases may increase the repertoire of interventions of all personnel.
- Impetus toward greater professionalism may occaionally encourage general and special education personnel to return to college, or to attend workshops for additonal knowledge and skills in new areas.

Federal and state laws, rules, and regulations that govern special education seek to ensure the placement of children in the LRE to support their educational needs. Thus monitoring of placement decisions and careful review of a child's needs for special education services are essential. Projects are being initiated in all areas of the country to determine how such services can be delivered effectively to students with the least disruption in their general education schedules. It is particularly important that such innovative projects be mindful of the safeguards listed above so that they are in place before program or placement modifications are made.

A special emphasis on accountability is crucial for quality service delivery to special education students. Special education services are expensive and large-scale plans to revamp a system must be examined carefully for ulterior financial motive. Professionals working with children with disabilities must ensure that safeguards are in place in the federal, state, and local levels before major changes are attempted so that services are not curtailed to the most vulnerable of children.

School social workers have a special opportunity to make the educational process more viable and benefical to children. Let us be aware of the challenge and sharpen our skills to meet this challenge. There are rights that cannot be denied. The issue for school social workers is not whether the intent of the law—educating each child of school age in the least restrictive environment possible—should be translated into practice, but to what extent the school social worker can effectively contribute to this process in serving the best interests of children with disabilities.

REFERENCES

Ferguson, D. 1995. The real challenge of inclusion. *Phil Delta Kappan,* 77(3):281–287.

Illinois Office of Education. 1979. *Rules and regulations governing special education.* Springfield, IL: Author.

Illinois State Board of Education, Division of Educational Programs, Department of Special Education. 1989. *Illinois special education policy and procedures training manual.* Springfield, IL: Author.

Janney, R. E., Snell, M. E., Beers, M. K., and Raynes, M. 1995. Integrating students with moderate and severe disabilities into general education classes. *Exceptional Children* 61(5):425–439.

Roach, V. 1995. Supporting inclusion. *Phi Delta Kappan* 77(3):295–299.

Stainback, W., Stainback, S., Courtnage, L., and Jabel, T. 1986. Facilitating mainstreaming by modifying the mainstream. *Exceptional Children* 52(2):144–152.

U.S. Department of Health, Education, and Welfare. 1977. 121a, 441.

Welsh, B., and Goldberg, G. 1979. Insuring educational success for children-at-risk placed in new learning environments. *School Social Work Quarterly* 1(4):271–284.

Will, M. 1986. *Educating students with learning problems—A shared responsibility. A report to the secretary* [Monograph]. Washington, DC: U.S. Department of Education, Office of Rehabilitative Services.

Wilmette School District Pilot Project. 1990. Report presented at Illinois Education Partners, Skokie, IL.

FURTHER READING

Algozzine, B., Christenson, S., and Ysseldyke, J. E. 1982. Probabilities associated with the referral to placement process. *Teacher Education and Special Education* 5(3):19–23.

Christenson, S., Ysseldyke, J. and Algozzine, B. 1982. Institutional constraints and external pressures influencing referral decisions. *Psychology in the Schools* 19: 341–345.

Gartner, A., and Kerzner-Lipsky, D. 1989. *Beyond separate education: Quality education for all.* Baltimore: Brookes.

Graden, J. L., Casey, A., and Christenson, S. 1985. Implementing a prereferral intervention system: Part I. The model. *Exceptional Children* 51(5):377–384.

Graden, J. L., Casey, A., and Bonstrom, O. 1985. Implementing a prereferral intervention system: Part II. The model. *Exceptional Children* 51(6):487–496

Illinois State Board of Education. 1988. *Relationship partnerships for achievement* [Draft]. Springfield, IL: Author.

Illinois State Board of Education. 1989. Serving those with severe handicaps: Interview with Ed Sontag, state superintendent. *Illinois Special Education Forum* 2(2): 1–6.

National Council on Disabilities. 1989. *The education of students with disabilities: Where do we stand?* Report to the president and Congress of the United States. Washington, DC: Author.

Wang, M., and Birch, J. 1984a. Comparison of a full time mainstreaming program and a resource room approach. *Exceptional Children* 51:33–40.

Wang, M., and Birch, J. 1984b. Effective special education in regular class. *Exceptional Children* 50:390–399.

Ysseldyke, J. E., Thurlow, M., Graden, J., Wesson, C., Algozzine, B., and Deno, S. 1983. Generalizations from five years of research on assessment and decision making: The University of Minnesota Institute. *Exceptional Children* 4:75–93.

CHAPTER 21

School Social Work Consultation and Collaboration

Christine Anlauf Sabatino
Assistant Professor, National Catholic School of Social Service,
Catholic University of America

- Defining Consultation
- Consultation Literature
- Stages in the Consultation Process
- A Theoretically Based and Empirically Based Model of School Social Work Consultation
- An Application of Mental Health Consultation
- Consultation and Collaboration: Team Building

Today's teachers face a student population with an enormous variety of personal and social problems that create barriers to learning and academic success. Alcohol and substance abuse, domestic and community violence, family instability, physical and sexual abuse, poverty, pressure to drop out, racism, and teen pregnancy are all barriers to learning and threaten the health, welfare, and education of America's youth (Keys and Bemak, 1997). In addition, there is an increasingly diverse student population—linguistically, culturally, economically, and racially (Dupper and Evans, 1996). As political, fiscal, and administrative pressures increase in school systems, children's educational prospects decline and teachers are caught in the middle (Shaw and Replogle, 1996). It is unfair and detrimental to the educational enterprise to expect classroom teachers to be solely responsible for an ever increasing array of students without designing and implementing support service delivery systems that address all the complexities students bring with them that affect education. How can school social workers support classroom teachers in the teaching-learning process and be most effective in meeting the current needs of students at risk?

One traditional answer to this question has been a *consultation model* that supports school personnel. Consultation has proved to be a stable and enduring approach to school service delivery, providing a depth and breadth of intervention unusual for an indirect service practice model (Freeman,

1996). The historic relationship between school social work practice and consultation can be traced back as far as the turn of the twentieth century (Oppenheimer, 1925). Over the past quarter-century, consultation has been consistently empirically documented as an important school social work task (Costin, 1969; Carr, 1976; Meares, 1977; 1982; Timberlake, Sabatino, and Hooper, 1982; Lambert and Mullaly, 1982; Allen-Meares, 1994).

Given these barriers to learning and the historical and empirical foundation for school social work consultation, this chapter synthesizes the literature on consultation theory, research, and practice from a variety of professions. A theoretically based and empirically tested model of school social work consultation is then presented for use by school social workers in a variety of settings—regular education, special education, and early intervention, whether class-based or home-based programs. Recommendations for recalibrating the model to apply to interprofessional collaboration also are given.

DEFINING CONSULTATION

Consultation is a specific and unique method of intervention. Although there are a variety of theories and techniques of intervention applied to this method, there is general agreement that all types of consultation have the following similar characteristics: (1) it is a problem-solving process; (2) it takes place between a professional consultant and a consultee, who has responsibility for direct service to a client; (3) it is a voluntary relationship; (4) the objective is to solve a job-related problem of the consultee; (5) the consultant and the consultee share in solving the problem; and (6) consultation helps the consultee become better prepared to deal with similar problems in the future (Caplan and Caplan, 1993; Kadushin, 1977; Meyers, Parson, and Martin, 1979; Zischka and Fox, 1985). In other words consultation is an interactional process that takes place between a help-giver and a help-seeker who is experiencing difficulties in performing professional functions with a client, group, or organization.

How is consultation distinguished from therapy, supervision, or education? Although there is some disagreement on this question among experts (Bergen, 1977; Caplan, 1970; Carlson, 1972; Curtis and Zins, 1981; Kaplan, Turner, Norman, and Stillson, 1996; Lippitt, 1959) the answer is important because it guides the consultant's activities. For example, in consultation, discussion material is often delicate in nature, personal to the teacher, and risky to share with others. In order to meet the agreed-upon goal of solving job-related problems, it is not appropriate for the consultant to examine or highlight unconscious material, or to foster the development of a therapeutic relationship. In fact, these traditional elements of psychodynamic intervention distract the consultant and the teacher from their central task of focusing on the educational problem.

In a supervisory relationship the supervisor holds an administrative position of authority in the agency hierarchy, a positions that requires an ongoing relation. Nor is an agenda brought by the consultant. However, an agenda is expected to develop during the consultation process.

In a school setting the consultation relationship is best defined as a coordinate, nonhierarchical relationship wherein two differently prepared professionals concentrate on helping students reap the full benefit of their education. The teacher is viewed as an entirely competent professional who retains full authority and responsibility for the student. The teacher is free to accept or reject the consultant's ideas and recommendations, even though assistance has been invoked. Advice giving is avoided becaise it implies some level of ignorance on the part of the consultee and it may be seen as a devaluation of the consultee's abilities. To reinforce this coordinate relationship, it is important to develop a joint language for communicating with each other about a student's difficulties by exploring the semantic meanings of the teacher's narrative (Saleeby, 1994) and by using language that is understandable and acceptable to the teacher. The nature of the concepts communicated must fit the culture of the school and teacher (Caplan and Caplan, 1993). The goal it to enable the teacher to deepen his or her understanding of those aspects of the presenting problem that are puzzling. Although the consultant may cover a broad domain of psychosocial knowledge, jargon is avoided.

CONSULTATION LITERATURE

For the serious student of consultation, it is important to understand that it is a specialized method of intervention. Many professionals assume that practice experience in a particular profession is adequate preparation to be a consultant. Training and certification in one's own profession does not translate inot competence in consultation knowledge and skills. Helping others with their work problems is a much more complex process than working directly with one's own cases. Specialized preparation is needed so that one understands the consultation process, consultation phases, different models of consultation, and the unique functions of the consultant's role.

A review of the consultation literature reveals that one may study it in the context of a specific profession, a field of practice or setting, or by types of models of consultation. An exhaustive bibliographic reference and descriptive review of much of the consultation literature may be found in three federal government publications: Mannino, MacLennan, and Shore (1975), Grady et al., 1981; Mannino et al. (1986). These books contain material on the definition of consultation from the perspective of a community mental health center, an annotated bibliography of materials categorized as mental health consultation models and approaches, and consultation by fields of practice, by practice settings, the process of consultation, together with research on mental health consultation.

The professions of social work (Kadushin, 1977), psychiatry (Caplan, 1970; Caplan and Caplan, 1993), psychology (Brown, Pryzwansky, and Schulte, 1987), school psychology (Gutkin and Curtis, 1990), education (Dinkmeyer and Kinkmeyer, 1978), nursing (Robinson, 1986), and business (Schein, 1969) have all developed a consultation literature base.

The school setting in particular has provided the foundation for a wealth of consultation theory, practice, and research (Alpert 1982; Alpert and Silverstein, 1985; Conoley and Conoley, 1982; 1988; Curtis and Zins, 1981; Drapela, 1983; Gallassich, 1982; Meyers et all., 1979; Newman, 1967; Sarason et al., 1966; West and Idol, 1987; Zins and Ponti, 1990). Consultation literature has been developed in relationship to regular education, special education school groups, and early intervention programs (Drisko, 1993; Early, 1992; Sabatino, 1986; Wesley, 1994). Finally, Gallessich's book (1982) remains one of the seminal texts that synthesize and analyze the various types of consultation models.

When studying the literature, it is important to know that consultation is presented at the highest level of knowledge development when it contains (1) a clearly defined theory base, (2) a clearly described practice model that may be replicated, and (3) descriptions of process issues, research components, and outcome evaluations (Mannino, 1981).

Consultation Theory

"Consultation theory is in the 'preparadigm' stage of scientific development in which numerous approaches or perspectives exist, each looking at somewhat different aspects of the problem, with no one perspective more encompassing than another" (Meyers et al., 1979, p. 39). There are a number of theoretical frameworks for different models of consultation. Behavioral theory, systems theory, organizational development theory, group theory, psychoeducational theory, and psychodynamic theory have all been used as the foundation for practice models. It is recommended that readers identify their preferred type of consultation model, given those presented in this chapter, and pursue the rich literature base that exists generally for the theory and specifically with the chosen type of consultation model. This preparation work is critical when developing research.

Consultation Research

A national survey reveals that between 1968 and 1978, 209 research articles were published in the area of consultation in mental health and related fields. During this same time frame, 208 consultation dissertations were written. The greatest percentage (74.6 percent) of these dissertations were conducted in school settings; only 4 percent were conducted by students in graduate schools of social work (Mannino and Shore, 1980). Meares (1982) studied the content of fifty-seven professional school social work articles and found a "marked increase" in the amount of material on "consultation with school personnel." The strengths and weaknesses of consultation research have also been examined by Alpert and Yammer (1983), Meyers et al. (1979), Medway (1982), and Kenney (1986).

Unfortunately, twenty years later, there is very little school social work consultation research by school social workers. A review for articles on consultation of the past thirteen issues of *Social Work in Education* (January 1995 through January 1998) reveals not a single research article on consultation published and only one on practice models (Kaplan et al., 1996) and one narrative account of a practice experience involving consultation (Freeman, 1995).

Solid consultation research requires a clear definition of the type of consultation be to tested, the specific techniques employed, and the specific variables under examination. It also requires the clarification the relationship between the theoretical approach and the outcome variables chosen. Hypothesis testing and experimental control are additionally needed. Analysis of change can take place through a combination of methods: self-report measures, objective indicators, observational techniques, and behavioral inventories. Change can be measured in relation to (a) the consultee, (b) the consultee's interactions and interrelations with those in the work environment, or (c) movement of the consultee's client or client systems. Additional factors to examine include input variables, process variables, and outcome variables. Input variables include consultee characteristics, consultant characteristics of the setting, and types of problems presented by the consultee. Process variables refer to elements that take place during consultation, such as warmth, empathy, and freedom to accept or reject the consultant's recommendations. Outcome variables are changes resulting from consultation, such as behavior, attitude, knowledge, or perception.

At the onset of consultation research efforts, it is important not only to delineate the most recent and sophisticated consultation research designs but also to link present research with previous work in the field. Consultation researchers must recapitulate what has already been learned in their own area of research and in relevant but unrelated areas. In this way there would be a synthesis of comparable data and the development of a powerful school social work consultation research literature base.

Consultation Practice: Alternative Types of Consultation Models

Gallessich (1982) provides a very informative framework for analyzing different consultation models using specific dimensions. Information applicable to one dimension naturally leads to and fits with data from other dimensions to build an internally consistent specific model of consultation. Clarifying one's thinking on a few of these dimensions leads the practitioner toward or away from choosing one type of consultation model rather than another for implementation. These dimensions are the following:

- The conceptualization or formulation of the problem,
- The overall or broad goal of consultation,
- The major methods used by the consultant,
- The consultant's assumption about change,
- The consultant's role or source of power, and
- The underlying value of the model.

Six different types of consultation models are compared and contrasted here using these dimensions. The purpose is to assist educational and pupil personnel to choose the most appropriate consultation model to consult with school-based and community-based programs and families as a result of P.L. 105-17.

Education and training consultation.   In the model of education and training consultation, the assessed problem is the consultee's lack of technological knowledge, information, or skills. The consultant's goal is to provide the needed knowledge, information, or skill. Methods used may include lectures, multimedia, learning materials, structured laboratory experiences, small-group discussion, modeling, and feedback measures. The consultant assumes that the consultee changes through cognitive learning. The consultant is viewed as an expert who values the growing fields of information and technology services to sustain the future of an organization, agency, or program. This model assumes that, in a school, the administrators have conferred with the faculty and reached mutual agreement that staff may benefit from the proposed education and training.

Clinical consultation.   In the model of clinical consultation due to the consultee's lack of technical expertise in the identified problem area, the need is for an expert diagnosis and authoritative recommendation regarding a client's disease or dysfunction. The consultant's goal is limited to the diagnosis and amelioration of a particular set of problems in order to restore normal social functioning or remediate symptoms in a case situation. The methods include diagnosis, prescription, and treatment. It is assumed that the diagnosis is outside the consultee's range of competencies; therefore, the consultant's expertise is essential for providing knowledge to bring about change. The consultant may be collegial or directive in relating to the consultee, but in either case, the consultant values the healthy functioning of the client. This model assumes that the student's problem is so complex it requires a specialist for evaluation, disposition, and management.

Mental health consultation.   In the model of mental health consultation, the problem is defined as the consultee's lack of knowledge, skill, self-confidence, or objectivity. The consultant's goal is to increase competencies and strenghten the consultee's professional functioning, with improvement in the client as a side effect. Although methods differ for each of these four problem categories, all use education, facilitation, and support. The model assumes that the consultee has the capacity to solve the work problem with cognitive and emotional support. The consultant brings many sources of power to the role and becomes a model teacher, resource, collaborator, and encourager. The consultant's primary underlying value is the infusion of mental health concepts and principles as a form of mental health prevention. This model assumes that there is administrative sanction and support that provides the consultant and the consultee with the necessary time to analyze the identified problem, plan, and implement interventions.

Behavioral consultation.   In the behavioral consultation model, the problem is formulated in terms of dysfunctional behavior. The goal is to reduce or eliminate undesirable behaviors and replace or increase the frequency of desired behavior. The method used is the systematic application of cognitive learning principles. It is similar to methods of clinical consultation with its case-centered focus on the methods of diagnosis, prescription, and treatment. The method involves the following elements: The problem is defined in behavioral terms. Behaviors are observed and recorded. Antecedents and consequences are analyzed. Reinforcement contingencies are designed and implemented. When this takes place, the consultant withdraws and the consultee assumes responsibility for the client's behavioral management program. The model assumes that change is possible with the consultant's empirical and rational expertise, which is the consultant's source of power. The behavioral consultation model places great value on technology and the scientific method. It assumes that the teacher is willing to collaborate with the consultant in the recording of observed behaviors, implementation of behavior modification strategies, evaluation of behavior changes, and integration of a new behavioral management program in the appropriate setting.

Organizational consultation.   Problems in the organizational consultation model may fall into several domains. These are technology, structural, managerial, and human relations. The goal is to increase organizational productivity and morale. The methods used by organizational consultants vary widely depending on the domain of concern. In some instances, teams composed of consultants with certain specialities are used. Consultants assume change is brought about by empirical knowledge and reeducation. The consultant's authority comes from expert knowledge. In addition, the consultee usually identifies with the consultant's area of expertise and the consultant's role performance. Organizational consultants base their models on the values inherent in technological information and human development services. As with education and training consultation, this model assumes that members of the organization agree that the services of a consultant are of value.

Program consultation.   Program consultation formulates the problem in terms of a lack of expertise needed to successfully carry out specialized services designed to benefit a target population. Methods used vary considerably due to the diversity of programs. Generally, they include some or all of the following progression: needs are assessed; clear goals are delineated; methods to achieve identified goals are selected. Then resources are identified, benefits assessed, and constituencies identified. Administrative procedures are defined. Staffing needs, conforming to funding guidelines, are determined. Later outcomes are evaluated and new programs integrated with existing services and agencies. The consultant assumes that theory and research is the foundation which changes are made to alter or plan a program. The consultant is viewed as an expert who values the scientific approach to program planning or the values reflected in the program.

Curtis and Zins (1981) use another framework to identify and contrast different consultation models. To understand and compare the type of model the consultant is using, it is useful to ask the following questions: what is to be changed (value orientation), for whom is change intended (target), through whom is change brought about (operational level), how will change take place (consultative methods), and what is the style of interpersonal interaction between the consultant and the consultee (consultant role)?

STAGES IN THE CONSULTATION PROCESS

Regardless of the theoretical base or type of consultation one chooses to use in practice, all consultation programs have a common set of stages or phases. Each stage needs to be explored in relation to both the school social worker's and the teacher's commitments and responsibilities. Each stage may have several subphases, and there is fluidity among the stages. The value of acknowledging and discussing these stages and subphases is that it gives the consultant and the consultee a common framework for reference if the process becomes unfocused, thereby helping the program remain productive.

Gallessich (1982) identifies the following phases of the consultation process. Awareness of these phases helps keep the consultant and the consultee focused and productive. There is fluidity among these phases, and a phase may have several subphases. Each of the phases is presented with a series of questions that Gallessich might pose to help the consultant with his or her thinking while developing a consultation program.

1. Preliminiary exploration
   What are the agency's needs?
   What are the consultant's qualifications regarding these needs?
   Is there a satisfactory "fit"?
   Are there any value conflicts among the parties?

2. Negotiation of a contract
   What are the terms for working together?
   Is this a formal or legal contract?
   Is this an informal or oral contract?
   Does the contract include consultation goals, length of contract, consultant responsibilities, agency responsibilities, consultant's role, and evaluation or termination procedures?

3. Entry
   Where will consultation take place?
   What physical barriers to entry are encountered?
   What social-psychologial barriers to entry are encountered?
   What agency dynamics might be a barrier to being trusted and accepted in this social system?
   What tensions arise in the course of building a relationship with the consultee?

4. Diagnosis of problems or needs
   Do consultant and consultee collaborate in data collection?
   Is diagnosis seen as an ongoing activity?
   Has the entire context been scanned or is the assessment narrowly focused on the presenting problem?
   Have "hard" data and "soft" data been used?
   Has more than one theoretical perspective been used to sort and analyze the problem?
   Is further data gathering required?

5. Goal setting
   Who has proposed the goal(s)?
   Have the merits of a number of goals been weighed?
   Are there realistic solutions to the problem?
   If not, is the consultant prepared to terminate the consultation?
   Can the goals be reached by the staff without consultation?
   How urgent is it to achieve a goal?
   How successful might this goal be?
   How feasible is a goal?
   What is the cost of this goal in time and money?

6. Exploration of intervention alternatives and selection of one or more intervention strategies?
   What is the best method for achieving the goal?
   Have alternatives been generated and examined?
   Is there a clear definition of the objective?
   Is there a clear plan of action to reach the objective?
   What problems are anticipated?
   Which people are responsible for which actions?
   Have the consultant's role, function, and responsibility been delineated from those of the consultee's?

7. Implementation of intervention
   Does implementation involve the consultant?

8. Evaluation of outcomes
   To what degree have the goal(s) been achieved?
   Is evaluation one of the consultant's functions?
   What factors contributed to the positive and negative outcomes?
   Is the evaluation informal and anecdotal?
   Is the evaluation formal and quantifiable?
   Has the consultant's performance been evaluated?

9. Institutionalization of changes
   Have new procedures or behaviors been incorporated and routinized in the agency?
   Does this change require additional training and monitoring, or that incentives be institutionalized?

10. Termination of consultation
    What are the criteria for termination?
    What are the emotional reactions surrounding the termination?
    Will termination occur through a series of steps?
    Are there follow-up plans to termination?

The interpersonal relationships established during these proceedings will be crucial to the success of the consultation program. It is important for the teacher to feel comfortable, accepted, and respected. The consultant may help to establish this atmosphere by being trustworthy, accepting, respectful, nonjudgemental, and collegial.

Throughout these stages, it is important to remember that it takes time for a teacher to build a relationship, to understand what consultation is, and to learn how to use it. Teachers need to learn how to present relevant information about a child, what kind of help to expect from the consultant, and what the consultant has to offer. Sometimes the teacher will have a hidden agenda in consultation. The consultant might be invited into a conflict as an "expert" to support one person's viewpoint about a child and family. The consultant might be expected to share the emotional burden of making a difficult decision, or to enable someone to abdicate responsibility in a difficult case. Sometimes the principal may wish to substitute consultation for administrative support or supervision.

In any case, there may need to be several preliminary meetings if the teacher is to understand the processes and use them effectively. It is important that the teacher understand what consultation is and how it is to be used. As Caplan and Caplan (1993) noted "resistance" may only be a lack of professional preparation for consultation. Or it may signal the belief that asking for consultation is an admission of professional incompetence. To overcome these barriers, the teachers may be reminded that students' problems are often complicated and confusing and that the request for consultation services is a sign of professional competency. Most difficult, though, is helping teachers understand that no significant problems can be managed hurriedly.

A THEORETICALLY BASED AND EMPIRICALLY BASED MODEL OF SCHOOL SOCIAL WORK CONSULTATION

Reid (1979) defines a practice model as rules for practitioners in defining and assessing target problems delineating sequences of interventions to be used in attempts to alleviate problems. A model organizes discrete principles, methods, and procedures into coherent strategies. Models are a bridge between theory and practice, the translation of theory onto how-to-do-it descriptions of activities.

Although consultation models have been presented in the literature for many years, they have seldom been expressed in true model form. Published reports have tended to emphasize the theory base of the model without concomitant stepwise procedures for implementing the practice of the model. Mannino (1981) states, "There is a broad array of theoretically and technically diverse approaches under the consultation label. It is, therefore, essential that the type of consultation studied be clearly described and defined" (p. 149). Meyers, Friedman, and Gaughan (1981) state, "There have not been enough clear descriptions of procedures that could be replicated readily by researcher or practitioners in the school."

AN APPLICATION OF MENTAL HEALTH CONSULTATION

The following mental health consultation model has been adapted for school social workers from Caplan and Caplan's (1993; Caplan, 1970) research- and practice-based model for providing remedial and preventive services to populations. This model complies with all the recommended elements for designing, implementing, and researching practice models. That is, it has a clearly articulated theory base; it specifies assessment concepts and recommends specific intervention practice techniques; it allows one to study consultation on multiple levels—the process, the content, and the outcome for the consultee and the client; it is easily replicated in practice and for research; and it lends itself to research on a variety of dependent outcome variables.

Specifically, this model builds on consultee-centered case consultation, one of Caplan's four specific categories of mental health consultation. According to Caplan's consultee-centered case consultation category of mental health consultation theory, there are four reasons why a teacher might have a problem with a student: need for knowledge, need for skill, need for self-confidence, and need for objectivity (Caplan, 1970). These four reasons provide the core concepts of this suggested model of school social work consultation. Each is presented here in greater detail along with recommended techniques of intervention. Case examples are given for each one.

Need for Knowledge

The school social work consultant is able to assess the need for knowledge as the problem in a teacher's professional functioning when, due to lack of specific psychosocial knowledge or the issues involved, erroneous understandings or conclusions are drawn about a student's puzzling behavior. In some instances, the teacher possesses the theoretical knowledge necessary to understand the situation but does not see its relevance or application to this particular child and problem. Interventions consist of imparting missing general information or sharing specialized expertise in an area.

Caplan takes the position that the need for knowledge should be the least frequent reason for consultation because the consultee is a trained professional. In a regular classroom setting, however, the teacher's primary training is in elementary or secondary education, not in mainstreaming special education students. Sometimes teachers are lacking in complex theoretical knowledge about the cognitive, emotional, social, or interactional processes that accompany a child's problem in the teaching-learning process. Other times a specific problem arises that would rarely be part of a teacher's training or expertise. It is inevitable that teachers will be confronted with experiences for which they are ill trained or undertrained. Psychological, social, and interactional processes related to social problems that accompany a child's presenting problem are not a routine part of teacher education. Incidents of child physical and sexual abuse are obvious illustrations. Teachers may hesitate to identify a child for reporting because they are unsure whether the assorted and myriad information they possess fits together cohesively as the profile of an abused child. Another example of need for knowledge would be the difficulties the teacher may encounter in building a home-school relationship to discuss student needs in the context of today's diversity in the school population. Cultural issues, refugee experience, immigration status, literacy, previous experience with school personnel, role and norm expectations, and relationship to authority may be real barriers to understanding. In such instances, the task of the consultant is to impart the missing information in the most economical manner. This may call for continued individual consultation, but also lends itself to inservice workshops that disseminate information more broadly and may benefit the entire faculty and administration.

Need for Skill

Sometimes the consultant will become aware that the teacher possesses the requisite theoretical knowledge to understand the presenting problem but does not possess the ability to apply appropriate skill to solve it. It is one thing to cognitively discern the difficulty but quite another matter to call forth and exercise the appropriate problem-solving skill. The main task for the consultant is to explore with the teacher how he or she might develop skill using the existing resources in the school. The best intervention involves assisting the teacher to invoke the assistance of colleagues, the principal, or a specialist. By offering to teach or model skill development there is a risk that the school social work consultant may threaten the collegial relationship and be perceived to be violating the norms of the role. The consultant might take on the role of supervisor and threaten the collegial relationship. The social work consultant may want to suggest to the teacher that he or she review the case with the principal who can supervise techniques of intervention. In some instances, however, the social worker is the ideal staff person for skill development.

For example, the Individual Family Service Plan for eligible infants and toddlers and their families, mandated by the Individuals with Disabilities Education Act, calls for assessment of family priorities, resources, and concerns. In many school districts, teachers who often lack basic intervention skills are expected to assist in the completion of this section of the document. For even the most competent mental health professional, the tasks of interviewing families and gleaning their personal issues connected with their children's developmental delay would be challenging. They would demand a complex array of theoretically grounded practice skills. In this instance, imparting basic interviewing techniques may be necessary. There are instances when the type of skill required does not fall under the category of elementary or secondary education. One illustration of this involves modifying instructional designs, methods, and learning skills for managing a mildly autistic child placed in the regular classroom.

Need for Self-Confidence.

There are instances when the consultation reveals that the teacher does demonstrate adequate psychosocial knowledge and skill performance but does not use it due to personal insecurities or lack of self-confidence. This problem may be detected in the teacher's tentativeness and uncertainty, or worse, in feelings of incompetence and worthlessness. In this case, the consultant listens to the teacher describe how the situation was handled and provides support for these work efforts. Another intervention centers on assisting the teacher to seek out senior or experienced faculty members who have had similar experiences and, thereby, engender the very powerful support of the "all in the same boat" phenomenon.

A heartrending illustration of this concept can occur when a student suddenly dies. As part of the debriefing process for a school, one often hears teachers recount catastrophic losses they have suffered, where they were when it occurred, what they thought, how they felt, how they reacted, what was helpful, and what was not helpful. In many cases, their students experience the same range of reactions. However, in the course of the grieving process, teachers are often very reticent to use their personal knowledge and experience as a framework for their class. Bringing together the teachers in a group offers them a way to support each other and gain confidence in using themselves effectively to help students express their feeling and perceptions and mourn.

Need for Objectivity

Lack of objectivity is defined as the teacher's loss of professional focus by becoming too close or too distant from the child or the family. When this occurs, conscious or unconscious factors invade the teacher's role functioning, distort perception, and cloud judgment. Five causes for loss of objectivity are (1) direct personal involvement, (2) simple identification, (3) transference, (4) characterological distortions, and (5) theme interference (Caplan, 1970; Caplan and Caplan, 1993).

Direct personal involvement takes place when the teacher's professional relationship evolves into a personal relationship. The teacher receives personal satisfaction rather than professional satisfaction in relation to the child. The task of the consultant is to help the teacher control the expression of personal needs in the workplace and develop professional goals and a professional identity. Modeling empathy while maintaining appropriate distance is one technique of intervention to be used. Another is to recount a similar experience the consultant has had in mastering personal feelings. When it is not feasible to discuss directly the teacher's overinvolvement and the difficulties that come from that, the problem can be reversed and reframed. What would the teacher do if the child or family might wish to have a personal relationship with him or her to the exclusion of classmates? It is easier to discuss the ramification of a direct personal relationship in this way.

When the teacher describes a problem in such a way that one person is perceived in glowing positive terms and the other person is perceived in derogatory, stereotypic terms, a tendency toward overidentification with a pupil might be evident. One might expect the teacher to possess some similar characteristics or experiences to the person seen in sympathetic terms (Caplan, 1970; Caplan and Caplan, 1993). The task of the consultant is to weaken the identification by having the teacher reanalyze the data about the entire situation. As this process unfolds, the consultant helps the teacher to see the actors as separate and unique people rather than extensions of the teacher.

Transference problems occur when the teacher imposes a preordained set of attitudes, perceptions, or expectations derived from the teacher's own life experiences that block an objective assessment and work with the child and family. The danger is that the teacher will use the child to act out or resolve the teacher's own unconscious conflicts or fantasy. One way to detect this problem is the teacher's paucity of data to back up assertions made about the child. The consultant identifies the conflict that has stimulated the teacher's transference reaction then asks the teacher to observe the child more closely in this area of conflict. Sometimes the newly collected observational data will help the teacher identify the conflict. In other cases, the best the consultant can do is to offer emotional support, allow the teacher to vent feeling, and steer the teacher toward more appropriate outlets for the conflict.

In all professions, some members have serious psychiatric problems that Caplan and Caplan (1993, p. 119) labels "characterological distortions of perception and behavior." In other words, the work-related difficulty is largely due to the teacher's own mental health problems. The task of the consultant is to support the teacher's defense structure and lower anxiety so that the teacher maintains an optimal level of professional functioning. The goal is to inhibit regression and help the teacher maintain control over impulses, fantasies, and regression and develop appropriate role boundaries.

One of the most interesting and useful concepts and intervention strategies in this model is theme interference. This is marked by a teacher's temporary ineffectualness in a limited segment of the work field. The teacher is suddenly confronted by a situation that is confusing and upsetting. Caplan and Caplan (1993, p. 122) postulates that an unresolved life experience or a fantasy persists in the consultee's "preconscious or unconscious as an emotionally toned cognitive constellation . . . a theme." A major component of the theme is its repetitive quality that links an initial category to an inevitable outcome. The teacher is reminded of an unresolved conflict and associates it with the current situation. This condition is perceived to lead to one particular outcome, usually involving pain and suffering. For example, a teacher may say, "Children whose parents neglect them [initial category] often fail later in life [inevitable outcome]."

One technique to use with theme interference is to influence the teacher to change his or her perceptions about the child so as to remove the initial category. This "unlinking" frees the child from the inevitable outcome. An unintended consequence of the technique, however, may be the consultee's displacement of the conflict onto another child. To avoid this problem the consultant can use a technique called "theme interference reduction." The consultant accepts the placement of the child in the initial category but, through examination of the specifics of the child's case, influences the teacher to see that the inevitable outcome is only one of several possible outcomes for the child. In fact, the data often suggest a different outcome.

The author has found the theory and practice of this consultation model were easily transmittable in staff development workshops to groups of school social workers. The most frequent teacher need in the process of consultation was for knowledge and skill. After the school social worker would receive training in this model, each worker offered to meet with individuals or groups of teachers for six weeks to consult with them about a student of their choice. An experimental research design revealed that changes in the teacher's perceptions of the child's classroom behavior were statistically significant (Sabatino, 1986).

CONSULTATION AND COLLABORATION: TEAM BUILDING

Interdisciplinary Collaboration

School-linked services (Hare, 1995; Briar-Lawson et al., 1997) and full-service schools (Dryfoos, 1994) are two prominent movements that currently hold promise as paradigms for integrating education, health, and social services through community building, partnerships, alliances, and networks. Integrated services delivery systems require specialized helping professionals to coordinate and blend various intervention approaches offered to children and families. Bridging traditional organizational and professional boundaries and building well-functioning teams is a complex effort that is well guided by the principles and practices of collaboration.

Mulroy (1997) notes that to understand collaboration "one must understand coordination, a concept that assumes different forms depending on its intended purpose." From the point of view of planning in an organization, collaboration may be viewed as an intervention method used to coordinate activities across various administrative hierarchies. From a different perspective, it may also mean a sense of cooperation among individuals in a system working on a common task. School social workers seek this sense of cooperation, which we can call interprofessional collaboration and team building, and it is this last view of collaboration that is offered here as a framework.

Certain assumptions are posited for this framework. Collaboration contributes to the growth and well-being of each team member. The process enhances the professional capabilities of each team member. Problem-solving efforts and service delivery systems planned and implemented by teams reflect and capture more of the complexities faced by the team. The team has more of an opportunity to deal with the whole picture. The members' knowledge base expands as they become familiar with the understanding of their teammates. In turn, mutual understanding and shared goals provide a powerful model for future work by all school personnel (Radin, 1992).

No one discipline can meet the diverse needs of today's student body. A collaborative approach acknowledges the interrelationship between various disciplines. Joint planning naturally builds interest, motivation, partnership, and consensus. Shared service delivery systems break through categorical approaches to services. By challenging isloated work efforts, there is a shift from policy and procedure to holistic student well-being. Finally, there is a deliberate pooling of effort that challenges members to go beyond their traditional roles.

Guidelines for Effective Teamwork

Successful interdisciplinary work does not magically emerge because different professional meet in a conference room. Gallessich (1982) offers the following guidelines to help teams function effectively.

1. *Structure.* Each team member brings a set of professional discipline, knowledge, values, and skills. Efforts to blend interprofessional strategies may give rise to fear that one's own profession will get "washed out" or that there will be "turf" battles. The philosophy of collaboration calls for various disciplines to plan to act together. In some instances this requires revisions in policy, job descriptions, leadership structure, and accountability requirements, and these often support a different work culture. Roles and assignments must be agreed upon and explicated. Goals and methods must be clarified. Certain unresolved conflicts will result in high tension.

2. *Openness.* A culture of trust between team members as well as the administration and frontline workers is necessary to develop and maintain flexible team work. This requires recognizing each others competencies, trusting each others communications, and relying on each others work (Roberts, 1996). Mutual respect and understanding of each other's values and orientation to service is a precondition to successful team work.

3. *Self-examination.* The team must commit itself to systematically reviewing and studying its own process. Successes and accomplishments

as well as failures require review and exploration. These efforts ensure accountability, for it is one thing to conceptualize collaboration and team work and another to implement it.

4. *Heterogeneity*. Including different professions with different styles and perspectives strengthens joint planning, shared decision making, supporting the school's mission, maximizing resources, and generating new paradigms for assessment, service, referral, and follow-up. These differences must not be so great that they interfere with the structure, openness, and process of the group. Blending and meshing different professional values and philosophies, however, guards against excessive specialization and fragmentation.

Shared Responsibilities and Serving the Host Agency

In recent years, Caplan and Caplan (1993) has added the "complementary" technique of mental health collaboration to his formulation of the theory and practice of mental health consultation. Collaboration adheres to the basic theoretical and practice principles of consultation but allows school social workers to recalibrate their role in response to the institution's particular needs. In collaboration, unlike consultation, the school social worker plays an active part in problem identification, data collection, assessment, treatment planning, and service delivery.

In collaboration, the school social worker's expertise is integrated into the overall mission of the institution. They continue to work toward the general improvement of the mental health culture of the school *and* accept some responsibility for the development and implementation of pupil service outcomes (Lim and Adelman, 1997). They develop partnerships with a network of professionals in a host setting, who are all tied to the well-being of the institution and the client. All are compelled by a shared responsibility to overcome the barriers to a student's education. An example of this type of collaboration is the development of the social development study for the Individualized Education Plan and for the Individual Family Service Plan.

With the rise in integrated services, new practice models and organizational relationships must be developed. There is no one correct way to implement consultation, collaboration, and team work. Each model and interprofessional team will be unique and emerge from the ecological context of its school and from the composition of its team. It is difficult to recommend precise plans in an imprecise world. However, improving the lives of children and families is a professional imperative. Therefore, consultation, collaboration, and team work is not a choice; it is a necessity and obligation for school social work practice (Corrigan and Bishop, 1997).

REFERENCES

Alpert, J., and Associates 1982. *Psychological consultation in educational settings.* San Francisco: Jossey-Bass.

Alpert, J., and Silverstein, J. 1985. Mental health consultation: Historical, present, and future perspectives. In J. Bergan (ed.) *School psychology in contemporary society.* Columbus, OH: Merrill.

Alpert, J. L., and Yammer, M. D. 1983. Research in school consultation: A content analysis of selected journals. *Professional Psychology: Research and Practice* 14(5): 604–612.

Allen-Meares, P. 1994. Social work services in schools: A national study of entry-level tasks. *Social Work* 39:560–565.

Bergen, J. R. 1977. *Behavioral consultation.* Columbus, OH: Merrill.

Briar-Lawson, K., Lawson, H. A., Collier, C., and Joseph, A. 1997. School-linked comprehensive services: Promising beginnings, lessons learned, and future challenges. *Social Work in Education* 19(3):136–148.

Brown, D., Pryzwansky, W. B., and Schulte, A. C. 1987. *Psychological consultation: Introduction to theory and practice.* Needham Heights, MA: Allyn & Bacon.

Caplan, G. 1970. *The theory and practice of mental health consultation.* NY: Basic Books.

Caplan, G., and Caplan, R. 1993. *Mental health consultation and collaboration.* NY: Jossey-Bass.

Carlson, J. 1972. Consulting: Facilitating school change. *Elementary School Guidance and Counseling* 7:83–88.

Carr, L. D. 1976. *Report on survey of social work services in schools.* Washington, DC: National Association of Social Workers. Mimeograph.

Conoley, J. C., and Conoley, C. W. 1982. School consultation: A guide to practice and training. NY: Pergamon.

Conoley, J. C., and Conoley, C. W. 1988. Useful theories in school-based consultation. *Remedial and Special Education* 9:14–20.

Corrigan, D., and Bishop, K. K. 1997. Creating family-centered integrated service systems and interprofessional educational programs to implement them. *Social Work in Education* 19(3):149–163.

Costin, L. B. 1969. A historical review of school social work. *Social Casework* 50(8): 439–453.

Curtis, M. J., and Zins, J. E. (eds.). 1981. *The theory and practice of school consultation.* Springfield, IL: Thomas.

Dinkmeyer, D., and Dinkmeyer, D., Jr. 1978. Consultation: One answer to the counselor role. *Elementary School Guidance and Counseling* 13(2):158–162.

Drapela, V. J. 1983. The counselor as consultant and supervisor. Springfield, IL: Thomas.

Drisko, J. 1993. Special education teacher consultation: A student-focused, skill-defining approach. *Social Work in Education* 15(1):19–28.

Dryfoos, J. 1994. Full-service schools: A revolution in health and social services for children, youth and families. San Francisco: Jossey-Bass.

Dupper, D., and Evans, S. 1996. From band-aids and putting out fires to prevention: School social work practice approaches for the new century. *Social Work in Education* 18(3):187–191.

Early, B. 1992. An ecological-exchange model of social work consultation within the work group of the school. *Social Work in Education* 14(4):209–214.

Freeman, E. M. 1995. School social work overview. In R. L. Edwards (ed.-in-chief). *Encyclopedia of social work* (19th ed., Vol. 3, pp. 2087–2099). Washington, DC: NASW Press.

Freeman, E. M. 1996. Everything I know about consultation. *Social Work in Education* 17(1):3–5.

Gallessich, J. 1982. *The profession and practice of consultation.* San Francisco: Jossey-Bass.

Grady, M. A., Gibson, J. J., and Trickett, E. J. *Mental health consultation, theory practice, and research 1973–78. An annotated reference guide* (DHHS Publication No. ADM 81-948. Rockville, MD: National Institute of Mental Health.

Gutkin, T. B., and Curtis, M. J. 1990. School-based consultation: Theory, techniques, and research. In T. B. Gutkin and C. R. Reynolds (eds.). *The handbook of school psychology* (2nd ed.). New York: Wiley.

Hare, I. 1995. School-linked services. In R. L. Edwards (ed.-in-chief). *Encyclopedia of social work* (19th ed., Vol. 3, pp. 2100–2109). Washington, DC: NASW Press.

Kadushin, A. 1977. *Consultation in social work.* NY: Columbia University Press.

Kaplan, C., Turner, S., Norman, W., and Stillson, K. 1996. Promoting resilience strategies: A modified consultation model. *Social Work in Education* 18(3):158–168.

Kenney, K. C. 1986. Research in mental health consultation: Emerging trends, issues, and problems. In F. V. Mannino et al., (eds.). *Handbook of mental health consultation* (DHHS Publication No. ADM 86-1446). Rockville, MD: National Institute of Mental Health.

Keys, S. G., and Bemak, F. 1997. School-family-community linked services: A school counseling role for changing times. *School Counselor* 44:255–263.

Lambert, C., and Mullaly, R. 1982. School social work: The congruence of task importance and level of effort. In R. T. Constable and J. P. Flynn (eds.). *School social work: Practice and research perspective* (pp. 72–84). Homewood, IL: Dorsey.

Lim, C., and Adelman, H. S. 1997. Establishing school-based, collaborative teams to coordinate resources: A case study. *Social Work in Education* 19(4):266–278.

Lippit, G. L. 1959. A study of the consultation process. *Journal of Social Issues* 15:43–50.

Mannino, F. V. 1981. Empirical perspective in mental health consultation. *Journal of Prevention* 1(3):147–155.

Mannino, F. V., et al. 1986. *Handbook of mental health consultation* (DHHS Publication No. ADM 86-1446). Rockville, MD: National Institute of Mental Health.

Mannino, F. V., MacLennan, B. W., and Shore, M. F. 1975. *The practice of mental health consultation* (DHEW Publication No. ADM 74-112). Rockville, MD: National Institute of Mental Health.

Mannino, F. V., and Shore, M. F. 1980. History and development of mental health consultation. Washington, DC: National Institute of Mental Health.

Meares, P. A. 1977. Analysis of tasks in school social work. *Social Work* 22(3):196–201.

Meares, P. A. 1982. A content analysis of school social work literature, 1968–1978. In R. T. Constable and J. P. Flynn (eds.). *School social work: Practice and research perspectives* (pp. 38–41). Homewood, IL: Dorsey.

Medway, F. J. 1982. School consultation research: Past trends and future directions. *Professional Psychology* 13:422–430.

Meyers, J., Friedman, M. P., and Gaughan, E. J. 1981. The effects of consultee-centered consultation on teacher behavior. In M. J. Curtis and J. E. Zins (eds.). *The theory and practice of school consultation*. Springfield, IL: Thomas.

Meyers, J., Parsons, R. D., and Martin, R. 1979. *Mental health consultation in the schools*. San Francisco: Jossey-Bass.

Mulroy, E. A. 1997. Building a neighborhood network: Interorganizational collaboration to prevent child abuse and neglect. *Social Work* 42(3):255–264.

Newman, R. G. 1967. *Psychological consultation in the schools*. NY: Basic Books.

Oppenheimer, J. J. 1925. *The visiting teacher movement with special reference to administrative relationships* (2nd ed.). NY: Joint Committee on Methods of Preventing Delinquency.

Radin, N. 1992. A peer feedback approach to assessing school social workers as team members. *Social Work in Education* 14(1):57–62.

Reid, W. J. 1979. The model development dissertation. *Social Service Research* 3(2): 215–225.

Robinson, L. 1986. Nursing and mental health consultation. In F. V. Mannino et al. (eds.). *Handbook of mental health consultation* (pp. 145–158). Rockville, MD: U.S. Department of Health and Human Services, Public Health Service. Alcohol, Drug Abuse, and Mental Health Administration, National Institute of Mental Health.

Sabatino, C. A. 1986. The effects of school social work consultation on teacher perception and role conflict—Role ambiguity in relationship to students with social adjustment problems. *Dissertation Abstracts International* 46(1).

Sarason, S. B., et al. 1966. *Psychology in community settings*. New York: Wiley.

Saleeby, D. 1994. Culture, theory, and narrative: The intersection of meanings in practice. *Social Work* 37:351–359.

Schein, E. H. 1969. *Process consultation: Its role in organization development*. Reading, MA: Addison-Wesley.

Shaw, K. M., and Replogle, E. 1996. Challenges in evaluating school-linked services: Toward a more comprehensive evaluation framework. *Evaluation Review* 20(4): 424–469.

Timberlake, E. M., Sabatino, C. A., and Hooper, S. N. 1982. School social work practice and P.L. 94-142. In R. T. Constable and J. P. Flynn (eds.). *School social work: Practice and research perspectives* (pp. 49–71). Homewood, IL: Dorsey.

Wesley, P. W. 1994. Innovative practice: Providing on-site consultation to promote quality in integrated child care program. *Journal of Early Intervention* 18(4):391–402.

West, J. F., and Idol, L. 1987. School consultation (part I): An interdisciplinary perspective on theory, model and research. *Journal of Learning Disabilities* 20: 388–408.

Zins, J. E., and Ponti, C. R. 1990. Best practices in school-based consultation. In A. Thomas and J. Grimes (eds.). *Best practices in school psychology-II.* Washington, DC: National Association of School Psychologists.

Zischka, P. C., and Fox, R. 1985. Consultation as a function of school social work. *Social Work in Education* (2):69–79.

CHAPTER 22

Perspectives on Groups for School Social Workers

Edward J. Pawlak
Professor of Social Work, Western Michigan University

Danielle Wozniak
Assistant Professor of Social Work, Western Michigan University

Michele McGowen
Graduate Assistant, Western Michigan University

- Examples of School-Based Groups from the Literature
- It Takes at Least a Whole School to Educate a Child
- When to Use Groups in Schools: The Case of a Bereavement Support Group
- Group Structure
- Normative Structure

Schools can be viewed as organizations consisting of small groups: *administrative or programmatic task groups* such as curriculum committees, an Individualized Educational Program (IEP) team, a PTA executive committee, and a crisis management team that deals with student fights or student deaths; *educational program groups* such as the student council, the Spanish language club, and the chemistry club; *social and recreational clubs* such as hiking and skiing clubs; *athletic program groups; counseling groups* such as a children-of-divorce support group, a bereavement support group, and peer relations, self-esteem, and problem-solving enhancement groups; and *natural groups* such as gangs, cliques, and friendship groups of students or teachers. This chapter concentrates on counseling groups, since these are the groups that school social workers are most likely to form and serve. We begin our discussion with an overview of the literature on the use of counseling groups in schools to inform readers about the variations in practice among school social workers. We then turn our attention to the unique opportunities and challenges in the use of counseling groups in schools. Although school social workers are more likely to work with counseling groups, and some task and natural groups, the other types of groups are likely to be engaged as practitioners work on behalf of their student clients.

To be an effective practitioner with all types of school groups, school social workers must be able to assess and understand their structures. Thus we end our discussion with an examination of frameworks that are useful in analyzing group and normative structure and demonstrate their application to groups in schools.

EXAMPLES OF SCHOOL-BASED GROUPS FROM THE LITERATURE

The journal *Social Work in Education* was reviewed for articles published during the past ten years on the use of groups in schools. The selections reported here reveal that school social workers engage in group work that is rich, varied, and designed to address a wide range of human needs.

Groups for Parents of Students

Greif (1993) formed a school-based drop-in support group for African-American parents in an urban neighborhood depicted as unsafe. The group served as a medium for discussing parenting concerns and providing mutual support and coaching related to the difficulties of raising children. Vayle (1992) established a group for mothers from multicultural families who had recently immigrated to America. These mothers provided a support network that enabled them to be effective advocates for their children as their families made the often difficult transition to American culture. Gonzalez-Ramos (1990) also used school-based groups for recent immigrants, specifically Hispanic families, who underutilize other traditional mental health services. In a study conducted with Puerto Rican mothers, Gonzalez-Ramos found that they overwhelming chose the school as the place they would prefer to go for help with their children's problems.

Groups for Students Who Are Parents

Bennett and Morgan (1988) suggest using groups to teach adolescent mothers effective interaction skills with their infants, reinforce feelings of competence, and lessen anxious and helpless feelings through peer influence. A group for adolescent fathers was designed to provide support, parenting education, and motivation to stay in school (Anthony and Smith, 1994). Seven of the eight fathers in the program completed the school year, and the average GPA for the group improved from 2.07 to 2.17.

Groups for Students Whose Families Are Experiencing Divorce

Admunson-Beckman and Lucas (1989) used groups for children of divorce to address children's feelings of isolation, loss, anger, guilt, and helplessness. The groups also provided a support network, and opportunities to share feelings with children in similar circumstances and rehearse new coping skills. Mervis (1989) involved children's groups in the production of a video on coping with divorce. The children videotaped themselves or puppets and then invited parents to watch the "premiere." Strauss and McGann (1987) developed a support group for children coping with divorce that included a parent group that met several times concurrently with the children's group. Teachers and parents reported an increase in communication between the home and school, and some parents reported that their children were more able to discuss issues about the divorce than they were before participation in the group.

Groups for Students Dealing with Substance Abuse Issues

Beaudoin (1991) established an aftercare support group for students returning to school from inpatient substance abuse treatment. The group was designed to provide peer support to recovering students and a place to learn new coping strategies as they encounter situations where old responses are expected of them. McElligatt (1986) described the CASPAR program, an after-school group in secondary schools providing a forum for students concerned about parental substance abuse.

Groups for Students with Attention Deficit Hyperactivity Disorder

A support group for teenagers with attention deficit hyperactivity disorder focused on self-esteem, feelings, behavior change, communication, conflict, friendship, anger, and problem solving (Timmer, 1995). A two-year follow-up with approximately half the parents of teens found that they had graduated or were going to graduate and had improved behavior and compliance with community rules.

Groups for Trauma-Related Recovery

Pope, Campbell, and Kurtz (1992) discussed two groups formed in a school after nine students were held as hostages by a student with a gun. One group was for middle school students exhibiting symptoms of post-traumatic stress disorder who requested help from the counselor, and a high school support group was created for the former hostages. The group helped the middle school students return to a precrisis level of functioning. The students in the group for hostages, however, achieved an even higher than precrisis level of functioning.

Groups for Students At Risk of Dropping Out

Charney (1993) used groups in a dropout prevention program for low achievers (GPA less than 2.0) in the second to sixth grades. These groups helped students learn to handle behavior problems that impeded their academic progress by incorporating students with GPAs of 3.0 or above as role models within the group. At termination, 30 percent of the underachieving students had attained a C average, and another 37 percent improved in smaller increments. Balsanek (1986) used short-term groups with seventh- and eighth-grade males who had failed at least two subjects during the preceding grading period but had achievement test scores showing above average scholastic ability. All participants improved at least one letter grade in the subsequent marking period, and most improved by two or more letter grades. The participants also displayed increased peer collaboration behaviors and verbalized many positive self-comments. Carley (1994) created a group for marginalized, hostile high school students at risk for dropping out involving the active participation of adults within the school system. Students and interested staff were asked to metaphorically recreate the story of how they wished to be perceived at school. Reputations could be rewritten to include new possibilities that shifted beyond hostility or authoritarianism. Teachers reported changes in students' attitudes and that they were easier to deal with. There was also an increase in rapport with administrators.

Groups Addressing Stress, Grief, and Loss Issues

Fisher (1989) used "magic circle" groups in a school with fourth-grade students whose teachers had miscarriages within one week of each other. The groups were formed to let the students explore their feelings and fears about death and loss. The farm crisis of the 1980s led Staudt (1987) to form a group for children to deal with the fear, loss, and change associated with the ways the crisis was affecting their families and the community. A group for children whose families had recently relocated to the community was formed by Bloomfield and Holzman (1988) to help the children adjust to their new environment and to cope with the change and losses incurred by moving.

Groups Addressing Socialization and Peer Interaction Skills

Lee and Lee (1989) successfully used group work to help students who are trainably and educably mentally retarded learn age-appropriate behaviors, become more expressive, and feel better about themselves. Students were able to transfer these new behaviors to situations outside the group.

Owen and Anlauf Sabatino (1989) worked with first- and second-grade children displaying cognitive developmental delay, withdrawn behaviors, or aggression. Each group focused on only one of these issues. The first group worked on strengthening deficient cognitive skills to improve classroom behavior, and the other two groups worked on verbalizing feelings to problem solve and become aware of the effects of their behavior socially and academically.

Groups Addressing Racial and Cultural Issues

Student forum groups were used by McGary (1987) in a high school that was experiencing interracial violence. Most of the group participants were considered high risk for behavioral deficits and poor achievement. The six groups, generally composed of students of similar racial backgrounds, set goals related to stopping the violence in the school and addressing racial issues that had surfaced. In the year and a half forum groups were in place, interracial fighting stopped, there was student-initiated elimination of institutionalized racist practices, and standardized test scores increased, especially for minorities. Also, positive responses to postforum survey questions increased significantly (e.g., "I feel safe in school" and "Adults in this school are willing to help me with my personal problems"). Congress and Lynn (1994) carried out a group for urban elementary school immigrants to help them adjust to life in the United States.

IT TAKES AT LEAST A WHOLE SCHOOL TO EDUCATE A CHILD

Forming Counseling Groups

School settings provide social workers with unique advantages while forming counseling groups. These advantages are both part of the organizational structure of schools and an important part of the school social worker's intervention process. For example, practitioners can observe the behavior of prospective group members in structured settings such as physical education, English, and music classes, and in unstructured settings such as lunch and recess. Observations made in these settings provide an empirical basis for deciding the composition of counseling groups to include members with complementary characteristics and to avoid imbalances, for example, too many acting-out members.

School social workers can also gather information about a student's behavior from several different sources (e.g., teachers in different classes, custodians, food service workers) to find out with which people and in which settings the student does well or poorly. Their observations often yield information that is essential for an accurate assessment and an effective treatment plan. For example, personal observations and information received from teachers are helpful in assessing students' strengths and areas in need of development, as well as understanding how various problems are manifested or exacerbated. This information is useful in guiding group composition and focusing content during group counseling sessions. Information gleaned from observations can be reflected back to the student in the context of the therapeutic relationship and incorporated in a student's self-assessment of his or her own difficulties and strengths. For example, students who have low self-esteem, poor impulse control, and poor peer relations might be expected to have a more difficult time in unstructured settings like recess or lunch time. Teachers' complaints about the student might include classroom disruption and management issues. However, on closer inspection, the student's difficulties might be limited to unstructured classroom activities exacerbated by arguments and fights occurring during recess. Intervention for that student might include both group counseling and work with teachers to restructure the child's day, alleviating many unstructured activities until the student has gained greater proficiency and comfort with them.

Collaboration with School Personnel

Another advantage to counseling groups in schools is that teachers, social workers, school administrators, and parents can participate in the therapeutic process together. The African proverb "It takes a whole village to raise a child" is particularly applicable when thinking about school-based counseling or support groups. Groups are most effective when the school social worker has the support and understanding of teachers and administrators. School social workers must enlist the direct help of classroom teachers, guidance counselors, parents, and administrators and consider them integral parts of the therapeutic process. Such collaboration can be achieved by establishing and maintaining good communication between teachers and social workers, and educating personnel about what constitutes helpful exchange. One way to begin this process is to ask teachers what kind of information or feedback they would find helpful and to tell teachers what kind of information school social workers find useful. This is a good time to educate professionals about what practitioners and student group members are expected to keep confidential about group discussions. The requirements and opportunities for collaboration abound, and we address them in the context of other issues that school social workers must address in their use of counseling groups in schools.

"What the Heck Goes on in Those Groups Anyway?"

The importance of educating school personnel about group process deserves attention. What do school social workers do with students? What do students work on? How? If the group has a curriculum, it might be helpful to share with teachers the topics of each group session. This can be done individually or as an inservice training presentation at a staff meeting. Preemptively educating school personnel about group processes eliminates unprofessional communication. For example, complaints about student behavior or inquiries about "what was discussed in group" can be recontextualized from deviant, bad, or troublesome to behavior that is amenable to intervention and improvement. Strong teacher–social worker communication also helps school personnel to own some aspects of the problem, to become invested in the solution, and thus to work *with* school social workers and students toward problem resolution. In this respect, intervention is a shared process and not simply a "pull out" program where the social worker meets students at the classroom door, conducts a group session, and returns them forty-five minutes later magically "fixed" or at least "made better."

Good teacher–social worker communication around therapeutic intervention issues begins with careful explanation of what the group is, what school social workers hope to attain, what the benefits are to students, and what behaviors (either improvements or potential problems) school personnel can and should watch for. Practitioners should regularly ask for feedback from teachers regarding student behavior and progress and provide information to teachers about the issues the group is working on. This can be done in general terms without breaking the confidence of group members. For example, teachers might be told that "this week the divorce support group is talking about how they first learned about their parents' divorce, and how the students felt it affected them. This is an exercise requiring introspection and looking directly at a painful time in their lives. Sara may be quieter than usual, more sensitive, more prone to tears or intolerant of frustration right after the group meeting." Through a therapeutic alliance, teachers can spot potential problems arising in the classroom and bring them to the school social worker's attention immediately. Informed teachers can also support group counseling efforts with follow-up classroom activities. For example, if the group is working on issues of self- or impulse control, an informed teacher can acknowledge times when students participating in the group show improvement. Teachers also can structure student activities to provide "moments of success."

Good communication is also important when informing teachers that what looks like fun and play is really a developmentally appropriate way of tackling some tough or sensitive problems. Communication and education about the group process helps teachers understand and appreciate the social worker's role in therapeutic groups. Practitioners must share their vision of the therapeutic process. Perhaps most important, the exchange provides opportunities to discuss the ways in which life trauma or stress that initially appears unrelated to academic achievement or performance is really intricately related to students' ability to benefit from their education and function in the school environment. That is to say, a strong teacher–social worker alliance helps teachers and social workers explore the relationship between life crises and a child's school performance. Many school social workers reported that most teachers involved in this discussion see a life-crisis (e.g., divorce) as one that would affect a child's ability to concentrate in school, complete assignments, or interact successfully with peers. Many teachers who interacted with children of divorce felt they could benefit from intervention by the school social worker and stated affirmatively that such children were in need of intervention. By understanding the nature of trauma inherent in a divorce, and the resulting sense of isolation and depression, teachers favored using the school setting to run divorce support groups.

Sometimes parents and teachers have difficulty understanding the treatment focus of some groups, especially when meetings involve participation in activities. When counseling groups are viewed as social or recreational groups, some parents want siblings to join the group, or teachers withhold a student's participation in a group meeting to discipline him for disruptive, unruly classroom behavior. These moments should be seized to interpret the counseling focus of group meetings, and the relationship of the service to school problems and performance. Teachers can be helped to understand that students with emotional impairments often do not simply have fun during group meetings but are working on important issues in a developmentally appropriate context. One school social worker described an outing to a public pool, in which five ten-year-old students spent as much time out of as in the water. He and the lifeguard had to issue many time-outs and restrictions for safety and rule violations.

Group counseling in schools provides members with access to services and school social workers with reasonable assurances that students will be present at group meetings and on time. However, when students are released from class to attend group meetings, and the discussion or activity becomes turbulent, the conflict may carry over into the classroom on the student's return. This situation creates management problems for teachers and increases their skepticism about the merits of in-school, on-school-time counseling groups. Sometimes group meetings can be scheduled at the end of the school day or after school. However, strong teacher–social worker communication can either quickly resolve problems that carry over into the classroom or prevent them from occurring.

The role of school administrators should not be overlooked. Principals, vice principals, and house masters are regularly in the position of doling out punishments or consequences to students who are not complying with school rules. However, many are eager to expand their role and their interaction with children. Involving administrators in therapeutic conferences, and keeping them informed of group activities and goals, enables them to interact with students positively. For example, students who are working in a group on impulse control in unstructured settings can be "caught being good" by informed administrators. Students who are often sent to the principal's office because of misbehavior can be sent to the principal's office for rewards, positive feedback, and praise. As allies, school administrators can often help the social worker overcome administrative or scheduling impediments to group counseling. For example, socialization groups ideally can be lunch-time groups, unless prospective student group members eat lunch on different shifts. Administrative understanding and support can make an insurmountable structural problem into one that is easily corrected.

"You Want to Pull My Kid out of Class and Put Him in a Group for Bad Kids?"

Parents may have mixed responses about their children's participating in an in-school therapeutic group. They may fear that their children will be stigmatized and consequently teased by other children, or that their children will get behind in their work. On the other hand, they may be relieved to know that they are no longer dealing with difficult social and emotional problems alone and finally have support and help for their children's problems. Again, communication and education about group purposes, benefits to students, and measures to protect students' confidentiality and to ensure that they will not fall behind academically can go a long way toward reassuring parents and ensuring their support. Another concern parents often express is that "my child doesn't have problems." When this sentiment is expressed, explanations of group purpose and process are used to help parents accept their child's difficulties, service from the school social worker, and collaboration with other school personnel to work toward resolution of problems. Often parents' denial is a part of the overall problem experienced by the child and the school community. Helping parents work through their feelings is an important component of a child's successful participation in school-based group counseling.

"How Do You Make Sure No One Talks about What We Talk About?"

There are some special considerations that one must entertain when working with groups in schools. One is the issue of confidentiality. Confidentiality of membership in a counseling group may be virtually impossible if students are released from class to participate in group meetings. The importance of confidentiality to students should be addressed directly with them in the group context. Some students will find confidentiality of membership very important and will want to develop some strategies for maintaining their confidentiality, or at least reducing the obviousness of their participation. In other groups, this will be a moot point or membership in the group will be a point of pride. Confidentiality of discussions that take place during group meetings must be pursued but cannot be assured. Some members may not be vigilant about confidentiality as they disclose their group experience to peer confidants or inquisitive fellow students. Student peers can be empathic, supportive, and understanding, but they can also be cruel. Breaches of confidentiality may have serious social and psychological consequences for members whose disclosures have been revealed. Affected students could be tormented, taunted, teased, shunned, or the object of whispered conversations. Members of student counseling groups sometimes "feel paranoid" that "others know" and devote energy to image and identity management, damage control, and public-presentation-of-self issues, even when confidentiality is maintained.

Group members should be told that confidentiality is a condition of participation. Groups may want to deal directly with their fears or concerns that confidentiality will not be maintained or with how they hope to be their own enforcers. In one group of second-grade girls who were working on self-esteem and peer relationship issues, the group identified one girl whom they feared would not keep their confidence. This quickly became a group issue. The girl acknowledged that she sometimes used group information as a way to gain friendships with children outside the group. In a controlled setting, the group showed their disapproval with this friendship-gaining strategy and helped her devise alternative strategies to making and keeping friends, as well as group strategies to help her maintain confidentiality. These activities were ultimately in service of the group's general goals, which were to strengthen peer relationship and problem-solving skills. Thus potential problems may be important therapeutic issues and can become a beneficial part of the therapeutic process. Finally, however, if confidentiality remains an issue or is continually breached, school social workers in collaboration with relevant others should evaluate whether some student problems are best treated in individual counseling sessions.

"I Don't Wanna Be in Your Group"

Stigma associated with membership in particular counseling groups may contribute to student resistance or refusal to participate. For example, one student who was being interviewed by a school social worker for possible inclusion in an after-school activity group asked, "Is this a group for crazies?" The social worker led the student into an exploration of the characteristics and behavior of other students who were being invited to join the group. The student said that a couple of kids were "crazy," and he explained what he meant by saying "they act-up, they're wild," and he didn't want to be in a group with crazies. However, he also recognized that one boy was sad, another did not have many friends, and some "don't stick with their work." Considering the discussion, the school social worker said that the "crazy" characterization of the group was not appropriate and asked the student to reframe his perception of the group. He responded by saying, "It's a do-better group." This student figured out how he would explain his membership to inquiring peers. However, others may not be so insightful and clever. Thus school social workers should help student members of counseling groups formulate a way of explaining membership in a counseling group and managing identities associated with such affiliation. Sometimes stereotypes of counseling groups develop because many referrals are understandably students who are behavioral management problems in the classroom. On the other hand, developmentally, adolescents tend to be self-conscious and wary of being singled out or made different. Calling a student out of class to engage in individual counseling is often an embarrassment. Group intervention allows students *not* to feel singled out, but to feel included and supported in a peer setting.

WHEN TO USE GROUPS IN SCHOOLS: THE CASE OF A BEREAVEMENT SUPPORT GROUP

When should one consider forming a group? How do issues of context, which is the unique social and structural environment of schools, pose both impediments and provide unique supports for forming a group? What other issues are important to consider? The following is an analysis of important considerations revolving around the formation of a bereavement support group by a school social worker. These considerations include case management issues, group themes, student's developmental issues, evaluating sound intervention strategy, setting group goals, and thinking about the benefits of a group to students with whom practitioners are working.

Case Management

One of the authors was a school social worker in a high school of approximately 800 students with two school psychologists and eight guidance counselors. The staff were regularly faced with a serious problem—caseloads were extremely high. Often the need to contact students and their families to begin intervention was urgent since problems faced by adolescents are seldom those that can wait three weeks for an appointment. Traditional models of intervention such as individual counseling or even home visits and family counseling were not always feasible. As we began to think and talk about alternative, yet effective interventions, we began to think about the context in which we were providing service. Most students placed themselves in groups and spent most of their waking hours living in intentionally created groups. Individual counseling, while essential for some students, had traditionally been the preferred and only mode of treatment selected by mental health professionals in the schools. Yet this was neither effective nor possible given our high caseloads. Based on case management constraints we began to think about the feasibility of groups.

Group Themes

At the high school we regularly had team meetings with all social service personnel to discuss the students who had been referred to us by teachers, parents, administrators, or guidance counselors. In discussing how to best serve the needs of students who had been referred for social work or psychological services, we began to look at the common issues each student was dealing with. We were startled to find fourteen students who had been referred to us over the previous two months had lost a parent. We were even more startled to find after talking to each student's guidance counselors and teachers that each was described in very similar terms. Each was truant from school, often spent most of each day in the nurse's office complaining of somatic illness, was involved to a greater degree than other students in substance abuse, mostly alcohol abuse, was emotionally withdrawn and depressed, had poor or tumultuous peer relationships, and was often desribed as a "loner." It was with this information that we began to think about a group, not about how to form one or even whether we should, but about formed and natural groups as *concepts to think with*, and thus to change the way we thought about our students, their troubles, and our approach to them. Common problems or life themes, or even difficulty with similar developmental tasks, made students at our high school little more than aggregates, or "collections of people who share a common circumstance or condition" (Longres, 1995, p. 319). However, thinking about students' shared concerns and shared developmental tasks became one way to think about how peers could potentially be brought together to form groups that could help, buoy, and strengthen each other. From this perspective, support groups, problem-solving groups, and issue-directed therapy groups made sense not only because they allowed us to provide services to larger numbers of students but because group counseling represented a sound intervention strategy for particular groups of students.

Thus we began to think about forming a group based on themes that were relevant to students. To the fourteen who had lost a parent, loss and bereavement were the hallmarks of their existence. We began to gather information about the students who should be invited to participate in the bereavement support group. We also shared with teachers our idea about forming the group, especially since we knew that to get fourteen high school students released from class once a week was going to take cooperation. Teachers reported that each student's academic performance, ability to concentrate, and attendance was an issue. Many teachers expressed frustration with these students' lack of communication and their academic failure. Since for many of these students their loss was not in the recent past, teachers needed to understand that without effective intervention students' feelings of bereavement would not just go away. Since teachers saw that we were addressing the "root causes" or etiology of academic and adjustment problems, they were supportive of our efforts, pledging their willingness to release students from class and help them make up missed work. Contexualizing the student's alienating, depressed, or antisocial behaviors in terms of life trauma that could be resolved or worked with had an impact on how teachers defined and then related to their students. We found that no longer were students "blamed" for their high absenteeism or failure to turn in work on time. Instead, teachers were more inclined to take an empathic approach to students, to extend additional help and support, and work with students and with group coleaders. The changed response from school personnel had the benefit of reducing student alienation and hostility and created an atmosphere in which students could reengage in the academic process. That is to say, students who were overwhelmed emotionally by feelings of depression relating to their loss felt support and empathy from their teachers. Thus students began to look at school as "not a total failure" and began to engage more in their work. This pattern continued as students progressed through the group, dealing in a supportive context with the painful issues of death, loss, and unresolved, and for the most part, unabating grief.

Therapeutic Goals

While part of evaluating whether a group is a sound intervention strategy includes an analysis of the setting and the potential issues students are facing, another component has to do with the therapeutic issues and goals. From this perspective, the most salient question becomes, based on your knowledge of students' issues and needs, and sound intervention strategies, does it make sense *therapeutically* to place students in a group or to form a group to deal with their issues? For example, in the bereavement support group, one reaction to a dramatic life event is to feel a sense of isolation from others and a sense of alienation from familiar settings and friends. Based on our review of the literature and our assessment of students' needs, a small group designed to reduce isolation and increase support was deemed beneficial. Other groups with similar goals might include alcoholism support groups, groups dealing with gay and lesbian sexual identity, and groups for students who have experienced sexual abuse.

Developmental Issues

A third consideration was developmental issues. We began by asking, *developmentally*, where are these students functioning? What are the important issues in their lives? Are those issues amenable to processing in a group? Can group work ease the processes by which students work through developmental issues? For the adolescents coming together to form a bereavement support group, constructing a sense of identity was one task with which they struggled. Another was to gain a sense of identity concerning a peer group. The social class and ethnic composition of the bereavement support group was primarily Euro-American, working- and middle-class males and females, generally from two-parent families. Establishing identity for these students was at times a tumultuous process and was often enacted through challenging parental rules, talking back to their parents, pushing boundaries, and creating distance between themselves and their parents in favor of peers. It was not uncommon in the general community for parents and adolescents to describe their relationships with each other as conflicted, problematic, and painful. It was in the middle of this process that fourteen of these students lost a parent. From a developmental perspective, one aspect of each teenager's story was to talk about the argument, the disagreement, the battle he or she was in the middle of when his or her their parent died. Students talked about their sense of regret, shame, and guilt. Sharing these feelings in a group normalized their experiences and reduced their anxiety and isolation by placing them within a context of developmental issues shared by other students.

Developmental issues are a part of larger questions: How do individuals arrange themselves and what issues are most salient to them? Are these issues a part of the way they group themselves? These questions often point to issues of identity or to a sense of goals and purpose. For example, students who identify themselves as "Hispanic" in a predominantly Anglo-American high school may be a part of a natural friendship network whose purpose is to support each other and share interests and activities based on a common sense of culture, family, values, and life ways. In this case, the way in which students see themselves has a direct relationship to the way in which they group themselves. Friendship networks can be supported, enhanced, and often used to form the foundation for treatment, education, or task groups. For example, Hispanic friendship networks can be used to increase Hispanic pride, to educate Euro-American students about Hispanic culture, and to help Hispanic students to find a comfortable place in a predominantly Anglo-American setting. The students in the adolescent bereavement group did not naturally form a group. Yet, individually, an important part of their "identity" was as someone who had lost a parent. Thus it made sense to bring these students together with others who identified themselves in a similar way, and to help them form friendship networks with students who shared a similar experience.

GROUP STRUCTURE

Group structure refers to stable patterns of interaction among group members at a point in time (Johnson and Johnson, 1997, p. 19). School social workers must discern these patterns in groups to understand and influence them. Group structure may be assessed in terms of *formal structure*, relationships among positions, and *informal structure*, relationships among individuals. We turn to a discussion of different types of formal and informal group structure, and then we explore their relevance and application to school social work.

Formal Structure: Relationships among Positions

Relationships among positions may be classified according to formal authority/leadership, communication, tasks, and mobility. *Authority/leadership structure* refers to group hierarchical positions that have been legitimated by members or officials. Examples of such structure include chairperson, president, vice president, coordinator. Teams elect captains or cocaptains; counseling groups may rotate the roles of convener or facilitator among members. *Communication structure* refers to required or expected patterns of exchange of information, viewpoints, or feelings between group members. Examples of such structure include committee deliberations regulated by parliamentary procedure, rules regarding timely advance notice of group meetings and circulation of the agenda, procedures governing recording and circulation of minutes of meetings, and guidelines that specify who is supposed to be informed about what, and who is supposed to send information to whom. Even counseling groups establish formal communication patterns when members agree to decision making by consensus in selecting topics to be explored. *Task structure* refers to legitimated distribution of the group's work among members. Examples of such structure include treasurer, recorder, corresponding secretary, membership secretary, faculty advisor to the student council, and representative to the IEP team. Counseling groups may rotate initiation of self-disclosure and first respondent among group members (note this is an example of both task and communication structure). *Mobility structure* refers to the patterns of movement in and out of group positions. Examples of such structure include term limits on occupancy in a group position; rules that govern eligibility for group positions (e.g., only seniors who were group members during their junior year may serve as president), and rules about succession (e.g., the vice chair is the chair elect).

This framework can be used in several ways as school social workers approach or work with groups in schools. For example, before attempts are made to help a social isolate join a hiking group, practitioners would be wise to learn about the group's leadership and authority structure and the role of the faculty advisor. The student may have to be coached about the appropriate ways of approaching student leaders and faculty advisors. In working with IEP teams, the group's task and communication structure must be understood if school social workers are to understand their roles and effective ways to influence members on behalf of students. Sometimes cliques dominate the leadership structure of educational program, recreational, or social groups, and some students never have an opportunity to be in leadership or task roles. To alter these patterns, the mobility structure of groups must be understood. School social workers may have to help school administrators, staff, teachers, students, or parents understand the formal structures of groups to help them learn how to maneuver within them. As one begins to understand group structure, one can figure out who should be approached in what ways to accomplish particular objectives. Furthermore, school social workers cannot influence what they cannot see and understand. The framework for assessing formal structure serves as a lens to discern prescribed patterns of group interaction.

Informal Structure: Relations among Individuals

Relations among individuals may be classified according to power, communication, task, affection, and status. *Power structure* refers to relationships based on ability to influence and affect the decisions or behavior of others. There are four types of power: reference, expertise, reward, and coercive (French and Raven, 1968). Referent power refers to the influence members have because they are liked; expertise power refers to the influence members have because they have knowledge and skill that is valued by others, such as knowledge of math or skill in photography; reward power refers to the influence members have because they positively reinforce others and are supportive; and, coercive power refers to the influence members have because they can impose their ideas on others, gain compliance, or require particular behaviors through psychological or physical force. *Communication structure* refers to the nature (e.g., hostile, friendly, attentive) and frequency of exchanges among members, who talks to whom, and communication roles members play in groups (e.g., listener, initiator). *Task structure* refers to the roles of members in carrying out the work of the group—for example, who volunteers to do what? *Affectional structure* refers to patterns of social acceptance and rejection, and preferences members have for each other. *Status* refers to the location of members on a hierarchical scale according to dimensions that are important to the group (e.g., physical strength, intelligence, sense of humor, ability to get along with others; Johnson and Johnson, 1997, p. 21).

This framework can be used in several ways as school social workers approach or work with various groups in schools. For example, although school task groups may have formal leaders, other members may have substantial power because they have expertise or are well liked. Both formal and informal leaders have to be considered when practitioners attempt to influence the group. In counseling and natural groups, it is imperative to assess the types and distribution of power. Practitioners must harness, redirect, or change the group's power structure if they intend to use the group as a means of influence. An assessment of communication structure in counseling groups is important because members are often referred to the school social worker for their troublesome patterns of communication.

Discussion

Within and between both types of group structure, members are likely to occupy several positions (for example, members of the formal task structure might also be members of the formal leadership structure; some members are likely to be a part of the informal affectional and informal power structure; members who are part of the informal affectional structure may also be members of the formal authority structure. Both types of group structure may affect the members' feelings toward each other, their attraction to the group, their commitment to group purposes, the level of conflict within the group, and the potential of the group as a means of influence on members. Effective social work in schools requires practitioners to discern and assess the structures and processes of small groups that might have a bearing on their clients' school adjustment and performance. The results of such assessments must be used to modify group structure and guide group processes. Such modification is essential to influencing group and individual goal achievement, whether it is behavioral change in a student, unruly school behavior of a clique, or modification of decision making by an IEP team.

Group structure can be viewed as a factor that can affect members' behavior through alterations of the dimensions identified above—for example, by altering the task structure of the group, practitioners might change a member's group status, or by modifying group mobility structure, practitioners might alter leadership opportunities and the confidence and self-esteem of some members. Group structure can also be viewed as a factor that can be affected by factors such as group composition (e.g., removal of a bully from the group), auspices (e.g., groups with or without a faculty advisor), program activities (e.g., competitive vs. cooperative activities), physical setting (e.g., off-campus vs. on-campus group meetings), and in-group and out-of-group interventions by the school social worker.

NORMATIVE STRUCTURE

Norms can be set formally or informally. Formal norms are prescribed standards of behavior that have prescribed consequences for failures in compliance (e.g., standards of conduct when school groups make field trips). Informal norms are also standards of behavior, but they are regulated by shared feelings of approval or disapproval among group members (e.g., group members' approval of taking turns or disapproval of horseplay that disrupts a group meeting; Johnson and Johnson, 1997, pp. 21–22).

Among students, group norms have powerful influences on imitation, compliance, conformity, the ability to exercise independence, and respect for one's own and others' individuality. Discussions about norms are inevitable in group counseling in schools. For example, normative discussions are likely about relations with teachers, school officials, fellow students, parents, law enforcement personnel, and others. Among junior and high school students in some counseling groups, normative discussions are likely about respect, race relations, use of substances, dating, and sexual activity. Norms about levels of effort to be expended on schoolwork and after-school employment are also topical. Violations of school norms are often reasons for referral to the school social worker and the focus of individual and group counseling discussions. Group norms also have powerful influences on teachers, school officials, and parents. For example, these groups make normative judgments that may be convergent or divergent about student discipline, parental involvement, teacher commitment, and equal opportunities participate in school activities.

Group normative structure can be assessed in several ways:

- The scope of behavior that is approved or disapproved,
- The intensity of the group's feelings about norms,
- The degree of agreement about norms among members,
- Peer pressure for conformity,
- Reference groups, and
- Congruence of group norms with those of relevant others in the group's life space (Johnson and Johnson, 1997, pp. 432–436; Radin and Feld, 1985, pp. 56–61).

School social workers can involve members from all types of groups in assessing their norms, the consequences of compliance and noncompliance, and conformity and nonconformity. Members might explore methods of coping with pressures for conformity with questionable norms. Alternative normative reference groups might be presented to group members.

A final consideration when thinking about groups in schools is what course of action would be most beneficial to the group of individuals with whom you are working? In the case of students, this might be how you can best enhance the problem-solving skills of a class of special education students who are struggling to learn self-control and impulse control. When working with naturally formed faculty groups such as all the third-grade teachers at a particular school, the issue might be how you help them coalesce into a task group that can effectively address curriculum changes to meet the increasingly culturally diverse needs of students. When you begin to think about the formed and natural *groups* that exist in schools rather than thinking about how can to make *individuals* function better, the question becomes, How can I help these groups of individuals meet their goals? This approach is one that automatically requires the social worker to examine the social and cultural context within which individuals live and work, as well as to integrate into an intervention strategy the culture of a particular group. Thinking with group concepts also broadens the definition of school social work. Practice shifts away from the social worker as only a provider of treatment to individuals who are in some way functionally impaired or having problems, an approach that reproduces the individual psychopathology model of intervention that arguably may have a limited place in contemporary school social work. Practice also shifts toward a model of intervention that is inclusive and strengths based. That is to say, social work is defined as services that can enhance the functioning and cooperation among people who see themselves as connected through the experience of interdependence, through a working structure, through a common identity, or through the delimitation of boundaries. In this respect, social work services are provided to various systems within the organization of the school and thus enhance the overall functioning of the school community.

REFERENCES

Admundson-Beckman, K., and Lucas, A. R. 1989. Gaining a foothold in the aftermath of divorce. *Social Work in Education* 12(1):5–15.

Anthony, I., and Smith, D. L. 1994. Adolescent fathers: A positive acknowledgement in the school setting. *Social Work in Education* 16(3):179–184.

Balsanek, J. A. 1986. Group intervention for underachievers in the intermediate school. *Social Work in Education* 9(1):26–32.

Beaudoin, E. 1991. Assessment and intervention with chemically dependent students. *Social Work in Education* 13(2):78–79.

Bennett, T., and Morgan, R. L. 1988. Teaching interaction skills to adolescent mothers. *Social Work in Education* 10(3):143–151.

Bloomfield, K. M., and Holzman, R. 1988. Helping today's nomads: A collaborative program to assist mobile children and their families. *Social Work in Education* 10(3):183–197.

Carley, G. 1994. Shifting alienated student-authority relationships in a high school. *Social Work in Education* 16(4):221–230.

Charney, H. 1993. Project Achievement: A six-year study of a dropout prevention program in bilingual schools. *Social Work in Education* 15(2):113–117.

Congress, E. P., and Lynn, M. 1994. Group work programs in public schools: Ethical dilemmas and cultural diversity. *Social Work in Education* 16(2):107–114.

Fisher, H. A. 1989. Magic circle: Group therapy for children. *Social Work in Education* 11(4):260–265.

French, J. R. P., and Raven, B. 1968. The bases of social power. In D. Cartwright and A. Zander (eds.). *Group dynamics* (3rd ed., pp. 215–235). NY: Harper & Row.

Greif, G. L. 1993. A school-based support group for urban African American parents. *Social Work in Education* 15(3):133–139.

Gonzalez-Ramos, G. 1990. Examining the myth of Hispanic families' resistance to treatment: Using the school as a site for services. *Social Work in Education* 12(4): 261–274.

Johnson, D. W., and Johnson, F. P. 1997. *Joining together* (6th ed.). Boston: Allyn & Bacon.

Lee, B., and Lee. S. 1989. Group therapy as a process to strengthen the independence of students with mental retardation. *Social Work in Education* 11(2):123–132.

Longres, J. S. 1995. *Human behavior and social environment.* Itasca, IL: Peacock.

Marsiglia, F. F., and Witt Johnson, M. 1997. Social work with groups and the performing arts in the schools. *Social Work in Education* 19(1):53–59.

McElligatt, K. 1985. Identifying and treating children of alcoholic parents. *Social Work in Education* 9(1):55–70.

McGary, R. 1987. Student forums addressing racial conflict in a high school. *Social Work in Education* 9(3):159–168.

Mervis, B. A. 1989. Shaggy dog stories: A video project for children of divorce. *Social Work in Education* 12(1):16–26.

Owen, M. C. and Anlauf Sabatino, C. 1989. Effects of cognitive development on classroom behavior: A model assessment and intervention program. *Social Work in Education* 11(2):77–87.

Pope, L. A., Campbell, M., and Kurtz, P. D. 1992. Hostage crisis: A school-based interdisciplinary approach to posttraumatic stress disorder. *Social Work in Education* 14(4):227–233.

Radin, R., and Feld, S. 1985. Social psychology for group practice. In M. Sundel, P. Glasser, R. Sarrik, and R. Vinter (eds). *Individual change through small groups* (pp. 50–69). NY: Free Press.

Staudt, M. 1987. Helping rural school children cope with the farm crisis. *Social Work in Education* 9(4):222–229.

Strauss, J. B., and McGann, J. 1987. Building a network for children of divorce. *Social Work in Education* 9(2):96–105.

Timmer, D. F. 1995. Group support for teenagers with attention deficit hyperactivity disorder. *Social Work in Education* 17(3):194–198.

Vayle, M. R. 1992. International Women's Group: A bridge to belonging. *Social Work in Education* 14(1):7–14.

CHAPTER 23

Social Skills for the Twenty-First Century

Craig Winston LeCroy
Professor, Arizona State University

Janice M. Daley
Project Coordinator, Arizona State University

Kerry B. Milligan
L & M Associates

- The Development of Social Skills Programs in the Schools
- Group Format and the Social Skills Training Method
- Social Skills Training Illustrated

School is the major socializing institution for children; in school, children develop social behavior as well as learn academic skills. Elias and Clabby (1992, p. 7) note that there is an "inextricable bond linking personal, social, affective, and cognitive development" in children. Although schools focus on children's educational and cognitive skills and capabilities, an important but neglected area of concern is the healthy social development of children (Benson, 1997). The National Mental Health Association Commission on the Prevention of Mental-Emotional Disabilities recommended that "programs should be developed in schools (preschool through high school) that incorporate validated mental health strategies and competence building as an integral part of the curriculum" (Long, 1986). Our schools must begin to acknowledge the importance of instructing students in a new set of basics: social skills. Children need social skills.

The socialization and academic education of children can be facilitated by offering various social skills programs within the school setting. Social skills classes can equip children with prosocial skills to help them replace aggressive or withdrawn behaviors with appropriate coping strategies. Interpersonal skills can be taught to enhance communication with peers, parents, and authority figures. Numerous opportunities exist for the implementation of various skill-based programs that can help facilitate the successful socialization of children and adolescents in our schools. School social workers can play an important role in the design and implementation of social skill programs that (1) enhance children's ability to learn and interact successfully with others and (2) enable teachers to focus on and better accomplish educational goals.

THE DEVELOPMENT OF SOCIAL SKILLS PROGRAMS IN THE SCHOOLS

Clinical observation and research in recent years have found a relationship between poor peer relationships and later psychological difficulties (Hartup, 1983). In fact, disturbances in peer relationships are among the best predictors of psychiatric, social, and school problems. Research strongly suggests that social competence is essential for healthy normal development (Hartup, 1983). Child developmentalists stress that it is through a child's interactions with peers that many of life's necessary behaviors are acquired. For example, children learn sexual socialization, control of aggression, expression of emotion, and caring from their families and in friendship through their interaction with peers. When children fail to acquire such social skills, they are beset by problems such as inappropriate expression of anger, friendship difficulties, and an inability to resist peer pressure. It is this understanding that has led to the present focus on changing children's interpersonal behavior with peers. Since many of a young person's problem behaviors develop in a social context, the teaching of social skills in the classroom or in small-group sessions elsewhere is one of the most promising approaches in remediating children's social difficulties.

Defining and Conceptualizing Social Skills

Social skills can be defined as a complex set of skills that facilitate successful interactions between peers, parents, teachers, and other adults. *Social* refers to interactions between people; *skills* refers to making appropriate discriminations—deciding what would be the most effective response and using the verbal and nonverbal behaviors that facilitate interaction.

The conceptualization of social skills as training suggests that problem behaviors can be viewed as remediable deficits in a child's response repertoire (Asher, 1983; Hops, Finch, and McConnell, 1989; King and Kirschenbaum, 1992; see also LeCroy, 1983, 1992; Jackson and Hornbeck, 1989; Hops, 1982). This perspective focuses on building prosocial responses as opposed to eliminating excessive antisocial responses. Children learn new options in coping with problem situations. Learning how to respond effectively to new situations produces more positive consequences than past behaviors used in similar situations. This model focuses on the teaching of skills and competencies for day-to-day living rather than on the understanding and elimination of defects. It is an optimistic view of children and is implemented in an educative-remedial framework.

An Application

A classic social skills training study by Oden and Asher (1977) sought to improve the social skills and peer relationships of third- and fourth-grade children who were identified as not well liked by their peers. The social skills program taught the following four skills: participation, cooperation, communication, and validation/support. The intervention consisted of a five-week program whereby each skill was (1) described verbally, (2) explained with examples, (3) practiced using behavior rehearsal, and (4) refined through feedback, coaching, and review of progress. This study found that the children increased their social skills and that they had improved significantly more than a group of elementary school children who did not participate in the program. Particularly impressive was the finding at one-year follow-up that the children showed gains in how their classmates rated them on play and peer acceptance.

Having defined social skills and established one successful application of this method, it is important to describe in greater detail how social skills groups are conducted.

GROUP FORMAT AND THE SOCIAL SKILLS TRAINING METHOD

Social skills training is usually conducted in a group format that provides support and a reinforcing context for learning new responses and appropriate behaviors in a variety of social situations. The group is a natural context for social skills training because of the peer interactions that take place as the group members work together. Additionally, the group allows for extensive use of modeling and feedback, critical components of successful skills training. Costin (1969) argued more than twenty-five years ago that there should be a broader application of group work method in the school setting.

Practical Considerations in Conducting Social Skills Training Groups

Conducting group prevention and intervention services is an efficient use of a school social worker's time, as several students can be seen at one time. But groups must be recruited and constructed with certain key factors in mind. Recruitment for social skills training groups will depend on the goals of the particular program. It may be necessary to limit the number of participants involved, in which case procedures must be used to help identify students most likely to benefit from the program. This screening process can be accomplished by administering assessment devices, identifying students who meet specified risk criteria, conducting pregroup interviews, or designing a referral system for teachers and other professionals to use to refer children directly to the group. Since the social skills group affects parental roles, a collaborative relationship and permission for entry into the group needs to be developed with the parents.

Group composition will be influenced by factors such as how well the group participants know one another, how heterogeneous the group is, and how large the group is. LeCroy (1994) notes that too much intergroup familiarity can lead to problems with control and that a preponderance of "good" friends in a single group may be counterproductive. Another important consideration in constructing groups is group size and ratio of group leaders to participants. Because it is important that all members of a group have the time and attention they need to practice skills and receive important feedback, social skills groups are most effective with six to ten members, and there should be a low leader-to-participant ratio. Two group leaders are recommended, especially if the group has as many as ten participants.

Development Program Goals and Selecting Skills

The first step in the development of a successful social skills training program is to identify the goals of the program based on the needs of the target population. For example, a program goal might be for withdrawn children to be able to initiate positive social interactions. Once the goals of the program are clearly defined, the next step is to select the specific skills that are to be taught.

Research has been helpful in identifying skills by studying behaviors that contribute to healthy social functioning in children and adolescents. Depending on the type of problem to be addressed, a number of different skills may be appropriate. Skills for withdrawn and isolated children include greeting others, joining in ongoing activities, starting a conversation, and sharing and cooperation about both things (e.g., toys) and ideas (King and Kirschenbaum, 1992; LaGreca and Santogrossi, 1980; Ladd, 1981; Hops, Walker, and Greenwood, 1979). As a specific example, Gilchrist and Schinke (1983) elaborate assertiveness skills needed for preventing teen pregnancy, including refusing unacceptable demands and problem solving. The basic principle is to break the preferred behavior down into a number of skills and assist the group in practicing them, while the members support each other's efforts.

The process of social skills training requires continual attention to refining each skill that is to be taught. After identifying the broad social skills, it is important to divide each broad skill into its component parts so that they can be more easily learned. For example, LeCroy (1994, p. 136) breaks down the skill "beginning a conversation" into six component parts:

1. Look the person in the eye and demonstrate appropriate body language.
2. Greet the person, saying one's own name.
3. Ask an open-ended question about the person. Listen attentively for the response.
4. Make a statement to follow up on the person's response.
5. Ask another open-ended question about the person. Listen attentively to the response.
6. Make another statement about the conversation.

It is important to construct realistic social situations that demand the use of social skills being taught. It is preferable that the social situations and skills be determined empirically. For example, Freedman, Rosenthan, Donahoe, Schlundt, and McFall (1978) constructed problematic situations that delinquents were likely to encounter, elicited responses to these situations, and then had the responses rated for effectiveness. This gives a clear indication of the types of situations that are problematic for delinquents and the responses considered appropriate in those situations. However, most practitioners must develop their own problematic situations or elicit them from the group during social skills training. For example, a substance abuse prevention program could address the following problem situation:

> You ride to a party with someone you've been dating for about six months. The party is at someone's house; their parents are gone for the weekend. There is a lot of beer and dope, and your date has had too much to drink. Your date says, "Hey, where's my keys—let's get going."

This situation ends with a stimulus for applying the skills of resisting peer pressure. An effective response to this situation would include the steps involved in resisting peer pressure: name the trouble, say no quickly, suggest alternatives, and leave the situation. (For additional information on assessment and selection of skills, see Cartledge and Milburn, 1980; Goldstein, Sprafkin, Kershaw, and Klein, 1983; King and Kirschenbaum, 1992).

Successful development of a social skills program will depend on its actual usefulness within a given setting. The age-related, developmental capabilities of participants must be considered. For example, one consideration in planning a series of social skills groups would be children's ability for language acquisition, which would have an impact on the program. School social workers must also cultivate acceptance and support for programs they implement. Although provided in a group setting, social skills training should be sensitive to both individual and familial needs. Effective programs require good communication with students, teachers, and parents and make modifications based on their feedback.

Social skills programs also must be sensitive to racial and ethnic considerations. A standardized social skills program may not work for a Native

American child living on a reservation or a Mexican-American child who speaks Spanish. The selection of social skills must be tailored to be an effective social interaction in a variety of cultures. If we remain sensitive to these issues, social skills training can help promote successful interactions in a variety of circumstances.

Guidelines for Practitioners

After program goals are defined and skills are selected, there is a sequential process for teaching social skills. The following seven basic steps delineate the process that leaders can follow (based on LeCroy, 1994). These guidelines were developed for social skills groups with middle school and high school students. Social skills groups with younger children would use modified guidelines (see King and Kirschenbaum, (1992) for guidelines with younger children). Table 1 presents these steps and outlines the process for teaching social skills. In each step there is a request for group member involvement because it is critical that group leaders involve the participants actively in the skill training. Also, such requests keep the group interesting and fun for the group members.

TABLE 1   Steps in Teaching Social Skills Training

1. Present the social skill being taught.
   A. Solicit an explanation of the skill.
   B. Get group members to provide rationales for the skill.
2. Discuss the social skill.
   A. List the skill steps.
   B. Get group members to give examples of using the skill.
3. Present a problem situation and model the skill.
   A. Evaluate the performance.
   B. Get group members to discuss the model.
4. Set the stage for role playing the skill.
   A. Select the group members for role playing.
   B. Get group members to observe the role play.
5. Have group members rehearse the skill.
   A. Provide coaching if necessary.
   B. Get group members to provide feedback on verbal and nonverbal elements.
6. Practice using complex skill situations.
   A. Teach accessory skills, e.g., problem solving.
   B. Get group members to discuss situations and provide feedback.
7. Train for generalization and maintenance.
   A. Encourage practice of skills outside the group.
   B. Get group members to bring in their problem situations.

1. Present the social skill being taught.   The first step for the group leader is to present the skill. The leader solicits an explanation of the skill, for example, "Can anyone tell me what it means to resist peer pressure?" After group members have answered this question, the leader emphasizes the rationale for using the skill. For example, "You would use this skill when you're in a situation where you don't want to do something that your friends want you to do; you should be able to say no in a way that helps your friends to be able to accept your refusal." The leader then requests additional reasons for learning the skill.

2. Discuss the social skill.   The leader presents the specific skill steps that constitute the social skill. For example, the skill steps for resisting peer pressure are good nonverbal communication (includes eye contact, posture, voice volume), saying no early in the interaction, suggesting an alternative activity, and leaving the situation if there is continued pressure. Leaders then ask group members to share examples of times they used the skill or examples of times they could have used the skill but did not.

3. Present a problem situation and model the skill.   The leader presents a problem situation. For example, the following is a problem situation for resisting peer pressure.

> After seeing a movie, your friends suggest that you go with them to the mall. It's 10:45 and you are supposed to be home by 11:00. It's important that you get home by 11:00 or you won't be able to go out next weekend.

The group leader chooses members to role play this situation and then models the skills. Group members evaluate the model's performance. Did the model follow all the skill steps? Was his or her performance successful? The group leader may choose another group member to model if the leader believes they already have the requisite skills. Another alternative is to present videotaped models to the group. This has the advantage of following the recommendation by researchers that the models be similar to trainees in age, sex, and social characteristics.

4. Set the stage for role playing of the skill.   For this step the group leader needs to construct the social circumstances for the role play. Leaders select group members for the role play and give them their parts. The leader reviews with the role players how to act out their roles. Group members not in the role play observe the process. It is sometimes helpful if they are given specific instructions for their observations. For example, one member may observe the use of nonverbal skills; another member may be instructed to observe when "no" is said in the interaction.

5. Have group members rehearse the skill.   Rehearsal or guided practice of the skill is an important part of effective social skills training. Group leaders and group members provide instructions or coaching before and during the role play and provide praise and feedback for improvement. Following a role play rehearsal the leader will usually give instructions for improvement, model the suggested improvements, or coach the person to incorporate the feedback in the subsequent role play. Often the group member doing the role play will practice the skills in the situation several times to refine the skills and incorporate feedback offered by the group. The role plays continue until the trainee's behavior becomes more and more similar to that of the model. It is important that "overlearning" takes place, so the group leader should encourage many examples of effective skill demonstration followed by praise. Group members should be taught how to give effective feedback before the rehearsals. Throughout the teaching process the group leader can model desired responses. For example, after a role play the leader can respond first and model feedback that starts with a positive statement.

6. Practice using complex skill situations.   The last phase deals with more difficult and complex skill situations. Complex situations can be developed by extending the interactions and roles in the problem situations. Most social skills groups also incorporate the teaching of problem-solving abilities. Problem solving is a general approach to helping young people gather information about a problematic situation, generate a large number of potential solutions, evaluate the consequences of various solutions, and outline plans for the implementation of a particular solution. Group leaders can identify appropriate problem situations and lead members through the above steps. Problem-solving training is important because it prepares young people to make adjustments as needed in particular situations. It is a general skill with large-scale application. (For a more complete discussion on the use of problem-solving approaches, see Elias and Clabby, 1992).

7. Train for generalization and maintenance.   The success of the social skills program depends on the extent to which the skills young people learn transfer to their day-to-day lives. Practitioners must always be planning for ways to maximize the generalization of skills learned and promote their continued use after training. There are several principles that help facilitate the generalization and maintenance of skills. The first is the use of overlearning. The more overlearning that takes place, the greater likelihood of later transfer of skills. Therefore, it is important that group leaders insist on mastery of the skills. Another important principle of generalization is to vary the stimuli as skills are learned. To accomplish this, practitioners can use a variety of models, problem situations, role-play actors, and trainers. The different styles and behaviors of the people used produces a broader context in which to apply the skills learned. Perhaps most important is to require that young people use the skills in their real-life settings. Group leaders should assign and monitor homework to encourage transfer of learning. This may include the use of written contracts to do certain tasks outside of the group. Group members should be asked to bring to the group examples of problem situations where the social skills can be applied. Last, practitioners should attempt to develop external support for the skills learned. One approach to this is to set up a buddy system whereby group members work together to perform the skills learned outside the group (for examples see Rose and Edelson, 1987).

SOCIAL SKILLS TRAINING ILLUSTRATED

This methodology may be applied to a whole range of problem areas. Social skills training is being applied to many different child and adolescent populations, including delinquents, behaviorally disordered children, and developmentally delayed children. Social skills training is also used extensively in prevention programs. As such, skills are reinforced for children in the general school population. Table 2 illustrates some common focus areas for social skills training in the schools, along with general skills to be developed and resources for more specific information about these focus areas.

While the examples in table 2 examine particular aspects of social skills training interventions, many practitioners use multiproblem social skills training in groups with children experiencing a variety of problems. For example, groups could include children with such problems as acting-out behavior, withdrawn behavior, fear, and so forth.

In groups designed for prevention purposes the goal is to promote positive prosocial alternative behaviors (LeCroy, 1994; LeCroy and Rose, 1986). Such programs may be tailored to meet the needs of specific populations. While social skills training will likely be the major component of the treatment, other treatment procedures also can be used; for example, a social skills training program may be enhanced by the addition of a psychoeducational component. A specific example of the development of one such prevention programs follows.

A Prevention Program for Early Adolescent Girls

A social skills training psychoeducational prevention program called "Girls Together" (LeCroy, Daley, and Leybas, 1998) was developed specifically for early adolescent girls. Program goals were identified through empirical investigation of problems common to this population and through direct interaction with middle school girls. In response to these identified problems, a group of "core" social skills—for example, assertiveness skills and basic conversational skills—are presented and taught during the first half of a twelve-session program. Participants are then asked to build on the

TABLE 2   Problem Behaviors and Related Social Skills Training

Type of Program and Resources	Social Skills Focus
Aggressive behavior Bierman and Greenberg, 1996 Elder, Edelstein, and Narick, 1979 Feindler and Guttman, 1994 Goldstein and Glick, 1987.	*Skills to work on* 1. Recognizing interactions likely to lead to problems. 2. Learning responses to negative communication. 3. Learning to request a behavior change.
Withdrawn and isolated behavior Gottman, 1983 Greenwood et al, 1982 Hops, Walker and Greenwood, 1979 Paine et al., 1982	*Skills to work on* 1. Greeting others. 2. Joining in ongoing activities. 3. Starting a conversation. 4. Sharing things and ideas.
Substance abuse prevention Botvin, 1996 Hohman and Buchik, 1994 Pentz, 1985	*Skills to work on* 1. Identifying problem situations. 2. Learning effective refusal skills. 3. Making friends with nonusing peers. 4. Learning general problem-solving techniques.
Teen pregnancy prevention Barth, R. 1996. Schinke, Blythe, and Gilchrist, 1981	*Skills to work on* 1. Identifying risky situations. 2. Refusing unreasonable demands. 3. Learning new interpersonal responses. 4. Learning problem-solving techniques.
Peer mediation for interpersonal conflict Schrumpf et al., 1991	*Skills to work on* 1. Learning communication skills. 2. Focusing on common interests. 3. Creating options. 4. Writing an agreement.

core skills by applying them to more specific situations—substance abuse refusal, for example—during the latter half of the program.

Identifying a problem area and selecting appropriate skills.   Consider the following information:

- A national survey by the American Association of University Women revealed that both boys and girls believed that teachers encourage more assertive behavior in boys and that, overall, boys received the majority of their teachers' attention (Orenstein, 1994).

- Girls are beginning to experiment with alcohol, tobacco, and other drugs at earlier ages than ever before, and teen pregnancy rates in the United States are among the highest of the Western industrialized countries (Barth, 1996).
- At all grade levels, girls have lower self-esteem than boys, and this difference increases by 30 percent from sixth to seventh grade. Girls who make the transition from grade schools to middle schools show the most severe drops in self-esteem (Simmons and Blyth, 1987).

One potential conceptualization of this "cluster" of information would be that girls could resist these problems better if they were equipped with the social skills to augment their assertiveness and ability to form new friendships during the middle school transition period. Thus two important program goals for Girls Together are to equip girls with assertiveness skills and to equip girls with the skills to build healthy peer relationships.

Building a solid foundation of skills.   We have already discussed the importance of overlearning in social skills training. The Girls Together program is designed to increase the odds of participants' overlearning by selecting key skills that girls need to learn and building participants' confidence and mastery of these skills over several sessions. For the focus area of "assertiveness," for example, the Girls Together program provides three sessions that help girls to learn this skill. In one of the early group meetings, girls are introduced to the general concept of assertiveness and are given practice using this skill. In two later sessions, girls are given additional practice using assertiveness skills in the context of refusing substances and unwanted sexual advances.

As the program progresses, girls are able to combine several of the core social skills they learned in early sessions to help them deal with more specific problem areas in the later curriculum. For example, by the time participants reach the curriculum section dealing with substance abuse, they have already completed sessions on the core social skills of assertiveness and starting conversations. They can draw from both of these areas in learning to effectively deal with peer pressure to use drugs. Table 3 illustrates how social skills may be combined in a complementary fashion to help participants build strengths.

As school social workers work toward the goal of enhancing the socialization process of children, methods for promoting social competence, such as social skills training, have much to offer. Social workers can make an important contribution to children, families, and schools through preventive

TABLE 3   Girls Together Skill Building

Girls Together Program Goal	Related Social Skills Training
Core skill: assertiveness Goal: To teach girls to act assertively rather than passively or aggressively. Rationale: Teaching basic assertiveness skills to girls will help them speak up in classrooms and withstand peer pressure and will serve as a foundation for learning more specific refusal skills.	1. Discuss the skill of assertiveness. 2. Group leaders demonstrate assertive, passive, and aggressive responses to sample situations. 3. Group members practice identifying assertive behavior. 4. Group members practice assertiveness skills. 5. Group leaders and other members provide feedback. Sample scenario: You are in science class, and the boy you are partners with tells you that he wants to mix the chemicals and you can be the secretary. What do you do?
Core skill: Making and keeping friends. Goal: To equip girls with the tools they need to establish and maintain healthy peer relationships. Rationale: Disturbances in peer relationships are among the best predictors of psychiatric, social, and school problems. Teaching friendship skills can reduce these problems.	1. Discuss the components of a successful conversation, including the beginning, middle, and end. 2. Group leaders demonstrate both ineffective and effective conversational skills. 3. Group members practice identifying effective conversational skills such as making eye contact and asking questions of the other person. 4. Group members practice conversation skills in role-play situations. 5. Group leaders and other members provide feedback. Sample scenario: It is your first day of junior high and you don't know anyone in your homeroom. Start a conversation with the girl who sits next to you.
Specific skill: Avoiding substance abuse Goal: To teach girls coping strategies and skills they may use to avoid using alcohol, tobacco, and other drugs. Rationale: More girls are using drugs, and at earlier ages, than ever before. Early drug use may place girls at risk for serious health and psychological problems.	1. Discuss the reasons why some girls use drugs. (Reasons may include: They don't know how to say no, they don't have friends and get lonely, etc.) 2. Discuss reasons why some girls don't use drugs. 3. Group members practice refusing drugs in role-play situations. They build on the core skill of assertiveness learned earlier. 4. Group members list coping strategies they can use instead of turning to drugs. They build on the core skill of starting conversations, by recognizing that they can build healthy friendships with nonusing friends to help them stay drug free.

and remedial approaches like those described in this chapter. As we have seen, children's social behavior is a critical aspect of successful adaptation in society. The school represents an ideal place for children to learn and practice social behavior. It provides the needed multipeer context and offers multiple opportunities for newly learned behaviors to be generalized to other situations and circumstances.

Social skills training provides a clear methodology for providing remedial and preventive services to children. This direct approach to working with children has been applied in numerous problem areas and with many child behavior problems. It is straightforward in application and has been adapted so that social workers, teachers, and peer helpers have successfully applied the methodology. Although we have emphasized the group application, social skills training also can be applied in individual or classroom settings. In general, research has supported the efficacy of social skills training; it is perhaps the most promising new treatment model developed for working with children and adolescents.

REFERENCES

Asher, S. R. 1983. Social competence and peer status: Recent advances and future directions. *Child Development* 54:1427–1434.

Barth, R. P. 1996. *Reducing the risk: Building skills to prevent pregnancy STD and HIV* (3rd ed.). Santa Cruz, CA: ETR Associates.

Benson, P. L. 1997. *All kids are our kids*. San Francisco: Jossey-Bass.

Bierman, K. L., and Greenberg, M. T. 1996. Social skills training in the fast track. In R. D. Peters and R. J. McMahon (eds.). *Preventing childhood disorders, substance abuse, and delinquency*. Thousand Oaks, CA: Sage.

Botvin, G. J. 1996. Substance abuse prevention through life skills training. In R. D. Peters and R. J. McMahon (eds.). *Preventing childhood disorders, substance abuse, and delinquency*. Thousand Oaks, CA: Sage.

Cartledge, G. and Milburn, J. F. 1980. *Teaching social skills to children*. NY: Pergamon.

Costin, L. B. 1969. An analysis of the tasks of school social work. *Social Service Review* 43:247–285.

Elder, J. P., Edelstein, B. A., and Narick, M. M. 1979. Modifying aggressive behavior with social skill training. *Behavior Modification* 3:161–178.

Elias, M. J., and Clabby, J. F. 1992. *Building social problem-solving skills*. San Francisco: Jossey-Bass.

Feindler, E. L., and Guttman, J. 1994. Cognitive-behavioral anger control training. In C. LeCroy (ed). *Handbook of child and adolescent treatment manuals*. NY: Lexington.

Freedman, B. J., Rosenthan, C., Donahoe, C. P., Schlundt, D. G., and McFall, R. M. 1978. A social-behavioral analysis of skill deficits in delinquent and nondelinquent adolescent boys. *Journal of Consulting and Clinical Psychology* 48:1448–1462.

Gilchrist, L. D., and Schinke, S. P. 1983. Coping with contraception: Cognitive and behavioral methods with adolescents. *Cognitive Therapy and Research* 7:379–388.

Goldstein, A. P., and Glick, B. 1987. *Aggression replacement training.* Champaign, IL: Research Press.

Goldstein, A. P., Sprafkin, R. P., Gershaw, N. J., and Klein, P. 1983. *Skill-streaming the adolescent.* Champaign, IL: Research Press.

Gottman, J. M. 1983. How children become friends. *Monographs of the Society for Research in Child Development* 48:410–423.

Greenwood, C. R., Todd, N. M., Hops, H., and Walker, H. M. 1979. Behavior change targets in the assessment and behavior modification of socially withdrawn preschool children. *Behavioral Assessment* 4:273–297.

Hartup, W. W. 1983. The peer system. In E. M. Hetherington (ed). *Handbook of child psychology: Vol. 4. Socialization, personality, and social development.* NY: Wiley.

Hohman, M., and Buchik, G. 1994. Adolescent relapse prevention. In C. LeCroy (ed.). *Handbook of child and adolescent treatment manuals.* NY: Lexington.

Hops, H. 1982. Children's social competence and skill: Current research practices and future directions. *Behavior Therapy* 14:3–18.

Hops, H., Finch, M., and McConnell, S. 1989. Social skills deficits. In P. H. Bornstein and A. E. Kazdin (eds.). *Handbook of child behavior therapy.* Homewood, IL: Dorsey.

Hops, H., Walker, H. M., and Greenwood, C. R. 1979. PEERS: A program for remediating social withdrawal in school. In L. A. Hamerlynch (ed.). *Behavior systems for the developmentally disabled: I. School and family environments.* NY: Brunner/Mazel.

Jackson, A. W., and Hornbeck, D. W. 1989. Educating young adolescents: Why we must structure middle grade schools. *American Psychology* 44:837–840.

King, C. A., and Kirschenbaum, D. S. 1992. *Helping young children develop social skills.* Pacific Grove, CA: Brooks/Cole.

Ladd, G. 1981. Social skills and peer acceptance: Effects of a social learning method for training social skills. *Child Development* 53:171–178.

LaGreca, A., and Santogrossi, D. 1980. Social skills training with elementary school students: A behavioral group approach. *Journal of Consulting and Clinical Psychology* 48:220–228.

LeCroy, C. W. 1983. Social skills training with adolescents: A review. In C. LeCroy (ed.). *Social skills training for children and youth* (pp. 91–116). NY: Haworth.

LeCroy, C. W. 1992. Promoting social competence in youth. *Structuring change* (pp. 167–180). Chicago: Lyceum.

LeCroy, C. W. 1994. Social skills training. In C. LeCroy (ed.). *Handbook of child and adolescent treatment manuals.* NY: Lexington.

LeCroy, C. W., Daley, J., and Leybas, V. 1998. Girls together: Building strengths for the future. Paper presented at the Society of Research on Adolescence, San Diego, CA: February 27.

LeCroy, C. W., and Rose, S. D. 1986. Evaluation of preventive interventions for promoting social competence in adolescents. *Social Work Research and Abstracts* 22:8–17.

Long, B. B. 1986. The prevention of mental-emotional disabilities: A report from a National Mental Health Association Commission. *American Psychologist* 41: 825–829.

Oden, S. L., and Asher, S. R. 1977. Coaching low accepted children in social skills: A follow-up sociometric assessment. *Child Development* 48:496–506.

Orenstein, P. 1994. *School Girls.* New York: Doubleday.

Paine, S. C., Hops, H., Walker, H. M., Greenwood, C. R., Fleischman, D. H., and Guild, J. J. 1982. Repeated treatment effects: A study of maintaining behavior change in socially withdrawn children. *Behavior Modification* 6:171–199.

Pentz, M. A. 1985. Social competence skills and self-efficacy as determinants of substance use in adolescence. In S. Shiffman and T. A. Wills (eds.) *Coping and substance use.* NY: Academic Press.

Rose, S. D., and Edelson, J. L. 1987. *Working with children and adolescents in groups.* San Francisco: Jossey-Bass.

Schinke, S. P., Blythe, B. J., and Gilchrist, L. D. 1981. Cognitive-behavioral prevention of adolescent pregnancy. *Journal of Counseling Psychology* 28:451–454.

Schrumpf, F., Crawford, D., and Usadel, H. C. 1991. *Peer mediation: Conflict resolution in the schools.* Champaign, IL: Research Press.

Simmons, R. G., and Blyth, D. A. 1987. *Moving into adolescence: The impact of pubertal change and school context.* Hawthorne, NJ: Aldine.

CHAPTER 24

Student Forums: Addressing Racial Conflict in a High School

Retired School Social Worker, Fairfax, Virginia, Public Schools

- Theory and Research
- Objectives
- Strategies
- Results
- Implications for Social Work

During the 1984–85 school year, Falls Church High School, in northern Virginia, was the setting for serious racial incidents. The school's population of 1,612 students included three American Indians, 83 Hispanics, 139 blacks, 326 Asians, and 1,061 whites. Racial tension between black and white students developed in the 1960s as the county schools implemented their desegregation plan. By the mid-1970s, confrontations between blacks and whites abated, and although traces of institutionalized inequity may have continued, these were either tolerated or ignored for much of the decade between 1973–83.

An influx of immigrants from Southeast Asia, Central and South America, and Korea has rekindled racial tensions in the community. In general, the newly arrived minority groups have not been welcomed by the established residents. This has been especially true among the low socioeconomic groups, who perceive the new arrivals as competitors for resources and jobs. The immigrants, unsettled in a new environment, have not always known how to address their changed situation. Intergroup conflict ensued, and feelings of anger and frustration articulated at home have been acted out at school. Overt racial altercations reached alarming proportions by the spring of 1984.

In late February 1984, a serious altercation between two adolescents— one black and one Korean—occurred on the basketball court of a nearby

SOURCE: Reprinted with permission from *Social Work in Education*. Vol. 9, No. 3, 1987.

elementary school. This was the first of several racial confrontations that occurred over the next three months. Students polarized along racial or ethnic lines, and weapons were brought into the high school. The school took action. Two police officers worked with the Korean group and the author, a social worker, was asked to work with the black group. The incident on the basketball court culminated—as did several subsequent altercations—in formal mediation between the groups. Mediation as a method to address conflict was selected because the facilitators of both groups believed that its formal and controlled attributes were necessary to initiate and maintain communication among students who did not ordinarily interact. The facilitators provided training in communication and mediation. Five student representatives from each group were selected by their peers. Three sessions were held, the last being a social event. These sessions proved successful in eliminating conflict between the two racial groups.

From this beginning, with the school social worker acting as a catalyst, student forums were created. During the 1984–85 school year, six such groups existed. With the exception of one group that met for only two months, the groups met weekly throughout the year. Approximately seventy students participated. Four guidance counselors served as cofacilitators with the social worker. There was a forum for black male students; black female students; Hispanic students, coed; Korean students, coed; a group of representatives from the above four groups; and a group of white male students.

THEORY AND RESEARCH

The leaders used a sociological/anthropological approach that focused more on group activity than on individual behavior. They taught some theoretical concepts to students and simply included other concepts in their repertoire of techniques and strategies. The following considerations were especially helpful:

1. Adlerian psychological theory—particularly the concepts that all children's misbehavior has a purpose and does not occur ordinarily out of meanness or badness and that misbehavior is frequently a function of habit and habits can change. These two ideas served to prevent adults from making premature judgments about the behavior of the student participants.[1]

2. Small-group theory—especially the concept that groups, as human systems, have a life of their own and often must change before change in individuals can occur. Understanding such group attributes as group leadership roles, norms, goals, coherence, deviance, and juncture was a necessary part of this program. Only by focusing on the group as a

system could the idiosyncratic behavior of the students be interpreted accurately.[2]

3. Analysis of the relationship between the helper and the person being helped—which needed conscious shaping in view of the stratification issues inherent to the problems (that is, child/adult, minority/majority, nonwhite/white). Freire's analysis of the relationship between oppressor and oppressed provided the direction needed to establish productive dialogue within and between groups and with school personnel.[3]

4. The active involvement of the principal—which was crucial. Experience showed that the principal was the school person who could listen to the students' needs and have those needs acted on. Without this involvement, the rest of the program would have only been an exercise.[4]

OBJECTIVES

The immediate objective was to stop the violence but not to bury the racial issues in the process. Long-term objectives revolved around addressing the racial issues that had surfaced. The school provided a time and a place where students or groups of students could come to construct their own definition of themselves, clarify their needs and their goals, and, through the group process, have their needs acted on by significant others.

The objective here was not to stop the fighting per se. To suppress reactive behavior toward perceived inequity completely would be poor mental health practice. Instead, forums were used to look for less debilitating forms of resistance, if resistance was indeed necessary.

STRATEGIES

Certain students, usually the ones with the most visibility as leaders in times of conflict, were invited to talk to the author about what was going on at school. The first encounter involved two or three students, usually youngsters who were friends. At that first meeting, the need for more dialogue was rapidly established. The students agreed to come to a second meeting and to bring other interested students with them. From that point on, selection of students for participation was totally student-managed, with the result that friendship groups or gangs, as a unit, came to the forums. Friendship groups at Falls Church High School, no different from many other integrated high schools in the country, generally form along patterns of total or near-total resegregation.[5] Therefore, students who participated in a particular forum were, with a few exceptions, of the same race. Most of the participants were considered at high risk for behavioral deficits and poor achievement. In addition, the groups were already organized informally and group attributes and characteristics were fairly well set. Indeed, in most of the groups, coherence and norms were so strong as to preclude individual thought or movement.

Attendance

The groups met weekly. Regular attendance was not obligatory. Teachers were advised to keep their students in class if the group meeting conflicted with an important academic activity such as a test. It was understood that the purpose was to talk. There were no games and no lectures. Few students were absent from the meetings. Peer leaders maintained control and discipline, sometimes in creative ways. One group, for example, handled the disruptive behavior of some of its younger, lower status members by inviting more serious students to attend, thereby diluting the disruption. Meaningful deliberation, not a highly developed skill in the participants, came about very slowly, but it did occur and goal setting became possible. Some students attended a few meetings and used the forums to work out specific interpersonal conflicts, placing the other members in the role of mediators. The conflict was resolved after one or two sessions, and these students did not return.

Goal Setting

Students generated their own ideas for effecting change in themselves, their group, and/or the school environment. The minority student groups adopted the two-pronged goal of (1) removing violence from their lives and (2) avoiding suspensions from school. The white students' group was too invested in racial fighting as a pastime to want to give it up, indeed to arrive at any goal. Group meetings were used to provide insight into their emotions and behavior and to develop an understanding of the consequences of their behavior to themselves and to others. The leaders' agenda for all the groups was to help the students achieve their newly set goals and, looking beyond fighting, to help students become part of the mainstream as well as to maximize their engagement in the learning process. Initially, discussion centered around the ongoing conflicts and the latest confrontations and altercations. Gradually, discussion began to focus on why the fights were occurring. Social dynamics, intragroup and intergroup, were studied, both theoretically and from the students' experiential vantage point. The concept of displaced aggression clarified many reasons why minority students were fighting. They began to see that they were allowing others, either nonminority students or students from other ethnic/racial groups, to provoke them into fights and that their own frustration over perceived inequities provided the fuel for them to accept the challenge. They quickly realized that this reactive behavior was futile and could not improve their situation. They had to rethink the causes of their discontent and look for alternative behaviors. The group process entered its second phase.

Dialogue

Group meetings, in the second phase, while still focusing mainly on specific conflicts among peers, began to include dialogue on perceived racial discrimination at school. What the students reported as racist acts were studied and clarified. Discussion on the need for change and how to effect it was initiated by the group facilitators. The discussion included talking about the work of Dr. Martin Luther King, Jr. King's powerful methods of nonviolent revolution were compared historically to the methods of other revolutionaries (that is, the fathers of the American Revolution, and more recently—and of interest to the Hispanic students—Che Guevara in South America who believed that armed revolution was the only option for his time and place).

As the students broadened their perspective and their understanding of racial conflict, they devised new ways of addressing issues. The turning point occurred in the aftermath of an especially violent confrontation between groups of Vietnamese and white students. The next day, both sides were regrouping for another fight and both sides approached the black male group for reinforcement. The black group refused to participate and the fight did not occur. The black students were jubilant as they realized that the critical thinking they had engaged in had helped them assume some degree of control over their environment. They realized that proaction was just as effective as reaction.

It was at this juncture that the group facilitator's role expanded as well. Until this time, participants had been contained within the group and the adult leaders were mainly in the role of teacher and facilitator of the group process. However, the students' new awareness produced new behaviors. These behaviors began to make demands on the school. Their need to talk to the administration became very pressing. The adult leaders became enablers and negotiators to bring that about. Student conflict needed to be managed. The adult leaders served as mediators, sometimes with the help of administrators. The adult leaders also became chaperons or sponsors for some group projects. It was at this time that the involvement of the school principal became crucial. Students met with the principal to discuss relevant issues. They prepared for this by role playing how to communicate with authority figures. The principal, in turn, listened to the students and acted on their needs. Change occurred. This process soon replaced the students' original method of using physical force to maintain control over their lives at school.

RESULTS

Results of intervention with groups are not always tangible or measurable. Change does not occur immediately, nor is it the result of only one effort.

Nevertheless, in the year and a half that the student forums operated, change was evident and positive effects on the students' lives were discernible. For one thing, interracial group fighting stopped. Students prevented rumbles from escalating. This work was done in the forums, sometimes at special meetings. As important as eliminating overt conflict, however, and certainly more far reaching, was the elimination of some institutionalized racist practices. Black male students played a leading role in rooting these out. For example, they addressed the practice that sent them to only one person, the black administrative aide, when they had any kind of concern or problem. They said that this practice deprived them of the help of other professionals and served to isolate them and make them feel different from the rest of the student body. This situation was discussed with the principal. Human-relations awareness training was given to faculty in the guidance department and the aforementioned practice was reduced significantly in the last half of the 1984–85 school year. Minority students received more attention and service from the grade administrators, the guidance counselors, and student services personnel. One sensed a change of attitude in these professionals as well.

A second issue addressed was the students' perception that black students were suspended from school more frequently and for longer periods of time than were other students. This perception was supported by national statistics, and it demanded investigation.[6] Using their new interactional skills, the students invited the administrators who they thought were perpetuating this practice to their meetings and discussed specific cases with them. This was helpful both to the students and to the administrators. (It is significant to note that the suspension rate dropped the next school year for all students.)

A third need surfaced quite unexpectedly. One of the forums had pressed for a school-sponsored college tour to a predominantly black college. This was arranged and, to everyone's surprise, 113 students, mostly minority students, signed up to go. When asked why they had signed up, many said that this was the first field trip they had had access to so far in their high school careers. The message was clear: low-track students, as many of them were, do not have field trips in their curriculum.

Another identified concern was the unique problem of Hispanic students who did not find a fit either in the Spanish curriculum or the Spanish Club. The Hispanic forum articulated a pressing need for the school to provide a Spanish curriculum for students whose first language is Spanish and to assist Hispanic youths in making a cultural contribution, jointly with non-Hispanic students, to the Hispanic activities of the school. At the time of this writing, the Spanish curriculum and extracurricular activities are for students who are learning Spanish as a second language. Thus, students from Vietnam or Afghanistan fit satisfactorily in these activities, because Spanish is a second language for them. This situation devalues the Hispanic student and must be addressed. Dialogue about this startling situation has already started, and the school is eager to search for a solution.

Other conditions and attitudes changed as well. Standardized test scores have gone up. The school now ranks third from the bottom out of twenty-five high schools, an improvement from ranking lowest for the previous three years. The test scores of minority students, particularly those of black girls, have gone up. Individual students have taken positive steps to invest more of their time and effort in learning. The school climate is calm, and one senses a new awareness. A survey taken by the Human Relations Department at the end of the 1984–85 school year showed a marked increase in positive student responses over the responses of 1983. Two items especially must be pointed out because the principal of the school attributes much of the increase to the student forums. The survey item "Adults in this school are willing to help me with my personal problems" went from 13.5 percent in 1983 to 69.9 percent in 1985 for black students and from 22.2 percent in 1983 to 63.6 in 1985 for Hispanic students. Another item, "I feel safe at school," was 55.9 percent in 1983 and 72.3 percent in 1985 for white students, 36.4 percent in 1983 and 69.9 percent in 1985 for black students. Most important, the school has taken new directions and acquired new sensitivities to the needs of minority students and majority students as well.

The process is evolving. Many of the students who participated in the forums have gone on to more mainstreamed activity and have less time to devote to the forums. Those students now understand that a multicultural school is not a static condition. Rather, it begs for the dynamic interchange that will make us all multicultural in the measure that we are able to interact with persons of cultures different from our own. The students who have reached this level of understanding agree that the forums must continue to provide service to students who need this type of intervention and to monitor the emotional climate of the school. Although constraints may prohibit their full participation in the forums, all want to assist the groups and the school in some way .

IMPLICATION FOR SOCIAL WORK

Student forums strengthened the social functioning of the participants, both within their groups and in the mainstream. They did not interfere with the participants' goals as minority students in a predominantly white society. The intervention at Falls Church High School benefited from, and owed much of its success to, social work concepts for practice. Identifying life tasks and then learning how to deal with one's life tasks, long the approach of the social work profession, served as the base for both the conceptualization and actualization of the students' involvement.[7] This project also supported the research of Slavin and Madden, which has shown the necessity of direct student involvement to affect interracial attitudes and behavior within a school environment.[8]

Finally, this endeavor represented a shift in social work practice from traditional casework to direct involvement in the internal life of the school. Although still using the casework method when indicated, the worker's role expanded to advocacy for minority students in their attempt to set a course of action for themselves. The student forums have been an effective tool toward providing equal treatment for all students and helping every person at Falls Church High School to become multicultural.

REFERENCES

1. For the application of individual psychology to adolescents, see D. Dinkmeyer and G. D. McKay. 1983. *Step/teen, systematic training for effective parenting of teens*. Circle Pines, MN: American Guidance Service.

2. Shepherd, C. R. 1964. *Small groups; some sociological perspectives*. NY: Chandler Publishing Co.

3. Freire, P. 1970. *Pedagogy of the oppressed*. NY: Seabury Press.

4. As an example of the principal's participation in programs to ensure success, see the following 1978 report to Congress: National Institute of Education. 1978. *Violent schools—Safe schools*. Washington, D.C.: U.S. Government Printing Office.

5. Cusick, P. A., and Ayling, R. 1982. Racial interaction in an urban secondary school. In J. W. Schofield and W. D. Francis, (eds.). An observational study of peer interaction in racially mixed "accelerated classrooms." *Journal of Educational Psychology* 74(5):p.724.

6. Several statistical studies confirm the disproportionate suspension rate for black students. Jurisdictions in suburban Washington, D.C. generally point to a ratio of 3 to 1. For national statistics the reader is referred to the Office for Civil Rights. 1980. *1980 Elementary and Secondary School Civil Rights Survey*. Washington, D.C.: Department of Education.

7. Bartlett, H. M. 1970. *The common base of social work practice*. NY: National Association of Social Workers.

8. Slavin, E., and Madden, N. E. 1979. School practices that improve race relations. *American Educational Research Journal* 16 (Spring): 169–180.

CHAPTER 25

School-Based Crisis Intervention for Traumatic Events

Jay Callahan

Associate Professor, Loyola University, Chicago

- Social Work Involvement
- Definitions
- Type I versus Type II Traumas
- Common Posttraumatic Reactions
- Predictors of Distress
- Trauma versus Grief
- Definitions of Crisis and Crisis Intervention
- Crisis Team and Levels of Crisis
- Crisis Plan
- On-Scene Interventions
- Team Activation
- Teachers' Meeting
- Notification of Students
- Support Services
- Critical Incident Stress Debriefing
- Ongoing Support Groups
- Consultation and Assistance to Faculty
- Ongoing Tracking and Review
- Media
- Community Meeting
- Rumor Control Mechanisms
- Reducing Suicide Contagion

In a small Arkansas town in March 1998, two schoolboys dressed in fatigues and hid in the woods near their middle school, armed with several semiautomatic rifles. The boys, ages eleven and thirteen, set off a false fire alarm and then fired twenty-seven shots at students and teachers who came out on the playground. They killed four young girls and a teacher and wounded ten others (Bragg, 1998).

Early one morning in the mid-1990s, in a small town west of Chicago, a substitute school bus driver drove across a pair of railroad tracks and stopped for a red light. Distracted by the noise of the engine and the students in the bus, she was unaware that the rear of the bus was hanging over the railroad tracks. A commuter train plowed into the bus, killing five high school students and injuring thirty others. Virtually everyone in their high school was traumatized (Washburn and Gibson, 1995).

In the late 1980s in a small town in southeastern Michigan, during the summer a ten-year-old boy committed suicide by hanging. Just after school began in the fall, a twelve-year-old girl from the same neighborhood also committed suicide, also by hanging. The middle school in that neighborhood was thrown into crisis. Friends and acquaintances of the second suicide victim attempted to cope with her death, while faculty, parents, and administrators feared that additional suicides would occur (Callahan, 1996).

It has become quite clear in recent years that schools are not immune to the traumatic events that occur in all facets of our society. Traumatic events take place in schools, on the way to and from schools, and in the communities to which schools belong. Many of these situations precipitate crises for schools and their surround communities. In this chapter we will discuss traumatic events and the crises that they often precipitate, as well as crisis intervention techniques to respond to these traumatic situations.

SOCIAL WORK INVOLVEMENT

In all of these cases, and in many others, school social workers have been central to the interventions that have followed these traumatic events. As individual professionals, and as members of school crisis teams, social workers are frequently leaders in providing crisis intervention to traumatized schools, faculty, and students. By virtue of training and education, social workers are often better prepared to respond appropriately than other school professionals. However, this is not to imply that all school social workers have an adequate background in crisis intervention and responding to traumatic stress; indeed, the purpose of this chapter is to outline this advanced level of training. Nonetheless, social workers are ideally suited to provide crisis intervention activities in the aftermath of a traumatic event.

DEFINITIONS

Traumatic events are extraordinary situations that are likely to evoke significant distress in almost anyone. Such events involve the threat of death or serious physical injury. They include homicide, suicide, or accidental death, specific examples include gang-related violence, the abrupt heart attack and death of a teacher, and an auto accident in which students are seriously injured. A *traumatic stressor* is defined by the American Psychiatric Association as

> the person experienced, witnessed, or was confronted with an event or events that involved actual or threatened death or serious injury, or a threat to the physical integrity of self or others [and] the person's response involved intense fear, helplessness, or horror (American Psychiatric Association [APA], 1994, p. 431).

Traumatic events are individual incidents that are traumatic stressors, although certain ongoing or chronic circumstances are also categorized as traumatic stressors. Other terms that are synonymous with traumatic stressor are psychic trauma, psychological trauma, and emotional trauma.

It has only been in the past fifteen years that empirical studies of children's and adolescents' response to traumatic stressors have been carried out. Prior to the early 1980s, a few psychoanalytic case studies existed, but little research was done. In 1980, the American Psychiatric Association's DSM-III was published (APA, 1980), which included a new category entitled *posttraumatic stress disorder* (PTSD). Although the impetus for this inclusion was the experience of Vietnam veterans, it soon became evident that other traumatic events and stressors also could lead to PTSD. Moreover, it was also evident that children and adolescents frequently experienced a variety of traumatic events and exhibited reactions that could be understood, not as manifestations of previous psychopathology, but as responses to the trauma (Pynoos and Nader, 1988; Terr, 1991). PTSD was conceptualized as a syndrome of persistent reactions following a traumatic stressor that was fairly similar among children, adolescents, and adults. A new disorder, *acute stress disorder* (ASD), was included in the DSM-IV in 1994. ASD is essentially PTSD in the short term—that is, less than one month; PTSD can only be diagnosed when the symptoms have persisted for one month or more. In this chapter we will not focus on diagnosable disorders, but rather on the spectrum of posttraumatic reactions and phenomena in general, which will be labeled *traumatic stress.* Even though traumatic events are defined as extraordinary situations that are likely to evoke significant distress in almost anyone, victims can exhibit a wide range of reactions. Even in highly stressful events, reactions range from mild to severe.

TYPE I VERSUS TYPE II TRAUMA

Traumatic stressors can take many forms. One helpful distinction is between acute, "single-blow" traumatic events and multiple or long-standing traumas (Terr, 1991). Multiple or long-standing traumas for adults include experiencing combat, concentration, and prisoner-of-war camps and being the victim of political torture. Among children and adolescents, prolonged childhood physical and sexual abuse are the primary examples. Type II traumas are multiple or continuous and occur in a context of physical or psychological captivity. Crisis intervention, such as the activities that will be described in this chapter, is not appropriate for Type II traumas. In these situations, the full nature of the trauma is frequently not evident to authorities and individuals in a position to intervene until months or years of abuse have passed. After such continued trauma, much more extensive treatment is required than the relatively brief interventions described here for Type I individual traumas.

Type I traumas that affect a school community include suicides, homicides, and sudden accidental deaths of faculty members; transportation accidents; significant violence occurring in the school; and disasters in the surrounding community, such as tornadoes, hurricanes, earthquakes, and wildfires. Rare but overwhelming events include hostage situations and sniper attacks on school grounds. Occasional national disasters, such as assassinations and the explosion of the space shuttle *Challenger*, can also have a powerful impact on a school community.

COMMON POSTTRAUMATIC REACTIONS

Although many social workers may think of the word "posttraumatic" as shorthand for posttraumatic stress disorder, the word means "after a trauma." Therefore, in discussing common posttraumatic reactions, no implication is intended that these are symptoms of PTSD. Posttraumatic relations occur on a continuum, as noted earlier, and span many different aspects of human functioning; only in the most severe cases is it appropriate to assign a diagnostic label. Moreover, the negative sequelae of trauma include depression, maladaptive alcohol and drug use, somatic symptoms such as headaches and muscle aches, and various manifestations of anxiety. It is also important to remember that the crisis initiated by a traumatic event can, at least in some cases, lead to adaptive and constructive psychological growth. Receiving appropriate support and intervention is frequently crucial in producing these positive outcomes.

The most common posttraumatic symptoms can be conceptualized as occurring in four major categories. These four clusters of reactions are (1) intrusive thoughts and images that are frequently reexperienced, (2) purposeful avoidance of places, people, and situations that remind the individual of the traumatic stressor, (3) dissociative phenomena, and (4) increased anxiety and autonomic arousal. These are described below, along with some consideration of the different reactions of children and adolescents. Adolescents' reactions tend to resemble adult reactions in most ways.

Reexperiencing

Reexperiencing phenomena include intrusive thoughts about the event that occur unbidden, and usually unwanted, and are relatively resistant to conscious control. Adults and adolescents may experience "flashbacks," in which they visualize the trauma and feel as if it is happening again. Children do not seem to experience flashbacks in the same way, although they may visualize images or hear sounds briefly (Pynoos and Nader, 1988). "Flashbulb memories" are so traumatic and dramatic that the individual retains the image like a flash photograph. Powerful and painful images of this kind that accompanied the explosion of the *Challenger* have been described among children of Concord, New Hampshire, who attended the school in which Christa McAuliffe taught (Terr et al, 1996). Dreams and nightmares are common, and children often incorporate trauma themes into their play (Terr, 1991).

Purposeful Avoidance

The second cluster of symptoms consists of conscious and purposeful avoidance of situations, places, and people that remind a victim of the traumatic event. Adolescents as well as children are reluctant to return to places where traumas occur, including school or home. In the aftermath of a sniper shooting at a school in Los Angeles, daily absenteeism increased to a peak of 268 per day from its normal level of 64 and remained elevated for a month (Pynoos et al, 1987). In addition, some individuals consciously avoid talking about the event, so as not to stir up strong feelings that may be overwhelming; such avoidance has been termed "affect avoidance." Because children often have even more difficulty tolerating strong feelings than adults do, affect avoidance may be particularly persistent in children.

Dissociation

The third cluster of symptoms refers to mild to moderate kinds of dissociation. Usually these experiences are described as "emotional shock" or "numbing of responsiveness." In this instance individuals report a variety of experiences such as "it didn't seem real" or "I couldn't believe it was actually happening." Dissociation is the structured separation of normally integrated functions of memory, emotion, consciousness, and identity (Spiegel and Cardena, 1991). Dissociation of memory is the common experience of being unable to remember all the details of a traumatic event afterwards, or of having "patchy amnesia." Dissociation of emotion is the frequent experience of feeling numb or of feeling nothing immediately after a trauma. Dissociation of consciousness is the feeling of unreality or disbelief that many individuals have during and after a traumatic event. Finally, dissociation of identity is the extreme separation of an individual's personality into several partial personalities. This extreme form sometimes occurs in the aftermath of chronic and severe sexual and physical abuse and has previously been labeled "multiple personality disorder."

Dissociation has received a renewed attention in recent years, and it has become increasingly clear that not only is dissociation a frequent consequence of a trauma, it is a marker or indicator of distress. The common conception of emotional numbing, or feeling of unreality, for example, is that it is a protective mechanism in the aftermath of a traumatic event that shields the individual from the full realization of the horror that has taken place. However, recent research has overwhelmingly demonstrated that individuals who make frequent use of dissociation fare poorest in the long run (Griffin, Resick and Mechanic, 1997; Marmar et al., 1994; Marmar, Weiss, Metzler, Ronfeldt, and Foreman, 1996). During the occurrence of an emotional trauma, victims frequently experience dissociation of consciousness, in which the passage of time seems altered (usually slowed down), the world seems unreal, the event seems to not really be happening, and similar phenomena. Dissociation at the time of the trauma is termed "peritraumatic dissociation," and a variety of studies have shown that victims who experience peritraumatic dissociation have the highest probability of developing PTSD (Griffin et al., 1997; Marmar et al., 1994, 1996).

Hyperarousal and Anxiety

The fourth symptom cluster is that of hyperarousal or heightened anxiety. In the aftermath of a traumatic stressor, people very frequently report difficulty sleeping, an increased startle reflex, jumpiness or a sense of being "keyed up," and anxiety in general. One particular aspect of this anxiety is fear of recurrence of the trauma; it is as if one occurrence, no matter how rare, suggests that the event could happen again. Similarly, the experience of being exposed to one trauma opens up the possibility of other traumas happening as well. For example, individuals of all ages who lose a family member or friend to sudden illness worry that others may die in car accidents.

Guilt is another common reaction and can have many referents. Frequently individuals who have been present when others were killed or injured feel guilty that they were not able to prevent or lessen the loss, or that there is no discernable reason that they survived while others died.

PREDICTORS OF DISTRESS

Since there are many different types of posttraumatic reactions, the general term "distress" is used here to indicate the severity of possible symptoms. Although a traumatic event is distressing to most everyone, some people react more intensely than others. Recent research has sought to clarify the factors that are associated with the severity of response. Across virtually all studies, for adults, adolescents, and children, the amount of exposure to the trauma is the single most powerful predictor of the intensity of the posttraumatic reaction. A helpful example, empirically validated, has been presented by Pynoos et al. (1987). Near the end of a school day, a sniper opened fire on a school playground in Los Angeles from a nearby apartment building window, killing one child and one adult and wounding thirteen others. He was found to have committed suicide when the police broke into his apartment. A group of 159 children were studied, and exposure to the gunfire was found to be the strongest predictor of distress. Children who were actually on the playground, who saw others being shot and heard the gunfire, were most severely affected. Children who were still in school at the time, and who were kept in their classrooms by their teachers, who feared an assault on the school, were next most affected. Children who had already gone home for the day were less affected. Finally, children who were "off track" in their twelve-month school schedule, who were not attending school that month, were least affected. The degree of exposure to the violence and the threat of death was the most powerful variable.

However, other variables have been shown to make significant differences in the severity of distress. The meaning of the event to the individual is perhaps one of the most important (Webb, 1994). In the situation described above, a twelve-month follow-up found that the children who were in the school building during the sniper attack, who feared that armed men would storm the school and kill students and teachers, had reappraised their risk. That is, in the days following the event it became evident that the gunman acted alone, that he shot from an apartment window across the street, and that the fear of an armed assault on the school was groundless. Consequently, many of the children revised their appraisal of risk and altered the meaning of the event to them, now concluding that they were never in any danger. As a result, their level of distress decreased markedly, whereas the children who were on the playground continued to have high levels of anxiety and other posttraumatic reactions a year later (Nader, Pynoos, Fairbanks, and Frederick, 1990).

Traditionally, theories of stress have included the concept of appraisal (Lazarus and Folkman, 1984). That is, the meaning that the individual attaches to the event is paramount in predicting and understanding his or her response. Controlling for the amount of loss of life and property damage, natural disasters are usually less distressing than human-caused accidents, and accidents are less distressing than incidents caused by human malevolence. These distinctions are thought to be due to most people's attributions that conscious human intent to harm others, such as the Oklahoma City bombing, is considered more preventable and less understandable than a human-caused accident, such as the crash of Northwest Flight 214, which was due to pilot error. Human error is thought to be preventable in theory, but most people realize that it is impossible to prevent 100 percent of accidents. Finally, natural weather disasters are considered inevitable, not preventable; they simply happen.

Another aspect of meaning is the possible violation of basic assumptions about life and the world. According to Janoff-Bulman (1985), and other theorists, adolescents and adults from all Western cultures share a small number of common, unstated, but deeply believed assumptions. One primary assumption is that the world is predictable, which gives rise to long-standing searches to find an understandable meaning. Survivors of trauma struggle to understand *why* it happened to them. Many people believe "everything happens for a reason" and that a victim "must have done something to have this happen to him," or they ask "what did I do to deserve this?" Of course, children may draw a variety of personal and malignant meanings from an event, partly due to cognitive immaturity.

Malignant meanings that individuals attach to events lead to higher levels of distress. Individuals who are able to find benevolent or positive meanings in events fare better. Furthermore, there appears to be a natural inclination to try to find some positive meaning in the aftermath of a trauma, and eventually many people find satisfaction in having survived, in having done the best they could under the circumstances, and similar conclusions.

Other factors that affect the outcome include prior trauma. As noted above, in the past theorists suggested that repeated trauma may provide a kind of "inoculation" against the destructive effects of additional trauma. However, recent research has indicated that multiple or continued trauma is harmful. For example, Vietnam veterans who were physically abused as children were more likely, given a certain amount of exposure to combat, to develop PTSD than those who were not (Pynoos and Nader, 1988; Schlenger et al., 1992). Clearly, this suggests that children and adolescents who have been victims of prior trauma are more likely to be severely affected by current trauma than those who have not. Family discord or a personal history of depression or other emotional problems are also associated with more negative outcomes.

Finally, social support plays an important role in shielding an individual from the most severe impact of traumatic stress. Numerous studies of stress, both normative and traumatic, have demonstrated that people with supportive family and friends cope with trauma better than those without. Especially important may be the initial response of significant others—the "homecoming" of Vietnam veterans and the initial response of the spouse of a woman who has been sexually assaulted (Johnson et al., 1997). In a trauma that affects a school, supportive and positive responses of teachers and staff to traumatized children are crucial.

TRAUMA VERSUS GRIEF

Death or the threat of death has a central role in many, perhaps most, of these traumatic situations. School social workers and other mental health professionals tend to conceptualize students' and teachers' reactions to death as grief or bereavement. However, such a conception is incomplete. Grief is the reaction to the death of a significant other, but posttraumatic reactions are a separate aspect and involve a variety of other symptoms and cognitive phenomena, which will be described below. Recent research suggests, in fact, that when both are present, posttraumatic reactions must be attended to first, before the grieving process can proceed (Nadar, 1997). Almost all deaths of young people, as well as unexpected deaths of adults, involve trauma as well as grief. Many of these deaths are by suicide, homicide, or sudden accidents, and many involve violence; these events evoke trauma responses as well as grief reactions.

DEFINITIONS OF CRISIS AND CRISIS INTERVENTION

A crisis is a period of psychological disequilibrium, during which a person's normal coping mechanisms are insufficient to solve a problem or master a situation (Callahan, 1994). A state of crisis necessarily persists for at least a few days, up to perhaps six weeks, during which the individual usually feels tense, anxious, depressed, and frequently overwhelmed. However, the disequilibrium and tension of the crisis state cannot last indefinitely; individuals naturally reach a new equilibrium. However, depending on a variety of actors, including the type and appropriateness of help received, this new equilibrium may be at a lower level of functioning than the person's previous level. Individuals may enter a state of crisis in reaction to a variety of precipitating events, including many that may be thought of as normative or common. For example, parental divorce may precipitate a crisis for many children and adolescents. Although "traumatic" in the ordinary sense of the word, a divorce is not a traumatic stressor in the sense that we have been describing here, there is no threat of death or serious physical injury, and divorce does not necessarily evoke significant distress in almost anyone.

Many crises are precipitated by traumatic stressors. In fact, in particularly severe events, most people experience a state of crisis. This does not mean that they necessarily qualify for a diagnosis of ASD, but it does mean they are significantly distressed, do not function at their normal levels, and are in danger of ongoing dysfunction—which may eventually justify a diagnosis of ASD or PTSD—if appropriate help is not received in a timely fashion.

In a similar way, a system may be thought of as being in a state of crisis when many of its members experience tension, anxiety, and depression and when the system as a whole does not function at its normal level and in its normal fashion. A school as a whole may experience a crisis after a traumatic event, and its continued health and ability to function effectively may depend on receiving appropriate help in a timely fashion.

CRISIS TEAM AND LEVELS OF CRISIS

The school social worker is often one of the primary professionals who can offer this help. In fact, a team of professionals is necessary to offer intervention to a school in crisis, and usually this team is designated the "crisis team" or the "traumatic event response team." The remainder of this chapter will consist of guidelines on responding to traumatic events, along with suggestions on how to decrease the possibility of cluster or contagious suicide when the original event is a student suicide.

It is helpful to conceptualize a variety of levels of severity, usually corresponding to the nature and breadth of impact of the event itself. A common typology defines three levels of crisis:

- *Level I*—a personal tragedy for one individual or a threatening incident primarily affecting a student, teacher, or administrator at one site. Examples are the death of a parent or family member, the serious illness of a student or faculty member, a suicide threat in school, or a student bringing a weapon to school.

- *Level II*—a major personal crisis or a major threatening incident at a single school, or a major disaster elsewhere that affects students and teachers. Examples include the death of a student or teacher while not in school, an accident with severe injuries, a student abduction, or gang violence.

- *Level III*—a disaster or threatened disaster that directly affects one or more schools. Examples include a tornado or flood, the taking of hostages or sniper fire at a school, an air crash, explosion, or fire at or near the school, cluster suicides, or a death at a school.

A graded series of interventions should be planned, corresponding to the level of crisis. A Level I crisis can often be responded to by one or two school social workers or other school mental health or health professionals and may not require the active intervention of a larger team. In contrast, a Level II or Level III crisis clearly requires a crisis team, made up of at least six to eight individuals, and may require additional help from other schools or the community (Dallas Public Schools, 1997; Smith, 1997).

CRISIS PLAN

Each school, and each school district, should have a carefully designed and periodically updated crisis plan. Such a plan would indicate a variety of activities, described below. Annual inservices for all faculty and staff should be provided, so that the plan is not simply filed and forgotten. In many schools, a school social worker is the director or leader of the crisis team; in any case the school social worker usually has an important role in the development of the crisis plan. Members of the crisis team usually include the school nurse, the school psychologist, and several volunteer teachers who are interested. A Level I crisis can usually be managed by just a few members of the team. Six to eight members on the crisis team is enough to provide most of the leadership and actual coverage in a Level II crisis. With a Level III crisis, outside help will always be necessary. It is always advisable to include at least one school social worker or other school mental health professional from another school in the same district, or an outside mental health consultant. In certain crises, in which the members of the crisis team are personally affected, or in which teachers need particular attention, the use of a consultant or professional from outside eliminates the undesirable situation in which the school social worker needs to provide personal support and intervention to faculty members who are his or her peers during regular school days. Such dual relationships should be avoided if at all possible.

ON-SCENE INTERVENTIONS

The vast majority of social work interventions for school crises take place in the aftermath of the traumatic event, that is, after the event itself is over. "Postvention" is another term for these responses, which indicates the timing of the activities, relative to prevention and intervention activities (American Association of Suicidology, 1997). Rarely does the event last long enough or occur in a place close enough for school personnel, including the school social worker, to become actively involved while the event is still unfolding. In the case of the sniper who fired at children on a school playground described above, teachers and other school personnel were involved in the traumatic situation itself. In fact, several hours passed after the gunfire stopped before it became clear that the sniper had killed himself and that it was safe to leave the school building. In other cases, such as fires or suspected fires, parents may arrive at the school and congregate on the playground or in the parking lot, and it may appear that some kind of intervention by the social worker is indicated.

During the event, no psychological interventions should be attempted. The only activities that are appropriate in this kind of situation are keeping order, providing information, and responding to rumors. Occasionally, social workers have attempted to engage parents or students in discussions of their feelings and thoughts at the time of an incident, before it is resolved. Such attempts are ill advised. Until the safety of everyone concerned is assured, parents and students are in a psychologically vulnerable state and are primarily experiencing fear, anxiety, and a sense of vulnerability. It is not appropriate to engage them in a discussion of these fears and anxieties when the outcome is unknown. In such situations parents and students have not explicitly or even implicitly agreed to such a discussion. Providing information about support activities and debriefings that will be scheduled for the near future is appropriate, as are periodic informational updates and rumor control. The only possible exception would be to provide informal support on a one-to-one basis with an individual who is obviously upset.

TEAM ACTIVATION

Many traumatic events, fortunately, take place away from school. As soon as knowledge of such an event becomes known to anyone on a school staff, the crisis team and the principal should be notified. If the school social worker is the leader of or a member of the crisis team, it may be his or her responsibility to coordinate a meeting of the crisis team either late on that same day, if staff are still at school, or early the next morning. Most school crisis teams meet early in the morning prior to school, and before a special teachers' meeting that itself is scheduled for thirty or forty-five minutes prior to the opening of school. In the crisis team meeting, the current situation and the crisis plan are reviewed, and a general approach to the current crisis is outlined. If no representative of administration is on the team, close communication with administration must be established and maintained.

As part of team activation, the principal of the school or superintendent of the school district should confirm the details of the event. Most often this entails talking to the police, or a hospital, or the medical examiner, or the family of the individuals affected by the traumatic event. Although most of the details of these situations may be confidential, authorities usually understand that the event will have a powerful impact on the school and that accurate information is essential in order to plan an effective response. Confirming the names of the deceased, for example, is often the central issue in a traumatic death.

With Level II and Level III crises, crisis team members need to spend most if not all of their time for at least several days responding to the traumatic event. Teachers who are team members will need to be replaced by substitute teachers, and school social workers will rarely be able to carry out many of their regular responsibilities.

TEACHERS MEETING

Using a "phone-fan-out" system or other emergency notification system, teachers are notified as soon as possible about the crisis situation, and are asked to attend a special meeting. This special meeting is usually held thirty to forty-five minutes before school begins the next morning. At this meeting, the principal usually briefs the faculty on the nature of the event and then turns the meeting over to the crisis team leader. The team leader describes the range of reactions expected from students, notes interventions and activities to be held over the next few days, and provides an opportunity for faculty to ask questions. If possible, an expert in the specifics of the traumatic event can be brought in to provide more detailed information. However, the range of reactions to almost all traumatic events is similar enough that general knowledge of the nature of traumatic stress is usually sufficient. In addition, a later voluntary meeting or other opportunity for faculty to talk with the crisis team and each other is essential. Faculty and staff cannot effectively help students if they are themselves distracted and preoccupied by their own reactions to the tragedy.

It is strongly recommended that information about the event be communicated to students through a prepared statement written by the crisis team and read to first-period classes by each teacher. Therefore, the written statement is prepared and duplicated by the crisis team in advance and distributed to the faculty at the early morning meeting. The written statement should include only information that has definitely been confirmed. Distributing a vague and generic announcement is not useful; by the time school has begun, many students will know more details about what happened than most of the faculty, and if the school does not appear knowledgeable, the crisis team and the faculty in general will lose credibility. If the death is a suicide and the family has indicated that they do not want this fact to be announced, the school should gently suggest to the family that little is gained by trying to conceal the manner of death and that the school must abide by the ruling of the medical examiner or coroner. If the medical examiner or coroner does not provide a definitive decision (in some cases, a decision with regard to mode of death is not available for some weeks), the statement should simply indicate that no ruling has yet been reached.

NOTIFICATION OF STUDENTS

As noted above, notification of students should take place in a personal manner, with teachers reading the statement previously prepared by the crisis team and administration. Announcements over the public address system are impersonal and inevitably poorly received, whereas classroom-by-classroom notification by teachers is usually appreciated by students. Inevitably, time for discussion must be provided immediately, and little normal work will be accomplished. In a Level II crisis, there are usually some students and some classes that are not intensely affected by the event, and discussion can be brief. In cases where students knew the victims well, much more time will be needed.

If a student or students have died, a member of the crisis team should attend each of the deceased student's classes throughout the day and assist the teacher in structuring the discussion.

SUPPORT SERVICES

Throughout the first few days of a Level II or Level III crisis, a school "drop in" center or centers should be established. These centers are easily accessible offices or rooms where students are encouraged to go if they feel the need to talk about the traumatic event or other related concerns. Drop-in centers should be staffed by members of the crisis team, with extra assistance if needed. Group or individual discussions should be conducted. Some experts in the field of traumatic stress have recommended that individual sessions be emphasized (Leenaars and Wenckstern, in press), but the consensus of the field is that group sessions are preferable and more practical, given the limitations of time and staff.

In a Level II crisis, students are typically permitted to leave their regular classes without an excuse to go to these drop-in centers for the first two or three days. After two to three days, school should begin to move back toward "business as usual." Many students will not be intensely affected and deserve to have their education continue with as few interruptions as possible. In a Level III crisis, return to normalcy may take considerably longer. Limiting the availability of the drop-in centers is also appropriate given some students' tendency to become emotionally involved in the trauma in a melodramatic fashion. Such students seem to be "seduced" by intense emotions and seem to unconsciously desire to continue the crisis state intensity as long as possible (Callahan, 1996). In addition, it is possible that some students will simply take advantage of the opportunity to miss class and to do something else that appears to be more interesting, whether they really need to or not.

CRITICAL INCIDENT STRESS DEBRIEFING

For some students in a Level II crisis, and for many students in a Level III crisis, a structured opportunity to discuss the event and their reactions is helpful. One such structured mechanism is critical incident stress debriefing (CISD), a one-session group process that has recently been used extensively with emergency services personnel (police, fire, emergency medicine) and in occupational settings (Bell, 1995; Mitchell and Bray, 1990; Mitchell and Everly, 1995). This model structures the group discussion along seven steps: introduction, fact, thought, feeling, symptom, teaching, and reentry. It also provides a forum for group support, normalization of traumatic stress responses, education about traumatic stress, and frequently socialization to the norm that talking about personal reactions to difficult situations and experiences is an adaptive and positive coping technique.

This technique has only been used with adolescents and adults and appears not to be appropriate for children. In the aftermath of the Waco Branch Davidian disaster, child care workers in Texas attempted to create a "debriefing game" to allow children to share their feelings about the fire and deaths of their friends and family members, but it was unsuccessful (Perry, 1994).

Debriefing sessions, or similar structured group discussions, should be arranged with all naturally occurring groups who were strongly affected by the traumatic incident. Homogenous groups are preferable. For example, one group might be made up of the close friends of any students who died, with a separate group of peers from classes. A third group might be composed of an athletic or extracurricular group of which she or he was a member.

ONGOING SUPPORT GROUPS

In some cases, especially with the group that consists of the close friends of a student who died or was killed, a one-session debriefing is clearly sufficient. This limitation has not always been acknowledged by many practitioners who are experienced in the CISD process, many times "the need for follow-up" is simply mentioned as an afterthought. However, in many Level II crises there are a small group of affected individuals who need more than a few conversations in a drop-in center and a group debriefing.

Support groups are ideal for this purpose. A typical group might meet a half-dozen times on a weekly basis, with a stable and fixed membership. The group leader should be a social worker or other school mental health professional who is experienced in group process. Support groups are not therapy groups: the material discussed is at a conscious level; the leader does not interpret hidden feelings or unconscious motivations. However, support groups can be very powerful and, in a Level II or III crisis, can grow naturally out of a debriefing session. Like debriefings, support groups should be held at a time and place where there will be no interruptions, and the content of the group must be kept confidential (although the usual exceptions apply). Because support groups usually continue for six weeks or so, there is often a rich opportunity to more fully process the traumatic material. In addition, since support groups normally include the students most affected by the trauma, the social worker can observe how well or poorly individuals are processing and coping with the incident and is in a unique position to recommend additional individual help if necessary.

CONSULTATION AND ASSISTANCE TO FACULTY

As noted above, in many situations faculty members are deeply affected and distressed themselves. A meeting, debriefing, or other structured discussion with faculty is an important aspect of crisis team functioning, although it is frequently overlooked. This session should be conducted by a school social worker or other mental health professional from outside the school in question, or an outside community professional, so that the teachers are not put into a position of talking about their personal emotional reactions with the school social worker they work with as a peer on a daily basis.

The school social worker and crisis team can also assist teachers in small ways. For example, some teachers are so distressed that they have difficulty reading the prepared statement to their first-period classes in the immediate aftermath of the traumatic event. A crisis team member could accompany them to class, read the announcement, and cofacilitate the ensuing discussion.

ONGOING TRACKING AND REVIEW

As the first few days of the crisis unfold, periodic feedback needs to be established, so that the crisis team and the social worker can make corrections as needed. A combined teachers and crisis team meeting after school on day 2 or 3 is quite helpful; the experience up to that point can be reviewed and changes can be made if necessary. It may be time to suspend the drop-in centers, for example, or it may be decided to continue them for another day. Specific students who are particularly distressed can be discussed, and in some cases, plans can be made for the social worker to speak to those students individually, or call their parents. If faculty are still distressed themselves, their difficulties can be addressed individually.

MEDIA

Especially in a Level III crisis, print and electronic media may be present at the school and demand information, access to witnesses, or statements from children. One member of the crisis team, or one member of the administration, should be designated the media representative, and everyone else should refuse to comment. Students should be informed that they are not obligated to speak to media personnel and that in fact the school suggests that they do not. Media representatives can be quite persistent and will often cite the illusory "public's right to know," which has no legal standing at the time of a crisis. For example, during a Level II crisis in a midwestern middle school in which five members of one family were killed in a fire, TV reporters (with cameras and microphones) walked uninvited into the school that the remaining child attended and attempted to interview his classmates. They refused to leave the building until directed to by the police and then set up their cameras on the sidewalk, just off school property (P. Reese, school psychologist, personal communication, 1990).

The media representative should provide information and answer questions concerning the school's response to the traumatic event. No information about the actual event—what happened, who was injured, who was killed—should be provided; this information should properly be obtained from the family, or from legal authorities. The media representative should be straightforward and nondefensive, even in response to what might be perceived as provocative questions. The most effective way to respond to media inquiries is to provide the information that the school wants to provide, regardless of the question asked.

COMMUNITY MEETING

Within a few days of the traumatic incident, a community meeting for parents and others should be held. This meeting should normally take place in the school auditorium on a weekday evening, and it should be led by the principal. Representatives of the crisis team should also attend. They will frequently be called upon to explain the details of the school's response to the traumatic event. Community members and parents can be confrontative and demanding at community meetings, and staff speaking to them must be prepared. If the community turnout is large, as it may be for a Level III crisis, it is helpful to present some information in a large group but then to break down into small discussion groups, each led by a crisis team member or teacher who is knowledgeable about traumatic stress and the school's response. If the community includes a group whose native language is not English, it is helpful to have one or more group facilitators who are fluent in that language.

RUMOR CONTROL MECHANISMS

Throughout the period of crisis, numerous rumors will be circulated among students, parents, and the community in general. Frequently these rumors represent peoples' fears about additional trauma, or their attempts to find a "cause." For example, in the aftermath of an adolescent suicide, and especially following two suicides, rumors of additional "suicide pacts" are extremely common, even though actual suicide pacts are quite rare (Gibbons, Clark and Fawcett, 1990). Similarly, after an accidental death, whatever the circumstances, rumors may circulate that the driver was drunk, or that this student was walking on that road because she had been thrown out of her parents' house, or that that student was secretly a gang member.

Various procedures to attempt to defuse and debunk these rumors can be useful. Foremost among these is frankly answering questions from students and parents as they arise, and explaining that there is no basis in fact to a particular rumor. Making announcements to large groups or to the media that a particular rumor is untrue is often not effective; in this era, a denial of a rumor that some people have not yet heard is, unfortunately a very effective way of promoting that rumor. On the other hand, debunking rumors when meeting with small groups of students or parents is usually effective.

REDUCING SUICIDE CONTAGION

When the traumatic event is a student suicide, which is usually a Level II crisis, school officials and community members are frequently concerned about the possibility of suicide "clusters." This is the phenomenon of one suicide's leading to other "copycat" suicides, and it has been observed in groups such as schools and hospitals. After one suicide, especially of a well-known or popular student, additional suicides are a possibility, although the number of actual suicide clusters in the United States has been fairly small (Davidson, Rosenberg, Mercy, Franklin, and Simmons, 1989; Gibbons et al., 1990).

The only research that has demonstrated the contagious nature of suicide has been carried out using the United States as a whole, following heavily publicized suicides of famous people. Only on such a large scale can a statistically significant increase be convincingly demonstrated. In these situations, some celebrity suicides have been shown to result in an increase in suicide over a three to four week period, primarily among adolescents and young adults (Phillips, Lesyna, and Paight, 1992).

Other studies have focused on specific cases with small numbers of subjects. One well-conducted study of specific individuals followed fifty-eight friends and acquaintances of ten different suicides for a six-month period. These friends and acquaintances had no more thoughts of suicide or suicidal behavior than a control group but did have significantly higher rates of depression, which may have represented complicated grief (Brent et al., 1992). These same researches also studied twenty-eight high school students who witnessed another student committing suicide on a school bus, after accidentally shooting another student while taking out his gun. In this report, the witnesses did not develop suicidal behavior themselves but did develop posttraumatic symptoms (Brent et al., 1993). These studies suggest that after an adolescent suicide, grief, depression, and trauma are much more likely to occur than additional suicides.

Nonetheless, the prospect of cluster suicides is anxiety-provoking (Centers for Disease Control, 1988). In fact, when a traumatic event is a completed suicide, the goals of a school's crisis intervention program are frequently not only to assist students to process the trauma but also to forestall additional suicides. Many of the crisis intervention activities already described are also useful in reducing suicide risk, in that they provide arenas for students to voice their concerns and feelings and give and receive support. These activities also provide opportunities for the crisis team members and the faculty to observe students for signs of unusual distress, and therefore for intervention. However, above and beyond these standard activities, there are a number of other steps that can be taken to lessen the possibility of contagion.

Perhaps most important is undermining the tendency of students to identify with the deceased suicide victim. Although cluster suicides are not well understood, it appears that the primary mechanism of the contagion is identification and imitation in someone already experiencing suicidal impulses. Adolescents are prone to perceive the world in rather judgmental and rigid categories and frequently see themselves and their friends as heroes and heroines attempting to combat an evil and corrupt adult society. Thus a teen suicide is often viewed as a defiant gesture by a heroic individual who was beaten down by powerful but destructive adult forces. The story of Romeo and Juliet exemplifies this concept, and adolescents' tendency to view a suicide as a "romantic tragedy" (Smith, 1988) could set the stage for a possible cluster suicide.

The key to prevention, therefore, is to undermine the atmosphere of romantic tragedy. One clear way to do this is to portray the deceased student, in all announcements and especially in small-group and individual discussions, as a troubled or depressed or substance-dependent isolated young person who made a bad decision. This portrayal must of course be done with sensitivity and tact and must remain sympathetic, but it will counter students' tendency to idolize and make heroic what is almost always a result, in part, of psychopathology.

Other activities can also help prevent additional suicides. Any student with a history of serious depression, previous suicide attempts, or suicide in the family must be sought out and interviewed individually by a member of the crisis team. Many of these students may benefit from a debriefing or support group, even if they do not belong to any of the naturally occurring groups for whom sessions will have already been planned. Alternatively, many of these students may need to be referred to a community mental health professional for traditional outpatient treatment.

A confidential list of students thought to be at risk for suicidal behavior should be prepared and maintained by the crisis team or school social worker. In addition to students with histories of suicidal behavior, the close friends of the victim should be considered at risk, along with any other students who appear to be strongly affected. Every student on this list should be interviewed privately by a mental health professional experienced at suicide risk assessment, and in any instances in which more than trivial risk exists, parents should be contacted and asked to come to the school and arrange suitable community treatment, outpatient or inpatient, with the assistance of school staff.

Although it may seem counterintuitive, the resumption of business as usual in a school is also an antidote to possible suicide contagion. The structure of the school routine is comforting and helpful to most students (and faculty). A long-lasting crisis atmosphere, in which usual classes or programming is canceled or altered, can easily contribute to an atmosphere of romantic tragedy and artificially elevated melodrama.

A more detailed discussion of reducing suicide contagion may be obtained in the author's case study of a "postvention" program that appeared to inadvertently worsen the situation (Callahan, 1996).

Traumatic events lead to crises in many school and for many students, but it must be remembered that a crisis manifests both "danger" and "opportunity" (Slaikeu, 1990). The danger in a crisis, of course, is that an individual will be unable to cope effectively with the traumatic stress involved and that the lack of resolution will result in long-term distress and a reduced ability to function. This long-term psychopathology typically takes the form of PTSD, major depression, alcohol or drug dependence, or some other disorder.

On the other hand, the opportunity is due to the uncharacteristic openness that individuals exhibit while experiencing a crisis. During a crisis, people are much more open to considering and trying out alternative coping techniques than they are at any other time, since (by definition) their customary coping mechanisms have not worked to resolve the current situation (Golan, 1978). Thus, with appropriate assistance, such as that provided by an effective school crisis team, an individual may work through a crisis and adapt new coping techniques, such as self-reflection, realizing the value of talking with friends and family about important and personal matters, the ability to tolerate strong feelings, and adoption of a more adaptive worldview, and the like. When a crisis leads an individual to adopt these or other new coping techniques, he or she becomes stronger, more capable, and more resilient than before the crisis. Many survivors of traumatic events feel "if I survived that, I can survive anything." This sense of confidence and mastery is especially important for children and adolescents, who may otherwise begin to perceive themselves as generally helpless and prone to victimization. The growth that students can build out of tragedy is one of the most gratifying processes that a school social worker can experience.

REFERENCES

American Association of Suicidology. 1997. *Suicide postvention guidelines* (2nd ed.). Washington, D.C.: Author

American Psychiatric Association. 1980. *Diagnostic and statistical manual of mental disorders* (3rd ed.). Washington, D.C.: Author.

American Psychiatric Association. 1994. *Diagnostic and statistical manual of mental disorders* (4th ed.). Washington, D.C.: Author.

Bell, J. L. 1995. Traumatic event debriefing: Service Delivery designs and the role of social work. *Social Work* 40:36–43.

Bragg, R. 1998. Arkansas boys held as prosecutors weigh options. *New York Times*, March 26, pp. A1, A20.

Brent, D. A., Perper, J., Moritz, G., Allman, C., Friend, A., Schweers, J., Roth, C., Balach, L., and Harrington, K. 1992. Psychiatric effects of exposure to suicide among friends and acquaintances of adolescent suicide victims. *Journal of the American Academy of Child and Adolescent Psychiatry* 31:629–640.

Callahan, J. 1994. Defining crisis and emergency. *Crisis* 15: 164–171.

Callahan, J. 1996. Negative effects of a school suicide postvention program: A Case example. *Crisis* 17:108–115.

Centers for Disease Control. 1988. CDC recommendations for a community plan for the prevention and containment of suicide clusters. *Morbidity and Mortality Weekly Report* 37 (Suppl. S-6):1–12.

Dallas Public Schools. 1997. *Crisis management plan: Resource manual.* Dallas: Author.

Davidson, L. E., Rosenberg, M. L., Mercy, J. A., Franklin, J., and Simmons, J. T. 1989. An epidemiologic study of risk factors in two teenage suicide clusters. *Journal of the American Medical Association* 262:2687–2692.

Golan, N. 1978. *Treatment in crisis situations.* NY:Free Press.

Gibbons, R. D., Clark, D. C., and Fawcett, J. 1990. A statistical method for evaluating suicide clusters and implementing cluster surveillance. *American Journal of Epidemiology* 132 (Supp. 1):S183–S191.

Griffin, M. G., Resick, P. A., and Mechanic, M. B. 1997. Objective assessment of peritraumatic dissociation: Psychophysiological indicators. *American Journal of Psychiatry* 154:1081–1088.

Janoff-Bulman, R. 1985. The aftermath of victimization. Rebuilding shattered assumptions. In C. R. Figley (ed). *Trauma and its wake* Vol. 1, pp. 15–35). New York: Brunner/Mazel.

Johnson, D. R., Lubin, H., Rosenheck, R., Fontana, A., Southwick, S., and Charney, D. 1997. The impact of the homecoming reception on the development of posttraumatic stress disorder: The West Haven Homecoming Stress Scale (WHHSS). *Journal of Traumatic Stress* 10:259–277.

Lazarus, R., and Folkman, S. 1984. *Stress, appraisal, and coping.* NY:Springer.

Leenaars, A. A., and Wenckstern, S. In press. Principals of postvention: Applications to suicide and trauma in schools. *Death Studies.*

Marmar, C. R., Weiss, D. S., Metzler, T. J., Ronfeldt, H. M., and Foreman, C. 1996. Stress responses of emergency services personnel to the Loma Prieta earthquake Interstate 880 freeway collapse and control traumatic incidents. *Journal of Traumatic Stress* 9:63–85.

Marmar, C. R., Weiss, D. S., Schlenger, W. E., Fairbank, J. A., Jordan, B. K., Kulka, R. A., and Hugh, R. L. 1994. Peritraumatic dissociation and posttraumatic stress disorder in male Vietnam theater veterans. *American Journal of Psychiatry* 151: 902–907.

Mitchell, J. T., and Bray, G. P. 1990. *Emergency services stress.* Englewood Cliffs, NJ: Prentice-Hall.

Mitchell, J. T., and Everly, G. S. 1995. *Critical incident stress debriefing: An operations manual for the prevention of traumatic stress among emergency services and disaster workers* (2nd ed.) Ellicott City, MD: Chevron.

Nader, K. O. 1997. Childhood traumatic loss: The interaction of trauma and grief. In C. R. Figley, B. E. Bride, and N. Mazza (eds.). *Death and trauma* (pp. 17–41). Washington, DC: Taylor & Francis.

Nader, K., Pynoos, R., Fairbanks, L., and Frederick, C. 1990. Children's PTSD reactions one year after a sniper attack at their school. *American Journal of Psychiatry* 147:1526–1530.

Perry, B. 1994. *Response to the Waco incident.* Paper presented at the national conference of the International Society of Traumatic Stress Studies, Los Angeles, October.

Phillips, D. P., Lesyna, K., and Paight, D. J. 1992. Suicide and the media. In R. W. Maris, A. L. Berman, J. T. Maltsberger, and R. I. Yufit (eds.). *Assessment and prediction of suicide* (pp. 499–519). New York: Guilford.

Pynoos, R. S., and Nader, K. 1988. Psychological first aid and treatment approach to children exposed to community violence: Research implications. *Journal of Traumatic Stress* 1:445–473.

Pynoos, R. S., Frederick, C., Nader, K., Arroyo, W., Steinberg, A., Eth, S., Nunez, F., and Fairbanks, L. 1987. Life threat and posttraumatic stress in school-age children. *Archives of General Psychiatry* 44:1057–1063.

Schlenger, W. E., Kulka, R. A., Fairbank, J. A., Hough, R. L., Jordan, B. K., Marmar, C. R. and Weiss, D. S. 1992. The prevalence of posttraumatic stress disorder in the Vietnam generation: A multimethod, multisource assessment of psychiatric disorder. *Journal of Traumatic Stress* 5:333–363.

Slaikeu, K. A. 1990. *Crisis intervention: A handbook for practice and research* (2nd ed.) Boston: Allyn & Bacon.

Smith, J. 1997. *School crisis management manual: Guidelines for administrators.* Holmes Beach, FL: Learning Publications.

Smith, K. 1988. *One town's experience with teen suicide.* Presentation at the annual meeting of the Michigan Association of Suicidology, Lansing, MI, October.

Spiegel, D., and Cardena, E. 1991. Disintegrated experience: The dissociative disorders revisited. *Journal of Abnormal Psychology* 100:366–378.

Terr, L. C. 1991. Childhood traumas: An outline and overview. *American Journal of Psychiatry* 148:10–20.

Terr, L. C., Block, D. A., Michel, B. A., Shi, H., Reinhardt, J. A., and Metayer, S. 1996. Children's memories in the wake of the *Challenger. American Journal of Psychiatry* 153:618–625.

Washburn, G., and Gibson, R. 1995. Ride to school ends in tragedy. *Chicago Tribune,* October 26, p. 1.

Webb, N. B. 1994. School-based assessment and crisis intervention with kindergarten children following the New York World Trade Center bombing. *Crisis Interventions* 1:47–59.

CHAPTER 26

Conflict Resolution: An Overview

Shirley McDonald
Clinical Associate Professor, Jane Addams College of Social Work,
University of Illinois at Chicago

Anthony Moriarty
Principal, Homewood–Flossmoor High School, Flossmoor, IL

- Culture and Conflict
- Conflict and Emotional Expression
- Skill Building for Resolution
- Process of Conflict Resolution
- Special Student Populations
- Problem Solving Process
- Adapting the Process to Your Setting
- Evaluation

Conflict resolution—the skills needed to become an effective resolver of conflict and the learning of a formalized process of coming to resolution—has recently become recognized as a core social skill. These skills are now viewed as fundamental for effective participation in ordinary day-to-day negotiations between people, and also for negotiating those sometimes more serious, but hopefully less frequent, episodes in our lives which threaten to create major disruptions if not resolved. For elementary and high school students these skills play a major role in confirming their sense of social competence and, although some students seem to possess these skills naturally, most need some training and additional practice to be able to use them effectively (Moriarty and McDonald, 1991). The formal process of conflict resolution builds on the fundamental practice skills of social work. Since such skills are already part of our professional repertoire, the preparation required for teaching these skills is only the time required to learn the process of conflict resolution. This chapter will discuss a variety of methods for resolving conflicts, both formally and informally, and the skills necessary to achieve such resolutions. Finally, attention will be given to issues of training special student populations to become proficient in both the skills and the process. Such school programs already in place are widely recognized as having a positive impact on individual student's lives, as well as a positive impact on the climate of the school (South Suburban Peer Network, 1993). When these skills are learned and modeled by teachers, administrators, parents, and community members, the process and skills learned are greatly reinforced, thereby producing family and community benefits.

CULTURE AND CONFLICT

How conflicts are handled in any society depends on community cultural norms, as well as individual perceptions of threats to personal safety in case of unsatisfactory resolution of the conflict (Combs and Snygg, 1959). For example, in many Asian cultures a third person is used as a go-between. Thus, the disputants need never directly acknowledge to each other that there is a difficulty, and may continue civil behavior as negotiations over the difficulty are in process (Sue and Sue, 1990). Clearly, the person acting as go-between will be selected because of a reputation for possessing skills of fairness, clear communication, and creative problem solving, all of which have the potential for obtaining a mutually agreeable solution. Peace may be preserved and the disputants can discard the previous concerns without acknowledging their feelings about the problem directly to the other. While the skills needed for an effective go-between in such cultures closely mirror the skills which describe an effective mediator in Western culture, the potential for problems with such a process may occur if the go-between is not perceived as fair, or may not communicate well in a particular dispute, and consequently, the outcome may or may not bode well for the concerned parties. Since the motivation for using a go-between is to resolve a dispute without the parties confronting each other directly, they are of course not able to hear the discussion with the go-between and the other disputant. Without this knowledge a process of checks and balances for correcting possible misinformation may be lacking. In Western society there is perceived honor in directly confronting one's accusers or provocateurs. Certainly, this direct confrontation has many pitfalls and often follows similar patterns of avoiding direct confrontation, not dissimilar to those of Eastern cultures, but with no recourse to a go-between. Perhaps there is a combination of these two cultural patterns for solving conflict that draws on the best attributes of each.

Day-to-day attitudes toward conflict in most Western societies tend to be those of avoidance, despite the perceived honor of confronting one's foes or potential foes. This avoidance takes many forms. Some of these, as already discussed have cultural roots, some are socially driven, but all seem to have the common theme of desiring painless resolution of the dispute. Unfortunately, once it is clear that a controversy will not dissipate or dissolve, there seem to be very few alternatives but to stand one's ground and defend it, aggressively if needed (Fisher, Ury and Patton, 1991). One can avoid the difficulty if possible, at least for the immediate present, then stand firm against any challenges if the dispute does not dissipate.

CONFLICT AND EMOTIONAL EXPRESSION

Real feelings often are not easily expressed in our society, at least publicly. Revealing emotions may be perceived as being overly sensitive, insecure, unsure, vulnerable, or manipulative. Each of these traits has its positive and negative attributes, but the interpretation of them, that is, the expression of emotion, is dependent upon the relationship of the person displaying the emotion and the interpreter of the experience. The potential is great for misunderstanding, and may leave the person showing emotion vulnerable to another's interpretation. Unfortunately, emotional displays are often discounted, apologized for, and perceived to be a weakness. Such negative interpretation is portrayed routinely in the media. The lesson learned most often is to withhold expression of feelings until one is in the safety of one's own space. For a child this is likely to be his/her home, room, or special secret hideaway.

An alternative reaction is to overreact aggressively early in the dispute's development as a warning that further incidents or perceived threats will not be taken lightly. This behavior can have the effect of rapidly escalating the emotional reaction to the dispute and physical aggression may be reverted to, especially by children and adolescents unless they are taught alternatives. In any case, the decision to warn of potential confrontation, or not to warn, has its own cultural and personal pressures. Societally, we continue to struggle with honest expression of feelings versus a sense of extreme vulnerability when emotional expression is experienced. This reluctance to confront negative reactions to others' behaviors exacerbates the difficulty of confronting others when their perceived actions cause discomfort. As school social workers, we routinely help students become more comfortable with their emotions and the productive expression of emotional responses. This skill must be achieved before a student is likely to profit from the process of conflict resolution.

Additionally, students need to be supported in demonstrating empathy to others' emotional responses. Next, there is a great need to explore mutually advantageous ways to defuse aggressive responses and to resolve the underlying problems before such potential conflicts escalate to physical assault. Finally, the social worker must incorporate teaching, coaching, reinforcing, and supporting of students in their ongoing use of conflict resolution skills.

A crucially important skill for a person in conflict is to learn to identify his or her feelings, and to be able to have sufficient empathic sensitivity to others' feelings, by observing their words, facial expression, tone of voice, body posture, and body language. This mutual ability to interpret emotional expression allows accurate communication to occur (Fast, 1970).

SKILL BUILDING FOR RESOLUTION

Once students show competence in the communication of feelings, the next step is expressing accurately how one feels, and communicating such feelings with nonpejorative language, such as "I messages" (Gordon, 1975). This gives the disputant the proper language and format with which the disputant can describe how she or he feels when the other disputant behaves in certain ways. This process has three parts:

1. State the behavior that affects you.
2. State the feeling that this behavior creates in you.
3. State the effect of the behavior on you (your feeling reaction).

For example:

1. Problem behavior: ignore me
2. Feeling created: worry
3. Effect: afraid you don't like me anymore

Using this formula, the following "I message" might be created: "When you ignore me I feel worried because I am concerned that you may not like me anymore." This nonaccusing language may allow enough communication to occur so each disputant may experience how the other is feeling.

Listening skills are not natural talents for all people, certainly not for all young people. Unfortunately, they are seldom taught. The cliché "Just because you said it, does not mean she/he heard it" is testament to the ability to hear words, without "getting" the intended meaning. The child's game of telephone where a circle of children attempt to pass a message successfully around the circle without the message being changed is a second illustration of social awareness that messages are frequently distorted. Often the results are funny and seldom does the message stay intact around the circle. Therefore, real listening skills need to involve dialogue designed to "check out" the meaning of what was stated, such as "Can you be more specific," "Can you say that in another way," or the Rogerian reflective listening, "Let me tell you what I think I just heard you say, correct me if I am wrong. . . ."

Staying with one subject is also difficult for some children. They are easily distracted, either by something said or by their own thoughts. Teaching phrases such as "How does that relate to" (what the original subject was) may be helpful to reconnect the dialogue to the stated problem to be solved. However, validating the student's new area of concern is critical, so that she or he does not feel belittled or marginalized. This can be dealt with by teaching children to give assurances that the new topic will be returned to once the current topic is resolved.

Role playing is another aid in developing good listening skills once the skill has been taught and modeled by the instructor. Making up scenarios for role plays can be an enjoyable and useful exercise and personalizes the activity for the students. For younger children the use of puppets may be helpful to begin a dialogue leading to role playing.

Self-talk as a phenomenon can be good, neutral, or negative. However, self-talk can be an impediment to successful conflict resolution, especially if the participant is nervous. Keeping the dialogue focused on the subject is essential to the process, and staying on task can be confounded by emotionality. It will be helpful to coach children to avoid negative self-talk, that is, statements one thinks silently, "I'm getting nervous" or "I hope s/he still (likes me) (doesn't get angrier) (doesn't tell my friends), etc." To counteract negative self-talk, children can be encouraged to repeat phrases to themselves, such as "Keep it up" or "Did I make that point clearly?" Being their own coaches through the use of positive, constructive self-talk statements is another powerful skill that will serve them well through their lives.

PROCESS OF CONFLICT RESOLUTION

The actual process of conflict resolution has several components: (1) identification of the problem in specific language; (2) brainstorming possible solutions; (3) agreeing on a solution; (4) confirming intent to make the resolution work.

First, the student needs to learn to identify problems. They must specify problems, avoid general terms and "fuzzy" language (Moriarty, 1992), and then prioritize the problems according to the level of seriousness or, in some cases according to level of likelihood of being resolved. This is a personal skill that will serve the student in many arenas. To acquire this skill at a useful level:

1. Students need to be able to state the present problem as specifically as possible and then
2. Identify the most troublesome parts of the problem.

At this point, it is important to introduce the idea of formulating what they feel they need from an agreement, if they are able to reach one. (This is crucial if each disputant is going to be able to accept the outcome as fair.) This process usually involves several components:

1. The student needs to reconfirm his or her desire for a solution, that he or she wishes this solution to occur with a problem-solving process and that this process may involve compromising on some points.

2. Next, it is important for the student to determine his or her "position," the problem, and, indeed, what the "bottom line" is—what is not negotiable (Fisher, Ury, and Patton, 1991). The student must learn that it is better to argue from a bargaining position that has some maneuverability.

3. The next skill that students find difficult is focusing on the important issues—not getting sidetracked. When people get into arguments they normally have a sense of being threatened, and when this threat becomes too great, it is very common for the disputant to divert the argument by introducing extraneous information or additional complaints not directly related to the argument. Role plays are probably the most effective tool to demonstrate and practice the skill of staying with core concerns.

4. Control of emotions is a skill that needs to be emphasized during the actual resolution process. It can be difficult, especially for younger students, but coaching students as they practice can quickly help them see how much control may often operate to their advantage if the real goal is resolution of the dispute.

SPECIAL STUDENT POPULATIONS

One fundamental reason for diverting arguments or at least getting off the subject is the fear of being exposed, either for faulty thinking, or over-emotionalism. These threats are often intensely felt by children who struggle in school because of developmental delays, learning disabilities, attention deficit disorder, or emotional disturbance/behavior disorders. Such children are already accustomed to being ridiculed for not succeeding, especially in cognitive areas, and for many, over-emotionalism is a persistent struggle as they attempt to become empowered. They need extra support in learning to sort the important from the unimportant and to stay with the main theme of the dispute. These students sometimes retain linear thinking processes longer than their age-mates who are not so disabled, and thus extra support in brainstorming for solutions may be necessary. This is not to say that such populations cannot benefit from conflict resolution training; in fact, the opposite is true and these students have some amazing assets and insights into the process, making them ideal candidates for such training.

Another population of students who need extra support are the students struggling with poor self-concepts and general problem-solving skills, sometimes identified as "at-risk" students. These students tend to cave in quickly to any challenge and are more likely to have difficulty staving off emotional responses that overwhelm their ability to think through problems clearly. However, the skills of conflict resolution can also enhance their sense of competence once they have successfully mastered them, and their ability to identify their "bottom line" needs in a dispute may be valuable to help them understand their rightful position in social encounters.

PROBLEM SOLVING PROCESS

The final skill that students need is a formalized process of problem solving to keep them on track to the end point of reaching an agreement. Problem solving is both a natural and a formal process. Most people go through a process of looking at a few options before making even small day-to-day decisions. This process may be barely conscious. A few options are considered and all but one ruled out. This becomes this person's decision about taking action or beginning an activity. This process works well if conflicting emotions are not significantly involved, and/or if the stakes are not very high. However, as the *outcome* of a decision increases in importance, the *process* becomes more important, and emotions are more likely to come into play, complicating the ability to think clearly and creatively. Also, the extent of an individual's routine use of formal operations in thinking patterns may further determine the "goodness of fit" of the resolution to the problem. Teaching a formal method of problem solving will certainly enhance the quality of life of students who receive such training, by giving them tools to use when under pressure to resolve a conflict at an early age. Such skill will carry over to their adolescent and adult years.

The steps to the problem solving process are these:

1. Identify the specific problem needing resolution;
2. Brainstorm potential solutions without criticizing any suggestions including some which may initially seem frivolous. All ideas are acceptable;
3. Discuss the positives and negatives of each possible solution that may have some potential;
4. Agree on one solution that has the most potential for satisfying both parties to the dispute, and that has the greatest potential of succeeding;
5. Agree on a timeline for trying the solution, even if it does not seem to be working very well at first. Stay with the proposed solution to give it a chance for success;
6. Evaluate whether the solution is meeting the needs of each disputant in resolving the identified and agreed upon problem, or whether some modifications need to be made or a new solution proposed.

Once the potential solution has been agreed to, the disputants and anyone helping to guide them through the process should congratulate each other on a successful outcome of the dispute. Older students will often shake hands as a sign of agreement. There should also be an understanding about not talking about the disagreement with outside parties, so that the privacy of all is respected (confidentiality).

ADAPTING THE PROCESS TO YOUR SETTING

Schools use conflict resolution in a variety of ways, but the process outlined above is essentially the same. The details are often quite different.

Some school districts have instituted system-wide training in conflict resolution skills but have no formal program, such as a trained team of mediators or conflict resolvers. Other districts do some training with all students, but also train a cadre of students who are available in more difficult situations, especially when emotions are running high, or when there seems to be an imbalance in power and, therefore, care is required to ensure that each party to the dispute is respectful to the other. These specially trained students are often identified as a team and have regular meetings. Younger students may wear special vests on playgrounds and in lunchrooms, or during special functions where students are not being closely supervised. Other schools have students identified in each classroom who are the designated conflict resolvers and who may hold such dispute resolution sessions in the classroom, ideally in an area somewhat removed from the rest of the class. Other schools do not train all students, but rely on a cadre or team of conflict resolvers or mediators to deal with identified problems. In such schools there is likely to be a set policy regarding which types of problems are appropriate for referral to such specially trained teams. In all cases, the school must have a means to oversee the referral process so that mediators are at all times protected from serious problems or risks.

Any plan for using a formal conflict resolution program in schools needs administrative sanction and support, as well as occasional morale boosts in terms of recognition for a job well done. Any faculty or staff may choose to sponsor such efforts. The only real requirement for such sponsorship is that the adult be invested in conflict resolution and dedicated to the program.

EVALUATION

The usual measures to chart effectiveness of mediation programs have focused on one of three measures: 1) satisfaction of training as evaluated by the students who have been trained; 2) satisfaction ratings by disputants as they report back, usually a week or so after the conflict has been resolved (Moriarty, Marsfield and Leverence, 1992); 3) school impact studies measuring recidivism rates of individual students (whether the original identified problem has resurfaced, or not), or a global school profile regarding reduction of violent incidents and/or reduction in the number of disciplinary actions such as suspension rates (Tolson, McDonald and Moriarty, 1991).

Each of the above evaluations measure only part of the total impact of an established conflict resolution program. Perhaps a researcher in the near future will develop a more comprehensive method of evaluating the impact of such programs on students' lives, the climate of the school, and the contribution to the community made by graduating students who have developed skills in peacefully resolving conflicts.

Conflict resolution skills have proven to be basic, essential life skills that can be taught at all levels of school, and to children of both regular and special education categories. Teaching such skills includes: identification of actual problems amenable to being solved; helping student to control emotional reactions during the resolution process; identifying disputants' "bottom lines" or the basic, underlying problem of the dispute; and, finally, problem solving to find an acceptable solution. Fairness, the ability to compromise, staying on task, and the respect to all parties involved, as well as confidentiality, need to be addressed.

Conflict resolution is implemented in a variety of ways in different school districts. Some teach the same skills to all children. Some teach a modified curriculum to all and an enhanced training is then give to a selected group who are identified as conflict resolvers or mediators. Other schools only train a cadre of students who then are the designated mediators in specified categories that concern the school.

Teaching children such life skills serves them when they are students and later as adults. The school climate is enhanced when students better resolve their own personal problems, and a language of respect is developed when people in the school disagree. Thus, conflict need not be avoided as a personal threat and something dangerous, but conflict becomes an opportunity for positive change when the skills are at hand to resolve the conflict in a creative and lasting way.

The next chapter will address more specifically one approach to developing a conflict resolution program in a school setting. This more formal approach is frequently identified as "peer mediation."

REFERENCES

Combs, A., and Snygg, D. 1959. *Individual behavior: A perceptual approach to behavior.* NY: Harper & Row.

Fast, J. 1970. *Body language.* NY: Pocket Books.

Fisher, R., Ury, W., Patton, B. 1991. *Getting to yes.* NY: Penguin Books.

Gordon, T. 1975. *Parental effectiveness training.* NY: Bantam Books.

Moriarty, A. 1992. Training guide. Mimeograph.

Moriarty, A., Mansfield, V., and Leverence, W. M. 1992. Student satisfaction and peer-based mediation. *School Social Work Journal* 16(2): 32–35.

Moriarty, A., and McDonald, S. 1991. Theoretical dimensions of school-based mediation. *Journal of Social Work in Education* 13(3): 176–18.

South Suburban Peer Network. Susan Kamba and Frank DuBois. Steering Committee Coordinators, Homewood-Flossmoor High School, Flossmoor, IL. Organized 1993.

Sue, D.W., and Sue, D. 1990 *Counseling the culturally different.* 2nd ed. NY: John Wiley and Sons.

Tolson, E., McDonald, S., and Moriarty, A. 1992. Peer mediation among high school students: A test of effectiveness. *Social Work in Education* 14(2).

CHAPTER 27

Mediation as a Form of Peer-Based Conflict Resolution

Anthony Moriarty
Principal, Homewood–Flossmoor High School, Flossmoor, IL

Shirley McDonald
Clinical Associate Professor, Jane Addams College of Social Work, University of Illinois at Chicago

- Selection Criteria for Mediators
- Development of a Mediation Program
- Peer Mediation, and School Social Work

Increasingly large numbers of adolescents are becoming disenchanted with and alienated from the decision-making processes that are in common use in secondary schools (Rappoport, 1989). A major consequence of this disenchantment or outright alienation is an erosion of the student's personal investment in education. This takes place in large part because of students' inability to experience self-determination or to achieve self-responsibility, two powerful motivators for adolescents. If social workers are to play a significant role in helping schools to become more successful, they must assume much of the task of developing channels for school support systems which empower students (Germain, 1988). Rappoport (1989) suggests that in the general society today our accumulation of knowledge generates increasing numbers of experts and bureaucracies for the administration of this additional knowledge. The ordinary person becomes increasingly disempowered.

Possibly because of an emerging awareness of their perceived lack of power, and in a society driven by bureaucratic structures, students often are engulfed by a sense of personal disempowerment and subsequent alienation. They become increasingly vulnerable to a variety of adolescent problems, such as anxiety, stress, a sense of personal inadequacy, and low self-esteem. These alienated students frequently are involved in conflict and can be disruptive to the educational process. Social workers need to counter this alienation with strategies that reconnect and empower students in a positive manner.

430

Mediation is a structured attempt to involve individuals, in this case students, in the resolution of their own disputes.

There are many formats within which mediation can occur. Some are relatively structured and formal, especially those developed to intervene, and, it is hoped, prevent, legal confrontations, as in special education disputes (Gallant, 1982), or those developed for neighborhood or community disputes (Neighborhood Justice Center of Atlanta, Inc., 1982). The format used in our project, however, has been adapted to reflect the school milieu, the relative skill of secondary student mediators, and the types of disputes identified as amenable to student-to-student mediation. It is not the opinion of the authors, however, that there is significant difference in experience or quality of outcome of less-structured formats. In all cases, mediation is inherently democratic in its process, and it effectively balances concern for the needs of students with the needs of the institution.

Mediation is an effective model that provides a format for addressing problems that have a disruptive and negative effect on students' daily lives. Students, given the opportunity to pursue meaningful activity in school, are unlikely to experience the feeling of estrangement or alienation from that system. We have found that students who experience a personal sense of empowerment tend to demonstrate a greater capacity to assume responsibility for their own welfare than those who do not feel empowered.

Mediation helps keep students in school. If, alternatively, they are suspended, students are at increased risk for more serious problems, such as dropout or destructive behavior. They generally are without supervision either at home or in the community. They also are often angry at the school and cut off from social interaction with their peers. The dropout rate for students who have been suspended frequently significantly exceeds the rate of the general school population (National School Safety Center, 1988). Some authors believe that peer mediation in schools may be the most positive and effective means of intervention with students at risk for more serious problems (Wheelock, 1988). The process of mediation conveys a belief that students are indeed competent and therefore have the capacity and potential to resolve their own problems. School mediation significantly deters the serious side effect of alternative punitive interventions: student alienation.

Systems such as schools vary as to their receptiveness to change, and the organizational characteristics of the institution affect the degree to which mediation likely will function congruently within the school community. Systems in general are "open" or "closed," depending largely on the administrative ability to accept change. In a closed system, a rule infraction is dealt with according to a predetermined procedure and without a process of organizational reflection about possible change. In a more open system, rule infractions have prescribed consequences, but they also serve as an indicator of the effectiveness of the school's relationship with its students and the overall educational process. Consequently, in an open system, although infractions require a response, the school sees itself as capable of change and adaption to enable each individual student to better cope with the causes and circumstances of infractions. Mediation probably cannot function in an entirely closed school system. It requires a degree of flexibility and openness to creative problem solving. It also depends on the school philosophy reflecting a belief that everything that goes on between students in a school can be used for growth.

Peer mediation in the secondary school system significantly empowers students, but not without some reasonable control. A principle long recognized in government, and to some extent in industry, is that an individual's interpersonal conflicts are best resolved in a dialogue with his or her peers. Our judicial system is based on the principle that peers can make fair judgments on disputed questions. Secondary school students are at a developmental stage where they are interested in and value approval and sanction from their peers. Interpersonal disputes that appear to be unresolvable to the disputants often arise in a high school. Here, a growth-inducing settlement using peer mediation is more likely to have a positive long-term effect than a mandated solution imposed by an adult authority figure.

Mediation teaches the art of compromise, effective listening, judicious inquiry, rational thinking, and a skillful focus on areas of mutual concern and benefit. In an institution offering a dispute resolution program, assistance in the resolution of disputes is provided by trained peers who facilitate the resolution of problems brought to a neutral table. As a result, both the students who are trained as mediators and those who avail themselves of the process actively engage in a fundamentally democratic activity. In conflict resolution vernacular, the basic goal of mediation is to arrive at a "win-win" outcome rather than the traditional "win-lose" outcome of more closed styles of dispute resolution (Fisher and Ury, 1981). This process has proved to be an effective face-saving opportunity for students who find themselves caught in a web of peer conflict.

SELECTION CRITERIA FOR MEDIATORS

Mediation training does not require the teaching of entirely new skills. It is an inherently efficient process in that it redirects talents demonstrated by students. This is true especially of the talents developed in peer relationships. Mediation training builds on these demonstrated talents to develop the necessary elements of the mediation process. These skills are defined, identified, and sanctioned by the school as valuable and important. They are put to work for the greater good of the school community and the mediators themselves.

Identifying potential student mediators is a process that relies heavily on recognizing leadership traits and specific personal qualities. The students selected should be those who are sought out by others in times of personal difficulty, rather than those who have identified leadership characteristics resulting from academic, athletic, or social talent. Students who are able to serve effectively as mediators are found in every strata of student populations. They frequently are not well known to each other because they are the effective leaders of their separate social groups. Effective mediators do not emerge more frequently from any one particular type of activity or group in the school.

These students readily learn the fundamental interpersonal communication skills essential to the mediation process. Once students are selected for mediation training, the process of refining these preexisting skills begins. Indigenous leadership skills are shaped, and a degree of structure is imposed upon them. Thus, it is clear that teaching new skills is not a major focus of training. Training tailors skills students have brought with them to the job of conflict resolution.

DEVELOPMENT OF A MEDIATION PROGRAM

An example of a training program is the effort that began in the spring of 1988 to develop such a program at Rich East High School in Park Forest, Illinois and is still functioning. This effort was met with an impressive degree of acceptance by the students and an equal amount of success in its efforts to resolve interpersonal conflicts between students. The project was initiated in a two-day workshop for the students selected to serve as mediators. This training program described an approach to mediation that was a combination of several existing models. The specific components of this model will be described later.

The Selection Process

The first step in developing this specific model was a decision to proceed with the training program. Once this took place, students needed to be selected. It was important that students selected to be mediators should have "clout" with their peers. Such clout in a school has two relevant implications. First, it means influence or "pull"; and second, it implies power or "muscle." Deans and counselors were asked to recommend students they believed were sufficiently influential and whom they believed possessed clout. Surprisingly, the deans and the counselors largely recommended the same students, despite the seemingly vague definition of this criterion. All ten of the original nominees agreed to participate in the project. This level of agreement was a surprise to the project planners, who expected some students to decline to participate. However, the level of participation correlates with the characteristics of the students selected. When the general concept of the program was explained, all the students appeared to recognize the program to be a valuable contribution to the school, as well as an opportunity for personal growth and gain.

This group of students defied generalization. They were dissimilar in every category except that of age. Race, gender, grade-point average, extracurricular participation, and regular and special education defined no common characteristics. Some had problems themselves that had brought them to the deans' offices earlier in high school. Others were relatively unknown to the administrative staff. It soon was clear that students with identifiable clout came from a wide range of social and educational strata in the high school.

The Orientation Process

This group of fledgling mediators was given an orientation to the process of mediation and a series of structured steps to follow in the actual mediation process. Emphasis was placed on creating the proper atmosphere, personal demeanor, the structuring of the physical setting, and the preliminary remarks made by the mediators. Ensuring confidence and respect in the process by starting out with a well-delivered opening statement was seen as critical to the success of the experience. Consequently, time was spent helping each student develop the opening statement, make introductions, establish ground rules, and explain the process of mediation and rules of decorum. It also was essential that these content areas be explained in language compatible with each mediator's personal style.

Opening statements.   Several elements are necessary in an appropriate opening statement. First, mediators need to structure a win-win environment. The disputants are told clearly that no one comes out of mediation a loser. This stimulates student interest and also lets them know early on that they are being provided a face-saving opportunity. Second, the principle of confidentiality is defined and its application to the mediation process is clearly established. Third, it is emphasized during the training sessions that a commitment to neutrality needs to be made clear in the opening statement. This is important for two reasons: the students in dispute need to know that the mediators are not going to take sides; and it is important for the protection of the mediators to reinforce the fact that mediators will not have any involvement with disputants outside the mediation session, at least in regard to the issue in dispute. Mediators must make it very clear that they will have no involvement with the problem or its solution outside of the mediation session, including any follow-up.

Finally, rules of order are introduced in the opening statement. The mediator requires appropriate decorum and specifically states what is and what is not appropriate behavior. In the pilot project the mediators quickly realized that full control of the mediation session is most effectively accomplished by insisting that all conversation be directed to and through the mediator. This style, while allowing each of the disputants to listen to the other's story, establishes equality and fairness in the disputants' opportunities to present their positions, and helps prevent interruptions.

Interpersonal skills.   Disputes brought to mediation often are not thoroughly understood by the disputants. Mediation trainers need to discuss the concepts of "secondary" or "hidden" agendas and in this project there was concern that these concepts would be difficult for the students to grasp. The students quickly dissipated these worries. These ideas were readily grasped by the mediators, as were double-binding messages, reflective listening skills, and the general techniques of good therapeutic style, including the withholding of judgment, neutrality, the use of "I messages," and confidentiality. The students' affinity for these concepts seemed to be a natural by-product of their preexisting leadership abilities.

The skill-building component of the training focused on sharpening communication skills to serve the specific goals of the mediation process. The most effective mediators are those who are especially good at the use of reflective statements and those able to quickly ferret out hidden agendas. Reflective statements convey to the disputants that their issues are understood; the discovery of hidden agendas brings into focus why the disputants are clinging to their conflictual issues. The process transcends the angry and rigid presenting of positions and guides the students to their real agendas. In short, the mediators are learning basic techniques essential to good therapeutic intervention, and they come to appreciate and respect the power of good communication skills.

During the first year of this project, the mediators processed forty-seven referrals with a recidivism rate of zero. In every case, suspensions were prevented and the disputants eventually were able to take responsibility for the resolution of their own differences. Problems involved interpersonal relationships, space violations, and possession of property. Some issues were relatively minor. Others were potentially catastrophic. The significant point is that the students in dispute were themselves involved in developing the agreement that resolved the dispute. There was a follow-up component intended to monitor students' compliance with the terms of the agreements. Given meaningful responsibility, the students demonstrated an effective degree of competence and compliance.

PEER MEDIATION AND SCHOOL SOCIAL WORK

The philosophy and process of mediation are compatible with the same tenets in social work. The only distinguishing characteristics of mediation that separate it from the fundamentals of social work practice are the relative formality and the degree of personal distance maintained by the mediators, as opposed to that of the usual social worker's more empathic response level. Also, the practical restrictions placed on mediators regarding their involvement in cases after the mediation is completed differs from good social work practice, where follow-up of cases is indicated when the need for this extended involvement is apparent. The process of mediation serves to facilitate a continuing thrust toward system change and effectively enables students to acquire more self-responsibility and competent independence within a complex system, a goal highly compatible with good social work practice.

The implementation of a program of student mediation in a secondary school has several benefits that affect the operation of the school and the effectiveness of the social worker in the school setting. First, it is congruent with the goals of social work in general. A program of student mediation is an effective vehicle for the promotion of mental health issues. Social workers are under an ongoing pressure to reach more students, and mediation helps to achieve this outreach goal.

Second, mediation also serves to increase general awareness in the school of the social worker's availability and effectiveness in program development. Such awareness is a prerequisite to encouragement of appropriate referrals of students for whom early interventions may be appropriate.

Third, the position of the social worker from a political perspective can be enhanced significantly by the implementation of a mediation program. The social worker's role is made easier once a position of relative indispensability is developed in the school system. Mediation is on the forefront of innovations compatible with a systems approach to school management, and school administrators, seeing their social worker on the cutting edge of innovation, may further consider their services essential to the effective administration of their school.

Fourth, the skills learned during mediation training, as well as the experience of mediation itself, have excellent carry-over value to other life situations involving dispute resolution. The experience of the authors has been that mediators do not leave these skills at school. They have found them useful in dealing with problems at home and in the community; and they use them regularly and, they report, effectively in off-campus settings.

Fifth, mediation is proactive. It serves to intervene and solve problems before disciplinary sanctions are required by the school. Consequently, a mediation program reduces suspensions, enhances student morale, and contributes to the overall positive operation of the school system.

Finally, mediators provide a significant service to the school. Mediation is serious business; the school runs better because of it. Mediators have a powerful experience in the building of their personal levels of self-esteem because they feel important to the school. Being important and doing an important job raise self-esteem as effectively as any activity the school can provide.

REFERENCES

Block, A. W. (ed.). 1983. *Effective schools: A summary of research.* Arlington, VA: Educational Research Service Press.

Fisher, R., and Ury, W. 1981. *Getting to yes: Negotiating agreement without giving in.* NY: Viking/Penguin Press.

Gallant, C. B. 1982. *Mediation in special education disputes.* Silver Spring, MD: National Association of Social Workers.

Germain, C. B. 1988. School as a living environment within the community. *Social Work in Education* 10(4).

Johnson, D. W., and Johnson, R. T. 1989. *Leading the cooperative school.* Edina: Interaction Book Company.

National School Safety Center. 1988. *Increasing student attendance: NSSC resource paper.* Malibu, CA: Pepperdine University Press.

Neighborhood Justice Center of Atlanta, Inc. 1982. *Dispute resolution in education.* The NJCA Mediation Model.

Rappoport, L. 1989. Entering the sacred: Prologue to a theory of transcendent consciousness. *Theoretical and Philosophical Psychology* 9(1):12–19.

Slavin, R. E. 1989. Research on cooperative learning. *Educational Leadership* 47(4): 52–54.

Viadero, D. 1988. Peer mediation: When students agree not to disagree. *Education Week,* May.

Wheelock, A. 1988. Strengthening dropout prevention: The role of school mediation programs. *The Fourth R: Newsletter of National Association for Mediation in Education,* 16.

CHAPTER 28

The No-Fault School: Understanding Groups— Understanding Schools

Joy Johnson*
Professor Emerita, Jane Addams College of Social Work, University of Illinois at Chicago

- What Makes Groups Work
- An Ideal School
- The Value of Diversity
- A Challenge
- The Problem-Solving Process: Your Ally

Schools can be seen as complex organizations composed of groups. The education process takes place when loosely organized and often isolated groups of teachers interact with groups (called classes) of students within an administrative hierarchy. Surrounding these school-based groups are a wide variety of community organizations and families. Formal education clearly takes place in a multitiered social environment. The student is learning social skills concurrently with the academic content, and these skills are essential to satisfactory progress. In order to learn to function successfully in a setting almost entirely dominated by various group structures, essential learning must occur in the areas of communication, cooperation, consensus decision making, and democratic organizational structure in addition to the academic regimen.

This chapter examines the nature of group life in the education experience to discover how to use it constructively to create a more effective learning environment. Defining this experience adds another conceptual dimension to education from a social work perspective, and looking at the group process may assist in clarifying appropriate social work roles in these processes.

WHAT MAKES GROUPS WORK

I have consulted in numerous school systems with teachers, administrators, and pupil personnel team members about group issues. Usually I have been

*Revised and edited in collaboration with Shirley McDonald.

asked to assist with a group that was floundering. As I studied "what went wrong," I saw a pattern emerge that elucidated some of the factors that appear crucial to group performance. My thought was that if I could isolate the elements that were destructive, I might be able to formulate a conceptual structure of what makes groups work. Continuing in my attempt to move from what went wrong to how to make groups go right, I found my consultation moving from a problem-solving focus to a preventive one. For the past several years, I have been testing these formulations against actual groups—classroom and therapeutic, natural and formed—and have been able to find several consistent criteria for what it takes to make groups become cohesive, well-functioning units.

Perhaps the most important element in creating a positive group experience is the merging of purposes of why that group exists. The multiple goals of the various group members, of the group leader, and of the sponsoring school must be compatible. If these goals do not somehow mesh together, the group is doomed before it starts. That does not mean that the goals have to be the same, but they must be able to coexist. In one teachers' association there were some teachers who were power hungry, who needed to be recognized, who needed to be valued, and who very much wanted to take a strong leadership role to satisfy their personal needs. Although some teachers in that association looked for group cohesion and closeness with one another, others were interested in getting more pleasant working surroundings and higher salaries. These sets of goals, although very different, are compatible. They can exist together. One group may say to another, "Okay, you can have the power. We will help you feel important and significant if you also will keep our interests in mind."

Group composition is another important part of what makes groups work. Who are the members? How is the group composed? In a classroom group the composition frequently is arbitrary and you have little control. Understanding how the membership fits together is very important in any event. When you form groups yourself, either for therapeutic purposes or for task completion, you will want to think about some group process issues that will help you form efficient and compatible groups.

There are certain combinations of people that seem to work well together and others that do not. Before you compose a group you need to be aware of some general guidelines of composition. As you select your members, try to make sure that all of the basic maintenance roles are included—nurturer, subject changer, enabler, and leader. A group will not work well if everyone in the group tends to fulfill the same role. If you have a group of all leaders with no followers, that group is likely to be in a power struggle from beginning to end. If, on the other hand, you have a group of people who nurture a great deal but are not particularly strong leaders, people may feel good about each other but never get the task done.

There are some other basic issues with respect to composition for constructive group process. One is to try to avoid too many extremes; another is to try to avoid putting only one person from a particular category in a group. Let me explain what I mean. If I had a choice, I would never put just one poor child in a group of affluent children, nor just one black child in a group of white children, nor one girl in a group of boys, nor one slightly retarded child in a group of bright children. When one group member is quite different from the others, regardless of what the difference is, that person tends to be a built-in scapegoat and may get picked on or act out for the others. Whether you are composing a classroom, a therapeutic group, or a faculty committee, if you have a choice, try to find enough people who are representative of the various maintenance roles that are needed to form a helpful group and try to avoid setting up a situation that may inherently create one or more scapegoats.

There is another "golden rule" for forming a group in a school. Avoid putting people with similar problems together. This is true regardless of the type of group—whether it is a faculty committee or a therapeutic group of young people in a junior high school. If you put people with similar problems together, they will tend to integrate that problem as a group norm. Groups with members who have a variety of coping mechanisms greatly enrich the opportunities for members to view a variety of alternative behaviors. I was a member of a committee composed of people who all dealt with their frustrations by blaming the administration. We sat around and complained and nobody did anything to make it better. There was a dramatic change in that committee when we invited two people who were doers rather than complainers. They said, "Yes, you are right, it is intolerable, and what are we going to do about it?" This new, more active approach made all the difference in the world to the functioning of the committee.

Four Essential Qualities

Another consideration regarding what makes groups work is the issue of why, and when, people want to belong to a group. What are some of the qualities essential to voluntary participation in any group? What entices someone to decide to participate in group interaction? As I have studied groups, it has become clear that the qualities necessary for an individual to want to participate in a group are the very same qualities needed in a classroom for students to want to learn. These qualities are many and varied, and some differ from community to community and from person to person. Every socioeconomic and ethnic group represented in the schools with which I have worked has different expectations of the groups within their subculture and differing values for their members. However, there are four qualities that consistently are required for someone to want to participate in a group. The way these qualities are acted out may differ greatly, but the qualities themselves are universal.

Safety.   For anyone to want to participate, the group needs to be a safe place. By that I mean emotionally and physically safe for everyone present. In a school where knives and guns are prevalent, it may not be physically safe to set foot in the classroom, or the school at all, and peoples' fears greatly inhibit learning. On the other hand, the fear within a classroom that is not emotionally safe also strongly inhibits learning and group participation. In any unsafe group, the goal moves from participation to survival, and the energies and efforts of the participants are focused to that end—survival. Many a teacher has said to me, "My only goal is to survive the rest of the school year." There are many reasons why a classroom or school may not be a safe place, emotionally or physically or both. This article attempts to help everyone who comes in contact with groups assist in making those groups safe.

You may think I am putting too much emphasis on the quality of safety, because adults do not need that much safety, especially emotional safety. You may feel that adults can take care of themselves. And yet I wonder what it would be like if you and I were sitting across from each other in a group session, I had encouraged you to be open, and then the first time you asked a question, I ridiculed you. Perhaps I could have said, "Boy, that was the dumbest question I have ever heard! Any more stupid questions?" That interaction might have caused you to get your dander up and fight back and say, "Hey, you can't talk like that to me!" My hunch is that you would do as I would have done—shut up and say to myself, "I better keep my mouth shut in this group; it is not safe to open it." Then, if I had a chance, I would probably leave at the first opportunity.

Another interesting dynamic about group safety is that if the group is not safe for everyone it is safe for no one. If I put you down, not only would the group feel unsafe for you, but for the other group members as well. They might think, "Forget it, I'm not going to take a risk either." This dynamic occurs in classrooms, faculty meetings, and groups of all kinds in schools. Time after time I have known safety to be a core issue.

Safety, or the lack of safety, passes not only from the teacher, leader, or facilitator to the group member, but also exists among the members themselves. If a bully in a group makes it unsafe for another member and if that is allowed to continue, the group becomes unsafe for everyone there, including the bully. If group members feel safe with one another, they protect one another from attack, from the leader or other sources. As a leader, therapist, teacher, or principal, whatever your role is in the school system, you need to help the school to be a safe place.

Something for you.   Another dimension that makes one want to participate in a group is that the group provides something for all the members. If I am going to risk myself in my learning, in talking about myself, or in my teaching, there must be something in it for me. One of the first things that most people ask, whether they consciously think about it or not, is,

"What's in it for me? What do I get for making this investment?" In some classrooms what students get is teacher or parent approval or higher grades, and these certainly are of value. But there are additional things students can get out of learning. You may want to do some thinking about how you (being who you are) can help students make an investment in their learning. How can they get something back for themselves in addition to grades and approval? One of my prime goals as a teacher is to help each student find something that he or she can get excited about in whatever it is that I am teaching. This makes the learning itself inherently useful instead of merely a source of external recognition or rewards. I have what I call the "selfish approach" to learning and teaching. Everybody, including the teacher, ought to get something out of every learning experience.

That may be somewhat idealistic; there are courses, and some parts of most courses, that are not going to be exciting. Some material you have to learn just because you have to know it, and some content that is exciting to some students is boring to others. But, it is to be hoped, this is the exception to the rule. When the prevailing focus of a teacher is on motivating and exciting students about their learning, the more boring learning tasks do not loom as large. Other groups are also faced with unpleasant tasks at times, but you should not expect any member of a committee, any member of a therapeutic group, any member of a class, or anybody playing on the playground to participate constructively in the group unless there is something they get back for themselves; that is normal, natural, necessary, and, I think, kind of nice.

Something to contribute.   Every person in every group should feel he or she has something to contribute. It is not enough to just take; a group member must feel that he or she has something to give. I vividly remember meeting with some high school students who had been in a treatment group for the majority of their junior year. As we reviewed at the end of the year what it was that made the group so successful in the eyes of the members, a consistent response (which each gave in his or her own way) was, "When I joined this group, I felt pretty crummy about myself, but when I found that I could be helpful to other people—could give advice and support when other people were hurting—I knew I wasn't as bad as I thought I was." This ability to give to other people turned out to be one of the prime curative factors in that group.

This is not necessarily the case in every group nor for all people. Many of you have had members in your group or class who did not seem to want to give. One teacher described two such students: "They don't want to give. They just think about themselves. They don't care about anybody else!" It is very difficult to work with people who appear to have this attitude, but it is important to find creative ways to help them to give, for them and for you. I worked with a group of delinquents who "ripped off" everybody and everything in sight and whose negative feelings about themselves and others led to their pretending they did not care about anything. When they were hired to manage a shelter for injured animals, this antagonistic attitude turned to one of deep concern. Discovery of their ability to give lessened their need to act out.

We have a responsibility as school personnel to see not only that our group participants get something for themselves, but also that everybody contributes something. Sometimes this is harder than seeing that everyone gets something, but it is even more important.

Someone cares.   A final important quality is that every member in a group has to know that somebody cares whether he or she is there or not. As one teacher said, "There's nothing worse than being gone for a week with the flu and nobody noticing that you were gone." All of us need warm, caring relationships, both on and off the job, in and out of the classroom, whether we are teachers, administrators, or students. One of the things that makes it so hard for the young person in a classroom who is being made a scapegoat is that he feels that no one cares, and therefore he makes little investment in trying to get people to like him. Besides that, he probably does not like himself much either. My experience is that when caring can come through, when I am able to show a person who has no friends that I care, if indeed I do, then he has reason to think that he might be likable after all and may begin to care about himself, even just a little.

Striking a Balance

No group or class can always have all four qualities at one time. No class or group can always be safe, always have something in it for everyone, always help everybody contribute, and always help everyone feel cared for and significant. I have found, however, that when those qualities usually are present and the group is constructively functioning, during those rocky times when one or more qualities is missing, one of the others temporarily makes up the loss. In my own group treatment there were times when it was pretty scary, when it was not safe. At those times the caring that I experienced from the other members made that lack of safety temporarily manageable. Everyone has, at one time or another, sat through a boring, difficult lecture or class where there was absolutely nothing in it for you, but still you were required to be there. Perhaps you were able to tolerate it because you were sitting next to somebody you cared about with whom you exchanged complaining notes. I have gotten through many a faculty meeting or dull committee meeting by sitting with somebody I like.

Other Applications

Although this discussion has been related mostly to the classroom, the same dynamics are easily transferable to any other group within a school.

I wonder how many PTA presidents have thought of dealing with their dwindling attendance by asking all members to come to one meeting to discuss how to make it a more viable experience for everyone? How many principals, when things begin to go sour in the faculty, give the faculty the task of making it better for themselves? To do this, a principal runs the risk of getting honest feedback from the faculty about things he might be doing that get in the way of positive group functioning. (One of the problems of asking people what they think is that they might tell you.) My experience in a variety of settings shows that insistence on mutual assumption of responsibility and decision making is very important.

Your response to this discussion may well be, "It sounds very nice but what if it doesn't work? And what about the time that I get so angry I don't want to be rational?" These are good questions. You may want to find new ways to get yourself out of a bind you are in as well as try to stay out of the bind in the first place. As a teacher, I have my classes trained. If I temporarily lose control of myself or my feelings, or become irresponsible or irrational, the students not only let me know it, but they help me out. Even second graders can say, "Hey, Mrs. Johnson, you're yelling again." That can be a signal to me to take a look at what I am upset about. By sharing this with my class, I can then help them see what it is they are doing that gets me so angry. Then we can discuss what we can do about it to have a better day together.

A school is a system in which every individual who walks in the door ought to feel valued as a worthwhile human being. Too often, instead, people (students and faculty alike) feel that they are insignificant members of a huge bureaucracy. The groups of which you are a part contribute greatly to these positive and negative feelings. Your understanding of the dynamics and meaning of the things that happen in these groups is a key to making your life in school more satisfying.

Think about your school for a moment. Think of the number of groups that you are a part of, the number of different subgroups that you belong to, and think about what it does to you to be a part of these groups. Are there some groups in which you feel significant and valued? Are there others in which you feel frustrated and angry most of the time? When you close the door to your office, do you feel that the young people are expectant and excited about working with you? Or do you feel hostility as you close the door, both from you and from them? When you sit down in the faculty lunchroom, do you always sit with the same group of people? Do they make you feel valued and cared about? Are they people whom you trust? Can you take risks with them? Can you tell them where you "blew it" and still feel okay about yourself?

Now take a step back and look at your school as a whole. Which groups are functioning well? Which are having difficulty? What is it like to be in a faculty meeting in your school? A committee meeting? A curriculum planning meeting? A pupil personnel staffing? How are these groups functioning? What would you change if you could?

As you become more tuned into group dynamics, you will discover your power to help facilitate better group interaction. Every member of a group affects what is going on, whether he or she knows it or not. If you choose, you can play a conscious part in helping any group you are in to function in a more productive and satisfying way. You may also choose, as often as you like, to stay out of the group process and not try to help it function better. You may decide to protect yourself and avoid the pain of trying to interact. Or perhaps you do not know what would be most helpful. Whatever the reason, you have a choice once you understand what is happening within a group.

AN IDEAL SCHOOL

Knowing that it is an impossible one, let me share with you my dream of an ideal school. This dream has evolved over the course of ten years of consulting in different school districts and seeing some schools that function very well and others where the conflict and constant crises took so much time and energy that there was not much left over for teaching. My ideal school is a place where everyone's goal is to provide an environment in which growth and learning can take place, and where everyone who enters is respected for the contribution that he or she can make toward that goal. It is a school where people feel valued and significant and assume responsibility for helping others feel important. In the same way that I have advocated that school people work with students in cooperative ways, in this ideal school the principal respects the faculty, expects them to participate in the decision-making process, and freely shares with them his or her mistakes as well as his or her strengths. There is a mutual agreement that faculty will understand and support the principal's attempts to be a good administrator, in the same way they expect him or her to work with them regarding their strengths and weaknesses as teachers. If something goes amiss in this school, the parties involved meet together to figure out what went wrong and how they can work together to make it right.

The No-Fault School

This ideal school operates on what I would call a no-fault basis. The vast majority of schools I have visited are fault schools. In a fault school when something goes wrong, the important thing is to find somebody to blame. If there is a problem in the classroom, you try to find someone on whom to pin it. If you cannot find someone to blame, it might mean that there is something wrong with you, that it is your fault. Or perhaps the incident occurred because the principal did not give you enough support, so it is really his or her fault. This need to find fault that is prevalent in many schools is the essence of destructiveness when it comes to working cooperatively to provide a safe learning milieu.

In one high school where I was consulting, an incident occurred in which the fault finding progressed right down the line. A student made a remark that made the teacher extremely angry, and she threw the student out of class. Because she was so angry, the teacher immediately sent a "referral" down to the office requesting disciplinary action for that student. After class, the student came to the teacher, apologized for his behavior, and asked to be readmitted. Because this was a fault system, the teacher was in a bind. If she readmitted the student and withdrew the referral, she would be admitting that she had acted precipitously. Knowing how the vice principal had responded in the past to similar situations, she was afraid that he would judge her harshly. On the other hand, the teacher felt the student was genuinely sorry and deserved another chance. Not knowing what else to do, she let the student return to class and yet, feeling very guilty, allowed the referral to stand. The vice principal felt a responsibility to punish the young man in order to support the teacher, even though he felt the teacher was wrong. When I talked with the vice principal later about the incident and expressed my concern that the young person had been disciplined after the student and the teacher had already resolved the issue, he said, "Well, we have our eye on that teacher, and she may not have her contract renewed at the end of the year, but we have to support her in the meantime, even at the expense of the student."

It seems as if everybody lost and nobody won. Because the school environment did not permit mistakes, everybody got punished and everything that occurred was blamed on someone else. I wonder what might have happened if that same situation had taken place in a different school with a supportive environment? If the teacher had felt valued, she might not have lost control as quickly as she did over the insolence of the student. But if she had lost control and sent the referral prematurely, a supportive school system would have permitted her to go to the vice principal and say, "That student really got to me, but I don't think I want to continue with the referral. I'd like to work it out with him myself." That would have ended that administrative involvement and then she could have sat down with the student and talked with him about what had made her so angry. Instead of being punished, the student would have had to take responsibility for his own behavior and make plans to change the way he treated the teacher.

There is something about punishment that is positive and negative at the same time. On the one hand, particularly in a junior high school, some children need to have rules to test, to push against. For these situations, providing some form of repercussion may be helpful. On the other hand, punishment lets children "off the hook," and they may feel they do not have to assume responsibility for their behavior as long as they are willing to take the consequences.

I was amused one day when I walked into a junior high school and found a very angry principal walking up and down the hall among fifteen children who were sitting on the floor, writing fifty times each "I will not be tardy again." She had said that for every minute they were late they would have to write that sentence ten times. I found some young people outside plotting together about how many times they were willing to write that statement, so that they could be that many minutes late to school. One girl came in ten minutes late. She had written "I will not be tardy again" a hundred times at home so that she would have an extra ten minutes to finish watching a television show before she came to school. For her it was worth it.

You may think that behaving in this way is childish and irresponsible, and you may be right. But how many of us park in an illegal parking place because we are in a hurry, and it is worth paying the fine to have the convenience? I am not sure, but I think that kind of response to punishment is natural.

The School as a System—The Faculty as a Group

Because the tardiness in the junior high school in the above example was getting increasingly out of hand, I suggested to the principal that she inform the students that the punishment system was no longer in effect, and they would have to start coming to school on time. I also suggested that she ask each teacher to discuss with his or her class how frustrating it was to teachers when the students straggled in and to ask the students to assume responsibility for seeing that this did not continue to happen. With a great deal of skepticism, the principal agreed to try removing the punishment for students who were late and asked them to see that they came to school on time. Obviously, I would not have included this example if it had not worked so well. Within three days, instead of having fifteen students tardy, there were two or three with some very legitimate excuses, and peer pressure from class members helped these students get to school on time in the future. The fault system of schools, although it is a natural part of many bureaucracies, is not conducive to creating responsibility for behavior.

My ideal no-fault school is one where people share the excitement, planning, and responsibility. Students and faculty are free to make mistakes, and the expectation of the group members is that when someone makes a mistake, others will try to help, rather than sit back and blame. This attitude starts with the administration, and the sharing process of administrators and faculty needs to be two-way. A principal ought to be free to help faculty members who make errors in judgment and at the same time expect the staff to assist her or him if she or he gets into difficulty.

There are constructive ways to develop this mutual support system within a faculty group. An outside consultant is very helpful, but not essential. Principals or other administrators or school social workers can implement this process themselves. The no-fault system starts with the assumption that everybody who comes into the school is entitled to have a good day. Then the question is, what are some of the things that can help this come about? One principal asked this question on the first faculty institute day. In small groups the faculty was requested to draw up several sets of goals. One set included broad school goals. Another set of goals was for the faculty—what would make school a good place for them? Another set involved goals for the students—what is it that we want our students to learn? As the administrator helped the faculty outline these goals, she tried to assure that the four essential qualities for voluntary participation (safety, something for them, something to contribute, and someone caring) were all included, not only that day but in the future goal setting. These are just as important and significant for faculty and administration as for students. After she helped the faculty outline some basic goals and they decided what type of environment they wished the school to provide, they moved toward a plan of implementation by posing several questions:

1. What can we do together to develop these qualities?
2. What role do we want the principal to play?
3. What can each of us do to facilitate the desired outcome?
4. Knowing that it is going to take some time and that there is much that must be undone and begun, where should we start?

As these questions were discussed, the faculty developed a commitment to work toward a no-fault approach—a freedom to make mistakes as long as you learn from them—and a general agreement that faculty, staff, and students can support one another. This required some reworking of the old group norms that had operated in the faculty and had prohibited the openness discussed above.

Many faculties have norms, such as "Always be polite, even if you don't mean it," or "Never show a colleague how you really feel." These norms usually develop in a fault school where much of the complaining and arguing goes on behind people's backs. I can go into a school and in about thirty minutes tell you whether it is a fault or no-fault school. One of my prime diagnostic sources is the faculty lounge. In the faculty lounge I can see whether people are listening to one another, showing mutual concern, offering suggestions to teachers with problems, or whether it is a place where a great deal of nonproductive complaining and griping occurs with nobody offering any suggestions or attempting to make anything better. In the latter situation, if a teacher does something to make another teacher angry, the problem is rarely dealt with openly. The offended teacher usually goes to someone else to complain. How the faculty handles disagree-

ments with one another and with the administration is an important indicator of their ability to function cooperatively as a group.

I am not saying that all faculty members have to like one another,
socialize together, or be comrades and confidants. That is neither possible
nor desirable. There will always be subgroups of people who like each other
better than other people, and who trust each other more than the rest of
the faculty; however, it is extremely important that these natural social
friendships do not interfere with an overall atmosphere of mutual acceptance in the school.

The ladder concept.   Once you feel you can make a mistake and still
be valued as a teacher, you may want to think about developing the "ladder
concept" in your school. The ladder concept gives each person in the school
an imaginary ladder that can be used to help colleagues get down if they get
stuck "up a tree." I believe that working with human beings is an extremely
emotion-laden endeavor and that it is not possible to be a good teacher
without sometimes having emotions take over. The times when I temporarily lose control of myself are the times when I would love to have somebody
there with a ladder to help me get down out of the tree. That person must
be someone who is not caught up in the incident, and who cares enough
about me to see that I do not get myself further out on the limb than I
already am.

A fourth-grade teacher was out of control, temporarily, in her fury at
a girl in her class. This girl, Sara, had been irritating, insolent, and difficult
to work with from the first day of school. The teacher, Mrs. S., had tried
everything she could to reach Sara.

Sara not only seemed to be unreachable, but also able to make Mrs.
S. feel inadequate. Sara's message was, "I'm not responding because you
are not a good teacher," and there was a part of Mrs. S. that believed this,
although the girl was wrong. The last straw came one day when Sara was
late from recess, and Mrs. S. looked up as she came in asked her why she
was late. Sara's defensive response was, "There was no reason to come to
class—nothing interesting ever happens here." The teacher lost control,
took Sara out in the hall, and started screaming at her. This strong emotional
response was a very honest and natural one under the circumstances. How
many teachers could have taken this all year without at some point letting
it get to them?

A teacher who had been nearby realized that Mrs. S. was temporarily
out of control and that she needed a ladder to get down out of her tree
before she said or did something she would regret. Because this was a
no-fault school, the teacher who was not upset was able to extricate Mrs.
S. from the situation by going in and saying, "It looks like Sara has really
gotten to you. Why don't you let me take her off your hands for a while?"
This removed Sara from the wrath of Mrs. S. and gave each of them a

chance to calm down. The helping teacher, the one with the ladder, walked off with Sara and without having to punish her or bawl her out was able to calmly comment, "You really made Mrs. S. furious. Is that what you wanted to do?" She then talked for a few minutes with Sara about what her goal was in relation to that teacher. After their talk, Sara came and sat in her classroom for a while until Mrs. S. sent word that she was ready to have the girl return.

This approach differs vastly from one where a teacher, trying to be supportive by not interfering, lets another teacher go on until real damage is done; or a colleague attacks the child in a false need to protect the angry teacher. The ladder concept is possible only when faculty members agree that these outbursts are normal and natural, and act as helping agents rather than judges. The ladder concept can also work among students in a classroom. Children can learn to help one another, but the tone must be set within the faculty. The guideline is: the person who is in control is the one responsible for helping make the situation better. As faculty members master this approach, they can educate their students to do the same thing—to carry ladders to help both students and teachers down from "trees" when they begin to do something that could be destructive to themselves or somebody else.

Conflict management.   Even in an ideal school there will, of course, be conflicts. Some of these conflicts occur among subgroups; some of them may be theoretical in nature, others may be much more practical. Some conflict is healthy for a school and a good exchange of ideas and suggestions can be helpful. If conflicts are resolved in a supportive way, or there is consensus (or even agreement not to reach consensus), the school can exist with its conflicts without real difficulty. If, on the other hand, the conflicts are driven underground and acted out rather than talked out, there may be real problems with communication. If one conflict cannot be discussed openly, it is difficult for any conflict to be resolved. But because working in schools is emotionally laden, it is not unusual for a faculty not to want to have to deal with conflict. I talked with a teacher who said, "I just can't stand any more hassles. When two faculty members begin to argue, I want to get up and leave." I can certainly understand how she feels, and yet if a norm develops in that school that it is not acceptable to air differences, then the disagreements will be handled covertly, which will create another problem.

One district in which I consult has two high schools, each of which resolved the same conflict in a different way. The issue was whether or not to have a "smoking room" for students. Faculty differed greatly on the issue of students smoking in school. Some felt that smoking was dangerous and that to allow it was setting a bad example and was extremely destructive for students. Others felt that some young people were going to smoke anyway and rather than drive it into the washrooms, they would like to provide a smoking area on the condition that the students agreed (and kept the agreement) to confine all smoking to that one area. One of the reasons that this was a loaded issue was because there was conflict among the faculty themselves about whether or not they should smoke in school. Some teachers complained, "We can't even go into the teachers' lounge because the smoke is so heavy we have trouble breathing!" Others said, "Smoking is part of life and we ought to accept it."

In one of the two schools an agreement was reached that was satisfactory to everybody—something that everyone could live with—even though there were parts of the agreement that nobody liked. In the other school, a decision was made based on strong opinions that were expressed by a few vocal faculty members. Three-fourths of the faculty did not really agree; they were hesitant to challenge the other faculty, so they gave in rather than fight for their own beliefs. If I am pushed into acquiescing to a rule with which I really disagree, the likelihood that I will enforce it actively is not very great. Even though I know I should, I tend not to. In the school where the faculty really worked together to find a solution with which everybody in the school could live, all of the faculty supported the decision. In the other school, the solution worked only sporadically. Some faculty closed their eyes when they found children smoking and others became extremely rigid. There was no cooperative enforcement of the policy that had been developed in that school.

Now, exploration of the question of permitting smoking in school or anywhere else could easily fill another whole book. The point here is that the way the decision was made and the willingness and ability of the faculty to support it were inalterably intertwined.

THE VALUE OF DIVERSITY

This leads to the whole issue of how a school can accept and use differences among faculty to strengthen the program. One of the things that is exciting to me about some faculties is their diversity. I would hate to be in a school where everybody was the same and where norms were developed that said that we should all operate in the same mold. In my ideal school each faculty member would have some strengths and concerns of his or her own that would be known to and respected by other faculty members. Each faculty member would be free to develop his or her program, to utilize strengths, and to fit concerns within the broad overall curriculum and school goals. There would be a minimum of expectations for faculty members to act in the same manner. Of course fundamental school rules and state laws are mandates that all teachers have to enforce, but there are many rules that can differ from class to class. There is no reason why every classroom should have the same rules; in fact, there are contraindications for that structure.

Insisting that all teachers follow the same rules inhibits their freedom to teach in ways that are comfortable to them. Students know when a person is enforcing a rule in which he or she does not believe, and it can create mistrust in some students. On the other hand, students are able to adapt to different rules in different classrooms. They are not only aware of, but also responsive to, contrasting requirements of teachers.

One seventh-grade teacher said, "I know there is nothing wrong with chewing gum, but there is something about seeing all those young people with their mouths going all the time that drives me up a wall. I just can't stand it." Once she felt free enough to have her own particular bias, she was able to say to her students, "It may not make sense to you, but gum chewing is so annoying to me that when I see it I can't teach. I think more about your mouths going than I do about the subject, so in my class you can't chew gum." Of course, the students' immediate response was, "But Mr. Jones lets us chew gum in his class!" This teacher, fortunately, felt comfortable enough with herself, and Mr. Jones, to say, "Marvelous! I'm delighted that Mr. Jones lets you chew gum in his class. Chew all the gum you want there, but not here." It is this acceptance of yourself and your own expectations and desires in a no-fault school that frees you to set different rules for behavior in your classroom than there are in others. That is perfectly all right. What is not okay is for you to try to get *all* teachers to outlaw gum chewing because it is offensive to *you*. That is where schools run into difficulty. There are certain behaviors that some faculty expect from their students but others do not, and faculty members ought to have permission from one another as well as from the administration to formulate with their classes their own rules, based on the needs of the faculty member and desires of the students.

A CHALLENGE

Take a step back now and think about your school. What goes on in the teachers' lounge? What expectations do faculty have of one another and of the principal? What kind of support system exists? Do you have a desire to get away from backbiting and work toward mutual support? Is it possible for disagreements to be aired between the people who disagreed rather than pushed underground? These are all important questions and challenges. Take a look at your faculty as a group. How do you relate to one another, and how does the administration relate to you?

Such an analysis may seem like an overwhelming and insurmountable task. You might begin by asking yourself, "If I could walk into school tomorrow and have one thing different in the way the faculty relates to one another and to the administration, what would it be?" If you could only have one change, where would you start? Now think about whether you can go to school tomorrow and begin to effect that one change.

THE PROBLEM-SOLVING PROCESS: YOUR ALLY

One of the principles of "Human Education" is that children, teachers, principals, and school social workers are important human beings. Each is unique, special, and very human. Many schools give permission to children to be human, including the right to err. How many schools, however, see the teacher as having the right to make mistakes? One teacher bitterly stated, "I spend all day accepting both the strengths and weaknesses of the children in my class. I teach them, nurture them, value them, and help them learn from their mistakes. When is someone going to care about me? Why can't I make mistakes as the children do? I'm human too!"

Teachers do make mistakes, of course, as do administrators, psychologists, social workers, consultants, and all other people. The very human qualities that cause errors are the same ones that make teachers so responsive to the children. The ability to become involved with the children you serve is a great strength, and yet it leaves you vulnerable to being hurt, to letting your feelings get in the way, to err.

The problem-solving process is not for anyone who is perfect. It was designed to be used by those of us who make more mistakes than we choose to admit. Basically, it is an approach to problem resolution to use when difficulties occur between you and any other person or group of people within the school. The process assumes that most real problems are two-way, that both you and the other party are responsible. This means that you also have the power to use this process to change the way things are, to resolve the problem in some way or another.

Define the Problem

The first step in the problem-solving process is to define the various parts of the problem as you perceive them. What is wrong? What happened? How did it happen? How do you feel about what happened? What did it do to you as a person to have had this experience? You need to try to get in touch not only with the content of the problem and the process of how it happened, but also with your personal response to it. Then you can move beyond that to questions about the other people involved. What do you think happened to them personally? How do they feel?

One teacher kept a whole class after school because they had become "smart alecky" and defiant. Usually she could handle such an occurrence and settle the children down without becoming punitive. But this particular day she was feeling rotten physically, she had had a disagreement with her husband before school, and the material that she had carefully ordered for her lesson plan had not arrived. The combination of all of these aggravations, plus the obnoxious behavior of some of the children in the class, made her feel furious, sorry for herself, frustrated, and helpless. She was certainly entitled to those feelings. Her affective response was very real and relevant to the situation. But she felt bad about the way she had blamed and punished the children and asked me to help her understand what had happened. This incident had brought out a side of her that she did not like very much.

Sometimes keeping children after school can be helpful, but in this instance the teacher perceived it as her attempt to get even because the children had made her feel bad. When I encouraged her to take a look at the problem in its entirety, supporting her feelings both from within and without the classroom as being important, we were then able to move to another question. How could she help the children understand what had happened and regain a nonpunitive attitude in the classroom?

Accept Your Feelings and Fantasies

The second step of the problem-solving process is to accept your feelings and allow yourself to imagine what you would like to do. When the teacher was so angry, for instance, what would she have liked to do? Clearly, in this case, a part of the teacher wanted to get even because the pupils had hurt her feelings. Her desire to get even was perfectly natural. Many teachers, when they have been hurt, have vivid fantasies of methods of retaliation and relish them! Having fantasies is usually harmless yet potentially very helpful—it is what you do that matters.

I would like to digress a moment to talk about the tremendous therapeutic value for people within a school system of permitting themselves to have wild fantasies about ways to cope with disquieting situations. Fantasies do not cost anything, do not hurt, and can help a teacher experience his or her own legitimate feelings. Perhaps the teacher in the above illustration, had she allowed herself, would have fantasized some wicked way to get even with those demons in her class. One teacher used to enjoy fantasizing hanging pupils from the coat hooks in the closet. She never actually did this, but the fantasy helped her through some rough times with difficult children. Do not be afraid to have negative fantasies as well as positive ones and to allow yourself to experience your feelings.

Stop

Once you know what the problem is, once you know how you feel about it and have allowed yourself a fantasy, stop. Just stop. This is the third step in the problem-solving process. That pause gives you a chance to regain your equilibrium. Then, without giving up the relevance of your feelings, try to move beyond them and think about what it is that you would really like to have happen. What kind of rapport would you like to have with those young people? What kind of a relationship do you really want with your faculty if you are a principal? And in that stopping process, when your feelings are very evident and appreciated (but put aside for a few moments), you can set specific goals for what you would like to have happen next.

A word of caution. The goals you set must be limited enough so that they are attainable if you act in a different way. You cannot take a child who makes you furious when he continues to say how much he hates school and have as your goal to make him love school. This obviously is not realistic. But you may very well be able to take a small piece of that unrealistic goal and say, "Okay, if he hates school and I want him to like it, I'd like to start with finding out if we can have one good experience together in the classroom. Can we have a good day, or a good lesson, any one time that both of us would enjoy to set the tone for other things to come?"

Develop a Plan of Action

After you have set your limited goal, you then need to move to the fourth step, which is to develop a plan of action to attain that goal. Ask yourself, "If my goal is to help this youngster have a positive experience with me and for me to enjoy him, what are some of the things I can do to help that come about?" This is the time when you may want to pick up those feelings that you put aside in the "stop" phase and consider whether there is some way to use those feelings in a way to achieve your goal. Your plan of action should include helping the other people involved understand some of the things they did that upset you and what you can do to improve things together.

You, for example, in your anger and frustration at the boy who hates school might take him aside and share your frustration with him. Without blaming him, you can let him know that you are frustrated and that you know he must be too. Together you can develop a plan to try something new. Is it possible to have a good morning tomorrow? What could each of us do to enjoy our morning? This conversation might lead to some partialized, workable goals, agreeable to both student and teacher. The teacher who is so angry with her class that she becomes punitive may be able to use her anger in a helpful way. She might tell the class how angry she is, not blaming them, but as a way to get them involved. She can then ask them how they feel. What would they like to be different? After this mutual sharing of feelings, the students and teacher can put together what each of them can do to change the situation, or be ready for it if it begins to happen again.

Develop a Built-In Contingency Plan

The fifth step in the problem-solving process is what I call the "escape hatch." Suppose you get in touch with your feelings, you stop, you set a goal, you make a plan of action, and it falls flat. That is always a risk, so your next step is to ask, prior to putting your plan of action to work, "What if . . . ?" What if the plan does not work? What if the child does not respond? What if I cannot control my feelings? In this way you build in a contingency plan, which you can hold in reserve for use as necessary (as you would take a spare tire on an auto trip in case you need it).

Even if your plan of action does not work out the way you had originally intended, this contingency plan is a means by which most of your problem solving can be in some way successful. You will find as you begin to use this model that, in most instances, some of its methods work and some do not, and your contingency plan may help you cope with any negative outcomes.

Postpone Action

This problem-solving model works best when you are aware enough of your own feelings that you can creatively and spontaneously go through the process, which may take anywhere from thirty seconds to thirty minutes. There will be times, however, when your feelings are too intense, when you have been hurt too deeply, when you care too much to use this framework at the time. You may be too angry to care what the child thinks at that moment. You may be too hurt by another teacher to be able to understand how she feels. These are the times when the process needs to be put aside for a while. At these moments, the best and most helpful thing you can do is to acknowledge to yourself and to the people you are working with that you feel too intensely to make a decision right now about anything. That temporary inability to act is okay. In fact, when you feel that intensely, it is best not to act until things are in better perspective for you.

One faculty member, who had been called filthy names by a group of angry students, felt she had to act. She had tried very hard to reach these young people, and their abusive language hurt and upset her so much that she knew that to talk with them at that point would not be helpful to her or to the students. Instead, she said, "Kids, right now my feelings are so strong that I can't talk to you without saying some things I might be sorry I said. You've hurt me deeply, and we need to take a look at this and see what we're going to do about it. But I can't do it now. Come back after school, all four of you, and let's all sit down and see if we can figure out together what happened and how we can keep this from happening again. I don't like being hurt and I don't think you do either."

Not even that amount of objectivity showed a great deal of ability on the part of the teacher to share her feelings in a helpful way. Many of us cannot even say that much. We may just have to say, "Go away right now, I can't talk to you. Come back after school." Or, "I'll talk to you tomorrow." There are many ways a teacher or principal can create "cooling off time."

Sometimes it helps to ask the group of young people to write down what they think happened, using the time that they are writing as space to recoup, to get in touch with your feelings, and to get back into the problem-solving process.

Evaluate the Process

It is an impossible task to understand all of the things that go on in groups and also keep in touch with your own feelings and desires so as to be able to always use yourself in a helping way. Indeed, if you must succeed in order to feel good about your interventions, if they must work out the way you planned, then you may be frequently disappointed. In my own work in the schools with faculty and administrators, I have discovered that in order for this problem-solving approach to work, I have to change the way I evaluate myself. I used to evaluate my decisions and actions based on how successful I was at getting the outcome I desired. If noise was a problem in my class, I evaluated my success as a teacher by how quiet I was able to get the children to be. I do not do that anymore. Now I evaluate myself, not by the specific outcome, but by how much I am able to help the students in my class and myself find some common goal that all of us can support. This plan may not be the same as one I might develop on my own, but it is usually more successful because it was created by all of us together. I must, then, change my usual investment from the *end result* to the *process by which the result takes place.*

There are times, of course, when the end result becomes crucial and the process much less important. These are times when safety is involved, when prompt obedience and response is needed, or when the outcome is particularly important to the teacher or principal. If you are primarily a process person who lets your staff, students, or therapeutic group participate in the problem-solving process, the times that you have to say, "This is what it must be, you must follow me now," the group members will usually do so because they know you would not ask if it was not important. Because in the past they have not needed to act out against your authority, they probably will not need to now.

A further dimension involves how I evaluate myself overall in my role in school. As always, my prime measure is what people learn in an objective sense. But in other ways, I find I have to evaluate myself differently than I used to. I no longer can judge myself as a teacher by how perfect I am and how few mistakes I make. Instead, I evaluate myself based on how responsive I was to the class or to the staff. How well was I able to hear their point of view? How able was I to facilitate the respect for each other's rights, both theirs and mine? If I got into a power struggle, how quickly was I able to perceive that I was in a conflict with a student or students or other staff? How able was I to accept my piece of the power struggle?

How willing was I to be flexible so that it could be resolved? All of these questions are relevant to successful use of the problem-solving process in your work within a school system.

The roles of the school social worker, the teacher, the principal, the school secretary, the janitor, and the librarian are all different, but they all work together for and through one another to make the education process work, each contributing in his or her own unique way. When they do act, it is no longer a single role, but a cooperative effort whose success or failure will not be so much dependent on the talents of each person, but on their ability to interact and to work with each other. This is the quality about schools that is most often missed and, when missed, can lead to the breakdown of parts of, or all of, the process. The holistic perspective of the social worker can often make a more positive interaction possible and develop a living environment that can allow that which each person has to offer to be nurtured and supported.

CHAPTER 29

Peer Sexual Harassment and the Social Worker's Response*

Susan Fineran
Assistant Professor, School of Social Work, Boston University

Larry Bennett
Assistant Professor, Jane Addams College of Social Work,
University of Illinois at Chicago

- Introduction
- Sexual Harassment and Sex Discrimination
- Research on Peer Sexual Harassment
- Research Comparison
- Social Work and Peer Sexual Harassment
- Same-Sex Sexual Harassment among Peers
- School Policy and Implications
- School Social Work Approaches to Peer Sexual Harassment

Peer sexual harassment is an often overlooked problem for both girls and boys in the educational environment. This chapter provides an historical framework for defining peer sexual harassment as a sex discrimination issue and a description of peer sexual harassment as a potential mental health issue. The chapter also reviews the limited empirical research on teen peer sexual harassment, which has consistently revealed that nearly four of five adolescents are the targets of sexual harassment by their peers. The authors explore a theoretical context for the understanding of sexual harassment, policy implications for the schools, and implications for school social work practice.

INTRODUCTION

Peer sexual harassment is a problem for both girls and boys in the educational environment. This experience can affect students' lives negatively well past high school. Many students report school performance difficulties due to sexual harassment, including absenteeism, decreased quality of

---

*A version of this chapter first appeared in *Social Work* and is used with permission.

schoolwork, skipping or dropping classes, lower grades, loss of friends, tardiness, and truancy. These symptoms in turn can lead to ineligibility for specific colleges or merit scholarships and loss of recommendations for awards, colleges, or jobs. All of the above may lead to fewer career choices, decreased or lost economic opportunities, and possible job failure that can affect a student for the rest of her or his life (Strauss and Espeland, 1992; Stein, Marshall, and Tropp 1993).

Sexual harassment is part of the larger problem of interpersonal violence in schools. The escalating problems associated with interpersonal violence in schools have become very important both nationally and in the international education literature. Many schools, increasingly concerned about violence, have developed active measures to establish a climate of civility in trying to counteract this trend (Kauffman and Burback, 1997). As an example of this developing literature on bullying is summarized by Barone (1997). Measures to deal with interpersonal violence, suggested in this international literature and discussed at a later point in this chapter, are quite related to the problem of sexual harassment. Sexual harassment can be seen as one of a number of problems of interpersonal violence that creates a negative atmosphere in the school, leads to failure of the educational project, and results in severe damage to developing students, whether through bullying, or through forms of personal denigration, such as teasing, or sexual harassment. Most of the prevention work regarding peer sexual harassment has been targeted at high school students; however, research suggests that younger students in elementary and middle schools should begin with prevention programs on bullying and that this behavior is a precursor to sexual harassment and other forms of interpersonal violence (Stein, 1996).

Strauss and Espeland (1992), Stein et al. (1993), and the American Association of University Women (AAUW, 1993) have identified sexual harassing behaviors at the secondary school level. The AAUW report *Hostile Hallways* (1993, p. 5) listed fourteen types of sexual harassment and asked 1,600 high school students whether someone had done any of these things to them:

- Made sexual comments, jokes, gestures, or looks
- Showed, gave, or left you sexual pictures, photographs, illustrations, messages, or notes
- Wrote sexual messages or graffiti about you on bathroom walls, in locker rooms, etc.
- Spread sexual rumors about you
- Said you were gay or lesbian
- Spied on you as you dressed or showered at school
- Flashed or "mooned" you

- Touched, grabbed, or pinched you in a sexual way
- Pulled at your clothing in a sexual way
- Intentionally brushed against you in a sexual way
- Pulled your clothing off or down
- Blocked your way or cornered you in a sexual way
- Forced you to kiss him or her
- Forced you to do something sexual, other than kissing

Peer sexual harassment in high school can also include "spiking" or pulling down someone's pants, "snuggies" or pulling underwear up at the waist so it goes in between the buttocks, and being listed in "slam books" that identify students' names and have derogatory sexual comments written about them by other students (Strauss and Espeland, 1992, p. 8).

In the AAUW study, four out of five students reported being sexually harassed, and of those harassed, 79 percent stated it was by a peer. Most of the literature on sexual harassment indicates that over 90 percent of the time, males are the perpetrators of sexual harassment against females (Langelan, 1993: Strauss and Espeland, 1992; Stein et al., 1993). The AAUW study was the first to document a high level of sexual harassment experienced by boys as well as girls. While much discussion of sexual harassment has focused on the university and the workplace, these findings point out that sexual harassment is a very big problem in schools—precisely the places where developing human beings are most vulnerable. The university and workplace literature showed that 2 to 15 percent of men in the workplace or university have been sexually harassed, while for women the range is 40 to 53 percent (Fitzgerald et al., 1988; Pryor, La Vite, and Stoller, 1993: Metha and Nigg, 1983; Gutek, 1985; U.S. Merit Systems Protection Board, 1987). The emerging knowledge that both boys and girls are affected by peer sexual harassment in schools gives school social workers further impetus and possibly new directions to pursue. Researcher Susan Strauss has studied the high school experience in Minnesota. She observes that

> many students say that sexual harassment is the norm in their schools. There have been numerous reports of sexual assaults and rapes on school grounds and in school buildings. In an environment that condones sexual harassment, everyone is a victim, not just those who are direct targets of the harassment. All students come to see school as an unsafe place, hostile and intimidating. They may alter their own behaviors in an attempt to decrease their sense of vulnerability (Strauss and Espeland, 1992, p. 7).

School as a Normative Environment

Reaching back through several decades of educational research, some of the strongest findings on school effectiveness remain that the effective school is a normative environment of order with clear understanding and enforcement of expectations. One body of research points out that effective schools are places where principals, teachers, students, and parents agree on the content of schooling. They are united in recognizing the importance of a coherent curriculum, public recognition of students who succeed, promotion of a sense of school pride, and protection of school time for learning (Kyle, 1985; Finn, 1984; Purkey and Smith, 1983). Another body of research points out that these norms need to be clearly understood in fair and consistent discipline policies and codes (Goldsmith, 1982). Effective education thus occurs when there is a normative agreement among teachers, parents, and administrators on the content and process of education. Key norms focus on keeping the school from becoming a hurtful environment. From the prior description of peer sexual harassment, we can surmise that these behaviors create a hostile school environment that would challenge even the most gifted student's ability to learn. The creation of a toxic atmosphere for children keeps the school from carrying out its mission to educate. When students do not feel protected by the school environment, they receive the message that school is unsafe. This overwhelms other messages that the school desires to teach, and students end up feeling vulnerable. Not only is the child's education at risk but his or her development as a person is potentially harmed.

SEXUAL HARASSMENT AND SEX DISCRIMINATION

Despite the effects of sexual harassment and other interpersonal violence on individual students and on the school community, discussed above, schools and school communities are only gradually recognizing the inherent toxicity of this behavior for the security and development of individual students and for the school environment as a whole. Much of the literature focuses on sexual harassment as a legal problem and a problem of sex discrimination, rather than as a threat to the school environment or as something dangerous for individual students. Courts can only operate after abuse has occurred and even then in a highly imperfect manner. Whatever redress the courts can provide to persons who have faced such a damaging situation, will not undo the damage to students and to the educational environment and may only reinforce a sense of permanent damage. A brief history of the evolving awareness of peer sexual harassment from workplace to school is presented below.

Sexual harassment is a specific type of sex discrimination defined by the courts of the past thirty years. In general, the interpretation of what constitutes sexual harassment in the educational setting has followed the concepts developed under employment discrimination law. Title VII of the Civil Rights Act of 1964 provides the main framework prohibiting discrimination on the basis of race, color, religion, national origin, and sex. In 1972 Title IX of the Education Amendments Act sought to address the educational needs of minorities and women. Title IX requires that an institution receiving federal funds provide an environment free of discrimination. It also prohibits sexual harassment in education and directs educational institutions to maintain a grievance procedure that allows for prompt and equitable resolution of all sex discrimination, including sexual harassment.

In 1986 the U.S. Supreme Court identified two forms of sexual harassment: quid pro quo and hostile environment. *Quid pro quo* applies when a person in a position of power (a supervisor or teacher) makes decisions that affect an employee's job or a student's grade or other selection—such as team membership—based on whether the employee or student complies with his or her sexual demands. *Hostile environment* applies when the harassing behavior of anyone in the workplace (not only a supervisor or teacher) causes the workplace to become hostile, intimidating, or offensive, because of tolerance or even encouragement of such behavior by superiors, and unreasonably interferes with an employee's or students' work (Langelan, 1993).

It is the *hostile environment* definition that is most closely aligned to peer sexual harassment. Employers are currently responsible for the actions of employees with regard to sexual harassment. In education a school's responsibility has been expanded to include the actions of students as well as employees. It is of interest to note that most of the literature regarding sexual harassment pertains to the workplace and university and that sexual harassment legislation for the two settings has developed in parallel.

RESEARCH ON PEER SEXUAL HARASSMENT

Sexual harassment of students can be divided into two distinct types: adult to student or student to student. Much has been written regarding adult- (or professor-) to-student and peer-to-peer harassment at the university level (Dziech and Weiner, 1990; Fitzgerald et al., 1988; O'Gorman and Sandler, 1988); however, few studies have documented either type of harassment at the high school level.

Overall, there have been six surveys conducted on teen sexual harassment (Strauss and Espeland, 1992; AAUW, 1993; Stein et al., 1993; Roscoe, Strouse, and Goodwin, 1994; Permanent Commission on the Status of Women [PCSW], 1995; Fineran and Bennett, 1995). Four of the six surveys focused primarily on determining the incidence and or prevalence of sexual harassment in high school, while the other two surveys also addressed the types of relationships that the students had with one another and who experienced sexual harassment.

Strauss and Espeland (1992) surveyed student leaders from thirteen school districts at a Minnesota State Sex Equity Student Leadership conference in 1991. She also surveyed 250 female high school students from four school districts in Minnesota where "approximately 50% of the teenage girls reported having been verbally and physically harassed at school and another 30% stated they had been harassed at work" (Strauss and Espeland, 1992, p. 3). Both of these surveys used convenience samples and primarily asked whether sexual harassment occurred in the school, how often it occurred, and to whom. Specific sexual harassment behaviors were identified, and students were asked whether an adult or another student was involved. Some contextual issues were identified, such as when and where the harassment occurred.

The AAUW study *Hostile Hallways* was conducted by Louis Harris and Associates in 1993. It consisted of 1,632 questionnaires completed by public school students in grades 8 through 11, from seventy-nine schools across the continental United States. A random sample of schools was selected from the database of public schools at the National Center for Education Statistics. A proportionally drawn sample by grade and regional location was used, and the study can be generalized to all U.S. public school students in the eighth to eleventh grades. The survey consists of forty questions and addresses sexual harassment with regard to the following areas: frequency, type (physical and nonphysical), grade level of first experience, frequency of adult to student, frequency of peer to peer, location, impact on student's education (cutting classes or school absence) or emotional state, and behavior (avoiding the harasser). The AAUW study addressed both the perpetration and experience of sexual harassment.

Hostile Hallways documented that the majority of sexual harassment that occurs in American high schools is between peers. Eighty-seven percent of the girls and 71 percent of the boys reported being sexually harassed by a current or former student at school, while one in four girls and one in ten boys have been targeted by adult school employees. Sixty-six percent of all boys and 52 percent of all girls surveyed by the AAUW admit they have sexual harassed someone in the school setting. Only 4 percent of these boys and girls say they harassed an adult. Of the 59 percent of students who say they have sexually harassed someone in the school setting, 94 percent claim they themselves have been harassed (98 percent of girls and 92 percent of boys). The fact that 79 percent of students report being harassed by peers and 59 percent report harassing other students leaves a minority of students experiencing a stress-free secondary education.

The AAUW study yielded important information regarding the prevalence of sexual harassment within the school system. It clearly identified who is being sexually harassed, when, and where. Students who harassed were asked why they engaged in sexual harassment and which of the reasons listed below applied to their behavior:

1. It's just a part of school life / a lot of people do it / it's no big deal.

2. I thought the person liked it.

3. I wanted a date with the person.
4. My friends encouraged me / pushed me into doing it.
5. I wanted something from that person.
6. I wanted the person to think I had some sort of power over them.

Stein et al. (1993) and the Wellesley College Center for Research on Women conducted a survey, in conjunction with the National Organization for Women (NOW) Legal Defense and Education Fund, that was published in *Seventeen* magazine in September 1992. This endeavor resulted in the 1993 report *Secrets in Public: Sexual Harassment in Our Schools*. Over 4,200 girls returned the surveys. The girls ranged in age from nine to nineteen and were in grades 2 to 12. Ninety percent of the girls were in public schools, 6 percent attended private schools, and 3 percent were in parochial schools. Ninety-nine percent of the schools were coeducational. Eighty-nine percent of the respondents were white, 2 percent African American, 3 percent Latino, and the remaining 6 percent of other background. These percentages probably reflect the ethnic makeup of the readers of *Seventeen*. The girls' responses provided detailed information regarding their personal experience of sexual harassment.

The *Seventeen* survey consisted of six questions and addressed sexual harassment according to frequency (adult to student and peer to peer), type (physical and nonphysical), location (public or private), reaction to the harassment, and school response. The most common forms of sexual harassment girls experienced were hearing or seeing sexual comments, gestures, or looks and being touched, pinched, or grabbed. Thirty-nine percent of the girls reported they experienced these behaviors every day. Ninety-seven percent of the harassers were identified as male peers, and 1 percent were female (Stein et al., 1993).

The fourth study, conducted by Roscoe et al. (1994), surveyed 561 (281 females and 280 males) white students at a midwestern intermediate school. The students ranged in age from eleven to sixteen years. Students were asked about their experience of peer sexual harassment and their acceptance of sexually harassing behaviors. Forty-three percent of the students experienced peer sexual harassment (50 percent of females and 37 percent of males). Results also documented that both boys and girls were highly unaccepting of sexual harassment behaviors.

The fifth survey was conducted by the Connecticut Permanent Commission on the Status of Women (PCSW) in cooperation with the University of Connecticut School of Social Work. Five hundred and forty-seven public high school students in grades 10 through 12 completed surveys. Seventy-eight percent of students surveyed experienced sexual harassment (92 percent of females and of 57 percent males). Demographic characteristics described the same as 78 percent Caucasian, 8 percent African American, 6 percent Latino, and 4 percent Asian. This was a representative sample of male and female students from seven school districts determined by the Connecticut Department of Education and reflected the socioeconomic status and age composition of the Connecticut student population. Twelve percent of harassing events were perpetrated by students who were boyfriends or girlfriends, 35 percent were perpetrated by a schoolmate whom the student knew casually, and 9 percent were perpetrated by a schoolmate whom the student did not know. Half of the boys and 75 percent of the girls reported being upset by the experience of sexual harassment at school. The victims reported that 75 percent of the perpetrators were male and 25 percent were female, a clearly smaller difference between male and female perpetrators than in the other studies.

Fineran and Bennett (1995) surveyed 342 students in a large, midwestern, urban high school. Their convenience sample reflected a high minority student population of 43 percent African American, 14 percent white, 11 percent Asian, and 24 percent Latino. Students were asked about the experience and perpetration of sexual harassment, how upset or threatened they were by these behaviors, and the relationship between perpetrator and victim. Students also completed two scales measuring beliefs about personal and gender-based power. Eighty-four percent of the students experienced peer sexual harassment (87 percent of females and 79 percent of males), and 75 percent reported perpetrating sexual harassment. Results also documented that boys perpetrate sexual harassment twice as often as girls. Sixty percent of harassing events were perpetrated by a schoolmate the students knew casually, 15 percent by a schoolmate the student did not know, and 25 percent by students in dating or ex-dating relationships.

RESEARCH COMPARISON

The literature is rich with information regarding the individual areas of teen development, adolescent relationships, power, sexual harassment, and gender issues; however, there is no specific body of knowledge or research that intertwines these topics and relates them to teen peer sexual harassment. The literature provides numerous insights into male perpetration of sexual harassment in the workplace. The workplace research supports a low adult male victimization rate. However, there is no discussion of the teen experience of peer sexual harassment, where males and females are both perpetrators and victims. This may indeed be quite unlike the adult world. Further investigation of teen peer sexual harassment is needed in order to create a more complete understanding of the factors and context that contribute to and sustain it within the high school environment.

SOCIAL WORK AND PEER SEXUAL HARASSMENT

Understanding the dynamics of teen peer sexual harassment has important theoretical and practical implications for researchers and practitioners in educational and mental health environments. The broad issue of sexual harassment in the workplace and university setting has been understood as sex discrimination, and legal recourse is available. Peer sexual harassment in the high school has only recently been documented and viewed as being remediable through legal processes. However, legal solutions to peer interactions in high school are complicated by the time it takes to process a case through the legal system and by the illogical idea that relationships among teens can be legislated. Although a legal approach may be needed initially to focus school systems on peer sexual harassment as a problem, this would be an expensive effort. Litigation would cost school districts, and ultimately taxpayers, large amounts of money.

Most studies indicate that peer sexual harassment is a gender issue, so that girls in particular are targeted by this behavior. Gender, power, and hierarchy fall broadly under social justice issues where sexual harassment is viewed as sex discrimination and affects females negatively. The fact that peer sexual harassment can be viewed as supporting a gendered hierarchy contributes to the need for education and training that encourages a more egalitarian environment and discourages discrimination against girls. It is important to note, however, that *all* students are affected by these behaviors and that the focus on the problem could be broadened to include men and women, individual groups in the school environment, perpetrators and victims, and groups that victimize or are victims. Teachers who appear unaware, who are afraid, or who don't know how to intervene are as much a part of the problem as the policies that do not directly address sexual harassment or do not support intervention by a teacher. The entire school community needs to be educated that the problem exists and is taken seriously. School social workers have important work to do with victims, perpetrators, groups, teachers, and education administrators. By broadening the issue of sexual harassment, social workers will undoubtedly develop ways of educating administrators, teachers, and students about discrimination in general and about how power and gender issues create oppression in a school environment.

Another way to understand peer sexual harassment utilizes a mental health perspective. The AAUW (1993) and PCSW (1995) studies found that students who experience sexual harassment report more school absence, lowered concentration, and less participation in class. These studies also reported physical symptoms that included sleep disturbance and appetite changes. Overall students reported feeling angry, upset, and threatened by sexual harassment, all of which contribute to lowered self-esteem and confidence (Strauss and Espeland, 1992; AAUW, 1993; Stein et al., 1993; PCSW, 1995; Fineran and Bennett, 1995).

Given that these studies indicate that students experience peer sexual harassment as upsetting and threatening, school administrators may approach this problem in two ways. The first is to take steps again a hostile environment by setting school policy on peer sexual harassment and actively enforcing this policy. School social workers will be instrumental in the construction of such a policy and active in its deployment and evaluation. The second way administrators may intervene in a hostile environment created by peer sexual harassment is to develop supportive, direct services for students that address peer sexual harassment as a mental health issue. Again, clearly the role for school social workers here would be identifying and working with such students.

Peer relationships among teens also remain problematic and indicate yet another reason for identifying this as a school "climate" problem with mental health implications. Peer sexual harassment falls in the domain of gender harassment and violence and may contribute to an environment that supports negative images of women and promotes dating violence. More females than males experience peer sexual harassment from dating or ex-dating partners; in particular, females are more likely to experience the more physical forms of sexual harassment. Based on the number of students in dating or ex-dating relationships who identify themselves as having been sexually harassed, dating violence among high school students continues to be an area requiring active education and intervention (O'Keefe, Brockopp, and Chew, 1986; Bergman, 1992; DeKeserdy and Schwartz, 1994; Molidar, 1995). There have been no specific studies that tie dating violence and sexual harassment together. However the AAUW, PCSW and Fineran-Bennett studies all had questions regarding the physical forms of sexual harassment that include sexual assault. All three studies documented that 10 percent to 20 percent of students experience these behaviors and that girls experience these behaviors more than boys. Unfortunately the teen dating violence literature and teen sexual harassment literature remain separate. Future research should incorporate questions from both areas in order to illuminate their relationship or identify a continuum of violence.

SAME-SEX SEXUAL HARASSMENT AMONG PEERS

The majority of peer sexual harassment cases involve sexual harassment of females by males. However, a number of cases regarding same-sex sexual harassment are now coming before the courts. A 1998 Supreme Court decision confirmed that same-sex sexual harassment is covered under Title VII (*Oncale v. Sundowner*). This should contribute to further clarity in judicial decisions regarding same-sex sexual harassment, which in the past have ranged from ambiguous at best to denial that same-sex sexual harassment even exists. This landmark decision should decrease recent confusion regarding a school's response to this issue.

In the AAUW (1993) study 86 percent of girls and 71 percent of boys report being targeted at school by a current or former student, and of these students 53 percent report experiencing same-sex sexual harassment. Thirteen percent of girls report being sexually harassed by other girls, and 39 percent of the boys report being harassed by other boys. With regard to perpetration of sexual harassment, 15 percent of boys admit targeting other boys, while only 5 percent of girls report targeting other girls.

Shakeshaft et al. (1995) in her research of peer harassment found that adolescent girls and boys are harassed in different ways, but conformity to gender stereotypes was central for both. Shakeshaft found that three types of students reported more harassment than did others: girls viewed by peers as being physically well developed and pretty, girls who were considered unattractive and not dressing stylishly, and boys who did not fit a stereotype macho male image. Her findings and the same-sex sexual harassment cases that have been litigated lend credence that it is the emphasis on gender stereotypes that contributes to a toxic atmosphere in our society, posing a mental health risk to all developing young people in schools, but especially those who may not fit certain stereotypes or whose current development may leave them vulnerable.

For social workers dealing with same-sex peer sexual harassment in schools, this type of behavior is frequently not well understood by either administrators or students. The lack of research and information regarding same-sex sexual harassment has made it difficult for school social workers to practice constructively. Fineran and Bennett (1998) found differences between same-sex and opposite-sex peer sexual harassment. Girls and boys experienced and perpetrated significantly less same-sex sexual harassment than opposite-sex harassment; however, boys and girls subjected to same-sex harassment were most threatened and upset by the experience of sexual harassment.

The negative implications of this are clarified by the AAUW (1993) findings. Eighty-six percent of all students surveyed stated that being labeled as "gay" or "lesbian" created the most distress for them. For boys, this distress was particularly severe. The report stated "no other type of harassment, including actual physical abuse, provoked a reaction this strong among boys" (p. 20). It is also important to note that similar to the heterosexual population, we do not know whether the students who perpetrated same-sex sexual harassment did so in response to being harassed. Again, victims and perpetrators are indistinguishable from one another.

Same-sex sexual harassment may be more misunderstood than peer sexual harassment. It may be for the most part invisible to those not directly involved, especially to school administrators. Regardless, it remains important for social workers to be able to provide guidance and leadership to schools while guarding and promoting the rights of students and responding appropriately to their potential counseling needs following harassment. The issue needs to be defined, not as same-sex and opposite-sex peer sexual harassment, but in a more general way as a serious mental health problem that contributes to a hostile learning environment. Clinical implications for school social workers suggest focusing on the consequences of these harassing behaviors rather than on the gender of the students involved.

Fostering a positive school climate remains the primary approach to reducing peer sexual harassment. School administrators have the ability to implement programs that foster trust and respect among students who are together thirty hours or more a week. School social workers have the responsibility to advocate that students be educated in a positive, nurturing environment. Formulating peer sexual harassment as both a hostile environment and mental health problem at the high school level allows changes to be made that can affect students personally. However, accomplishing this task presents a challenge. School administrators have negotiated a variety of paths in their attempts to understand the problem and then adequately address it. The following discussion highlights some of the definitional problems school administrators face.

SCHOOL POLICY AND IMPLICATIONS

Defining a theoretical context in which to understand sexual harassment is difficult. Lee, Croninger, Linn, and Chen (1996) outline four cultural theories of sexual harassment: Freudian, structural, critical, and ethical. How a school administrator chooses to view sexual harassment will influence the type of policy a school will develop to address this issue.

In brief, from Lee et al.'s perspective the *Freudian* cultural approach views sexual harassment as a failure of the culture to repress sexuality, resulting in social breakdown and signaling a major threat to the social order. The existence of sexual harassment in schools is denied. The realities of teen sexuality are not dealt with. Teen programs advise students to "just say no."

The *structural* approach addresses school norms and seeks to address sexual harassment through formal programs such as the school's discipline code or a grievance procedure. Changing school norms may consist of decreasing the tolerance of school rituals such as hazing. The structural approach can be criticized for being too superficial and reactionary.

The *critical* theory approach looks at abuse of power within the school culture and relates sexual harassment to violence and aggression in the larger society. Schools have the option of providing a less hostile climate in which students and staff become involved in discussing issues of oppression and its alleviation. Detractors of the critical perspective see the school culture as a reflection of the larger society and regard attempts to address oppression at the high school level as futile.

The *ethical* approach contemplates the importance of shared values and ethical or moral concepts that bind members together as a community.

Lee et al. (1996) state that "those who support a cultural theory organized around ethical or normal concerns would see sexual harassment as a sign of the failure of existing organizations to instill ethical coherence and integrity in their members" (p. 389). This approach assumes that the schools do take responsibility for teaching the basic tenets of democracy.

Keeping these four very different understandings of sexual harassment in mind let us turn to some pragmatic examples of schools dealing with this issue. Stein (1995) points out that dealing with the problem in an arbitrary way in itself becomes problematic. One school district banned all physical touching after numerous complaints from female students about being sexually assaulted by a football player. Stein also points out that the "school as courthouse" approach may also be questionable. Although demonstrating such democratic ideals as a "jury of one's peers," there can be a problem of victim blaming by popular vote. A popular student accused of sexual harassment will frequently gain status as a victim while the student who points the finger becomes the accuser and is blamed for provoking the behavior.

Another way of responding to sexual harassment is to have victims or targets write letters to the perpetrators. This intervention can be viewed by the student as a therapeutic or empowering experience. However, this "one on one" encounter does not involve the other students who may have witnessed the event, nor does it contribute to fostering a positive school environment. Although it may be a positive move to foster mental health in the individual, it does not afford the possibility of addressing sexual harassment as a large social issue within the school. It is simply defined as a private trouble rather than a public issue. Many school officials try to maintain the privacy of the people involved, but frequently rumors of the event, especially if it was witnessed by other students, may have worse consequences.

Many schools have developed sexual harassment policies and procedures that focus on an individual grievance and punishment process. These are more reactive than proactive. They place the burden directly on the student to file a complaint and face the response. They use the victim-perpetrator model, which presents difficulties when the majority of students are both perpetrator and victim (AAUW, 1993; Fineran and Bennett, 1995). Lee et al. (1996) state that "it is difficult to think that a policy of punishing the perpetrator and protecting the victim will be effective in eliminating [peer] sexual harassment in schools" (p. 408).

For school administrators and school social workers these arguments are important when considering school policy. Sexual harassment is a complex phenomenon that requires a complex response. There is no tried and true way to deal with this problem in the K–12 school setting, and the framing of the issue is very important. Sexual harassment has been identified as an abuse of power (MacKinnon, 1979). Lee et al. (1996) discuss the abuse of organizational power where a power differential exists between people's roles (e.g., teacher-student, supervisor-employee). The abuse-of-power theory responds well to a structural approach that defines a perpetrator-victim relationship. These circumstances could exist in a school environment where school personnel are sexually harassing students. However, the majority of sexual harassment in schools is peer to peer and requires a different, less punitive response.

Lee et al. (1996) support a cultural theory approach utilizing ethical dimensions where "more discussion of basic democratic values" is encouraged and "moral and ethical questions are hotly debated" (p. 409). Stein and Sjostrom (1994) believe that sexual harassment needs to be considered as "a matter of social injustice" and that schools should promote democratic principles.

This review of sexual harassment policy is not at all exhaustive and serves only to highlight the complexity of the issue. It would appear that school administrators need to utilize a number of responses that support a legal and democratic understanding of sexual harassment while insuring that individual students are protected and a positive learning environment is encouraged. This is a particularly large order since there is scant research on the efficacy of any of these approaches for administrators to rely on for guidance. Although some schools have instituted preventive training for sexual harassment through workshops, there are no longitudinal studies demonstrating the long-term effect of these workshops. There is, however, a large body of international research on the larger problem of interpersonal violence, and this research could be quite useful in the discussion of peer sexual harassment (Brendtro and Long, 1995; Fukuyama, 1995; Goldstein, 1988, 1995; Kikawa, 1987; Mellor, 1980; Sprick, Sprick, and Garrison, 1992; Sutter, 1995).

Summaries of the literature on interpersonal violence and bullying in schools provide a variety of recommendations that follow some of the findings cited above from the effective schools movement. The school must enunciate a clear policy on interpersonal violence. The policy must be enforced. There must be education of students, parents, and staff, since often the greatest problem is that people are oblivious of the problem and consider it "normal" behavior. Intervention must be swift and clear, but also fair. In one emblematic approach to bullying Stuart Greenbaum (1987) lists ten prevention and intervention strategies:

1. Use a questionnaire to determine the scope of the problem.
2. Communicate clear standards of behavior and consistently enforce them.
3. Monitor playgrounds closely.
4. Establish a recording system for incidents of bullying.
5. Provide children with opportunities to discuss bullying.

6. Never overlook intentionally abusive acts.

7. Contact the parents of both the victims and the bullies when a problem occurs.

8. Establish intervention programs.

9. Encourage parent participation.

10. Provide support and protection for victims.

Greenbaum's approach to bullying can be applied without much change to other interpersonal violence or intimidation, such as peer sexual harassment. The biggest part of the problem may be a matter of implicit acceptance of such behavior by students, teachers, and parents, or perceived helplessness to do anything about it.

SCHOOL SOCIAL WORK APPROACHES TO PEER SEXUAL HARASSMENT

Building on the determination of the school community that it be a safe place for vulnerable young people, the school first of all needs to develop policies that recognize the problem and put the resources of the school behind the effort to create a safe environment. School social workers can then find a variety of roles for themselves within this broader commitment of the school. These roles could be divided into (a) contributions to school policy development, (b) development of grievance and mediation procedures, (c) consultation with teachers and administrators, (d) work with groups in school and in the community, and (e) work with victims and perpetrators of interpersonal violence.

Although schools want to offer support to students affected by peer sexual harassment, dealing with this issue solely from a victim-perpetrator perspective complicates the situation enormously. A more direct course is for social workers to work closely with teachers and to support immediate intervention when they observe harassing behaviors occurring between students. One of the main complaints from students experiencing sexual harassment is that it occurs in front of school personnel who do nothing to stop it (AAUW, 1993; Stein et al., 1993; PCSW, 1995). Teachers may hesitate to intervene unless they are sure that consequences for the behavior are in place and will be enforced.

The first direction for the social worker is in the development of school policies. As a normative community the school's effectiveness rests on recognizing problems of serious interpersonal violence and preventing them from taking over the school normative climate and damaging students. To be successful the school needs to develop and carry out clear expectations. Rather than approaching this from a negative perspective, the school must affirm that a basic principle underlying membership in the school community is that persons respect each other, their rights, and their dignity. Persons, including pupils, who do not respect others can lose membership in this community. They may only return when there is assurance that they will not endanger the safety of others. This principle, now applied to guns, can be applied to other acts that endanger others and undermine education. The social worker, who is often the member of the school community most aware of interpersonal violence and its effects, can consult and assist in the development and implementation of school policies. School social workers can provide consultation to administrators and to the board of education on the development of such policies. Policy issues involve possible levels and types of removal from the educational environment. Perpetrators need to demonstrate their readiness to return without creating further danger in the environment. Teachers need the support of policy, as do social workers. No further approach to these problems is possible without explicit policies.

Identifying and setting consequences for interpersonal violence will create the need for grievance and mediation procedures. Mediation procedures reinforce norms that apply to everyone. They avoid making faculty alone responsible for norm development. They are crucial for a whole-school approach to the development of "civility." School social workers currently are developing mediation programs to enable a return to a respectful "civil" environment. By implication these programs reinforce norms of respect for others. The school social worker's role in the development of these are described in chapters 26 and 27. Assisting teachers in situations of interpersonal violence in class, gym, and hallway situations will demand a more developed consultative role, together with some possible group facilitation of teachers' problem-solving efforts.

In another approach social workers can encourage students to move away from their role as "participant-observer" when they see sexual harassment occurring. Students need to band together and call their peers on sexual harassment. Civil rights attorney Catherine McKinnon (1979) noted of sexual harassment victims, "The un-named should not be taken for the non-existent." Students and teachers should be encouraged to name this behavior and not accept it as "normal adolescent behavior."

Social workers can work with students individually or in groups. They may work with victims to help them deal with their loss of self-efficacy and allay the certain damage. Such victims may need help to restore their normal, but damaged, assertiveness and feelings about their gender and emergent sexuality. Social workers may work with perpetrators to help them return to a civil and respectful environment. Social workers may deal with groups to help the group feel safe again, or may help teachers to do this.

For most adolescents, the high school experience is critical to their personal development and readiness to become part of the adult world. Peer sexual harassment interferes with and inhibits this important developmental process. Social workers who are able to clearly identify the problems associated with peer sexual harassment strengthen their positions as advocates for improved school environments. Hostile school environments are a serious social problem with negative mental health and legal ramifications. In the past, sexual harassment was generally viewed as just "teasing" or "good natured fun." This "typical adolescent behavior" needs to be reframed as behavior that hurts both males and females in the education setting and reinforces discrimination against women in society at large.

REFERENCES

American Association of University Women Educational Foundation. 1992. *How schools shortchange girls.* Washington, DC: Wellesley College Center for Research on Women.

American Association of University Women Educational Foundation. 1993. *Hostile hallways: The AAUW survey on sexual harassment in America's schools* (Research Report No. 923012). Washington, DC: Harris/Scholastic Research.

Barone, F. J. 1997. Bullying in school: It doesn't have to happen. *Kappan* 79(1):80–82.

Bergman, L. 1992. Dating violence among high school students. *Social Work* 37: 21–27.

Brendtro, L., and Long, N. 1995. Breaking the cycle of conflict. *Educational Leadership*, February, pp. 52–56.

The Civil Rights Act of 1964, 42 U.S.C.

The Civil Rights Act of 1964, Title VII, 42 U.S.C. 2000e-2(a).

DeKeseredy, W. S., and Schwartz, M. 1994. Locating a history of some Canadian woman abuse in elementary and high school dating relationships. *Humanity and Society* 18:49–63.

Dziech, B. W., and Weiner, L. 1990. *The lecherous professor: Sexual harassment on campus (2nd ed.).* Urbana, IL: University of Illinois Press.

Fineran, S., and Bennett, L. 1995. Peer sexual harassment. Paper presented at the Fourth International Family Violence Research Conference, University of New Hampshire, Durham, NH, July.

Fineran, S., and Bennett, L. 1998. *Social work practice implications of peer sexual harassment between same-sex teens.* Presentation at the International Conference on Research for Social Work Practice, Miami, Florida, January.

Finn, C. E., Jr. 1984. Toward strategic independence: Nine commandments for enhancing school effectiveness. *Kappan* 65(8):513–524.

Fitzgerald, L. F., Shullman, S., Baily, N., Richards, M., Swecker, J., Gold, Y., Oremerod, A. J., and Weitzman, L. 1988. The incidence and dimensions of sexual harassment in academia and the workplace. *Journal of Vocational Behavior* 32: 152–175.

Fukuyama, F. 1995. *Trust: The social virtues and the creation of prosperity.* NY: Free Press.

Goldsmith, A. H. 1982. Codes of discipline: Developments, dimensions, directions. *Education and Urban Society* (pp. 185–298). ERIC Document No. RJ 260 932).

Goldstein, A. P. 1985. *The EQUIP program: Teaching youth to think and act responsibly through a peer-helping approach.* Champaign, IL: Research Press.

Goldstein, A. P. 1988. *The prepare curriculum.* Champaign, IL: Research Press.

Greenbaum, S. 1987. What can we do about school yard bullying? *Principal.* November, pp. 21–24.

Greenbaum, S. 1989. *Set straight on bullies.* Malibu, CA: National School Safety Center.

Gutek, B. A. 1985. *Sex and the workplace.* San Francisco: Jossey-Bass.

Kauffman, J. M., and Burback, H. J. 1997. On creating a climate of classroom civility. *Kappan* 79(4):320–325.

Kikawa, M. 1987. Teachers opinions and treatments for bully/victim problems among students in junior and senior high schools: Result of a fact-finding survey. *Journal of Human Development* 23.

Kyle, R. (ed.). 1985. *Reaching for excellence: An effective schools sourcebook.* Washington, DC: U.S. Government Printing Office.

Langelan, M. J. 1993. *Back off.* NY: Simon and Schuster.

Lee, V. E., Croninger, R. G., Linn, E., and Chen, X. 1996. The culture of sexual harassment in secondary schools. *American Education Research Journal* 33(2): 383–417.

MacKinnon, C. A. 1979. *Sexual harassment of working women.* New Haven, CT: Yale University Press.

Mellor, A. 1990. *Bullying in Scottish secondary schools.* Edinburgh: Scottish Education Department.

Metha, A., and Nigg, J. 1983. Sexual harassment on campus: An institutional response. *Journal of the National Association for Women Deans, Administrators and Counselors* 46:9–15.

Molidor, C. E. 1995. Gender differences of psychological abuse in high school dating. *Child & Adolescent Social Work Journal* 12:119–134.

O'Gorman, J., and Sandler, B. R. 1988. *Peer harassment: Hassles for women on campus.* Project on the Status and Education of Women. Association of American Colleges, Washington, DC.

O'Keefe, N. K., Brockopp, K., and Chew, E. 1986. Teen dating violence. *Social Work* 31:465–468.

Oncale v. Sundowner Offshore Services, Inc., No. 96-568, 1998 WL 88039 (U.S., March 4, 1998).

Permanent Commission (CT) on the Status of Women. 1995. *In our own backyard: Sexual harassment in Connecticut's public high schools.* Hartford, CT: Author.

Pharr, S. 1988. *Homophobia: A weapon of sexism.* Inverness, CA: Chardon.

Pryor, J. B., La Vite, C. M., and Stoller, L. M. 1993. A social psychological analysis of sexual harassment: The person/situation interaction. *Journal of Vocational Behavior* 42:68–83.

Purkey, S. C., and Smith, M. S. 1983. Effective schools, A review. *Elementary School Journal* 83(4):427–452.

Shakeshaft, C., Barber, E. Hergenrother, M. A., Johnson, Y. M., Mandel, L., and Sawyer, J. 1995. Peer harassment in schools. *Journal for a Just and Caring Education* 1(1):30–44.

Stein, N. 1995. Sexual harassment in K–12 schools: The public performance of gendered violence. *Harvard Educational Review* 65(2):145–162.

Stein, N. 1996. *Bullyproof*. Wellesley, MA: Wellesley College Center for Research on Women.

Stein, N. Marshall, N. L., and Tropp, L. R. 1993. *Secrets in public: Sexual harassment in our schools*. Wellesley, MA: Wellesley College Center for Research on Women.

Stein, N., and Sjostrom, L. 1994. *Flirting or hurting? A teachers guide on student to student sexual harassment in schools*. Washington, DC: National Education Association.

Sprick, R., Sprick, M., and Garrison, M. 1992. *Establishing positive discipline policies*. Longmont, CO: Sopris West.

Strauss, S., and Espeland, P. 1992. *Sexual harassment and teens*. Minneapolis: Free Spirit.

Sutter, R. C. 1995. Standing up to violence. *Kappan*, January, pp. K1–K12.

Title IX. Education Amendments of 1972. *Federal Register, Part II Department of Education* 45:30955–30965.

U.S. Equal Employment Opportunity Commission. 1980. Guidelines on discrimination because of sex. *Federal Register* 45:74676–74677.

U.S. Merit Systems Protection Board. 1981. *Sexual harassment of federal workers: Is it a problem?* Washington, DC: U.S. Government Printing Office.

U.S. Merit Systems Protection Board. 1987. *Sexual harassment of federal workers: An update*. Washington, DC: U.S. Government Printing Office.

U.S. v. Virginia et al., 116 S. Ct. 2264, 135L. Ed.2d 73 (1996).

CHAPTER 30

New Tasks and Old in Resource Development

Richard S. Kordesh
Visiting Lecturer in Community Development and Family Policy,
Jane Addams College of Social Work, University of Illinois at Chicago

Robert Constable
Professor Emeritus, Loyola University of Chicago

- The Continuing Challenges in Resource Development
- School-Community Relations
- Interagency Agreements
- Case Management
- The Transagency Team in the Schools
- Emerging Roles in Resource Coordination
- Wraparound Services
- School-Based Family Empowerment as Community Resource Development
- Possible Future Scenarios for Social Workers as Resource Developers

Given his or her unique relationship to the central institutions in a child's social ecology—the family and the school—the school social worker often plays the role of resource developer. This has been true since the New York Public Schools began school social work by hiring settlement house staff to work with vulnerable children. Now, with greater awareness of children's vulnerability, with the increased fragility of the child's ecology in a postindustrial society, and with the broadening scope of schools, resource development has become an even more critical task. As Chapter 6 related, this new school-based institution building has been prompted in part by reform movements taking place in education and in human services. Yet the new developments are the bearers of some familiar traditions. However innovative the reforms might be, they also constitute conscious efforts on the part of their framers to renew principles reflective of traditional social work practice. Thus resource development and coordination for school social workers remain a continuing domain of practice, even as they signal an emerging set of opportunities.

THE CONTINUING CHALLENGES IN RESOURCE DEVELOPMENT

From the very beginnings of practice school social workers had to find resources, get clients connected with them, make sure they were providing appropriate services, work out difficulties between different service providers, and develop new services or fight for their accessiblity. The more severe the disability or the gap between home and school, the greater the need for complex and individually constructed supportive resource systems. This component of practice has always been understood by school social workers. The movement to include more severely disabled youngsters in public education has created an even greater need for professionals who can develop these support systems. The current mandate of the school for provision of special education and related services creates a situation in which the school is an even more important part of the network of services for children with disabilities. The schools are only now beginning to address the implications of their centrality in services for children with disabilities. There is an opportunity now for the school social worker to reaffirm an historic commitment and to develop a long-standing skill.

There are a number of long-standing reasons for the importance of resource development and coordination of services for school social workers. The service delivery system is segmented, divided by special functions within health care, child welfare, vocational rehabilitation, educational systems, mental health, and so on, in a seemingly unlimited array of services, each with a particular function, mission, and rationale for helping. Although family and school both have concerns that transcend the segmentation—with the whole child and his or her environment—both have natural roles in addressing the difficulty in accessing services for vulnerable children. The more vulnerable the child, the greater the need to coordinate services from different service providers and the greater the potential damage if something goes wrong. The more services involved, the greater the likelihood that something will go wrong, and thus the greater the need for a problem-solving professional to address the configuration and delivery of services. The school is central to the child, and the school social worker is directly in the middle as the person most likely to coordinate services and provide case management services.

Resource development and coordination of services is recognized as crucial in working with diverse populations with profound and ongoing needs: the elderly, the physically disabled, the developmentally disabled, the chronically mentally ill, children experiencing neglect or abuse, and so on. Each area has developed a literature of its own in the areas of integration of services, coordination of services, and case management. In the schools there have been particular concerns for young children with severe disabilities and older disabled youngsters nearing transition from the world of the schools into the world of work. With both populations, some case management is mandated, but with neither of these populations can effective service be provided without the larger structure of interagency agreements and the smaller structures of case management that appropriately involve the family as well as resource persons in individual case plans.

The initial and continuing development of the NASW *Standards for Social Work Services in the Schools* (1978) and its subsequent review by school social work practitioners throughout the country confirmed this historical continuity of role. The essential skills of the school social worker include implementing referrals to resources in the community, collaborating with agencies to solve specific problem situations, and developing new resources for pupils and their parents. A taxonomy of tasks for social work services in schools was divided into three areas—services to pupil and parents, work with school personnel, and school community relations. Because they are directly relevant to resource development and coordination, the list of school-community relations tasks are worth reviewing in their entirety. The standards were most recently updated in 1992.

SCHOOL-COMMUNITY RELATIONS

Remedial

Identify children or target groups of children needing alternative educational planning or programs and support services.

Consult and collaborate with community representatives to identify effects of interacting school, community, and pupil characteristics and develop resources to meet needs of child or target group.

Collaborate with community agencies in the development of alternative education programs and support services.

Clarify and interpret specific roles and responsibilities of the community in promoting school attendance.

Set objectives, monitor progress, and measure outcomes of service.

Crisis Resolution

Collaborate in community planning for crisis intervention services—drugs, rape, abuse and neglect, suicide, runaways, family violence, and so forth.

Set objectives, monitor progress, and measure outcomes of service.

Developmental

Aid in identification of child or target group of children needing preventive social services.

Aid in development of preventive social services to meet needs of child or target group.

Aid in collaborative planning to provide full range of services to target group.

Set objectives, monitor progress, and measure outcomes of service.

Resource development and coordination of service is clearly a part of the school social worker's function for several very practical reasons. First of all, the school and family often cannot really accomplish their own functions without specialized help from other agencies. These agencies might provide health services, counseling services, concrete assistance, respite care, summer camp, or other services necessary in modern society. School pupils may be involved with other systems in our society that have deeper claims on them, such as the juvenile justice system or the child welfare system.

INTERAGENCY AGREEMENTS

As schools have become more central to service provision to severely disabled children of all ages, but particularly the very young and those transitioning into the world of work, the demand for case management is accompanied by the need for interagency collaboration. Schools only gradually are seeing themselves, not as a world of their own, but as members of a larger community of services. They are not accustomed to thinking of themselves in terms of interagency coordination, although efficiency of service provision and indeed the effectiveness of any case management attempts will demand agreements reached beforehand among various agencies serving particular populations. Some of these agencies are large public agencies with complicated structures, and some are small grass-roots operations. LaCour (1982) cites some of the difficulties in developing agreements:

- Lack of clarity on "first dollar" responsibility,
- Lack of coordination of agencies' priorities,
- Lack of coordination between state and local agencies,
- Failure to coordinate budgets with service mandates,
- Inconsistent service standards, and
- Conflicting views of constraints on confidentiality of information.

He suggests that efforts to overcome these barriers be based first of all on an understanding of pertinent law and regulations. With this understanding the social worker needs to develop a network of informal connections to the leadership of the involved agencies. This task may not be so formidable when the school social worker is well connected with people in the school district administration, who often are in contact with their counterparts in the involved agencies. In addition, the social worker's parallel relation with these agencies at the direct practice level also affords entry into the organization and an understanding of how the service is working in specific cases. The social worker needs to know how the agency is working from the inside. This knowledge allows the social worker to identify the resources to be exchanged and point out the benefits of a resource exchange to the participating agencies. Building on reciprocity, an agreement can then be drafted.

A good interagency agreement needs to be written in simple and clear language. It should contain sections that (a) describe the reason for writing the agreement, (b) identify the responsibilities of each agency and the method for performing those responsibilities, (c) identify the standards each agency must meet when performing an activity, (d) describe the process of exchanging information on common clients, and (e) describe the method for modifying the agreement. The agreement should be flexible, focusing on the desired outcome rather than on the process of getting there. It should not jeopardize an agency's funding or turf. Instead, the agreement should seek to clarify these issues. Finally, and obviously, the mutual benefit should be evident, enhancing the opportunity for future agreement as well as the full implementation of the current agreement (LaCour, 1982).

The paradox of service provision is that the more severe the need, the more difficult and complex the access. Children and parents often have multiple, complex involvements with these systems. When these systems provide resources at all, access is difficult and complicated and is accompanied by multiple and conflicting behavioral demands of the potential clientele. The more generally vulnerable the pupil, particularly the handicapped pupil, the greater the needs for external services, the greater the difficulty in getting these services, and, finally, the greater the likelihood of family breakdown in the face of these difficulties. Often parents are not even aware of what systems exist. Any commitment to vulnerable children places the school in the difficult and unwanted position of having to interact with community agencies in complex planning efforts. Educators generally are unprepared for this task. The school social worker is frequently the only member of the school team whose orientation and general skill development does include interaction with community agencies, and so any coordination, if it is done at all, is and should be done by the school social worker. The social worker's investment of time in informing parents, removing barriers to service obtainment, and helping parents utilize services has a high payoff in the child's adjustment to a learning situation.

Resource development and coordination is particularly important for the child with disabilities. These children often have difficulty and special needs in coping with other areas of their environment as well as school. The family's attempts to support the youngster and compensate for gaps in socialization and capability places it under pressure, particularly where the family is already under strain. Family units such as the single-parent household or the household where both parents work are particularly vulnerable. Whatever takes place in the family inevitably will affect what the pupil is able to do in school, and so it is artificial to draw a sharp boundary between what is educational and what is noneducational. The law has recognized to a degree the legitimacy and necessity of services that will help the child with disabilities benefit from special education. Recent court interpretations around related services reveal a similar difficulty in distinguishing between educational and noneducational services. Related services are defined as services that are required to assist a child with disabilities to benefit from special education. Furthermore, the law, in firmly placing the responsibility for free appropriate public education of the child on the school, also places the school in the position of having to support more expensive and more restrictive alternatives for placement of the child with disabilities if the network of family, informal support systems, and formal community resources breaks down. The need for coordination and service integration is dictated by the belief that it is better that children with disabilities remain with their families, and by simple economics, which makes remaining at home a less expensive educational alternative. Given the scarcity of regular and special education resources within school districts, the school faces the complex problem of bringing children and educational resources together in an appropriate environment and maintaining a support system.

Resources in the community can be divided into two groups: (a) services available from formally constituted organizations, often purchased by either family or school, and, if not purchased, subject to complex eligibility determinations for entitlement, and (b) informal, helping networks of neighbors, community people, relatives, members of church and civic groups, local merchants, and other schoolchildren who may be willing and able to help in a variety of ways.

It would be unrealistic to assume that formal organizations by themselves will be able to meet the complex needs of children with disabilities and their families. The social worker may locate and help the family communicate with a variety of informal, helping networks that may exist in a community. Possible uses of such networks are almost limitless. The social worker will often maintain an ongoing consultative relationship with some network members so that they do not become disappointed or confused at the initial response of the child with disabilities or his or her family. The authors have used volunteers, police officers, and a wide variety of other persons in many ways to provide structure, an element of caring, and vitally needed help for the handicapped child and his or her family.

New structures for collaboration are needed among public and private agencies having resources for handicapped children, with particular focus on the family of the disabled. A mixture of hard services (programs and tangible resources) and soft services (counseling, access to psychological support, and information), which help people to deal with stress, is needed. Traditional services for children with disabilities have been quite segmented and competitive, with different agencies dealing with different aspects of the disabled child's needs. Continuing this segmented system or dumping the responsibility on the school would be grossly dysfunctional.

Because a variety of resources are being brought to bear on an individual child, the management problem is also quite different from the traditional model of educational administration, involving a building, an administrative hierarchy, a faculty, a group of pupils, equipment more or less in one place, and transportation primarily from home to school. With the decentralization of specialized personnel and equipment, the logistical problems faced by the school district or intermediate unit are complex. Proper utilization of resources both in and outside of school demands that the services be coordinated over a large area, that the services be integrated according to the needs of each child, and that there be accountability to assure that the services promised in the Individualized Education Program actually are delivered.

In Illinois the assumption of increased responsibility by the schools in the wake of P.L. 105-17 seems to have led to a lessening of responsibility for these children by other state agencies, if there is a possibility of school support for these services. The response of the state education agency to this increased burden has been to develop a mandate for collaborative planning among agencies, each taking responsibility for its own area of service. Necessary services are in theory available at no cost to the parents. Such a directive from the state level is necessary to conserve resources and to prevent unnecessary movement of children to more restrictive placements. It could not be implemented in the absence of structures on the local and regional level that develop the necessary interagency agreements. On the other hand, such fragile networks of agency agreements are not workable without state support.

For these networks to be viable, they have to include a commitment on the state level, a means of communication, and development of network agreements on the local or regional level, as well as practitioners equipped to implement and coordinate service agreements on the direct practice level.

The movement to services based on legal entitlement has taken place, not only in the schools, but in most other agencies serving children with disabilities. In order to cope with the implications of this entitlement, laws have prescribed or agencies have developed case management approaches to the widened range of available services. These case management approaches have become instruments of compliance and management tools for assuring that clients are getting what they are entitled to and have the opportunity to be active, rather than passive, consumers of services. The approaches to case management are fairly similar. Each involves an individu-

TABLE 1   Seven Case Management Approaches

Case Management Approach	Entitling Legislation or Framework
The Individualized Habilitation Plan	P.L. 94–103, for developmentally disabled
The Individualized Education Program	P.L. 105–17 for all children with disabilities
Individualized Written Rehabilitation Program	Rehabilitation Act of 1973
Individualized Service Plan	Title XVI for children with disabilities eligible for social security income
Individualized Care Plan	For Title XIX Medicaid
Individualized Program Plan	Mandated by Joint Committee on Accreditation of Hospitals
Individualized Program Plan	Title XX, purchase of service

alized plan founded on a data-based assessment of needs. They are driven by specific objectives to be attained, placed in a time frame with a date for specific initiation and duration of services, and given expectations for evaluation and review and participation in setting objectives and deciding on appropriate resources. Table 1 illustrates six major case management approaches coming out of different enabling legislation or frameworks.

It is ironic that these case management approaches continue to segment services now under the grandiose label of a "plan." Although such plans are worthwhile instruments for assuring appropriate service delivery, the next step would be to develop a *single* individualized plan that brings together all of the services needed by the client, with one focal case coordinator from one agency who would ensure the client's access to other services. Such an approach would need support at higher policy-making levels than any one agency could provide and on the other hand would need to be closely related to the needs of the family. It should come out of a coordinating structure that is not attached to any one agency. Schools and school services would have to play a major role in the development of any service network addressed to families and children.

CASE MANAGEMENT

Case management is a commonly accepted approach in social work to the delivery of service to populations having ongoing or fairly complex needs, necessitating that different services work together. It is an approach that requires considerable skill, because the social worker is working simultaneously with pupil, parent, teacher, school, and a network of agencies. Indeed, from a systems perspective the combination of small changes in each sector often makes broader changes that no one sector—pupil, parent, teacher, school, or network—could ever accomplish on its own. Case management tasks described in the literature (Garland, Woodruff, and Buck, 1988; Compher, 1984, Kurtz, Bagarozzi, and Pullane, 1984; Eriksen, 1981; Austin, 1983; Frankel and Gelman, 1998) include the following:

1. Assessing client needs,
2. Developing service plans,
3. Coordinating service delivery,
4. Monitoring service delivery,
5. Evaluating services, and
6. Advocating on behalf of the needs and rights of the client(s).

In order to complete each step, the case manager needs to move beyond the confines of his or her agency or discipline. To coordinate the diverse segments of a service delivery system, the social worker needs to reach beyond the confines of agency and discipline and include other services with full respect for the differences they offer the totality. Two models of teamwork have emerged to meet the demands of case management: the transdisciplinary team and the transagency team.

Typically the *transdisciplinary team*, composed of the family and professionals from a variety of disciplines, collaborates in assessment and program planning. One individual, chosen from among the team members, works in consultation with colleague specialists to carry out the individualized plan. Together with the family, the case manager integrates the information and skills of the entire team to work with the child and family on goals established, to ensure coordination and communication among providers, and to monitor services to make sure that services planned are actually provided. In the transdisciplinary model the case manager typically is both the primary provider and the service coordinator.

The *transagency team* provides an alternative structure for case management, bringing together not only the many disciplines working with a single agency but also a variety of agency representatives to assess needs and plan services. These are models in which the transagency team is created specifically for the purpose of a particular population, and the agencies represented on the team are determined by the nature of the program (Garland, et al., 1988).

THE TRANSAGENCY TEAM IN THE SCHOOLS

Schools offer a natural setting for the coordination of services among agencies. Schools are the central public institution dealing with the normal needs of children, and schools are now central to children with disabilities and crucial to the development of mental health services. The transagency approach to services within school walls is a useful starting point for the development of more comprehensive models of service coordination and provision for children and families with complex needs.

We developed such a structure in the Chicago south suburban area. The area is heterogeneous, with patches of severe poverty mixed with blue-collar and middle-class suburbia. There are large populations of black and Hispanic minorities and white ethnics of Eastern or Southern European background. The area has experienced considerable development over the past twenty years, development that had outstripped the capacities of the traditional service resources and provided the opportunity for a fairly innovative type of planning effort. An independent committee was established, composed of the major public and private agencies that are resources to families of children with disabilities. The committee has been given the neutral name of Regional Community Integration Resource Committee (RCIRC).

The RCIRC reaches agreements on individualized service plans and provides a means of communication around resource issues affecting children with disabilities. A major focus of the committee is to develop agreements on individualized service plans for particular situations of need. With participation of the client, family, or informal resource network, one particular agency is designated the focal agency and a particular worker from that agency develops an agreement with the family about their overall goals and what resources they need to reach them. This agreement involves the client system, any appropriate informal support systems, and the committee. The social worker from the focal agency who works with the client, family, or informal support system needs to be sufficiently skilled to:

Help the client and family define the problem, some resultant goals, and what resources, services, and supports are needed;

Define with the family the supportive network available to the client;

Involve the client, family, or informal resource network in decision making by working with them individually, coordinating with other sectors, and bringing them together when they are ready to come to an agreement;

Identify formal resources needed, maintain a steady communication with the formal resource systems in the network, and do problem solving with these systems as questions arise;

Help the client or family and members of the informal resource network relate to the formal agency resources as collaborators, without a feeling of loss of dignity or control and with the assumption that agency actions must be related to client need;

Help client use the situation of receiving service to identify his or her own aspirations for change and to embark on a change process when his or her own aspirations or need to adapt to realities in the environment make evident a need for change in his or her attitudes or accustomed ways of relating to others.

In providing means of communication around issues of service development and planning among agencies working with a particular clientele, the RCIRC focuses on gaps in services, situations where the client is at high risk, has needs involving a number of agencies, and requires coordination of services. It cannot represent any one agency if it were to carry out its function.

The social worker is the crucial link between planning processes. There is a duality in the social worker's role: the social worker has, on the one hand, a close relationship with an individual client and his or her family or informal support system and, on the other hand, a working relationship with formal agency resources through the RCIRC. Members of the RCIRC generally do not have direct service responsibilities. They are to be far enough up the agency hierarchy to deal with potential resource commitments and close enough to practice and service delivery to communicate with the direct service level of the agency. Examples of these coordination arrangements can be given:

Doris is an eighteen-year-old, severely disturbed adolescent whose reactivity to a symbiotic conflict with her mother and resultant self-destructive behavior has led to several hospitalizations. The school had found itself reacting to the behavior and programming for Doris rather than getting the mother and daughter into contact with help. Mother and daughter have now begun with a social worker in private practice. The school will now bring Doris into a one-hour-per-day class in ceramics with only the instructor present. If this can be established without incident, Doris will be involved with a pet zoo run by another agency. Because the situation between mother and daughter is potentially explosive, a shelter arrangement with a relative to be used in a crisis will be worked out. This would keep Doris in the community as long as possible. If the social worker is able to make further gains with the mother and Doris' school adjustment stabilizes, the next step to develop a program with the Illinois Department of Vocational Rehabilitation. The state agency is involved in the plan and will give special consideration to Doris' needs.

Michael is a twenty-one-year-old severe and barely stabilized diabetic, legally blind, who lives in a nursing home because his single, working parent was unable to care for him. He is about to graduate from his special education program because of his age. A plan is developed in the RCIRC to make it possible for him to return home through utilization of public assistance, Medicaid, and homemaker and home health care services. Some further medical assessment is planned, and based on this assessment, some vocational assessment would be done. The social worker from the school will work with Michael and his mother, coordinating with other agencies, with the goal of passing on case management responsiblities to another agency when the two have solidified their own direction and connections with other services.

Although such cases present complex need, they are not particularly unusual. In both cases a combination of resources could prevent institutionalization or make movement from an institutionalized setting possible. Furthermore, none of the hard service provision, no matter how flexible, could have been effective or even possible without the soft services to parent and child that helped them deal with the situation and link their processes and needs with programs and resources. To make complex plans for families without their choice, involvement, and participation, indeed not to make the individual-in-family-unit the center of the decision process, is to court disaster and set up an unproductive struggle around power and control.

EMERGING ROLES IN RESOURCE COORDINATION

Issues about power and control have surfaced repeatedly in the broader policy reforms that are now changing the school environment for social services. Indeed, the power of the school social worker is shifting as the new reforms come into play in many school settings. New roles in resource coordination are emerging. School social workers will face important choices in constructing their own roles in this changing context.

WRAPAROUND SERVICES

"Wraparound" planning has become part of the new lexicon of human service reform. In general, the term refers to the involvement of multiple formal and informal resources in all phases of service delivery to particular clients. Often these clients, if not served by a more complex network of family, community, and social services, would face institutionalization (or are returning into the community from institutional settings). Wraparound planning is a process that takes the interagency professional team another step toward comprehensiveness by involving, when necessary, family members, friends, neighbors, pastors, or other significant persons in a client's life in problem definition, goal setting, implementation and evaluation of services, and relating these informal resources to the formal social agency and school systems. It also stresses the importance of involving the client as part of the deliberation and "treatment" team. These emphases on comprehensiveness, the integration of formal and informal resources, and client empowerment all reflect the policy reforms discussed in chapter 7.

To some school social workers, the components that define wraparound planning might not sound so new. In essence the components do affirm many of the principles espoused in traditional, generalist models of social work practice. Indeed, many proponents of wraparound and the broader reforms in which wraparound is nested recognize this legacy in classical social work. Wraparound planning is rather a response to the growing awareness of the need for community alternatives to institutionalization as well as a recognition of the continuing work, despite obstacles from community and school fragmentation, toward developing comprehensive, family-centered, ecologically based practice for vulnerable people in the community. Obstacles include policy fragmentation, overspecialization in treatment, services that neglect the family context, and a growing disassociation of clinical practice from community practice.

Eber, Nelson, and Miles (1997) describe the uniqueness of the wraparound approach as it is utilized in a school-based setting for students with emotional and behavioral challenges:

> An important characteristic separating wraparound plans from other types of student plans is that they are driven by needs rather than by the parameters of programs currently available. In contrast to the traditional practice of evaluating student needs on the basis of available educational placements, existing program components and services are analyzed and employed according to their usefulness in meeting student needs. Services are not based on a categorical model (i.e., services are embedded in a program in which "eligible" students are placed), but are embedded or created on the basis of specific needs of the student, family, and teacher. The child and family team consists of persons who know the student best, and who can provide active support to the student, his or her teacher and family. Extended family members, neighbors, family friends, and mentors also are frequently participants in child and family teams (pp. 547–549).

Eber illustrates wraparound planning as a process in Table 2. The diverse perspectives recruited into the child and family team ensure that diverse domains of a student's life will be viewed as a whole. Specialists are challenged to open the boundaries of their own vision as well, working collaboratively to formulate strategies to resolve the difficulties students face academically as well as socially.

Wraparound is intrinsically a resource development method. It creates a new avenue for the school social worker to engage in mobilization activities on behalf of children in school. The very commitment by a school to wraparound will usually trigger a more intensive outreach effort to families, friends, kin, and neighbors. Thus resource development activities for the school social worker who participates in, or leads, a wraparound effort will similarly begin with the formation of the child-family team. It will continue through the assessment, planning, and implementation phases as the team identifies additional resources needed to "wrap around" the child, forming new supports for him or her and bolstering the child's chances for school success.

TABLE 2 Community-Based Wraparound Planning Steps

Step	Definition	Purpose
Issue identification	Prior to the team meeting, facilitator contacts key stakeholders, which include, at minimum, the parents, child, and significant others (e.g., agency providers, relatives, community mentors).	• Identifies issues that might affect outcomes of the plan, as well as concrete steps that must be taken immediately. • Identifies strengths of the child, parents, and others to use as a foundation for future planning. • Builds a sense of being listened to and heard by the persons most involved in the child's care. • Prepares facilitator to understand system and personal issues affecting the child's performance. • Develops knowledge of the situation as seen by the persons most involved in the child's care. • Allows the facilitator to understand points of agreement and disagreement between the parents and providers. • Allows the facilitator to develop immediate crisis response, if needed, prior to the first meeting.
Introductions and agenda setting	Facilitator allows participants to identify their roles and relationship to the student and sets expectations for the product to be developed in the meeting.	• Allows meeting participants to understand their relationship to the family. • Sets expectations against which the process can be measured (i.e., building practical support plan that will produce better outcomes for the child). • Begins to build a sense of team as well as communicating to the parents that they do have access to support in their care for the child. • Builds a sense of hope about the capacity for improved outcomes if all team members can agree on areas for improvement.

TABLE 2 Community-Based Wraparound Planning Steps—(Continued)

Step	Definition	Purpose
Strengths presentation	Facilitator presents a summary of family, student, and other participants' strengths as developed from conversations in the issue identification step.	• Begins to build appreciation across meeting participants relative to the family strengths we well as provider capacities. • Identifies strengths as the foundation for strategy and plan development. • Allows persons in attendance to move from the role of meeting participants to team members. • Builds an alliance between the parents and providers in appreciating each other's strengths. • Allows team members to commit to the possibilities of improved outcomes and creates a sense of commitment to the child. • Allows team members to see providers as both assets and as persons in need of support.
Goal setting and needs identification	Facilitator leads team through goal-setting exercise, focusing on present performance levels of a typical child. Information is presented and commented on by team members. When goals have been set, parents and significant others are asked where strategies need to be developed to bring the child's functioning level to the defined "typical" functional level.	• Allows team members to set realistic outcomes that are easily understandable to all team members. • Builds a framework in which team members can pinpoint areas of need as measured against the description of a typical child. • Builds an alliance between parents and providers as they begin to view their similarities in terms of needs statements. • Allows participants to voice expectations and feel "heard" by other team members.

Needs prioritization	Facilitator asks parents and providers to identify needs that must be addressed first. Prioritized needs are limited to no more than five per meeting. Other team members are asked if other areas are seen as needing to be addressed first.	• Allows the team to break the need for interventions into manageable parts. • Creates the expectation that other team members will provide support to the persons most closely involved with the child's daily life. • Solidifies the team's commitment to working together, creating interventions, and building a commitment to improved outcomes. • Strengthens alliance between parents and providers. • Expectations for future planning around other need areas often are set, in order to foster the expectation that when first priority needs are met, others will be added.
Strategy development	Facilitator leads the team through a brainstorming process in which strategies to meet identified needs are developed. Members are asked to be as specific as possible. Suggestions do not focus solely on linking traditional services or settings. The facilitator continually verifies with the parent whether the strategies suggested might be helpful for the child.	• Allows team members to create a plan that is tailored to the needs of the child as well as building team ownership of the action plan. • Sense of ownership is likely to pay off in terms of task completion and follow-through. • Allows team members to identify creative strategies that are tailored to the needs of the child rather than the programs or services currently in place. • Allows the team to specify target behaviors, potential reinforcement strategies, as well as support activities implemented by certain adults involved in the planning.
Securing team member commitments	After needs have been brainstormed and listed on a flip chart, team members are asked to commit to certain strategies.	• Builds a sense of public commitment to specific action steps by team members. • Allows the team to move toward self-management by requiring the facilitator to wait for their commitment. • Gives the team a sense of direction and response in building a student support plan.

TABLE 2 Community-Based Wraparound Planning Steps—(*Continued*)

Step	Definition	Purpose
Follow-up communication	As the plan is formalized, the facilitator identifies a communication plan by which team members can have contact with each other. Team members are encouraged to commit to contact other participants. The facilitator commits to contact stakeholders regarding the child's progress.	• Builds a sense of team functioning that is likely to occur between meetings. • Allows team members to build alliances and communication protocols apart from formal team meetings. • Creates an environment of volunteerism among team members when participants commit based on their ability to follow through rather than on their job descriptions. • Allows parents and other providers to feel supported and that help is nearby.
Process evaluation and closure	Facilitator checks with stakeholders regarding whether the plan developed will be helpful, whether the meeting was productive, and whether participants felt their ideas were heard. A follow-up meeting is scheduled within the next five weeks. Procedures for calling an emergency meeting are identified.	• Allows the team to gain ownership by evaluating the process. • Parents feel supported and heard in the teaming process. • Communicates a sense that help is available regarding day-to-day needs. • Allows the facilitator to set expectations regarding communication and crisis as well as establishing action steps to determining their efficacy.

SCHOOL-BASED FAMILY EMPOWERMENT AS COMMUNITY RESOURCE DEVELOPMENT

While wraparound planning brings the school social worker into resource development, another trend that broadens the school social worker's resource development activities is multifaceted family empowerment projects in schools. As related in chapter 6, one type of project that will vastly increase the potential for school-based family empowerment is the family resource center in the school. Through school-based family resource centers, school social workers will confront many new challenges for mobilization of community assets. These will be assets critical for family support and for bolstering the productive roles families might play in the community.

School-based or school-linked family resource centers have become critical components of community revitalization strategies in impoverished neighborhoods. Although such centers represent innovations in school-based institutions, they are also grounded in classical social work principles. As Dupper and Poertner (1997) put it, "The school-based, family resource center movement is a promising model for improving results for children and families through reshaping the service delivery system in impoverished communities. Although this movement is relatively new, the concept is deeply rooted in social work."

After a national study of exemplary family support programs, the Family Resource Coalition of America (FRCA, 1996) issued guidelines for practice that illustrate how intrinsically important resource development is to empowering families. While phrased to pertain to community-based family support programs in schools and outside of schools, the principles reveal the practical opportunities for working with community assets that will emerge for school social workers. The FRCA's guidelines for practice in condensed form are as follow:

> Guideline A: Program facilitate a sense of belonging and a connection to the community among program participants (Practices include encouraging community participation by families, encouraging positive relationships among diverse cultural groups, ensuring accessiblity of school-based programs.
> Guideline B: Programs identify and develop networks of support in the community that are available to participants. (Practices include identifying support systems for families, helping families get in touch with support systems.)
> Guideline C: Programs respond to community issues and engage families as partners in this process. (Practices include assessing community issues, helping ensure responsiveness of school-based programs to community issues, preparing parents to become effective advocates and leaders, promoting public awareness of community issues that bear on family well-being.)
> Guideline D: Programs work to develop a coordinated response to community needs. (Practices include participating in community-wide planning, facilitating interagency collaborations in the school and community, promoting accountability of school-based programs to families and community, working

to ensure sufficient funding and policy supports exist to support the healthy development of children and families.)

Through family resource centers, school social workers will find more support in reaching the families, neighbors, and agencies who can be helpful in working with their own students. Moreover, it will be possible to engage in more family practice. In addition, new opportunities for empowering families to wield more influence in the school and the community will emerge. Schools will be taking on this broader community focus partly because of the presence of family resource centers in the schools.

POSSIBLE FUTURE SCENARIOS FOR SOCIAL WORKERS AS RESOURCE DEVELOPERS

Whatever the future holds for new school-based services, it certainly will continue to call for the many traditional resource development activities that social workers have conducted. School social workers will continue to serve as facilitators of school-community relations. Such activities will remain as varied as organizing services around particular children, building collaborations with agencies in the school, and monitoring the quality of service. Remedial, crisis-oriented, and preventive methods will endure as well.

Moreover, negotiating, facilitating, drafting, and brokering interagency agreements will remain a resource development task of the school social worker. Fashioning such agreements will at times take place through the function of case management, at other times through participation as a member of an interagency team.

The future is not as certain with respect to social worker roles in the wraparound process. In fact, the future scope of wraparound in the school remains somewhat murky. Two scenarios seem possible for the roles of school social workers in wraparound. One scenario holds the lead role for the school social worker. Leading a wraparound team (or "wrap" team, as it is sometimes called) would engage the social worker in a more diversified, perhaps more strengths-based, model of case management for clients. A second scenario places the social worker into the wraparound as one of the resources on the team. As a member of a wraparound team, the school social worker might take more narrow roles, such as conducting social histories, negotiating referrals, or providing counseling as part of the wraparound's overall plan.

The expanded family support and empowerment programs that will grow in schools will also structure different possible scenarios for the resource development activities of school social workers. At a minimum, one might imagine school social workers conducting case management with some of the families present in the school due to the family resource center. More broadly, one might envisage school social workers helping families form their own empowering associations, which could be either school based or school linked. Family empowerment associations will enable families to deliver more support to one another, exercise stronger roles as coteachers through tutoring and mentoring, and exercise more influence over school governance. In short, many experiments with family-based institutions in schools will take place. Some school social workers will likely lead in their design and formation.

Finally, new scenarios for resource development will also arise as a result of the expanded community-building activities that will take place through schools. One entry point through which school social workers will participate in this trend will be the wraparound process. Or, it might be through an expansion of the interagency brokering roles school social workers have traditionally played. New school-based collaborations around violence prevention or dropout prevention might create leadership vacuums in school settings that school social workers would appropriately fill. The possibilities are not all clear, but it is clear that there will be new roles. These roles will carry forward traditional social work practices in schools into new institution-building initiatives.

REFERENCES

Austin, C. 1983. Case management in long-term care: Options and opportunities. *Health and Social Work* 8(1):16–30.

Compher, J. V. 1984. The case conference revisited: A systems view. *Child Welfare* 63(5):411–418.

Dupper, D., and Poertner, J. 1997. Public schools and the revitalization of impoverished communities: School-linked, family resource centers. *Social Work*, (September): 415–422.

Eber, L., Nelson, M. C., and Miles, P. 1997. School-based wraparound for students with emotional and behavioral challenges. *Exceptional Children* 63(4):539–555.

Eriksen, K. 1981. *Human services today* (2nd ed.). Reston, VA: Reston Publishing.

Family Resource Coalition of America, 1996. *Guidelines for family support practice.* Chicago: Author.

Frankel, A., and Gelman, S. R. 1998. *Case management.* Chicago: Lyceum.

Garland, C., Woodruff, G., and Buck, D. 1988. Case management. Division for Early Childhood White Paper. Reston, VA: Council for Exceptional Children.

Kurtz, L. F., Bagarozzi, D. A., and Pollane, L. P. 1984. Case management in mental health. *Health and Social Work* 9:201–211.

LaCour, J. A. 1982. Interagency agreement: A rational response to an irrational system. *Exceptional Children* 49(3):265–267.

National Association of Social Workers. 1979. *NASW standards for social work services in schools.* NY: Author.

National Association of Social Workers, Education Commission Task Force. 1992. *NASW standards for school social work services.* Washington, DC: Author.

SECTION FOUR
Research and Evaluation

CHAPTER 31

Research and Evaluation of Practice and Services in the Schools

John P. Flynn
Professor Emeritus, Western Michigan University

- Differential Uses of Research and Evaluation
- Influences Demanding Research and Evaluation of Practice and Services
- Four Uses of Research and Evaluation
- Support for Research and Evaluation

We have saved this section on research and evaluation for the end, but in reality, the integration of clinical issues and techniques and service interventions are, of course, inextricably interwoven with research and evaluation. Ideally, the range of professional practice is iterative and circular, with each aspect of practice informing the others. Research undergirds policy and program development, discussed in section II, and practice methods, discussed in section III.

DIFFERENTIAL USES OF RESEARCH AND EVALUATION

Research and evaluation are two distinct approaches that use the scientific method to examine practice and services. Some would say that evaluation is merely a subset of techniques under the more general rubric of research, mainly because the major elements (problem specification, assessment or identification, sampling, data collection and analysis, reporting, and the like) are commonly shared. Perhaps that is so; however, we choose to define our conception as follows: *Research* is used to discover the *state* or *nature* of a particular activity. *Evaluation* is used to determined the *value* of a particular activity. Both employ a disciplined approach suggested. Stated simply, research helps us to determine the size and shape or the present dimensions of a condition; evaluation helps us to determine whether our values lead us to accept or reject that nature or state of whatever we have systematically observed. As in all life, dichotomies and other classification schemes are never perfectly adequate to explain reality. In real life, research and evaluation usually go hand in hand, except when a project is aimed particularly at one or the other research or evaluation objective. It is a matter of what the emphasis is at any moment in time or in any project at hand.

INFLUENCES DEMANDING RESEARCH AND EVALUATION OF PRACTICE AND SERVICES

A number of influences create demand for research on and evaluation of social work practice and services in the schools. First, the age of accountability continues. Stakeholders in America's institutions, education included, demand that the outputs (activities) and outcomes (results) of their investments be made known. The utility and effectiveness of services supported by both private and public resources are constantly questioned. Available resources and automatic patronage continue in short supply. The findings of reputable research and evaluation can, at times, provide credible evidence that satisfies the questions of those who might offer such support.

Second, the mandate of the profession itself is to integrate research and evaluation with the conduct of professional practice. Competition for support means that practitioners must find ways to confirm their credibility and viability. Practice research and program evaluation can substantiate a profession's claims for status and legitimacy; hence, social work as a profession has its own interest in mind (and, by extension, the good of its clientele) when seeking to advance its "scientific" stature. The professional's approach to practice and to research and evaluation have much in common. As noted above, the similarities include specification of problem situations, objective means for assessment or problem identification, sampling of events or people or information, various means of data collection, and techniques for analysis and reporting that objectify the statement of findings and conclusions. Indeed, the practice of social work has now moved from having research and evaluation as ancillary functions of professional practice to using research, evaluation, and sound practice as a triumvirate that guides the fundamental orientation of a responsible professional person. Research and evaluation, once add-ons to practice, are becoming key elements in an amalgamated model of the researcher-practitioner.

A third influence is the ethical mandate embraced by all human services professions to take ongoing responsibility to improve their practice methods and examine the impact of their services. This mandate has to do with a profession's obligation to police itself, not only to guard against malpractice and the errors of its own members but to constantly question and challenge its past and current practices.

A fourth influence comes with the ever increasing problems that different professional disciplines have in communicating with one another and their publics in the modern world. In education, as in all modern institutions, there is a constant tendency toward particularistic and specialized approaches to problem solving. This tendency is evidenced by the presence of elementary-level teachers, secondary-level teachers, special education and regular education teachers, school nurses, psychologists, social workers, occupational therapists, audiologists and speech therapists, and the like and, of course, subspecialties within all of these categories. The methods and techniques of research and evaluation provide a *common language* that facilitates shared dialogue and a *common platform* for the problem-solving tasks shared in the schools.

FOUR USES OF RESEARCH AND EVALUATION

There are at least four pragmatic uses for the methods of research and evaluation in school social work. The first use might be called the *codification of practice*. That is, the methods of research and evaluation are used to identify what social workers do and what works best under what conditions or at what particular times. Research and evaluation validate, through systematic and aggregated examination, what phenomena exist and which phenomena might be meaningfully correlated, even if it is not possible to distinguish antecedent causes, and resultant effects.

A number of task analyses have been conducted over the years pointing out that social work's role in the ecology of schools has changed over time, shifting from a focus on individual children, to targeting at-risk populations, to the provision of program development and consultation as means of providing maximum impact with minimal resources. Now the focus has shifted (perhaps back to the original intent of social work services in schools) to examining the school system's impact on and the relationship with the family and the community. At the present time, the volume of research aimed at codification is increasing rapidly. The codification of practice focuses on the building of a *professional knowledge base*, a repertoire of knowledge and skill, so that the accumulated and verified experiences of professionals can be captured, communicated, and passed on to those now in the field and to those yet to come.

A second use, and very close to the codification of practice, is the *development of guidelines for practice.* This activity might be seen as one step below codification. Guidelines are, as the word implies, *guides to practice* in which practice wisdom not yet subjected to rigorous examination enters the portfolio of "tricks of the trade." More explicit use of research and evaluation then helps the practitioner to begin systematically examining these hunches or intuitive interventions and moving their tests into the category of codification.

A third use of research and evaluation is the *evaluation of progress* or *performance*—measuring an activity and determining how things are going, particularly in relation to how one (or someone) *desires* things to go. That is, this use tends to focus more on *evaluating*, or on what one might prefer. While codifying practice or developing guidelines for practice might emphasize value-free preferences for intervention, this third use explicitly examines what the practitioner or the service might value, or rank-order, or prefer, or desire compared to other possible activities or outcomes of service or practice. This use is more likely associated with program evaluation projects and with studies of service effectiveness.

Finally, a fourth use of research and evaluation is *for their own sake*. Research and evaluation are *in themselves* a method of practice and a method of service. Social workers are generally thought to engage primarily in clinical or interventive modes of professional presence in the schools. They do things with teachers, other school personnel, children, parents, or members of the community in which activity is aimed at intervening for the purpose of change directly with or on behalf of an individual client or group. On the other hand, social workers (like other professionals) can also engage in the methods of research and evaluation as the major emphasis of their role in the schools; however, this orientation of social work practice is rare. The reality is, hopefully, an integration of clinical or interventive practice and research and evaluation practice.

As noted above, we fail when we try to organize thoughts by classification schemes. Divisions of reality are always false, but they do help us to communicate similarities and differences. The differences here are based on the emphasis given to the type of professional activity seen in a particular use of research and evaluation; the similarities are found in the fact that all approaches are aimed at emphasizing what exists and what works. They all seek to improve the ability of practice and services to support the educational process for children and to improve the school's contribution to the life of families and the community.

SUPPORT FOR RESEARCH AND EVALUATION

The field presently faces a dilemma, however. The age of accountability and the presumed return to basics by our sponsors and patrons demand that the schools, social work services included, provide evidence of soundly guided practice and of practice and service effectiveness. Yet, it is rare to see a line item in a school budget for any significant level of funding for research and evaluation of social work services. This dilemma also, then, seemingly presents a contradiction between expectation and support. Given this reality, the creative professional must redefine both the situation and the response.

One approach is to take steps consciously to more fully integrate research and evaluation with everyday practice. School social workers, like other school staff, are now generally overburdened with expectations, increasing caseloads, and broadened territorial responsibility. There is no recourse but to again redefine the nature of practice in the schools. The integrative approach suggested here is not only not radical, it is reasonable and consistent with the direction of the field.

Given the busy nature of today's life for student support personnel in the schools, it is no wonder that the rate of research production on practice outside of the school is greater than the rate of research consumption or utilization within the schools. This imbalance, along with the lack of budgetary or people-power supports and the demand for accountability, suggests that modest, gradual, and targeted integration of practice with research and evaluation is needed. One reasonable strategy is to use single-subject case studies or metaanalysis of completed or existing project or program evaluations having some similarity in sampling or intervention method. School social workers can also define more practical research and evaluation goals. We need not focus on the grand interventions that solve most problems. Instead, we can focus on interventions that show promise of near-term or intermediate payoffs. These interventions can provide timely reality checks on what works and what does not. Another approach is to use data already available within the schools or the community, saving valuable time and obviating the need for additional resources for data collection. Yet another is to address needs currently being expressed by the community that may, in fact, force us to redefine our priorities within the schools— for example, spurring the development of new efforts at the cost of old routines. Some examples might be the need to respond to new levels of teen violence, the relationship (or lack thereof) of the employment community to the school population, or the conflict over inclusive education for the developmentally disabled. A current emphasis is on the need to organically integrate school social services with other community services through the "wraparound" approach, such as jointly pursuing community mental health, public health, and public assistance programs or services for the homeless or with children at risk in multiproblem families.

These possible changes have to do with more than proving the worth of social work practice in the schools. They have to do with sound ethical practice—using research and evaluation to guide and shape what we do and to form a professional style. In so doing, we build a habit of always examining our practice as social work makes its contribution to the education of the whole person-in-environment.

CHAPTER 32

Needs Assessment in a School Setting

Lyndell R. Bleyer
Director, Community Information System, Western Michigan University

Kathryn Joiner
Associate Director, Community Information System,
Western Michigan University

- What Is a Needs Assessment?
- Planning Your Needs Assessment
- Implementing the Assessment
- Analyzing Your Data
- Reporting Your Findings
- Sources for Data and Other Resources

Needs assessment is a crucial skill in school social work. It provides a systematic means of gathering data about a problem experienced by more than one student in the school. It provides a broader context for the problems which students are experiencing in school. It provides a data-based means of communicating about this broader context in a way school administrators, teachers, and community members can understand. It provides school social workers with a powerful, data-based means of custom-tailoring their roles to fit the needs of a particular school or district. In a time when such decisions are becoming increasingly decentralized to the school and to the district, it is clear that the skill of doing needs assessment will become an important component of every school social worker's professional responsibility. This chapter is intended as a jargon-free introduction to needs assessment for school social workers.

WHAT IS A NEEDS ASSESSMENT?

According to a 1975 report funded by the former U.S. Department of Health, Education and Welfare, a human need is any identifiable condition which limits a person as an individual in meeting his or her full potential. Human needs are usually expressed in social, economic or health related terms and are frequently qualitative statements. Needs of individuals may be aggregated to express similar needs in quantified terms (United Way of America, 1982).

Many have attempted to define human need, from *Erikson*'s (1968) eight critical stages of development, to *Maslow*'s (1970) concept of motivation based on a hierarchy of needs. *J. A. Ponsioen* (1962) stated that every society's first duty is to take care of the basic survival needs of its citizens, which include the biological, emotional, social, and spiritual aspects. According to this view, each society must establish a level below which no person must fall. These levels vary from society to society, and change over time within the same society (United Way of America 1982, p. 7). Therefore, "need" is a normative concept involving value judgements, and is greatly influenced by social, political, and economic conditions. The change in political power during the mid-1990s will challenge the standards established during the mid-60s War on Poverty. For example, according to the Center for Budget and Policy Priorities, if the proposed welfare reforms are implemented, more than five million children currently receiving assistance would be ineligible for benefits (Michigan League for Human Services, 1995, p. 1). This will place more responsibility for creative solutions and interventions on our communities and our schools.

A needs assessment is a data gathering and planning activity to inform decision making. The data describe the characteristics, achievements, knowledge, behaviors, desires, needs, and/or opinions of a group of persons or an entire community.

Why Conduct a Needs Assessment?

The data gathered in a needs assessment are used to:

- help understand the nature of a problem; its characteristics, magnitude, or consequences;
- provide clues about causes and possible interventions;
- compare your students with other students or other schools;
- document the need to be included in a problem statement of a grant proposal;
- convince school officials that a problem exists that warrants the allocation of resources;
- demonstrate the need for programs threatened by budget cuts;
- document the support for new programs or interventions;
- provide information to assist with planning or developing new services/programs;
- influence legislation or policy decisions.

A needs assessment can be as simple as examining existing data, or as complex as a multi-year, multi-phase study involving the design of questionnaires to collect new data. Designing and administering surveys is time-consuming and expensive. Explore and use existing data before considering any type of new data generation. Collecting existing data can be very effective and schools generally have a wealth of data on hand.

Types of Data

There are a variety of sources that form the substantive elements of need. Some examples are:

- *Characteristics* describe the group or population being studied and include ascribed characteristics like age, gender, and race, and achieved characteristics like family income, poverty status, highest grade completed, and so forth.

- *Counts and rates* provide data on the incidence and prevalence of conditions. For instance, the teen birthrate is a measure of the number of births to teenage mothers compared to the number of female teenagers, while prevalence is the total number of cases in a given population at a point in time, such as the number of suicides that occurred during a particular period in your community (Simons and Jablonski, 1990, p. 5).

- *Knowledge* might include reading comprehension levels, math proficiency, standardized test scores, or street-smarts, and so on.

- *Beliefs and opinions* range from concepts like self-esteem or knowing right-from-wrong and the value placed on education, to conceptions like believing boys are better at math and science.

- *Behaviors* might include: eating habits, use of alcohol, participation in sports, number of hours worked per week by full time students, absences, number of students suspended or expelled by reason, and so forth. Normative behaviors fall within expected/acceptable ranges.

- *Desires* are what people want (or think they want) but don't have, while *needs* can encompass things missing that are self-perceived or perceived by others. *Needs* might be determined by directly asking the intended audience, observed, or inferred from available data, whereas *desires and opinions* are usually gathered directly from questions on a survey and/or are gathered through observation, interviews, focus groups, or community forums.

PLANNING YOUR NEEDS ASSESSMENT

Determine What You Want to Know

The first step is determining what you want to know, then deciding what information you really need to make an informed decision. The second step is determining the best source, balancing accuracy and reliability against cost and time restraints. Often as you and/or a committee begin to explore doing a needs assessment, the list of questions to be answered keeps growing. To expedite the process, make a checklist and decide which data are critical to your goal, which data would be helpful to clarifying issues, which would be interesting to have, and which will not add any insight to the problem being studied. As part of your checklist, include a source column. This may help you narrow your choices. Remember to look at existing data first before gathering new data.

In the next example, a school district wants to know if a school breakfast program is a worthwhile pursuit. First, they need to know whether or not nutrition makes a difference in school performance, then what percent of the students currently do not eat a nutritious breakfast, what their current performance is, and perhaps, how many children would be eligible for a subsidized breakfast program.

Information which may be useful in planning school services or programs are:

- the number of children living in your community and the percentage that those children represent of the total population;
- how many children live in poverty; how many are homeless;
- how many have disabilities;
- how many live in single-parent families;
- mobility/consistency—what percent of students attend the same school in June that they attended in September;
- reported incidence of crimes by juveniles, violent, serious, and misdemeanor;
- the services and resources already available to meet the specific need you are addressing.

Discuss the project with school administrators, teachers, parent and student representatives to develop a clear idea of the purpose of the needs assessment and what you hope to learn/achieve. One way to encourage cooperation among all the involved parties is to form a small committee to help you formulate an action plan. In addition to promoting ownership of the project, involving others in the planning stage is a good way to make sure you have not overlooked important details. Having the scope of the activity agreed upon by a majority of those involved will reduce hurdles.

Write a Proposal or Plan

After you and/or your committee have determined the scope of the needs assessment, develop a written plan. In the proposal include the following:

TABLE 1   Types of Data or Questions and Associated Sources or Methods

Type of Data or Questions	Source and Method	Essential	Helpful	Interesting	No Use
Breakfast's impact on learning—does it make a difference?	Literature review via: State Dept. of Educ. U.S. depts. of Educ., Health & Human Serv.	✔			
How many of our children eat a nutritious breakfast?	Students and/or parents via log, diary, or question	✔			
What are eligibility guidelines for subsidies?	U.S. Dept. of Health & Human Serv.; census		✔		
How many of our school's children are eligible?	School records: i.e., now eligible for free milk or lunch subsidy; census data on poverty		✔		
Are there any differences in achievement between:	*Grades and test scores plus:*				
Our children who do and don't eat breakfast?	students &/or parents, teacher observation	✔			
Our children from single vs. two parent homes?	school records			✔	
Our children who get <7 vs. >7 hours sleep?	students &/or parents log/diary, teacher observation			✔	
Our children with parental review of homework?	parent signature on homework			✔	

- Methodology of the study.
- Tasks to be performed and by whom.
- Project time-line. Don't set short deadlines. Give yourself enough time to collect data, review it, and produce a well-written summary.
- Develop a budget for the project based on the activities and time needed to carry them out. In addition to personnel, other expenses might included copying of questionnaires and summary reports, computer time, phone, postage, and resource materials.

In writing your needs assessment plan, be realistic about whether or not you and other school staff have the time and the expertise to carry out *all* elements of the project and what level of data fit the time available and the need. Keep in mind the impact school breaks will have on your project. You may have a fairly good grasp of basic research concepts and techniques from your masters level courses. On the other hand it may be that you will want to perform certain tasks, but will need to engage additional help from other professionals to perform certain functions. If there are colleges or universities close by, you may be able to work out a plan for a graduate-level or upper-level undergraduate class to take on all or portions of your study as their semester project. Many colleges and universities have research centers that provide technical assistance and consultation to nonprofit organizations at cost. Large corporations may have research staff that they are willing to "loan" for committee work or consultation. If you intend to carry out the needs assessment yourself, consider whether or not you will need or can get release time.

IMPLEMENTING THE ASSESSMENT

Accurate information is key to successful planning. Having reliable data can help you prove your point and persuade others. Think of the group or groups which will be the beneficiaries of the needs assessment, and also think of the groups that will be potential funding sources or will make the decision to allocate resources to address the need. Gather data with both audiences in mind.

If, for example, you are concerned about the need for enhanced substance abuse prevention education, you could provide a number of statistics regarding substance use and abuse, e.g., the age at which children begin to smoke, use drugs and alcohol; the number of teenagers and young adults who smoke or use alcohol; gender differences in drug usage; changes in use/abuse patterns over time, the number of automobile accidents attributed to substance abuse by age of driver, and so forth. Existing data might be in previously compiled reports or could be gathered by observation. Some data may only be readily available at state or national levels. You may cite the data as found, or you can provide a rough estimation of local incidence by applying state or national rates to local populations.

Gathering *Existing* Data

Be sure to make use of your own organization. Most school districts have data on absences, suspensions, number of students repeating a grade, standardized test scores, student turn-over (migration in and out of school district or building), and immunization records. Also check with the regional or intermediate school district and the state department of education. Local libraries also provide a wealth of data. If materials are not available at your library, the librarian may be able to assist with interlibrary loans, searches of other libraries' catalogs, and computer searches of various databases. This provides access to many federal and state resources.

- Do a literature review or search to find out what other studies or data exist.
- Establish a profile of the student population affected by the problem.
- Determine if there are any programs/services currently in place to meet the need.
- Describe your organizational structure, goals, and objectives.
- List current programs, services, and resources.

Identify sources of existing data (see list at end of chapter for additional information):

Federal—U.S. Census Bureau, Department of Health and Human Services, Department of Education, and other federal agencies.

State—Department of Education, Department of Public Health, state data centers, state human service leagues, special interest/lobby groups, etc.

Local—Public, college and university libraries, police or public safety departments, chambers of commerce, school boards, technical consulting with local universities, computer-based search techniques via such systems as the Internet. Many hospitals maintain medical libraries which may be open to the public.

Other—Children's Defense Fund, Child Welfare League of America, and many non-profit foundations which fund programs and research about children and teens.

Other potential sources of data include: teacher and guidance counselor records, evaluation forms and reports done for accreditation review, and standardized test scores.

Gathering New Data

Exhaust existing sources of data before determining if you need to collect any new data. If you determine that you need additional data that can only be gathered firsthand, several methods are possible including: (1) observation, (2) focus groups, (3) key informant interviews, and (4) use of surveys. Surveys may be used with in-person or phone interviews, or can be distributed by mail, or at meetings or other gatherings.

As an example of data gathered through observation, one measure of cigarette use and/or exposure to second-hand smoke would be to count the number of students entering each homeroom that smell of smoke or have tell-tale nicotine-stained fingers. This measure would be crude, as it depends on the sensitivity and accuracy of the observer. Some might perceive observation as invasion of privacy.

Consider which of the following might be most successful and provide the best results for your specific project:

Focus Groups. These small informal groups, led by a facilitator, gather information from audiences similar to those who would fill out a questionnaire (teachers, students, parents, school administrators). You usually have a script or a short questionnaire to serve as a guide; however, the advantage of a focus group is that people build on the ideas of others (brain-storm, think-tank), and therefore, the group may explore ideas that you or the committee never anticipated.

Key Informant Interviews. Key informants are persons in a position to know or be aware of the problem you are studying. They may include the same people you would invite to a focus group: teachers, administrators, parents, other professionals, and/or students. A questionnaire is used, but the format enables the interviewer to follow-up and clarify responses, as well as explore areas that were not on the original questionnaire. This procedure is best when there are a limited number of issues to be discussed, a limited number of people to interview, and there are interviewers who are well-trained not to be judgmental or to allow their own opinions to influence the outcome.

Using Existing Instruments. If an appropriate instrument or questionnaire already exists and has been tested, it may be the best use of time to obtain permission to use that instrument.

Designing New Survey/Questionnaire Instruments (mail, phone, or in-person interviews and focus group scripts). If you decide to design a new instrument, develop your questions with data analysis and output in mind. Try to make it as easy as possible for respondents to answer. Keep in mind that a large number of open-end questions that require the person to write answers rather than circle answers on a provided list will add considerable time to your data analysis process. Then you will have to categorize and synthesize these responses. However, if you don't want to provide the respondent with answers, an in-person or telephone interview in which the interviewer reads the questions but not the checklist of answers is often a good compromise.

If time permits, pilot-test your questionnaire on a small group (12 to 20 people) to help you anticipate the range of responses for checklists, and to see if some questions are too ambiguous or poorly worded. At the very least, make sure the person analyzing the data looks at the questionnaire from that perspective.

Suggestions for getting the most out of each method. *Focus Groups*—Carefully identify those individuals you want included to be as representative as possible to reduce bias or skewing of results. Schedule in advance. Hold the sessions at a location convenient for those attending. Offer an incentive for attending. Have someone experienced lead the focus group. If possible, tape-record your sessions so you will not have to concentrate on note-taking and have a back-up tape recorder.

Key Informant Interviews—Schedule the interviews in advance and have your questions prepared. Let those being interviewed know how long the interview will take and stick to that time frame.

Mailed Survey—Allow adequate time for the return mail, and if possible, time for follow-up if the initial response rate is low. Including a "business-reply envelope" or stamped self-addressed reply envelope will increase the response rate. This method tends to be the least expensive. However, response rates are lower than other methods unless you offer an incentive or have a hot topic about which people want to express their opinion.

Phone Survey—Try to schedule phone calls at the most likely time to reach your specific population. For example, during the day for stay-at-home moms or retirees, or evenings for working parents. This method tends to be expensive, unless you have volunteers, such as PTA members to make the calls. Phone interviewers must be trained so that questions are asked in a standard format. You will need approximately ten phone numbers for every three surveys you hope to complete assuming that you attempt each phone number at least three times on different days and different times. It takes approximately six nights, with twelve interviewers to complete 300 to 350 four-page questionnaires.

In-person Survey—Use interviewers who are friendly and outgoing. Keep the questions short so those being interviewed do not have to remember long sentences or lists of things. Use 3 by 5-inch cards for answer scales, that can be handed to the person (i.e., 1 = strongly agree, 5 = strongly disagree). Do the surveys at a time when those you want to reach are not rushed. Pick your interview location carefully. For example, if you want to talk to students, a good place might be a quiet room near a study hall or the library. Bad timing for the survey would be during midterm or final exams.

ANALYZING YOUR DATA

Unless your study is funded by a major foundation or a federal or state agency which requires detailed documentation, you may be able to analyze your data by looking at the frequency or prevalence of conditions. How many students come from families with incomes below poverty? Where do they live? Or examine the frequency of opinions, such as, how many parents believe their children are receiving a strong foundation in the three R's. If, however, you need to provide more extensive data analysis, many of today's computerized software packages will provide you with an assortment of statistical measures and tests that are appropriate for various types of data. If you feel your data analysis skills are rusty, consider using a consultant to provide this level of analysis for you. However, it is important for the consultant to review your data collection methodology, including the questionnaire *before* you begin collecting data. Contact local colleges and universities for consultants within educational leadership, social work, statistics, and other disciplines that specialize in research.

Depending on the size of the sample, data can be hand-tabulated (under 50 respondents), or entered into a computer and analyzed by a statistical analysis software package such as SPSS (Statistical Package for Social Sciences), SAS (Statistical Analysis System), or other packages. For small sample sizes (50 to 200 respondents), manually enter the responses in a table or chart and calculate any desired percentages. For larger samples (over 200 respondents), consider using an optical scan form for questionnaire responses. With this method, answer sheets are optically scanned instead of manually input into a computer file. The optical scan format for data gathering and analysis generally saves time and money with large size samples. Customized scan forms which allow the respondent to read the question and make their answer next to each question have the highest degree of accuracy. However, the minimum fee for printing customized forms is often $1,000, making it more cost-efficient for surveys involving 500 or more respondents.

REPORTING YOUR FINDINGS

Reporting findings is a critical element to the success of your needs assessment. Present your results in a manner that is easy to understand. Do not lose sight of the audiences to whom you are presenting. Focus your attention on the specific issue you have studied, and use your data to show that the changes proposed will make a difference. If you want to convince your audience regarding effective programs or services, it is helpful to cite examples of other successful programs or efforts.

Many times lengthy narratives are not the best way to report findings. You may find that a simple summary accompanied by charts, graphs, or tables that show your data in easy-to-interpret formats is the best way to present the results. Table 2 illustrates one method of displaying standardized test scores. The key statistic is the percent of students with satisfactory test scores. School districts evaluate strengths and weaknesses in their curricula by looking at these data over time. Comparing your own school or school district with others in your county or state provides a measure of where your district stands in relation to others.

If, for example, you collected data on the number of children who ate breakfast before coming to school and the data varied widely by grade level, an effective way to display this result might be in a bar chart with each bar representing the number or percent of children in that grade level who

TABLE 2   Michigan Education Assessment Program (MEAP),
Fictitious County: 1993–94

	Students with Satisfactory Scores		
Grade Level	*4th*	*7th*	*10th*
Reading	47.5%	44.2%	43.5%
Math	49.9%	46.8%	33.0%
Grade Level	*5th*	*7th*	*11th*
Science	70.0%	61.9%	58.1%

do not have breakfast. Instead of wading through paragraphs of narrative, the reader could see at a glance that the problem is not common across all grade levels and then you may be permitted to target limited resources where they are most needed.

Needs assessment is a systematic data collection and analysis process. Its purposes are (1) to discover and identify the resources and services the community is lacking in relation to generally accepted standards and (2) the transmittal of that information to those who make resource allocation decisions (United Way of America 1982, p. 10).

The choice of data-gathering methods will depend on both data availability and on the topic of need being explored. Using existing data will help conserve time and funds. Using focus groups and/or key informants will provide information on the level of support and help rank needs by your audience's opinion of their importance. Questionnaires, while more costly and time intensive, enable you to directly measure the desires, beliefs, knowledge, and opinions of your intended beneficiaries and benefactors.

SOURCES FOR DATA AND OTHER RESOURCES

The Internet has a wealth of information, including results of studies, how-to guides, and data. Many reports are available on the World Wide Web, some of which can be downloaded. Often the reports are in Adobe or *PDF* format. You can download the Adobe Reader software at the *census.gov* site and many of the sites that publish reports in the Adobe format. If you do not have a computer with a Web browser, try your school library or computer lab, your community's public library, or a local college or university computer center.

Available on the Internet

Assessments and evaluation via Education Resources Information Center
http://www.cua.edu/www/eric_ae/intbod.htm#AA
or if you don't mind frames, *http://ericae.net/intass.htm*

Center for the Future of Children
http://www.futureofchildren.org/

Demographic data via the Census Bureau
http://www.census.gov

Indian Health Service
http://www.tucson.ihs.gov/

Library of Congress homepage
http://www.loc.gov/

National Center for Educational Statistics
http://nces0.1.ed.gov/NCES/indihome.asp

Office of Minority Health—Resource Center
http://www.omhrc.gov/welcome.htm#TOC

Social Statistics Briefing Room
http://www.whitehouse.gov/fsbr/ssbr/html

Survey development assistance via Community Information System and Research Services
http://www.wmich.edu/cisrs/

United Way of America—Outcome Evaluation Measures
http://www.unitedway.org/outcomes/

Web addresses for state government Internet sites
http://fic.info.gov/

Youth CrimeWatch (violence prevention programs)
http://www.ycwa.org/

Youth Info Website of the U.S. Department of Health and Human Services
http://youth.os.dhhs.gov/

Youth Risk Behavior Surveillance System—Centers for Disease Control
http://www.cdc.gov/nccdphp/dash/yrbs/ov.htm

National and Federal Sources

U.S. Census Bureau Customer Services. Bureau of the Census, Washington, DC 20233-8300. (301) 457-4100. Customer services has phone numbers for the following data sources:

Depository libraries. 1,400 libraries (college and public) that have selected publications and some computer files on CD-ROM from the U.S. Government Printing Office and Census Bureau.

State data centers. Usually state government agencies (and assorted affili-
ates, often state universities) with data services. Centers receive Census
Bureau data for their areas and make them available to the public.
Found in all states.

U.S. Census Bureau publications.

1990 Census of population reports, characteristics of the population. (There
are several different volumes in this series: General Social and Economic
Characteristics, Detailed Population Characteristics; Living Arrangements
of Children and Adults, Household and Family Characteristics; Money Income and Poverty Status in the United States.) The population census is
conducted once every ten years; 1990 is the most recent. Most likely the
data for the census conducted April 1, 2000 will be available in 2003.

> *County and city data book: [recent year].* Provides selected characteristics
> about counties and cities above 50,000 in population. Anticipated re-
> lease date of recent edition is May 1998.
>
> *Statistical abstract of the United States: 1997.* 1,040 pages, $32. PB94-20985
> National Technical Information Service. Also available on line at cen-
> sus.gov/publications/
>
> *More education means higher career earnings.* 2 pages, single copy free.
> SB-94-17

Other publications.

National Center for Education Statistics. *Digest of education statistics.* Gives
per pupil expenditures.

National Foundation for the Improvement of Education and National Education Association. *Teacher centers and needs assessment.* Washington, DC.
25 pages. LB1745.E32.

U.S. Department of Education. *State education performance chart.* Washington, DC. Shows percentage of students who graduate from high school.

U.S. Department of Health and Human Services, Public Health Service,
Centers for Disease Control, National Center for Health Statistics. *Vital
and health statistics.* Washington, DC.

U.S. Department of Labor, Bureau of Labor Statistics. *Employment and
earnings.* Washington, DC.

United Way of America. *Needs assessment: A guide for planners, managers
and funders of health and human care services.* Alexandria, VA, 1982.

Private and Nonprofit Sources

Catholic Relief Services.   *Participatory program evaluation: A manual
for involving program stakeholders in the evaluation process.* By Judi Aubel,
1993.

Children's Defense Fund.   25 E Street NW, Washington, DC 20001, (202) 662-3652.

The adolescent and young adult fact books, 1991. Comprehensive reference on America's ten-to twenty-year-olds. Includes family income, family types, health status, school enrollment, causes of death, sexual activity, and more.

The state of America's children yearbook 1997. Annual analysis of the status of children.

Where to find data about adolescents and young adults: A guide to sources, November 1989. CDF's Adolescent Pregnancy Prevention Clearinghouse report.

Council of Chief State School Officers.   One Massachusetts Avenue NW, Suite 700, Washington, DC 20001. *Family support, education and involvement: A guide for state action,* 1989.

Harvard Family Research Project.   Cambridge, MA 02138.

Weiss, H. B. *Raising our future: Families, schools, and communities, joining together: A handbook of family support and education programs for parents, educators, community leaders, and policy makers,* 1992.

Weiss, H.B., et al. *Innovative models to guide family support and education policy in the 1990s: an analysis of four pioneering state programs—Connecticut, Maryland, Minnesota, Missouri,* 1990.

Weiss, H. B., and Halpern, R. *The challenges of evaluating state family support and education initiatives: An education framework,* 1989.

Books on Evaluation, Needs Assessment, or Survey Design by Individuals

Chelimsky, E. and Shadish, W. R. 1997. *Evaluation for the 21st century.* Thousand Oaks, CA: Sage.

Herman, J. L., Morris, L. L., and Fitz-Gibbon, C. T. 1987. *Evaluator's handbook.* Thousand Oaks, CA: Sage.

Patton, M. Q. 1997. *Utilization-focused evaluation—The century text* (3rd ed.). Thousand Oaks, CA: Sage.

Posavac, E. J. 1997. *Program evaluation: Methods and case studies* (5th ed.). Englewood Cliffs, NJ: Prentice-Hall.

Rossi, P. H., and Freeman, H. E., 1993. *Evaluation: A systematic approach* (5th ed.). Newbury Park, CA: Sage.

Salant, P. and Dillman, D. 1994. *How to conduct your own survey.* NY: Wiley.

E-Mail and News Groups

Contact with individuals or organizations known to be associated with programs or issues of concern to someone engaged in needs assessment can sometimes be easily made by obtaining the e-mail addresses of those persons or organizations. If e-mail addresses are not known, it is sometimes possible to obtain e-mail addresses via "Yellow Pages" or "White Pages" on the Web.

Another way to get some feedback on questions or ideas is to log into one of the millions of "news groups" or "discussion groups." This approach may or may not be successful, however, depending on the discipline and focus to be found in any particular group and how expert the discussion or information might actually be. However, such groups may be helpful in citing examples or suggesting new ideas.

Listservs.   "Listservs" is jargon for getting one's own e-mail address onto a list whereby current news releases or ongoing discussions are automatically sent to one's e-mail address. Listservs facilitate dialogue among and within particular interest groups, such as program evaluators in elementary education, advocates for special education services in public schools, or issues of gender or race in school programs. Listservs range from electronic support groups to professional information-sharing networks. These are places to look for information, ask questions, and hopefully receive useful responses. Connecting with a listserv requires learning how to register one's address, and one must be convinced of its value before being flooded with a myriad of unwanted communications.

REFERENCES

Erickson, E. H. 1968. *Identity, Youth and Crisis.* New York: W. W. Norton.

Maslow, A. H. 1970. *Motivation and Personality.* New York: Harper & Row Publishers.

Michigan League for Human Services. 1995. *The Human Services Connection.* January, p. 1.

Ponsioen, J. A. 1962. *Social Welfare Policy: Contributions to Theory.* Publication of the Institute of Social Studies, Vol. 3. The Hague: Mouton & Co.

Simons, J., and Jablonski, D. 1990., *An Advocate's Guide to Using Data.* Washington, D.C.: Children's Defense Fund.

United Way of America. 1982. *Needs Assessment: A Guide for Planners, Managers and Funders of Health and Human Care Services.* Alexandria, VA: November, p. 8.

CHAPTER 33

Practical Approaches to Conducting and Using Research in the Schools

Sung Sil Lee Sohng
Associate Professor, University of Washington School of Social Work

Richard Weatherley
Professor, University of Washington School of Social Work

- Research in the Schools
- Applications of School-Based Research
- How to Get Started
- Low-Cost, Straightforward Methods

The purpose of this chapter is to demystify a process generally considered the exclusive domain of professionally trained researchers and to suggest low-cost research approaches that can be carried out by school-based practitioners. Practitioner research is a unique genre of research. Experimental researchers strive for valid and reliable measures in order to assure generalizability of their results; naturalistic researchers seek trustworthiness and authenticity in order to uncover the social rules for the situations they describe. In contrast, practitioner researchers seek to understand the individuals, actions, policies, and events in their work environments in order to make professional decisions. Practitioner research has gained legitimacy during the past ten years. It has contributed to professional development, school restructuring, and curriculum reform and has fostered social and political change.

Several concurrent forces have helped to make this happen. First, the conduct of research has been linked to the professionalization of social work practice. Second, after the postmodern challenge to "objective truth" narratives, self-studies, cases, vignettes, and other writings were recognized as potentially significant sources for the knowledge base (Harold, Palmiter, Lynch, and Freedman-Doan, 1995; Holland, 1991; Shulman, 1992). Third, the interest in practitioner research has also increased in response to the movement to create reflective, critical practitioners (Altrichter, Posch, and Somekh, 1993; Cochran-Smith and Lytle, 1992). Fourth, educational reformers have recognized that the success of reforms depends on an understanding of the context in which they are to be implemented. Practitioners, with the use of inquiry processes, can adapt the reforms to suit particular work situations (Calhoun, 1994). Finally, a link has been forged between practitioner research and critical pedagogy through the work of Paolo Freire and others (Carr, 1995; Hick, 1997; Nofke and Stevenson, 1995; Sohng, 1996). Practitioner inquiry and other forms of action research are seen as emancipatory tools to help practitioners become aware of the often hidden hierarchical institutional structures that govern their work.

Following an introductory discussion of research in the schools, we consider a range of alternative applications and discuss their relevance for the school-based practitioner. We outline guidelines for initiating research, and we identify several low-cost methods for gathering and using research.

RESEARCH IN THE SCHOOLS

Research is something done more often to school personnel than by them. The growth of social programs in the 1960s spawned a new evaluation and research industry. While in the popular view research is the product of the curiosity of individual academics, in reality the bulk of current research, evaluation, and data-gathering efforts in the schools is a response to federal and state legislative mandates. Legislative bodies demand strict accounting for the funds they appropriate, and even while decrying the regulations and paperwork, legislatures also contribute to the paperwork by imposing heavy reporting and evaluation requirements.

The volume of research and data-gathering activities in public schools has reached such proportions that the federal government has found it necessary to impose some restrictions. There are rules to protect the research subjects, both students and personnel, from inappropriate intrusion by researchers. There have also been efforts to restrict the volume of research through federal review by the Office of Management and Budget (OMB). Federally mandated research must first be cleared by the OMB as well as by the Education Data Acquisition Council, composed of representatives of federal education agencies and members of the Chief State School Officers Association. Their task is to make sure that proposed research is relevant and necessary and does not duplicate other ongoing or past research.

The impact of the research explosion on local schools is, of course, well known to practitioners. It shows itself in constantly growing paperwork requirements. School personnel at all levels spend much of their time completing forms and reports, a good deal of them seemingly irrelevant to day-to-day work concerns. The usual research role of school-based personnel is that of provider of data for research conducted elsewhere. Adding to the frustration of having to spend time completing forms is the fact that the information is seldom of direct use to the practitioner, furthermore, the practitioner rarely has any knowledge of why the data are needed or how they are to be used. From the local school's perspective, much of this data-gathering effort appears to be little more than busy work.

Research tends to be defined as something that is done exclusively by academics, whose specialized langauge and methods are assumed to be necessary conditions for scientific validity. The use of complex statistical methods often limits the communication of research results, shutting out practitioners and the public. While methodological rigor is to be admired, all too often esoteric language and methods are worn as a badge of expertise and rationalized as necessary for scientific precision.

Local school personnel are themselves rarely involved in research design (let alone the parents, students, or local community members), in assessing research products, or in suggesting applications. More often they are considered instruments for achieving organizational objectives. They are in this sense passive receivers of information and objects of administrative control. Research designs and instruments are too frequently developed without regard for the cultural diversity of school and community. Furthermore, even the most rigorous research, designed from afar, may yield statistically significant findings that have little practical application (Oja and Smulyan 1989; Sirotnik, 1987).

APPLICATIONS OF SCHOOL-BASED RESEARCH

If as suggested, externally driven research is so often irrelevant to practice, why should the practitioner be concerned with research at all? There are compelling reasons for school social workers and others to conduct their own research. Like it or not, this is the age of accountability. Schools are under pressure to demonstrate increased effectiveness, even without additional resources. Those who wish to regain some measure of control over their work environment must, of necessity, speak the language of accountability.

There are both defensive and affirmative reasons for conducting school-based research. Locally initiated practitioner research can ward off top-down bureaucratic forms of accountability. Hierarchical management systems have proved inadequate for producing significant changes in program delivery at the school site (Elmore and McLaughlin, 1988; Sarason, 1971). Practitioner-based research can support a bottom-up change process and a collegial form of accountability. Recent educational reforms emphasize working toward institutionalization of cooperative principles as the focus of school renewal (Calhoun, 1994; Holy, 1991; Reed, Mergendoller, and Horan, 1992). Rather than being passive consumers of clients, parents and community members can also become active partners in the collaborative network. Studies of educational innovations suggest that involvement of the local school community in research helps mobilize the capacity for internal regeneration of policies and strategies for school-driven improvement (Barth, 1988; Jones, 1991; Sirotnik, 1989).

Since school personnel spend their working lives with students, they are in an excellent position to identify educational issues firsthand. They are interested in what works and are sensitive to the practical constraints of school settings in ways that outside researchers may not be. The utilitarian, participatory, and localized nature of school-based research significantly reduces the gap between the discovery of what works and practical applications of this knowledge (Elliot, 1991).

School-based research is the antithesis of externally generated and externally imposed change. Just as administrators and policymakers use research as a political resource, school social workers can do the same. Research in this sense is not the search for "objective" knowledge, but a political resource and adjunct to practice offering more immediate payoffs. Practitioners, including regular and special class teachers as well as school social workers, psychologists, and others, can use research to ward off new programs and requirements that are unfeasible, impractical, or harmful to students. On the other hand, they can use research in a positive way to gain support for new program initiatives, to demonstrate the effectiveness of their services, to obtain additional resources, or to find out what kinds of interventions work best. School social workers can use research to move beyond traditional clinical roles to enlarge the arena of practice. Research can be used as an adjunct to consultation and as a way of demonstrating the potential of a broader social work role adapted to its environment.

School social workers are in an especially advantageous position to develop collaborative school-based research. The profession has long been interested in effecting change through the empowerment, participation, and action of the people involved. The collaborative approach to research calls on interactive skills, cultural sensitivity, group decision making, and conflict management skills necessary for negotiation among diverse constituents and interests. This kind of collaborative research is characterized by (1) participation in problem posing, (2) practitioner participation in data gathering that answers questions relevant to *their* concerns, and (3) collaboration among members of the school community as a "critical community." Here research is aimed at generating data that can guide and direct planned change. It involves observation, assessment, interviewing, reading and analyzing reports and documents, and writing findings. These skills are already within the behavioral repertoire of school social workers. Below we will review how to do it. But first we examine some of the uses and potential benefits by practitioner-initiated school-based research.

Developing Multicultural Resources

Consciousness of multiple realities lies at the heart of postmodern thinking. Schools must incorporate diverse voices into their curricula, with particular attention to those who have been silenced (Banks, 1996; Sleeter, 1996). The key concept in this endeavor is the deliberate, thoughtful development of research that allows for the diversity of perspectives and interests. School-based research can offer a promising vehicle for assessing cultural diversity in curriculum, classroom, and school practices and improving the campus climate for a diverse student body. You might, for example, take a look at how the composition of the student population at your school has changed over the years. A good place to begin would be the office that tracks student characteristics. To get an overall picture of changes, you might examine the past ten years, comparing two different years for which you can get good demographic data. In considering diversity at your school, you should also familiarize yourself with both official and informal institutional policies and procedures, academic programs, and instructional support. Have these policies and programs kept pace with the changing student population? Another approach is to conduct a student survey on demographic and cultural backgrounds, financial status, living and working conditions, and curricular progress and problems. This can be an effective way to engage students and teachers in examining the implications of diversity. Social workers can also collaborate with teachers in a self-study investigating structures and processes within their schools, such as placement of students (by race and sex) in remedial and special education and the representation of diverse groups in the curriculum. Out of such research the team can develop a profile of students as a basis for organizing student mentoring, tutoring, and support programs.

Connecting to Unrecognized Constituencies

The constituent base of multicultural education consists of disenfranchised people in this society, particularly parents and children of color or of low-income backgrounds; immigrants and refugees; children who are disabled, gay, or lesbian, and their parents or adult supporters. However, in many arenas of multicultural activity, the professionals sometimes act as if *they* were the constituents. Professionals can certainly be allies, but they need to recognize their power and their self-interest, which may lead them to shape multicultural education to fit their own needs. A growing literature on multicultural education is directed toward professionals, often substituting for dialogue between school personnel and community people (Sleeter, 1996). Redirected toward parents and community activists from diverse groups, research can serve as an empowering resource for those who are often unheard and uninvolved. A community needs assessment, for example, provides an instrument whereby community people can make their educational needs known, expressing an action agenda for school change. (Delgado-Gaitan, 1993; Williams, 1989).

Demonstrating the Effectiveness of Services

As practitioners, we generally know, or think we know, the effectiveness of the services we provide. We sometimes assume that because we are professionals, others should take us at our word when we make claims about the needs for and benefits of our services. However, in the absence of convincing evidence, such claims may be dismissed by others as self-serving.

One female school social worker, for example, was valued by the principals and teachers of the schools she served for her effectiveness in handling crisis situations—episodes of students acting out, students' threatening violent and destructive behavior, and confrontations between students and teachers. She was frequently called on to handle emergencies. She felt that this disruption of her regular work schedule was well worth the price, since her availability to handle crises gave her the credibility needed to get into the schools to do some of the more routine work. However, her crisis work was not officially recognized. It was not part of her job description, nor was it generally known by her superiors how much time it took or how much it was appreciated by the principals. Had she taken the time to document the number of such cases per month, to describe the circumstances and outcomes, and to record the feedback from the student and teachers, she could have used these data to gain official acknowledgement of an enlarged work role. She might also have gained greater insights into her work, recognition of her contribution, additional resources or decreased demands, or authorization for training school personnel in crisis intervention. As it stood, her work was appreciated by many but unacknowledged and unrewarded by administrators.

Fostering Collegial Accountability

School-based research conducted by practitioners on practical concerns can foster a greater congruence to building greater collegial, shared accountability. Let us assume, for example, that a social worker and a group of teachers have developed an alternative tutorial strategy, adding adult helpers to the classroom to work with a group of students, rather than taking these students out of class for remedial instruction. The team wants to examine the effect of this experiment. The results would be subject to some outcome measures, such as the students' progress, increases or decreases in tutoring time spent with each student, and the students' and teachers' assessment of the new procedures. Here the purpose of research does not necessarily require rigorous research procedures but calls for collegial problem identification and problem solving. The process of observing students and gathering data may also be an occasion for team members to examine and reflect on their interaction and behaviors with students. By having the opportunity to experience and experiment with the research process, the team members may gain an increased appreciation of research and come to demand more of themselves, for example, to be more parsimonious and specific in the data they collect and clearer about learning objectives.

Expanding Students' Involvement

Involving students in a research project can provide an excellent learning experience and meaningful participation in the school community. In Denmark, for example, one of the authors observed a high school class research project on birth control practices. The students had surveyed the student body, presented the findings to their peers, and then, working with the school administration, helped design a sex education program. Similarly, peer counseling programs have gained in appeal in the United States as they involve students in real-world concerns that are important to them. Students might, for example, participate in the assessment and evaluation of peer mediation programs with school staff. Guided by school staff, a group of students (or a class) might develop questionnaires then collect and analyze data about specific school problems experienced by students. The process, as well as the findings, could serve as the basis for further joint student-teacher problem solving around these issues.

Establishing the Need for New Services

Arguments for the establishment of new services are all the more persuasive when supported by research data. Reluctant school administrators have become staunch supporters of services for pregnant students when staff demonstrated the increased state funding generated for average daily attendance by retaining students who might otherwise drop out (Weatherley, Perlman, Levine, and Klerman, 1986).

Let us assume, for example, that the social worker and teachers feel that there is a need for a school breakfast program. This is variously resisted by school administrators, who are concerned about the cost as well as the administrative problems of implementing a program for which there may be little constituent demand. Requests for the program from teachers and social workers can easily be deflected by administrators in the absence of any other compelling reasons. When the request is accompanied by data showing the support from students and parents, the number of children who come to school without breakfast, well-documented reports of behavioral problems and the lack of attentiveness of such children, information on effects of nutritional deficits on learning, and data on the costs of the program, the request would be more seriously considered.

Establishing the Need for Additional Resources

School personnel constantly seek increased resources or reduced workloads in order to accomplish their work in keeping with professional standards. Administrators hear such requests so often that they are routinely discounted. Administrators like to sidestep conflicts between professional standards or official policy requirements and the limited resources available to meet them. This forces the practitioner to reconcile conflicting demands as best he or she can. For example, with the requirements of the Individuals with Disabilities Education Act, school social workers, psychologists, special class teachers, and other educational specialists are often expected to carry out their regular work while accommodating time-consuming and cumbersome assessment and paperwork requirements for increased numbers of children. Administrators, themselves caught between federal and state requirements and limited resources, often thrust the problem downward, leaving it to school-based personnel to figure out how best to meet the new demands. School personnel work harder, taking paperwork home with them, forgo planning and preparation time, or routinize work tasks.

Another more proactive approach is to conduct team-based data gathering, documenting carefully the time required to perform specific tasks, thereby demonstrating the impossibility of completing them without sacrificing quality and deferring other responsibilities. Furthermore, the group involved in such data gathering and analysis can identify ways to reduce duplication and redundancy and can recommend new procedures more relevant to the school community.

Fostering Collaborative Practice among Staff and Students

In settings where representatives of several different professions work together, professional dominance hierarchies develop, reflecting the respective status of the professions. The prototypical dominance hierarchy is that of doctors over nurses, social workers, and other professionals in medical settings (Friedson, 1974). In schools, social workers find themselves in a host setting administered and dominated by educators; social workers occupy a somewhat tenuous position. Their unique competencies are often neither recognized nor appreciated.

The use of research to demonstrate the effectiveness of services has already been mentioned. Advocating and organizing an interdisciplinary research project may be another way of highlighting the unique contribution of social workers. For example, a team consisting of the principal, social worker, counselor, and classroom teachers conducts focus group interviews of seventh graders near the end of the first middle school year. The students, selected to reflect the composition of the class in terms of ethnicity and ability, are asked what the school could do to help students make a more comfortable transition from grade school to middle school. The results are discussed by the team and reported to the faculty. Based on further faculty input, changes are made in the orientation and follow-up program for entering seventh graders.

Testing New Programs or Procedures

Often, new procedures are developed by administrators in response to mandates from Congress, the state legislature, or the local school board. This top-down approach, while customary, often results in the imposition of new requirements with insufficient sensitivity to actual conditions within the schools. School-based personnel cope as best they can. However, it makes more sense to test new programs and procedures before they are implemented throughout the system. As an advocate for and participant in pilot tests, the school social worker can expand his or her role while indirectly contributing to the empowerment of all school-based staff.

Illuminating Practices Normally Hidden from View

In all organizations, schools being no exception, there generally are some practices tacitly accepted but at variance with official policy and not openly discussed. Research offers a way of bringing such practices out into the open by guaranteeing anonymity and confidentiality, thereby depersonalizing what may be very emotional issues. Examples include disciplinary practices, cultural sensitivity, or concerns about student-to-student sexual harassment and harassment of gay and lesbian students. Teachers may be reluctant to discuss their own practices because they may violate official policy or because of the divisive nature of the issue. Such emotion-laden issues may be driven underground and beyond the scope of discussion. An anonymous survey might elicit responses that would never be brought out in open discussion and could serve to bring to the attention of administrators practices of which they might otherwise prefer not to know.

Forestalling the Implementation of an Undesirable Policy

A favorite method of politicians to avoid taking action is to call for a study of the issues. While outright opposition to an undesirable policy may be viewed by the administration as insubordination, proposing a study is a more constructive and conciliatory step that is harder for recalcitrant administrators to oppose. If, in fact, a study is undertaken, the results may help resolve differences about implementing a proposed policy.

HOW TO GET STARTED

We have discussed a number of ways that research can be used to enhance the role of the school social worker and to support organizational change

initiated from below. We turn now to the more difficult question of how
to do it. In this section, we offer guidelines for getting started and suggest
ways to augment limited resources. The concluding section provides a discussion of readily available data sources and methods of conducting research
that do not require special research training.

Be Clear about Objectives

The first step in contemplating any research is clarity of objectives,
both political and substantive. Are there specific group or organizational
goals to be accomplished by undertaking the research? Will these objectives
be realized if the research is carried out? What are the costs in terms of
both resources and possibly strained relations? If, for example, the objective
is to encourage the implementation of a free breakfast program, would
research findings in fact bring about that result?

It is important to distinguish between fairly broad goals and more specific objectives. A very useful resource in this regard is the now classic book
by Mager (1984) on preparing instructional objectives. A frequent error of
field researchers is to undertake a study with only vague objectives, hoping
to make some sense out of the findings later. This approach is time consuming and wasteful for researcher and subjects alike. For example, in approaching the issue of corporal punishment, one could try to find out about
teacher, student, and parent attitudes as well as actual practices in the
schools. But if current practices are the focus of concern, that is what should
be studied. If teachers' support for a particular policy is at issue, then their
attitudes and opinions may be a more appropriate focus. The objectives,
framed as precisely as possible, should determine the direction of the research, not vice versa.

Don't Try for Too Much

When thinking in research terms, everything becomes a potential subject of research. One must guard against being overly ambitious and be
realistic about the adequacy of the resources available to do the job. If one
is planning to do a study without additional help, how much time can
realistically be spent? Will this be sufficient to complete the study? One
should estimate the time needed to accomplish each specific step. Even
if it can be done, are the results likely to be worth the effort? If the answer
to the latter two questions is no, then the research should not be undertaken.

Ask for Help

One way of extending available resources is to get additional help. This
might mean seeking released time or volunteer assistance from colleagues

and students. The greatest possible involvement of both colleagues and school community is desirable if the research objective is to bring about change.

Additional resources are available outside the school system. These include academics, student researchers, and advocacy groups. Advocacy groups have their own particular interest in practices within the schools, although their advocacy position may itself increase the suspicions of administrators. Academics are often interested in consulting on practical issues and may even be willing to undertake the research themselves if offered an interesting research issue and access to a site. Students are often available from a number of academic disciplines—social work, education, psychology, sociology, political science, and public administration—to carry out research that satisfies their practicum requirements under academic supervision.

Involve Others at an Early Age

There are two reasons to involve others at an early stage of a project. First, some might feel slighted, and justifiably so, if asked to join a project after the major directions have already been decided by others. Second, and more important, the contributions of others enlarge the scope of issues considered and provide an essential source of new ideas. On the one hand, group process may complicate the orderly achievement of objectives, and groups are subject to groupthink, which may constrain the consideration of alternatives. On the other hand, research aimed at changing current practices should be undertaken with a view to building constituencies of support to help implement the findings.

LOW-COST, STRAIGHTFORWARD METHODS

Most social research is an extension of logical processes used in everyday life. In shopping for new clothes, getting estimates for car repair or home improvement, or planning a vacation, the customary first step is to gather data on the reliability of the seller, the quality of the merchandise or service, and its availability and price. Prior to the data-gathering stage, there may be some assessment of the need and ability to pay. Similarly, when contemplating research in the work setting, a first step is to specify the objectives of the research and then develop a research plan. This involves a determination of the information needed, its availability, the methods required to obtain it, and the relative costs of time, materials, and other resources.

There are several research approaches that require a minimum of time, some of which may be undertaken using readily available data. (On the use of existing data sources, see Webb, 1981.) While it is generally desirable to enlist the support of administrators and colleagues in undertaking research, there occasionally may be situations in which administrators are threatened by the proposed research and withhold permission or seek in other ways to block it. In such instances, it is still possible to gather data using records and documents that are public information available to any citizen.

Perhaps the most straightforward kind of research involves the analysis of existing data. Schools are constantly compiling reams of data on every conceivable activity. Much of this information is funneled to state and federal agencies to meet reporting requirements but is not necessarily analyzed for local administrative purposes. Examples include aggregate data on pupil characteristics, family income, attendance, grades, achievement test scores, the numbers receiving free lunches, the incidence of visual or dental problems, the prevalence of handicapping conditions, the numbers in special classes or programs, the incidence of problems requiring disciplinary action, and so forth. Other data are available with respect to class size and caseloads of social workers and other educational specialists. Frequently, when caseload sizes are examined in relation to performance requirements, a discrepancy between expectations and the reality of the workload is immediately apparent. The fact that a class for children with special needs contains fifteen children of differing ages and levels of ability and is taught by one teacher with no aide offers prima facie evidence of a resource deficiency. Or if a particular school has an unusually high incidence of violence, there may be cause to investigate further.

Another invaluable source of information is the school district's budget. The budget is a planning document that gives a good picture of what the district actually does and what its priorities are, as represented by the commitment of resources. An examination of the budget permits a comparison of the stated objectives with the actual allocation of resources to achieve those objectives.

Other public documents that may shed light on local practices are federal and state laws, administrative codes and regulations, court decisions, state agency policy and procedural statements, and state and local education agency reports. (Such documents and data are increasingly available on the World Wide Web.) A reading of the state or federal requirements may reveal a discrepancy between these requirements and local practices. Some administrators intentionally keep information about the specific state and federal requirements from those school personnel who must implement them. Knowledge of deliberate violations of law can give school-based staff a powerful tool for advocating change. School practices with regard to discipline, suspensions and expulsions, and the notification and involvement of parents in placing children in special programs may be at variance with the law or district policy. If so, change can be encouraged by a range of interventions, all the way from judicious questioning to encouraging advocacy groups to file suit.

Another powerful kind of analysis is estimating the costs of procedures and practices. For example, it is a humbling exercise to calculate the cost of a single meeting in relation to its objectives and results. When one counts the dollar value of the participants' time, the costs can be quite substantial. Certain reporting requirements are costly, yet the costs are rarely calculated. In processing paperwork, one must consider both the actual cost of completing the forms and reports as well as other hidden costs. These include the costs of printing the forms, moving the paper through the organization, handling and storing it, and the time of those who must read it, comment on, and analyze it. Cost comparisons of alternative procedures can be used to support one alternative rather than another.

Chances are good that most problems have been encountered elsewhere and subjected to some kind of analysis or research. Therefore, a good starting point in any research activity is the library and the Web. University librarians are generally helpful in locating studies and reports. There are now a number of excellent computerized reference files that can produce a list of titles and abstracts on specific subjects at nominal cost.

Academic specialists in schools of education and social work, and departments of psychology and sociology may be familiar with specific bodies of literature and be willing to share their expertise with practitioners. For just about any problem that can occur in a public school setting, there are likely to be some interested specialists. In addition to academic departments of universities, educational specialists are found in the federal Department of Education, in state departments of education, in contract research firms, and on the staffs of interest groups such as state chapters of the Children's Defense Fund, Council for Exceptional Children, National Association of School Boards, Council of Chief State School Officers, National Association of Social Workers, and so on. A few phone calls are generally sufficient to access such networks and learn what work has already been done in a specific problem area. For example, if one is investigating student discipline, the Children's Defense Fund may be able to provide a number of references to completed studies, summaries of legal opinions and pertinent laws, and suggestions about model programs. The state teachers' union may maintain a research staff and have access to information on many school issues. Newspaper articles provide another source of data about school policies. In larger cities, local newspapers often have reporters who specialize in educational concerns and who develop expertise in particular educational areas. The papers themselves frequently maintain clipping files, as does the school administration. This is an important documentary record that should not be overlooked. The school board minutes are available to the public and also supply a documentary record of actions taken and contemplated.

Other methods for gathering data about school activities include surveys, structured observation, interviews and on-line databases. Questionnaires are advantageous for gathering information that safeguards anonymity and providing a structured format for analysis of responses. The disadvantages are that they restrict the amount of data that can be gathered and analyzed, and questionnaire responses may be at variance with actual behavior. Face-to-face interviews offer an opportunity to gather information in greater depth. The interviewer can probe, ask additional questions, and clarify responses. Furthermore, some structure may be maintained through the use of an interview schedule, a listing of topics or questions.

Structured observations are those in which there is some purposeful gathering of data according to predetermined categories. Observational techniques can get very sophisticated and complicated, as with the use of interaction scales to record information about who initiates and responds in a group meeting. More straightforward, simple observational methods will usually suffice. Very simple categorization and computations will sometimes reveal profound meanings. In research by one of the authors on Individualized Educational Programs (IEPs), the number of participants in, as well as the duration of, IEP meetings were counted and recorded. It was observed that in one school system, the meetings lasted several minutes and involved only three to four participants, whereas in another system, the meetings averaged nearly an hour and involved six or seven individuals (Weatherley, 1979). This difference in itself revealed a great deal about the quality of the assessments in these two school systems. Sometimes it is also possible to enlist others in making observations. For example, all school social workers may agree to keep records of certain activities or to record observations of meetings in which they participate for subsequent analysis.

Using On-Line Databases

We need to conceptualize research beyond paper and pencil, and into cyberspace, the virtual village, and the information highway. These avenues offer important, free information that can be accessed by the nonspecialist. On-line databases offer a variety of information for conducting research. Using on-line databases, practitioners from large and small schools, from urban and rural communities, can gain access to a range of popular and specialized periodicals, government publications, historical resources, and newspapers. There are a number of excellent directories of on-line databases and CD-ROM resources (Paris and Jones, 1988).

New generations of computers hold the promise to transform everyday life as immense databases become accessible through wireless communication of voice, text, and images (Jones and Maloy, 1996). Low-cost access to information and global communications can foster the multiple perspectives of our postmodern age. Today's smart machines manage production and integrate knowledge—thereby redefining educational strategies and structures. Computers and electronic media facilitate the storage, transmission, and manipulation of information. However, individuals will select what messages they receive and decide how to interpret the data and what actions to take. The role of the practitioner-researcher is still to build confidence by fostering collaboration, by acknowledging multiple truths (realities), and by making relevant knowledge accessible to others.

A final stage in the process is the compilation of data and the preparation of a report or position paper. The format will depend on the purpose of the research and the objectives sought. If one is attempting to block the initiation of a new policy or procedure, the report would necessarily differ from that used in attempting to compare two alternative procedures, neither of which is particularly preferred. The guidelines offered earlier for initiating the research will also serve in planning the report: be clear about objectives, avoid being overly ambitious, keep it simple, involve others, and seek the help of those with expert knowledge. In writing the report one should avoid pejorative language, cast the findings in objective or neutral terms, and let the facts make the argument. Brevity and clarity are the watchwords. Graphic programs and materials, music, and multimedia sources enhance research presentations. Using technology can make dry materials interesting, colorful, and appealing. Dissemination of research reports to the constituent communities through community centers and local organizations are important to enlist their involvement with the school.

Research is too important to be left entirely to researchers. This chapter shows some of the ways practitioners can conduct and use research and, in the process, enhance their practice roles. Perhaps the most difficult step is getting started, particularly in view of the widely held perception that the proper conduct of research requires expertise that comes only from years of specialized training and experience. Such a view effectively rules out many of the more relevant applications of research in schools. However, as shown in this chapter, the school-based practitioner can rescue research from researchers and, by so doing, assume a more affirmative role in fostering collaboration, making space for diverse perspectives, and shaping school policy.

REFERENCES

Altrichter, H. Posch, P., and Somekh, B. 1993. *Teachers investigate their work: An introduction to the methods of action research.* New York: Routledge.

Banks, J. (ed.). 1996. *Multicultural education, transformative knowledge and action.* New York: Columbia University, Teachers College.

Barth, R. 1988. School: A community of leaders. In A. Lieberman (ed.). *Building a professional culture in schools* (pp. 129–147). NY: Teachers College Press.

Calhoun, E. 1994. *How to use action research in the self-renewal school.* Alexandria, VA: Association for Supervision and Curriculum Development.

Carr, W. 1995. *For education: Towards critical educational inquiry*. Bristol, PA: Open University Press.

Cochran-Smith, M., and Lytle, S. 1992. *Inside/Outside: Teacher research and knowledge*. New York: Columbia University, Teachers College.

Delgaro-Gaitan, C. 1993. Researching change and changing the researcher. *Harvard Educational Review* 63(4):389–411.

Elliott, J. 1991. *Action research for educational change*. Milton Keynes, UK: Open University Press.

Elmore, R. F., and McLaughlin, M. W. 1988. *Steady work: Policy, practice and the reform of American education*. Santa Monica, CA: Rand Corporation, February.

Freidson, E. 1974. Dominant professions, bureaucracy, and client services. In Y. Hasenfeld and R. A. English (eds.). *Human service organizations*. Ann Arbor, MI: University of Michigan Press.

Harold, R. D., Palmiter, M. L. Lynch, S. A., and Freedman-Doan, C. R. 1995. Life stories: A practice-based research technique. *Journal of Sociology and Social Welfare* 22:23–44.

Hick, S. 1997. Participatory research: An approach for structural social workers. *Journal of Progressive Human Services* 8(2):63–78.

Holland, T. P. 1991. Narrative, knowledge and professional practice. *Social Thought* 17(1):32–40.

Holy, P. 1991. From action research to collaborative inquiry: The processing of an innovation. In O. Zuber-Skerritt (ed). *Action research for change and development* (pp. 36–56). Brookfield, VA: Gower.

Jones, B., and Maloy, R. 1996. *Schools for an information age*. Westport, CT: Praeger.

Jones, J. 1991. Action research in facilitating change in institutional practice. In O. Zuber-Skerritt (ed.). *Action research for change and development* (pp. 207–223). Brookfield, VA: Gower.

Mager, R. F. 1984. *Preparing instructional objectives* (rev. 2nd ed.). Belmont, CA: Lake Management & Training.

Nofke, S., and Stevenson, S. 1995. *Educational action research: Becoming practically critical*. NY: Teachers College Press.

Oja, S., and Smulyan, L. 1989. *Collaborative action research: A developmental approach*. NY: Falmer.

Paris, L., and Jones, V. 1988. *Directory of online databases and CD-ROM resources for high schools*. Santa Barbara, CA: ABC-Clio.

Reed, C., Mergendoller, J., and Horan, C. 1992. Collaborative research: A strategy for school improvement. *Crossroads: The California Journal of Middle Grades Research*. spring: 5–12.

Sarason, S. B., 1971. *The culture of the school and the problem of change*. Boston: Allyn & Bacon.

Shulman, J. 1992. *Case methods in teacher education*. NY: Teachers College Press.

Sirotnik, K. A. 1987. Evaluation in the ecology of schooling. The process of school renewal. In J. I. Goodlad (ed.). *The ecology of school renewal: Eighty-six yearbook of the National Society for the Study of Education* (pp. 41–62). Chicago: University of Chicago Press.

Sirotnik, K. A., 1989. The school as the center of change. In T. J. Sergiovanni and J. H. Moore (eds.) *Schooling for tomorrow: Directing reforms to issues that count* (pp. 89–113). Boston: Allyn & Bacon.

Sleeter, C. 1996. *Multicultural education as social activism*. Albany, NY: State University of New York.

Sohng, S. 1996. Participatory research and community organizing. *Journal of Sociology and Social Welfare* 23(4):77–97.

Weatherley, R. 1979. *Reforming special education: Policy implementation from state level to street level*. Cambridge, MA: MIT Press.

Weatherley, R., Perlman, S. B., Levine, M. H., and Klerman, L. V. 1986. Comprehensive programs for pregnant teenagers: How successful have they been? *Family Planning Perspectives* 18:73–78.

Webb, E. J. 1981. *Nonreactive measures in the social sciences* (2nd ed.). Boston: Houghton Mifflin.

Williams, M. R. 1989. Neighborhood organizing for urban school reform. NY: Teachers College Press.

CHAPTER 34

Research in School Social Work: Catching Up and Moving On

Christine Anlauf Sabatino
Assistant Professor, National Catholic School of Social Service,
Catholic University of America

Elizabeth March Timberlake
Ordinary Professor, National Catholic School of Social Service,
Catholic University of America

- Contextual Challenges of Public Law Mandates
- Value and Ethical Challenges
- Research Questions and Paradigms
- Outcome Effectiveness
- Methodological Challenges
- Methodological Guidelines
- Substantive Challenges
- Policy and Program Impact Studies
- Epidemiological Planning Studies

Population trend estimates for the year 2010 suggest that there will be 62,644,000 children under age eighteen with no one racial/ethnic or cultural majority (National Center for Education Statistics, 1993). Their opportunities for success in school will depend not only on their own academic talents, competencies, resiliencies, and vulnerabilities but also on how the contextual factors of their lives enable them to meet their ordinary needs. These needs include, for example, family support systems, economic security, access to physical and mental health care, and opportunities for positive peer relationships, healthful recreation, and constructive work experiences. Yet population trend estimates suggest that besides being culturally diverse, the child population of the early twenty-first century is likely to experience life contexts in which:

- 51,368,080 (82 percent) children will have working mothers (Wetrogen, 1989);

- 26,310,480 (40 percent) children will live in poverty (Huston, 1994);
- 18,793,200 (30 percent) children will live in single parent, female-headed households (Betson and Michael, 1997); and
- 6,264,400 (10 percent) children with disabilities will need specialized education and support services (Lewit and Baker, 1996).

Traditionally, school social workers have addressed the needs, vulnerabilities, resiliencies, and competencies of children in their life contexts through services based within the boundaries of the school setting. Increasingly, they are being asked to extend their professional role responsibilities and service models across the boundaries of the school and incorporate community-brokered and school-linked service arrangements (Franklin and Streeter, 1995, 1998; Lee, 1998). Given the political and fiscal conservatism of the times, it is not surprising that school social workers are being asked to meet children's needs more effectively and efficiently with fewer resources and greater accountability.

In the face of the changes, challenges, and problems facing schools and the social work profession in this era of uncertainty and rapid change, it is imperative that school social workers substantiate what they do in a format meaningful to their host setting and document their practice effectiveness and efficiency. To assist school social workers in these tasks, this chapter highlights the critical role of program evaluation and practice research in enabling school social work to catch up and move on into the twenty-first century. In doing so, the chapter first grounds school social work practice and research within the contextual challenges of public law mandates for education before addressing value and ethical, methodological and substantive challenges in school social work practice research and program evaluation.

CONTEXTUAL CHALLENGES OF PUBLIC LAW MANDATES

As late as a generation ago, the teaching-learning process was designated for the regular education teacher and the classroom student. Education was confined to the classroom, which was in effect a closed system wherein all informational input and educational output was centered. During the last quarter of this twentieth century, however, public laws have fundamentally altered the scope and boundaries of public school education. The federal response to schoolchildren with special needs has precisely defined the rights and dramatically increased services to these children.

Initially, the 1975 Education of All Handicapped Children Act (P.L. 94-142) set the platform for a challenging and complex array of legal mandates that forever changed the target population, curriculum programs, curriculum goals, interprofessional collaboration, funding streams, governance, and the sheer scale of public education. With the passage of this law, the classroom student-teacher dyad was no longer the operative paradigm for a large population of students. Decision-making and service models were extended beyond the boundaries of the school system. The school population was redefined to include both regular education and special education students. All children, regardless of disability, are now entitled to a free appropriate public school education in the least restrictive environment.

Ten years later with the passage of the 1986 Education for All Handicapped Children Amendments, Part H (P.L. 99–457), the eligible target population was further expanded in categorical definition and chronological age with the creation of early intervention programs for infants and toddlers. Now, children from birth to age twenty-one make up the public school population.

The explosion of legally mandated functional and categorical definitions of public school students brought about requisite changes in many other areas. For example, curriculum development requires comprehensive and coordinated programs and a variety of related services. Curriculum goals include not only standards of learning but also efforts to enhance child development and minimize potential delays, codified in the Individualized Education Plan (IEP) and the Individualized Family Service Plan (IFSP). Furthermore, because federal regulations require a comprehensive multidisciplinary evaluation and assessment procedure by appropriate qualified personnel to determine eligibility, school districts are compelled to develop interprofessional collaboration systems.

Most revolutionary of all is the concept that non-school-based personnel have a role to play in decision-making and service delivery. Specifically, public law mandates the inclusion of families in the eligibility procedures through the IEP and grants them due process appeals procedures when disagreements occur. The IFSP documents the use of the family and the community in the administration and provisions of early intervention with infants and toddlers. Both home-based and class-based services now are mandated to work with the family as the basic service medium through which a child's developmental delays are addressed. Today, coordinated interagency and community-based programs play a new pivotal role in service delivery and require a sophisticated level of community partnership between school and community institutions.

Finally, coordination of federal and state funding sources is designed to provide a broader financial base for local school districts to comply with new federal regulations. These dollars, however, also bring concomitant governance requirements in planning, development, implementation, and monitoring. While the intent of these legal mandates is to build on existing school system structures, increased costs and rising expenditures are the unintended result of compliance with federal standards.

Any one of these areas of change—population, programs, goals, collaboration, funding, governance, or scale—lend itself to systematic empirical study of its underlying assumptions, organizational mechanisms for implementation, and impact on school social work service delivery. It is essential that school social work research on the effects of educational policies on children and their families go beyond head counts of affected children and their families. What are the outcome criteria by which program success is evaluated? Do programs effectively achieve these outcomes? What are the actual experiences of children and their families in accessing and utilizing legally mandated services? What is the impact on child development, school attendance, and school achievement?

VALUE AND ETHICAL CHALLENGES

Value Issues

In the early years, part of the mission of public education was the socialization of immigrant children and, thereby, the shaping of a uniform American values structure for individual children, their families, and their communities. As the nation has become more diverse linguistically, economically, culturally, and racially, there have been many efforts to open up the value base of the educational environment and establish a value-neutral climate accepting of diversity. However, the public debates about regular educational initiatives, elementary school guidance services, English as the official language, health and well-being programs, and core knowledge versus critical thinking skills programs point to a growing mismatch between the efforts of the educational system and those of conservative coalitions, advocacy groups, and religious parent groups. These interacting oppositional forces have resulted in the "unbundling" of the moral and ethical values operative within the nation's school system and attempts to sort out which values are the province of the family and which are ceded to the classroom teacher. The result is a shifting gray value line that, unbidden, may bend and settle in ways that influence policy, program goals and practice models, selection of evaluation methodology and outcomes, choice of measurement domains, and types of analysis used, to name a few.

Problems arise when the dynamic ever present value beliefs and biases remain covert and are neither acknowledged nor controlled. Thus, to carry out their research agenda in an ethical way, school social workers must clarify its ideological, social, and moral underpinnings and support a value diversity, rather than a value-neutral, stance. For example, whose point of view is the research likely to support? Who will the findings of the research empower? In other words, who benefits? Simply making this information explicit provides a powerful means for addressing the research issues of value and bias conceptually and pragmatically.

Ethical Commitments

The value base, ethical commitments, and expected professional behaviors of school social workers are spelled out in multiple ways. They are
mandated as legal rules of behavior by state licensure or certification laws,
codified as canons in a professional code of ethics (National Association of
Social Workers [NASW], 1996). and prescribed as practice conventions and
research regulations by the accountability structure of the educational institutions in which they practice.

At times, these multiple values, behavioral rules, and ethical commitments are congruent; at other times, they conflict. All, for example, would
concur that school social workers have a professional duty to (a) define
their intervention models, procedures, and projected outcomes precisely,
(2) routinely engage in the evaluative process by documenting intervention
process and collecting outcome data in an objective and systematic manner,
and (3) protect clients by being accountable for their practice and following
value conventions such as:

- Concern for the dignity and privacy of all participants;
- Protection of participants from discomfort, danger, and deprivation;
- Explication of risk-benefit consequences for voluntary, informed parental consent and child assent to participation in school social work
  services;
- Assurance of confidential handling of information and security of
  file information, paper-and-pencil tests, and computerized data;
- Protection of child and family participants and educational staff from
  value influences and biases in biopsychosocial assessment, direct
  child and family intervention, and teacher consultation;
- Development and testing of assessment and intervention models
  that incorporate the best empirical evidence of effectiveness;
- Recognition of value influences and bias embedded in evaluation
  research methodology, outcome documentation, and interpretation
  of findings; and
- Assurance of fairness in participant access to and utilization of research and demonstration service projects with documented evidence of effectiveness.

The principles of ethical reasoning and decision-making that underlie these
value conventions for everyday practice and research activities include,
among others, truthfulness, full disclosure, quality of life, least harm, and
acceptance of divergent perspectives of human behavior (Holland and Kilpatrick, 1991).

Both the social work profession and the educational institution would
also concur that children have the right to receive school social work services

and would question whether the anticipated benefit of long-range improvement of children's well-being through the research structure of experimental design would ever justify delaying service provision, even in the short term. Thus comparison group research designs addressing the question "Which treatment works better?" would be preferable to experimental designs with treatment groups and no-treatment control groups that address the question "Does treatment work better than no treatment?" However, in those instances where school social workers cannot provide services to all children—in-need, wait-listed children may be asked to serve first as a control group and later receive treatment in a replication study (*albeit* with the slight modification of having been wait-listed).

By contrast, value conflicts may arise in the biopsychosocial assessment, planning, and referral process because of differences in the ways social work and education conceptualize practice. A case in point, P.L. 105–17, the Individuals with Disabilities Education Act, presents an instrumental value dilemma at the point of initial service—the point of individualized educational assessment and planning. The law specifies that families have a right to obtain a copy of all public school system evaluations of their children but does not specify the method of providing this information. It is this method that may become a source of value conflict among multidisciplinary team members. For example, some team members emphasize the content and substance of the report, believing that furnishing a written copy of an evaluation report satisfies the legal requirements and constitutes the whole point of the initial service. School social workers, by contrast, traditionally have placed emphasis on both content and process. They value the professional intervention process of assessment, planning, and reporting as the whole point of the initial service. In other words, school social workers value the family's right to participate in and respond to the evaluation process, findings, and recommended plan. To explore this professional value dilemma in service delivery, school social workers might pose the following research questions: Do different styles and levels of family participation in individualized assessment and planning affect their response to and use of the process, findings, recommendations, and outcomes? If so, which families are affected?

Informed Consent

To protect the rights of participants in practice research, program evaluations, and demonstration projects, potential subjects are informed of the purpose, goals, procedures to be followed, issues of confidentiality, possible risk and benefits, the right not to participate, and the right to withdraw at any time. In turn, potential subjects signify their willingness to participate by signing a consent form detailing this information. The intent behind informed consent is to ensure that research participants truly understand that to which they are consenting.

However, issues of client competence, knowledge, and volition make this ethical imperative of ensuring the protection of human subjects more complex in educational settings that it may initially appear. Competence, for example, refers to the subject's ability to make a well-reasoned decision to participate on the basis of the information provided, that is, to give *meaningful* consent. However, to protect minor children's rights, parents—as legal guardians—must provide written consent before their children may participate. Older children and adolescents then are asked to sign a form to confirm their understanding of the project and indicate their willingness to participate. In this way, children give meaningful assent. Knowledge refers to the subject's understanding of the purpose and nature of the research, the facts, sources of discomfort and possible risks and benefits. With children and adolescents, the task is to convey the information as clearly and simply as possible in age-appropriate language that ensures their understanding. With parents and other adults, the task is to frame and convey the information at the appropriate level of comprehension. Volition refers to the basis on which the subject agrees to participate, that is, provision of consent and assent willingly with no coercion and no fear of penalty.

RESEARCH QUESTIONS AND PARADIGMS

Research questions and the methodological paradigms selected for exploring them are based in the school social work researcher's professional and personal value system. That is, the choice of question and paradigm grows out of the school social worker's preferred conceptualizations of children, families, schools, and school-linked services; preferred instrumentalities for assessing and intervening with children, parents, educators, and educational systems, and preferred outcomes for school social work practice (Levy, 1973). A review of the past thirteen issues of *Social Work in Education* (January 1995 through January 1998) illustrates the value choices some school social workers have made as they systematically explored research issues associated with their practice.

During this three-year period, a dozen articles reported quantitative (9) and qualitative (3) studies of school-related problems of children and youth that have the potential to facilitate development of intervention models at some later date. The focus of the quantitative studies ranged from the extraordinary to the ordinary practice problem: stress, stressors, and coping strategies (De Anda et al., 1997); perspectives of childhood trauma after a residential fire (Greenberg and Keane, 1997); deaf children, self-esteem, and parents' communication patterns (Deselled and Pearlmutter, 1997); peers and social development (Hepler, 1997); and assistance with homework as an indicator of natural support strengths (Delgado, 1998). The three qualitative studies explored issues of family adaptation and assessment: adaptation of families of children with disabilities (Bennett, Luca, and Allen, 1996), portfolios as assessment tools (Franklin and Karoly, 1996), and community asset assessments (Delgado, 1996).

Another dozen articles in this same time period reported quantitative (5) and qualitative (7) school social work program evaluation studies. The quantitative studies focused on promoting prosocial school behavior and achievement: strengthening personal and social competencies (De Mar, 1997), employing strengths-based substance abuse prevention (Delgado, 1997), promoting educational achievement (Aguilar, 1996), and improving school attendance (Ford and Sutphen, 1996). The qualitative program evaluation studies explored concepts such as empowerment, resiliency, social support, and getting better and their connection with change: for example, facilitating teacher self-efficacy and empowerment (O'Connor and Korr, 1996), supporting and empowering families (Dunlap, 1996); the getting better phenomenon (Carley, 1997); promoting resiliency (Kaplan, Turner, Norman, and Stillson, 1996); and social support and school completion (Rosenthal, 1995).

Only one article was identified that clearly reported practice process and outcome. This research study explored the treatment of a student with autism and attended to decelerating self-stimulating and self-injurious behaviors (Early, 1995).

As a body of work, these twenty-five articles reflect attention to children, youth, and teachers in their social environments—their schools, communities, families, and cultures. Thus these studies clearly conveyed school social work researchers' incorporation of the social work profession's preferred value paradigm of person-in-environment into their research efforts. Since 63 percent of the articles under review were authored by a team of two or more school social work researchers, this body of work also reflected the value of the team approach in educational settings. In addition, the articles suggested that school social work researchers viewed both quantitative and qualitative research methodologies as valuable tools in producing usable knowledge about the outcomes of their programming efforts and for developing future intervention programs. By contrast, the paucity of research articles focused on individual treatment of children and youth appeared at first glance to reflect a less valued practice issue—but whether less valued by school social work practitioner-researchers, this particular journal, or the structure of school social work programming and service delivery efforts remains an open question.

OUTCOME EFFECTIVENESS

High standards and rigorous assessment of student learning and achievement are being promoted nationwide in an effort to establish both the overt and hidden costs and benefits of all educational services. Yet a central question about school social work outcomes remains: How are program and practice outcomes of school social workers to be defined and rigorously assessed? As practitioner-researchers, school social workers face the difficult task of identifying outcomes that are meaningful to the children, families, schools, and communities served; are based on social work goals and objectives in a host setting, address the individual and group behavior of child-in-environment; and go beyond individual client-level outcomes to include the broader spectrum of environmental and community-level outcomes inherent in social work practice. In other words, school social work practice and program outcomes need to reflect the complexity of the interpersonal, behavioral, and empowerment interventions used with person-in-environment practice models and the multidisciplinary service context in which school social work practice occurs. Much of the time in educational settings, outcomes also need to reflect multidisciplinary team contributions with attribution to teamwork rather than to a single intervention.

One part of this outcome issue is clearly accountability to whom—child, parent, school, school social work service, or school system? Another part involves establishing practice standards and exploring costs and benefits in relation to service quality. At this time, school social workers have rejected the option of allowing others to set standards for them and have accepted the challenge of specifying their own practice standards and goals, developing ways of evaluating the outcomes of their practice, establishing ways of assessing costs and benefits, and conducting program and practice evaluations. This choice clearly places school social workers in a better position to take responsibility for explicating the scope, costs and benefits, and quality of service offered; establishing accountability criteria for the public and private resources absorbed; and making the case for increased resource allocation as indicated by the data.

As a tool for the improvement of service quality, program evaluation research requires multidimensional measurement of outcomes in a way that captures the full scope of the school social work program's intent. The ideal program evaluation resarch plan would include, for example:

- *Service outcomes* that provide data about the intentions of the school social work service provider and the way the intervention was delivered. The emphasis is on service availability, accessibility, and comprehensiveness; the practice model and techniques selected; the context of service delivery; and the amount of intervention provided.

- *Cost outcomes* that focus on quantity of service and cost containment. Ideally, cost and effectiveness outcomes are viewed in tandem.

- *Satisfaction outcomes* that refer to the user's contentment with the quality of service provided and the outcome achieved. As a measure of success, satisfaction reflects service acceptability and is thought to correlate with client retention and clinical change.

- *Clinical intervention outcomes* that refer to changes made and reflect intervention effectiveness as perceived by children, parents, teachers, and school social workers.

Taken together, this array of outcome measures answers questions such as which service programs and intervention processes are most effective? Which children need a different array of services? How well do school social workers follow administrative expectations? What is the cost effectiveness of school social work service delivery?

METHODOLOGICAL CHALLENGES

Professional Knowledge Base

Throughout the twentieth century, social workers have debated the usefulness, credibility, and hierarchical status of professional knowledge derived through practice wisdom and disseminated through the oral tradition of supervision and professional knowledge obtained through scientific method and disseminated through publications (Richmond, 1917; Flexner, 1915). Although appearing in various forms, the core of the debate has centered around three questions: (1) Is scientific practice knowledge about treatment effectiveness generated by empirical research more valid and reliable than cumulative practice wisdom about what works? (2) Which is more credible, relevant, and useful in the real world of practice? (3) Which establishes the credibility of the social work profession with consumers and with colleagues in other professions? In recent years, social workers appear to have tacitly accepted the need for a scientific knowledge base for the profession and have virtually ignored practice wisdom. Yet neither type of professional knowledge by itself is adequate for practice. Nor does this tacit resolution appear to have addressed the place of theory in professional practice. Thus, for the foreseeable future, the professional knowledge base for school social workers is perhaps best defined as comprising a network of propositions that have originated in practice experience, theory, and research. These propositions are grounded in both the social work profession and the school practice setting. For school social work practitioner-researchers, the knowledge development issue thus becomes: What constitutes credible social work knowledge and validly informed social work practice in the face of constantly evolving state-of-the-art knowledge and an uncertain practice context?

Paradigm Debate

Today, social workers acknowledge the different purposes and strengths of quantitative and qualitative paradigms in contributing to the school social work knowledge base and exploring issues of practice accountability (Guba, 1992; Hudson and Nurius, 1994; Luborsky, Crits-Cristoph, Mitz, and Anetbach, 1988). In the ideal more than the reality of actual research efforts, the value of multimethod research designs is increasingly acknowledged. These designs employ multiple theoretical perspectives, embedded or nested designs, multiple measures, multimodal analyses, and within- or across-group replications to offset the weaknesses of one approach with the strengths of another (Brewer and Hunter, 1989; Timberlake and Sabatino, 1994). These validity and reliability debates and the multimethod solution, however, beg the critical issue underlying the choice of design in school social work research. Rather than being chosen simply to cross-validate findings through a counterbalancing of methodological strengths and weaknesses, a research design is ideally selected because it (1) best enables the researcher to address the research problem and question at hand, (2) provides a means of corroborating the findings, (3) generates evidence that fills in knowledge lacunae, and (4) permits the researcher to build explanatory and intervention models that are adequate, acceptable, accessible, and accountable to the multiple stakeholders in the outcomes of school social work practice—child and parent consumers, social work service providers, educator colleagues, boards of education, and the tax-paying public. For, it is increasingly clear that professional truths in explanation and intervention are established by agreement among constituent communities of consumers, practitioners, and payors rather than by the research community alone.

Generating Meaningful Data

In that social workers employ different criteria and measures than educators in evaluating outcomes, it has been difficult to document service effectiveness. For example, educators use educational measures and outcomes such as ability tests, performance measures, report card grades, and attendance—outcomes directly associated with their services and only indirectly associated with school social work services. School social workers, by contrast, conceptualize and reframe observed changes in psychosocial functioning in education-related terminology and outcomes to evaluate and report their service outcomes as:

- Higher levels of social support and school completion (Rosenthall, 1995),
- Improved appropriateness of classroom behavior and lowered probability of identification of students as academically deficient (Owen and Sabatino, 1989),
- decreased separation anxiety and improved school adjustment in transitioning from home to school, or
- age-specific task achievements and developmental phase-specific accomplishments associated with increased attention to the teaching-learning process

It is important to note that, although school social work practice models may vary over time, desired outcomes change little. Rather, they remain closely tied to the ultimate outcome measure driving all professions employed in the school setting—the success or failure of a child's classroom performance.

When the research paradigm is an integral part of school social work service design and delivery, practice research and program evaluation questions are concerned with the impact of the specified intervention on outcomes meaningful to the school setting—changes in children's attitudes and behaviors in the classroom, environmental structures and processes in the school setting, the fit of children with their classroom environments, and the ultimate outcome for the host setting of improvement in academic achievement. In framing the question, the choice of specific outcome (or dependent variable) depends on the practice problem addressed, the purpose of the study, the phase of service provision being explored, and the explanatory and intervention theories employed.

The goal of school social work practice research and program evaluation is capturing the reality of what actually happens in service delivery, but doing so often proves difficult. For example, the theoretical orientation of the research may not take into account the actual experiences of the children, the parents, or the teachers. Lack of cultural understanding or insensitivity to diversity in the schools might impose dominant cultural norms on the data collected (Marin and Marin, 1991). Data collection tools may not capture the specificity of the behaviors, attitudes, and situations that are the foci of intervention (Mullen and Magnabusco, 1997). The measurement or observation procedures may miss important aspects of children's classroom behavior or well-being in school that are affected positively or negatively by the intervention. Or the assumptions in the selected measures may differ from those in the practice intervention. In these instances, the research does not measure what the school social worker thought it would measure and provides invalid answers to the questions asked. In other instances, the demonstration project and outcome research may not yield the same answers on repetition and, thereby, may raise reliability issues of intervention replicability as well as issues about stability, accuracy, and error of measurement. Thus it is clear that conceptualizing, implementing, and assessing school social work practice is a matter for careful clinical framing, operationalization in practice, and systematic evaluation.

METHODOLOGICAL GUIDELINES

In the face of the profession's thrust toward documenting its theory and practice and the federal laws that increasingly affect social work practice in the schools, school social workers are moving forward in developing a theoretically framed and empirically based practice. As they do so, it is important that their research studies in the aggregate:

- Employ valid and reliable single-subject and larger scale experimental research designs in actual educational settings;
- Develop and test social work intervention models that represent discrete points of service responsive to specific problems and target populations of interest to both social workers and educators;
- Develop and test social work intervention models that variously incorporate child-focused, family-focused, and community-focused approaches germane to educational settings;
- Develop and test social work intervention models that represent discrete points of service responsive to specific problems associated with organizational development, empowerment, advocacy, school reform, and policy development;
- Develop and test individual and group intervention models for psychosocial dysfunction, psychoeducational models for normative problems as well as empowerment, consultation, collaboration, and mediation practice models;
- Explore and refine the change processes occurring within social work intervention models;
- Select problem explanations and intervention methodologies that are appropriate, theoretically driven, based on conceptually integrated evidence (as opposed to eclectic summarizations), and germane to the educational setting;
- Use theoretical frameworks and research methodologies sensitive to cultural, socieconomic, age, and gender diversity in order to build a body of knowledge that translates into increased understanding of school population heterogeneity, expanded social work service technology and skills, and additional ways to facilitate school personnel's understanding and handling of classroom diversity.

However, a word of caution is in order. Unless the research problem and proposed interventions can be described and discussed in terminology meaningful to the mission of this host setting, the outcomes of school social work services cannot be assessed by administrative, instructional, or special education personnel in terms of their cost-benefit ratios—their usefulness, effectiveness, efficiency, and financial outlay. Nor can they be used as justification for allocating scarce resources to school social work.

SUBSTANTIVE CHALLENGES

Intervention Outcome Effectiveness Studies

Today's accountability paradigm with its underlying conservative philosophy makes it clear that school social workers no longer have the luxury of simply describing and conceptualizing what they are doing and accomplishing in their espoused models of practice. They must increasingly move toward greater specificity in what they actually do and routinely test for practice effectiveness.

In providing services in this host setting, school social workers are accountable not only to their clients, themselves, and their profession but also to the school as an educational institution within which their practice occurs. As competent practitioners, they are responsible for providing adequate evidence of the extent to which their clients have benefited from intervention and of ongoing efforts to improve their practice. That is, they are responsible for establishing the effectiveness of both service delivery programs and individual practice efforts.

Studies of program effectiveness establish the degree to which a particular school social work program meets its goals and objectives in terms of types of problems addressed, number of clients served, barriers to service utilization, overall results achieved, cost-benefit ratio, and congruence of results with the core educational mission of the school setting. Since school social work programs are continually evolving entities, establishing their effectiveness is not a one-time event. Rather, program evaluation is an ongoing dynamic process. Decisions about actual service delivery should be based on evidence, not arguments of ideology, theory, or authority (Hasenfeld, 1992). In program evaluation, clinically and statistically significant evidence is based on information derived from (1) substantive programmatic variables that operationalize multidimensional service structures, staffing patterns, practice activities, and client outcomes; (2) contextual variables such as program history, educational and social work norms, community expectations, and political pressures; and (3) client variables such as demographic characteristics, diversity, and family involvement. For example, Timberlake, Sabatino, and Hooper (1979) explored decisions about the educational placement of handicapped children in order to understand the contribution of the social case history to multidisciplinary team decision making and evaluate the effectiveness of this practice tool. O'Donnell, Michalak, and Ames (1997) assessed the degree to which after-school peer programs promoted bonding and reduced risk of poor school performance among inner city children.

Studies of practice effectiveness address the outcomes expected when intervention is provided under the real-world conditions of school settings and with all of the variations apparent among children, families, educators, and school social workers. Practice effectiveness studies link substantive questions of service provision, conceptual issues of explanatory and change theories, intervention practices, and specific outcome questions. For example, Early (1995) linked behavioral intervention with outcomes of decelerating self-stimulating and self-injurious behaviors of a student with autism; De Mar (1997), examined group intervention which strengthened personal and social competencies in latency-age children. Few practitioner-researchers have also linked cost-benefit analyses. In services research, it is important to go beyond simply counting and ask questions that provide adequate empirical evidence useful in making practice decisions. For example, does early intervention improve elementary school attendance for at-risk children (Ford and Sutphen, 1996)? It then becomes the practitioner's task to translate the meaning of the evidence to parents, educators, and children. For example, Drisko (1993) developed but did not test a conceptual model of school social work consultation that profiled student skills and special education teacher intervention strategies while enhancing teacher empathy and understanding. Sabatino (1986), by contrast, not only developed a conceptual model of school social work consultation but also incorporated an effectiveness measure as a major component of the model. Using a quasi-experimental design with pre and post measures of teacher perception of children's classroom behavior, she provided teacher-centered mental health case consultation services and found statistically significant differences between teachers who received consultation services and those who did not. Additionally, she found that children whose teachers received consultation earned statistically significant higher report card marks for nonacademic performance of "listens to and follows teacher's directions."

In sum, program and practice effectiveness research involves assessing both the statistical significance and the clinical meaningfulness of the findings obtained. It also involves systematic data collection that draws on explicit practice models and intervention techniques and uses sound research design.

POLICY AND PROGRAM IMPACT STUDIES

According to Prigmore and Atherton (1979), policy decision making requires choosing from among various alternatives that reflect social values and preferences. In this way, public values heavily influence how politically viable and publicly acceptable, a particular social policy will be. The new accountability paradigm with its underlying conservative philosophy makes it clear that school social workers no longer have the luxury of simply relying on federal policies as the legal basis for practice in school settings. They must move toward policy analysis guided by social work, economics, and educational precepts and provide an evidentiary database for policy decision making and refinement. In such an approach, a policy impact assessment would, at minimum, focus on analyzing each of the four elements of entitlements, goals, service delivery, and financing (Chambers, 1993) from a perspective that takes into account social work, education, and economic factors. While heavy emphasis would be placed on economic cost-benefit analysis, such analysis would be framed and anchored within the philosophy, values, and goals of the school social work mission.

Childhood educational disability legislation provides a case in point. As noted in the *Washington Post* ("Special Education Students," 1994), the Department of Education reported that in 1992–93 nearly 95 percent of the nation's 5,017,000 students with disabilities received education and related services in a regular school setting for some part of the day. Of these disabled students aged six to twenty-one, 52.4 percent were assessed as having specific learning disabilities, 22.2 percent speech or language impairment, 10.9 percent mental retardation, and 8.3 percent emotional disturbance. These figures, however, are flat and yield minimal information about programmatic successes or failures. On the one hand, they suggest that the educational system is providing comprehensive assessment services and, by extrapolation, that the system is moving disabled children toward normalization in the regular classroom. On the other hand, the psychosocial and economic cost and benefits were not discussed. Without cost-benefit data, practitioners and planners have no nuanced evidentiary base for evaluating the policy's operationalization into programming and practice in keeping with the best interests of all children.

For example, Seligman and Darling (1989) assert that (1) the availability of supportive community resources is the most important determinant of normalization for most families of disabled children and (2) the ability of children to achieve a normalized lifestyle is determined by their access to resources, their opportunity structure. Although it is clear that 95 percent of these children now spend part of their time in mainstream classrooms, school social workers do not know whether schools and families see this as a supportive resource and as normalization of children's lives. In addition, during the past decades, major pieces of federal legislation sought to remove barriers to normalization in the schools. Specifically, P.L. 94–142, P.L. 99–457, P.L. 102–119, and P.L. 105–17 mandated that preschool and school-age children with targeted disabilities receive a free and appropriate public education in the least restrictive environment. Policy impact studies, however, have not yet assessed the degree to which the promise of normalization within the least restrictive environment has become reality and at what educational, psychosocial, and financial costs with what educational, psychosocial, and financial benefits.

In the past ten years, full-service schools and school-linked services have increased from 32 programs in 1985 to 574 in 1993 (Adler, 1994). This growth appears to be based more on the assumptions that school-linked models decrease social service fragmentation, increase service accessibility, and increase child and family well-being. After a review of the literature and evaluative studies of eighteen school-linked service sites, Shaw and Replogle (1996) concluded that empirical examination of these program assumptions is inadequate and key questions remain unanswered. For example, how do service delivery patterns within school-linked models differ from those in school-based models? Do their outcomes differ?

EPIDEMIOLOGICAL PLANNING STUDIES

Philosophically, school social workers espouse universal social work services to address the psychosocial problems of children and youth that interefere with school learning and performance. With conservative economic and social policies, however, programs and services are likely to be based on local and state school priorities and available funding sources. The actual scope of need and the school social work services provided must be made clear: Who is being served? For what problems? Under what circumstances? At what costs and with what benefits? And, conversely: Who is not being served? For what problems? At what costs?

An epidemiological planning study, for example, might address the question of children's needs for school social work services, including the nature and severity of the problem and the numbers of children involved. One such study (Sabatino, Timberlake, and Zajicek-Farber, 1992) found no difference on these key variables when comparing inner city and suburban elementary school students. This finding and others served to undo the stereotype that inner city children were experiencing more problems of psychosocial dysfunction in the classroom and pointed to functional strengths in the coping resourcefulness of inner-city children. A second study (Timberlake and Sabatino, 1994) explored the nature and severity of the problem of homelessness to children and found that school attendance mediated their self-esteem and loneliness. Recent studies have explored stress, stressors, and coping strategies among middle school adolescents (De Anda et al., 1997); effects of economic stress on high school students' views of work and the future (Jones, Agbayani-Siewaert, and Friaz, 1998); community asset assessments by Latino youth (1996); and problems of inner city children (Gerdes and Benson, 1995). The findings of these studies provide an empirical base for program development to meet identified service needs.

School social workers also need an epidemiological database to help in predicting child and parent behavior that is likely to be dangerous to self or others. Community and administrative pressure and growing legal liability are pressing school social workers to pay increased attention to their clinical data, inferred practice implications, and predictions about the future behavior of children, youth, and parents (Gambrill, 1990; Murdock, 1994). For example: Is this child likely to attempt suicide? Is this parent likely to abuse? Is this adolescent likely to harm another child? School social workers are accustomed to making clinical predictions informed by social case history, current behavior patterns, and psychosocial assessment. They are not, however, accustomed to using a template whose aggregate data provide information about the statistical likelihood that certain behaviors will occur. Such aggregate databases can facilitate more systematic clinical prediction and decision making by expanding the profession's practice knowledge base and identifying harmful behavioral outcomes likely to be associated with:

- Historical behavior patterns—degree to which history of assault is predictive of future violent behavior in school or the community or a history of suicide threats is predictive of a future suicide attempt; or

- Demographic factors—degree to which age, gender, race, diagnosis, and family status are predictive of destructive behavior in school.

While data that can function as useful indicators or predictors have been compiled into actuarial tables for use in selected mental health situations calling for clinical judgment, such tables have not yet been developed for school social work.

In addition to programmatic needs assessment and clinical prediction, epidemiological research sets the stage for long-range planning. By juxtaposing a broad-based client characteristics and needs data set, a school social work service provision data set, and a data set of school social work services utilized, epidemiological research can provide both the desired specificity about and fuller understanding of school social work practice.

This consideration of critical issues, unproven assumptions, published research, and unanswered questions highlights the paucity of sound empirical study of school social work intervention and raises grave concern. As a practice profession, social work needs service models that are not only experimentally grounded in practice wisdom, contextually anchored, and theoretically framed but also empirically grounded as to their quality and effectiveness through sound services research. In this era of outcome-driven service delivery, school social work and the profession's other fields of practice need services research designed to provide empirically grounded evidence about specific features of the specialized practice as well as practice impact on psychosocial and educational outcomes, thereby providing the advocacy tools to advance their preferred educational policies and practices.

REFERENCES

Adler, L. 1994. Introduction and overview. In L. Adler and S. Gardner (eds). *The policies of linking schools and social services* (pp. 1–18). Washington, DC: Falmer.

Aguilar, M. 1996. Promoting the educational achievement of Mexican American young women. *Social Work in Education* 18(3):145–156.

Bennett, T., De Luca, D., and Allen, R. 1996. Families of children with disabilities: Positive adaptation across the life cycle. *Social Work in Education* 18(1):31–44.

Betson, D., and Michael, R. 1997. Why are so many children poor? *Future of Children* 7(2):25–39.

Brewer, J., and Hunter, A. 1989. *Multimethod research.* Newbury Park, CA: Sage.

Carley, G. 1997. The getting better phenomenon: Videotape applications of previously at-risk high school student narratives. *Social Work in Education* 19(2):115–120.

Chambers, D. 1993. *Social policy and social programs*. NY: Macmillan.

De Anda, D., et al. 1997. A study of stress, stressors, and coping strategies among middle school adolescents. *Social Work in Education* 19(2):87–89.

Delgado, M. 1996. Community asset assessments by Latino youths. *Social Work in Education* 18(3):169–178.

Delgado, M. 1997. Strengths-based practice with Puerto Rican adolescents: Lessons from a substance abuse prevention project. *Social Work in Education* 19(2):101–112.

Delgado, M. 1998. Puerto Rican elementary school-age children: Assistance with homework as an indicator of natural support lengths. *Social Work in Education* 20(1):49–54.

De Mar, J. 1997. A school-based group intervention to strengthen personal and social competencies in latency-age children. *Social Work in Education* 19(4):219–230.

Deselle, D., and Pearlmutter, L. 1997. Navigating two cultures: Deaf children, self-esteem, and parents' communication patterns. *Social Work in Education* 19(1):23–30.

Drisko, J. 1993. Special education teacher consultation: A student-focused, skill-defining approach. *Social Work in Education* 15:19–28.

Dunlap, K. 1996. Supporting and empowering families through cooperative preschool education. *Social Work in Education* 18(4):210–221.

Early, B. 1995. Decelerating self-stimulating and self-injurious behaviors of a student with autism: Behavioral intervention in the classroom. *Social Work in Education* 17(4):244–255.

Flexner, A. 1915. Is social work a profession? In *Procedures of the National Conference of Charities and Corrections*, (pp. 576–590). Chicago: National Conference of Charities and Corrections.

Ford, J. and Sutphen, R. 1996. Early intervention to improve attendance in elementary school for at-risk children: A pilot program. *Social Work in Education* 18(2):95–102.

Franklin, C. and Karoly, J. 1996. Using portfolios to assess students' academic strengths: A case study. *Social Work in Education* 18(3):179–186.

Franklin, C., and Streeter, C. 1995. School reform: Linking public schools with human services. *Social Work* 40(6):773–782.

Franklin, C., and Streeter, C. 1998. School-linked services as interpersonal collaboration in student education. *Social Work* 43:67–69.

Gambrill, E. 1990. *Critical thinking in clinical practice*. San Francisco: Jossey-Bass.

Gerdes, K., and Benson, R. 1995. Problems of inner-city schoolchildren: Needs assessment by nominal group process. *Social Work in Education* 17(3):139–147.

Greenberg, H., and Keane, A. 1997. A social work perspective of childhood trauma after a residential fire. *Social Work in Education* 19(1):11–22.

Guba, E. 1992. *The paradigm dialog.* Newbury Park, CA: Sage.

Hasenfeld, Y. 1992. *Human services as complex organizations.* Newbury Park, CA: Sage.

Hepler, J., 1997. Social development of children: The role of peers. *Social Work in Education* 19(4):242–256.

Holland T., and Kilpatrick, A. 1991. Ethical issues in social work: Toward a grounded theory of professional ethics. *Social Work* 36(2):138–145.

Hudson, W., and Nurius, P. 1994. *Controversial issues in social work research.* Boston: Allyn & Bacon.

Huston, A. 1994. Children in poverty: Designing research to affect policy. *Social Policy Report* 8:2.

Jones, L., Agbayani-Siewaert, P., and Friaz, G. 1998. Effects of economic stress on high school student's views of work and the future. *Social Work in Education* 20(1):11–24.

Kaplan, C., Turner, S., Norman, E., and Stillson, K. 1996. Promoting resilience strategies: A modified consultation model. *Social Work in Education* 18(3):158–168.

Koppich, J. 1992. Choice in education: Not whether, but what. *Social Work in Education* 14(4):253–257.

Lee, W. 1998. Balancing the educational needs of students with school-based or school-linked services. *Social Work* 43(1):65–66.

Levy, C. 1973. The value base of social work. *Journal of Social Work Education* 9:34–42.

Lewit, E., and Baker, U. 1996. Children in special education. *Future of Children* 6(1):139–151.

Luborsky, L., Crits-Cristoph, P., Mintz, J., and Auerbach, A. 1988. *Predicting therapeutic outcomes.* New York: Basic Books.

Marin, G., and Marin, B. 1991. *Research with Hispanic populations.* Newbury Park, CA: Sage.

Mullen, E., and Magnabusco, J. (eds.) 1997. *Outcomes measurement in the human services: Cross-cutting issues and methods.* Washington, DC: NASW Press.

Murdock, A. 1994. Avoiding errors in clinical prediction. *Social Work* 39:381–386.

National Association of Social Workers. 1996. *Code of Ethics.* Silver Spring, MD: Author.

National Center for Educational Statistics, 1993. *Digest of education statistics.* Washington, DC: Author.

O'Connor, R., and Korr, W. 1996. A model for school social work facilitation of teacher self-efficacy and empowerment. *Social Work in Education* 18(1):45–51.

O'Donnell, T., Michalak, E., and Ames, E. 1997. Inter-city youth helping children: After-school programs to promote bonding and reduce risk. *Social Work in Education* 19(4):231–241.

Owen, M., and Sabatino, C. 1989. Effects of cognitive development on classroom behavior: A model assessment and intervention program. *Social Work in Education* 11:77–88.

Prigmore, C., and Atherton, C. 1979. *Social welfare policy: Analysis and formulation.* Lexington, MA: Heath.

Richmond, M., 1917. *Social diagnosis.* NY: Russell Sage Foundation.

Rosenthal, B. 1995. The influence of social support on school completion among Haitians. *Social Work in Education* 17(1):30–39.

Sabatino, C. 1986. The effects of school social work consultation on teacher perception and role conflict-role ambiguity in relationship to students with social adjustment problems. *Dissertation Abstracts International* 46:11.

Sabatino, C., Timberlake, E., and Zajicek-Barber, M. 1992. Psychosocial coping of urban children. *Social Thought* 17:35–47.

Seligman, M., and Darling, R. 1989. *Ordinary families, special children.* NY: Guilford.

Shaw, K., and Replogle, E. 1996. Challenges in evaluating school-linked services. Toward a more comprehensive framework. *Evaluation Review* 20(4):424–469.

Snyder, T. (ed.) 1993. 120 Years of American education: A statistical portrait. Washington, DC: National Center for Education Statistics.

GLOSSARY

ACLD—American Council on Learning Disabilities

Adaptive Behavior Assessment—Standardized instrument measuring seven areas of functioning other than educational achievement

ADD—Attention Deficit Disorder

ADHD—Attention Deficit Hyperactivity Disorder

AFT—American Federation of Teachers

AIDS—Auto-immune deficiency syndrome

Annual Review—Interdisciplinary yearly meeting required under Public Law 94-142, and subsequently Public Law 101-476, to review progress of each identified student needing special education services.

Anorexia—Eating disorder marked by serious distortion of body perception and excessive avoidance of food. Intense fear of becoming fat.

Autism—Distortion of skills and function marked by social non-responsiveness, impaired or peculiar language, and bizarre responses to the environment.

BD—Behavior Disorder—characterized by difficult to manage acting-out behaviors

Case Study Evaluation—An educational evaluation of a child referred for possibility of receiving special education services which includes among other components a Social Development Study

CEC—Council for Exceptional Children

Confidentiality—Social work value respecting and guaranteeing privacy of client communication, within the parameters of the law.

DD—Developmental Disability

DSM-IV—Diagnostic and Statistical Manual, Fourth Edition (published by the American Psychiatric Association)

ED—Emotional disturbance

EH—Educationally handicapped

EMH—Educable mentally handicapped

EMI—Educably mentally impaired (same as EMH)

GED—General equivalency diploma

HHS—U.S. Department of Health and Human Services

HI—Hearing Impaired

Host Setting—Setting in which social work is a support service, rather than the primary service

ICD-X—International Classification of Diseases, Tenth Edition

IEP—Individualized Education Program

IFSP—Individualized Family Service Plan

IGAPP—Iowa General Assessment of Pupil Performance

Inclusion—Movement which grew from the REI (Regular Education Initiative) concept, placing all students possible in regular education classrooms in their home district

LD—Learning disability

LEA—Local Education Agency (school district)

Low Incidence—Disabilities which affect fewer than one-tenth of one percent of the population (.1% or fewer)

LRE—Least Restrictive Environment—Educational placement most closely resembling a regular education placement, in which student may maximize his/her educational experience

Mainstreaming—The practice of placing students from self-contained classrooms into one or more regular education classrooms for regular education instruction

MBD—Minimal brain dysfunction

MDC—Multi-disciplinary conference—mandated conference to determine a student's eligibility for special education programming

Mediation/Conflict Resolution—Process of identifying real issues in a dispute and discovering acceptable compromise solutions to original conflict

MLD—Moderate learning disability

MMI—Moderately mentally impaired

MR—Mental Retardation

Multipli-Disabled—More than one significant disabling condition affecting a person

NEA—National Education Association

OT—Occupational therapist

Peer Support—Any of a variety of programs using a teaching/learning model which relies on student-to-student communication

PH—Physically handicapped

P.L. 94–142—The Education for All Handicapped Children Act of 1975, amended as:

P.L. 99–457—Early Childhood Amendments, and

P.L. 101–476—Individuals with Disabilities Education Act (IDEA)

PMI—Profoundly mentally impaired

PT—Physical Therapy

REI—Regular Education Initiative—movement to integrate special education students into the regular educational environment

Related Services—Instruction given a student by specially trained professionals within the special education domain, not primarily related to regular educational instruction

Resource Room—A separate environment within a regular education setting within which the student receives special education services on a limited basis

Resource Services—Services delivered to a student who spends more than 50 percent of his/her time in a regular education classroom

Self-Contained—Classrooms in which students designated as special education students receive over 50 percent of their daily educational instruction

SDS—Social developmental study, includes an assessment of adaptive behaviors and assessment of cultural environment, as mandated by P.L. 94–142 and P.L. 101–476

SLD—Severe learning disability

SMI—Severely mentally impaired

SSWAA—School Social Work Association of America. National association, organized officially in 1994, to support national legislation, sponsor national conferences focused on issues relevant to school social work, to support the formation and particular interests of regional state organizations, and to support the professional needs of individual school social workers.

Standard Education Placement—Placement in a regular education school setting

TMH—Trainable mentally handicapped

VI—Visually impaired

INDEX

postponing action, 456–57
skill development for, 383
stopping when you know what the problem is, 454–55
procedural due process. *See* due process
professional values, 59
profiles, 309
program consultation, 341
property taxes, 111
psychotherapy, 82, 173, 181*n*13
public education
attacks on, 26
characteristic focus of social worker in, 45–63
mandate of, 11
the social development study in, 278–80
socialization as early mission of, 541
See also free appropriate public education; schools
public law mandates, 539–41
punishment
in junior high schools, 446–47
objectives in research on, 530
as the teacher getting even, 453–54
pupils. *See* students
pupil services, 118
purposeful avoidance, 403

qualitative paradigm, 547
quantitative paradigm, 547
questionnaires, 513, 533–34

race
adaptive behavior assessments as nondiscriminatory, 287
demographics, 102
discrimination as reinforced in public schools, 26
and dropping out, 106
GRADES test, 142
groups addressing issues of, 360
and organizational culture, 159
and poverty, 102
in social skills programs, 380–81
student forums in addressing racial conflict, 391–98
and violence, 106
reexperiencing, 402–3
reform, school. *See* school reform
reform, social. *See* social reform programs

Regional Community Integration Resource Committee (RCIRC), 487–89
Regular Education Initiative (REI)
encouraging movement back to regular classroom, 78
and Will's report, 322–24
Rehabilitation Act of 1973, 485
related aids and services, 81
related services, 171–72
clean intermittent catheterization as, 174
defined, 81
educational and noneducational, 82, 483
in Individualized Education Program, 294
psychotherapy as, 82
as a right, 81–82
social workers as, 118–19
social work services, 171
what services schools must provide, 172–74
remedial programs, 480
research. *See* school social work research
resource rooms, 320
resources, 52
for children with disabilities, 482–85
concepts for analyzing, 56–58
continuing challenges in development of, 479–80
development of, 478–97
emerging roles in coordination of, 489
integrating for IEPs, 292–93
interagency agreements in development of, 481–85
networks of, 57
in policy analysis, 143–45
school-based family empowerment as, 495–96
school social workers as, 61–62
school social workers as developers of, 496–97
types of community resources, 483
wraparound services, 489–94
return to basics, 504
Richmond, Mary, 19–20, 34
Rochester, New York, 25
role conception, 14
role development, 13–14
role perception, 14
role playing, 382, 425, 426
roles, expectations as grounded in, 52–53
Rowley, Amy, 180*n*4
rumor control, in period of crisis, 415